HOW TO FIND THE RIGHT PLACE

ILLUSTRATED GUIDE TO BRITAIN'S COAST divides the coastline into 145 sections, each of which corresponds with a box on the endpaper maps at the front and back of the book. The number in each box indicates the number of the page on which the description of each section of coastline begins. The numbering starts at the Severn Bridge, near Bristol, and the guide proceeds anti-clockwise round the entire coast of Britain and the main offshore islands.

CHANNEL ISLANDS

Alderney 76

Guernsey 78   Sark

Jersey 76

FRANCE

ISLE OF WIGHT

READER'S DIGEST

ILLUSTRATED GUIDE TO
BRITAIN'S COAST

Published by the Reader's Digest Association Limited
LONDON · NEW YORK · SYDNEY · CAPE TOWN · MONTREAL

EDITOR
Henrietta Heald

DEPUTY EDITOR
Beverley Jones

ASSISTANT EDITORS
Marion Moisy
Charles Phillips
Karen Waldron

ART EDITOR
Colin Goody

DESIGNERS
Vanessa Marsh
Megan Huston

PICTURE RESEARCHERS
Rosie Taylor
Julie McMahon

CARTOGRAPHIC EDITOR
Alison Ewington

CARTOGRAPHIC ASSISTANTS
Vanessa Gale
Sally Gable
Charles Jordan

EDITORIAL ASSISTANT
Stacey Mendoza

EDITORIAL DIRECTOR
Robin Hosie

EXECUTIVE EDITOR
Michael Davison

MANAGING EDITOR
Paul Middleton

ART DIRECTOR
Bob Hook

RESEARCH EDITOR
Prue Grice

PICTURE RESEARCH EDITOR
Martin Smith

EDITORIAL GROUP HEADS
Julian Browne
Noel Buchanan
Cortina Butler
Jeremy Harwood

CONTRIBUTORS

WRITERS
Joe Barling
John Booth
Mike Briggs
Anthony Burton
Jane Egginton
David Finlay
Ross Finlay
Peter Gutteridge
Derek Hall

Tim Locke
John Man
Derrik Mercer
John Miller
Hamish Scott
Helen Spence
Keith Spence
Richard Tames

PHOTOGRAPHERS
Neil Holmes
Ian Howes
Andrew Lawson
Colin Molyneux
John Sims
Patrick Thurston
Trevor Wood
Jon Wyand

ARTISTS
David Atkinson
David Baird
Peter Barrett
Owain Bell
Trevor Boyer
Colin Emberson
John Francis
Tony Graham
Nicholas Hall

Hayward &
Martin
Norman Lacey
Josephine Martin
Liz Peperall
Gillian Platt
Andrew Riley
Gill Tomblin
Adrian Williams

The publishers would also like to thank Doug Baird,
Geoff Crellin, William Geddes and Clive Mumford

Front cover: Bedruthan Steps, Cornwall
Back cover: Maldon, Essex
This page: Crinan Harbour, Strathclyde
Pages 2-3: Formby Dunes, Lancashire
Pages 6-7: Tor Bay from Fishcombe Point, Devon

Contents

Coast of Contrasts

From the tempestuous seas around Cape Wrath, at the north-west tip of the Scottish mainland, to the gentle creeks and estuaries of East Anglia, Britain's coastline offers an inexhaustible range of dramatic contrasts. Whether you are looking for peace and solitude or all the fun of the fair, the *Illustrated Guide to Britain's Coast* will lead you there – to remote sandy coves or lofty clifftop viewpoints, or to the world's tallest, fastest roller coaster at Blackpool.

Starting from the Severn estuary, near Bristol, this unique guide takes you on a journey of discovery round the entire coast of England, Scotland and Wales, observing the changing scenery, and evoking the character of more than 1500 places of interest. With the help of easy-to-follow maps, it explains how to get there, and describes the type of beaches you will find, and the variety of activities to choose from, when you arrive. It identifies castles and stately homes to visit, nature reserves to explore, exhilarating coast walks to discover, and places where you may simply prefer to sit back and relax. The book is packed with anecdotes that bring history and legend to life, and special features cover subjects as varied as smuggling and the birth of the seaside holiday.

The guide can be read page by page as a continuous journey; but the key-maps on the end-papers, showing the way the coast has been divided, enable you to arrive instantly at any area you choose. Most of the historic buildings and other attractions included are open to the public, unless otherwise indicated, but check opening times with local tourist offices, as these may vary from year to year. Some attractions are open only during the summer season, which generally runs from Easter to the end of October.

Resorts and a seafarers' city by the Severn estuary

Sandy beaches flanked by bold headlands give way east of Weston-super-Mare to mud and shingle foreshore. Inland is the spectacular Avon Gorge, and a city that was once one of the world's greatest ports.

① WESTON-SUPER-MARE

Between the prominent headland of Brean Down and the wooded ridge of Worlebury Hill are 2 miles of sand bordering a busy resort. Among Weston's attractions are the Tropicana Pleasure Beach, a Sea Life Centre with an aquarium and the Grand Pier with its busy fair. The Woodspring Museum includes a 19th-century house whose rooms are furnished as they would have been in 1901. Boat trips leave from the northern end of Weston Bay, and there are donkey rides along the beach. At low tide the sea is more than a mile from the promenade, and it is dangerous to walk out too far because of the mud that lies below the sand. The southern end of the bay marks the start of the 30 mile West Mendip Way to Wells in Somerset.

② SAND BAY

Flanked by Worlebury Hill and Sand Point is a wide sandy beach backed by caravans. An Iron Age hill fort stands in the ancient woods that cover Worlebury Hill, at the western end of which a car park looks onto tiny Birnbeck Island.

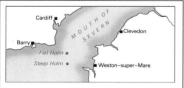

TWO ISLAND NATURE RESERVES
Nature reserves occupy two islands in the Bristol Channel. Steep Holm, which can be visited by boat from Weston-super-Mare, has a 2 mile nature trail that takes in Britain's only wild clumps of the Mediterranean peony, introduced by monks in the 12th or 13th century. Flat Holm can be visited by arrangement with South Glamorgan County Council.

Wild peony
Paeonia mascula
April–May

③ SAND POINT

The narrow headland that leads to Sand Point provides panoramic views of Exmoor and the Bristol Channel. Grassy slopes stretch northwards to seaweed-covered rocks and mud flats, and southwards to Sand Bay. The point is reached from a car park at the north end of Sand Bay, which is also the starting place for a 2 mile walk to Woodspring Priory. Founded in 1210, the building was a farmhouse for more than 400 years; it has been restored, and one of its rooms is a museum displaying finds from the site. The priory can also be reached by road from Worle.

④ CLEVEDON

The charm of this sedate seaside town lies in its many Georgian and Victorian buildings, and in its restored pier and seafront with bandstand and bowling greens. Poet's Walk, whose name recalls Clevedon's links with literary figures such as Tennyson and Coleridge, follows the clifftops past the 12th-century St Andrew's Church. Lovers' Walk leads north-east to the rocky cove of Ladye Bay. Clevedon's beaches are rocky, with low-tide mud. Boat trips and sea-fishing trips are available.

Clevedon Court (NT), a 14th-century manor, is where William Thackeray wrote a large part of his novel *Vanity Fair*; the house has a fine collection of glass made in the nearby town of Nailsea. Glass engraving and wood-turning are among the crafts demonstrated at Clevedon Craft Centre.

⑤ PORTISHEAD

Near the centre of this busy town lies Lake Grounds, a beach-side area with parkland, a cricket ground, a boating lake and a golf course. It is dangerous to venture onto the low-tide mud that can be seen

SEASIDE VICTORIANA *Clevedon's restored wrought-iron pier, built in 1869, juts out some 850 ft into the Severn estuary.*

beyond the shingle shoreline. At Battery Point shipping passes close to the land on its way to Avonmouth docks.

⑥ AVON GORGE

The narrow, steep-cliffed Avon Gorge is spanned by the magnificent Clifton Suspension Bridge, built by Isambard Kingdom Brunel in 1864, which soars 245 ft above the river. Leigh Woods, clothing the west side of the gorge, are a popular walking area; one path forms part of the 30 mile Avon Walkway that follows the river inland. A nature reserve supports several rare plants such as the Bristol whitebeam, which is

Clifton Suspension Bridge

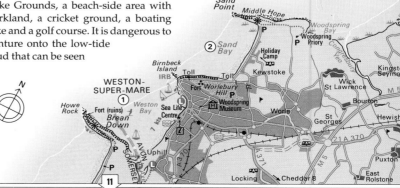

clear that Avonmouth could not cope with ever-larger container ships. Royal Portbury Dock remains a lively commercial shipping centre, handling bulk carriers of up to 120 000 tons, and importing vehicles, timber products and coal. The docks are closed to the public.

⑨ SEVERN BEACH

Low tide at Severn Beach reveals the English Stones reef, beneath which the Severn Tunnel has provided a rail link between the two banks of the Severn since 1885. South of the tunnel a new road bridge has been built to relieve the first Severn Bridge, 3½ miles upriver.

PLACES TO SEE INLAND

Blaise Castle Estate, 3½ miles NW of Bristol city centre. Late 18th-century house with museum of everyday life; hamlet of cottages by John Nash.

Cheddar Gorge, 10 miles SE of Weston-super-Mare. Gorge, caves and heritage centre.

Dyrham Park (NT), 12 miles E of Bristol. 17th-century house; gardens and deer park.

TOURIST INFORMATION

Bristol (0117) 926 0767; Weston-super-Mare (01934) 626838

---

unique to the gorge. There are dramatic views of the gorge from Clifton, with its wealth of elegant 18th-century houses.

⑦ BRISTOL

The tall Cabot Tower near the centre of the city commemorates the 1497 voyage of John Cabot, one of several explorers whose expeditions opened up new markets for Bristol's trade. There are excellent views of the city from the top of the tower. In the 17th and 18th centuries Bristol was one of the world's great ports, its prosperity based on sugar, rum, tobacco and slaves. Now its harbour warehouses shelter the Arnolfini Art Gallery, cinemas and museums. Brunel's SS *Great Britain*, the world's first propeller-driven, ocean-going iron ship is open to the public in the dry dock where she was launched in 1843. A 3 mile heritage walk passes by the 18th-century St Nicholas Market, the Georgian Corn Exchange and four late 16th-century 'nails', or brass pillars used as trading tables, and climbs Christmas Steps, a narrow street 'steppered' in 1669 by a rich wine merchant. Bristol's many other historic buildings include the Georgian House, furnished in the style favoured by an 18th-century merchant's family, the Red Lodge, with 16th-century carved panelling and plasterwork ceilings, and the original terminus of Brunel's Great Western Railway, which houses the Exploratory, a 'hands-on' science centre.

⑧ AVONMOUTH

In the late 19th century Avonmouth took over from the city docks, 8 miles upriver, as the hub of Bristol's shipping activities. The Royal Portbury Dock, on the western side of the river mouth, was built in the 1970s when it was

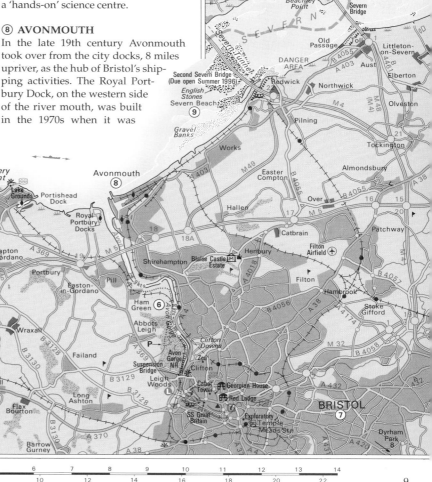

Beaches and mud flats round Bridgwater Bay

Low tide in Bridgwater Bay exposes vast mud flats where sea birds congregate. Sandy beaches fringe the eastern shore; to the south, below the steep-sided Quantock Hills, there are low cliffs and small bays.

① EAST QUANTOXHEAD
Stone cottages, some thatched, stand near a duck pond in this attractive village below the Quantock Hills. East Quantoxhead is dominated by Court House, the home of the Luttrells who once owned Dunster Castle, and who have owned the village since it was granted to an ancestor by William the Conqueror. The house is not open to the public. A 10 minute walk along a path behind the pond passes through fields to crumbling cliffs and a shingle shore.

QUANTOCK'S HEAD *Crumbling cliffs near East Quantoxhead mark the northern end of the rolling, wooded Quantock Hills.*

② KILVE
The ruins of a 13th-century chantry stand beside the lane from Kilve, with its duck pond and thatched cottages, to the sea. Cars can be parked round the corner from the chapel. A 5 minute walk following the stream leads to the shore, where fossils may be found in the shale among the huge rocks that lie at the bottom of the cliffs.

South-west of Kilve, paths scale the Quantock Hills. The high moorland ridge, densely wooded on its eastern side and dotted with the remains of ancient cairns and tumuli, affords magnificent views westwards to Exmoor and northwards across the Bristol Channel to south Wales.

③ LILSTOCK
Narrow lanes wander towards the scattered hamlet of Lilstock, from where a 2 minute walk leads to a shingle beach with some low-tide sand. The view along the grass-covered clifftops to the east is dominated by the squat grey buildings of Hinkley Point power station, 2½ miles away; visitors to the site can see the nuclear reactor and giant turbines, and follow a nature trail.

④ COLERIDGE COTTAGE
From 1797 to 1800 the poet Samuel Taylor Coleridge lived in the quiet village of Nether Stowey, in a cottage that is now owned by the National Trust. Coleridge wrote nearly all his finest poems there, including *The Rime of the Ancient Mariner* and *Kubla Khan*.

⑤ STOLFORD
A winding lane leads down through farmland to this isolated hamlet on the shore of Bridgwater Bay, where low tide exposes a vast expanse of glistening, treacherous mud. Cars can be parked on a grassy area behind the high pebble bank that lines the shore.

The mud flats north and east of Stolford are visited by many wildfowl and waders. Ducks, including wigeon and teal, winter there, and in summer large numbers of shelduck gather to moult. The area is a national nature reserve. The reserve's car park is in the village of Steart, 5 miles east of Stolford.

⑥ COMBWICH
Grassy slopes, a children's play area and two nearby pubs make Combwich a popular spot for visitors. The village is set on the western shore of the River Parrett, which at low tide is reduced to no more than a narrow channel flowing between high banks of glistening mud.

⑦ BRIDGWATER
Once a busy port on the River Parrett, the town was linked to the Bridgwater and Taunton Canal by docks which are now used by pleasure craft. The small Admiral Blake Museum is named after one of Cromwell's commanders during the Civil War, and occupies the house where Blake was born. It contains relics from the Battle of Sedgemoor, fought 3½ miles to the east, which in 1685 ended the West Country's 'Pitchfork Rebellion' of the Duke of Monmouth and his supporters against Charles II. Bridgwater's annual Guy Fawkes Carnival travels to local towns and villages.

⑧ BURNHAM-ON-SEA
At the start of the 19th century the enterprising Reverend David Davies sank wells on the shore at Burnham in an attempt to create a spa town. The spa was not a success, but the venture established Burnham as a seaside resort. On the sandy beach is a distinctive wooden lighthouse on stilts. Behind the long promenade is the 14th-century Church of St Andrew. Inside are carved figures of cherubs and angels originally from the chapel in London's Whitehall Palace, which was destroyed by fire in 1698. The Apex Leisure and Wildlife Park, at the southern end of the town,

BEACH BEACON *The unique nine-legged lighthouse at Burnham-on-Sea was built in 1832 to warn ships of sandbanks.*

FISHING BY 'MUD HORSE'
Fishermen at Stolford have traditionally used a unique wooden-framed vehicle called a 'mud horse' to reach their nets, positioned far out on the mud exposed at low tide. Without a mud horse to support him, the fisherman could not travel quickly with the day's catch and reach the shore before being engulfed by the incoming tide.

'Mud horse'

area, and a walk along the ridge brings into sight the Bristol Channel and, on a clear day, the hills of South Wales.

⑪ BREAN

High dunes back the wide stretch of sand at Brean, whose holiday parks attract young families. Brean Leisure Park has indoor and outdoor swimming pools, a funfair and a golf course. Cars can be driven right onto the sand at the more northerly of the two beach car parks. Brean's 13th-century St Bridget's Church is thought to have been built on the site of a church founded by Irish monks in the 6th century.

⑫ BREAN DOWN

A steep path leads to the crest of this bold, mile-long finger of land that juts out into the Bristol Channel. Peregrine falcons, gulls and cormorants may be seen on the headland, and ducks, geese and waders visit the nearby mud flats at low tide. The fort at the seaward end of Brean Down was built in 1867, when there were fears of a French invasion.

BREAN DOWN *The headland towering over the north side of Bridgwater Bay is one of Somerset's most prominent coastal features and gives views of South Wales and Exmoor.*

has a large lake, and fishing and picnic areas. A cattle market takes place every Monday at nearby Highbridge.

⑨ BERROW

The small village of Berrow lies behind sand dunes and the sandy stretch of Berrow Flats, which extend northwards to Brean Down. Low tide on the beach reveals the remains of a Norwegian ship wrecked in 1897. East of Berrow is the grassy cone of Brent Knoll; the outlines of an Iron Age fort are clearly visible on its 450 ft summit.

⑩ BLEADON HILL

According to legend, the hill was originally known as 'Bleed Down' after a bloody fight between local people and Danish raiders in about AD 800. A footpath to the top of the hill from the nearby village of Loxton offers magnificent views of the surrounding

---

PLACES TO SEE INLAND

Fyne Court, 8 miles SW of Bridgwater. Woodland walks, nature trails, information centre.

Secret World, 4 miles SE of Burnham-on-Sea. Farm animals, badgers, exhibition of farming on Somerset Levels, nature trail through wetland.

TOURIST INFORMATION

Bridgwater (01278) 427652 (summer); Burnham-on-Sea (01278) 787852; Sedgemoor Services, M5 (01934) 750833

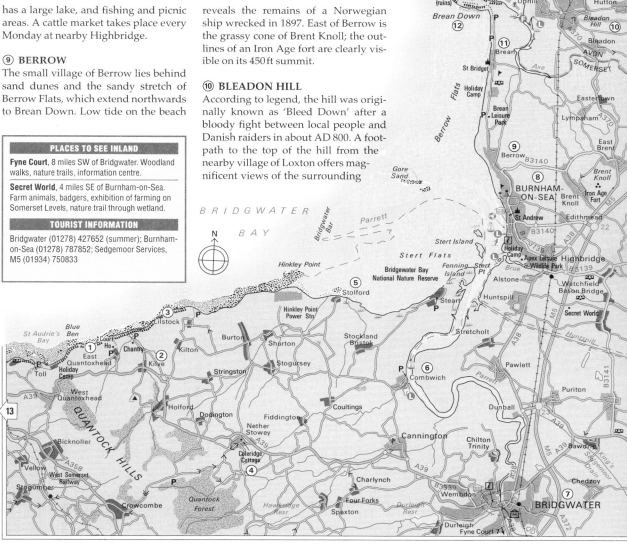

Wooded hills behind Minehead's holiday coast

Along the sand and shingle shore are harbours where pleasure craft have replaced cargo vessels. West of Minehead, hills slope steeply down to the sea, and inland is a group of carefully preserved villages.

① CULBONE CHURCH
A 2 mile walk from Porlock Weir leads up through dense oak woodland to a quiet combe and the isolated Culbone Church, England's smallest complete parish church. Only 34 ft long and 12 ft wide, St Beuno's can seat about 30 people, and is still used for services. The walk may be shortened by following the coast path from a roadside parking area on the toll road which climbs up Ashley Combe. Not far from the road are the overgrown remains of tunnels that once formed part of a house built for the daughter of the poet Lord Byron, in the style of an Italian castle.

② PORLOCK WEIR
A sea-driven bank of shingle encloses a narrow inlet where a small port developed in the 15th century. Pleasure craft now moor in the harbour, and houses and a pub cluster on the tiny quayside. A crescent of shingle stretches eastwards to Hurlstone Point, but strong currents make swimming dangerous anywhere in Porlock Bay.

③ PORLOCK
The white stone buildings of Porlock, a mile from the sea, lie at the foot of Porlock Hill, down a road which descends the wooded slopes of Exmoor

at a one-in-four gradient. At the east end of Porlock is the 15th-century Doverhay Court, which houses a small museum and information centre. The 13th-century Church of St Dubricius takes its name from a saint who, according to legend, crowned King Arthur and married him to Guinevere.

④ SELWORTHY
Clinging to a hill on the edge of Exmoor, Selworthy is a village of cream-walled and thatched cottages surrounding a green. From the largely 14th-century Church of All Saints, which overlooks the village, there is a good view of Dunkery Beacon, at 1705 ft Somerset's highest peak. One of the cottages has been converted into a National Trust information centre; behind it a path climbs up through woods to Selworthy Beacon, whose 1013 ft summit gives superb views northwards across the Bristol Channel and inland over Exmoor.

Thatched cottages can also be seen in several neighbouring hamlets, including Allerford, where there is a packhorse bridge and a museum of rural life, and the long village of Bossington, which has a farm park. Bossington is also the starting place for walks to Hurlstone Point and Porlock Bay. At nearby Lynch there is a 16th-century chapel of ease, constructed for the convenience of parishioners living some distance from their parish church.

⑤ MINEHEAD
A long esplanade with many amusement parks, nearly a mile of sandy beach and a funfair are Minehead's most distinctive seaside features. But a walk through Blenheim Gardens, where Sunday concerts are held in summer, leads to the quieter, older part of the town, and to the harbour, which was busy with ships in the 17th century. Fishing trips and boat trips are available. The eve of May Day each year is the start of a three-day festival, in which the Sailors' Hobby Horse, shaped like a horse and draped with ribbons, dances around the streets accompanied by a drum. Rising up behind the harbour are the slopes of North Hill, where there are walks and a nature trail. The South West Coast Path climbs the hill at the

OLD MINEHEAD *The stone quay and whitewashed cottages by Minehead's harbour date from the 17th century, when local ships traded as far away as Africa and North America.*

STEAM POWER *The 20 mile West Somerset Railway runs along the coast, then inland between the Quantock and Brendon hills.*

start of its 600 mile course to Poole, in Dorset. A road leads over North Hill and on to Selworthy Beacon.

Minehead is the western end of the West Somerset Railway, whose steam trains stop at restored stations such as Blue Anchor and Watchet, on their way to Bishops Lydeard, near Taunton.

⑥ DUNSTER

The village's broad high street is lined with well-preserved buildings, some of which date from the 13th century, and is dominated by a 17th-century yarn market at one end and the towers and turrets of Dunster Castle at the other.

The castle, which stands on a steep hill, was remodelled in 1870, but still has an oak staircase and plasterwork dating from the 17th century. Magnolias, fuchsias and rhododendrons

grow on the slopes below the castle. Two gateways and part of the walls of the original village of Dunster are still standing, along with a 12th-century church, priory and gardens; nearby are an old tithe barn and monks' dovecote. By the river, and near the medieval Gallox Bridge, is a 17th-century watermill which produces flour. A 19th-century hymn writer, Mrs C.F. Alexander, is believed to have been inspired to write the hymn 'All Things Bright and Beautiful' while walking on Grabbist Hill, which rises behind Dunster.

The shingle-and-sand Dunster Beach is a mile from the village, and is overlooked by Conygar Hill, whose wooded summit is crowned with a folly tower. In Dunster Forest, south of the A396, several waymarked walks start from Nutcombe Bottom car park.

The Yarn Market, Dunster

SKYLINE BATTLEMENTS *Dunster village is dominated by the castle, which belonged to the Luttrell family from 1376 to 1976.*

⑦ BLUE ANCHOR

A long open beach of sand below a narrow strip of shingle is backed by cliffs in places, and elsewhere by rows of caravans. From the beach there are good views along the sweep of Blue Anchor Bay, and coast walks towards Dunster Beach to the north-west, and Watchet to the east. The Blue Anchor Railway Museum, which is open to the public on summer Sundays and Bank Holidays, tells the story of the Great Western

Railway. Visitors to nearby Home Farm can observe pygmy goats and other animals, and follow a woodland walk.

⑧ CLEEVE ABBEY

'Gate be open, shut to no honest person,' reads the greeting on the carved stone gatehouse of Cleeve Abbey (EH), which includes some of England's most complete cloister buildings, as well as the remains of the refectory and other living quarters. The abbey was once occupied by monks of the austere Cistercian order; an exhibition explains their way of life and the abbey's history.

⑨ WATCHET

The harbour town of Watchet is almost certainly the place where the poet Samuel Taylor Coleridge met an old sailor whose seafaring tales inspired *The Rime of the Ancient Mariner*. The Market House Museum tells the story of the ancient seaport, which was so important in Saxon times that it was made the site of a royal mint.

A 2½ mile walk from Watchet to Washford follows the track of a railway line built in the 1850s to provide a link between iron ore mines in the Brendon Hills and Watchet harbour.

⑩ ST AUDRIE'S BAY

A holiday camp stretches along the top of the high, crumbling, multicoloured cliffs that rise behind St Audrie's Bay, where a waterfall plunges onto shingle and sand. The beach is reached by a toll road leading to a car park. There are remains of a harbour where coal from South Wales was once landed.

PLACES TO SEE INLAND

Combe Sydenham Country Park, Monksilver, 5 miles S of Watchet. Courtroom of Elizabethan manor, woodland paths, restored corn mill.

Tropiquaria, 2 miles SW of Watchet. Birds, animals and reptiles in a jungle setting.

TOURIST INFORMATION

Minehead (01643) 702624

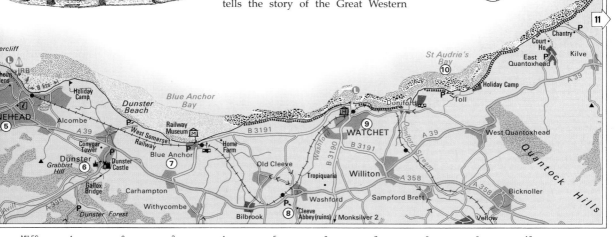

High cliffs and deep valleys on the edge of Exmoor

The best of the scenery is reserved for walkers on the ridge of steep cliffs that rises either side of Lynton and Lynmouth. Deep, wooded combes wriggle inland towards Exmoor and the land of the legendary Doones.

① COMBE MARTIN

Strung out along a deep valley, Combe Martin has a village street which at some 2 miles long is said to be the longest in England. The street leads down to a sand and shingle beach, on one side of which is a concrete path giving views of large clear rock pools. The village was formerly a centre of silver and lead mining, and a seafront museum explains its industrial and agricultural history.

British motorcycles and old garage equipment are displayed at the Combe Martin Motorcycle Collection, and on the town's outskirts is the Wildlife and Dinosaur Park with snow leopards and birds of prey, and life-size models of dinosaurs. A cliff walk leads eastwards past the secluded Wild Pear Beach and climbs to fine viewpoints at Little Hangman and 1043 ft Great Hangman.

A narrow road from Combe Martin to Hunter's Inn skirts the 1146 ft summit of Holdstone Down, which can be reached on foot from a roadside car park.

② HEDDON'S MOUTH

A mile walk down a deep valley, its sides covered with scree, leads to Heddon's Mouth, a small shingle cove that is dominated by the remains of an 18th-century limekiln. The kiln was used for burning limestone brought from Wales in an attempt to neutralise Exmoor's acid soil and make it suitable for agriculture. The walk starts at a car park at Hunter's Inn; a 2½ mile path eastwards from there to Woody Bay passes the site of a Roman fort constructed as a defence against tribes from Wales.

③ WOODY BAY

From the coast road a steep track zigzags down through dense oak woodland to the rocks and sand of Woody Bay. The walk takes about 25 minutes; wood warblers and pied flycatchers can be seen in the woods.

④ LEE BAY

High, tree-clad slopes shelter Lee Bay's beach of sand and large boulders, where a river seeps through the rocks. Fast-flowing tides can trap walkers exploring the foreshore, and strong currents sweep past the bay's headlands. The tiny cave-like chapel on the beach is owned by a Christian community which also owns nearby Lee Abbey, built in the 1840s as a private house and now a conference centre.

STONE SENTINEL *Castle Rock, the loftiest feature of the Valley of Rocks, plunges almost vertically into Wringcliff Bay.*

⑤ VALLEY OF ROCKS

East of Lee Bay, the toll road along the coast enters the 1½ mile long, riverless Valley of Rocks, named after its jagged pinnacles of sandstone. Castle Rock is said to be the site of an ancient castle haunted by the devil, and Rugged Jack, the main ridge separating the valley from the sea, is topped by tors and screes. Wild Cheviot goats graze on the cliffs, where sea birds such as guillemots and razorbills make their nests.

⑥ LYNTON

High cliffs and roads resembling mountain passes led the Victorians to call the area round Lynton and Lynmouth 'Little Switzerland'. In August 1952 Lynmouth suffered a disastrous flood which swept away trees, buildings and bridges, and claimed 34 lives. The Rhenish tower on the harbour wall is a

SITE OF A TRAGEDY *Lynmouth's harbour has been carefully rebuilt since 1952, when a cloudburst over Exmoor caused a huge surge of floodwater down the West and East Lyn.*

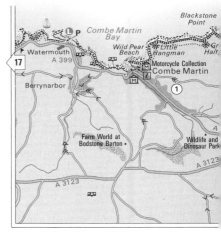

built in 1832 at the junction of the rivers is now a National Trust tea room and shop with a huge old Monterey pine on the lawn. Some of the many footpaths through the surrounding woods and farmland were originally mule tracks used by workers in the charcoal and tanning industries.

⑧ COUNTISBURY COMMON
A car park next to the A39 is the start of a 1½ mile walk across Countisbury Common to the lighthouse at Foreland Point. The walk passes through a churchyard to a hair-raising path cut into 991 ft gorse-covered cliffs and gives a bird's eye view of the Bristol Channel, and of Lynton to the west.

⑨ OARE
It was in the small, plain 12th-century Church of the Blessed Virgin Mary at Oare that Lorna Doone, the heroine of R.D. Blackmore's novel, was shot during her wedding by Carver Doone. Blackmore's grandfather was rector of Oare from 1809 to 1842, and the surrounding moors and valleys are rich in associations with the legendary 17th-century outlaws known as the Doones on whom Blackmore based his story.

The car park on the A39 at nearby County Gate is the starting point for a 3 mile nature trail to Glenthorne, where trees shelter the beach.

CLIFF RAILWAY *Linked by pulleys, the two cars each have a water tank that is filled at the top of the hill and emptied at the foot.*

reconstruction of a 19th-century tower used to supply a local home with sea water for baths. Boat trips and fishing trips are available.

Lynton, on a plateau 500 ft above the harbour town, is reached by a road with a one-in-four gradient or by a two-car cliff railway powered by two 700 gallon water tanks. The Lyn and Exmoor Museum, in a restored 17th-century cottage, has exhibitions of local history and traditional arts and crafts, and nearby Hollerday Hill has woodland walks and a path to the Valley of Rocks.

⑦ WATERSMEET
The East Lyn River joins the Hoaroak Water in a series of small waterfalls as it flows down a deep wooded gorge towards Lynmouth. A fishing lodge

---

PLACES TO SEE INLAND
Arlington Court (NT), 5 miles SE of Combe Martin. Regency house, Victorian garden, carriages, Shetland ponies.
Exmoor Steam Railway, 9 miles SE of Combe Martin. Narrow-gauge steam railway.
Farm World at Bodstone Barton, 3 miles SW of Combe Martin. Nature trail, horses, country museum, children's playgrounds.

TOURIST INFORMATION
Combe Martin (01271) 883319; Lynton (01598) 752225

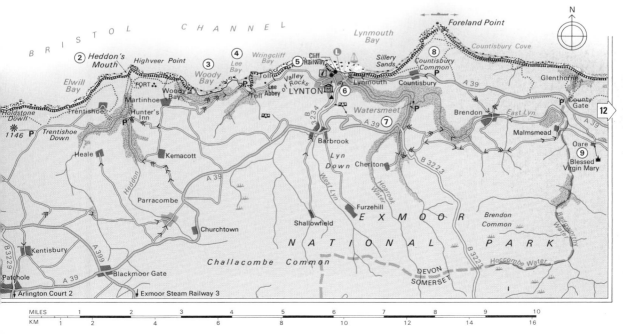

Surf-pounded beaches, and two sheltered harbours

Formidable cliffs on the Bristol Channel coast are broken by coves and sheltered inlets. South of Morte Point, surfers ride the long Atlantic rollers onto sandy beaches; the island of Lundy lies 20 miles offshore.

WATERMOUTH CASTLE *Sited by a narrow inlet, the castellated mansion is home to one of Devon's largest theme parks.*

① WATER MOUTH

Small boats fill the narrow sheltered inlet of Water Mouth, where low tide reveals sand and shingle. A short walk to the headland at the mouth of the inlet starts at the yacht club; beyond the headland, the path continues for a farther 1½ miles to Hele Bay. Watermouth Castle, built in 1825, has a museum of working Victorian pier machines, a smugglers' dungeon and a wide variety of children's amusements, including an 'Enchanted Walk' through the gardens.

The coast from Combe Martin, just east of Water Mouth, to Morte Point, is a voluntary marine reserve whose aim is to promote awareness of North Devon's marine wildlife, which includes dolphins, porpoises and basking sharks. Guided shore walks are available.

② HELE BAY

Caravans on the grassy cliffs overlook a beach of shingle and coarse sand where a stream flows into the sea. A path from the western end of the beach leads to Hillsborough Nature Reserve, which includes Bronze Age and Roman sites. A 16th-century watermill on the edge of the village of Hele has a restored 18 ft water wheel. It produces flour and is open to visitors in summer.

③ ILFRACOMBE

Ilfracombe's harbour, one of the few refuges for boats on this stretch of coast, was busy with fishing vessels long before the town became a holiday resort in Victorian times. St Nicholas's Chapel, on a crag at the harbour entrance, contains a small maritime display. Pleasure craft use the harbour, and in summer there are boat and fishing trips along the Exmoor coast, and day cruises to Swansea and Lundy.

The town is built on steep slopes that rise from a shore of rocks and coarse grey sand. At the Tunnels Beaches are two large tide-filled pools that were built in Victorian times for single-sex bathing, but are now open to all. Ilfracombe Museum, on the promenade, has displays of local and natural history, as well as agricultural and military exhibits. The Torrs Walk skirts the edge of clifftops west of the town; walkers can continue to Lee, 3 miles away, along a track which was once the main route between Ilfracombe and Lee.

To the south of Ilfracombe, the Cairn Nature Reserve consists of 2 miles of disused railway line and the wooded slopes surrounding the rocky outcrop of Cairn Top. Jays, buzzards and woodpeckers may be seen there, along with green hairstreak and painted lady butterflies. At nearby Bicclescombe Park are a restored 18th-century watermill, water gardens and a boating lake.

④ LEE BAY

The small scattered village of Lee sits in a deep wooded vale known as Fuchsia Valley because of its abundance of fuchsias. A stream runs down from the valley to Lee Bay, a cove of rocks, seaweed and low-tide sand, which was once used regularly by smugglers.

⑤ MORTEHOE

Mortehoe's 13th-century St Mary Magdalene Church has a barrel roof and fine Tudor bench ends. The village, perched on a hill on the edge of Woolacombe, is the starting point for walks over the headland to Morte Point. From there a 2 mile stretch of the coast path leads round Rockham Bay, where steps descend to a strip of rocks and a sandy beach, and on to Bull Point lighthouse.

⑥ WOOLACOMBE

The spectacular sweep of Woolacombe Sand, popular with surfers and swimmers, is backed by high dunes. A car park runs the length of the dunes, and walkways lead across them to 2 miles of open beach. Barricane Beach, north of Woolacombe village, consists almost entirely of shells carried over by sea currents from the Caribbean. Putsborough Sand, another surfing beach, at the southern end of Morte Bay, is reached by a narrow lane from Croyde.

⑦ CROYDE

A stream runs next to the high street in Croyde, whose thatched cottages and shops selling clotted cream attract many visitors. The village's Gem, Rock and Shell Museum has exhibits from all over the world. Small, sandy Croyde Bay is often used for surfing, but swimming can be dangerous at low tide and near the rocks. The village also has a leisure pool with water rides. The National Trust car park at the northern end of Croyde Bay is the start of a popu-

UNDER THE LANTERN *The cliffs form a dramatic backdrop to Ilfracombe's harbour. Since 1320 the Chapel of St Nicholas, above the pier, has shone a lantern to guide mariners.*

LIFE ON LUNDY ISLAND

Lundy means 'puffin island' in Norse, but the bird is just one of the 280 species recorded on the island. Sika deer, wild goats, ponies and Soay sheep live there, and grey seals bob up out of the sea. The centre of the 3 mile long island is a flat plateau about 400ft high, with cliffs on all sides. Lundy's own ship, *Oldenburg*, ferries visitors from Bideford all year round, and from Ilfracombe in summer. Owned by the National Trust, the island has a castle built by Henry III in 1244. The waters around Lundy form Britain's first statutory marine nature reserve, where fishing and watersports are restricted by bye-laws and a system of 'zoning' to protect the wide variety of plants and animals that flourish there.

The puffin gave Lundy Island its name.

lar 1 mile clifftop walk to Baggy Point, where gulls, fulmars, shags and kestrels breed on the steeper slopes. Baggy Erratic, under the low cliff at Baggy Point, is a 50 ton boulder carried by glaciers from western Scotland during the last Ice Age.

⑧ SAUNTON SANDS

The 3 mile expanse of sand is backed by the grass-tufted dunes of Braunton Burrows and dominated by a large white hotel on the cliffs at the northern end. Surfing, watersports and sand-yachting are popular, but strong currents round Bideford Bar make swimming unsafe at the southern end of the beach, and the rocks below Saunton Down should be avoided.

⑨ BRAUNTON BURROWS

A vast wilderness of sand dunes, some 100ft high, lies behind Saunton Sands. The southern part is a national nature reserve, and among the 400 species of flowering plants that grow there are purple thyme and yellow birdsfoot, as well as the rarer sand pansy and sand toadflax. Newts and frogs gather round

ponds that have been dug to ensure that water is present in summer. The dunes are occasionally used for military training; at such times access is restricted.

⑩ BRAUNTON

A wide main road, lined with shops selling surfing equipment, contrasts with the narrow, quieter streets in the old part of Braunton, said to be the largest village in England. The Braunton Museum explains the life and work of local farmers and fishermen. Close by is St Brannock's Church, whose oldest parts date from the 13th century.

South-west of the village is Braunton Great Field, where narrow strips of cultivated land, separated by lines of grass, are a rare surviving example of the medieval open-field system. Braunton Marsh, south of the Great Field, was drained in the early 19th century and is now grazed by cattle. The marsh has several small circular buildings, or linhays, built to provide shelter for livestock in the 19th century.

⑪ BARNSTAPLE

The 'capital' of north Devon, on the tidal River Taw, was well established by the time of the Norman conquest, and in the late 16th century became a major port, trading with the new settlements in America. The town's history is chronicled at a heritage centre housed in St Anne's Chapel, one of the town's oldest buildings. It was used as a school from

the 16th century until 1910 and contains displays of 17th-century schooling. A Heritage Trail starting at the chapel passes a Norman castle mound, the 13th-century Long Bridge, and almshouses founded in 1627. The Pannier Market, a general market open on Tuesdays, Fridays and Saturdays, takes its name from the panniers from which market traders once sold their wares. The Museum on the Square displays local pottery, and uniforms and equipment of the Royal Devon Yeomanry.

At the Butterfly House, north-west of the town, visitors can see eggs, caterpillars and chrysalises, as well as tropical butterflies. Barnstaple is the centre of the Tarka Trail, a 180 mile walk through country that inspired Henry Williamson's 1927 novel *Tarka the Otter*. The trail traces a rough figure of eight, passing through Lynton, Woolacombe and Braunton Burrows, and reaching as far south as Okehampton.

PLACES TO SEE INLAND

Brannams Pottery, 2 miles SW of Barnstaple. Tours and museum; visitors can make pots.

Cobbaton Combat Collection, 5 miles SE of Barnstaple. Includes World War II armoury.

Marwood Hill, 3 miles N of Barnstaple. Gardens with lake, camelias, rare shrubs and exotic trees.

TOURIST INFORMATION

Barnstaple (01271) 388583; Ilfracombe (01271) 863001; Woolacombe (01271) 870553 (summer)

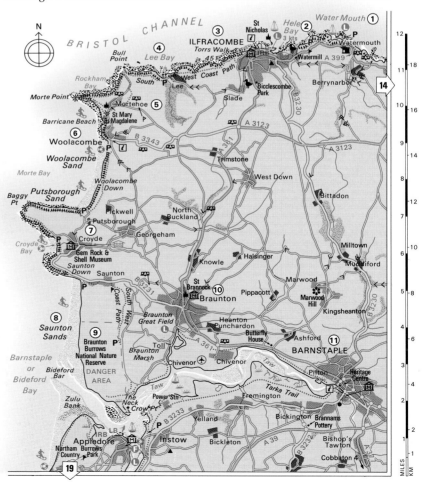

Cobbled streets in Clovelly flanked by dramatic cliffs

One of the few roads to the coast in this part of Devon leads to the pretty harbour village of Clovelly, which must be explored on foot. To the east, in contrast to the grandeur of lofty cliffs, are the sands of Westward Ho!

① HARTLAND QUAY

Dark jagged cliffs slide into the sea at Hartland Quay, whose small harbour was built by Raleigh, Drake and Hawkins as a safe haven for boats on this hazardous stretch of coast. The harbour was almost destroyed by storms in the 19th century. The only buildings are a hotel converted from coastguard cottages, and a museum devoted to seafaring history and local wrecks, some of which can be seen at low tide.

The South West Coast Path follows high cliffs southwards to Speke's Mill Mouth, where a waterfall tumbles in stages down to a pebble beach. Walkers should keep to marked paths, as the unstable cliffs can be dangerous.

The road to Hartland Quay passes through the hamlet of Stoke, where the 14th-century St Nectan's Church has a 130ft tower that was built as a landmark for sailors. In the churchyard is Stranger's Hill, where some of the victims of local shipwrecks were buried.

Nearby Hartland Abbey, a family home since the 16th century, contains Victorian and Edwardian photographs, and has a woodland walk through the grounds to the coast. The house, open on Wednesday and Sunday afternoons in summer, was extensively rebuilt in the 18th century on the site of a monastery founded soon after 1157.

② HARTLAND POINT

A toll road leads to the craggy headland that the Romans called the 'Promontory of Hercules'. Almost hidden on a plateau near the base of the cliffs is a white lighthouse with a helicopter pad.

From the headland's car park, walkers can follow the clifftop path eastwards, passing a Ministry of Defence radar station and the pebble beach of Shipload Bay. Beyond the bay the path continues along 6 miles of coast, accessible only on foot, to Clovelly.

③ CLOVELLY

Donkeys and sledges are the only form of transport in Clovelly's steep, cobbled main street, flanked by whitewashed cottages. The street leads down to a small harbour, once the base of a fishing fleet, which prospered in the 18th and

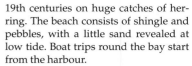

HARTLAND POINT *From its cliff perch, the lighthouse sends out one of the strongest beams on the British coast. The point shelters Shipload Bay from Atlantic gales.*

19th centuries on huge catches of herring. The beach consists of shingle and pebbles, with a little sand revealed at low tide. Boat trips round the bay start from the beach.

Cars must be left in the car park outside the village, where a visitor centre has an audiovisual display explaining Clovelly's history. In summer a Land-Rover ferries visitors between the top of the village and the harbour, using a route that avoids the main street.

If time seems to have stood still in Clovelly, it is mainly due to Christine Hamlyn, who owned the village from 1884 to 1936 and devoted her life to protecting its buildings and beauty. Descendants of the Hamlyn family live at Clovelly Court, on the edge of the village, which is not open to visitors.

The most attractive way to approach Clovelly is along the 3 mile wooded toll road known as the Hobby Drive, which leaves the A39 at Hobby Lodge. At The Milky Way, 1½ miles to the south of the village, visitors can see birds of prey and displays of falconry, as well as farm animals and sheep dogs.

④ BUCK'S MILLS

The narrow village street leads down to a pebble-and-sand beach and the ruins of a large ivy-covered limekiln. According to legend, the villagers of Buck's Mills are descendants of the survivors from a 15th-century Spanish shipwreck. The tree-clad cliffs that rise up behind the beach extend westwards as far as Clovelly, and eastwards for nearly 2 miles. To the west of the village, the coast path passes through Buck's and Keivill's Wood, part of an extensive woodland area that supports stunted mature oaks and mature sycamores.

⑤ WESTWARD HO!

Founded in 1863, Westward Ho! is a relative newcomer in an area of old-established towns and villages. The small resort, which has holiday camps, beach huts and amusements, takes its name from Charles Kingsley's seafaring adventure story, written in 1855. Rising to the west is the bracken-covered

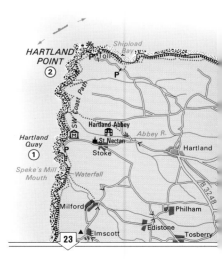

SLOPING STEEPLY *Whitewashed cottages line Clovelly's main street, built on a dry stream bed, and known as Up-a-long or Down-a-long according to which way one is going.*

Bridge, which is 677 ft in length with 24 arches, has spanned the Torridge since the Middle Ages. It has now been joined by a second road bridge that bypasses the town to the north.

On Tuesday and Saturday mornings local artefacts and produce are sold at Bideford's Pannier Market, continuing a tradition that dates back to 1272, when the first market charter was granted. Eight cannons in Victoria Park, known as the Armada Guns, are said to have come from a 16th-century Spanish wreck. A cycleway, forming part of the 180 mile Tarka Trail, through countryside that inspired Henry Williamson's novel *Tarka the Otter*, follows the course of a disused railway line to the north and south of the town.

⑧ INSTOW

A wide expanse of sand, backed by dunes at the northern end, stretches out in front of the peaceful village of Instow, from where there are views across the sheltered Torridge estuary to Appledore. The village is popular with waterskiers, sailors and artists.

PLACES TO SEE INLAND

Dartington Crystal, Great Torrington, 7 miles SE of Bideford. Factory visits, shop.

Rosemoor Garden, nr Great Torrington, 8 miles SE of Bideford. RHS garden.

Tapeley Park, 2 miles S of Instow. Italian gardens; 17th-century house with collection of William Morris furniture.

TOURIST INFORMATION

Bideford (01237) 477676

Kipling Tor, where footpaths offer a choice of walks. The hill was named after Rudyard Kipling, who was a pupil at the United Services College in Westward Ho! from 1878 to 1882, and recalled his time there in *Stalky and Co*.

North of the town is a 2 mile sweep of sand backed by a huge bank of pebbles. Behind the pebble bank is Northam Burrows Country Park, an area of sand dunes, salt marsh and pasture populated in winter by a wide variety of birds, including cormorants, eider ducks and Brent geese.

⑥ APPLEDORE

Tudor buildings constructed from ships' timbers stand alongside colour-washed fishermen's cottages in Appledore, whose seafaring traditions go back more than a thousand years. Boatbuilding has been important there since the 15th century, and continues at a

yard on the water's edge. The quay, used by many sailing ships until the 1930s, overlooks a muddy estuary where strong currents make bathing unsafe. The North Devon Maritime Museum explains the nautical history of the area. Fishing trips for cod, bass, skate and other fish start from the harbour; in summer, a ferry crosses the estuary to Instow. A path from the old custom house and lifeboat station leads to Northam Burrows Country Park.

⑦ BIDEFORD

A long quay, built in the 17th century when wool was imported from Spain, recalls the days when Bideford was one of Britain's busiest ports. Fishing and cargo boats, and pleasure craft, come and go from the quay, and there are day excursions to Lundy Island throughout the year. The Long

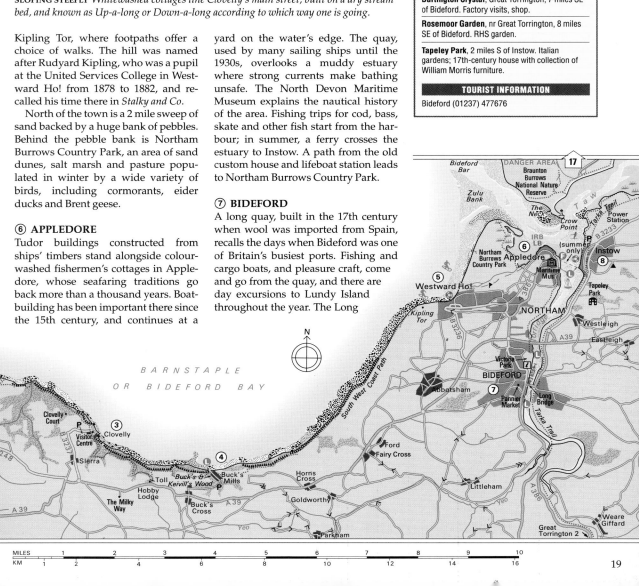

PROUD VICTIMS OF THE CRUEL SEA

*F*ROM LAND'S END TO SCAPA FLOW, Britain's coastal waters are littered with shipwrecks. Driven by the fury of Atlantic gales onto the deadly reefs of the west coast, or foundering in the shifting sandbanks and icy waters of the North Sea, generations of ships have met their doom. Many shipwrecks are from the days of sail, but the toll did not end with the arrival of steam: the seabed is scattered with liners, steamers and battleships, as well as Spanish galleons, English men-of-war, clippers and fishing smacks.

Several dramatic wrecks in recent years have involved oil tankers. When the *Torrey Canyon* was gashed open on a reef off Bryher on the Isles of Scilly in 1967, some of the tanker's 120 000 tons of crude oil drifted onto Cornish beaches, even though the wreck was bombed to burn off the oil flow. In 1993, the *Braer*, carrying 84 000 tons of oil, was stranded in rough seas off Shetland; an ecological disaster threatened as oil started to seep from the hull, before the ship finally sank and broke up on the seabed.

Many wrecks and wreck sites provide as much historical insight as castles or battlefield sites on land, as shown by the discovery of Henry VIII's flagship *Mary Rose*, which sank off Southsea, Hampshire, in 1545, while engaging the French fleet. After the main wreck site was located about 1970, more than 16 000 items were brought ashore, including pewter plates and cutlery, clothes and surgical instruments; the artefacts combined to convey a vivid impression of life aboard a 16th-century warship. Scientific analysis even identified the maggots and vermin that infested the food stores.

Particularly hazardous areas for shipping include the Isles of Scilly, the rocky northern shores of Devon and Cornwall, and the waters around the Goodwin Sands, a 12-mile-long sandbar off the Kent coast. Countless vessels have foundered on these treacherous shifting sands and been sucked down,

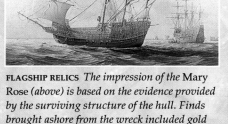

FLAGSHIP RELICS *The impression of the* Mary Rose *(above) is based on the evidence provided by the surviving structure of the hull. Finds brought ashore from the wreck included gold coins such as nobles and sovereigns (top left), a brass syringe and bleeding bowl (top right), and wooden blocks from the rigging (right).*

STRANDED ON THE SANDS *The South Goodwin lightship capsized on the Goodwin Sands during a gale in November 1954, with the loss of her crew of seven. By next morning the ship was half buried in the sands.*

FATE OF AN EAST INDIAMAN *Many ships of the East India Company, which plied the trade routes to the East in the 17th and 18th centuries, were wrecked in British waters. The* Halsewell *(above) sank off the Isle of Purbeck in 1786.*

never to be seen again, giving the Goodwin Sands the gruesome nickname of 'The Ship Swallower'.

The sea continues to claim a regular toll of victims. A familiar pattern was repeated in December 1982 when the Dutch coaster *Johanna* was pounded by furious seas and broke up on the jagged reefs below Hartland Point in north Devon. Though there was little of any genuine value aboard, a crowd stripped the vessel of everything that could be removed, following the tradition of the infamous 'wreckers' of earlier centuries. The use of lights to lure ships onto rocks is not well documented, but there is no doubt that the cargoes of wrecks were rapaciously plundered. When the East Indiaman *Amsterdam* ran aground near Hastings in 1749, after leaving the Netherlands with a cargo that included 28 chests of silver ingots, hundreds of people descended on the wreck in search of rich pickings. The silver was found and returned to the Netherlands, but some items disappeared, including thousands of boxes of French wine. New plundering of the *Amsterdam* by modern-day treasure-hunters

PERILOUS ISLAND REEFS *The barque* Maipu *ran aground in 1879 off Bryher, in Scilly, notorious as a sailors' graveyard.*

was among the thefts that prompted the introduction in 1973 of the Protection of Wrecks Act. Since then underwater archaeologists have identified more than 40 historic wreck sites, which can be explored only by special licence.

Some sites have been found by chance after lying unnoticed for centuries on the seabed. A 16th-century Portuguese vessel carrying a cargo of silver and copper ingots was discovered in 1981 at Mount Bay, Cornwall, after a holidaymaker picked up an ingot on the beach. In 1974 members of the Dover subaqua club came across Bronze Age artefacts in the waters outside Dover harbour. Other divers and fishermen have made similar discoveries. Finds of any items from wrecks, valuable or not, are required by law to be reported to the Receiver of Wreck, who can be contacted through coastguard centres.

ATLANTIC BREAKERS *North Cornwall's long list of shipping tragedies grew in May 1995, when the 137-year-old* Maria Asumpta *was wrecked off Padstow (above), with the loss of three lives. Farther north on the same stretch of coast, the battered shell of the grain carrier* Johanna *(left) was still visible a year after she foundered near Hartland Point in 1982.*

Rocky ramparts between the beaches of Bude Bay

The mighty Atlantic pounds the crumbling cliffs of this harsh coast, where hundreds of ships perished in the days of sail, but there are wide expanses of smooth sand onto which surfers can ride the rolling waves.

① WELCOMBE MOUTH

A steep lane, narrowing to a bumpy track, leads to a slate-grey shingle beach framed by cliffs. On a bright summer's day, with the sea washing gently over the rocks, it is hard to imagine the cove as it was in the 19th century – a grave-yard for ships and a haunt of wreckers. In the days of sail, any vessel coming too close to this coast with an onshore wind was almost certain to founder on the jagged rocks.

Set back from the shore is the small nature reserve of Welcombe and Marsland Valleys, whose forested slopes are alive with butterflies in summer. A footpath runs southwards from Welcombe Mouth to the rock and pebble beach at Marsland Mouth, where a stream marks the boundary between Devon and Cornwall. The coast path between here and Bude, some 9 miles away, has many steep gradients, but offers superb views over Bude Bay.

② MORWENSTOW

A colourful 19th-century churchman, Robert Stephen Hawker, dominates the history of this isolated hamlet. Hawker was vicar of Morwenstow for 40 years, and achieved some success as a poet. He built the vicarage, whose curious chimneys represent the towers of churches he had known.

The sturdy wooden hut in which Hawker wrote some of his poems can be reached down 17 steps from the top of precipitous Vicarage Cliff.

The fine Norman Church of St Morwenna, notable for its stone carvings and 16th-century carved bench ends, is dedicated to a 9th-century Celtic saint. More than 40 seamen are buried in its churchyard, and the figurehead of the *Caledonia*, wrecked in September 1843, is a memorial to some of them. The land between the church and the cliffs is National Trust property dedicated to Hawker's memory.

③ STANBURY MOUTH

The secluded beach is reached by a 15 minute walk from the car park, along a path overshadowed by the great white dish aerials of a Ministry of Defence communications tracking establishment. The grassy path, lined with banks of gorse, follows the course of a bubbling stream. As the descent grows steeper, the path becomes rocky, leading over several makeshift bridges as it twists down to the shingle shore.

④ DUCKPOOL

A pool of fresh water, contained by a natural dam of pebbles, and fed by a stream from the Coombe Valley, gives this cove its name. A National Trust car park overlooks a sandy, shingle-backed beach littered with evidence of rock falls from the crumbling cliffs. Swimming is unsafe from parts of the beach.

A mile inland is the enchanting village of Coombe, a huddle of thatched cottages reached across a ford. The woodlands of Coombe Valley support a rich variety of plants, birds and small mammals. Walks start from the car park at the east end of the valley. Nearby is Stowe Barton Farm (NT), built in 1793 using materials from the 17th-century mansion of Stowe, which stood on this site; it is not open to the public.

⑤ SANDY MOUTH

The popular holiday beach, backed by high, seamed cliffs, is reached by a short stroll from a National Trust car park and cafe. At low water the sands run southwards all the way to Bude. Walkers must check the state of the tide before setting out, because the unstable cliffs offer very few escape routes.

NATURAL SCULPTURES *At Sandy Mouth, jagged pinnacles of rock, shaped by the sea and the winds, rise starkly above the sands like the gaunt ruins of an ancient abbey.*

CANAL BY THE SEA *Lobster pots stand on the quay of the 35 mile Bude Canal, of which just 2 miles are navigable today.*

⑥ NORTHCOTT MOUTH

A large parking area overlooks an isolated beach, whose sand is strewn with large heaps of dark, rocky rubble from cliff landslips. Northcott Mouth is an easy walk over the cliffs from Bude. It can also be approached by road from Poughill, pronounced 'Poffle', whose 14th-century Church of St Olaf is notable for its colourful interior and its 78 carved-oak bench ends.

⑦ STRATTON

During the Civil War, Stratton was the base of Royalist forces who won a victory at nearby Stamford Hill in 1643. Surrounded by new buildings, the old

---

ECCENTRIC POET-PRIEST

The Reverend Robert Stephen Hawker, vicar of Morwenstow from 1834 to 1875, made a lasting contribution to the Church by originating the Harvest Festival. Inspired by Cornish legend, and by the many shipwrecks along this coast, he composed poems, and smoked opium, in a hut on the cliffside. Hawker was known for salvaging corpses from shipwrecks to give them a Christian burial.

Reverend Robert Hawker and his driftwood hut.

---

village of thatched houses survives, including the Tree Inn, which was the headquarters of the Royalist commander, Sir Bevil Grenville. Grenville is not as well remembered today as his servant, the so-called 'Cornish giant' Anthony Payne, who was 7ft 4in tall, and whose life-size portrait can be seen in the inn's courtyard.

⑧ BUDE

Dolphins can sometimes be seen off the flat sandy beaches of Summerleaze and Crooklets, from where, at low tide, there are exhilarating walks along the shore. Between the two beaches is a natural seawater pool washed daily by the tides. Although best known as a beach resort, especially for surfing, Bude is a quiet town, separated from the sea by a wide band of springy turf. Bude Castle, designed by the 19th-century inventor Sir Goldsworthy Gurney, and now used as local council offices, is thought to have been the first building in Britain constructed on sand, using a concrete raft. Gurney's achievements are explained at Bude Museum, which also has exhibits on Bude Canal.

⑨ BUDE CANAL

The sea lock marking the entrance to Bude Canal is one of the last working locks of its kind in Britain. It is also the only working lock on this remarkable waterway, which ran for 35 miles from Bude to Launceston and rose to a height of 350ft in 6 miles. The change in levels was achieved by inclined planes, or ramps, between each different level and wheeled tub-boats which were pulled up the ramps on metal rails.

Opened in 1823, Bude Canal was the longest tub-boat canal ever built. It carried lime-rich sea sand for fertilising inland farmlands, and on the return trips brought oats and slate to the trading vessels in Bude harbour. Today the waterway is used by rowing boats, canoes and small pleasure craft. It is navigable only as far as Helebridge, whose picnic area and old wharf

buildings can be reached by a 2 mile walk from Bude, which leads past the Bude Marshes Nature Reserve.

⑩ WIDEMOUTH SAND

This holiday beach, set in a wide curving bay of flat sand with a domed headland on each side, is popular with families and surfers. A car park on Penhalt Cliff to the south gives an almost aerial panorama of the bay.

⑪ MILLOOK HAVEN

The narrow undulating road from Widemouth winds steeply through a series of S-bends to Millook, which consists of no more than a few houses and a tiny cove. The peaceful, pebbly beach,

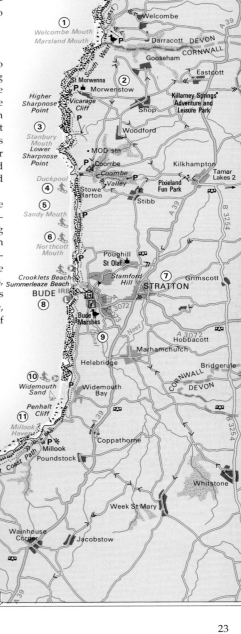

THE EVER-CHANGING COASTLINE *At Sharpnose Point, near Morwenstow, boulders strewn at the foot of crumbling cliffs and outcrops of harder rock formed into tiny islands show that the northern Cornish coast is gradually losing ground to the rollers' pounding.*

approached through a wooden gate, is notable for the zigzagging layers of rock visible on the cliff face, caused by massive upheavals of the earth millions of years ago. There is parking space at the roadside for only two or three cars.

⑫ CRACKINGTON HAVEN

The shingle and sand beach at the foot of towering, unstable cliffs is peaceful and unspoiled. Set back from the coast, at the end of a no-through road, with views of the sea across a well-wooded stretch of countryside, stands the Church of St Gennys, whose tower has served as a landmark for centuries. The graveyard has memorials to some of the seamen who, in spite of the landmark, lost their lives in the tempestuous waters below, including the crew of the Swedish brigantine *William*, wrecked in the haven in 1894, and seven others

who were drowned six years later when storms claimed the steamer *City of Vienna* and the barque *Capricornia*.

The clifftop path from Crackington Haven to Cambeak and beyond provides some of the most majestic coastal scenery in Britain, but walkers must take extreme care to keep clear of the crumbling cliff edge.

Wave-lashed crags beside the palace of King Arthur

Legends about a king and knights enrich this wild, rugged coast, with its high cliffs and bays reached only on foot. The fishing village of Port Isaac is one of the few places where buildings run right down to the sea.

① THE STRANGLES

The path to this remote beach with its sinister name winds steeply down 450 ft of rocky hillside, zigzagging in the last stages. Low tide in the bay reveals large patches of sand between mounds of rocks, but swift currents and strong undertows make swimming unsafe. In the 1820s more than 20 sailing ships perished in one year on the rocky shore.

The 15 minute walk to the beach starts opposite a parking area just south of solitary Trevigue Farm. An alternative walk follows the clifftop southwards for about a mile to High Cliff, Cornwall's highest cliff at 731 ft, from where there are spectacular views.

② BOSCASTLE

The narrow, winding inlet of Boscastle harbour provides rare shelter for boats on this intimidating stretch of coast. Tourism is the main activity today, but in the 19th century Boscastle was a busy commercial port, importing coal and timber and exporting slate and china clay. Ships had to be towed in by eight-man rowing boats because of the dangerous harbour entrance. A blowhole in the outer harbour sometimes sends out plumes of spray.

A mile walk eastwards along the South West Coast Path leads to Pentargon, a small bay where a waterfall cascades over sheer black cliffs.

③ ROCKY VALLEY

The 10 minute stroll down deep Rocky Valley, which starts east of Bossiney on the Boscastle to Tintagel road, begins through a small forest before becoming more rocky as it descends. Two bridges cross a stream which deepens to meet a stony cove between seamed cliffs. The cove's many large, flat stones make it an ideal spot for picnics.

④ BOSSINEY HAVEN

The clifftop gives spectacular views of Bossiney Haven – a small, sheltered beach that is sandy at low tide and surrounded by a semicircle of cliffs. The view alone is worth the 10 minute walk along a signposted path from the village of Bossiney, but only fit and agile visitors should attempt the hazardous scramble down to the beach.

TINTAGEL'S OLD POST OFFICE *Stout chimney-stacks cap the crazily irregular roof of the 14th-century manor house.*

⑤ TINTAGEL

Tintagel fully exploits the legends made popular by Lord Tennyson's mid 19th-century *Idylls of the King*, which made much of the village's supposed links with King Arthur and his Knights of the Round Table. Nothing, however, can trivialise the awesome impact of the reputed site of Arthur's court – a craggy headland, called The Island, but in fact connected to the mainland by a strip of wave-lashed land.

A winding wooden stairway of some 300 steps, which can be treacherous when wet, clings to the sheer rock face as it climbs to the top of The Island. Ruins rising from the steep slopes are those of the 13th-century Tintagel Castle (EH). There is no evidence that Arthur actually lived there; however, the 'island' fortress had been a stronghold of Cornish kings for centuries before the castle was built, and even earlier may have been the site of a Roman signal station and a Christian monastery. There is a good view of The Island from the clifftop to the south, where the Norman Church of St Materiana stands apart from the rest of the village of Tintagel. In the church is an inscribed Roman milestone.

The weather-beaten Old Post Office (NT), a manor-in-miniature on the village's main street, dates from the 14th century and was first used as a post office during the 19th century. King Arthur's Great Halls nearby were built in the 1930s from 52 different types of Cornish granite, and have more than 70 stained-glass windows telling the story of Arthur and his knights.

⑥ TREBARWITH STRAND

Two large car parks on the approach to Trebarwith Strand testify to the popularity of its sandy beach. The sand lies beyond a scattering of large, lumpy rocks; signs warn of the potential danger to swimmers, and of the risk of being swept off the rocks by giant waves. The crumbling cliffs that back the beach were once quarried for slate.

Nearly 2 miles inland, near the hamlet of Trewarmett, is a picnic area from where a short nature trail leads through a disused slate quarry.

⑦ DELABOLE

The vast crater at Delabole, 500 ft deep and half a mile wide, is a slate quarry that dates back to the 11th century and has been worked continuously since the early 17th century. A pool of vivid blue-green, the colour created by natural minerals, lies at the bottom of the crater, and a fenced walk runs for 1½ miles round the quarry. Until the railway arrived in the 1890s, slate was shipped out from Portgaverne and Boscastle; now it is moved by road.

North-east of the quarry are the 10 tall wind turbines of Delabole Wind Farm, which produces enough power each year to meet more than half of Delabole's and Camelford's annual electrical consumption. The wind farm has a visitor centre.

A KING AND HIS CASTLE

The legend of King Arthur is a fascinating blend of fact and fiction. According to the 12th-century writer Geoffrey of Monmouth, Arthur was crowned King of the Britons at the age of 15 and won many battles against the invading Anglo-Saxons. Many historians believe that the real King Arthur was a 6th-century British chieftain and was probably born in the West Country. The deeds of chivalry and heroism associated with the king and his Knights of the Round Table stem from the works of later writers, notably Sir Thomas Malory's *Le Morte D'Arthur*, published in 1485, and Tennyson's *Idylls of the King*.

A 14th-century stone carving represents the shadowy Arthur.

Tintagel Castle was, according to legend, the seat of King Arthur and his knights.

HAVEN FROM THE WAVES *Port Isaac's tight huddle of buildings flank a maze of tiny lanes and stepped paths leading down to the harbour, where fresh fish is regularly sold.*

⑪ PORT ISAAC

Unusually for the north Cornwall coast, Port Isaac is a working fishing village where fish are sold in the cellars and restaurants beside the small, 60 ft wide slipway. Cars can be parked on the beach at low tide, but the best approach to Port Isaac is on foot from a car park above the village, taking the route which overlooks the sea and the headland to the west. Boat trips and fishing trips for mackerel, cod and other fish start from the harbour. Flower-filled hanging baskets decorate the cottages in Port Isaac's maze of narrow alleyways; among these is Squeeze-ee-belly Alley, whose name may strike a warning note about the dangers of too many creamy Cornish delicacies.

⑧ CAMELFORD

The small market town of Camelford is a good centre from which to explore both the coast, to the west, and Bodmin Moor, to the south-east. The North Cornwall Museum in the town centre has a reconstruction of a late 19th-century moorland cottage, as well as old tools and domestic equipment and a collection of Cornish and Devonshire pottery. Just north of Camelford is a museum of the history of cycling.

Camelford is often claimed to be the site of King Arthur's Camelot and near Slaughterbridge, north of the town, is an inscribed stone about 8 ft long called Arthur's Grave. The slab can be reached by a slippery path leading off the marked private road to a trout farm at Worthyvale Manor.

⑨ TREGARDOCK BEACH

Secluded Tregardock Beach, with its great slabs of shining grey rocks and low-tide sand, can be reached only on foot. The path to the beach starts from a lane at Tregardock, where roadside parking is very limited, and descends a gentle, gorse-covered valley which becomes rocky, and is slippery in wet weather. A notice warns of hazardous swimming and unstable cliffs.

To the south, the path along the top of the cliffs to Portgaverne passes a collapsed tunnel known as Barrett's Zawn, through which slate was once hauled.

⑩ PORTGAVERNE

The village lies close to a natural harbour protected by long arms of rocky land. In the 19th century Portgaverne was a thriving fishing port, and its fish cellars, or 'pilchard palaces', processed up to 1000 tons of pilchards in a season. The stone buildings still stand behind the pebbled beach. A hundred ships a year used to call at Portgaverne to pick up slate from the Delabole quarry.

Tourism is now the village's main business, and most of the pilchard cellars have been converted into visitor accommodation. Parking is limited, and it is advisable to use the car park on top of the hill at nearby Port Isaac.

PLACES TO SEE INLAND

The Tamar Otter Sanctuary, North Petherwin, 15 miles E of Boscastle. Otters in natural enclosures, as well as waterfowl, owls and deer.

TOURIST INFORMATION

Bude (01288) 354240; Camelford (01840) 212954 (summer)

Headlands and wide bays near the Camel estuary

North Cornwall's rugged coast of high cliffs is broken by enticing bays onto which Atlantic rollers break. Broad sands line the sheltered mouth of the River Camel, bright with boats during the holiday season.

① TREYARNON
A lane leads north-west from the B3276 towards a small hamlet, beyond which high headlands enclose a broad and shallow sandy bay. Slabs of dark rock line much of the beach, and low tide reveals a large natural pool in the rocks on the northern side of the bay. Ample car parking makes the beach popular with young families. Conditions are often ideal for surfing. Strong currents can make swimming hazardous.

② CONSTANTINE BAY
Marram grass and tamarisk shrubs cover Constantine Bay's sand dunes, and long, flat, dark-grey rocks edge the sandy beach, creating numerous pools at low tide. Bathers and surfers should beware of strong currents. The South West Coast Path skirts the popular bay and heads northwards over low cliffs towards the quieter beach at Booby's Bay before continuing to Trevose Head.

③ TREVOSE HEAD
A toll road leads to a jagged headland, where grassy picnic areas provide magnificent views north-east to Pentire Point and south to Newquay. At the tip of Trevose Head, the round white tower of a lighthouse stands on sheer granite cliffs, its lantern 204 ft above the sea.

Padstow's lifeboat is based in rocky Mother Ivey's Bay, on the eastern side of the headland. The station was moved

HEAD LIGHT *The gleaming lighthouse on Trevose Head, built in 1847, has a beam that is visible 27 miles out to sea.*

here in 1967, after Padstow had lost three lifeboats on the treacherous sandbars of the Camel estuary.

④ HARLYN BAY
A stream trickles out into the popular half-mile sandy crescent of Harlyn Bay, on the sheltered, eastern side of Trevose Head. The beach is backed by dunes and fields, and low cliffs stretch eastwards towards Trevone. Harlyn Bay was the site of an Iron Age cemetery, relics of which can be seen at the Royal Cornwall Museum in Truro.

⑤ TREVONE
A large beach of flat, firm sand is the focal point of the quiet village, bordered to the west by Newtrain Bay, where rock pools form at low tide. One of these pools, some 500 yd west of the car park beside Trevone beach, is about 6 ft deep and its still water makes it popular with swimmers. Strong tides can make bathing in the sea hazardous. A clifftop walk leads north past Round Hole, a collapsed sea cave.

⑥ HAWKER'S COVE
Low tide exposes wide stretches of sands on the western side of the Camel estuary, where Hawker's Cove is a popular place from which to watch pleasure craft negotiating their way past the Doom Bar sandbank. The coast path from Padstow heads north to Stepper Point, a lofty promontory crowned with a tower built as a landmark for sailors.

⑦ PADSTOW
The popular holiday resort retains the character of a working fishing port. The 15th-century Church of St Petroc stands amid Padstow's network of narrow streets, which converge on the harbour, a pleasing clutter of boats, lobster pots and ropes. The town was well known by Elizabethan sea captains – Sir Walter Raleigh spent much time there when Warden of Cornwall in the late 16th century – and it was a thriving commercial port in the 19th century. The Doom Bar sandbank at the mouth of the Camel prevented the passage of larger modern vessels, and the harbour is now the embarkation point for fishing expeditions and pleasure cruises. The history

of the port is illustrated in a little museum above the library, and the Shipwreck Museum on South Quay displays items recovered from wrecks around the Cornish coast.

Next to the Shipwreck Museum are lobster tanks owned by Trevose Foods; the warehouse, which also stores crabs, conger eels and other marine life, is open to visitors. The town is at its most traditional during its May Day festival, when a figure in black tarpaulin and a grotesque mask, dubbed the 'Obby 'Oss, parades through the town followed by a crowd of dancers and musicians. At the end of the day the 'Oss is ritually 'done to death'.

On the northern edge of Padstow is 16th-century Prideaux Place, whose mansion, dairy, formal gardens and woodland are open to visitors during the summer. South of the town is the starting point for the Saints' Way, an ancient route used by travellers making their way from Brittany to Ireland. The path climbs up Dennis Hill and passes a monument to Queen Victoria before carrying on to Fowey, 25 miles away on Cornwall's south coast.

The Padstow 'Obby 'Oss

⑧ WADEBRIDGE
Since 1993 the busy market town's 14-arched, 15th-century bridge has had a rival: a viaduct spanning the River Camel which is part of the town's bypass. Wadebridge's days as a port were ended by the silting of the river and the coming of the railway in 1899. The line,

---

CORNISH GIANT AND WESTERN STAR

The perennial Babington's leek grows up to 6 ft high on stout, round stems and is found on cliffs and waste places in Cornwall and the Isles of Scilly. In spring, grassy cliffs on the western coasts are studded with the bright blue stars of spring squill, a bluebell-like flower with narrow leaves.

Babington's leek
Allium babingtonii
July-Aug

Spring squill
Scilla verna
April-May

ANCESTRAL HOME *Prideaux Place, in Padstow, is still the residence of descendants of the Prideaux family who built it in 1588. Gothic features were added in Georgian times.*

meet the cliffs at Lundy Bay. At the bottom of a short flight of steps, large flat boulders form comfortable seats from which to view the rocky bay. In the cliffs above the beach, a collapsed sea cave known as Lundy Hole gives glimpses of the sea churning between splintered rocks below at high tide. The coast path continues eastwards across a narrow stream towards the neighbouring secluded cove of Ebbhaven.

⑫ PORTQUIN

The tiny hamlet by a small shingle cove, uninhabited for many years in the 19th century, has been restored as holiday cottages by the National Trust. On Doyden Point, a short walk to the west, stands a squat 19th-century castellated folly known as Doyden Castle, now also renovated as a holiday house. A 2 mile clifftop walk to the east ends in a descent of 80 steps to Port Isaac.

About 2 miles south-east of Portquin, outside the village of Trelights, are a large maze and a 'secret garden' at Long Cross Victorian Gardens. A 6th-century Christian burial stone stands at the crossroads outside the grounds.

closed in the 1960s, now forms the 17 mile Camel Trail to Wenfordbridge in the foothills of Bodmin Moor. The 5 mile stretch west of Wadebridge along the Camel to Padstow is rich in wildlife, with large populations of wading birds such as herons. The Royal Cornwall Show is held at Wadebridge in June.

⑨ ROCK

The large village of Rock is strongly nautical, with a sailing club and sailing and waterskiing schools, and Porthilly Cove is packed with pleasure craft in summer. The sandy beach, just north of the cove, is the departure point for a passenger ferry to Padstow. During the winter, the ferry can be summoned from Padstow by waving a flag left for the purpose at the ferry point.

⑩ POLZEATH

Surfers and other holidaymakers flock to Polzeath and the spacious, flat sands of Hayle Bay. The coast path north of Polzeath leads to the cliffs and farmland of the Pentire peninsula and

Rumps Point (NT), where there are traces of the banks and ditches of an Iron Age fort.

South of Polzeath at Trebetherick is the long sandy beach of Daymer Bay, which gives views across the Camel estuary to Stepper Point. The simple Church of St Enodoc, surrounded by a golf course, is the burial place of the poet Sir John Betjeman, who loved Cornwall and celebrated it in verse. In the 19th century the church was almost completely buried by sand, but it was restored in the 1860s and is now used for regular worship.

⑪ LUNDY BAY

About 1½ miles north-east of Polzeath, a path starting from a National Trust car park winds through a grassy valley to

---

PLACES TO SEE INLAND

Mellingey Mill Willow Craft Centre, St Issey, 3 miles SE of Padstow. Basket-weaving workshop based in old watermill complex; exhibitions on local history and wildlife, nature trail.

Pencarrow House and Gardens, nr Bodmin, 7 miles SE of Wadebridge. Georgian mansion.

Shire Horse Centre, Tredinnick, 4 miles SE of Padstow. Daily parades of shire horses, owl sanctuary, nature trail.

TOURIST INFORMATION

Padstow (01841) 533449

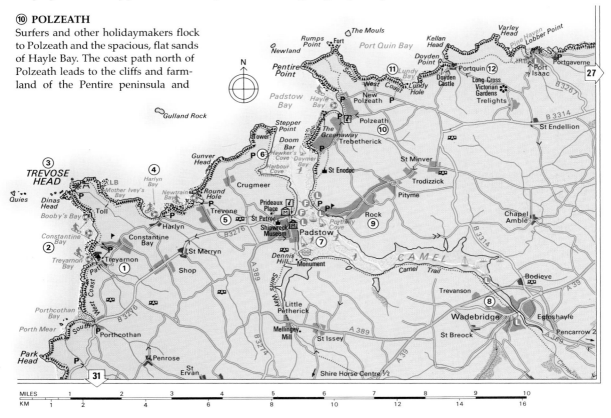

Golden sands, and a surfers' paradise at Newquay

Superb surfing beaches, seen at their most dramatic when mighty waves thunder ashore, stretch from north of Newquay to Perranporth. In some places the sand has invaded the land and created extensive dunes.

IN A GIANT'S FOOTSTEPS *Local legend says that Bedruthan's huge slate stacks, detached from the mainland by wave erosion, were steppingstones used by a Cornish giant.*

① PORTHCOTHAN
The sandy beach at Porthcothan is backed by dunes, among which visiting families, protected by windbreaks, sit on summer days. Currents sweeping past the headlands at each end of the beach make it dangerous to swim at low water. A short walk over the low southern headland leads to Porth Mear, a secluded cove made up of rock and low-tide shingle; beyond the cove is the low plateau of Park Head, whose defensive banks and ditch are believed to date from the 1st century BC.

② BEDRUTHAN
The massive slate rocks on the beach, called Bedruthan Steps after a legendary Cornish giant, make up one of the most dramatic features on the Cornish coast. One rock, Samaritan Island, is named after a brig that was wrecked there in 1846; her cargo of silks and satins was 'rescued' by local people, who used the luxurious materials for dresses and quilts. Another has been christened Queen Bess Rock, but its supposed likeness to the profile of Queen Elizabeth I has been lost through

erosion. The best view of the rocks is from the grassy clifftop above the beach. A long, steep flight of steps has been rebuilt. It leads down to the beach, where an expanse of sand is exposed at low tide; bathing is unsafe.

③ MAWGAN PORTH
A small group of beach shops stands beside a bridge over the stream that runs into the horseshoe-shaped sandy bay at Mawgan Porth. The stream flows down the deep Vale of Mawgan. St Mawgan village, 2 miles upstream from the bay, provides an oasis of calm. Its 13th-century church has an early 15th-century lantern cross in the churchyard and some attractive 15th and 16th-century brasses. A bonsai nursery is another distinctive feature of the village.

St Mawgan's cross

④ WHIPSIDERRY
A steep descent down 134 rocky steps, with a reassuringly substantial iron handrail, leads to a sandy cove fringed by tall, dark cliffs. To the north is Watergate Beach, a 2 mile sweep of sand, which is popular with surfers.

A 10 minute walk to the west is Trevelgue Head, whose ramparts and ditches are the remains of large Iron Age fortifications; a burial mound there dates from the Bronze Age.

⑤ NEWQUAY
Cornwall's biggest resort has a number of different sides to its character. Around Fistral Beach is Surf City, the scene of international surfing championships, while the sandy beaches to the east of Towan Head are busy in summer with hundreds of families enjoying a traditional seaside holiday.

In the harbour, where lobster pots are stacked up high, fishermen continue Newquay's traditional occupation: long before the first holidaymakers arrived the town was a thriving fishing community. It also exported metal ores.

Just above the harbour is the Huer's House, where a lookout man scanned the sea for shoals of pilchards, netted in vast quantities in the 18th and 19th centuries. The cliff path to the west of the Huer's House provides good views of the Tea Caverns, excavated by miners quarrying the cliffs for metal ores, and later used by smugglers who used to hide contraband tea there.

Newquay's wide range of holiday attractions includes a zoo called Animal World, a boating lake among the lushly subtropical vegetation of Trenance Gardens, a Sea Life Centre with an underwater see-through tunnel, and a pool at the Blue Lagoon Leisure Centre. Fishing trips for mackerel, bass and pollock are available, and there is fishing from the shore in winter.

Porth, which has become an extension of Newquay, once had its own separate identity, with shipbuilding yards and pilchard cellars – buildings in which the fish were salted to preserve them. The main attraction of the village today is a wide sandy beach; swimmers should avoid the north side of the sands, where a river takes a course past Trevelgue Head and into the sea.

⑥ CRANTOCK BEACH
The beach is a tempting sight when viewed from Pentire Point West. The broad stretch of sand is backed by high dunes and an undulating grassy plateau known as Rushy Green. It can be reached from the National Trust car park at the lower, older part of Crantock village. Swimming is banned at the northern end of the beach, which is the mouth of the River Gannel. At low tide, the river estuary can be crossed by two bridges that are exposed as the sea retreats; in summer a rowing-boat ferry operates at high tide.

SHELTERED HAVEN *Still used by small craft, Newquay's old harbour dries out at low tide, leaving a sandy bathing beach.*

⑦ PORTH JOKE

The unspoiled sandy cove of Porth Joke can be reached only on foot, but the route from West Pentire requires a mere 5 minute stroll beside a field ablaze with poppies in early summer. The cove is known locally as Polly Joke. The name Joke comes from the same source as the word chough, denoting the Cornish red-legged crow which is extinct in the wild in Cornwall. A rocky islet called The Chick stands off Kelsey Head, which is situated to the west.

⑧ HOLYWELL BAY

Caravan parks, a golf course and an army training area border the resort of Holywell. A stream crossed by a wooden bridge meanders past steep sand dunes, and a slithering scramble over the dunes is rewarded by a view of nearly a mile of golden sand. Dolphins sometimes appear round the two Gull Rocks in the bay. The location of the holy well which gave the bay its name is not clear – it may have been within a cave, which can be visited at low tide, on the northern side of the bay.

FISHERMEN'S WATCHTOWER

Until the late 19th century, the huer was an important person in Newquay. From the Huer's House he would alert fishermen to signs of pilchard shoals – flocks of gulls over the sea, rippling of the surface and a red tinge to the water – by shouting 'Heva! Heva!', meaning 'Found! Found!'. His name and the call may derive from the French *huer*, meaning 'to shout out'.

The Huer's House overlooks Newquay Bay.

---

⑨ ST NEWLYN EAST

In the 19th century, lead mines flourished near St Newlyn East, which is grouped about the handsome Church of St Newlina. To the east of the village the narrow-gauge Lappa Valley Steam Railway is laid on the track bed of a mineral line that opened in 1849 to connect the East Wheal Rose mine with Newquay. The 10 minute railway journey ends at a country leisure park on the site of the mine; the engine house has been restored, and other attractions include a lake and a maze. East Wheal Rose was in 1846 the scene of Cornwall's worst mining disaster, when a freak cloudburst flooded the mine and caused the deaths of 39 miners.

Trerice (NT), an Elizabethan manor house north-east of St Newlyn East, has fine 17th-century English furniture, an orchard of old varieties of fruit trees, and a museum of lawn mowers.

⑩ GEAR SANDS

A simple stone marks the place where the 6th-century St Piran's Oratory lies buried in Gear Sands, a rather eerie area of steep, grass-covered sandhills. The small church was founded by St Piran, patron saint of tinners, who arrived in Cornwall from Ireland in the 6th century. Shifting sands have alternately buried and revealed the oratory over the centuries, but it has remained buried since 1980. A 15 minute walk to the oratory site starts from the Perranporth to Mount road, and is marked by white stones. A large holiday camp can be seen within the dunes.

⑪ PERRANPORTH

Two miles of sand, backed by dunes, sweep northwards from the popular resort of Perranporth, a former fishing and mining community where old

mine workings stretch beneath the town. Swimmers should keep away from the southern end of the beach, where streams running into the sea past Chapel Rock create treacherous currents. Chapel Rock has a natural tidal swimming pool, reached by a scramble over the rocks. Sea fishing for bass, pollock and mackerel is available at Perranporth, and there is coarse fishing at nearby Bolingey. Sedge warblers and reed buntings are among the birds that can be spotted in the reed beds of the Nansmellyn Marsh Nature Reserve.

PLACES TO SEE INLAND

World in Miniature, 3 miles E of Perranporth. Scale models of the Taj Mahal, the Pyramids and other landmarks set in 12 acres of gardens.

TOURIST INFORMATION

Newquay (01637) 871345

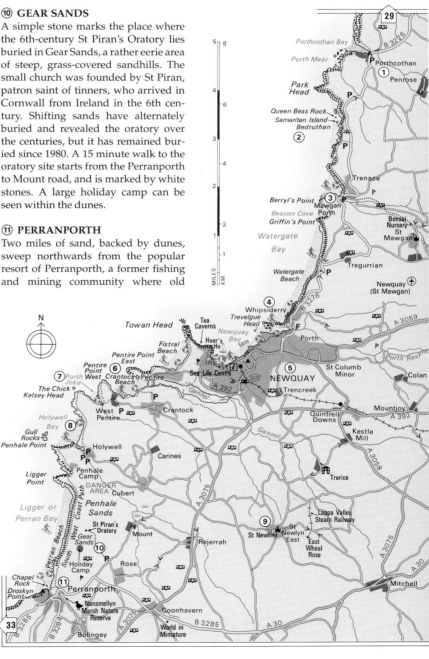

Villages where fortunes were made from mining tin

Imposing cliffs loom over placid bays and jagged rocks along a coast that is benign and fierce by turns. Old mine buildings and chimneys bear silent witness to the source of Cornwall's former prosperity.

① TREVELLAS PORTH
The road from Trevellas village, sign-posted Cross Coombe, winds down a shaded, leafy, narrow tunnel of a road to the disused Blue Hills Mine. In the 19th century the whole of this quiet coombe, known locally as Jericho Valley, was thick with the dust and noise of tin mining; today the shingle cove is silent apart from the noise of the waves. Erosion makes the cliffs treacherous, and bathing is dangerous because of strong currents.

② TREVAUNANCE COVE
A road at the northern end of St Agnes village descends to a car park above the small Trevaunance Cove, which has a wide expanse of sand at low tide. To the east is a jumble of craggy outcrops. The beach is popular with surfers, and fishing from the shore yields mackerel, pollack and bass. Trevaunance Cove was the main harbour for the mines of St Agnes. Coal and other imports were winched up the hill using horses, and outward cargoes of ores were poured down chutes to the harbour. A few granite blocks are all that now remains of the harbour, which was torn apart by a fierce storm in 1915.

③ ST AGNES
St Agnes is sleepy and calm today, but the gaunt outlines of former mine buildings rising above its streets are evidence of the days when up to a thousand people were employed in local tin and copper mines. The local museum illustrates with the aid of displays and film the mining history of St Agnes, and

Stippy Stappy cottages in St Agnes

also the village's associations with the sea. A path beside the Church of Our Lady, Star of the Sea, leads to the engine house of Wheal Friendly Mine, now used as holiday accommodation, and Trevaunance Cove. Wheal is the Cornish word for 'work' or 'mine'.

At the bottom of the village is a stepped terrace of cottages, some dating from the 18th century, called Stippy Stappy. A path from there winds its way up to the extensive buildings of Wheal Kitty, an important copper and tin mine until it closed in 1930. Wheal Kitty gives views of several former mine buildings that rise above green hills; one, the Polberro Mine, was once Cornwall's richest source of tin.

④ ST AGNES BEACON
From St Agnes Beacon, 629 ft above the sea, may be seen 30 parish churches, both coasts of Cornwall and, at night, the beams of 12 lighthouses. A footpath that starts opposite a car park on the seaward side of the Beacon climbs through gorse and heather to the exhilarating open landscape around the summit. It is claimed that in 1588 fires blazed there to warn of the approach of the Spanish Armada; more fires were lit in 1977 to celebrate the Silver Jubilee of Queen Elizabeth II.

⑤ CHAPEL PORTH
From the approach road, Chapel Porth appears as a blue wedge of sea between heather-covered hills. The lane ends in a National Trust car park at the head of a sandy, shingle-backed beach flanked by rocks which provide many suntraps. Swimmers and surfers should beware of currents and undertows.

In a steep valley south-east of the cove are the ruined engine house and chimney of the Charlotte United mine, one of several tin and copper mines that flourished round Chapel Porth in the 19th century. To the north are the buildings of Wheal Coates tin mine, which was worked from at least the 17th century until its closure in 1889. Dramatically positioned on the edge of a cliff is the Towanroath engine house, constructed in 1872 to house the pumping engine that was needed to keep Wheal Coates free of water.

⑥ PORTHTOWAN
A long, steep hill winds down to the sea at the holiday resort of Porthtowan, where a small cluster of shops and cafés and an amusement arcade overlook a sandy, gently shelving beach. The 19th-century engine house of a copper mine is now a private dwelling. More dramatic evidence of local mining can be seen just over a mile inland, at Tywarnhale, where there are the remains of old copper-mine buildings.

⑦ PORTREATH
Today's cheerful holiday bustle around Portreath's harbour and sandy beach, popular with surfers, makes it hard to imagine that in the 19th century the

ABANDONED MINE *The Towanroath engine house and chimney-stack of Wheal Coates mine stand over a 600 ft deep shaft.*

PERILOUS WATERS *Buttresses of rock check the path of the racing tide and churn the sea to flying spume between Godrevy Point and the lighthouse on Godrevy Island.*

⑨ BASSET'S COVE

The stretch of coast between Portreath and Navax Point is a place to enjoy for its stimulating views, and for bracing walks along the flat-topped cliffs.

A series of coves at the foot of the cliffs, inaccessible from the coast path, includes the chillingly named Deadman's Cove and Hell's Mouth. Basset's Cove, littered with fearsome, steep-sided rocks, is overlooked by a car park which can be reached by following an unsignposted rough track opposite an entrance to Tehidy Country Park. The park provides woodland walks, a lake and nature trails.

⑩ GODREVY POINT

Low cliffs rise above the flat rocks, dappled with low-tide pools, which flank the dangerous channel between Godrevy Point and Godrevy Island. Although popular, Godrevy Point does not become overcrowded because visitors disperse to the headland's many paths and picnic spots, or to the long, sandy beach to the south.

The lighthouse on the island – which is a useful navigational guide for motorists as well as for sailors – is thought to be the one referred to in Virginia Woolf's novel *To The Lighthouse*.

village was a busy port, exporting 100 000 tons of copper a year and importing vast amounts of South Wales coal to feed mining engines. Even in the 1960s, the present beach car park was a coal depot. The remains of the ramp used to transport cargoes up and down the hill can be seen from the harbour.

⑧ REDRUTH

In the 19th century, Redruth and the neighbouring town of Camborne were surrounded by as many as a hundred tin and copper mines, one of which, the Dolcoath Mine, was more than 3000 ft deep. Two great beam engines, once used to pump water from mines, can be seen at Cornish Engines (NT). The Geological Museum of the Camborne School of Mines displays rocks and minerals from all over the world, including yellow sulphur from Sicily and pale green fluorite from Cornwall.

Carn Brea, between the two towns, rises to 738 ft. On its windswept summit is a huge cairn of boulders built in ancient times, and a monument to the 19th-century mine owner Francis Basset, Lord Dunstanville. A bumpy track from Carnkie, on the hill's south side, leads to the summit with views of old mine workings in every direction.

TOURIST INFORMATION

Helston (01326) 565431; St Ives (01736) 796297; Truro (01872) 74555

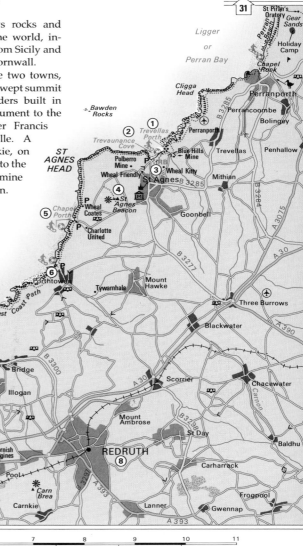

Relics in stone, and an artists' retreat at St Ives

The past is commemorated in stone in this area: in the ancient stones of prehistoric settlements, in the granite 'hedges' lining the fields, and in the crumbling engine houses and chimneys of disused mines.

① TREWELLARD

An unmarked road starting opposite the Trewellard Hotel leads to Levant in Steam (NT), where the country's oldest steam engine has been restored and housed in the engine house of the old Levant tin mine. The mine was the scene of a disaster in 1919 when the 'man engine', which carried the miners, collapsed and 31 men died. Botallack Mine, where old engine houses crouch on a ledge close to the sea, lies to the south. Among the buildings is a 1908 'calciner' used to refine tin ore and to produce arsenic, the smell of which still hangs in the old flues.

② PENDEEN WATCH

The lighthouse standing on a slate promontory above a sandy cove has guided ships for almost a century. From the eastern end of the car park near the lighthouse, a 15 minute walk leads to Portheras Cove, where a perfect semicircle of sand is revealed at low tide.

A mile inland in the village of Pendeen, Geevor Tin Mine, which ceased production in 1990, is now a museum. Its displays include a model of the ill-fated man machine from Levant and a dazzling collection of iridescent minerals found in the mines. Underground tours can be arranged.

③ ZENNOR

The village is surrounded by small fields separated by granite 'hedges' up to 7 ft thick, some of which date back to the Bronze Age. The serene 12th-century Church of St Senara has a chair from the 4th century with carvings of a mermaid illustrating a local legend of tragic love between a man and a mermaid. The Wayside Museum, in a former mill beside a stream with a turning waterwheel, tells the village's history and includes exhibits on tin mining, milling and fishing. Outside is a plague stone, which during outbreaks of cholera was filled with vinegar to disinfect the money passed between outsiders and villagers. D. H. Lawrence and his German wife Frieda lived in Zennor in World War II. He worked on *Women in Love* there until the couple were ordered to leave because of suspected pro-German sympathies. This incident was later recalled in his semiautobiographical novel, *Kangaroo*.

An hour's walk along a track southeast of the village leads across moorland to the largest surviving chambered tomb in Britain, dramatic Zennor Quoit. Dating from the early Bronze Age, it measures 18 ft by 9½ ft.

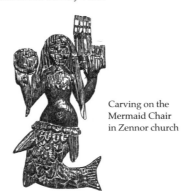

Carving on the Mermaid Chair in Zennor church

④ CHYSAUSTER

Chysauster Ancient Village (EH) consists of eight houses in two rows of four along what is said to be the oldest identifiable street in England, built about 2000 years ago. The houses are virtually identical with rooms grouped around courtyards. In one of the dwellings, which has been partially reconstructed and given a roof of straw, a hearth can be seen and even a 'back door'. The hilltop settlement is reached from a car park on a narrow lane, from which it is a 250 yd walk up a steep path.

⑤ ST IVES

The town has been an artists' colony since the 1880s, attracting talents as diverse as James McNeill Whistler, Patrick Heron and Walter Sickert. Trewyn Studio, where the sculptor Barbara Hepworth used to work until her death in 1975, is now a memorial museum to her. Among some 30 art galleries, the Tate Gallery, on a hillside above the surfing beach of Porthmeor, displays the work of 20th-century painters and sculptors, and offers wide views of the Atlantic.

Its narrow, winding streets and sandy beaches have made St Ives popular with tourists, but fishermen still use the harbour. Visitors can arrange their own fishing trips from the quayside. Although cars are restricted from entering the town in high summer, there is extensive parking overlooking the bay. An unusual and attractive way to approach St Ives is to park at Lelant and go by train, from which there are spectacular views of the coast on the way to Porthminster's golden beach.

⑥ CARBIS BAY

A 2 mile walk over the cliffs from St Ives leads to a privately owned beach, bordered by gentle hills, where visitors are welcome. Low tide exposes some eight acres of sand; at certain states of the tide it is possible to walk along the sand to Lelant and the Hayle estuary, about 1½ miles to the south-east.

⑦ LELANT

The popular resort prospered as a port until gale-driven sands started to choke the Hayle estuary in the 15th century. A

WONDERS IN STONE

Among the stone antiquities dotting the moors of Cornwall is Lanyon Quoit, near Pendeen, a 'gallery' grave, or chambered cairn, erected around 2500 BC. Nearby is Chun Castle, an Iron Age hill fort overlooking Chun Quoit, which is believed to be 5000 to 6000 years old. The Nine Maidens, south-west of Zennor, is a true circle of stones, some of which lean at precarious angles.

The gallery grave of Lanyon Quoit was once the heart of a huge mound.

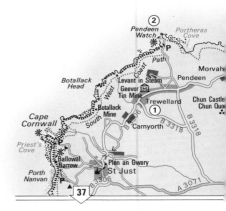

path beside the village's 15th-century Church of St Uny leads across a golf course and dunes to the flat, golden sweep of Porth Kidney Sands.

⑧ HAYLE
Sandy beaches are the main attraction of this former industrial town and harbour. Machines for the Cornish mining industry, including the engine at the Levant Mine near Pendeen, were made in the foundries of Harvey & Co until the early 20th century. Paradise Park, in the western part of the town, is devoted to the conservation of rare and endangered species, including the Cornish chough, a red-legged crow now extinct in the wild in Cornwall. Peregrines, kingfishers and great northern divers are among the rare species that draw birdwatchers to the Saltings, at the head of the Hayle estuary.

⑨ THE TOWANS
The 3 mile stretch of sand between Hayle and Godrevy Point includes a beach known as The Towans, meaning 'sand dunes'. The sand is wide and flat, and there are rocky pools to investigate at low tide. Cars can be parked close to the beach, the route to which lies through a village of holiday chalets.

PAINTING THE TOWN *Mediterranean light qualities give St Ives an ever-changing appearance and have, since the 19th century, inspired an international colony of artists.*

⑩ GWITHIAN TOWANS
A lane from the charming village of farmsteads and thatched houses descends southwards to a 3 mile stretch of sand. The steep, grassy dunes that back the beach are threaded with dozens of well-trodden footpaths and provide natural picnic areas. There are fine views north towards Godrevy Island and its lighthouse.

TOURIST INFORMATION
St Ives (01736) 796297

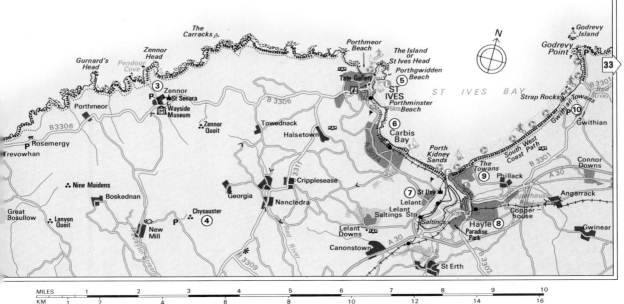

Land's End, where Atlantic breakers meet granite cliffs

West of Penzance are the battered cliffs of Land's End, and sheltered coves reached by lanes or from the coast path. Artists have been drawn to the area since the 1880s, and actors perform in an open-air theatre.

① CAPE CORNWALL
The narrow road from St Just to Cape Cornwall passes a tall chimney, all that remains of what was Britain's most westerly tin mine when it was worked in the 1870s. From the headland – the only one in England and Wales to bear the name 'Cape' – there are views of Land's End, which extends 1000yd farther westwards than Cape Cornwall, and of the Longships lighthouse.

On the southern side of the headland, a short walk from the car park descends to the quiet, boulder-strewn Priest's Cove. The South West Coast Path continues southwards past Ballowall Barrow (EH), an unusually elaborate Bronze Age burial chamber.

Beyond the burial chamber is Porth Nanven, where a stream runs through boulders to a seaweed-scattered shore of rocks and low-tide sand, backed by high grassy cliffs. The cove can also be reached by road from St Just, the westernmost town in England, which was a thriving tin-mining centre in Victorian times. At its centre is a natural grass-covered amphitheatre called Plen an Gwary, meaning 'playing place', where medieval miracle plays were performed until the 17th century. The much restored Church of St Just includes two medieval wall paintings and a 5th-century burial stone.

② SENNEN COVE
The great sweep of Whitesand Bay, a surfing beach more than a mile long and backed by steep grassy cliffs, is the focus of Sennen Cove. South of the beach is a huddle of cottages, a lifeboat station, two slipways and a harbour with a huge granite breakwater.

Land's End can be reached by a half-hour walk starting near the harbour car park. The coast path climbs to the headland of Pedn-mên-du, and continues south past a Bronze Age barrow and the remains of Britain's earliest known cliff castle, dating from before 300 BC.

③ LAND'S END
Known to the Romans as Belevian, or 'Seat of Storms', the wave-lashed granite headland of Land's End is the most south-westerly point on the British mainland. From Land's End, there are views to the Longships reef and its lighthouse, a mile offshore; on the horizon lie the Isles of Scilly and in between, according to legend, is the lost land of Lyonesse. Visitors pay a charge to enter the area, where there are restaurants, craft shops and displays of Cornish history and legends using special sound and lighting effects. In summer, RSPB staff are on duty at birdwatching sites.

④ PORTHGWARRA
A steep cobbled slipway runs down to a snug cove with a beach of sand and bladderwrack flanked by sheer cliffs. The cliff on the eastern side is pierced by a tunnel, beyond which are dark granite rocks with low-tide pools. A huge hole in the headland just west of Porthgwarra drops the full height of the cliff, and the sea can be seen rushing in at the bottom. No roads touch the remote, unspoilt coastline between the cove and Land's End, and the rugged terrain poses a challenge to walkers.

⑤ PORTHCURNO
Porthcurno's tiny triangle of beach, made up of ground-down shells, was once known as the 'centre of the universe', for the cove was the landing place for undersea cables that linked Britain to the world telegraph network. The first cable was laid in 1870.

Just south of the cove is the open-air Minack Theatre, an amphitheatre cut into the high cliffs. Completed in 1932, the theatre stages performances in summer, and has an exhibition centre explaining its history.

Half a mile west of Porthcurno is 13th-century St Levan's Church, which dominates the tiny scattered village of St Levan. Across the road from the church, a short path to Porth Chapel ends with a difficult climb down to a small sandy beach, sheltered by cliffs.

A mile walk along the coast path eastwards from Porthcurno leads to the headland of Treryn Dinas, where a huge earth and stone rampart is all that remains of one of Cornwall's most substantial Iron Age promontory forts. Nearby Logan Rock is a granite boulder estimated to weigh more than 60 tons and once balanced in such a way that it could be made to rock or 'log'. In the 1820s a group of high-spirited sailors dislodged the stone, but were unable to restore it to its original position. Treryn Dinas can also be reached by a 15 minute walk across fields from Treen.

⑥ PENBERTH COVE
A stone slipway serves the small fishing fleet based at the tiny, rocky Penberth Cove, which is described by its owner, the National Trust, as 'the most perfect of Cornish fishing coves'. There is parking space for a few cars in the leafy lane that follows a stream down to the cove, past rose-covered cottages and a scattering of stone houses.

ATLANTIC RAMPART *The battered granite cliffs at Land's End, 200ft high, are the roots of a mountain chain which once extended from the Isles of Scilly to Brittany and beyond.*

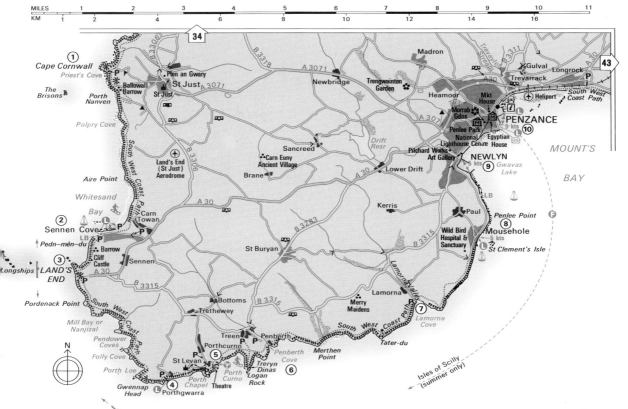

Map labels:

① Cape Cornwall — Priest's Cove
The Brisons
Porth Nanven
Polpry Cove
Ballowall Barrow
Plen an Gwary
St Just
St Just
A 3071
Madron
Newbridge
Trengwainton Garden
Heamoor
Mkt House
Morrab Gdns
Penlee Park
National Lighthouse Centre
Pilchard Works
Art Gallery
Egyptian House
PENZANCE
NEWLYN ⑨
Gwavas Lake
Gulval
Trevarrack
Heliport
South West Coast Path
Longrock
MOUNT'S BAY
Land's End (St Just) Aerodrome
Aire Point
Whitesand Bay
Sancreed
Carn Euny Ancient Village
Brane
Drift Resr
Lower Drift
A 30
② Sennen Cove — Pedn-mên-du
Carn Towan
Barrow
③ LAND'S END — Cliff Castle
Longships
Pordenack Point
Sennen
Kerris
St Buryan
Paul
Penlee Point
Mousehole ⑧
St Clement's Isle
Wild Bird Hospital & Sanctuary
Mill Bay or Nanjizal
Pendower Coves
Folly Cove
Porth Loe
Gwennap Head
④ Porthgwarra
St Levan ⑤
Porth Chapel Theatre
Porthcurno
Porth Curno
Treen
Penberth
Treryn Dinas Logan Rock ⑥
Penberth Cove
Merthen Point
Bottoms
Trethewey
Merry Maidens
Lamorna
⑦ Lamorna Cove
Tater-du
Isles of Scilly (summer only)

N

MINACK THEATRE *An ocean backdrop and a granite stage grace productions of opera, Shakespeare, musicals and modern drama.*

⑦ LAMORNA COVE

A steep, narrow lane runs down to a tiny harbour where, in the 19th century, ships loaded high-quality granite from nearby quarries. From about 1880 to 1910, the village and the surrounding area attracted many artists. Now the seaweed-covered rocks and small area of sand are used as a base for divers exploring local reefs and wrecks. The cove is privately owned, and there is a charge to enter and park.

A mile west of Lamorna are standing stones known as the Merry Maidens, and along the coast path to the west of the cove is the Tater-du lighthouse.

⑧ MOUSEHOLE

The little port, whose name is pronounced 'Mowzull', was described by Dylan Thomas as 'the loveliest village in England'. Houses crowd around a harbour with curving stone quays, where a small area of sand is revealed at low tide. Mousehole was a major pilchard port until nearby Newlyn developed in the 19th century; now pleasure craft and fishing boats use the harbour, and shark and deep-sea fishing trips start there. Dolly Pentreath, a Mousehole fishwife who died in 1777, was thought to be the last woman to speak Cornish as her native tongue; a plaque marks the site of her cottage.

Steep Raginnis Hill to the south of the harbour leads to the Wild Bird Hospital and Sanctuary, which is open to visitors; the hill is also the starting point for an exhilarating 2 mile walk to Lamorna.

⑨ NEWLYN

Narrow streets of stone cottages wind down to the harbour, which is the base of a 120-strong fishing fleet and overlooked by a fish market. In the town, the last working pilchard-pressing factory in Cornwall opens in the summer as a museum. A beach north of the harbour consists of shingle leading down to sand and scattered rocky outcrops. Artists started going to Newlyn in the 1880s, attracted by the special quality of light in this part of Cornwall. The Newlyn Art Gallery, opened in 1895, exhibits work by living artists.

⑩ PENZANCE

In the 19th century, nearly half Cornwall's tin was shipped from Penzance. Though it has long ceased to be a major port, the town has a harbour used by fishing boats, pleasure craft, and summer passenger ferries to the Isles of Scilly. Fishing trips start from the harbour.

The Trinity House National Lighthouse Centre illustrates the history of lighthouse-keeping. A town trail begins at the granite Market House, in front of which is a statue of Sir Humphry Davy holding the miner's safety lamp that he invented. Davy was born in Penzance in 1778. In Chapel Street is the arresting Egyptian House, built in 1835 and now a National Trust shop. The nearby maritime museum includes a re-creation of an 18th-century man-of-war with four decks. Palms, camellias and magnolias are among the plants in Morrab Gardens, where a Georgian-style house built in 1841 is now a private library.

CORNISH WHIMSY *Fanciful columns and cornices adorn Penzance's Egyptian House, modelled on an Egyptian temple.*

PLACES TO SEE INLAND

Carn Euny Ancient Village (EH), Sancreed, 6 miles W of Penzance. Iron Age village with burial chamber.

Trengwainton Garden (NT), 3 miles NW of Penzance. Walled gardens with rhododendrons, magnolias and many plant species from Assam, Burma and the Himalayas.

TOURIST INFORMATION

Penzance (01736) 62207

A Prosperous Trade in Contraband

*F*ROM THE EARLY MIDDLE AGES until the 19th century smuggling was a way of life along many parts of Britain's coast. In the south, every port from Penzance to Margate had boats that combined fishing or legitimate trade with smuggling; in coves and quiet creeks barrels of spirits were secretly brought ashore and buried in the sand for later collection.

As far back as Saxon times, duty was levied on goods imported from across the Channel. But it was not until after 1275, when Edward I created a permanent customs system to solve his financial problems, that smugglers really came into their own. Edward began by introducing an export tax on wool and hides. By the time George III came to the throne in 1760, about 800 items carried customs duty, and during his reign 1300 further items were added.

Most dutiable commodities had originally been luxuries, but they quickly

ARTFUL DODGING *Inns such as the Mermaid at Rye (above) were favourite smugglers' haunts. Rye had houses with linked attics, allowing goods to be shifted from one to another in emergencies. Before coming inshore, contraband-laden ships waited for the all-clear from a 'lander' (right).*

came to be seen as necessities, and few people cared about the illicit origins of smuggled goods. Squires and magistrates turned a blind eye – and took their cut, as did some customs men – and farmworkers supplemented meagre wages by 'moonlighting'.

The north-east coast was dotted with smuggling ports, including Robin Hood's Bay and Staithes in Yorkshire, but south-east England was particularly attractive to illegal traders because of its proximity to the Continent. During smuggling's heyday, in the 18th century, the area around Rye, on the border of Sussex and Kent, was home to the savage Hawkhurst Gang, who in the 1740s conducted a reign of

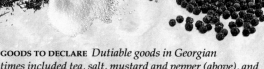

GOODS TO DECLARE *Dutiable goods in Georgian times included tea, salt, mustard and pepper (above), and even such unlikely items as coffin nails and playing cards.*

RISKY BUSINESS *A lonely rocky cove was the ideal place to bring ashore smuggled goods, as seen in George Morland's painting of 1792 (right), but bloody battles often broke out if smugglers were intercepted by excisemen (above).*

TOOLS OF THE TRADE *Barrels of spirits, concealed under water (left), were recovered with grappling hooks (top), and often hidden in caves. By the mid 18th century smuggling was so rife that bounties were offered (right) for the betrayal of suspects.*

terror along the south coast, until in 1749 ten of them were tried and hanged. Nearby Deal was known for two kinds of smuggling vessels that were built there: the large Deal lugger, which had two or three masts and carried up to ten cannons, and the long and narrow Deal galley, which was rowed by a crew of four to ten men. So successful were these galleys that in 1764 they were made illegal. The West Country, with its hundreds of rocky coves, was ideal smuggling terrain. At ports such as Polperro and Penzance, most of the inhabitants took part. Polperro's shipwrights built boats fast enough to outstrip any pursuing excise craft. One of them, the *Unity,* made 500 successful smuggling trips before being captured in 1802. A customs officer noted in 1769 that the mayor of Penzance had been bound over for smuggling. The town's notoriety as a smugglers' haven inspired the Gilbert and Sullivan opera *The Pirates of Penzance.* Smuggling was often a family affair, as it was with the three Carter brothers, of Prussia Cove, Mounts Bay. The cove was honeycombed with caves, some linked by secret passages to the Carters' clifftop house. The brothers put off curious excisemen by deploying a battery of cannons along the rim of the cliff.

A 'tubman' carrying barrels

Boats used for smuggling were fitted with false bottoms or cabin ceilings; tobacco was plaited into ropes and coiled to look like part of the rigging. Smugglers were warned of approaching excisemen by 'flashers' – men on shore carrying lanterns with long spouts to direct the flame's stream of light. Once landed, the cargo was taken inland for distribution, often from public houses such as Jamaica Inn, on Bodmin Moor, on which Daphne du Maurier based her novel of the same name. 'Batmen' armed with cudgels kept watch, while goods were carried from the beach by 'tubmen' laden back and front with barrels in a special harness.

For hundreds of years, because of public contempt for the taxation system, dealing in contraband had been regarded by many as an acceptable form of robbery, but in the 19th century people increasingly saw it as theft from the community and a new era in the fight against smugglers began. In 1816 the Royal Navy took over the revenue cutters and blockaded the coast, and in 1831 the Coastguard service was established. The forces of law and order became better paid and better at their job, and excise duties were steadily reduced, making smuggling less profitable. The last armed clash between smugglers and coastguards took place at Pevensey Bay, in Sussex, in 1833.

SLIPPERY CUSTOMERS *To make them harder for excisemen to catch, animals used in smuggling were shaved and covered with grease. Horses were taught deceptive commands, and would run off at the traditional stopping shout 'Whoa!'.*

Palm trees and white sands on the Isles of Scilly

About 28 miles south-west of Land's End are well over 100 islands and islets with a mild, sunny climate and miles of sandy beaches. The islands, part of the Duchy of Cornwall, are a paradise for birdwatchers.

HUGH TOWN *St Mary's Church contains a wooden lion recovered from the flagship of Sir Cloudesley Shovell, wrecked in 1707.*

① ST MARY'S

Around three-quarters of Scilly's population of just over 2000 lives on St Mary's, the largest island, measuring roughly 2½ miles across at its widest point. Gently undulating fields and low, bracken-clad headlands are surrounded by an easily explored coastline with several sandy beaches and many rocky coves. Pelistry Bay on the east coast becomes dangerous at high tide when currents sweep over the sandbar between St Mary's and Toll's Island.

The 'capital' of Scilly, Hugh Town, stands on a narrow strip of land between the sands of Town Beach and Porth Cressa beach. Its main street, flanked by buildings of gale-defying granite, leads to a harbour where trawlers and visiting yachts mingle with private craft, and with the sturdy passenger launches which take about 20 minutes to reach the outlying islands of St Agnes, Bryher, Tresco or St Martin's. The launches provide opportunities to observe grey seals and a great variety of sea birds at close quarters. In summer there are gig races, contested by long open boats pulled by crews of six people. Fishing trips and

boat trips are available. Hugh Town developed under the protection of Star Castle, an eight-pointed fortress completed in 1593 when a second Spanish Armada was feared. Now a hotel, the fort forms part of The Garrison, the headland to the west of the town, which in the first half of the 18th century was surrounded by stone ramparts.

A walk along the well-preserved ramparts, the Garrison Walls (EH), is particularly rewarding towards sunset. The beams of eight lighthouses – the Bishop Rock, Round Island, Peninnis, Wolf Rock, Longships, Pendeen, Tater-du and Lizard – are visible from The Garrison on a clear night.

The history and natural history of the islands are illustrated in Hugh Town's museum by exhibits spanning more than 6000 years. The museum's outstanding features include the pilot gig *Klondyke* built in 1873, and a superb bronze gun recovered from the wreck of the 90-gun *Association*, the flagship of Rear-Admiral Sir Cloudesley Shovell, which sank in 1707 after striking the Gilstone reef, in the Western Rocks. Scattered reefs and rocky islets round the Isles of Scilly have for centuries taken a grim toll of shipping.

Old Town is an attractive cluster of stone cottages; its sandy, rock-studded bay curves round to the Old Church, shaded by palm trees and with the date 1662 carved above its door. Many victims of the *Schiller* disaster of 1875 are buried in the graveyard: the German liner was on a passage from New York to Germany when she struck a reef in fog and went down with all but 37 of her 372 passengers and crew.

Porth Hellick, a very sheltered bay of sand framed by seaweed-draped rocks, is the starting point for one of two way-marked nature trails. The other runs from Old Town Bay to the A3111 near Sandy Banks Farm.

The turf-topped Porth Hellick Down Burial Chamber (EH) dates from the Bronze Age, and is one of Scilly's many tangible links with prehistory. Another burial place, Bant's Carn (EH), is on the north-western rim of St Mary's and overlooks the granite hut circles of a Romano-British village that was inhabited almost 2000 years ago.

② GUGH

The little island – its name pronounced to rhyme with 'Hugh' – has only two houses and is linked to St Agnes by a sand-bar that is covered at high tide. There are sandy beaches on either side of the bar at low water, but the incoming tide creates dangerous currents as it sweeps over the barrier. The Old Man of Gugh, a 9ft standing stone, was erected by the island's Bronze Age inhabitants.

③ ST AGNES

A patchwork of tiny fields, sheltered by lofty hedges, is overlooked by the disused 17th-century St Agnes lighthouse, whose portly white tower dominates the little island.

A road just wide enough for a single vehicle runs from the quay at Porth Conger to the sand-and-shingle beach at Lower Town, half a mile away on the opposite side of the island, whose population numbers fewer than 100. The east window of St Agnes Church is dedicated to crews who manned the lifeboat based nearby from 1891 to 1920. A church plaque records the loss in 1907 of the American schooner *Thomas W. Lawson*, which foundered off the nearby island of Annet. Sixteen people died, including a member of the lifeboat's crew who went aboard to act as a pilot.

Troy Town Maze, on the western side of the island, measures 30ft across and consists of ankle-high stones set into the ground. Who laid out the maze is a mystery; one theory is that it was made by a lighthouse keeper, but another is that it dates from Celtic times.

Annet, just over half a mile off St Agnes, is a bird reserve where puffins and Manx shearwaters breed. Boat trips from St Mary's take visitors near the island, but do not land there.

The Bishop Rock lighthouse stands sentinel over the south-west tip of the Isles of Scilly, 4½ miles from St Agnes. Its light has a range of nearly 30 miles.

ROCKY PILLARS *Granite outcrops, eroded into monumental forms by the waves, fringe the south-west coast of St Agnes.*

④ SAMSON

Small, humpbacked Samson has been uninhabited since 1855 and is now a breeding ground for lesser black-backed gulls. The island's population never recovered from a tragedy during

TROPICAL TRESCO *Exotic plants flourish in Tresco Abbey Gardens. Many were brought from afar by ships' captains and grow nowhere else in the Northern Hemisphere.*

bottlebrush, an Australian shrub. Tresco's beauty is enhanced by two lakes, Great Pool and Abbey Pool, where coots, moorhens, mute swans and other birds nest amid the reeds.

A fort known as Cromwell's Castle (EH) was built in 1651 when the Royalist islands finally capitulated. From the fort it is only a short walk to the ruined King Charles's Castle (EH) which, despite its name, was built 100 years earlier than Cromwell's Castle.

The island has much to offer the walker, as well as an art gallery, and superb beaches for visitors seeking nothing more than relaxation. Helicopters from Penzance land at the heliport on the Abbey Green, which doubles as the island's cricket pitch.

⑦ ST MARTIN'S

Around 110 people live on the 2 mile long St Martin's. Its 'capital', Higher Town, has a sailing centre and is overlooked from the east by a steep little hill whose striped Daymark Tower has been a landmark for sailors since the 17th century. The island has several beautiful beaches. The sands at Porth Morran on White Island, linked to St Martin's by a natural, tide-covered causeway, lead to pits where seaweed was once burned to produce an alkali used in the manufacture of soap and glass. This was an important source of income in the islands during the 17th and 18th centuries.

the Napoleonic Wars that claimed the lives of most of the young islanders. They captured a French ship and were sailing her to the mainland when she foundered on the Wolf Rock off Land's End with the loss of all hands. Boat trips from St Mary's land on Samson between April and October; ruins of islanders' cottages can still be seen.

⑤ BRYHER

Bryher's western coast, battered into weird shapes by the awesome power of Atlantic storms, contrasts with the sheltered beach which faces Tresco and the tranquillity of Rushy Bay, at the southern end of the island. The bay's sands are overlooked by Bronze Age cairns on Samson Hill. About 80 people live on the island. A new quay was built in 1993 as a result of the television programme 'Challenge Anneka', and is known locally as 'Anneka's Quay'.

⑥ TRESCO

The second biggest island, with a population of 160 or so, Tresco is a private estate leased to the Dorrien Smith family by the Duchy of Cornwall since

1834. The first of the line, Augustus Smith, built Tresco Abbey near the site of the island's medieval priory and created its luxuriant subtropical gardens, which are open to visitors. In the grounds are Canary Island palms, brightly coloured proteas from southern Africa, ironwoods from New Zealand, and the colourful

Jagged rocks and secluded coves in Mount's Bay

Shipwrecks were once common in this sweeping bay, bounded east and west by two islands. Beaches and quiet coves lie between the cliffs, and a long shingle bank shelters a tranquil lake which probes inland.

① MARAZION

The narrow streets of Cornwall's oldest town snake down to the sea. Marazion was granted a charter by Henry III in 1257, and its tin and copper were exported until the late 19th century. A museum in the old fire station tells some of the town's history.

The quiet waters of Marazion's sandy bay make for good sailing and windsurfing. On the north-western outskirts of the town is Marazion Marsh RSPB reserve, where breeding colonies include grey herons, and aquatic warblers visit from the Mediterranean.

② ST MICHAEL'S MOUNT

The great granite crag rising from the waters facing Marazion has a spectacular battlemented castle, built in the 14th century on the site of an earlier monastic shrine. The island and its buildings are now in the care of the National Trust, and a large part of the castle is open to the public, including an armoury and a priory church which is still in use. At low tide a half-mile causeway joins the mount with Marazion; small boats provide a link with the mainland when the causeway is covered.

③ PERRAN SANDS

A steep flight of stairs leads down from a small village to Perran Sands, a beach of rocks and sand. A sandbank which sometimes forms just off the beach can make swimming hazardous. To the south-east the cliffs wind their way to jagged Cudden Point (NT), on whose rocks many ships have foundered.

FRENCH CONNECTION *The priory incorporated into the castle that crowns St Michael's Mount was founded by Benedictine monks from the Mont St Michel in Normandy.*

CORNWALL'S MINES

The chimneys and engine houses of long-disused tin and copper mines stand on the rugged Cornish coast from The Lizard peninsula to Newquay. In the early 19th century, around three-quarters of the world's copper was mined in Cornwall. The industry declined in the 1920s, ending a practice that had its origins in the 5th century BC.

The Wheal Prosper engine house stands on Rinsey Head.

④ PRUSSIA COVE

A narrow winding lane leads from Rosudgeon to a private estate which includes the clifftop settlement of Prussia Cove, named after a notorious 18th-century smuggler who modelled himself on Frederick the Great. From the car park it is a 10 minute walk to a group of old cottages and houses standing on the top of a dark rockface that slides ominously into the sea. The path runs behind the cottages to a slipway which crosses the small shingle beach. To the east, above Kenneggy Sands, the cliff path passes the dumps of a disused tin and copper mine.

⑤ PRAA SANDS

Two headlands and high dunes enclose the mile-long crescent of sand and its holiday village. The western end of the beach is sheltered from westerly winds by the cliffs of Hoe Point; but strong currents make bathing unsafe at low tide. The coast path leads eastwards from the often crowded beach towards rugged Lesceave Cliff (NT).

⑥ RINSEY HEAD

A high-hedged lane from Ashton opens out into a hamlet, from which a very rough track leads to a car park. Fulmars nest on the rockface near the bracken-clad headland where waves pound the granite cliffs. Just to the east is Wheal Prosper (NT), the restored 19th-century engine house of a disused tin and copper mine. Half a mile farther east along the coast path are the ruins of Wheal Trewavas copper mine.

⑦ PORTHLEVEN

Steep narrow streets lead down to a deep harbour, built by London industrialists in 1811 primarily to export tin and import mining machinery. Boats can be launched at high tide, but the harbour dries out at low tide. Sunken wrecks and a local reef make the area

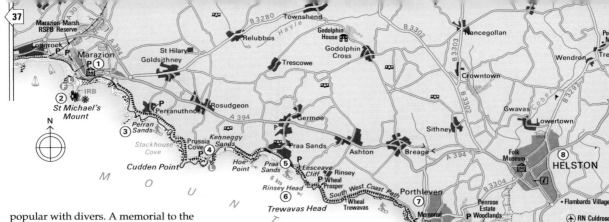

popular with divers. A memorial to the many sailors who have lost their lives in the bay stands on the western cliff.

⑧ HELSTON

Developed as a port in Roman times, Helston became in the 14th century one of four stannary towns in Cornwall where local tin was tested for quality. Helston's yearly festival, Flora Day, one of the oldest in Britain, is usually held on May 8. To mark the coming of summer, the town is wreathed in flowers, and hundreds of dancers weave in and out of houses along the hilly streets performing the 'Furry Dances'. A small folk museum in the old butter market explains the history of the market town and the surrounding area.

South-east of the town is Flambards Village theme park, a re-creation of a Victorian village with other family attractions, including a display of aircraft covering the history of aviation.

⑨ THE LOE

The large freshwater lake, surrounded by the woodlands of the Penrose Estate (NT), is separated from the sea by the large shingle barrier of Loe Bar. A network of footpaths includes a 5 mile circuit of The Loe and Carminowe Creek. The marshes and tangle of water-tolerant trees at the northern end of the lake are a winter refuge for wildfowl such as teals and coots, and cormorants and herons can also be seen.

The coast off Loe Bar is dangerous for swimmers and shipping. Many ships have come to grief there, including the frigate *Anson*, which was beached in 1807; a memorial marks the spot where more than a hundred men died while a crowd watched helplessly from the land. The cliff path leads south-east to Gunwalloe Fishing Cove (NT). The cove's pebble beach can be reached by road from the village of Berepper, but parking space is limited.

⑩ CHURCH COVE

A small stream cuts through a sand and shingle beach backed by the rounded cliffs of Castle Mound. At the foot of the mound is the predominantly 15th-century Church of St Winwaloe, whose detached bell tower is built right into the rock. Ancient Winnianton Farm, beside the National Trust car park, is the only evidence of the large settlement that existed here from the 9th to the 11th centuries. The soft, low-lying rock which forms the mound is severely eroded, and granite has been deposited in an attempt to prevent the sea from isolating the church.

⑪ POLDHU COVE

This popular square of sandy beach, almost entirely edged by a low stone wall, is backed by a small stream where the National Trust has erected staves to stabilise the sands. A clifftop walk leads southwards to the Marconi Memorial, erected near the spot from which the first radio message across the Atlantic was sent in 1901.

⑫ POLURRIAN COVE

From a large clifftop hotel, reached by a path from Mullion's St Melan's Church, steep steps lead down to a sandy surfing beach. The coast path south of Polurrian Cove passes a lookout with views over Mount's Bay to Penzance, some 14 miles to the north-west.

⑬ MULLION COVE

Giant greenstone rocks face the walls of the old harbour and a few ancient buildings. Most of the shore around the small cove is owned by the National Trust, as is Mullion Island, a nesting site for guillemots and kittiwakes that is closed to the public. The slipway leads to an area of sand from which a tunnel through the rocks leads to another tiny beach. A 1½ mile circular walk climbs south over Mullion Cliff before joining a valley lane back to the harbour.

CHURCH ON THE BEACH *The church of St Winwaloe, in Church Cove, has a separate belfry some 200 years older, built into the cliffs 14 ft away from the chancel.*

PLACES TO SEE INLAND

Culdrose Airfield, 1 mile SE of Helston. Large helicopter base with viewing enclosure.

Godolphin House, 5 miles NW of Helston. Tudor mansion. Some afternoons in summer.

Poldark Mine, Wendron, 3 miles N of Helston. Mine, heritage collection, amusements.

TOURIST INFORMATION

Helston (01326) 565431; Penzance (01736) 62207; Truro (01872 74057)

A mariners' graveyard off the remote, rocky Lizard

Sunken lanes lead to small coves to the east of the Lizard peninsula, whose tip is mainland Britain's most southerly point. Many ships have been wrecked round the Lizard, and on The Manacles reef offshore.

SOUVENIR OF LIZARD *Serpentine rock, mottled and veined in a variety of colours, is named for its similarity to snakeskin.*

① KYNANCE COVE

Huge outcrops of serpentine rock shelter the popular beauty spot, where the pale golden sands are completely covered at high tide. The cove is best visited within 2½ hours of low tide, when it is possible to explore the caves to the west, including the Devil's Bellows, which is transformed into a spectacular blowhole by the surging sea. One of the giant mounds of rock on the beach is known as Albert Rock, after a visit in 1846 by Prince Albert and the royal children. The ebb tide is very strong and swimmers should not venture farther out than Asparagus Island, which is so named because wild asparagus used to grow on its slopes. Kynance Cove is reached by a toll road and a 5 minute walk from a National Trust car park.

The South West Coast Path leads southwards past Lion Rock, where many birds gather, and slopes down to tiny Caerthillian Cove before continuing round Lizard Point. Cornish heath, unique to Cornwall, is among the wild flowers that flourish in the Lizard National Nature Reserve.

HIGH DRAMA *Kynance Cove exemplifies the rugged grandeur of the western coast of the Lizard peninsula, where a flat hinterland gives way to plunging 200 ft cliffs.*

② LIZARD

The scattered village of Lizard, standing on a lonely plateau, is a centre for polishing and fashioning the local serpentine rock into ornaments. The richly coloured stone became very popular in the 19th century, after Queen Victoria visited Cornwall and ordered serpentine items for Osborne, her new house on the Isle of Wight.

A narrow lane from the village leads southwards through farmland for half a mile to the tip of the Lizard peninsula. Far below the high cliffs stands the dilapidated former lifeboat station at the shingle beach of Polpeor Cove.

The flat-topped peninsula is lashed on three sides by waters that have been the cause of many shipwrecks. Near the end of the road is a lighthouse dating from 1751. It succeeded a structure which was built in 1619, and whose proposed erection had drawn protests from local people afraid of losing a major source of revenue from looting wrecks.

At tiny, rocky Church Cove, to the east of Lizard village, there is just room for a slipway and an old boathouse. The cove was once the site of a pilchard fishery, and fish cellars built around a courtyard beside a stream can still be seen. Cars can be parked by St Wynwallow's Church; from there, it is a 5 minute walk to the cove, along a lane lined with thatched cottages.

A footpath southwards from Church Cove leads past the lifeboat station at Kilcobben Cove to the slopes of Bass Point, which offers views of the cliffs.

③ CADGWITH

A prime example of the 'ideal' Cornish fishing village, tiny Cadgwith has thatched stone cottages sitting in a narrow valley, and small boats, used by fishermen who catch lobsters and crabs, on the shingle beach. Visitors' cars must be left in the car park 2 minutes' walk from the shore. The small hut on the cove's northern side was built in the late 19th century as a coastguard lookout.

A turf-topped mushroom of land, known as The Todden, separates the

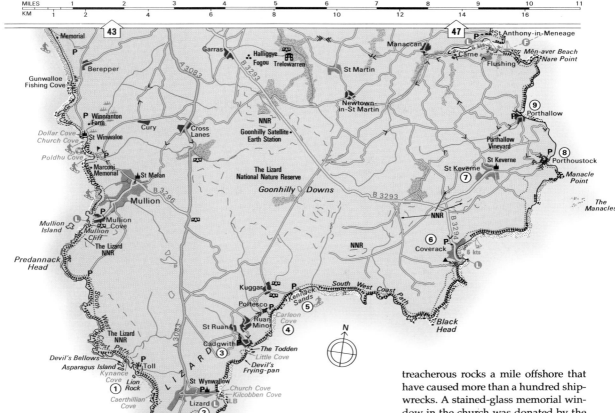

(Map of the Lizard peninsula, Cornwall, with locations including Gunwalloe Fishing Cove, Mullion, Lizard Point, Cadgwith, Coverack, St Keverne, Porthoustock, Porthallow, Goonhilly Satellite Earth Station, and The Manacles)

CORNISH PASTIME *In season, boat trips are on offer at Cadgwith, as they are at many other harbours on the Cornish coast.*

main cove from Little Cove, to the south. A steep 5 minute walk up the southern slopes of Little Cove passes rare dwarf elms and leads to the Devil's Frying-pan, where at high tide waves foam through a natural rock archway and into a collapsed cave.

④ CARLEON COVE

It is hard to imagine the deserted cove, a 10 minute walk from Poltesco, as it was in the 19th century, humming with industry. A pilchard fishery operated in Carleon Cove until the mid 19th century, when the building became a factory for working serpentine rock. The pilchard cellar buildings were extended to accommodate a steam engine, used to power machinery for cutting and polishing the stone, and a stream was deepened to allow flat-bottomed barges to ferry the products out to waiting ships. All that remains of the works is the shell of the warehouse. Finished items included shop fronts, which were made for businesses in London and Paris. The car park makes a useful starting point for walks southwards into Cadgwith, which has little parking space; the coast path follows a section of track along which rock used to be taken to the serpentine works at the cove.

⑤ KENNACK SANDS

From the wide sandy beach, the largest and one of the most popular on the Lizard peninsula's east coast, visitors may see seals, sharks and dolphins offshore. There are holiday parks on the narrow lane to the beach from Kuggar.

⑥ COVERACK

Crab, mullet and monkfish are landed at the harbour in Coverack, a fishing village that was once a busy pilchard port and the haunt of smugglers. There is a sweeping bay of sand and shingle, sheltered by a promontory. A coastal walk of about a mile leads southwards to the 230 ft cliffs of Black Head.

⑦ ST KEVERNE

By a village square, rare in Cornwall, stands the 15th-century Church of St Keverne. The village stands on the high plateau of the Lizard, and the church spire has long been a landmark for ships negotiating The Manacles, the treacherous rocks a mile offshore that have caused more than a hundred shipwrecks. A stained-glass memorial window in the church was donated by the owners of the *Mohegan*, wrecked in 1898 with the loss of 106 lives; a large granite cross in the churchyard marks the mass grave of her passengers and crew. A smaller stone identifies the graves of nearly 200 Cornish emigrants drowned in 1855 after their ship struck The Manacles on the way to Canada.

⑧ PORTHOUSTOCK

Stone was shipped from Porthoustock until the local quarry closed in 1972, and the huge rusted loading stations continue to overshadow the bay. Boats are beached, and cars parked, on the grey shingle and stone shore, where sand is exposed at low tide. The beach is used by divers as a base from which to explore ships that have been wrecked on The Manacles reef.

⑨ PORTHALLOW

Porthallow's north-facing gravelly beach looks across Falmouth Bay to the lighthouse on St Anthony Head. The hamlet's inn displays relics of the *Bay of Panama*, wrecked in 1891 at Nare Point, about a mile north of Porthallow. Porthallow Vineyard, south-west of the village, offers wine and cider tastings.

PLACES TO SEE INLAND

Goonhilly Satellite Earth Station, 4 miles NW of Coverack. Telecommunications station; visitor centre; bus tours of the site.

Halliggye Fogou (EH), 7 miles NW of Coverack. Iron Age underground chamber.

Trelowarren, 7 miles NW of Coverack. Mansion in Elizabethan and Georgian styles.

TOURIST INFORMATION

Helston (01326) 565431; Truro (01872) 74057

Tranquillity on the wooded inlets of the Helford River

Plants thrive in a mild climate on the northern side of the Helford estuary, whose narrow creeks probe far inland between wooded banks. The South West Coast Path traces an intricate, mostly level course.

① SWANPOOL BEACH
Caravan parks line the road down to the popular sandy beach with its cluster of brightly coloured beach huts. Swan Pool, bordering the Falmouth road, is encircled with reeds and, true to its name, patrolled by swans.

② MAENPORTH
The sheltered sandy beach has a water-sports centre where diving equipment, sailboards, snorkels and boats can be hired. Cars may be parked on the beach. The South West Coast Path leads south-wards over clifftops carpeted with blue-bells in spring, and continues to the fist of Rosemullion Head, from where there are fine views over Falmouth Bay.

③ MAWNAN
The 13th-century church of St Mawnan, near the tiny hamlet of Mawnan, stands on high ground. Its tower has been a landmark for sailors for centuries, and in times of war lookouts have been placed there to watch for the coming of invaders. The coast path leads west-wards through fields and along oak-covered cliffs to Toll Point, from where there are magnificent views across the mouth of the Helford River. Eastwards, the path cuts through the shade of steeply sloping woodland, and contin-ues to Rosemullion Head. There is lim-ited parking space by the church.

④ DURGAN
For centuries the daily catch of fish was transported from Durgan to Falmouth in donkey panniers. Tin was also once exported from Durgan, now a peaceful waterside hamlet, much of which is owned by the National Trust. Visitors must park at the top of the hill, from where a 10 minute walk leads to cot-tages beside a sand and shingle shore. Sailing and motor boats can be hired.

To the west, Glendurgan Garden (NT) straddles a valley running down to the Helford River. Planted at the be-ginning of the 19th century, the garden includes tulip trees as well as a cherry laurel maze and arrays of azaleas, camellias and hydrangeas.

Nearby is Trebah Garden, planted in a ravine whose slopes descend steeply to a private sandy beach, which may be

SUBTROPICAL DELIGHTS *At Trebah Garden, near Durgan, agapanthus blooms in front of a verdant canopy of tree ferns.*

used by visitors to the garden. Palms and 100-year-old tree ferns flourish there, along with exotic water plants, giant Brazilian rhubarb and rhododen-drons towering to 60 ft. A path zigzags through a rare and beautiful collection of Mediterranean plants.

⑤ HELFORD PASSAGE
Houses stand by the sand and shingle beach at Helford Passage, a hamlet that looks across the estuary towards the village of Helford and its frame of green hills. Cars may be left in the lane lead-ing into the village, from where it is a 10 minute walk to the shore.

A ferry runs across the estuary in summer. The north and south banks of the Helford River have been linked by ferry since the Middle Ages. Until around 1910 a cart would have been carried across by boat while the horse, tied to a rope, swam alongside.

Helford Passage is one of many pop-ular mooring spots on the river. Sailing boats and motor boats can be hired, and river trips can be arranged. 'Trigging', or digging for cockles, takes place on the foreshore on Good Friday.

⑥ PORTH NAVAS
The sleepy hamlet, at the head of its own creek, is the centre of the Duchy of Cornwall's oyster fisheries. The beds

THE CORNISH LANGUAGE
The Iron Age Celts who settled in Cornwall from about 500 BC introduced a Celtic language that survived the coming of the Anglo-Saxons and was spoken until the 18th century. Since the 19th century there have been attempts to revive the ancient tongue, whose legacy is apparent in countless place names.

aber river	*men* ancient stone
als cliff	*morva* seaside
bal mine, tinwork	*pen* head, top
brea hill	*pol* .pool, anchorage
chy house	*porth* harbour, cove
dynas hill fort	*pras* pasture
efan spacious, vast	*towan* sand dune
eglos church	*tre* home, village,
glyn deep valley	town
hayl estuary	*tyr* land
leven smooth	*wheal* a minework

cover the lower reaches of Porthnavas and Polwheveral Creeks, and nearby stretches of the Helford River.

⑦ GWEEK
In Roman times traders called at Gweek, which stands on a creek at the head of the Helford estuary. From the 14th century it was a busy port, where timber, coal, lime and other cargoes were exchanged for tin and produce from local farms. In the 19th century thousands of Cornish emigrants, bound for North America, embarked there. Now pleasure boats are overwin-tered and maintained in the village. Gweek's Cornish Seal Sanctuary, the largest in Europe, cares for sick, injured and starving seals before returning them to the wild. Visitors can see the animals being fed, and there is an underwater observatory. An interpreta-tion centre has exhibits of marine life.

SAVING THE SEAL *This grey seal is typical of those found stranded on Cornish beaches and taken to the Seal Sanctuary at Gweek.*

⑧ TREMAYNE WOODS
The winding ribbon of woods can be explored by following a 1½ mile foot-path starting from the Mawgan to Man-accan road, where there is limited parking. The path leads down a valley to a creek and along the Helford to Tremayne Quay. The quay was built in the 1840s for a planned visit by Queen Victoria that never took place.

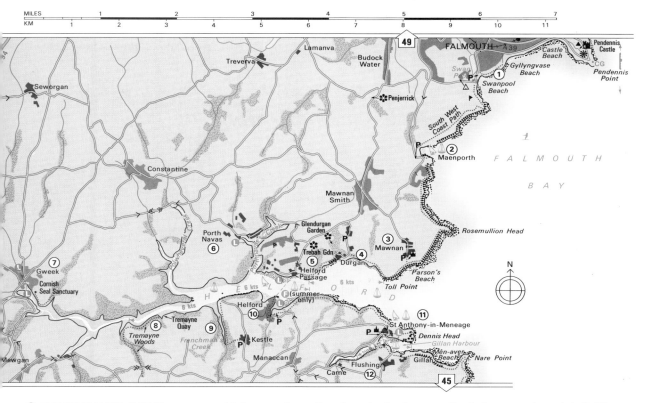

⑨ FRENCHMAN'S CREEK

Perhaps best known as the subject of Daphne du Maurier's novel of the same name, the isolated inlet with its overhanging trees is more reminiscent of an Amazonian backwater than a Cornish creek. Local people insist that its waters are haunted, and even in high summer the creek can be deserted. Herons, cormorants and kingfishers are among the birds seen there. Frenchman's Creek can be reached on foot from Helford, or by a 10 minute walk from Kestle, where parking is limited.

⑩ HELFORD

The quiet village, hugging an inlet on the Helford estuary, has thatched cottages and gardens that are ablaze with colour in summer; in spring the nearby woodlands have swathes of daffodils and primroses. A passenger ferry runs to Helford Passage in summer, when visitors' cars must be left in a car park 2 minutes' walk from the village. Sailing and motor boats can be hired.

⑪ ST ANTHONY-IN-MENEAGE

According to tradition, the Church of St Anthony-in-Meneage (pronounced 'meneeg'), at the centre of the tiny village, was founded by shipwrecked Normans grateful to have reached dry land. There may be some truth in the legend, for the church tower is built of granite found in Normandy but not in Cornwall. It overlooks a small beach, of sand and shingle, where sailing boats and sailboards can be hired. Behind the church a path leads to the promontory of Dennis Head, which was fortified against Spanish attack in Elizabethan times. St Anthony-in-Meneage stands on Gillan Harbour. It is possible to wade across the creek upstream within one hour of low tide.

⑫ FLUSHING

Not to be confused with Flushing on the River Fal, the hamlet lies on a hillside that slopes down to Gillan Creek. A lane leads to a beach of shingle and sand; there is no parking space at the far end. Similar beaches to the east, at Mên-aver and Gillan, can be reached on foot.

PEACEFUL WATERS *At Porth Navas, stone cottages cluster around berthed yachts on a tree-lined creek that leads into the Helford River and fills and empties with the tides.*

PLACES TO SEE INLAND

Penjerrick, Budock Water, 3 miles SW of Falmouth. Valley garden with rhododendrons and ponds. Two afternoons a week in summer.

TOURIST INFORMATION

Falmouth (01326) 312300; Helston (01326) 565431 (summer); Truro (01872) 74057

A maze of quiet creeks off Falmouth's broad harbour

Between the ancient port of Falmouth and the bustling town of Truro is a landscape of gentle, wooded hills and tranquil tidal waterways, where small villages dot the shores and pleasure craft bob at their moorings.

① FALMOUTH

Near the colourful ranks of pleasure craft in Falmouth's harbour, tall cranes rise from the docks area, where ocean-going vessels ride at anchor. Narrow, crowded streets run behind the busy port, which faces the sheltered waters of Carrick Roads, the estuary of the River Fal. On one of these streets is Falmouth's oldest surviving domestic building, the 16th-century Arwenack House. The low stone mansion has been converted into private apartments. To the south, stately hotels line the cliff walk, overlooking the popular, spacious sandy beaches.

Falmouth's Maritime Museum has a wealth of displays explaining the activities of the mail-carrying packet ships that brought prosperity to the town during the 18th and 19th centuries. At Custom House Quay is the 'Queen's Pipe', a freestanding, brick-built incinerator in

The Queen's Pipe in Falmouth

which seized contraband tobacco was burned; dating from the early 19th century, it was first called the 'King's Pipe'.

Pendennis Castle (EH), one of the many castles erected by Henry VIII against the French, remains a brooding presence on the headland, reached by a half-hour walk eastwards from the town centre. A nearby leisure complex has a swimming pool with water rides.

There are passenger ferries from Falmouth to Flushing and St Mawes, and summer cruises up the River Fal to Truro, 12 miles inland, and to the Helford River, to the south-west.

② PENRYN

A 19th-century clock tower and town hall stand isolated between two roads at the centre of the small, granite-grey town at the head of Penryn creek. A thriving port long before the development of Falmouth, Penryn has a quiet dignity. Some of the locally quarried granite shipped from the town quay in the 19th century was used in the building of London's Central Criminal Court at the Old Bailey. The creek is now used by private craft and a few fishing boats.

③ FLUSHING

The small village, in which a sign warns of swans crossing the road, comes to life with the arrival of the passenger ferry from Falmouth. Tourism, boat-building and fishing are the

principal sources of income at Flushing, a prosperous port in the 17th and 18th centuries. Elegant houses, which were once the homes of naval officers and captains of packet boats, line the waterfront. Riverside walks lead west to Penryn and north to Mylor Churchtown.

④ MYLOR BRIDGE

Two villages blend into one another on the south side of Mylor Creek, both of which are popular mooring spots for pleasure craft. From Mylor Bridge, a lane leads along the southern shore of the creek to the busier harbour of Mylor Churchtown and the Norman Church of St Mylor. In the churchyard is a fine Celtic cross. A footpath follows the north shore of the creek and continues along Carrick Roads to the narrow channel at Restronguet Passage, a quiet hamlet with an old riverside inn.

⑤ LOE BEACH

A steep road from Feock village ends at a small bay where a sand and shingle beach is exposed at low tide. Loe Beach, whose name derives from the Cornish word for rock and harbour, is home to a watersports centre and a boatyard. The beach faces due south, giving good views down Carrick Roads towards Falmouth. From Feock, a lane leads southwards through fields to the rocky tip of Restronguet Point.

⑥ TRELISSICK

Bounded on three sides by the River Fal and two of its many creeks, the estate of Trelissick (NT) encompasses rolling parkland, landscaped gardens studded with subtropical shrubs, and woodland plantations. The 18th-century mansion is open to visitors on a few days each year. There are 5 miles of paths around the estate, including a riverside woodland walk which passes the embarkation point for the King Harry Ferry, a car ferry pulled across the Fal by a diesel-powered chain drive. The channel, though narrow, is deep enough to be used by big ships waiting for a berth at Falmouth docks or making their last voyage to the scrapyard. Neither side of the river has parking space for traffic that is not using the ferry.

⑦ TRURO

The tall towers and spires of Truro Cathedral, completed in 1910, rise above the handsome market town's web of streets. In the 14th century Truro became one of Cornwall's 'stannary' towns, where tin had to be brought for testing and stamping, and the town developed as a port until the 17th century, when much of its shipping trade was lost to Falmouth.

There is still some commercial activity on the Truro river, but the waterway is now used mainly by pleasure craft. Mining continued to bring prosperity to the town, however, as reflected in its many fine Georgian buildings, which

SAFETY FAST *The* Elizabeth Ann, *Falmouth's Arun-class lifeboat, can travel at 18 knots, and has a range of more than 200 miles. It can be visited on certain days in summer.*

include the Royal Cornwall Museum, containing Stone and Iron Age relics and a collection of Cornish minerals. There are summer cruises to Falmouth.

⑧ MALPAS

The tiny village, located at the tip of a headland where the Truro and Tresillian rivers meet, acts as a ferry stage for the Falmouth-Truro service when tidal conditions prevent landing at Truro. At such times, a bus carries passengers along the wooded riverside road between Malpas and Truro, 2 miles to the north-west.

A summer ferry usually links Malpas with the opposite banks of the Truro and the Tresillian, enabling walkers to reach isolated hamlets such as Old Kea and St Michael Penkevil. There is no public access to the private woodland and shore south of St Michael Penkevil.

⑨ ST CLEMENT

A 1 mile footpath heads north from Malpas to a sleepy hamlet by the Tresillian, whose 14th-century Church of St Clement is a favourite subject for photographers and painters. St Clem-

ROSELAND'S TOWER *Warm in the midday sun, the ancient grey stones of the tower of St Just's Church look down on the still waters of St Just Pool, a creek off Carrick Roads.*

ent's unusual lich gate has an upper room said once to have served as the village school. Near the church porch is a stone dedicated to Isniocus Vitalis, a 3rd-century Roman, and bearing inscriptions in the ancient Celtic ogham alphabet. A similar stone, dedicated to the father of Isniocus, can be found in the churchyard at Yealmpton, Devon.

⑩ TURNAWARE POINT

From the B3289 north of St Just in Roseland, a lane leads down past privately owned Commerrans Farm to a secluded National Trust headland. Splendid views towards the mansion and landscaped parkland of Trelissick to the north and the rolling fields edging Carrick Roads to the south make Turnaware Point an ideal area for picnics, but parking space is very limited. The remains of a concrete dock are evidence that the spot was used by Allied troops in the run-up to the D-Day landings of 1944, which are commemorated by an obelisk.

⑪ ST JUST IN ROSELAND

The evocative name of the hilltop hamlet comes from the Cornish word *ros*, or *roos*, meaning promontory. The 13th-century Church of St Just, whose lich gate stands level with the top of its tower, overlooks the pleasure craft in St Just Pool and the big ships in Falmouth harbour. The path to the church is flanked by granite tablets carved with verses, and subtropical plants such as Chilean myrtle and Chinese fan palms tumble down to the waterside.

Most of the land surrounding the coastal path south to St Mawes, which starts from the boatyard at the bottom of the lane beside the church, is owned by the National Trust.

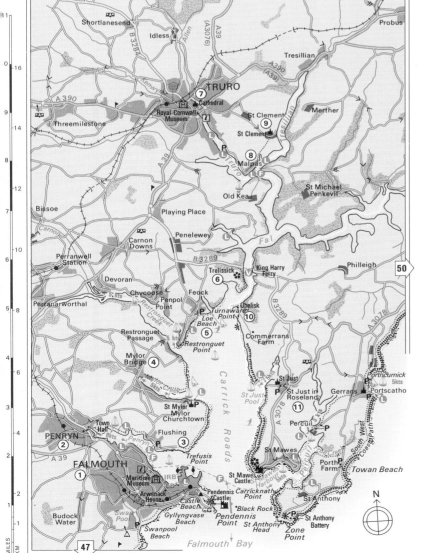

PLACES TO SEE INLAND
Probus Gardens, 5 miles NE of Truro. Gardens, horticultural trial centre and gardening techniques demonstration centre.
Trewithen Gardens, Probus, 5 miles NE of Truro. Woodland parkland and landscaped gardens noted for rhododendrons, azaleas and magnolias.
TOURIST INFORMATION
Falmouth (01326) 312300; Truro (01872) 74555

Sheltered bays and green fields east of St Mawes

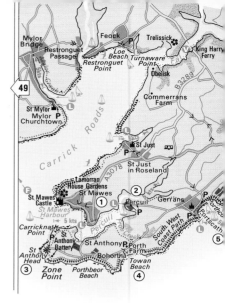

From the tranquillity of the Roseland peninsula, bordering the Carrick Roads waterway, winding lanes lead over grassy headlands to sandy bays, small fishing villages and the bustling resort of Mevagissey.

① ST MAWES

Set on steep slopes at the end of a peninsula flanked by Carrick Roads and the Percuil river, St Mawes clusters around a harbour busy with fishing boats and pleasure craft, where in summer many day visitors arrive by the ferry from Falmouth. The narrow winding road which forms a triangle around the town passes St Mawes Castle (EH), built in the mid 16th century to a clover-leaf design of three bastions around a low tower. The castle faces Falmouth's Pendennis Castle on the opposite side of Carrick Roads, and its grounds provide a splendid vantage point from which to watch big ships ease into the waterway. Nearby are the Lamorran House Gardens, where subtropical plants and water gardens cover precipitous hills. The gardens are open two days a week from spring to early autumn, but are closed in August. Seals are occasionally seen close to St Mawes harbour in the early morning.

St Mawes Castle

② PERCUIL

Once a busy trading port, Percuil is now a hamlet with a tiny harbour dominated by a boatyard and pleasure craft. A National Trust picnic area located on a shoulder of land above the creek offers peaceful views and waterside walks along the Percuil river.

③ ST ANTHONY HEAD

The squat headland, at the foot of which a lighthouse marks the entrance to Carrick Roads, affords superb views of Falmouth Bay and the surrounding countryside. At low tide, stretches of sand appear along the shore between St Anthony Head and Carricknath Point to the north. On the cliff behind the lighthouse are concrete remains of

BRIGHT LIGHT *The 225 000 candlepower lighthouse on St Anthony Head has guided ships into Falmouth harbour since 1835.*

the St Anthony Battery, in military use until the 1950s. The old officers' quarters have been converted by the National Trust into holiday cottages.

④ TOWAN BEACH

A short walk from a discreetly sited National Trust car park at Porth Farm leads to a sweeping half-circle of sand. Although *towan* is the Cornish word for sand dune, there are no dunes at Towan Beach today. They may have disappeared through erosion, or because the sand was removed by farmers and mixed with seaweed to enrich agricultural soil, a common practice at one time. The peaceful sandy beach of Porthbeor, a mile to the south, can be reached by the coast path or by an unmarked track from Bohortha, where there is limited roadside parking.

⑤ PORTSCATHO

Sturdy stone-built houses are gathered around Portscatho's small harbour. The coast path leads south to secluded rocky coves. To the north is the sandy beach of Porthcurnick, where a large car park gives wide-ranging views across Gerrans Bay. The trim, brightly painted Methodist and United Reform chapel overlooking Portscatho harbour was built by a local fisherman in 1822.

⑥ PENDOWER BEACH

At low tide Pendower Beach (NT) and Carne Beach become one long stretch of sand. At its western end Pendower Beach is crossed by a stream which flows down the wooded Pendower Valley. By a lane to the north-east is Carne Beacon, one of the largest Bronze Age barrows in Britain and reputed to be the grave of a Cornish king. Inland is the village of Veryan, distinguished by its thatched round houses, designed by a 19th-century vicar to stop the Devil from lurking in corners.

⑦ NARE HEAD

The headland rises to more than 300 ft, but the 15 minute walk from a National Trust car park above Kiberick Cove to jagged Nare Head is a gentle stroll through open fields. Wide-ranging sea views take in Gull Rock, a nesting site for sea birds such as kittiwakes and guillemots, about half a mile offshore.

⑧ PORTLOE

Fishing boats, winches, lines and lobster pots abound in the unspoiled village's tiny harbour. In stormy weather the narrow gap in the towering rockface is impossible for boats to negotiate. The village's large inn reflects its appeal to tourists. There are memorable walks along the cliffs south-west to Nare Head and east to Porthluney Cove.

⑨ PORTHLUNEY COVE

The wide expanse of sand facing south-west is part of the Caerhays Castle estate, whose grounds can be seen from the beach. The privately owned castle, dating from the early 19th century, is the work of the architect John Nash, whose works include Brighton's Royal Pavilion and London's Marble Arch. The gardens are open to visitors from Easter to early May, and part of the castle is often open during that period.

A pleasant 1 mile stroll west along the coast path leads to the twin villages of East and West Portholland, each set in its own valley behind a shared beach and joined by a winding clifftop road.

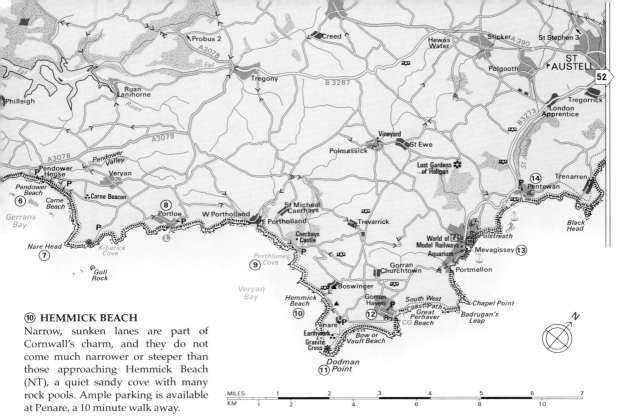

⑩ HEMMICK BEACH

Narrow, sunken lanes are part of Cornwall's charm, and they do not come much narrower or steeper than those approaching Hemmick Beach (NT), a quiet sandy cove with many rock pools. Ample parking is available at Penare, a 10 minute walk away.

⑪ DODMAN POINT

The 20 minute walk from Penare to this striking headland follows the course of a massive Iron Age earthwork. The tree-lined track then joins the coast path, which continues south to a granite cross built in 1896 as a navigational aid. The view inland includes the white 'lunar' landscape of the china clay workings near St Austell, 10 miles to the north.

⑫ GORRAN HAVEN

Tourism plays a large role in this former fishing village, where boats housed in the old pilchard-curing cellars offer cruises and angling trips. There is a fine sandy beach which at low tide connects with the longer and sheltered Great Perhaver Beach to the north. Half a mile to the south-west, a very steep path descends to Bow or Vault Beach, a sweep of sand and shingle at the foot of bracken-clad cliffs.

⑬ MEVAGISSEY

Restaurants, bars, pubs and shops line the village's only through street, reflecting its popularity with holidaymakers. Mevagissey's heart is the large harbour where fishing boats and pleasure craft mingle. Its attractions include an aquarium and a small museum displaying photographs covering a century of local history. Nearby is the World of Model Railways, with more than 40 working model trains. The steep, narrow streets of Mevagissey are unsuitable for cars, and visitors are directed to large car parks at the edge of the village.

To the south is the former fishing and boat-building village of Portmellon. Seen on a sunny day in summer, the cove has a serene quality, but high tides and strong easterly winds sometimes lash the shore, sending spray into the streets. As a defence against the sea, the houses are protected by stout shutters and fronted by concrete walls 3 ft thick. From Portmellon, paths head inland along a stream which flows through a quiet narrow valley.

About 2 miles north-west of Mevagissey are the Lost Gardens of Heligan, where a long-neglected 19th-century garden has been carefully restored to feature summerhouses, a crystal grotto, rockeries and a jungle-like ravine.

⑭ PENTEWAN

The St Austell river reaches the sea at Pentewan, crossing the northern end of a long sandy beach. The harbour has been silted up for decades but it was once the centre of a thriving port. Local stone was quarried in the 18th century, and later the harbour was used for shipping coal, timber and clay. A 2 mile stretch of strenuous coast path leads east to the promontory of Black Head.

PLACES TO SEE INLAND

Automobilia, St Stephen, 10 miles N of Mevagissey. Motor museum.

Polmassick Vineyard, 3 miles W of Mevagissey. Vineyard trails, tastings.

TOURIST INFORMATION

Falmouth (01326) 312300; Fowey (01726) 833616; Mevagissey (01726) 842266

WILD ISOLATION *Arms of rock enclose the wide bay at Polstreath, just north of Mevagissey. The beach is reached by steep steps from the clifftop path.*

Beaches on a sandy bay, and a busy china-clay port

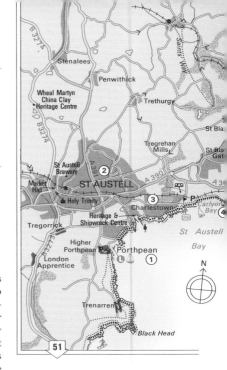

East of Gribbin Head, the sandy sweeps of St Austell Bay give way to a series of little beaches backed by massive cliffs, and lively villages such as Polperro and Looe. At Fowey, huge ships overshadow pleasure craft.

① PORTHPEAN

A narrow lane drops steeply from the neat little village of Higher Porthpean to a car park near a sheltered sandy beach, with fine views across St Austell Bay. The village was once a fishing community, and the old fish cellars are now used by the local sailing club.

② ST AUSTELL

The busy market town owes its development to the discovery in the mid 18th century of kaolin, or china clay, used in the making of paper and porcelain. To the north of St Austell, near the white 'moonscape' formed by the quarry spoil-heaps, is the Wheal Martyn China Clay Heritage Centre. The restored 19th-century site includes an 18 ft water wheel, historic and nature trails, and two working clay pits.

In the town centre, narrow streets spread out from the Italianate market hall, built in the 1840s. The nearby Holy Trinity Church has a carved 15th-century tower, and its central aisle was constructed in a sharp curve. Guided tours are available of the St Austell Brewery, founded in the 1850s.

③ CHARLESTOWN

The town is named after Charles Rashleigh, a local mine-owner who built the harbour in the late 18th century. Copper was the main export for several years, but Charlestown grew prosperous from the export of St Austell's china clay. Better port facilities at Fowey, Par and Plymouth led to the decline of Charlestown's docks at the close of the 19th century, and tourism has largely replaced shipping.

On the edge of the docks area is the Heritage and Shipwreck Centre, which houses an extensive collection of shipwreck artefacts and traces the history of deep-sea diving with audiovisual displays; the centre's square-rigged tall ships, in the inner harbour, can be visited. On either side of the harbour are two small pebbly beaches.

④ CARLYON BAY

A leisure complex, cafés and a range of amusements line much of a long beach, overlooked by a private estate with hotels and a golf course. The shore is backed by craggy cliffs, and at the bay's eastern end is a private naturist beach.

⑤ PAR SANDS

Sand dunes line a large, flat beach that at low water extends seawards for half a mile. To the west are the slender chimneys of Par's clay-processing plant, and to the east is an opening in a low rocky cliff, known as Little Hell Cove, which can be reached when the tide is out.

⑥ POLKERRIS

A narrow lane leads south from the A3082 to a peaceful harbour, where a curving breakwater shelters a sandy, west-facing beach hemmed in by rocky cliffs. From the beach there is a distant view of the smoking chimneys of the clay-processing plants at Par.

⑦ GRIBBIN HEAD

A 20 minute walk south from a car park at the privately owned Menabilly Barton farm leads to a craggy headland,

TRANQUIL COVE *Polkerris's harbour wall dates from the 19th century, when the village was a fishing port. The castle-like structure of the former pilchard cellars still stands.*

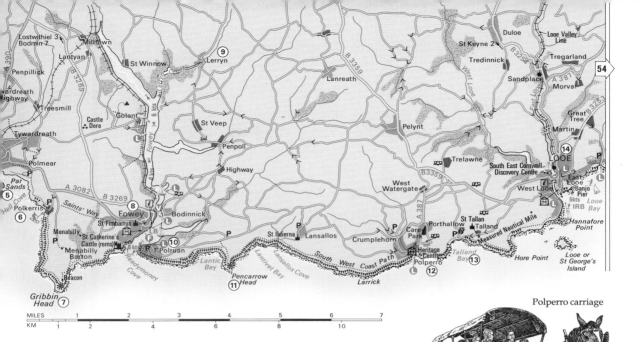

MARINERS' MARK *The beacon on Gribbin Head was built in 1832 to help seafarers to identify the approach to Fowey harbour.*

at the tip of which stands an 84 ft high, red and white landmark for sailors. The footpath skirts the private grounds of Menabilly, which was Daphne du Maurier's home for many years and the 'Manderley' of her novel *Rebecca*.

⑧ FOWEY

The estuary of the River Fowey is a busy waterway, used by ferries, water taxis and pleasure craft, as well as by huge ships making their way to the china clay docks north of Fowey. On the waterfront, shops, restaurants and pubs trade under the shadow of the Church of St Fimbarrus, rebuilt in 1460 after a fire, and houses cover the steep hills behind the ancient port. A small museum has displays on the china clay industry and local shipbuilding. To the south of the town is sandy Readymoney Cove, from which a wooded path climbs up to the remains of 16th-century St Catherine's Castle (EH). Parking is severely restricted in Fowey, but there are large car parks on hills above the town.

The coast path leads south-west to Gribbin Head, and sea and moorland views can be had from the Saints' Way, which runs for 26 miles to Padstow, on the north coast of Cornwall. About 2 miles north-west of Fowey are the Iron Age earthworks of Castle Dore.

⑨ LERRYN

Once a busy river-port, the sleepy creekside hamlet is a good starting point for several walks. Much of the land around Lerryn Creek's thickly wooded slopes, said to have inspired some of the river scenery in Kenneth Grahame's *The Wind in the Willows*, is owned by the National Trust.

⑩ POLRUAN

The passenger ferry from Fowey provides a fine view of Polruan's cottages, stacked high above the village's waterfront. By Town Quay is a 15th-century blockhouse from which a heavy chain was connected to Fowey to seal off the river mouth; deep grooves carved by the chain can be seen in the rock. Cars are not allowed in Polruan during the holiday season.

⑪ PENCARROW HEAD

From a National Trust car park about 1½ miles east of Polruan, a track heads south to a broad headland crisscrossed with trails. West of Pencarrow Head is Lantic Bay, a sandy cove lashed by powerful currents, which is reached by a steep path. In the more sheltered Lantivet Bay to the east is the small shingle beach of Lansallos Cove. From the small village of Lansallos, a half-mile track, which starts beside 14th-century St Ildierna's Church, follows a tree-lined stream which falls to the shore as a small waterfall.

⑫ POLPERRO

Narrow streets, some only 6 ft wide, lead to a little harbour, which swarms with holidaymakers in summer. Non-resident traffic is banned in Polperro; but visitors can ride in a shuttle minibus or a horse-drawn carriage from the car park to the harbour. To the west of the harbour, a climb of some 40 steps leads to Chapel Hill, with its wide-ranging views. In the village is the Heritage Centre, where photographs illustrate

the history of the community. To the east of the museum, a 2 mile clifftop walk leads to Talland Bay.

⑬ TALLAND BAY

A sheltered shingle cove is overlooked by the 13th-century Church of St Tallan. The coast path leads east to the headland of Hore Point (NT), passing large black and white panels used for offshore speed trials by the Royal Navy.

⑭ LOOE

A narrow estuary separates residential West Looe from the popular waterfront and sandy beach of East Looe. The small streets around the Old Guildhall, built in 1500 and now housing the local museum, converge on Banjo Pier, where there is a fish market most mornings. Boat trips include a visit to privately owned Looe Island, a haven for sea birds that lies half a mile offshore. At the South East Cornwall Discovery Centre in West Looe there are video presentations and displays of local wildlife and scenery. The train station in East Looe is a terminus for the scenic 8 mile Looe Valley Line to Liskeard.

PLACES TO SEE INLAND

Lanhydrock (NT), 11 miles NE of Fowey. Victorian country house, long gallery, woodland walks.

Magnificent Music Machines, St Keyne, 6 miles N of Looe. Fairground, cinema and barrel organs.

Restormel Castle, nr Lostwithiel, 8 miles NE of Fowey. Medieval remains in a wooded valley.

TOURIST INFORMATION

Fowey (01726) 833616; Looe (01503) 262072

Polperro carriage

Two great bridges linking Devon with Cornwall

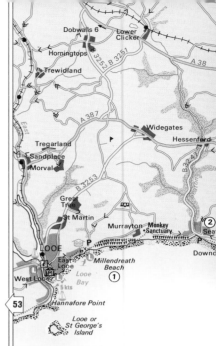

Warships mingle with ferries, fishing boats and yachts in Plymouth Sound, while the Cornish side of the Tamar is characterised by quiet, muddy creeks that are hard to reach by road, and long stretches of sand.

① MILLENDREATH BEACH
A small, sheltered beach of sand and fine shingle, backed by an indoor swimming pool, is the focal point of this holiday village. At the east end of the beach is an artificial pool filled by the tide.

② SEATON
At the mouth of the River Seaton lies a beach of coarse grey sand overlooked by holiday homes. To the west, on a hillside bordering Looe Bay, is the Monkey Sanctuary, where several generations of Amazon woolly monkeys, all bred in Cornwall, roam free in gardens or in outdoor enclosures. There are talks and exhibitions on the life of the monkeys.

③ DOWNDERRY
A large, straggling village, sandwiched between steep slopes and the sea, backs a beach of fine shingle, where low tide exposes a network of rock pools. The south-facing beach is sheltered from northerly winds by a towering sea wall.

④ WHITSAND BAY
East of the hamlet of Portwrinkle, some 4 miles of sands fringe a gently curving bay notorious for strong cross-currents.

The beach can be reached by paths which zigzag down slate cliffs more than 250ft high in places, but the area west of Tregantle Cliff forms part of a military firing range and is sometimes closed to the public. Along some stretches of the beach, high rocks create tiny sheltered coves, and large seawater pools form at low tide.

⑤ RAME HEAD
The southernmost point of Mount Edgcumbe Country Park is a headland of exhilarating beauty. On its tip stands the ruined 14th-century St Michael's Chapel, which originally had a beacon that was kept blazing to guide ships into Plymouth. The chapel is reached by a 10 minute walk from the car park near the coastguard station. The lane to the headland passes through the hamlet of Rame, whose Church of St Germanus is still lit by candles.

⑥ KINGSAND AND CAWSAND
Cawsand Bay was a magnet for smugglers from Tudor times until the 18th century, and the twin villages of Kingsand and Cawsand, with their narrow streets and colour-washed buildings, retain the character of smuggling haunts. Parking is very restricted in both villages. Their tiny sand and shingle beaches, sheltered from the prevailing winds by Rame Head, are good places from which to watch ships sailing in and out of Plymouth.

⑦ MOUNT EDGCUMBE COUNTRY PARK
Extending along the coast from Cremyll to Tregonhawke, the park combines woodland and rugged coastline with formal gardens and open grassy slopes that rise to 377ft above sea level. Its centrepiece is Mount Edgcumbe House, rebuilt in its original Tudor style after being destroyed by bombs in 1941. Exotic plants that thrive in the gardens include some 600 different species of camellia. The country park can be reached from Plymouth by passenger ferry to Cremyll or by car ferry to Torpoint.

⑧ TORPOINT
A frequent car-ferry service, giving views of the Devonport naval dockyard, operates all year round between Plymouth and the busy little town of Torpoint. To the south is St John's Lake, an inlet of tidal marshes and saltings.

A mile north-west of Torpoint is Antony House (NT), an 18th-century mansion with grounds designed by the landscape gardener Humphry Repton. Antony Woodland Garden is crisscrossed by waymarked walks.

⑨ SALTASH
A former fishing port, with narrow streets rising steeply from the riverbank, Saltash offers spectacular views of the Tamar's two mighty bridges. The Royal Albert Bridge, which carries the railway, was designed by Isambard Kingdom Brunel, and completed in 1859. It runs alongside the slender tollbridge for vehicles, built 102 years later.

FEATS OF ENGINEERING *When it opened in 1961, the Tamar Bridge, carrying road traffic alongside Brunel's rail bridge, replaced a ferry service dating from the 13th century.*

SUTTON HARBOUR *Fishing boats dock in Plymouth where Drake, Hawkins, Raleigh and Frobisher began their voyages.*

⑩ PLYMOUTH

An unusual modern landmark, the impressive Armada sundial, stands at the heart of Plymouth city centre, completely rebuilt after its devastation by air raids during World War II. A much older landmark, Smeaton's Tower, dominates the Hoe, the grassy expanse overlooking Plymouth Sound where Sir Francis Drake reputedly finished his game of bowls before sailing to meet the Spanish Armada in 1588. Built in 1759 by John Smeaton, the red and white tower was the third lighthouse to stand on the treacherous Eddystone rocks, 14 miles offshore, before it was moved stone by stone to its present site in 1882. Energetic visitors can climb the 93 steps to the top of the tower.

Just below the Hoe, the Plymouth Dome visitor centre brings the city's epic history to life with imaginative audiovisual shows and sound effects.

Nearby is the imposing Royal Citadel, a 17th-century fortress which can be explored by guided tour.

The citadel watches over Sutton Harbour, with its busy fish market, and the largely pedestrianised Barbican area, whose narrow cobbled streets retain many links with the past, including the Elizabethan House, furnished as it would have been in Drake's time. The Plymouth Gin distillery, where gin has been made to a special recipe for more than 200 years, offers guided tours. Island House is where the Pilgrim Fathers are believed to have lodged before sailing to North America in 1620. Their voyage is commemorated by the Mayflower Stone and Steps.

The Barbican includes an array of small art galleries, but the city's main Museum and Art Gallery is to the north, at Drake Circus. The Pavilions leisure centre includes a skating rink, and a swimming pool with a wave machine.

Boat tours of the warships and dockyards of Devonport naval base depart regularly from the Mayflower Steps, and occasional cruises venture up the Tamar as far as Calstock and Morwellham Quay. Morwellham, where visitors can walk around a reconstructed Victorian copper-mining village, may also be reached by train from Plymouth along the Tamar Valley Line.

⑪ JENNYCLIFF BAY

The clifftop car park above Jennycliff Bay offers wide views of Plymouth and Plymouth Sound. Steps cut into the chalk cliff lead to a small beach of shingle and rocks where the ebbing tide leaves many pools.

THE CIRCUMNAVIGATOR *A statue of Sir Francis Drake, one hand resting on the globe, looks out across Plymouth Sound.*

⑫ BOVISAND BAY

A sandy bay, flanked by low rocks, is overlooked by Fort Bovisand, the base of a large sub-aqua school. To the south, Wembury Point comes under the guns of HMS Cambridge, the Royal Navy's shore-based gunnery school. Red flags fly when firing is in progress.

PLACES TO SEE INLAND

Buckland Abbey (NT), Yelverton, 11 miles N of Plymouth. 13th-century monastery that became Sir Francis Drake's home.

Cotehele (NT), St Dominick, 9 miles NW of Plymouth. Medieval manor house and gardens.

Dobwalls, nr Liskeard, 12 miles W of Saltash. Family adventure park with miniature railway.

TOURIST INFORMATION

Looe (01503) 262072, Plymouth (01752) 264849 or (01752) 266030

CITY OF SEA DOGS AND ADVENTURERS

DRAKE, HAWKINS, FROBISHER, the Pilgrim Fathers, James Cook, Charles Darwin . . . Long and distinguished is the list of seafarers associated with Plymouth, whose historical pre-eminence was determined by its strategic position at the western end of the English Channel, and by the magnificent natural harbour of Plymouth Sound. From the late Middle Ages, Plymouth grew from the small fishing village of Sutton to become one of the greatest ports in the world and England's gateway to overseas expansion. During the 1530s, William Hawkins, from a celebrated Plymouth family of sailors and buccaneers, sailed south-west to Brazil and became the first Englishman to trade across the Atlantic. He returned from a journey to Africa with a tattooed tribal chief, to the surprise of Plymouth's citizens.

Plymouth reached its high point of maritime glory in the reign of Elizabeth I. Sir Martin Frobisher set out from the port in 1576 in a fruitless search for the North-West Passage, and Sir Humphrey Gilbert sailed from there in 1583 to take possession of Newfoundland. But of all the Elizabethan sea dogs it was Sir Francis Drake who most captured the public imagination. In 1566, still in his 20s, he left Plymouth on his first treasure-seeking expedition to the Spanish Main – the northern coast of South America. Drake's greatest moment as a navigator came in 1580, when he returned in triumph to Plymouth after a three-year voyage round

BIDING HIS TIME *A 19th-century drawing imagines Drake finishing a game of bowls on Plymouth Hoe before taking on the Armada. On Drake's left is Lord Howard, High Admiral.*

the world aboard the *Golden Hind*, laden with gold, jewels, spices and silks seized from the Spaniards. In 1587 Drake masterminded the sacking of Cadiz, home port of the Spanish treasure fleet, and the following year, as deputy to Lord Howard of Effingham, he led an English fleet out of Plymouth to help in routing the Spanish Armada. A generation later the town saw another historic departure, when the Pilgrim Fathers set out for the New World. Two ships, the *Mayflower* and the *Speedwell*, had left Southampton in June 1620, but *Speedwell* was found to be unfit for the 3000 mile voyage across the Atlantic, so *Mayflower* sailed alone from Plymouth.

The town had anti-Royalist leanings and sided with Cromwell during the Civil

*Charles Darwin,
1809-82*

A LAST FAREWELL *In September 1620, the* Mayflower *departed from Plymouth (right) for the New World. On board were 36 Puritan pilgrims hoping to escape religious intolerance, and 66 fellow emigrants seeking their fortunes. After a hazardous voyage, the travellers, who included 30 women, landed safely at Cape Cod, Massachusetts. The Mayflower Memorial (above), at Plymouth's Sutton Harbour, commemorates their journey.*

VICTORY OVER THE ARMADA *After the Spanish Armada was sighted in 1588, Drake sailed out of Plymouth Sound to join Lord Howard of Effingham's fleet, which harried the invading forces to destruction up the English Channel and beyond.*

War. In the 1660s, after the Restoration, when Charles II built the Royal Citadel on The Hoe, he made sure that it had gun positions pointing at Plymouth as well as out to sea.

In the early 18th century Devonport was founded as a major naval dockyard, and continued to thrive in that role for some 300 years, before falling victim to defence cuts. Later the same century Captain Cook sailed from Plymouth on his three voyages of exploration, taking in Australia, New Zealand and the Pacific. In 1831 Charles Darwin left Devonport aboard the *Beagle*, on the first of the long voyages that sowed the seeds of his evolutionary theory. By that time Plymouth had become one of the main ports for the transportation of convicts to Australia.

In the years between the two world wars, Plymouth played host to the great transatlantic liners, and in 1940 HMS *Exeter* returned there after taking part in the Battle of the

River Plate, the first major action of World War II. During the war old Plymouth was largely destroyed by German bombers. In the 1970s its maritime tradition was revived with the opening up of ferry routes to Roscoff in Brittany and to Santander in Spain.

LONE VOYAGER *Plymouth's tradition of great navigators was renewed in 1967, when Sir Francis Chichester sailed triumphantly into harbour aboard Gypsy Moth IV (far right, centre) after the first ever single-handed circumnavigation of the globe.*

Deep estuaries among the south Devon farmlands

The low rolling hills of south Devon are crisscrossed by narrow lanes which snake down to a coast of contrasts, where majestic cliffs give way to the softer, more serene beauty of tidal estuaries running far inland.

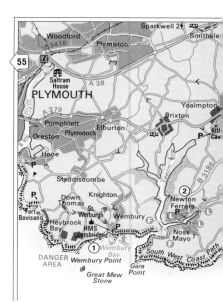

① WEMBURY BAY

The bay is part of a voluntary marine conservation area stretching from Fort Bovisand to Gara Point; Wembury Beach, where a warden conducts 'rockpool rambles' in summer, is used for the study of seashore life. The beach has patches of sand between the rock pools.

A large National Trust car park, overlooked by the Church of St Werburgh, is the starting point for two walks. The westward route gives good views over the mouth of Plymouth Sound and the steep-sided Great Mew Stone, lying within the danger area of the HMS Cambridge gunnery school on Wembury Point. The eastward route leads to the Yealm estuary, which can be crossed in high summer by ferry to Newton Ferrers and Noss Mayo.

② NEWTON FERRERS

Tucked away in the sheltered estuary of the Yealm, pronounced 'Yam', Newton Ferrers is a small sailing centre set on the edge of a creek and overlooked by the attractive village of Noss Mayo. From the mouth of the estuary there is a fine 6 mile walk eastwards over the cliffs to Erme Mouth and Mothecombe.

Three miles north of Newton Ferrers are the popular Kitley Caves, reached by a 15 minute walk from a car park. Excavations have uncovered Stone Age flint tools in the limestone caves, two of which are open to the public.

③ SHIRE HORSE CENTRE

Daily parades of the 'gentle giants' and flying displays by birds of prey are the focus of activities at the National Shire Horse Centre. Visitors can take a horse-drawn cart ride, or a farm walk by the Yealm. Stables and harness rooms are open to the public, and the centre includes a butterfly farm, a large pets area and a children's playground.

④ MOTHECOMBE

A 10 minute walk from the car park in this isolated hamlet leads to a long stretch of low-tide sands at the mouth of the Erme, which runs inland between wooded banks. Wonwell Beach, on the other side of the estuary, can be reached by wading across the river from Mothecombe an hour either side of low tide.

Flete House, set in extensive grounds at the head of the Erme estuary, is built largely in 19th-century Gothic style. It is open to the public on Wednesday and Thursday afternoons in summer.

⑤ BIGBURY-ON-SEA

A small resort, 2 miles seaward of the village of Bigbury, stands on low cliffs, with wide views over a sandy beach curling round to the mouth of the Avon. Burgh Island is joined to the mainland by sand at low tide, but can be reached at other times by sea tractor; the island's 14th-century inn was once a smugglers' haunt. At low tide walkers can follow a 'tidal lane', marked by a line of poles, for 4 miles along the west bank of the Avon from Bigbury to Aveton Gifford.

West of Bigbury-on-Sea is a beach of sand and fine shingle backed by the holiday village of Challaborough.

HIGH RIDE *An ungainly looking wheeled contraption known as a sea tractor links Burgh Island to the mainland at high tide.*

⑥ BANTHAM

Once the focus of a busy port, the quay at Bantham is now used by small-boat sailors. A path from the car park on the promontory leads to a sandy beach edged by marram-covered dunes, with pool-dappled rocks at its southern end.

⑦ THURLESTONE

A long, curving main street, lined by thatched cottages, leads to 13th-century All Saints' Church and a clifftop golf course fringed by sandy coves. Beyond is the sweep of South Milton Sands, favoured by surfers. Thurlestone Rock, a pinnacle holed or 'thirled' by the waves, lies just offshore.

DEVON THATCH *Cottages at Ringmore, near Bigbury-on-Sea, are typical of many that give the area an old-world flavour.*

⑧ HOPE COVE

The sandy, rock-flanked cove has a small harbour at its northern end. At Inner Hope, one of the cove's two hamlets, former fishermen's cottages cluster around a small cobbled square. There is a car park at Outer Hope.

⑨ BOLBERRY DOWN

This exhilarating expanse of turf, gorse and bracken is part of a strip of National Trust land that runs all the way from Bolt Tail to Bolt Head and on towards

---

A PLANT WITH NO LEAVES

The unusual plant called butcher's-broom has no genuine leaves; instead it has leaf-like structures called cladodes which are really flattened stems that bear flowers and berries. Branches are reputed to have been used by butchers for sweeping their meat-chopping blocks. Butcher's-broom is a woodland plant, but in Devon it also flourishes on rocky cliffs.

Butcher's-broom
Ruscus aculeatus
Jan-April

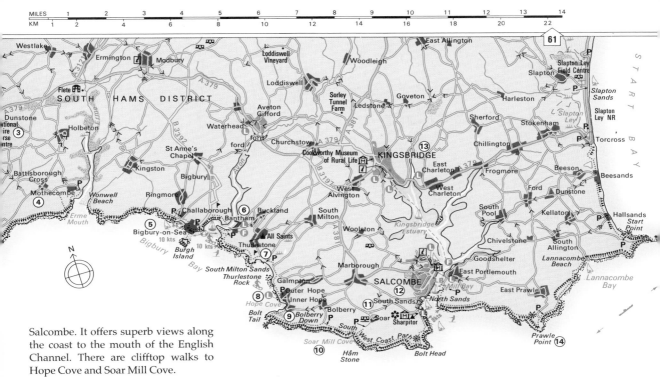

Salcombe. It offers superb views along the coast to the mouth of the English Channel. There are clifftop walks to Hope Cove and Soar Mill Cove.

⑩ SOAR MILL COVE

A steep 10 minute walk from the car park in Soar leads to a sheltered cove of sand and rock pools. The Ham Stone, a few hundred yards offshore, claimed the Finnish barque *Herzogen Cecilie* in 1936. She was one of the last sailing ships to be wrecked on Britain's coast.

⑪ SOUTH SANDS

The popular beach at the end of a wooded valley on the outskirts of Salcombe is backed by a hotel and leisure complex. A passenger ferry runs to Salcombe in summer. On the headland overlooking the beach is Overbeck's Museum and Gardens (NT) at Sharpitor, where palm trees, magnolias and other subtropical plants flourish in the mild climate. The museum explains the area's history, and has special attrac-

tions for children, including a secret room and a ghost hunt. The lane from South Sands to Salcombe passes North Sands, another popular beach framed by wooded cliffs.

⑫ SALCOMBE

A long-established haven for yachtsmen, Salcombe has one of the West Country's finest natural harbours and is the gateway to nearly 2000 acres of tidal creeks. Small boats can explore the tranquil waters as far inland as Kingsbridge. The town's narrow streets are packed with visitors in summer, when the estuary becomes a forest of masts and billowing sails. The Island Cruising Club, based in a converted Mersey ferry, is a sailing school open to day visitors. A maritime museum illustrates Salcombe's history as a sailing port, and as a US base during World War II.

⑬ KINGSBRIDGE

The hub of the South Hams district, Kingsbridge is a lively old town with steep streets leading down to the head of the estuary, where small boats anchor by the quays. Cookworthy Museum of Rural Life has a reconstructed Victorian kitchen and an Edwardian pharmacy.

A mile north of Kingsbridge is Sorley Tunnel Farm, a working farm where visitors may explore an eerie, 150 ft deep disused railway tunnel.

⑭ PRAWLE POINT

A sunken lane zigzags down from East Prawle to a car park, from where it is a short walk to Prawle Point, Devon's southernmost tip. From Salcombe visitors can take a passenger ferry to East Portlemouth and follow the coast path along the southern edge of the Prawle peninsula. At Mill Bay, trees shelter a sandy beach with fine views across the estuary to Salcombe. Between here and Prawle Point is rugged terrain for walkers, but breaks can be taken at secluded coves. East of the point the coast path takes a lower, gentler route, passing several more coves.

YACHTING HAVEN *In summer pleasure craft of all kinds crowd the Kingsbridge estuary and its sinuous creeks, whose sheltered waters are ideal for small-boat sailing.*

PLACES TO SEE INLAND

Dartmoor Wildlife Park, Sparkwell, 8 miles NE of Plymouth. More than 150 species of animals and birds; attractions include the West Country Falconry Centre.

Loddiswell Vineyard, 5 miles NW of Kingsbridge. Guided tours of vineyard, and wine tasting; children's play area.

Saltram House (NT), 3 miles E of Plymouth. Georgian mansion in wooded parkland; interior has well-preserved rooms by Robert Adam; walks beside the River Plym.

TOURIST INFORMATION

Kingsbridge (01548) 853195; Modbury (01548) 830159; Salcombe (01548) 843927

A sweep of shingle curving to the Dart's winding inlet

The grassy and wooded slopes of the Dart estuary contrast with the steeply shelving beaches that fringe the wide arc of Start Bay. Farther north are huge cliffs, and wide views over Tor Bay from Berry Head.

① BERRY HEAD
Berry Head lighthouse is said to be both the lowest and the highest in Britain – the building is only 15ft tall, but because of the height of the cliffs on which it stands the light is 200ft above sea level. Massive 19th-century fortifications on the headland, which gives superb views across Tor Bay, were built to defend the coast against Napoleonic forces. Berry Head is a country park and a nature reserve, and has a large breeding colony of guillemots, known locally as Brixham penguins.

② SOUTHDOWN CLIFF
The 350ft Southdown Cliff can be explored by following the South West Coast Path from Sharkham Point, where there is a car park. Some sections of the path are steep, including the descent from Southdown Cliff to the shingle beach at Man Sands.

To the north of Sharkham Point, steep slopes enclose the sand and shingle beach of St Mary's Bay.

③ KINGSWEAR
Kingswear faces Dartmouth across the Dart, and ferries for foot passengers and cars link the two, sharing the river with pleasure craft using the town's marina and with fishing boats landing crabs. The town is the southern terminus of the Paignton and Dartmouth Steam Railway, whose trains run beside Tor Bay and along the Dart estuary. The line was originally opened in 1864 as part of the Great Western Railway. At Coleton Fishacre Garden (NT), 2 miles east of Kingswear, tree ferns and bamboos flourish in the mild, humid climate, along with plants from many parts of the world including South America and China.

④ STOKE GABRIEL
The former port of Stoke Gabriel stands on sloping river banks above a narrow creek whose upper reaches have been dammed to form a tranquil pool. A magnificent yew tree flourishes in St Gabriel's churchyard; a local legend says that anyone who walks backwards round the tree three times and makes a wish will have the wish granted.

⑤ TOTNES
Elegant 16th and 17th-century houses, many with Georgian façades, climb a steep hill above the River Dart. The town's former East Gate straddles the High Street, and just below it a narrow flight of steps leads up to Rampart Walk, a lane following the line of the medieval town walls. The lane skirts the slate-hung Guildhall, built in 1553, and the 15th-century red sandstone Church of St Mary.

Totnes Castle (EH), at the top of the hill, is a perfect example of a Norman motte and bailey and, never having seen battle, is remarkably well preserved. The town's history is brought to life every Tuesday in summer when local people don Elizabethan costumes and the square is transformed into a bustling marketplace.

Totnes, standing at the highest navigable point on the Dart, was a flourishing port in the Middle Ages. River trips to Dartmouth start at the quayside,

Totnes vintages: 1950 Talbot Lago

1954 D-type Jaguar

which has been carefully renovated. An old cider warehouse on the eastern bank has been converted into a motor museum displaying vintage and sports cars; many of them are in working order and are raced regularly.

Bowden House and Photographic Museum, a mile south of Totnes, contains a large collection of early movie and still cameras. Guides to the house, which has a Queen Anne façade, wear costumes in the style of 1740, and 'ghosts' leap out to startle visitors.

SUNNY SLOPE *Facing south across the River Dart, Kingswear claims to be the sunny side of the estuary. Houses and hotels on the hillside take full advantage of the aspect.*

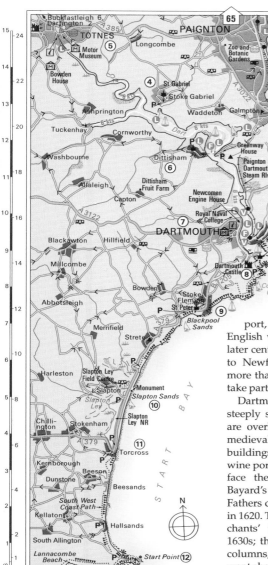

TOTNES
PAIGNTON
BRIXHAM
DARTMOUTH
Dartmouth Castle

and during the Civil War. There is a splendid view across the harbour from the castle roof. Artillery was concealed at Dartmouth Castle during World War II, and the harbour mouth was protected at that time by an anti-submarine boom which supported steel mesh reaching right down to the seabed.

The castle can be reached by boat from Dartmouth Harbour, as well as by road, though parking is very limited. The 17th-century Church of St Petrox, next to the castle, has some fine brasses.

⑨ BLACKPOOL SANDS
High wooded cliffs shelter the crescent of golden sand and fine shingle at the northern end of Start Bay which attracts many visitors in summer.

The village of Stoke Fleming perches 300 ft up on the cliffs above the beach. The tall tower of its 14th-century Church of St Peter served for centuries as a landmark for shipping.

⑩ SLAPTON SANDS
During World War II, US troops used Slapton Sands, and nearby villages, to rehearse for the 1944 D-Day landings. A granite monument overlooking the 3 mile arc of shingle records the US Army's gratitude to the local people. In April 1944, 749 US servicemen died when two of their craft were sunk during a practice exercise off Portland Bill, in Dorset, by German E-boats.

A busy road hugs the beach and for part of its length runs along the top of a narrow shingle bar, behind which is Slapton Ley, a shallow freshwater lake. The lake, and the neighbouring reed-beds, are a national nature reserve and the haunt of many birds, including great crested grebes and Cetti's warblers and, in winter, huge flocks of migrating wildfowl. The reserve's rich

⑥ DITTISHAM
Pronounced 'Ditsome' by local people, the village sits high above the broadest part of the Dart, its skyline dominated by the tower of the medieval Church of St George. Lanes run steeply down to the tidal shore, where a passenger ferry crosses to the jetty at Greenway Quay. Above the quay is Greenway House, the home of the crime writer Agatha Christie from just before World War II until her death in 1976. The house is not open to visitors.

Two miles south-west of Dittisham, at Capton, a Stone Age roundhouse has been reconstructed at Dittisham Fruit Farm. The site has been occupied for at least 8000 years, and many flint tools found there are on display.

⑦ DARTMOUTH
In the 12th century, Crusaders set sail from Dartmouth for the Holy Land. In Elizabethan times 12 ships sailed from the town's fine natural harbour to join the English fleet opposing the Spanish Armada. Down the centuries, Dartmouth grew prosperous as a trading

port, with merchants exchanging English wool for French wine and, in later centuries, venturing farther afield to Newfoundland. On June 4, 1944, more than 480 ships left Dartmouth to take part in the D-Day landings.

Dartmouth's narrow streets are steeply sloped or stepped, and many are overhung by the upper floors of medieval houses. Grapes carved on buildings reflect the town's days as a wine port. Elegant 17th-century houses face the waterfront at the cobbled Bayard's Cove, where the Pilgrim Fathers called on their way to America in 1620. The Butterwalk is a row of merchants' trading houses built in the 1630s; the upper floors, supported on columns, sheltered the traders as they went about their business below. One of the houses is now a museum which traces the town's nautical past and has a collection of model ships.

Thomas Newcomen, who invented the atmospheric steam engine, was born in Dartmouth in 1663; a late 18th-century model, very similar to his first engine of 1712, has been reconstructed at the Newcomen Engine House.

Riverboat cruises along the Dart give fine views of the Britannia Royal Naval College, which dominates the hill overlooking the harbour. Building of the college, which replaced training ships moored on the Dart, was completed in 1905. George V, George VI and the Prince of Wales all trained there.

⑧ DARTMOUTH CASTLE
Standing guard at the mouth of the Dart estuary, Dartmouth Castle (EH) dates largely from the late 15th century but has been added to and altered over the centuries. It was one of the first castles in Britain designed to take cannon. To defend Dartmouth harbour against invaders, a 750 ft chain could be stretched across the river to Kingswear on the opposite bank; the chain was used at the time of the Spanish Armada

HARBOUR GUARD *Built to deter 15th-century Breton raiders, Dartmouth Castle changed hands twice during the Civil War.*

NAUTICAL THEMES *The Britannia Royal Naval College at Dartmouth looks down over a tall ship in the deep waters of the harbour. The town hosts the Dartmouth Regatta in August.*

World War II tank at Torcross

plant life includes the rare strapwort, and fungi found only there. Slapton Ley Field Centre organises guided walks.

⑪ TORCROSS

The small resort and former fishing village of Torcross is sandwiched between Slapton Ley and Start Bay. Its shingle beach is backed by a strong sea wall built after storms washed away the village's defences in 1978-9. A Sherman tank behind the Start Bay Inn stands as a memorial to the US servicemen who lost their lives in the bay in April 1944.

⑫ START POINT

A 15 minute walk from a clifftop car park leads along a narrow, bracken-clad promontory to Start Point. The lighthouse at the tip of the promontory

warns of Black Stone rock, where five ships were wrecked during a single night in 1891. Currents swirling round Start Point make swimming dangerous.

Deserted ruins at the foot of a low cliff 1½ miles north-west of Start Point are the remains of the once-thriving fishing village of Hallsands, nearly all of which was destroyed by storms in 1917. The village had been left vulnerable to the sea and wind when some 650 000 tons of shingle were taken to

Plymouth at the end of the 19th century to make concrete for new docks at Devonport. A mile walk north along the coast path leads to Beesands, where a sea wall protects the line of cottages and a pub that make up the village.

The shingle beach, popular with fishermen whatever the weather, slopes steeply down to the sea. There is a wildflower meadow at the northern end. Beesands can also be approached by car along steep, narrow roads.

PLACES TO SEE INLAND

Buckfast Abbey, Buckfastleigh, 6 miles NW of Totnes. Benedictine monastery open to visitors.

Dartington Cider Press Centre, 2 miles NW of Totnes. Craft centre, glassware, woodland trails.

South Devon Railway. Steam railway along the Dart valley between Totnes and Buckfastleigh.

TOURIST INFORMATION

Dartmouth (01803) 834224; Kingsbridge (01548) 853195; Totnes (01803) 863168

Coves, sands and harbours on the English Riviera

Torquay, Paignton and Brixham, towns of very different character, frame Tor Bay, where palm trees grow along the seafront. As well as the popular beaches, there are secluded coves to be reached only on foot.

① WATCOMBE BEACH
High red sandstone cliffs protect the small, secluded beach at Watcombe, which is reached from the car park by a 5 minute walk down a very steep tarmac lane. A terrace with a shop and café overlooks the sand and shingle shore; there is good fishing from the rocks for dogfish and mackerel.

② BABBACOMBE
The village grew up as a winter resort in the early 19th century. Babbacombe Downs offer far-reaching views, and below them are the sandy Babbacombe and Oddicombe beaches. There is a steep path down to the beaches, and a cliff cable car to Oddicombe Beach. Visitors to Babbacombe Model Village can explore a thatched village, a modern town, an industrial area and a rural landscape – all scaled down to one-twelfth life size.

Bygones, a museum at nearby St Marychurch, has a full scale replica of a Victorian street, which includes shops, a pub and a forge, and has re-created smells. A dauntingly steep 10 minute walk from St Marychurch leads to the shingle Petit Tor Beach. Kents Cavern, a large cave system to the south of Babbacombe, has beautiful rock formations; finds from the caves, which were inhabited in prehistoric times, are displayed in Torquay Museum.

③ HOPE'S NOSE
A grassy slope dotted with pine trees sweeps down from the elegant Ilsham Marine Drive to Hope's Nose, a rocky headland marking the northern end of Tor Bay. Just off the Nose is Ore Stone, which has Devon's largest breeding colony of kittiwakes.

On the Torquay side of the headland is Meadfoot Beach, whose sands completely disappear at high tide.

④ TORQUAY
Described by the poet Lord Tennyson as 'the loveliest sea village in England', Torquay is a town of genteel Victorian terraces, manicured gardens and wide promenades. It became a fashionable resort in the early years of the 19th century, when war in Europe prevented wealthy people taking their holidays abroad.

The Mediterranean atmosphere of Torquay's spacious harbour, palm-fringed and choked with yachts and cabin cruisers, led to comparisons between the town and the French Riviera, and by the 1920s the trio of Tor Bay resorts – Torquay, Paignton and Brixham – were being dubbed 'the English Riviera'.

Torquay's first small harbour was established at the end of the 12th century by the monks of Torre Abbey, whose foundation dates from 1196,

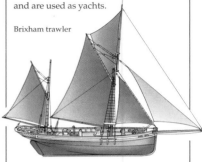
making it the town's oldest building. In the 18th century the abbey remains were incorporated into a Georgian mansion which now houses an art gallery, and has furnished period rooms and collections of glass, silver and porcelain. Within the Abbey Gardens is the Spanish Barn, which is so named because it was used to hold Spanish captives at the time of the Armada, in 1588. Sandy beaches lie to the west of Torquay's harbour, and shingle coves to the east. Boat trips start from the harbour.

A mile inland, and a sharp contrast to Torquay's elegant ambiance, is the village of Cockington, with its leafy lanes, thatched cottages and pretty gardens. Cockington Court, the village manor house, is set in an expanse of parkland and has a Norman church, a craft centre and organic and walled rose gardens. Visitors can tour the village by horse-drawn carriage.

⑤ PAIGNTON
The less grand neighbour of Torquay, Paignton has a long sandy beach, lined with brightly coloured beach huts and popular with young families. Boat trips and fishing trips start at the harbour – a reminder that Paignton was a small fishing village until well into the 19th century. The town's early patrons included Isaac Singer, the sewing machine manufacturer, who in the 1870s built the pillared Oldway Mansion; parts of its interior were inspired by the Palace of Versailles. Some rooms and the formal gardens are open to the public.

The town includes the northern terminus of the Paignton and Dartmouth Steam Railway, which runs along the coast and on to Kingswear. Paignton Zoo, set in botanical gardens, has some 1300 animals.

SECLUDED SHORE *Red sandstone cliffs tumble down to the sea at Watcombe Beach, and at several other small coves around Babbacombe Bay and Tor Bay.*

⑥ GOODRINGTON SANDS

The half-mile stretch of Goodrington Sands is one of Tor Bay's most popular beaches. Behind the beach is Shipwreck Island, a water theme park that includes water rides and slides.

⑦ BROAD SANDS

Steam trains chug along a viaduct behind popular Broad Sands, whose sandy beach slopes very gently to the sea's edge. A short walk over the cliffs from the car park leads to the relative seclusion of Elberry Cove, which has a shingle beach.

⑧ FISHCOMBE BEACH

Wooded red sandstone cliffs back Fishcombe Beach and the neighbouring shingle beach of Churston Cove. The nearest car parks are a few hundred yards away in Brixham. A path zigzags up through woods and leads to Elberry Cove, just over a mile away.

PAST AND PRESENT *Brightly painted houses climb the slopes behind Brixham harbour, in which a replica of Sir Francis Drake's* Golden Hind *is an eye-catching feature.*

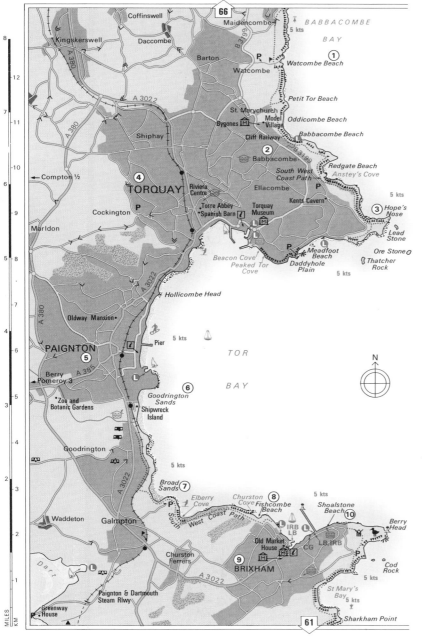

⑨ BRIXHAM

Narrow streets and attractive old buildings cling to the steep slopes which almost encircle Brixham's harbour, home of a large fishing fleet and the oldest town in Tor Bay. Pleasure trips start at the harbour. Yachts and cruisers are moored around a life-size replica of the *Golden Hind*, looking too small to sail round the world as it did under the command of Sir Francis Drake from 1577 to 1580.

The Old Market House, beside the harbour, houses an innovative museum called The Deep, where visitors can explore a sunken pirate ship, look into a mermaid's underwater cavern and descend towards the seabed in a bathysphere – a spherical deep-diving chamber.

Brixham Museum, housed in a former police station in the town centre, has exhibits on the fishing industry, the coastguard and boatbuilding. There is a collection of pictures that were embroidered by seamen on their long voyages.

⑩ SHOALSTONE BEACH

A small pebbly beach lies to the east of Brixham's long breakwater, and a few hundred yards farther is the shingle and rock Shoalstone Beach, a favourite place for rock-pool dabblers at low tide. There is an open-air seawater swimming pool.

PLACES TO SEE INLAND

Berry Pomeroy Castle (EH), 5 miles W of Paignton. Ruins of medieval castle and Tudor mansion on a wooded hillside.

Compton Castle (NT), 5 miles W of Torquay. Fortified manor house, with restored great hall, dating from the 14th to 16th centuries.

TOURIST INFORMATION

Brixham (01803) 852861; Paignton (01803) 558383; Torquay (01803) 297428

Red cliffs and sands, and the wide estuary of the Exe

TRADESMAN'S SIGN *One of Topsham's endearing oddities is a plaster relief of a bull's head above a butcher's shop.*

Vast numbers of birds visit the estuary formed by the River Exe as it flows into the sea south of Exeter. Sandstone cliffs the colour of mellow red brick flank the resorts of Dawlish and Teignmouth.

① LYMPSTONE

Low red sandstone cliffs flank a village of pastel-coloured cottages and narrow streets with cobbled pavements. The small harbour is used by fishing boats and pleasure craft, and is a good vantage point from which to observe the bird life of the Exe estuary.

② TOPSHAM

Attractive houses with Dutch gables and bow windows date from the 17th century, when Topsham was a busy port where merchants from Holland traded in Devon wool. The town was also a shipbuilding centre until the late 19th century. Topsham Museum, in a late 17th-century merchant's house, traces the town's maritime history and describes the wildlife of the Exe estuary.

③ EXETER

Dominating the city's skyline are the twin Norman towers of St Peter's Cathedral, a beautiful golden building with a wealth of carved stone and wood. The 300 ft nave has a soaring rib-vaulted roof decorated with ornately carved and coloured bosses. A 15th-century clock shows the Moon and Sun revolving round the Earth.

Exeter was founded by the Romans as Isca Dumnoniorum, and sections of the Roman city wall still stand. In the heart of the city, alleys which survived air raids in 1942 are overhung by the upper floors of half-timbered medieval buildings. Beneath the city's streets are the Underground Passages – medieval aqueducts built to bring water to the city. The passages may date from as early as the 12th century and can be visited, but are very narrow.

By the River Exe, boutiques, craft shops, pubs and restaurants line The Quay, where woollen cloth was once loaded onto ships. Exeter Maritime Museum, beside the river, is the world's largest collection of boats built for work; exhibits include a Chinese junk, a tiny Welsh coracle, African dugouts, an Iraqi boat built of pomegranate stalks and straw, and craft from Indonesia, Norway and Malaysia. Some boats are on the water, while others are displayed in former dock buildings.

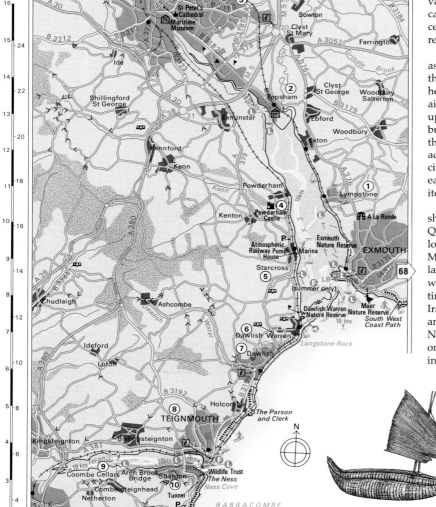

On show in Exeter is a reed boat from Lake Titicaca in South America (left).

Another exhibit at the Maritime Museum is St Canute, a Danish steam tug built in 1931.

④ POWDERHAM CASTLE

The battlemented Powderham Castle stands in a deer park beside the Exe. Built between 1390 and 1420, it was much altered and renovated in the 17th and 18th centuries after damage in the Civil War and has fine state rooms.

⑤ STARCROSS

In summer, a passenger ferry links the quiet village of Starcross with Exmouth, across the estuary. The tall building overlooking the jetty where the ferry starts was one of the pump houses built in the 1840s to serve the 'atmospheric' section of Isambard Kingdom Brunel's Great Western Railway between Exeter and Newton Abbot. Pumps evacuated air from a tube between the rails, creating a vacuum which 'pulled' a piston attached to the train. The system was abandoned in 1848.

⑥ DAWLISH WARREN

Chalets, amusement arcades and caravans make up the holiday resort at the landward end of Dawlish Warren, a 1¼ mile sandspit that juts out across the mouth of the Exe estuary. There are fast-flowing currents at the tip of the spit. A lane under the railway line leads to a car park, go-kart track and funfair, and a long sandy beach with abundant shells. The view to the south is dominated by Langstone Rock, a huge block of sandstone with a wave-carved arch.

Dawlish Warren Nature Reserve embraces an extensive area of mud flats and salt marsh, as well as dunes and sandy shore. The reserve attracts large numbers of waders and wildfowl, including dunlins, black-tailed godwits and Brent geese. Among its hundreds of flowering plants is the Warren crocus, whose lilac-blue flowers can be seen nowhere else in mainland Britain.

⑦ DAWLISH

At the centre of this family resort is The Lawn, an ornamental garden through which Dawlish Water flows over a series of small weirs. Black swans can often be seen on the water. A railway line runs right along the seafront, and a tunnel under the track leads to a long beach of deep red shingle and sand, typical of this part of Devon's coast. At the southern end of the beach, high cliffs shelter a cove which is the starting point for mackerel fishing trips, and boat trips to Brixham and Babbacombe. Charles Dickens was a regular visitor to Dawlish and set part of his novel *Nicholas Nickleby* there.

⑧ TEIGNMOUTH

A long beach of dark red sand is backed by a promenade with a bowling green, playgrounds and a miniature golf course. At the southern end of the beach, near the mouth of the Teign estuary, the shore shelves steeply and there are dangerous currents.

Teignmouth harbour exports ball clay from nearby quarries; the clay is used to make crockery and bathroom fittings. Dartmoor granite was shipped from Teignmouth in the early 19th century for the building of structures such as the former London Bridge, now in the USA, and the British Museum.

⑨ COOMBE CELLARS

Hidden away at the end of a narrow lane leading to the Teign estuary is a yacht club, and an inn once notorious for smugglers who were reputed to have eluded capture by using a secret passage leading under the estuary to the far shore. 'Cellars' is a corruption of *salaria*, the Latin word for salt; the Romans once panned for salt from the nearby marshland. From the shore there are good views of the granite outcrops of Hay Tor on Dartmoor. At lonely Arch Brook Bridge, half a mile to the east, waders flock onto the mud flats at low tide, and the skeletons of rotting rowing boats provide resting places for sea birds. There is a breeding colony of herons at Netherton, a mile south-west of Coombe Cellars.

⑩ SHALDON

Georgian cottages, shops and pubs surround the carefully tended bowling green in Shaldon, which overlooks the Teign estuary. A well-lit smugglers' tunnel through The Ness headland leads to Ness Cove, a sandy beach at the foot of high cliffs that is popular with young families. At the landward end of the tunnel is the Shaldon Wildlife Trust, a collection of small mammals, exotic birds and reptiles. A passenger ferry connects Shaldon and Teignmouth. Fast currents at the mouth of the Teign make bathing dangerous.

⑪ MAIDENCOMBE

A precipitous path and a long flight of steps lead down from Maidencombe's car park to a small secluded sandy beach framed by high red cliffs and fallen boulders. Visitors are warned not to climb at the foot of the cliffs because of the danger of rock falls.

PLACES TO SEE INLAND

Killerton (NT), 7 miles NE of Exeter. Late 18th-century house with costume collection; grounds with rhododendrons and rare trees.

Newton Abbot. Market town. Medieval church tower without a church; working malthouse open to public; lake and woodland walks in Decoy Country Park.

TOURIST INFORMATION

Dawlish (01626) 863589; Exeter (01392) 265700; Exeter Services (01392) 437581; Newton Abbot (01626) 67494; Teignmouth (01626) 779769

SEASIDE LINE *The railway line to Penzance, built by Brunel for the Great Western Railway, provides passengers with coastal views, and Dawlish with an unusual seafront.*

An elegant Regency town near quiet holiday villages

The coastline of east Devon is a feast of contrasting colours: burgundy red headlands at Sidmouth, honey-yellow sands at Exmouth and an abundance of lush green countryside descending to glistening blue seas.

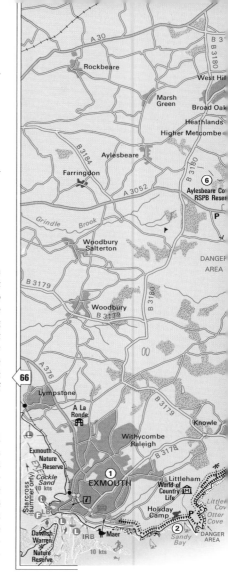

① EXMOUTH

The cliffs dominating the East Devon coastline give way at Exmouth to 2 miles of flat, sandy beach. The resort is stylish and spacious with immaculate gardens and parks, and attractions such as putting and a boating pool. From the old docks area there are magnificent views upriver towards Exeter. A summer foot ferry sails to Starcross on the opposite bank of the Exe estuary. Exmouth Nature Reserve encompasses Cockle Sand and the surrounding mud flats. From the footpath or the 'drive-in' path near the railway station, visitors may see redshanks, dunlins, and even sanderlings and grey plovers. Farther east an area of sand dunes and grassland forms Maer Nature Reserve, where around 400 species of plant grow.

On the northern edge of the town is A La Ronde (NT), a unique 16-sided house built in 1796, whose interior is encrusted with shells.

② SANDY BAY

The superb, sandy beach can be visited by car only after paying to go through a large holiday camp. Part of the cliff area is used as a military firing range and a red flag flies when it is in use. Vintage vehicles, farm animals and an adventure playground are among the attractions on offer at the World of Country Life, near the holiday camp.

③ BUDLEIGH SALTERTON

The River Otter reaches the sea at Budleigh Salterton, whose broad sweep of pink, pebbled beach is guarded to the west by 500 ft red sandstone cliffs.

The coast path can be followed with little interruption for 6 miles south-west to Exmouth and 6 miles north-east to Sidmouth. Budleigh's sea wall was the setting for Sir John Millais's painting 'The Boyhood of Raleigh'. Behind part of the wall stands the house, marked by a plaque, where the painter lived. One of the pews in All Saints' Church at nearby East Budleigh bears the coat of arms of the Raleigh family.

④ OTTERTON

A shimmering stream passes thatched houses in Otterton's main street. A signpost shows the way to Otterton Mill, a restored water mill that continues a tradition stretching back to the 11th century, when the original mill was built. There is a delightful 3 mile walk south through riverside meadows to Budleigh Salterton. Bicton Park, northwest of Otterton, has a woodland railway and themed gardens.

⑤ LADRAM BAY

The small bay can be reached only from the large parking area at the caravan park near Otterton village. Fulmars fly above the spectacular red cliffs, parts of which have been eroded by the sea into isolated columns, and cormorants hunt in the waters below. It is a good beach for fishing, particularly for mackerel.

⑥ AYLESBEARE COMMON RSPB RESERVE

Summer is the best time to visit the reserve, when birds such as curlews, nightjars and tree pipits can be seen, and the heath is at its most colourful, with the pinks and mauves of heather and the brilliant yellow of gorse. The entrance to the reserve is across the A3052 from a roadside car park a mile west of Newton Poppleford.

⑦ SIDMOUTH

When the weather is rough, the sea at Sidmouth is streaked with red from the sand of the crumbling, ruddy-coloured cliffs that rise on each side of the bay. The half-mile stretch of shingle beach is popular for sun bathing, sailing and fishing. Handsome hotels, many of them Regency or Victorian, line the esplanade, and a fine indoor swimming

pool lies at the eastern end. Peaceful gardens and clipped lawns stretch along the western end of the seafront. Overlooking the town, on Salcombe Hill, is the Norman Lockyer Observatory, which has a planetarium and two telescopes from the late 19th century.

THE BOYHOOD OF RALEIGH *Sir John Millais set his painting at Budleigh Salterton. His sons posed as the two boys.*

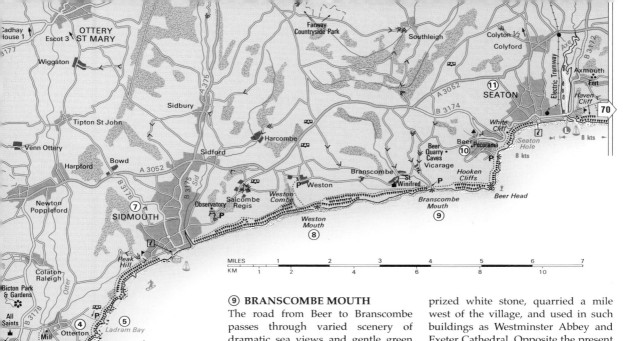

MILES   1   2   3   4   5   6   7
KM   1   2   4   6   8   10

⑧ WESTON MOUTH

There can be an almost eerie sense of isolation on the small, pebbly beach at Weston Mouth. Inaccessible by car, it is the most secluded of the bays in this area. A walk of about 15 minutes leads from a tiny, grass-covered parking area in the hamlet of Weston through woodlands and open fields, before descending to the beach by means of a flight of steps cut into the red hillside which flanks Weston Combe.

⑨ BRANSCOMBE MOUTH

The road from Beer to Branscombe passes through varied scenery of dramatic sea views and gentle green valleys, and narrows as it approaches the beach. There is a thatched café beside the car park on the sheltered, shingle shore with views to the east of the awesome columns of Hooken Cliffs, scene of a massive landslip in 1790. Branscombe itself is a pretty village with a thatched smithy, dating from Norman times, and a 12th-century church. St Winifred's has a triple-decker pulpit, one of only two in Devon, and the remains of a 15th-century mural.

⑩ BEER

Fishermen and fishing boats share the pebbly beach at Beer with holiday-makers and their deckchairs. A large car park on a grassy headland west of the beach provides spectacular views towards Lyme Regis. Similar fine views add to the pleasures of a trip on the miniature railway at the Pecorama fun park. Beer is famous for its highly prized white stone, quarried a mile west of the village, and used in such buildings as Westminster Abbey and Exeter Cathedral. Opposite the present quarry are the old workings of Beer Quarry Caves, where there are conducted tours of the immense halls and galleried passages that were first worked in Roman times.

⑪ SEATON

The sedate resort has a mile-long beach of shingle and pebbles that curves east from the bulk of White Cliff to Haven Cliff. Seaton's most popular attraction is its Electric Tramway, which has a fleet of nine trams, some open-top, and travels for 3 miles inland from Harbour Road to Colyton. The route is excellent for birdwatching as it runs beside the mud flats and marshes of the River Axe, where many waders and ducks feed and breed.

Seaton tram

SCENE OF A QUEEN'S GIRLHOOD Sidmouth retains much of its early 19th-century elegance. The future Queen Victoria lived there with her parents from 1819 to 1820.

PLACES TO SEE INLAND

Cadhay, 7 miles NW of Sidmouth. Tudor House.

Colyton, 3 miles N of Seaton. Village laid out in the Saxon pattern; St Andrew's Church, with carved Saxon cross.

Escot Aquatic Centre and Gardens, 8 miles NW of Sidmouth. Estate in parkland. Otters, wild boar, wilderness walks.

Farway Countryside Park, 7 miles NW of Seaton, nature reserve, farm animals, butterflies.

TOURIST INFORMATION

Budleigh Salterton (01395) 445275; Exmouth (01395) 263744; Seaton (01297) 21660; Sidmouth (01395) 516441

Golden sandstone heights east of Lyme Regis

The shifting shingle of Chesil Beach, the towering headland of Golden Cap and the crumbling, fossil-rich cliffs of Lyme Bay offer a fascinating series of geological contrasts along West Dorset's spectacular coast.

① AXMOUTH

One of the busiest ports in Britain in Roman times, Axmouth was described in the 16th century by the historian John Leland as 'an olde and bigge fischar toune'; it was also a centre for the export of West Country wool and iron. Over the centuries landslips have choked the mouth of the Axe, stranding the former port a mile from the sea. It is now a somnolent village of thatched cottages lying beside a marshy estuary that attracts curlews, redshanks, common sandpipers and many other birds. Stepps Lane winds up to Hawkesdown Hill, where there is an Iron Age fort and a path to the Undercliffs nature reserve.

② UNDERCLIFFS NATIONAL NATURE RESERVE

In 1839, in a huge landslide, some 20 acres of chalkland between Axmouth and Lyme Regis slid seawards, creating what is known locally as Goat Island. The landslip is now part of a national nature reserve called the Undercliffs, which stretches for 6 miles through some of the wildest, most unspoiled country in southern England.

A narrow footpath, part of the coast path, runs through the reserve, but it is rough and slippery in wet weather. There are no points of access from the path to the beach, or to the land on either side of the path, and only experienced walkers should attempt the full journey. But it is possible to walk for a couple of miles and enjoy the tranquility of this undisturbed countryside, where deer and badgers roam and 120 species of birds have been recorded. From Lyme the reserve is reached by a footpath from Holmbush car park at the top of Pound Street. Energetic walkers may enjoy the challenge of the climb to the car park from Monmouth Beach, where the grey, glutinous nature of the slips can be seen at close quarters.

③ LYME REGIS

Although the present Lyme Regis is a quiet and charming resort, it has a dashing, heroic past involving sea battles, smugglers and sieges. Many of these adventures centred on The Cobb, the 600 ft long stone breakwater protecting the harbour. The Cobb remains the focal point of the town today, with visitors enjoying the salty atmosphere of yachts and fishing boats. Lyme's attractions include a marine aquarium on The Cobb, and a Dinosaurland exhibition. The Philpot Museum has samples of

PORT ROYAL *A forest of bobbing masts fills the harbour at Lyme Regis. The town gained its suffix 'Regis' under Edward I, who used the port as a base for wars against the French.*

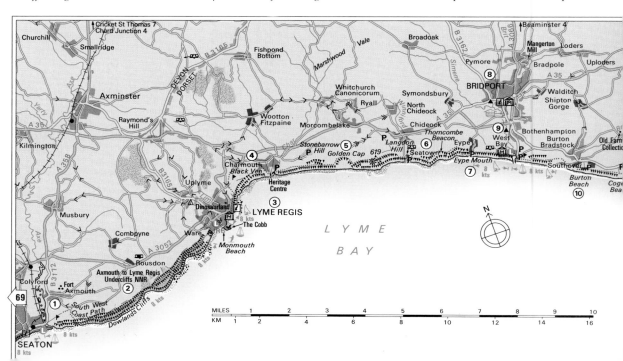

local fossils. Narrow streets lined with colour-washed houses climb steeply from the seafront, and there are several vantage points with fine views towards Golden Cap over Black Ven, the fossil-bearing cliffs between Lyme and Charmouth. These cliffs continue to slip, and the coast path over them is closed. The beach area is threatened by cliff falls, tides and mud flows.

④ CHARMOUTH

A popular resort, with a beach of shingle and low-tide sands, Charmouth is world famous for its abundance of fossils, exposed during centuries of cliff erosion. In 1810 the first complete fossil of an icythyosaurus, a meat-eating reptile resembling a giant porpoise, was discovered at Black Ven by 11-year-old Mary Anning. A heritage coast centre on the seafront gives information about the fossils, including where they can be found, preferably with the help of an expert guide. The cliffs and the tides are treacherous, and fossil-hunters should take extreme care.

THE COBB *Lyme Regis's harbour wall, looking out to Golden Cap, inspired scenes in two novels – Jane Austen's* Persuasion *and John Fowles's* The French Lieutenant's Woman.

FOSSILS FROM THE CLIFFS

The coast east of Lyme Regis is a happy hunting ground for amateur fossil collectors. Climbing the cliffs is dangerous, but among the stones on the beach below are the remains of animals that lived some 200 million years ago. The most common fossils found are those of extinct molluscs such as the spiral-shaped ammonite and the bullet-shaped belemnite.

Ammonites are distant ancestors of squids.

---

⑤ GOLDEN CAP

The golden-orange sandstone peak of Golden Cap soars to 619ft above sea level, making it the tallest cliff in southern England. Dramatic views from the top stretch as far as Portland Bill to the east and Start Point to the west. The cliff is part of a National Trust estate that embraces most of the coastal land between Charmouth and Seatown, and includes 18 miles of walks over terrain ranging from steep cliffs to undulating meadows and clumps of ancient woodland. Several paths lead to the summit of Golden Cap, but the shortest route is from the car park at Langdon Hill to the north-east. There is another car park and an information centre at Stonebarrow Hill, to the west.

⑥ SEATOWN

Reached by a lane from Chideock, this village with thatched cottages of honey-coloured stone has an open shingle beach which shelves steeply above low-tide sands. Golden Cap can be seen a mile to the west, while along the coast path to the east Thorncombe Beacon rises to more than 500ft.

⑦ EYPE MOUTH

A narrow lane winds steeply through the tiny village of Eype, pronounced 'eep', to a car park, from which steps descend to a small, secluded shingle beach backed by crumbling clay and sandstone cliffs. West Bay is a mile-long walk over the cliffs, or 3 miles by road.

⑧ BRIDPORT

Ropes and nets have been made in Bridport since the 13th century, with craftsmen adapting to changing social conditions. During the age of sail the town was so closely associated with rope-making that the hangman's noose was known as 'the Bridport dagger'. Modern workers, by contrast, use their skills to provide nets for snooker-table pockets. Bridport is now a busy shopping centre, with markets on Wednesdays and Saturdays. Among the town's interesting buildings are the Georgian town hall, and Britain's only thatched brewery, established in the late 18th century. The town's museum explores Bridport's local history.

On the northern side of the town is Mangerton Mill, a 17th-century working watermill and rural museum.

⑨ WEST BAY

Bridport's former harbour, where ships were built until 1879, is a mile from the centre of the town. At its eastern end is a beach of fine shingle backed by soaring, wind-sculpted, orange cliffs. West Bay, which marks the westernmost point of Chesil Beach, is now visited mainly by sunbathers, walkers and fishermen. The River Brit reaches the sea here, but silting has always been a problem at the man-made harbour, whose story is told at the Harbour Museum.

⑩ BURTON BEACH

The expanse of fine shingle and sand overlooked by the village of Burton Bradstock, though officially called Burton Beach (NT), is known locally as Hive Beach, and is signposted as such from the village. From the car park at the end of Beach Road, there is a grassy picnic area and a track to the beach,

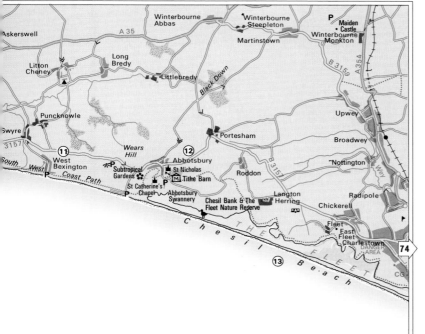

PORTLAND PROSPECT *Beyond the hilltop St Catherine's Chapel, the shingle bank of Chesil Beach (above) encloses The Fleet lagoon, whose eel-grass feeds swans at Abbotsbury. In Abbotsbury, the huge tithe barn (left) once stored local produce paid as tax to the Abbey of St Peter.*

where the erosion of soft layers in the cliffs creates the impression of an end-view of stacks of timber.

A rough track, for walkers only, leads down from a parking area next to the B3157 to the shingle bank of Cogden Beach (NT). The Old Farming Collection, on the road between Burton Bradstock and Litton Cheney, is a working farm on the River Bride, with displays of old farming equipment.

⑪ WEST BEXINGTON

The road through the small village ends by a steeply shelving shingle beach backed by a few beach huts and a car park used mainly by sea anglers. From the top of Wears Hill, a few miles to the east on the road to Abbotsbury, there are superb views of Chesil Beach and the Isle of Portland.

⑫ ABBOTSBURY

The Tithe Barn and the Abbotsbury Swannery are within easy walking distance of the car park in this village of honey-coloured houses. The large thatched stone barn, now a country

museum, was built in about 1400 to store the riches of the neighbouring Abbey of St Peter, one wall and an archway of which remain. The Swannery, founded by the abbey monks as a source of food, now gives sanctuary to hundreds of mute swans, which breed in the lagoon behind the shingle beach.

On a hill overlooking Abbotsbury is the 14th-century St Catherine's Chapel (EH), once used to store thatchers' reeds, but now in a state of disrepair. St Nicholas's Church has a pulpit pockmarked with shots fired during the Civil War, when the village fell to Cromwell's Parliamentarians.

Just west of the village are the subtropical Abbotsbury Gardens, set in a valley where a very mild microclimate allows exotic trees and shrubs to flourish out of doors all year round. The gardens include streams and ponds.

⑬ CHESIL BEACH

The billions of pebbles that make up Chesil Beach are naturally graded from west to east, the fine gravel at West Bay increasing gradually in size to large cobbles at Portland, 17 miles away. Chesil Bank, part of the beach east of Abbotsbury, rises to a height of 40 ft and protects a lagoon known as The Fleet. The lagoon forms a nature reserve that attracts swans, waders such as curlew and dunlin, and many wintering wildfowl. The Bank can be reached from car parks either end of the reserve at Abbotsbury and Portland. There is no pedestrian access along the beach between May and August to prevent the disturbance of breeding birds.

PLACES TO SEE INLAND

Beaminster, 6 miles N of Bridport. Parnham House and Gardens, with woodworking school; 16th-century Mapperton House and Gardens.

Crinkley Bottom TV Theme Park, Cricket St Thomas, 15 miles N of Lyme Regis.

Forde Abbey, Chard Junction, 13 miles N of Lyme Regis. Cistercian monastery converted into country house. Gardens.

Maiden Castle, 7 miles NE of Abbotsbury. Ancient grass-covered hill-fort.

TOURIST INFORMATION

Bridport (01308) 424901; Lyme Regis (01297) 442138

Sculptures in rock, and the wide bay of Weymouth

Between the two 'islands' of Portland and Purbeck, Dorset's chalk downs meet the English Channel in a series of high white cliffs, where over thousands of years the sea has created startling rock formations.

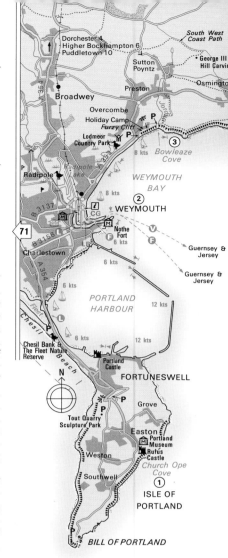

① ISLE OF PORTLAND

Stories of smugglers and shipwrecks abound in this dramatic rocky peninsula, which the writer Thomas Hardy described as 'the Gibraltar of Wessex'. Steep on its northern side and gently sloping to the south, the isle is pitted with quarries, several still producing the pale-coloured Portland stone from which both St Paul's Cathedral and Buckingham Palace were built.

At the southernmost tip, the fast-flowing currents known as 'Portland Race' have been responsible for many shipping disasters, including one that claimed the life of William Wordsworth's brother John in 1805. Portland Bill lighthouse looms above the rocky foreshore, and a short distance inland a white Trinity House tower is now used as an RSPB observatory.

Portland Castle (EH), built by Henry VIII, has an interior little changed since Tudor times. Cannons line the stone 'apron' that guards the harbour. From the shattered walls of the 11th-century Rufus Castle, named after the ruddy-faced William II, steep steps lead down to Church Ope Cove, a small beach lined with fishermen's huts. Nearby Portland Museum explores the island's history. Tout Quarry Sculpture Park uses a former quarry as a natural gallery for modern sculptures, many carved from the living rock. The wildlife information centre at Chesil Bank and The Fleet Nature Reserve is the starting point for two nature trails.

② WEYMOUTH

A long, wide, sandy beach is backed by an elegant curve of small hotels and boarding-houses, many dating from the late 18th or early 19th centuries. George III began to visit the town for his health in 1789, and established Weymouth as a fashionable resort. An ornate statue of him stands on the seafront. The nearby pinnacled clock tower was built in 1887 for Queen Victoria's Golden Jubilee. During 1869-70 Thomas Hardy worked for a Weymouth architect, and the town features in some of his writings as Budmouth Regis. The quays of Weymouth harbour are lined with fishing boats and pleasure craft.

At Brewers Quay, just south of the harbour, an 18th-century brewery now combines a period shopping village with attractions such as the Timewalk, illustrating six centuries of Weymouth's maritime past. Deep Sea Adventure, in a restored warehouse across the harbour, tells the story of global underwater exploration. Nothe Fort, built in 1860-72 as a bulwark against the threat of French invasion, has been converted into a museum of coastal defence. Radipole Lake is an RSPB reserve in the heart of the town, while Lodmoor Country Park, just north of the town, includes another bird reserve and a Sea Life park.

③ BOWLEAZE COVE

The cove, which is overlooked by part of a holiday camp, has a beach of sand, shingle and seaweed-covered rocks. Above it, the broad expanse of turf on Furzy Cliff, which is favoured by picnickers, offers exhilarating views over Weymouth Bay to the Isle of Portland. Limited car parking is available on the

NATURAL ARCH *Durdle Door is one of the most remarkable rock formations on Britain's coast. Durdle is derived from the Anglo-Saxon word* thirl, *meaning 'to pierce'.*

DORSET'S RARE SKIPPER

The dancing flight of the brown and black Lulworth skipper may be seen along the coast from Sidmouth to Swanage, and particularly on grassland slopes around Lulworth Cove, during July and August. The butterfly was first recorded more than a century ago, and is rare outside Dorset and Devon.

Lulworth skipper   Wing underside
Thymelicus acteon

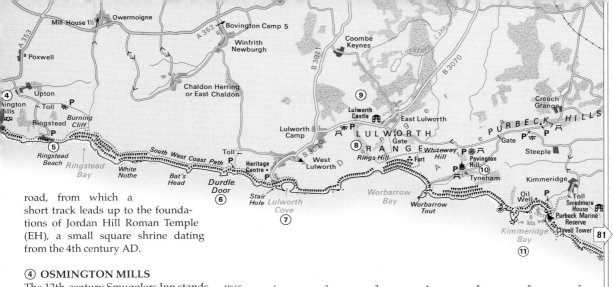

road, from which a short track leads up to the foundations of Jordan Hill Roman Temple (EH), a small square shrine dating from the 4th century AD.

④ OSMINGTON MILLS

The 13th-century Smugglers Inn stands at the top of a path leading down to a cove of shingle and rocks. North of Osmington village is a huge figure of George III on horseback, cut into the chalk slope in 1808.

⑤ RINGSTEAD BEACH

A narrow lane leads through the hamlet of Upton to a sloping shingle beach. This stretch of coast suffered serious erosion from winter storms in the 1980s. From the T-junction above Ringstead village, another lane leads over a cattle grid to a National Trust car park, beyond which the South West Coast Path takes walkers along the cliff to the imposing chalk headland of White Nothe, a mile to the east. Burning Cliff consists largely of oil-rich shales, which ignited in the 1820s and continued to smoulder for several years.

⑥ DURDLE DOOR

A spectacular limestone doorway, carved out by the sea, is reached by a steep track from the clifftop car park. On either side of the arch flights of steps lead to shingle coves. Both beaches are popular with swimmers and subaqua divers. Another, smaller hole pierced through the rock can be seen a little farther to the west, at Bat's Head.

⑦ LULWORTH COVE

High cliffs of crumbling chalk form a natural amphitheatre round a beautiful, oyster-shaped bay. Stair Hole, west of Lulworth, is a similar cove in the making. Lulworth Heritage Centre explains the area's geology and history.

⑧ LULWORTH RANGE

The coast from the east side of Lulworth Cove round to Kimmeridge Bay forms part of a Royal Armoured Corps tank and gunnery range, but the roads and paths are open to the public most weekends, and during the week in certain holiday periods.

A narrow lane runs east for 3 miles across the range from East Lulworth. The parking and picnic area on Povington Hill has fine views, northwards across heathland and forest and

CALM BAY *Waves attacking joints in the rock, creating arches and then breaking through the softer clays, formed Lulworth Cove, and Stair Hole in the foreground.*

southwards out to sea. Waymarked footpaths, including the South West Coast Path, cross the range.

⑨ LULWORTH CASTLE

Set back from the road on the edge of East Lulworth, the castle, now restored, was designed as a hunting lodge in the 17th century. There are superb views from the top of one of the 100 ft towers. In the park behind the castle is the Rotunda, built in 1786; it was the first Roman Catholic church built in England after the Reformation.

⑩ TYNEHAM

The village, tucked away in a valley, has been deserted since 1943, when the inhabitants had to quit their homes to make room for a wartime firing range. It is still used by the army, but is open to the public most weekends. A marked trail explores the eerie ruins. The valley's story is movingly told by displays in the church and school.

⑪ KIMMERIDGE BAY

A narrow lane switchbacks through the thatched village of Kimmeridge to the shingle beach, where a 'nodding

donkey' oil pump bobs on the unstable cliff. It produces about a million gallons of oil a year. A tower across the bay was built about 1820 by an amateur astronomer, the Rev John Clavell. Nearby Smedmore House, his family home, dates from the 1630s, and is open a few days each year. At the east end of the bay is Purbeck Marine Reserve and visitor centre, where marine life can be observed in a variety of habitats.

PLACES TO SEE INLAND
Athelhampton, nr Puddletown, 14 miles N of Weymouth. Medieval manor house.
Bovington Tank Museum, Bovington Camp, 7 miles N of Lulworth Cove.
Clouds Hill (NT), nr Bovington Camp, 9 miles N of Lulworth Cove. Lawrence of Arabia's home.
Dorchester. County Museum; Max Gate (NT), Thomas Hardy's home.
Hardy's Cottage (NT), Higher Bockhampton, 11 miles NE of Weymouth. The writer's birthplace.
Mill House Cider Museum, 9 miles NE of Weymouth. Displays of cider-making equipment.

TOURIST INFORMATION
Wareham (01929) 552740; Weymouth (01305) 785747

Well-fortified islands in the English Channel

Headlands of jagged rocks and sweeping sandy bays encircle Jersey, the largest of the Channel Islands, with its two proud castles. Smaller Alderney, just 8 miles from the French coast, is best explored on foot.

① ST HELIER

Pavement cafés and tree-lined squares give Jersey's capital a French flavour, but Jersey's mainland neighbour was not always friendly. Looming above the harbour is Fort Regent, built between 1806 and 1814 when Napoleonic France seemed poised to invade. The fort now contains a leisure complex, and its towering ramparts are topped by a modern roof. Nearby is the Jersey Museum, home to a large tapestry made by islanders, depicting life in Jersey under the German occupation in World War II.

On an islet in the bay, and reached by a low-tide causeway, stand a 12th-century hermitage and the 16th-century Elizabeth Castle, which has exhibitions on Jersey's military fortifications. St Helier's main buildings and attractions are linked by a town trail. A tape-recorded commentary chronicles the island's history, which includes the creation in 1768 of the first chamber of commerce in the English-speaking world.

Plaque in Royal Square

② HAMPTONNE

Set in hilly meadowland are several restored buildings that once formed part of a large estate, now a museum of country life. Buildings include a 16th-century Breton home and 17th-century Hamptonne House, set in a garden and amid valley woodland. The property is owned by the National Trust for Jersey.

③ ST AUBIN

Linked today to St Helier by a seafront road, promenade and cycle track, and lined with houses and hotels, St Aubin was Jersey's original port. In the narrow streets above the small 17th-century harbour are some of the houses built by merchants who used the port.

About a mile north of Beaumont, on the coast road skirting St Aubin's Bay, almost a mile of corridor was hewn from solid rock by forced labour during the German occupation to create an underground hospital; it is now a museum devoted to the Occupation.

④ PORTELET BAY

A steep flight of steps near the car park leads down wooded hills to a rocky shore, where rock pools and a sandy beach are exposed at low tide. Just off-shore is an islet, Ile au Guerdain, crowned by an 18th-century Martello tower, one of many built in the Channel Islands as defences during the Napoleonic Wars. At Noirmont Point, a bluff headland on the eastern side of the bay, is a World War II German command bunker, which can be visited one day a week during the summer.

⑤ ST BRELADE'S BAY

One of Jersey's most popular beaches, with a mile of firm, golden sand at low tide, is backed by an attractive promenade, gardens and fountains. Just to the south-west is Beauport, a small sandy beach sheltered by rocky headlands.

⑥ CORBIERE POINT

The barren peninsula's jagged, needle-sharp rocks are frighteningly impressive. A low-water causeway at the tip of the headland leads to Britain's earliest

---

FIGS AND FERNS

The Hottentot-fig, introduced from South Africa, grows in the Channel Islands but does not produce ripe seeds. Its flowers range from magenta to yellow. Jersey fern is the only annual fern in Britain. Its golden-green fronds are seen only in Guernsey and Jersey on damp, south-west facing hedgebanks.

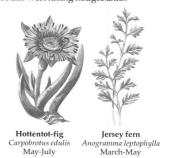

Hottentot-fig
Carpobrotus edulis
May-July

Jersey fern
Anogramma leptophylla
March-May

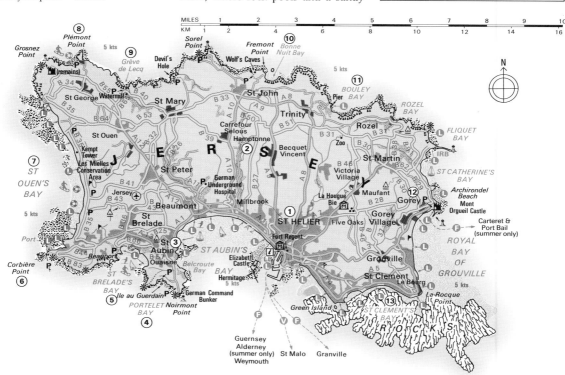

GOREY ALIGHT *At night, Mont Orgueil Castle takes on a fairyland appearance, the soft shadows of the floodlighting contrasting with the bright lights by the harbour's edge.*

concrete lighthouse, built in 1874. A siren is sounded 15 minutes before the fast incoming tide covers the causeway.

⑦ ST OUEN'S BAY

Jersey's finest beach stretches almost the full length of the island's western coast. When the tide is out, the water's edge almost disappears from view; when the tide comes in, it often does so in spectacular fashion, thundering over the sand in great curling arcs of water. St Ouen's Bay is very popular with surfers, and surfing competitions are held during the summer. Strong currents make bathing dangerous in certain spots, but stretches of the shore are designated swimming areas.

Behind the coast road, dunes stretching inland for almost a mile incorporate the Les Mielles conservation area. This is one of the most important dune systems in northern Europe, supporting hundreds of plant species, including wild orchids, sand crocus and autumn squill. There is an interpretation centre at Kempt Tower. Also in the area are putting greens and a golf course.

⑧ PLEMONT POINT

From a small car park, a rough track near the entrance to a holiday village leads down a steep flight of steps to a sandy beach with rocks and caves. To the west, on exposed Grosnez Point, are the remains of a medieval castle.

⑨ GREVE DE LECQ

The B40 to the beach at Grève de Lecq runs through a wooded valley, passing on its way an old water mill, which is now an inn. The small sandy bay has expanses of flat rocks at low tide and is sheltered by grassy cliffs. From a visitor centre, a coast walk leads east to Sorel Point, along the top of rugged rockfaces

falling sheer to the water. The path leads past the Devil's Hole, where the sea has cut through a huge rock and at high tide boils and booms in a rocky cauldron. The hole can be reached by car from a lane off the B33.

⑩ BONNE NUIT BAY

High cliffs shelter a fishing harbour and a small sandy beach. Around the headland of Fremont Point to the west are Wolf's Caves, which can be reached with care at low tide by a rough path.

⑪ BOULEY BAY

At the bottom of a winding road is a small pier used by lobster boats. Skin-diving lessons and equipment are available, but bathing in this mostly shingle bay is safe only for strong swimmers. To the east is the sandier Rozel Bay, a little fishing harbour by a wooded valley.

Inland from Bouley Bay, on the B31, is a zoo created by the naturalist Gerald Durrell in the 1960s, officially titled the Jersey Wildlife Preservation Trust. Rare animals bred in the zoo include Brazilian tamarins, a species of small monkey, and Mauritian pink pigeons.

BIRD ROCKS *Cliffs at the south-western tip of Alderney look out to the Garden Rocks, home to a large colony of gannets.*

⑫ GOREY

Overlooking the harbour at Gorey is Mont Orgueil Castle, with its magnificent 13th-century keep, Elizabethan tower and rambling outworks. The shingle Archirondel beach to the north offers a good view of the mile-long breakwater protecting St Catherine's Bay. To the south, the sandy beach of Royal Bay of Grouville sweeps down to La Rocque Point, winter home to large numbers of migrating waders such as turnstones and sanderlings.

About 2 miles west of Gorey, next to the archaeological and geological museums at the inland hamlet of La Hougue Bie, a medieval abbey crowns a Stone Age passage grave.

⑬ ST CLEMENT'S BAY

The long sandy beach is easily reached from St Helier, 2 miles to the west. The nearby Green Island can be reached at low tide, when the surrounding rocks offer a vast area for exploration.

⑭ ALDERNEY

There are few roads on the island, and the best way to get about is on foot or by bicycle. Rough tracks lead to magnificent viewpoints such as Giffoine, Telegraph Bay, and Essex Hill with its spectacular outcrop known as Hanging Rock. Sandy beaches include Corblets Bay, Arch Bay and Saye Bay. Dotted around the coast are fortifications built during the German occupation. Alderney's only town, St Anne, resembles a Normandy village with its tiny squares, pastel-shaded cottages and granite-cobbled streets. Pleasure cruises around the island are available.

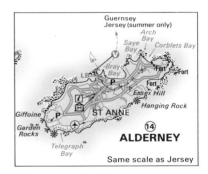

Quiet bays and headlands near the coast of France

Guernsey and its smaller neighbours Herm and Sark are no more than 8 miles apart, but each has its own way of life. Whereas Guernsey is a bustling centre, in Herm and Sark the peace is unbroken even by cars.

① ST PETER PORT

Guernsey's capital is a town of narrow, cobbled streets and solid grey-granite buildings clambering up a steep hill-side above the harbour. The town has a Continental flavour, but the architecture is predominantly English, from the Georgian, Victorian and Edwardian periods. Within the 18th-century Royal Court sits Guernsey's parliament, the States of Deliberation, for although the islands are Crown Possessions they are not part of the United Kingdom, and Guernsey's laws of government date back to Norman times.

In the harbour are three marinas, docks for car and passenger ferries, and three piers from which launches and hydrofoils cross to Herm and Sark. At the harbour entrance stands the 13th-century Castle Cornet, whose massive walls embrace three military museums and an art gallery. South of the harbour is the town beach, in Havelet Bay. The foreshore is shingle, with sand at low tide. The house in which the French novelist Victor Hugo lived from 1855 until 1870 is a museum displaying rooms and objects as he left them.

The cliff path from St Peter Port, joined at La Valette just south of the town, leads to Fermain Bay, where trees tumble almost to the water's edge. The beach, which has stretches of firm sand at low tide, can also be reached by a lane leading from the main coast road.

② MOULIN HUET BAY

Three sandy beaches are sheltered within rocky headlands linked by a coastal path. From the coast road, a lane ending at a small car park leads to Moulin Huet beach. Rocks are exposed at low tide, and there are caves in the cliffs. Petit Port is harder to reach, the final approach being down a long flight of steps. Saint's Bay is reached by a lane which runs through a wooded vale.

③ ICART POINT

One of many such rocky headlands on Guernsey's south coast, Icart Point has perhaps the finest views in the island. Westward lie La Bette Bay, Le Jaonnet Bay, Petit Bot Bay and Portelet Bay, with La Moye Point a craggy finger on the skyline to the west. Petit Bot is one of the few bays on the south coast that can be reached by road, and it is served by the local bus. The beach has a pebbly foreshore with sand and rocks exposed at low tide. A cliff path runs along the entire length of the south coast.

At Les Vauxbelets, north of Icart Point, stands the Little Chapel. This tiny church, encrusted with seashells and pieces of broken china, was built in the 1920s by a monk, who based it on the grotto at Lourdes in France.

④ ROCQUAINE BAY

The high cliffs of Guernsey's southern coast give way abruptly on the western side of the island to wide, flat bays of rock, sand and shingle. At Pleinmont Point, the south-westerly tip of the island, the cliffs overlook the large sandy beach of Rocquaine Bay. A small rocky peninsula, Pezeries Point, juts into the southern end of the bay, giving a good view of Hanois lighthouse about a mile offshore. Within the bay is the tiny fishing harbour of Portelet (one of two places so named on the island), which has a small sandy beach. At the end of a causeway is Fort Grey, a 19th-century fortification in which a maritime museum chronicles the many shipwrecks on this treacherous coast.

⑤ PERELLE BAY

A World War II lookout tower dominating this small rocky bay is one of many reminders of the German occupation. Below the tower a low-water causeway leads to Lihou Island and the ruined 12th-century priory of Notre Dame de la Roche. East of the lookout tower is Le Trepied, one of Guernsey's many dolmens, or prehistoric stone tombs.

⑥ VAZON BAY

The wide crescent of sand and shingle is popular with surfers, although they are restricted to the centre of the bay. The water is unsuitable for bathing at certain states of the tide.

⑦ COBO BAY

Rust-coloured rocks are exposed at low tide on this sand-and-shingle beach, home to a windsurfing school. About a mile to the north, high rocks flank the sandy cove of Port Soif, where the tide hurtles in fast and furiously. The Guernsey Folk Museum, run by the National Trust of Guernsey, is about half a mile south-east of Cobo Bay.

⑧ GRAND HAVRE

The coast road north from Cobo skirts the sand-and-pebble beaches of Port-infer and Pequeries before turning east-

HIGH HEADLAND *Icart Point is typical of Guernsey's remote south coast, which is punctuated by rocky promontories encompassing tiny coves and rugged bays.*

wards to follow the curve of Grand Havre, a fishing harbour set in a wide, irregular, sandy bay, where there are boat moorings and three slipways. There is a windsurfing school at Ladies Bay. A short distance to the east across the narrow headland is L'Ancresse Bay, a broad horseshoe of jagged rocks and shimmering golden sands that is considered to be one of Guernsey's best bathing beaches. Half a mile farther east is Beaucette Marina, a tiny haven flanked by high rocks.

⑨ ST SAMPSON

Tall cranes nod and bow at the dockside of the small commercial port of St Sampson. By contrast, a mile north of the docks, the fishing village of Bordeaux sits prettily by its harbour. The first part of the coast road south from St Sampson is lined with warehouses and oil storage tanks, but soon the wide beaches of Belle Grève Bay and the harbour walls of St Peter Port come into view.

⑩ HERM

Within this compact island, 1½ miles long and half a mile wide, lie towering cliffs, wooded valleys, sandy beaches and enough pastureland to support some 40 Guernsey cows. The island, which is a 20 minute boat trip from Guernsey, is leased from the States of Guernsey, and the Tenants live in the 15th-century granite-built Manor House. By the small harbour are a few pastel-coloured cottages, a hotel, a pub and a shopping square. There are no cars, or roads to drive them on.

North of the harbour are the sandy Fisherman's Beach and Bears Beach, beyond which a path cuts across heathland to the island's showpiece, Shell Beach. On a golden strand, millions of tiny shells have been washed up, some from as far away as the Gulf of Mexico. About 10 minutes' walk away is Belvoir Bay, small and secluded, and then the going gets tough as the path climbs and dips along the cliffs and valleys of Herm's southern half. Another walk, from Belvoir or from the harbour, leads to the tiny St Tugual Chapel, which dates from Norman times.

About half a mile off Herm's southern tip stands the island of Jethou, a desolate rocky cone divided from Herm around AD 700 by a great storm. It is privately owned and cannot be visited.

⑪ SARK

The island of Sark is still run along feudal lines, governed by a seigneur whose feudal rights date back to 1565, when they were granted by Elizabeth I. The gardens of La Seigneurie are open to visitors in summer.

No cars are allowed on Sark. Tractor-drawn trailers take visitors up the steep hill from the harbour; horse-drawn carriages can be hired for a leisurely drive around the island; and bicycles are available. But it is best to explore the island on foot, as paths that

FEUDAL MANOR *Since the early 18th century La Seigneurie has been the home of Sark's feudal lords, or seigneurs.*

lead down to the bays and beaches are often too steep for bicycles.

The island is about 3 miles long and 1½ miles across, and at the southern end is almost cut in two. The southern section, called Little Sark, is reached by a natural causeway of rock, 250ft above sea level, called La Coupée. Though some of Sark's bays can be reached without too much effort – Dixcart Bay and Grève de la Ville, for example – the island's glory is in the views from its headlands. From Havre Gosselin, on the west coast, the view extends across to the lonely, privately owned Brecqhou Island. Below the cliffs the sea licks hungrily around jagged rocks and probes the dark caverns of the Gouliot caves. Almost half of Sark's eastern side can be seen from Banquette, including the lighthouse at Point Robert to the south. On a clear day it is possible to see the coast of France, some 20 miles away.

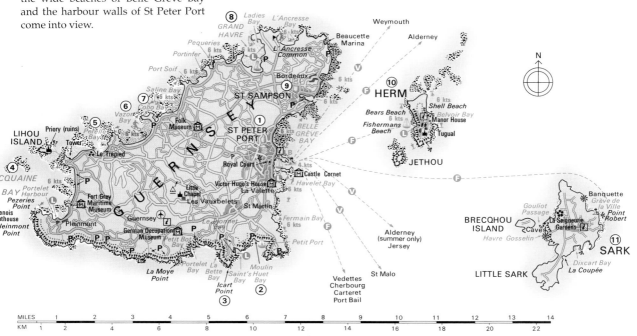

Purbeck's cliffs and heaths, and a vast natural harbour

Stone-built villages dot the hilly peninsula known as the Isle of Purbeck, whose cliffs are reached only on foot. To the north, low-lying pine woods and heathland flank Poole Harbour's deeply indented shore.

PRECARIOUS PILLARS *Waves battering The Foreland, near Studland, have eroded the chalk stacks of Old Harry and the slender Harry's Wife, both of which will eventually collapse.*

① POOLE

Tugs, fishing vessels and pleasure boats moor at Poole Quay, the departure point for boat trips to Brownsea Island and round Poole Harbour. The quayside is lined with Georgian buildings, including the Old Harbour Office and the Guildhall, which has a display of items relating to the town's history. At Poole Pottery visitors can try their hand at throwing and painting pots. The Waterfront Museum looks back on Poole's maritime history. Nearby is Scaplen's Court Museum, which was built in the 15th century as a merchant's house and has exhibits on domestic life through the ages. The Aquarium Complex offers a window onto the natural world, with displays of marine life, reptiles and insects.

Poole's long, sandy beaches lie some 3 miles south-east of the town centre. Strong currents make swimming dangerous near the entrance to Poole Harbour. A vehicle ferry from Sandbanks crosses the harbour mouth. Car ferries to France depart from the docks, to the south of Poole Quay.

Just inland from the beaches, there are Italian and Japanese gardens at Compton Acres. Close by is Branksome Dene Chine, a wooded valley with pine trees, rhododendrons and strawberry trees. On the west side of Poole, Upton Country Park has formal and landscape gardens round a 19th-century house.

② WAREHAM

Massive earthern banks, which are thought to date from Saxon times, surround three sides of the town. The River Frome, on the fourth side, was once busy with ships exporting clay from pits round the Blue Pool, near Corfe Castle. Inside St Martin's Church, which was built about 1020, is an effigy of T.E. Lawrence – Lawrence of Arabia – who spent his last years at Clouds Hill (NT), 6 miles west of the town. Wareham Museum displays photographs and other items relating to him. Outside Wareham, Hartland Moor and Morden Bog are areas of heath, designated as national nature reserves.

③ ARNE

China dolls, tin toys, musical boxes and games and puzzles can be seen at A World of Toys in the tiny hamlet of Arne. To the north lies Arne RSPB reserve. A trail within it leads through heathland, where the rare Dartford warbler may be seen, and proceeds along the coast, which is visited by terns in summer and by great crested grebes and goldeneyes in winter.

④ POOLE HARBOUR

With more than 90 miles of coastline and 14 sq miles of tidal water, Poole Harbour is one of Europe's largest natural harbours. Sailing clubs, marinas and boatyards are scattered along the northeast shore. Oil is extracted on Furzey Island, but trees mask the installations from the rest of the harbour.

⑤ BROWNSEA ISLAND

The patchwork of woods, grassland and heath on Brownsea Island (NT) is the home of many animals and birds, including sika deer, semi-wild peacocks and red squirrels. The northern half of the island is a nature reserve with a large heronry. Lord Baden-Powell held his first experimental Scout camp on Brownsea Island in 1907. The island is reached by passenger ferries from Poole Quay and Sandbanks.

⑥ STUDLAND

The village lies scattered round a network of lanes. St Nicholas Church is an exceptionally well-preserved Norman building. Close by is a sandy beach, backed by low cliffs that are made up of coloured sand and similar to those at Alum Bay on the Isle of Wight.

To the west of the village is Studland Heath National Nature Reserve, an area of heath, woods, mud flats and open water with two waymarked trails. Lizards and snakes, including adders, live on the heath, and roe deer in the woods. Paths from Studland and Knoll lead to the Agglestone, a 17ft high boulder of resistant sandstone.

The 594 mile South West Coast Path starts at the northern end of Shell Bay and follows the coast to Minehead in Somerset. A mile's walk along the path east of Studland leads to The Foreland, overlooking the offshore stacks known as Old Harry Rocks. Walkers can continue onto Ballard Cliff for a magnificent panorama of Swanage Bay.

⑦ SWANAGE

Sheltered within its wide bay, Swanage is a popular resort with a sandy beach and colourful gardens. Boats can be hired, and there are boat trips, fishing trips and a diving school. The lifeboat station is open to visitors.

Near the pier is the Wellington Clock Tower, which once stood at the southern approach to London Bridge and was moved to Swanage in 1867. It was originally intended to house a statue of the Duke of Wellington, but funds ran out. The carved stone façade of the Town Hall was formerly the front of the Mercers' Hall in the City of London.

Although much of the town centre has a distinctly Victorian look, Swanage has reminders of its village days around Church Hill, with a group of stone cottages huddling by a former mill house and millpond. Steam trains on the Swanage Railway run to Corfe Castle and through the Purbeck countryside.

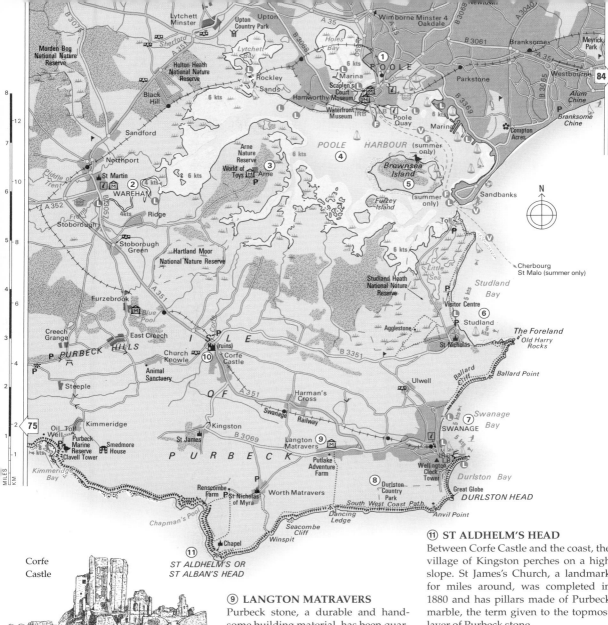

75

Corfe
Castle

⑪
ST ALDHELM'S OR
ST ALBAN'S HEAD

⑧ DURLSTON COUNTRY PARK

A 10 ft Portland stone globe, made in 1887, stands by the cliffs of the country park. The globe was the idea of George Burt, a stone merchant and amateur astronomer. The activities of a colony of guillemots are beamed back to the Park Centre, and an underwater microphone installed near Durlston Head enables visitors to hear the echolocation signals of offshore bottle-nosed dolphins.

---

⑨ LANGTON MATRAVERS

Purbeck stone, a durable and handsome building material, has been quarried since Roman times, and the village's little Coach House Museum explains the industry's history. At Putlake Adventure Farm, visitors can touch and feed the animals.

⑩ CORFE CASTLE

The awesome ruins of Corfe Castle (NT) stand high on a steep grassy slope above a gap in the Purbeck Hills. The castle dates from the 11th century onwards, but was partly destroyed by Cromwell's men after a siege in 1646. Below the shattered keep and crazily jagged towers are the cottages of the village of Corfe Castle, many of which were built of stones taken from the castle itself. A model village shows how Corfe Castle may have looked before 1646. At nearby Church Knowle, a sanctuary caring for sick and neglected animals is open to the public.

Two miles north-west of Corfe is the Blue Pool, a lake that formed in an old clay pit after mining ceased. The clay was used to make tobacco pipes. A museum has a model of the site as it is thought to have looked in about 1850.

⑪ ST ALDHELM'S HEAD

Between Corfe Castle and the coast, the village of Kingston perches on a high slope. St James's Church, a landmark for miles around, was completed in 1880 and has pillars made of Purbeck marble, the term given to the topmost layer of Purbeck stone.

A primitive 12th-century chapel stands on top of 300 ft cliffs at St Aldhelm's Head, at the southern tip of the Isle of Purbeck and reached only on foot. A 1½ mile track to the headland starts at a car park by Renscombe Farm on the west side of the stone-built village of Worth Matravers.

PURBECK STONE *Cottages at Kingston, on a hilltop near St Aldhelm's Head, are built of mellow limestone from local quarries.*

GLORIES OF NATURE FRINGING THE WAVES

*F*ROM SALT MARSHES TO MAJESTIC CLIFFS, from sand dunes to broad estuaries, nearly 950 miles of undeveloped coast in England and Wales have been given special recognition as a treasured part of our national inheritance. Since 1973 the Countryside Commission and the Countryside Council for Wales have identified 45 separate stretches of coastline as Heritage Coasts, with the aim of protecting their natural beauty and encouraging enjoyment of them in ways that do not threaten their conservation.

Although they have no legal safeguards, Heritage Coasts must be respected by local planners, and consent may be withheld for development that is not in harmony with the scheme's intentions. These special coastlines, which vary in length from 2½ to 60 miles, often overlap with Areas of Outstanding Natural Beauty or National Parks, where particular planning restrictions apply; and the stretches of Heritage Coast owned by the National Trust are protected from any development. The scheme involves 120 professional staff, more than 1000 volunteers and a collective annual budget of some £2 million.

Some Heritage Coast officers act as wardens, leading guided walks and giving advice to farmers, local people and landowners about conservation and access. The Purbeck shoreline of Dorset is typical of many Heritage Coasts in having several owners, including the National Trust, notably at Studland, a sandy shore that draws more than a million visitors a year. The owners have cooperated with Heritage Coast staff and conservation bodies to enhance Purbeck's natural attractions. The coastal footpath, part of the South West Coast Path, has been clearly signposted and maintained, car parks have been built, extended or screened, interpretive boards have been erected to highlight aspects of the shore, and eyesores have been removed. Durlston Country Park

RUGGED GRANDEUR *Lantic Bay in south Cornwall forms part of a Heritage Coast stretching east from Gribbin Head to Polperro. Characterised by remote rocky headlands that can be reached only on foot, this coast also includes the more subdued charms of the Fowey estuary.*

KEY TO MAP

Heritage Coast

National Park

North Northumberland

LAKE DISTRICT

St Bees Head

NORTH YORK MOORS

North Yorkshire & Cleveland

Flamborough Head

Spurn Head

Anglesey

Great Orme

North Norfolk

SNOWDONIA

Lleyn

THE BROADS

Ceredigion

Suffolk

PEMBROKESHIRE COAST

Pembrokeshire

Gower

Glamorgan

South Foreland
Dover-Folkestone

North Devon

Exmoor

Lundy

EXMOOR

Sussex

DARTMOOR

North & West Cornwall

East Devon

West Dorset

Purbeck

Isle of Wight

Isles of Scilly

South Cornwall

South Devon

ROCKY FASTNESS *The jagged outline of Dunstanburgh Castle is one of the many dramatic features along the wild and lonely shoreline of north Northumberland, the first Heritage Coast to be created when the scheme began in 1973. Offshore to the north are the magnificent National Nature Reserves of the Farne Islands and Lindisfarne.*

VIEW FROM THE HEATH *The wide sweep of Studland Bay (above) forms part of the Purbeck Heritage Coast, an area of international importance for sea birds and for plants such as the rare early spider orchid (left).*

near Swanage organises a 'coast watch' scheme to monitor the activities of fish and dolphins. Certain Heritage Coasts include visitor centres explaining what can be seen along the shore. Charmouth in west Dorset, for example, has an audiovisual show about local fossils, while the centre at Flamborough Head in Humberside offers birdwatching trips and seashore 'safaris'. Growing interest in marine nature conservation was reflected in 1991 by the creation of the first Marine Heritage Coast, on Cardigan Bay.

Many people visit the seaside to walk along coast paths or explore nature reserves; more want simply to relax on the beach. Others have active pursuits

such as rock climbing in mind. Reconciling clashes of interest is one of the main tasks of Heritage Coast officers. Coping with erosion is another; re-routing paths inland after a cliff collapse or moving stiles and signs may be necessary to ensure safety. Some officers act as auxiliary coastguards. Others can muster volunteers when problems strike; an oil slick off south Devon in 1991 was controlled with the help of a team from the Heritage Coast service.

ENTERPRISE NEPTUNE

In 1965 the National Trust launched a campaign called Enterprise Neptune to save areas of unspoilt coastline. Its success means that the Trust now owns some 550 miles of coast, and 120 000 acres of coastal land, none of which can be sold or developed in any way. Public access is allowed to most of this land, which is managed in the interests of nature conservation and to preserve and enhance scenic beauty.

GUARDIANS OF THE COAST *Neptune runs conservation projects for schoolchildren (left) and works to maintain traditional features (below).*

PEACEFUL HAVEN *Porth Oer is one of many sandy bays on the Lleyn Heritage Coast in north Wales. The Lleyn Peninsula is popular for watersports, but beach 'zoning' and a public information campaign have helped to safeguard its tranquillity.*

A prehistoric site between honey-coloured sands

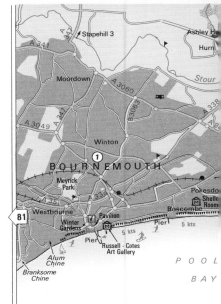

Sandwiched between the serene resort of Bournemouth and the broad arc of Christchurch Bay is the curving spit of Hengistbury Head, which is known to have been settled from the Stone Age to Roman times.

① BOURNEMOUTH

The sedate Victorian resort has two piers, a variety of seaside amusements and a long promenade bordering part of a 7 mile sandy beach. The 'Chines', natural pine-clad valleys once used by smugglers, cut through the sheltering cliffs to the shore. The Lower Gardens, with their aviary, lie behind the seafront and follow the Bourne Stream to Central Gardens and Upper Gardens. From there it is a short walk to Meyrick Park, a large pine-covered estate with walks and a golf course.

The Russell-Cotes Art Gallery and Museum in the town centre is an Italianate villa housing Victorian and Edwardian paintings, and Oriental and Victorian artefacts. The Shelley Rooms in Boscombe Manor contain a small museum and study room devoted to the poet Percy Bysshe Shelley, whose son lived in Bournemouth between 1849 and 1899. The Winter Gardens concert hall, first built in 1875, is the home of the Bournemouth Symphony

Orchestra; while the Pavilion, built in 1929, includes a theatre and ballroom. In summer there are day cruises from the pier to the Isle of Wight.

② HENGISTBURY HEAD

The narrow, hooked finger of land, made up of 2 miles of heath, woods, marsh and meadow, almost completely encloses Christchurch Harbour. From its southern side paths run to the 118ft summit of Warren Hill, an important archaeological site, where traces of Stone Age settlement have been found. There are superb views from the hill across the Solent to the Isle of Wight. Mudeford Sandbank is a strip of dunes at the head's tip, where beach huts can be hired. The sandbank can be reached either by ferry from Mudeford Quay, on the other side of the harbour mouth, or by 'land-train', a small mock train which runs on a path from Double Dykes, two defensive ditches built in Viking times. The head is an important wildlife conservation area, and a warden's headquarters at the dykes has information on a nature trail and details of the birds and insects that may be seen from it.

③ CHRISTCHURCH

Known in Saxon times as Twynham, 'the place between two waters', Christchurch lies at the meeting point of the Avon and Stour, which made it an ideal centre for smuggling in the 17th century. Christchurch's most notable feature is the imposing 11th-century Priory Church. At 312ft, it is the longest church in England, longer even than most cathedrals. The Priory Gardens in front of the church stand on the site of a Norman castle, of which only the ruined walls of the keep and the Constable's House remain. A short heritage trail takes in the church and the Georgian Red House Museum, which chronicles the borough's history from its earliest settlement. The trail leads down to the yacht-filled quay from where ferries leave in summer for Hengistbury Head and Mudeford. Near the quay is the world's only Tricycle Museum. The trail continues to the partially restored Place Mill, an Anglo-Saxon water mill built in one of the town's few remaining monastery

buildings. The Priory also marks one end of the Avon Valley Path, which can be followed for 34 miles northwards to Salisbury. On the harbour's northern shore is the small Stanpit Marsh Nature Reserve, an area of reed beds and salt and freshwater marshes, where birds such as curlews, whimbrels, redshanks and snipe congregate. A car park at the northern end gives access to several footpaths into the reserve.

④ MUDEFORD

A narrow stretch of water known as the Run separates Mudeford Quay from the tip of Hengistbury Head. The quay is the centre of the local fishing industry, whose salmon netting methods have changed little over 200 years. In spite of residential development a few old fishermen's cottages still remain, along with the original Haven House Inn, the site of a battle between smugglers and the Royal Navy in the 17th century. The harbour's sheltered waters offer ideal conditions for dinghy sailing and windsurfing, while Christchurch Bay is used for mackerel fishing and deep-sea fishing trips. Mudeford is linked to Hengistbury Head in summer by a passenger ferry. Avon Beach, to the east of Mudeford, has seaweed and pebbles at low tide, and a shore flanked by beach huts for hire.

⑤ HIGHCLIFFE

Just over a century old and originally known as Newtown, Highcliffe has expanded to become an attractive residential area. Highcliffe Castle, built around 1830 by Lord Stuart de Rothesay, replaced an earlier house constructed by his grandfather, the Earl of Bute, prime minister during the reign of George III. The dilapidated castle is undergoing long-term restoration and is being opened to the public in stages. From the car park near the castle, steps zigzag down to a sandy beach, hemmed in by green slopes. Farther east is a natural glen, known as Chewton Bunny, through which a stream flows. A double-tiered grassy bank descends

HENGISTBURY HEAD *The breezy mile-long promontory is dominated by Warren Hill, which gives views of the Isle of Wight.*

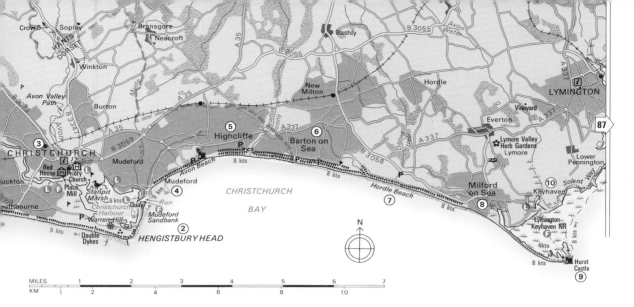

gently from the car park to a pebbled beach, and an unpaved track winds its way through the glen.

⑥ BARTON ON SEA

A cliff car park in this residential town on the border of Dorset and Hampshire adjoins a large, grassed area with many benches. Low cliffs and beach huts edge the shore of shingle and sand.

⑦ HORDLE BEACH

Favoured by walkers, this secluded, shingle beach is not accessible by car. It can be reached on foot along a short path that leads through farmland from a car park on the B3058. There are footpaths in both directions, to Barton on Sea and Milford on Sea, along the top of dramatically eroding cliffs, but walkers should take extreme care.

⑧ MILFORD ON SEA

The residential town's shingle beach is backed by a sea wall and beach huts with concrete porches. The seafront marks one end of the Solent Way long-distance walk, which can be followed for 50 miles east to Emsworth.

Lymore Valley Herb Gardens, a mile north-east of Milford, is set among Victorian farm buildings, with walled herb gardens and a nursery.

⑨ HURST CASTLE

Crouching at the end of a lonely spit, and only a mile from Cliff End on the Isle of Wight, Hurst Castle (EH) was built by Henry VIII between 1538 and 1540. It can be reached by a strenuous 2 mile walk across a pebble causeway that starts just outside Milford, or by a ferry in summer from Keyhaven. The castle has a 12-sided central tower, and on display are two Victorian 38-ton guns; an exhibition tells of the castle's history.

⑩ KEYHAVEN

The marshes of this quiet, sheltered inlet were once used for salt production, but they now form part of the Lymington-Keyhaven Nature Reserve. The reserve is visited by redshanks, dunlins, oystercatchers and curlews. There is a sailing club, and numerous yachts fill the small harbour. Summer ferries leave from the quay for Hurst Castle and the Isle of Wight. A sea-wall footpath from the harbour winds along the marshes for 4 miles to Lymington.

ANCHORAGE WHERE TWO RIVERS MEET *Overlooked by the 120 ft tower of the Priory Church, Christchurch Harbour offers safe moorings for a host of brightly painted boats.*

PLACES TO SEE INLAND

Moors Valley Country Park, Ashley Heath, 12 miles N of Bournemouth. Narrow-gauge steam railway, golf course and walks.

New Forest Owl Sanctuary, Crow, 9 miles N of Christchurch.

Stapehill Abbey, Crafts and Gardens, 8 miles N of Bournemouth.

TOURIST INFORMATION

Bournemouth (01202) 789789; Christchurch (01202) 471780; Lymington (01590) 672422 (summer)

A 'beautiful place' on the river, and marinas galore

In its heyday Southampton was home to transatlantic liners such as the Queen Mary *and the* Mauretania. *Ships from Nelson's fleet were built at Bucklers Hard. Now the area is surrounded by bustling marinas.*

GEORGIAN VIEW *The peaceful setting of Bucklers Hard belies its industrious past, when oaks from the New Forest lay on the grass ready to make men-of-war for England's fleet.*

① LYMINGTON

Historically a market town, granted a charter between 1184 and 1216, Lymington still hosts a Saturday market in its Georgian high street. Cobbled Quay Hill winds down from the bottom of the high street to a yacht-filled harbour from which there is a ferry service to Yarmouth on the Isle of Wight. The Royal Lymington Yacht Club marks the start of a 7 mile walk to Bucklers Hard; the path forms part of the Solent Way. Lymington Vineyard, on the south-east side of the town, offers walks among the vines and a herb garden.

② NEEDS ORE POINT

The eastern tip of the North Solent Nature Reserve, which covers most of the western shoreline of the Beaulieu River, is a haven for birdwatchers. The reserve, which includes Gull Island, has the country's largest population of black-headed gulls. Needs Ore Point is reached along a private gravel road, signposted Warren Lane, which begins 2 miles south of Bucklers Hard near the ruins of St Leonard's, a grange that once served Beaulieu Abbey. The road leads to isolated marshland and several hides. Entry to the reserve is by permit from the Beaulieu estate office, at the National Motor Museum.

③ BUCKLERS HARD

Two rows of 18th-century cottages and a grassy 'high street' sloping gently down to the Beaulieu River make up this beautifully restored, tree-lined village. Between 1698 and 1827 it was a busy shipbuilding centre. Two warships for Nelson's fleet were built there, *Agamemnon* in 1781, and *Euryalus* in

FLEET FIGUREHEAD

Among the exhibits in the Maritime Museum at Bucklers Hard is a replica of the figurehead from HMS *Gladiator*, launched in 1782. Although the *Gladiator* never saw action, it served as the home for convalescent seamen at Portsmouth before being broken up in 1817. Bucklers Hard was a busy shipbuilding centre between 1698 and 1827, and the museum contains models of ships constructed there, including those of Nelson's fleet.

The carved figure of a Roman gladiator once graced the prow of a British ship.

1803. A fee to enter the village includes admission to the Maritime Museum, where tableaux re-create 18th-century life in the village. There are river cruises from the jetty, and a 2½ mile riverside walk from the boatyard to Beaulieu.

④ BEAULIEU

The village of redbrick buildings, set amid woodland, and sitting at the head of the Beaulieu estuary, was originally known as Bellus Locus Regis. The monks who founded an abbey there in the 13th century changed the name to its Norman French equivalent 'Beau Lieu', meaning 'beautiful place' and now pronounced 'Bewley'. The remains of the abbey, together with Palace House, are part of a pleasure complex which includes picnic areas, a monorail and the National Motor Museum with its collection of more than 250 historic and vintage vehicles.

⑤ EXBURY GARDENS

Surrounded by woodland, the world-renowned Exbury Gardens were created by Lionel de Rothschild and his 150 gardeners before World War II. There are springtime displays of rhododendrons, azaleas and camellias, as well as a Winter Garden and a Rose Garden. Strolls along the river include a 1½ hour return walk from the main entrance to the 'Top Pond'.

⑥ LEPE COUNTRY PARK

The small park that covers a narrow stretch of the Solent coast is within an Area of Outstanding Natural Beauty. There are clifftop walks, picnic spots, and an information centre next to the car park. A shingle spit, where swimming is dangerous, is revealed at low tide. In winter Brent geese and many wading birds feed on the mud flats.

⑦ CALSHOT

A pebbly beach lined with bathing huts leads to a bleak spit overlooked by the 650 ft chimney of Fawley power station. Three sprawling hangars are the remnants of what used to be one of Britain's most important seaplane stations and maritime training bases, established in 1913. The airbase has been closed since the early 1960s. Tucked away behind the giant hangars stands Calshot Castle (EH), built by Henry VIII in 1539. The rippling coastline of Calshot Marshes, which snakes westwards to Fawley's oil refinery, forms a nature reserve, where black-tailed godwits and a variety of migratory birds can be seen.

⑧ HYTHE

At this industrial and residential suburb of Southampton, flying boats were designed and built between 1930 and 1940. Pointing out across Southampton Water is the long, thin finger of Hythe's 100-year-old pier, whose narrow-gauge railway carries passengers to the ferry terminal at Southampton.

⑨ SOUTHAMPTON

Britain's major passenger port has a nautical heritage stretching back more than a thousand years. The Museum of Archaeology shows how the port grew from a number of separate Roman, Saxon and medieval settlements, while the Maritime Museum has an exhibition on the *Titanic,* which set sail on its fateful voyage from the port in 1912. Although Southampton was heavily bombed in World War II, the towers of the 14th-century town walls remain, along with the 12th-century Bargate building and the 15th-century Tudor House Museum and Garden, which has displays of local history and Victorian and Edwardian life.

Ocean Village, at the southern end of Southampton, is a modern waterfront development where luxury yachts moor alongside wooden schooners dating from the 1920s. The last working coastal passenger and cargo steamer, SS *Shieldhall,* built in 1955, is permanently docked in the harbour, and is open to visitors. A passenger ferry operates to both Hythe and Town Quay, another harbour development, which has a Sunday market where traders from France sometimes set up their stalls.

The Lower Test Nature Reserve, on Southampton's western outskirts, has a nationally important population of Cetti's warblers. Footpaths and boardwalks from the car park lead to hides.

⑩ NETLEY

A pebbly shore leads east to the Royal Victoria Country Park, which is dominated by the remains of the country's first purpose-built military hospital, opened in 1856 by Queen Victoria to care for Crimean War casualties. All that is left of the Royal Victoria Military Hospital is a chapel, housing a museum of the hospital's history, and a tower, which can be climbed for panoramic views of the area. The park was once part of the grounds of nearby Netley Abbey (EH), built by the monks of Beaulieu in the 13th century. A mile walk follows the western shoreline of the park, and a narrow-gauge railway runs through it on a line formerly used to transport wounded soldiers to the hospital. Westwood Park, north-west of Netley, is an area of ancient woodland with grassland and stream-side walks. From the hillside slopes on which the park stands is a high viewpoint, which looks across Southampton Water and to the wooded expanse of the New Forest.

⑪ HAMBLE LE RICE

Known for many years as Hamble, meaning 'crooked river', the village has reverted to its original name, le Rice meaning 'in the brushwood'. It is predominantly a yachting centre, with five marinas. A pebble beach looks over Southampton Water to Fawley oil refinery and power station. There is a foot ferry to Warsash across the Hamble.

Hamble Common, south-east of the village, is an area of heath, salt marsh and woods which has a variety of wildlife, including nesting stonechats and linnets. Hamble Point, where a World War II anti-aircraft battery stands, is the site of an Iron Age fort.

CARS AT BEAULIEU *Veteran cars from the collection of historic vehicles in the National Motor Museum stand before Palace House, formerly the gatehouse of Beaulieu Abbey.*

PLACES TO SEE INLAND

Broadlands, Romsey, 7 miles N of Southampton. Former home of Earl Mountbatten of Burma.

Eling Tide Mill, 4 miles W of Southampton. Restored 18th-century mill.

Manor Farm, 6 miles SE of Southampton. Traditional working farm with blacksmith's forge.

Mottisfont Abbey Garden (NT), 10 miles NW of Southampton. 12th-century priory.

New Forest Nature Quest, 6 miles W of Southampton. British wild animals such as foxes and deer, seen in their natural habitat.

New Forest Museum and Visitor Centre, Lyndhurst, 8 miles W of Southampton.

TOURIST INFORMATION

Eastleigh (01703) 641261; Lymington (01590) 672422 (summer); Lyndhurst (01703) 282269; Southampton (01703) 221106

The heart of yachting on an island of fluttering sails

While yachtsmen flock to the international sailing centre of Cowes, thousands more visitors reach the Isle of Wight by ferry to enjoy lively resorts such as Ryde and the quieter charms of Seaview and Bembridge.

AT WIGHT'S WESTERN TIP *The sea constantly erodes the vulnerable Needles. In 1764 a stack, known as Lot's Wife, fell and the resultant crash was heard on the mainland.*

① THE NEEDLES
The three 100ft pinnacles are the remnants of a chalk ridge that used to join the Isle of Wight to the mainland. A Pleasure Park with funfair amusements and picnic areas stands on The Needles peninsula near a vast parking area. From here a walk of almost a mile over the headland leads past the Old Battery (NT), a restored Victorian fort complete with guns, to a closer, more spectacular view of The Needles.

Tranquillity can be found east of the peninsula on the grassy chalk ridge of Tennyson Down, named after the poet Lord Tennyson, who lived at nearby Farringford House. He walked on the down regularly, and declared the air there was worth 'sixpence a pint'. A monument to him was erected on the summit in 1897, five years after he died.

② ALUM BAY
The pebbly bay is backed by steep cliffs of coloured sands formed of white quartz, red iron oxide and yellow limonite. Visitors can reach Alum Bay by a chair lift from The Needles Pleasure Park, or by a nearby footpath and steep steps. Boat trips round The Needles can be taken from the beach.

③ TOTLAND BAY
A gently curving shingle beach lies at the foot of clay cliffs. Totland's pier and a mile-long esplanade are overlooked by a grassy picnic area with seats, and views west to Hatherwood Point.

④ COLWELL BAY
There is an air of seaside jollity about Colwell Bay, with its sheltered, sandy beach fringed by holiday houses. Golden Hill Fort, to the east of the village, is a monument to British fears of a French invasion in the 1860s. The fort's museum describes its history from the 19th century, when six 40lb guns bristled on the hill site, through World War II, to the 1980s when it was opened to visitors.

⑤ FORT VICTORIA
Built as part of 19th-century defensive measures against a French invasion, Fort Victoria is now occupied by a marine aquarium, a planetarium and a maritime heritage exhibition. Sconce Point, on which the fort stands, is an ideal place from which to watch shipping in the Solent. There is good offshore fishing from the sandy beach. Fort Victoria Country Park, which surrounds the fort, has a nature trail.

⑥ YARMOUTH
The home of the Royal Solent Yacht Club, Yarmouth is a charming village of stone quays and attractive, narrow lanes. There are two small beaches, one shingle, the other sand and shingle. The pier, built in 1876, is popular for fishing, and for its views across the Solent. Boat trips round offshore Hurst Castle (EH) and The Needles are available in summer, and a car ferry sails to Lymington, on the mainland. Behind the ferry port stands Yarmouth Castle (EH), built by Henry VIII in 1547.

⑦ NEWTOWN
A thriving port in the 14th century, Newtown retains little evidence of its former glory, apart from a restored 18th-century Town Hall (NT), which is open some afternoons in summer. There is a serene quality about the empty, reedy landscape of the Newtown estuary, on which the village stands. A footpath from a car park by the old coastguard cottage leads to the Newtown National Nature Reserve, and a catwalk crosses pools and streams to the water's edge, where Brent geese, teal and wigeon can be seen. Permits are required to enter the reserve.

⑧ COWES
East Cowes has a long promenade with a children's paddling pool and play area, and superb views of yacht racing outside the harbour. A chain ferry across the River Medina links the town to the world sailing centre of West Cowes, where colourful yachts ride at anchor in the bay below the headquarters of the Royal Yacht Squadron, and regattas take place in summer. A maritime museum is housed in the town's library. From the sailing club, a promenade leads west to Egypt Point,

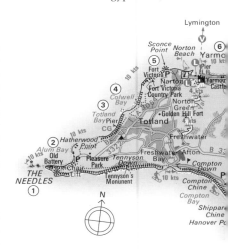

VICTORIAN RETREAT *Supervised by Prince Albert, Osborne House was rebuilt between 1845 and 1851 as 'a place of one's own, quiet and retired' for Queen Victoria's family.*

the northernmost point of the island. Travellers can cross to Southampton by ferry from East Cowes or by passenger hydrofoil from West Cowes.

⑨ OSBORNE HOUSE

Queen Victoria's retreat in the country, Osborne House (EH) provides an intimate glimpse of the monarch's family life, as it has been left almost unchanged since her death there in 1901. A grove of cork trees in nearby Barton Manor Gardens and Vineyards was planted by Queen Victoria's husband, Prince Albert. He also designed the flamboyantly Gothic Church of St Mildred at Whippingham, a mile south-west of the manor.

⑩ FISHBOURNE

Apart from its car ferry service to Portsmouth, Fishbourne has a pretty green and a small, shingle beach that faces Wootton Creek, a lively holiday centre attracting watersports enthusiasts. Visitors approaching

Fishbourne from the sea will notice the redbrick spire of Quarr Abbey, built in 1912. A path from its driveway, signposted on the A3054, leads to the ruins of a 12th-century Cistercian abbey.

⑪ RYDE

A broad esplanade between the sea and the Victorian hillside town gives the busy resort of Ryde a rather grand air. Golden sands stretch out on each side of the mile-long pier, which was built in 1813 and is thought to be the oldest in Britain. There are boating lakes, an ice-skating arena and a miniature train on the seafront, and to the east, in the landscaped gardens behind Appley Beach, is a heated swimming pool. Regularly departing hovercrafts and ferries carry foot passengers to Portsmouth.

Shire horses, miniature ponies, a children's farm and a collection of

horse-drawn carriages are among the many attractions at Brickfields Horse Country in Binstead, west of Ryde.

⑫ SEAVIEW

The sailing village of predominantly blue and white houses is aptly named. Its long, sandy beach gives broad views of the Spithead area of the Solent, and the four forts built at sea in the 1860s to protect the mainland harbours from feared invasion from France. A seawall walk of about a mile leads to Ryde. Flamingo Park, north-west of Seaview, has many species of waterfowl, and water-garden displays.

⑬ BEMBRIDGE

Houseboats line the village's wooded harbour, where yachts sail sedately in and out, and where there are moorings for small boats. Bembridge's small airport is used by light aircraft. The Shipwreck Centre is crammed with artefacts, including Spanish pieces of eight and cannons recovered from local shipwrecks. On the northern side of the harbour is St Helens Duver (NT), an area of gorse and open grassland on a narrow, sandy spit, that attracts migrant birds. There are also fine views of boats in the Yar estuary.

On the outskirts of the village is Bembridge Windmill (NT), the island's only surviving windmill, built in the early 18th century. The mill was the subject of a sketch made by the artist J.M.W. Turner in 1775.

PLACES TO SEE INLAND

Carisbrooke Castle, 2 miles SW of Newport. Impressive Norman castle where Charles I was imprisoned before being taken to London for trial and execution.

Isle of Wight Steam Railway, Havenstreet, 10 mile trip through countryside.

TOURIST INFORMATION

Cowes (01983) 291914; Newport (01983) 525450; Ryde (01983) 562905; Yarmouth (01983) 760015 (summer)

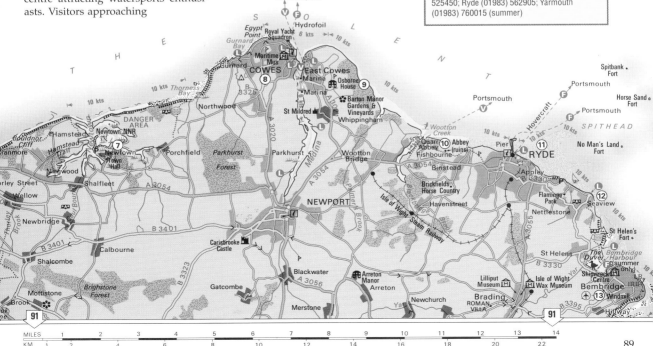

Grassy uplands, leafy chines and sandy bays

The Isle of Wight's southern coast is blessed with golden sands and has a sunny, equable climate. In places, landslips caused by geological weaknesses have given a dramatic shape to the chalk and clay cliffs.

① FRESHWATER BAY

Badly eroded chalk cliffs rise beside a curving sea wall and a steeply shelving pebble beach. Two chalk stacks, smaller versions of The Needles, stand in the bay, and another is being carved out of the cliff face by the relentless sea. Farringford House, on the western edge of Freshwater, was the home of the poet Lord Tennyson between 1853 and 1864. The house is now a hotel.

② BROOK

The hamlet of Brook marks the southern end of the Hamstead Trail, an 8 mile walk from Hamstead Ledge on the northern shore of the island. On the seaward side of the village is Brook Chine (NT), where a path from the car park leads to a sand and shingle beach, flanked by crumbling clay cliffs. Chine is the local name for a ravine caused by streams working their way to the sea. Other nearby chines include Shippards Chine and Compton Chine.

Compton Bay, north-west of Brook, is a sandy beach. Behind the 200 ft cliffs that back the bay soars Compton Down, popular with hang-gliders.

③ BRIGHSTONE

Typical of many of the Isle of Wight's villages, Brighstone has thatched cottages and tearooms. The Church of St Mary dates from Norman times. Inland from the village is Brighstone Forest, where there are several footpaths, one of which leads to the Long Stone, a 30 ft standing stone dating from between 3000 and 2000 BC. The stone can also be reached along a short path starting near Mottistone Manor Garden (NT), whose trim gardens are open to visitors. From Brighstone Down on the forest's eastern side there are fine views of the coast.

Yafford Mill, a mile south-east of Brighstone, is an 18th-century water mill in full working order. Among its attractions are a display of farm machinery, a nature trail and a narrow gauge railway. A road south from the mill leads to Dinosaur Farm where, in 1993, the skeleton of a giant sauropod dinosaur was unearthed. Visitors can see it there, along with other bones and fossils which have been discovered in the area's eroding sandstone.

④ WHALE CHINE

The long, deep chine got its name from an incident in 1758, when a 63 ft whale was stranded there. The chine's secluded rock and shingle beach can be reached down a footpath, leading from a car park on the A3055, a mile west of Chale. The path descends to a wooden staircase through Whale Chine's dark, damp walls. In the event of landslippage the path may be closed.

⑤ BLACKGANG CHINE

Landslips are common along this stretch of coast, and Blackgang has suffered many over the years. The movements are caused by layers of rock and earth lying on a bed of soft clay, known locally as blue slipper, sliding off into the sea when rain or spring water seeps through. The viewpoint overlooking Blackgang Chine gives an almost aerial vista of the contrasting chalk and clay cliffs of the south-west of the island. On a clear day it is possible to pick out the Isle of Purbeck, 28 miles away, and even Portland Bill, 50 miles distant. The area's main attraction is a fantasy theme park, which includes Dinosaurland, Fantasyland and Smugglerland. A 14th-century lighthouse base, known as the pepperpot, stands on the summit of St Catherine's Hill. It can be reached from a short walk that looks over the viewpoint car park.

⑥ ST CATHERINE'S POINT

Until the lighthouse was built in 1840, the sea around St Catherine's Point was a graveyard for many ships. Between 1748 and 1808 an average of ten ships a year came to grief. Visitors to the lighthouse, which is open at the discretion of the keeper, should park in Niton village to the north, and make the five-minute walk from there. The bracing, open headland of Knowles Farm (NT) lies to the west of the lighthouse.

HILLSIDE RESORT *Ventnor's villas perch on ledges, and roads zigzag down one-in-four gradients to the beach, sheltered from cold winds by the 787 ft crest of St Boniface Down.*

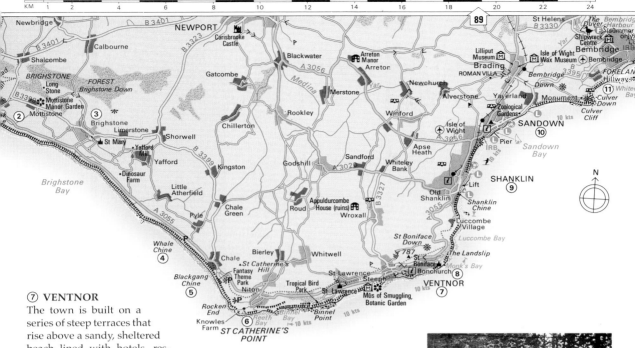

⑦ VENTNOR

The town is built on a series of steep terraces that rise above a sandy, sheltered beach lined with hotels, restaurants and shops. A waterfall cascades down a stepped garden to the beach, where a signpost indicates that France is straight ahead. In the battle against cliff erosion, 30 000 tons of Mendip limestone has been deposited on the shore to the west, and a mile-long sea wall has been built to the east, extending as far as Bonchurch. St Boniface Down, the highest point on the island, has good all-round views of the coast and inland hills. Smuggling was once a way of life in Ventnor, and a smugglers' pageant takes place in June.

A smugglers' museum is housed in the Botanic Garden, west of the town. The island's benign climate enables many subtropical plants to thrive in the gardens. From the main road that passes through them a footpath leads to the small, secluded beach of Steephill. Farther west, at St Lawrence, there is a Tropical Bird Park with some 300 exotic birds, including toucans and macaws. St Lawrence's Church, built in the 12th century, is one of Britain's smallest, measuring just 45 ft by 15 ft.

Appuldurcombe House (EH), 2 miles north-west of Ventnor, is a ruined baroque-style mansion, built in 1710, surrounded by ornamental gardens.

⑧ BONCHURCH

A fishing and quarrying hamlet during the 19th century, Bonchurch is reached by road, or by a mile-long walk along the sea wall from Ventnor. In a leafy setting stands the ancient Church of St Boniface, said to have been built in 1040 by monks from Normandy. A path runs from the church to the former home of the 19th-century poet Algernon Swinburne above Monk's Bay, where there has been extensive work to protect Bonchurch from the erosions caused by The Landslip. The slip was formed in the early 19th century when 30 acres, and later 50 acres, of land slid into the sea. More recently, a further 25 acres of earth has fallen away.

⑨ SHANKLIN

A largely Victorian seaside town blends into the scattering of thatched houses to the south that make up Old Shanklin. The old village overlooks Shanklin Chine, a deep, wooded ravine with a roaring waterfall. A walk through the chine passes a Victorian brine tub, in which heated seawater baths could be taken, and part of the PLUTO pipeline used in World War II to carry fuel under the Channel. Shanklin's other main attraction is a long, inviting, sandy beach at the foot of honey-coloured cliffs. The beach can be reached by a lift from Keats Green, named after the poet John Keats who stayed in the town in 1819. Shanklin is a good starting point for walks, including a steep climb to Luccombe Village, less than a mile to the south, and a sea-wall walk to Sandown, 1½ miles to the north.

⑩ SANDOWN

Sandown's pier has outlived those at Shanklin and Ventnor, lost in the 1980s to storm and fire respectively. The pier is a focal point for entertainment, with a theatre, sideshows and ranks of slot machines. The 5 mile long sandy beach stretching from Shanklin to Sandown and beyond is the longest on the island. At the northern end of the beach, a 19th-century fort is home to the Isle of Wight Zoological Gardens, which specialises in breeding endangered species.

⑪ CULVER DOWN

The stone needle on Culver Down is a memorial to the Earl of Yarborough, first commodore of the Royal Yacht

SHADY DELL *Ferns and mosses cling to the soft sandstone walls, and trees form a leafy canopy above the cleft of Shanklin Chine.*

Squadron. From this point walkers can pause to take in the spectacular views of the long, golden sands of Sandown to the west and Whitecliff Bay to the north. Bembridge Down, which has an orientation table identifying features of the surrounding view, merges with Culver Down to give a wide area for exhilarating walks. There is the added interest of watching light aircraft flying in and out of Bembridge airport.

PLACES TO SEE INLAND

Arreton Manor, 3 miles NW of Shanklin. Manor house of the Elizabethan and Jacobean periods.

Brading, 2 miles NE of Sandown. Lilliput Antique Doll and Toy Museum; Roman Villa, dating from around AD 300 with superb mosaic flooring; Wax Museum, collection of wax figures in town's oldest house.

TOURIST INFORMATION

Sandown (01983) 403886; Shanklin (01983) 862942; Ventnor (01983) 853625 (summer)

A great naval base that is part of England's history

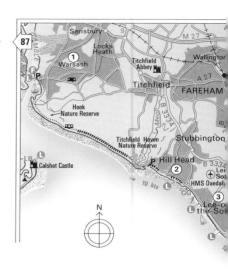

Ancient sea forts and castles line this strategically important stretch of coast, presided over by the fortress town of Portsmouth. The area's low-lying islands and peninsulas are separated by marshy creeks and inlets.

① WARSASH

A car park near the shore of this yachting village is the start of a 4 mile coastal path to Hill Head, which passes Hook Nature Reserve. The reserve is visited by oystercatchers, shelducks, linnets and meadow pipits. From the western end of Warsash a passenger ferry sails to the village of Hamble le Rice.

East of Warsash are the superb ruins of 13th-century Titchfield Abbey (EH), comprising the original priory buildings and a four-storey Tudor gatehouse.

Titchfield Abbey

② HILL HEAD

A promenade and large grassy area back the shingle beach of this old smugglers' haunt. Strong currents restrict swimming, but there is good fishing at the western end. Coast walks lead to Lee-on-the-Solent, a mile to the east, and to the Hamble estuary, 4 miles to the west. Permits are needed to enter the Titchfield Haven Nature Reserve, where hides give views of waders and wildfowl, especially wigeon.

③ LEE-ON-THE-SOLENT

The home of HMS Daedalus naval base and coastguard station, Lee-on-the-Solent is a mainly residential town with a neat area of grassland and a promenade running behind a shingle beach. A small amusement arcade lies at the eastern end of the beach, along with a sailing and an angling club.

④ GOSPORT

The history of this former fishing village is explained in the local museum. A ferry service to Portsmouth, which has run since the reign of Edward I, operates from the Ferry Gardens at the end of the high street. To the south of the town is HMS Dolphin naval base and the Royal Navy Submarine Museum, where visitors can board HMS *Alliance,* and *Holland I*, the navy's first 'submarine boat'. To the north is Fort Brockhurst (EH), built as a defence against invasion by Napoleon III, and used by the navy until World War II. Stokes Bay, to the south, has been well defended since Tudor times, and an early 19th-century battery, or gun emplacement, can still be seen at the western end of the 3 mile beach. The bay is now a popular centre for watersports.

'Little Woodham', on the western outskirts of the town, is a reconstruction of a 17th-century hamlet with timber-framed houses, which recalls life in the area before the Civil War.

⑤ PORTCHESTER CASTLE

The outer walls of Portchester Castle (EH) are those of a Roman fortress – the most complete surviving Roman fortress in Europe. The castle's Norman keep houses an exhibition of its history, and a path from the Water Gate leads to the shore and good views of Portsmouth Harbour. A coastal path heads west towards Fareham.

The chalk escarpment of Portsdown Hill, a mile north-east of Portchester, has footpaths and outstanding views across Portsmouth and the Solent. Fort

MAN-OF-WAR HMS Victory, *now in dry dock at Portsmouth, secured Nelson's triumph over Napoleon at Trafalgar in 1805, though the admiral himself was killed.*

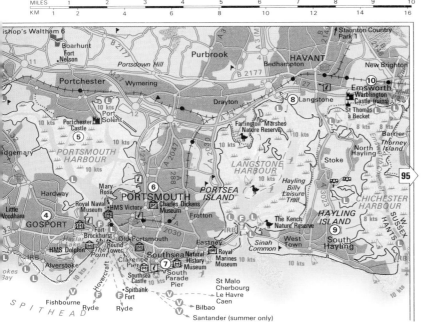

Nelson, built by Lord Palmerston in the 1860s, houses the Royal Armouries Museum of Artillery.

⑥ PORTSMOUTH

A fortress town since the 15th century, Portsmouth is England's most important naval base and the home of the Royal Dockyard founded by Henry VIII in 1540. Among the dockyard's Georgian storehouses is the Royal Naval Museum, together with Henry VIII's warship *Mary Rose* and Lord Nelson's flagship, HMS *Victory*. Visitors can also board HMS *Warrior*, which was the world's most advanced warship when it was launched in 1860, and is permanently docked in the harbour.

Old Portsmouth is the site of the City Museum and Art Gallery, and the 12th-century Cathedral of St Thomas of Canterbury. The Camber, in the western part of Old Portsmouth, where Sir Walter Raleigh landed with England's first supplies of potatoes and tobacco in 1585, was the city's original harbour.

Although still a working dockyard, fishing is its principal activity. The 15th-century Round Tower was built by Henry V to guard the harbour entrance.

On the northern side of the city is the Continental Ferry Port, where there are sailings to France and Spain. The nearby house where Charles Dickens was born in 1812 has been turned into a museum containing memorabilia of the novelist and the couch on which he died in 1870. Ferries to the Isle of Wight leave from a port near the train station. Port Solent, on the far upper reaches of Portsmouth Harbour, is a marina development with shops and restaurants.

⑦ SOUTHSEA

Though part of the City of Portsmouth, Southsea retains the character of a traditional seaside resort. It has a long shingle beach with patches of low-tide sand, two piers, and a string of seaside attractions, including a fairground, a D-Day Museum and the Pyramids leisure centre. Southsea Castle was built

by Henry VIII around 1544 to defend the Royal Dockyard. Its battlements offer good views of the Solent and of Spitbank Fort, a coastal defence which can be visited by ferry from Portsmouth's naval base. South Parade Pier, popular for fishing, marks the start of Southsea's esplanade, which is backed by the Rose Gardens and a boating lake. Behind the gardens is the Natural History Museum, including a butterfly house. At Eastney, at the east end of the beach, the Royal Marines Museum, is housed in Eastney Barracks.

⑧ LANGSTONE

The high street of this former fishing village ends at a small saltmarsh inlet where the Old Mill, once a smugglers' hideout and now a private residence, is said to be linked by tunnels to two waterside inns. Langstone Harbour is a Site of Special Scientific Interest that includes an RSPB reserve and also Farlington Marshes Nature Reserve, where many species of waders and wildfowl can be seen from a public footpath. Behind the mill, a path leads eastwards to the village of Warblington and the ruins of its 17th-century castle. The nearby Church of St Thomas à Becket has a Saxon tower and two 18th-century gravewatchers' huts, whose occupants once guarded against body-snatching.

⑨ HAYLING ISLAND

Linked to the mainland by a bridge, the island is fringed by marshes except on its southern shore, where there is a long stretch of sand and shingle. There are funfairs and amusement arcades along the seafront, as well as three yachting clubs, and a golf course on Sinah Common. The Hayling Billy Leisure Trail is a 3 mile coast walk from West Town, tracing the route of a former railway. This is the best place from which to view birds such as bar-tailed godwits and dunlins on the Kench Nature Reserve, which adjoins Langstone.

⑩ EMSWORTH

There are two old tide mills on the harbour of this former fishing port at the mouth of the River Ems. One of them houses the sailing club, which sits at the head of the harbour in front of a tidal pond. Its harbour wall, a delightful promenade, is the start of two long-distance trails, the 50 mile Solent Way west to Milford on Sea and the 90 mile Wayfarer's Walk inland to Newbury.

PLACES TO SEE INLAND

Bishop's Waltham Palace (EH), 9 miles N of Fareham. 12th-century ruins with Great Hall.

Staunton Country Park, near Havant, 8 miles N of Portsmouth. Ornamental farm and gardens.

TOURIST INFORMATION

Fareham (01329) 221342; Gosport (01705) 522944; Havant (01705) 480024; Hayling Island (01705) 467111 (summer); Portsmouth (01705) 826722

THEY ALSO SERVE *Destroyers await a call to service at the Royal Dockyard at Portsmouth, which has been Britain's largest naval base for nearly 500 years.*

Tidal creeks where small boats sail and birds flock

Market cross, Chichester

George V's convalescence in Bognor led him to confer the title 'Regis' on the town. Holidaymakers are its main visitors today, while sailors are drawn to Chichester Harbour, one of Europe's largest marinas.

INDOMITABLE WATERS *The creek at Bosham is said to be where King Canute commanded the tide to retreat, as a lesson to his courtiers who believed him to be all-powerful.*

① THORNEY ISLAND
The westernmost of three peninsulas in Chichester Harbour, Thorney Island is flat and featureless. The island is mostly the property of the Ministry of Defence, and the road south to the village of West Thorney is closed by a barrier.

The only part of the island that can be explored by visitors is an 8 mile footpath skirting the foreshore. There are good views of the harbour from the path, and Longmere Point, at Thorney's southern tip, overlooks the RSPB reserve of Pilsey Island.

② PRINSTED
A lane from the village of cottages that overlook tidal flats runs down to a shingle beach at the head of Thorney Channel. A small car park is a good starting point for walks in both directions round Chichester Harbour. Small boats can be launched near high water.

③ BOSHAM
One of the beauty spots of the south coast, the harbour village of Bosham, pronounced 'Bozzam', sits on a small wedge of land between two tidal creeks. Its sailing club is housed in an old quayside water mill in the marina. Quay Meadow (NT) is a grassy picnic area, beyond which rises the steeple of the Saxon Holy Trinity Church.

④ FISHBOURNE ROMAN PALACE
Seven years of excavation during the 1960s brought to light the remains of a magnificent palace on this early Roman site. The palace, built around AD 75, is thought to be that of the British King Cogidubnus, who had supported the Romans' invasion of AD 43, enjoyed their patronage and been allowed to rule on their behalf. The mosaics and the remains of luxurious chambers and corridors are protected beneath a modern building, which also houses a museum of the palace's history.

⑤ CHICHESTER
The typical Roman town-plan, distinguished by four main streets converging on a market cross, and partly surrounded by a circular wall, can still be seen in Chichester's centre. The town was founded by the Romans around AD 70. Building of the cathedral started in 1091, and continued until the early 15th century, when the detached bell tower, cloisters and spire were added. Nearby Pallant House is a restored 18th-century wine merchant's home with fine antiques and pictures. The late 13th-century Guildhall, once part of a monastery, has since served as both town hall and courthouse. Displays inside illustrate the building's history and that of Priory Park in which it stands.

A stroll around Chichester's old ramparts provides good views of the town and surrounding country. Performances of drama, opera and music are given throughout the year at the Festival Theatre. To the east of the town is the Mechanical Music and Doll Museum. To the north is the Royal Military Police Museum.

⑥ DELL QUAY
In the 18th century Dell Quay, together with neighbouring Apuldram, was the seventh most important port in England. It is now no more than a quiet sailing hamlet. Cottages are dotted along the narrow lane leading down to the quayside and yacht anchorages, where parking is very limited. Walks in

---

HISTORIC CHURCH

Bosham's church is featured in the Bayeux Tapestry, which depicts the Norman Conquest. Harold, the Earl of Wessex, who was soon to become King of England, set out from Bosham on his fateful voyage to Normandy. His oath of loyalty to Duke William triggered a chain of events that eventually led to William invading and conquering England.

Harold shown outside the church at Bosham.

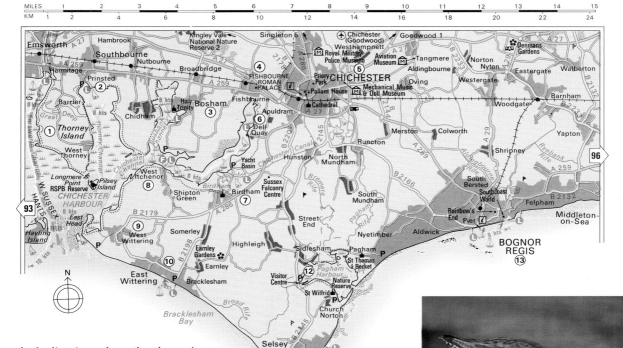

both directions along the shore give wide views over Chichester Channel, where wildfowl and waders abound.

⑦ BIRDHAM

With neat bungalows and cottages scattered about St James's Church and a green with its water pump, Birdham retains a village character. Close by lies the entrance to the Chichester Canal, which separates two huge marinas, Chichester Yacht Basin and Birdham Pool. Each has its own sailing club, boatyards and chandlers.

The Sussex Falconry Centre, east of Birdham, breeds and displays owls, kestrels, sparrowhawks and buzzards.

⑧ WEST ITCHENOR

Formerly a busy commercial port, West Itchenor is now a pretty sailing centre. The main road through the village leads to a shingle beach and a public jetty, from which boat tours of the harbour operate. In the summer a ferry runs across Chichester Channel to Bosham.

⑨ WEST WITTERING

The popular holiday village has a mile-long sandy beach fringed with dunes, reached by a signposted drive from the main street. The road ends at a large car park and picnic area.

West of the village, the shingle spit of East Head (NT) attracts birdwatchers and naturalists, who may spot ringed plovers, little terns and several species of butterfly on the tidal lagoon and among the dunes.

⑩ EAST WITTERING

Residential estates and holiday parks stretch for almost 2 miles along the seafront between East Wittering and Bracklesham. East Wittering's beach, where a large expanse of sand is revealed at low tide, can be reached either from Shore Road, which has no nearby parking, or from a car park

where the B2198 ends at Bracklesham. Various themed gardens, including a Scented Garden and a Seaside Garden, have been laid out at Earnley Gardens, north-east of Bracklesham. Tropical butterflies, exotic birds and farm animals can also be seen there.

⑪ SELSEY

Holiday homes and residential properties occupy the whole of Selsey's low-lying headland. From Selsey Bill there are fine views across to the Isle of Wight and eastwards along the coast. Sandy beaches stretch either side of the headland, where fast currents make bathing hazardous. Extensive parking behind the sea wall attracts most holiday-makers to East Beach, near the lifeboat station, where locally caught fish and shellfish can be bought.

⑫ PAGHAM HARBOUR

The former port is now a nature reserve. Dunlins, grey plovers, curlews and Brent geese are among the many species which gather on the mud flats, while much of the surrounding land is a haven for small mammals, insects and butterflies. The reserve is reached along a path from a visitor centre at Sidlesham, 2 miles north of Selsey.

The village of Pagham is centred on the seafront. The mainly 13th-century Church of St Thomas à Becket is one of the few signs of an earlier settlement. Pagham's sandy beach, backed by pebbles, is served by a car park and a collection of cafés and amusements. Two paths in the village lead to the harbour; one starts near the church, the other at Harbour Road behind the seafront. A path along the harbour's southern edge

SENTRY OF THE SHORE *The redshank feeds on invertebrates in the mud, but flies off with a loud alarm call when disturbed.*

leads across Church Norton churchyard, where there is a chapel dedicated to St Wilfrid, who brought Christianity to the South Saxons in the 7th century.

⑬ BOGNOR REGIS

One of the most popular resort towns on the south coast, Bognor Regis has sandy beaches, funfairs, bandstands and a pier with amusement arcades, cafés and a nightclub. Its holiday camps include Southcoast World, which is open to day visitors. The Rainbow's End children's adventure park offers circus shows, animated displays and a small farm. The leisure centre includes sunbeds and an indoor swimming pool.

PLACES TO SEE INLAND

Denmans Garden, Fontwell, 5 miles NE of Chichester. Shrubs and plants in a walled garden.

Goodwood House, 3½ miles NE of Chichester. 18th-century mansion.

Kingley Vale National Nature Reserve, 4 miles NW of Chichester. Europe's largest yew forest.

Tangmere Aviation Museum, Tangmere, 4 miles NE of Chichester. History of flying from 1917 at famous Battle of Britain airfield.

Weald and Downland Museum, Singleton, 6 miles N of Chichester. Historic buildings rescued and rebuilt.

TOURIST INFORMATION

Bognor Regis (01243) 823140; Chichester (01243) 775888

Long beaches that draw visitors to Worthing

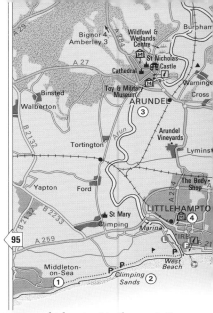

Towns and villages have spread out and merged along much of the coast near Worthing, but have not encroached on the shingle and dunes at Climping Sands. Inland, Arundel Castle rises above the River Arun.

① MIDDLETON-ON-SEA

Houses line the seafront in this predominantly residential area on the edge of Bognor Regis. Middleton was the site of a seaplane base during World War I; the present village developed largely between the wars. Several footpaths lead to the shingle and sand beach.

② CLIMPING SANDS

A large parking and picnic area behind the sea wall at Climping Sands is the start of foreshore walks in both directions along 2½ miles of undeveloped coastline. The walk eastwards, to the mouth of the River Arun, gives good views of the castle and cathedral at Arundel, and passes shingle colonised by sea kale and the yellow horned poppy. A few houses on the road to the shingle beach are all that remains of the village of Atherington, the rest of which was washed away in the 16th century.

The tower of St Mary's Church, almost 2 miles inland in the village of Climping, was built around 1170 and has a finely carved doorway. The rest of the church was built 60 years later and its structure is little changed since then.

③ ARUNDEL

The great battlemented castle at Arundel, its lofty rooms containing fine furniture, family portraits and armour, has been the home of the Dukes of Norfolk and their ancestors for more than 700 years. The castle is set in magnificent grounds overlooking the River Arun. Its keep dates from the 12th century, but most of the present castle was rebuilt in the 18th and 19th centuries. The tombs of the Dukes of Norfolk are in the Roman Catholic Fitzalan Chapel, which is at the east end of the Anglican parish church of St Nicholas, separated from the main part of the church simply by an iron grille. The chapel can be reached only from the castle grounds. There are fragments of interesting wall paintings dating from the 14th century in the parish church. Arundel's other most conspicuous building is the Roman Catholic cathedral, built on a hilltop site in French Gothic style between 1869 and 1873.

Exhibits and photographs in the Museum and Heritage Centre illustrate the history of Arundel. Dolls, dolls' houses, toy soldiers and games are displayed in the Toy and Military Museum. Boat trips on the river are available in summer. The Wildfowl and Wetlands Centre, beside the Arun a short distance outside the town, is home to ducks, geese, swans and other wildfowl from all over the world. At Arundel Vineyards, 2 miles south of the town, in the village of Lyminster, visitors can walk among the vines and taste the wines.

④ LITTLEHAMPTON

Sandy beaches have drawn visitors to Littlehampton since the late 18th century, and in the early 20th century the resort was promoted as 'the children's paradise'. The East Beach is backed by a wide green, and there is an amusement park on the western promenade. A footbridge and, in summer, a ferry cross from the town to the west bank of the Arun, where there are boatyards, marinas and a sailing club, and also the West Beach, backed by dunes. It is dangerous to bathe near the river mouth. The headquarters of the Body Shop company is just outside Littlehampton; tours explaining aspects of cosmetics production must be booked in advance.

⑤ RUSTINGTON

Rustington's old flint-walled cottages and its medieval Church of St Peter and St Paul have been engulfed by housing estates which extend to the coast. Steps from the promenade lead down to a beach of pebbles and low-tide sand.

Angmering-on-Sea, to the east, is a village of mostly private estates. Visitors can walk to the beach along paths between some of the houses.

⑥ FERRING

Fishing boats can often be seen drawn up on the shingle above the sandy beach at Ferring, which is separated from Worthing by fields and woods. Highdown Chalk Gardens, on the South Downs 2 miles inland from Ferring, has plants from all over the world, including Chinese maples and Indian chestnuts. The garden was established in 1910 by Sir Frederick and Lady Stern, who worked for 50 years to prove that plants would grow on chalk.

⑦ GORING-BY-SEA

A wide grassy area lies behind the seafront of this residential suburb of Worthing, laid out with plenty of open space. The beach is shingle, with low-tide sand. A mile inland, in Goring's modern English Martyrs Catholic Church, there is a copy of the ceiling painted by Michelangelo in the Vatican's Sistine Chapel. The painting was completed in 1993.

⑧ CISSBURY RING

One of Britain's largest Iron Age hill forts stands 600 ft up on the South Downs; oval in shape, it is nearly half a mile long and a quarter of a mile wide. Cissbury Ring was built about 300 BC, but flint was mined there 4000 years earlier and depressions in the ground are the filled-in mine shafts. From the hilltop there are fine views over Worthing to the sea.

⑨ WORTHING

Five miles of seafront, a wide promenade, colourful gardens, and a pier offering amusements and good fishing attract many holidaymakers to this large resort. The beach at Worthing is shingle with low tide sand; beacons and

HILLTOP FORTRESS *Arundel Castle was seriously damaged during the Civil War, but was later extensively restored.*

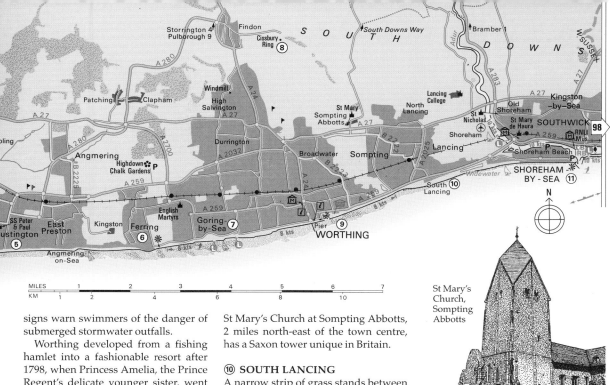

| MILES | | 1 | | 2 | | 3 | | 4 | | 5 | | 6 | | 7 |
| KM | 1 | | 2 | | 4 | | 6 | | 8 | | | 10 | |

signs warn swimmers of the danger of submerged stormwater outfalls.

Worthing developed from a fishing hamlet into a fashionable resort after 1798, when Princess Amelia, the Prince Regent's delicate younger sister, went there for her health. Some buildings from the town's early years survive. The museum and art gallery has a costume collection from 1700 to the present day.

On Worthing's northern edge is High Salvington Windmill, a black post mill completed in 1720 and now restored and producing flour. The mill is open on two Sundays a month in summer.

St Mary's Church at Sompting Abbotts, 2 miles north-east of the town centre, has a Saxon tower unique in Britain.

⑩ SOUTH LANCING

A narrow strip of grass stands between the coast road and a beach of sand backed by shingle. Lancing College chapel, 2 miles from the sea and started in 1868, is a landmark along the coast.

⑪ SHOREHAM-BY-SEA

The busy port of Shoreham lies astride the River Adur, at the point where the river turns sharply eastwards before

St Mary's Church, Sompting Abbotts

meeting the sea. The Church of St Nicholas at Old Shoreham, the original village and port, dates from Saxon times. By 1100 the Adur was silting up and the Normans chose a site farther south for their town of New Shoreham, with its 12th-century Church of St Mary de Haura, meaning 'of the harbour'. The Marlipins Museum, housed in an early 12th-century building, contains paintings and ship models.

A footbridge over the Adur from the town centre leads to Shoreham Beach, built on a shingle bank between the Adur and the sea. Widewater, a land-locked lagoon at the west end of Shoreham Beach, is home to herons, swans and ducks. Shoreham Airport, the oldest in Britain, has an art deco terminal building; pleasure flights and flying lessons are available, and there is a Museum of D-Day Aviation.

WILDE ABOUT WORTHING *It was while staying on holiday in Worthing in 1894 that Oscar Wilde wrote the play* The Importance of Being Earnest. *He gave the name John Worthing to its principal character, who was said to have been 'found in a handbag'.*

PLACES TO SEE INLAND

Amberley, 8 miles N of Littlehampton. Attractive village with thatched cottages; open-air industrial and craft museum in disused chalk pits; Amberley Wild Brooks is wetlands area.

Bignor Roman Villa, 10 miles N of Littlehampton. Mosaics, one 80ft long; hypocaust underfloor heating system; museum.

Bramber, 4 miles N of Shoreham-by-Sea. Remains of Norman castle (EH); 15th-century timber-framed St Mary's House with panelled rooms and painted wall leather.

Parham, nr Storrington, 11 miles NW of Worthing. Elizabethan house with displays of tapestries and needlework; gardens with maze.

Pulborough Brooks RSPB Reserve, 11 miles NW of Worthing. Wetlands area.

TOURIST INFORMATION

Arundel (01903) 882268; Littlehampton (01903) 713480 (summer); Worthing (01903) 210022

Seaside fun at Brighton, and breezy downs behind

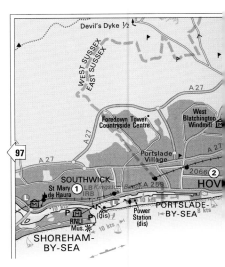

Lively Brighton and quieter Hove together form one of Britain's major seaside resorts. Rolling downland rises behind the coastal towns and villages, and cross-Channel ferries berth in the Ouse at Newhaven.

SEASCAPE *John Constable and his sick wife Maria visited the Hove area in 1824, and he painted this scene of the beach. He described it as 'a wonderful place for setting people up'.*

① SOUTHWICK

Traditional flint-walled houses stand round a spacious green in Southwick, an old village that has been engulfed by later development. To the south, a narrow inlet that runs to Hove contains Shoreham's marina, and forms the commercial, eastern arm of Shoreham harbour, flanked by Portslade-by-Sea. Facing the harbour entrance, Kingston Beach is a crescent of shingle with a disused lighthouse built in 1846, and the Shoreham lifeboat station. All that remains of the power station that once dominated the harbour is a tall chimney, used by ships as a landmark.

② HOVE

Wide expanses of lawn along the seafront give an open feeling to Hove, Brighton's sister resort and more sedate neighbour. Among the town's many elegant crescents and terraces is the monumental Brunswick Square, which dates from the 1820s and opens onto the seafront. Number 13 is being restored as a town house of the period and is open to the public by appointment. A Victorian villa houses Hove Museum and Art Gallery, which has paintings by British artists, together with ceramics, toys and clocks; there is also a section on early 20th-century commercial film-making in Hove. The beach consists of a broad bank of pebbles with a narrow strip of sand at low tide. The British

Engineerium, 1½ miles inland, is a restored Victorian pumping station with many full-size and model engines, and a huge beam engine that is 'in steam' some Sundays and on Bank Holidays. Nearby, West Blatchington, a downland village swallowed up by the expansion of Hove, is crowned by an early 19th-century smock windmill, containing a milling museum, open on summer Sundays and Bank Holidays.

High above the northern outskirts of Hove is Foredown Tower Countryside Centre, where a camera obscura focuses onto its white concave surface wide-ranging views extending over the South Downs and the English Channel.

③ BRIGHTON

The onion-domed Royal Pavilion forms an extraordinary centrepiece to the queen of British seaside resorts. Brighton's oriental fantasy, its interior as whimsical as its exterior, was the early 19th-century creation of the Prince Regent, who later became George IV. Fashionable society followed the prince to Brighton, and the town expanded steadily, its elegant terraces and squares surrounding the old fishing village of Brighthelmstone.

The narrow streets of the old village are now a pedestrianised shopping area known as The Lanes, which has many antiques, clothes and jewellery shops. Brighton Museum and Art Gallery,

housed in the former stables of the Royal Pavilion, traces Brighton's development into a major resort, and has Art Nouveau and Art Deco furniture.

Brighton's beach consists of pebbles leading down to a narrow strip of low-tide sand. The Palace Pier has amusements and a funfair; the West Pier has been closed to the public since 1975. Volk's Electric Railway, the first such railway in Britain when it was opened in 1883 by Magnus Volk, rattles along the seafront from Madeira Drive, the finishing point of the annual London to Brighton Veteran Car Run. The railway ends near the huge Brighton Marina, which has berths for up to 1700 boats, and pubs, restaurants and homes on the waterfront. There is a naturist beach to the west of the marina.

The Sea Life Centre and the Fishing Museum are both on the seafront, and 1½ miles inland are the Booth Museum of Natural History and Preston Manor, whose fully furnished interior has changed little since Edwardian times.

④ ROTTINGDEAN

The coast road between Brighton and Rottingdean skirts the cliff edge, giving good views over the English Channel. On the hill above the road is Roedean girls' school, built mainly in the 1890s.

Rottingdean has a small seafront, with a sea-wall promenade and a rocky beach. Old Rottingdean runs inland, and its narrow street of old flint-built houses opens out on to a green beside a village pond. The writer Rudyard Kipling lived in the village from 1897 to 1902, and the Grange Museum, housed in an 18th-century vicarage, has a collection of items relating to Kipling, including a replica of the author's study showing him sitting at his desk.

⑤ SALTDEAN

Estates of houses are grouped round Saltdean's oval recreation ground, at the seaward end of which is a fine example of a 1930s 'lido', or open-air swimming pool. From the car park, a

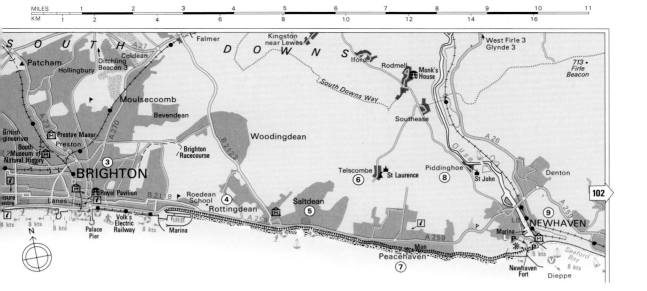

subway leads under the road to a concrete promenade. Steps descend to a rocky beach with patches of sand.

⑥ TELSCOMBE

Buried in a hollow in the downs, Telscombe is a remote hamlet of flint-walled houses with the tiny Norman Church of St Laurence. From the end of the lane, paths climb the downs and give expansive views over Saltdean, Peacehaven and the English Channel.

⑦ PEACEHAVEN

Houses and bungalows are laid out in a grid pattern in Peacehaven, which dates from soon after World War I. There was a plan to call the clifftop town Anzac-on-Sea, probably because troops from Australia and New Zealand were stationed nearby, but the name was changed to Peacehaven to commemorate the end of the war. A monument to George V is marked with the distances to towns of the British Empire. Steps lead steeply down to a pebbly beach.

⑧ PIDDINGHOE

Small boats in the Ouse and flint-walled cottages give Piddinghoe the appearance of a remote country village, though it is little more than a mile from the centre of Newhaven. Built of flint and stone, St John's Church has a round Norman tower, topped by a gilded weather vane in the form of a fish.

⑨ NEWHAVEN

Ferries to and from Dieppe, in Normandy, inch their way along the narrow River Ouse and berth on its eastern bank. The town centre is on the west bank, where there is also a marina, and a small shingle beach from which there are good close-up views of the ferries and other shipping.

Until 1579 the mouth of the Ouse was at Seaford to the east and present-day Newhaven was called Meeching, but that year a great storm changed the river's course, and the 'New Haven' was the result. Newhaven Fort, high above the western side of the river mouth, is one of a chain of 72 coastal defences built in the 1860s to withstand French attacks. The fort, which was garrisoned until 1956, has been restored and has displays on army life, the Royal Observer Corps and the 'Home Front' during World War II. On the ramparts, guns still point menacingly out to sea.

PLACES TO SEE INLAND

Devil's Dyke, 5 miles N of Hove. Steep valley associated with legends of the devil; hill fort with dramatic views; walks along South Downs Way.

Ditchling Beacon, 6 miles N of Brighton. High point on the South Downs; nature reserve and hill fort; 2 mile walk west to 'Jack' and 'Jill' windmills.

Firle Place, West Firle, 8 miles NE of Newhaven. Tudor and Georgian house with paintings by British and European old masters.

Glynde Place, Glynde, 7 miles N of Newhaven. Tudor house, panelled long gallery.

Monk's House (NT), Rodmell, 4 miles NW of Newhaven. Small weatherboarded country retreat of the novelist Virginia Woolf.

TOURIST INFORMATION

Brighton (01273) 323755; Hove (01273) 746100; Peacehaven (01273) 582668

FASHIONABLE STROLLING-GROUND *Brighton's Palace Pier is a well preserved example of seaside Victoriana; it replaced the earlier Chain Pier, destroyed by a storm in 1896.*

The Birth of the Seaside Holiday

*T*HE ENGLISH invented seaside holidays in the late 17th century, when 'taking the waters' was extended to mean bathing in and drinking sea water. One of the earliest resorts was Scarborough, a spa town which grew in popularity after 1660, when a local doctor, Robert Wittie, enthused about the medicinal benefits of sea bathing; by 1720 visitors to Scarborough were taking the plunge in large numbers. Thirty years later a Sussex doctor, Richard Russell, wrote a book extolling the virtues of imbibing and bathing in the sea water at Brighthelmstone, as Brighton was then called. His treatment drew many people to the town, including the Prince of Wales, later Prince Regent and George IV, whose frequent visits made Brighton a fashionable resort; the prince's father, George III, preferred Weymouth. By the mid 19th century seaside towns had no more need of royal patronage, as cheap rail travel had enticed hordes of day trippers.

BESIDE THE SEA *Several seaside resorts claim to be the first to have introduced bathing machines, and one was recorded in Scarborough as early as 1735. Brighton (above) was not slow to provide these mobile changing rooms for modesty-conscious Victorians.*

DOCTOR OF ENTERPRISE *Richard Russell practised as a physician in Lewes. His sea-water treatment made him prosperous enough to build a house in Brighton, on the site where the Royal Albion Hotel stands today.*

PRINCE OF FASHION *The Prince Regent first visited Brighton in 1783, and later built the Royal Pavilion, where he entertained lavishly.*

FANTASY PALACE *Brighton's Royal Pavilion began as a modest mansion designed by Henry Holland, but the Prince Regent's later obsession with oriental art led to the ornate building which John Nash completed in 1822.*

REGENCY TERRACES *The elegant houses of Regency Square, dating from between 1818 and 1824, are among many that rose in Brighton as wealthy aristocrats followed the Prince Regent to the seaside for their health and recreation.*

PUPPET SHOW *Pierrots, promenade shows and Punch and Judy have long been traditional seaside entertainments. Punch and Judy, and their dog Toby, date back to the 17th century and have their origins in Italian comedy.*

GRAND BY NAME, GRAND BY NATURE *When it was built in 1867, Scarborough's Grand Hotel was the biggest brick building in Europe, with 365 bedrooms, 52 chimneys, 12 floors and 4 turrets, representing the days, weeks, months and seasons of the year. An outdoor electric lift, which still survives, linked the hotel with the promenade.*

BATHING BELLES *In about 1910, when this hand-tinted photograph was taken, bathing costumes such as these would have been considered rather daring.*

'THE FINEST PIER IN THE WORLD' *Few argued with Brighton's proud boast when its Palace Pier was opened in 1899. The pier offered everything its Victorian visitors desired, on 1760 ft of promenade deck, with ornate domes and glass-covered sun verandahs.*

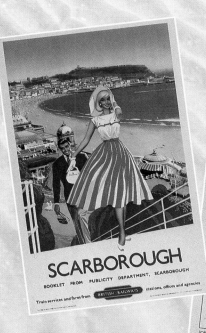

SUNSHINE LINE *The arrival of the railway paved the way for cheap excursions to the seaside. The London and North-East Railway, opened in 1845, did much to promote Scarborough's development as a resort. Between 1934 and 1972 the Brighton Belle took holidaymakers from London's Victoria station to what had become known as 'London-by-the-Sea'.*

Sheer chalk cliffs that drop to Eastbourne's seafront

The South Downs meet the sea in a wall of white chalk whose highest point is the bastion of Beachy Head. East of the cliffs, and the Victorian resort of Eastbourne, the flat Pevensey Levels back shingle beaches.

① SEAFORD

The shingle beach bordering the quiet, mainly residential seaside town shelves steeply, and at high tide the sea is suitable for strong swimmers only. A small local history museum is housed in a seafront Martello tower – the westernmost of the chain of circular, early 19th-century fortress towers that extends round England's east and south-east coasts. The Crypt, a restored 13th-century stone undercroft, is also open to visitors, and has an associated art gallery. From the car park at the western end of the seafront, a 15-minute walk along the shingle leads to the massive foundations of the Bishopstone tide mill, which harnessed tidal power to grind corn in the 19th century.

② SEAFORD HEAD
NATURE RESERVE

Behind the 282 ft cliffs of Seaford Head is a nature reserve where migrant birds, including willow warblers, chiffchaffs, whitethroats and redstarts, stop to feed while heading south in autumn. Ring ouzels and pied flycatchers may also be seen there, and nightingales are heard in spring. A clifftop path from Seaford to the headland gives spectacular views along the coast. The reserve can also be reached by car from Chyngton Road, which leads to a car park on the headland, with fine views. The path from the car park to Hope Gap gives a splendid view of the scalloped white wall of cliff known as the Seven Sisters.

③ CUCKMERE HAVEN

The tranquil River Cuckmere, whose name is pronounced 'Cookmere', makes a series of enormous loops through water meadows before reaching Cuckmere Haven, a gap in the chalk cliffs which 18th-century smugglers found ideal for landing cargoes of brandy, lace and other contraband from France. The main road is a mile inland, and the only way to the stone-scattered beach is by footpath along the valley. There is a large car park near the start of the walk, at Exceat, pronounced 'Ex-seet'.

The eastern side of the Cuckmere valley and the western end of the Seven Sisters cliffs make up a country park that includes meadows, downland,

chalk cliffs, salt marsh and shingle, and supports a variety of wildlife. Barns by the Seaford to Eastbourne road at Exceat house a visitor centre with exhibitions including The Living World, where stick insects, scorpions and butterflies can be seen, plus a display of seashore life. A 3 mile trail leads from the visitor centre to the cliffs and back.

④ ALFRISTON

Weatherboarded cottages and timber-framed inns line the streets of this pretty downland village. Carved figureheads on the outside of one inn are former ships' ornaments. The magnificent 14th-century Church of St Andrew stands by the village green. Beside the church, and also dating from the 14th century, is the thatched and timbered Alfriston Clergy House, which was bought by the National Trust for £10 in 1896 – its first purchase. The road

between Alfriston and Seaford rises steeply to the appropriately named High and Over, where a car park gives wide-ranging views over the South Downs towards the sea.

⑤ LONG MAN OF WILMINGTON

The gigantic outline of a man holding a staff in either hand stands out clearly on the chalk hillside south of the village of Wilmington. The earliest record of the 235 ft Long Man is a drawing made in 1710, but one local legend says that he was made as long ago as the Bronze Age or the Iron Age. Roman coins with similar figures suggest that he could be a Roman creation. Another theory is that he is the work of a monk from nearby Wilmington Priory and dates from somewhere between the 11th and 15th centuries. A well-trodden path to the Long Man leaves the minor road just south of the village.

SOUTH DOWNS GIANT *The origins of the Long Man of Wilmington continue to baffle historians. He has been explained variously as a god, as a fertility symbol, and as a folly.*

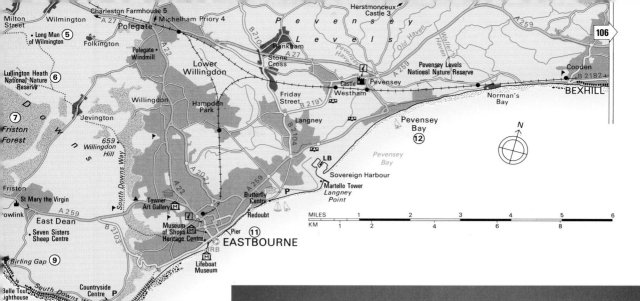

POMP AND CIRCUMSTANCE *Military music from a 1930s' bandstand on the seafront reverberates in the genteel Eastbourne air every day during the summer months.*

⑥ LULLINGTON HEATH NATIONAL NATURE RESERVE

One of Britain's largest remaining areas of chalk heath lies in the heart of the South Downs, between the villages of Litlington and Jevington. A mile walk from either village leads to the heath, which is a national nature reserve. In spring, nightingales and warblers nest in the scrub that covers most of the reserve; the more open areas are the haunt of butterflies including the chalk-hill blue and the dark green fritillary.

⑦ FRISTON FOREST

Dense forest, mostly of broadleaved trees, sprawls across the downs and can be explored by a 2¾ mile waymarked walk that starts at the car park at the west end of the forest. South of the coast road, a lane beside Friston's St Mary the Virgin Church leads down to Crowlink, where there are fine views towards the sea from the small car park.

⑧ SEVEN SISTERS

Between Cuckmere Haven and Birling Gap the striking vertical chalk cliffs rise and fall like the waves in the sea far below. Despite its name, there are in fact eight summits in the range, the highest of which is 253 ft.

⑨ BIRLING GAP

Like Cuckmere Haven, this narrow gap in the cliffs was once frequented by smugglers who used the flint-built village of East Dean, a mile inland, as their headquarters. Birling Gap's shingle beach is reached by steep steps down the 30 ft cliff, which is wearing away.

Visitors to the nearby Seven Sisters Sheep Centre can watch sheep-shearing and milking, and see 30 breeds of sheep, including older breeds not seen on modern farms. To the east of Birling Gap, the former Belle Tout lighthouse perches on the cliff edge; built in 1834, it is now a private house.

⑩ BEACHY HEAD

The Normans called it *Beau Chef*, meaning 'Beautiful Headland', and over the centuries the name of this colossal chalk rampart has been corrupted to 'Beachy'. The 534 ft cliff rises sheer from the rocky foreshore, and from its grassy summit the view on a clear day takes in the English Channel from Dungeness in the east to the Isle of Wight in the west.

A breezy path from the main car park leads past clumps of sea lavender and samphire to the cliff edge, from where there are good views of the red-and-white lighthouse near the foot of the cliff far below. Exhibits in the Beachy Head Countryside Centre include a rock pool with tides, and explanations of the downland's history, natural history and agriculture.

⑪ EASTBOURNE

A lively pier, and a turquoise-roofed bandstand where military bands play in summer, stand at the centre of 3 miles of seafront in Eastbourne, which has plenty of stuccoed Victorian buildings. Colourful public gardens that line the seafront include the Carpet Gardens, where flowerbeds are laid out in the patterns of Persian carpets. The beach is mainly shingle, with sand at low tide; fishing trips are available, and boat trips take visitors past Beachy Head and the Seven Sisters cliffs.

On the seafront is a restored Martello tower known as the Wish Tower. The neighbouring Lifeboat Museum is housed in a former lifeboat station. Eastbourne's heritage centre, a few minutes' walk inland, traces the town's growth since the 17th century, and the nearby Museum of Shops shows how people shopped and lived between 1850 and 1950. Farther east along the seafront are the Redoubt, a restored Napoleonic fortress housing military exhibitions, and the Butterfly Centre, where exotic moths and butterflies fly about the glasshouse gardens in specially recreated tropical conditions.

Inland, in the old town, a fine 18th-century manor house is now the Towner Art Gallery and Local History Museum, one of whose exhibits is a Victorian kitchen. Polegate Windmill, on Eastbourne's northern outskirts, is a restored tower mill built in 1817 and open to the public on summer Sundays and Bank Holidays, and on a few days

WALLS OF WHITE *From Cuckmere Haven, the chalk cliffs known as the Seven Sisters climb and dip for 5 miles to Beachy Head. The roller-coaster feature was formed from parallel valleys that once extended farther seaward. The South Downs Way follows the clifftop.*

in August. Between Eastbourne and Pevensey Bay is Sovereign Harbour, a large marina and leisure area.

⑫ **PEVENSEY BAY**
In 1066 William the Conqueror landed somewhere along this stretch of coast, although the precise spot is not known because the coastline has changed over

the centuries. Today, the shingle beach is fringed with chalets and small houses, which continue along the coast towards Norman's Bay, where there are more beachside homes.

The old village of Pevensey, a mile inland, is dominated by the mighty walls of Pevensey Castle (EH); the outer walls were built by the Romans as a

defence against Saxon raiders. Within them are the remains of a castle dating from soon after the Norman Conquest. From Pevensey, a minor road meanders across the flat grazing land of Pevensey Levels towards Bexhill. Part of the level is marshland and a national nature reserve. No paths cross the reserve, but from the roadside there are good views of its birdlife – yellow wagtails and reed and sedge warblers in summer, and golden plovers and lapwings in winter.

HEADY HEIGHTS *At the foot of the formidable Beachy Head is a 153 ft lighthouse built in 1902. To construct the lighthouse, Cornish granite was lowered from the clifftop by an aerial ropeway.*

Pebbly shore near the spot where William conquered

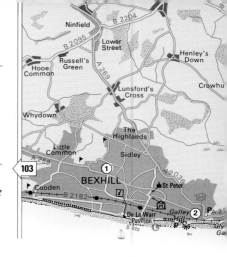

Breezy open clifftops and flat reclaimed land ablaze with yellow gorse lie to the east of the resorts of Bexhill and Hastings. The Normans of 1066 left their mark, and defences against later invaders can still be seen.

① BEXHILL

The quiet resort is dominated by the long, low lines and great sweeps of glass of the De La Warr Pavilion, which was built in 1935. Bexhill's beach is shingle, with a broad expanse of sand and rock pools uncovered at low tide, and was the first in Britain where mixed bathing was allowed, in 1901. Half a mile inland, a small group of weather-boarded houses and St Peter's Church, founded in 772, make up the old town of Bexhill. The former stable block of the old manor house nearby is now a museum with displays of costumes, dolls and Victorian kitchen equipment.

② GALLEY HILL

At the eastern end of Bexhill's seafront, the clifftop viewpoint of Galley Hill gives wide-ranging panoramas out to sea and round the coast. A short walk down the hill leads to the secluded shingle beach at Glyne Gap.

③ BULVERHYTHE

The long stretch of stone and shingle at Bulverhythe was once a favourite landing place for smugglers. A pub by the main road, the Bo-Peep, takes its name from the nursery rhyme which is said to have been written in the 18th century for the landlord's daughter. The sheep in the rhyme are supposed to have been smugglers, and their tails casks of smuggled French brandy. At very low tides the timbers of the *Amsterdam*, a Dutch merchantman wrecked in 1748, can sometimes be seen offshore.

④ ST LEONARDS

The planned seaside resort of villas and gardens, rising along the sides of a valley behind the seafront, was created between 1827 and 1837 by the architect James Burton and his son Decimus for wealthy visitors. Buildings dating from this period include the assembly rooms, now used as a Masonic hall, and the Royal Victoria Hotel, which is dwarfed by the huge white bulk of Marine Court, a block of flats built in the 1930s to resemble an ocean liner. St Leonards long ago coalesced with Hastings to form one uninterrupted built-up area.

⑤ HASTINGS

Although Hastings gave its name to the battle that took place in 1066, Duke William of Normandy actually defeated King Harold and his Saxon army 6 miles inland, at Battle. Hastings was already a flourishing harbour town when the Normans landed at Pevensey to the west, and in the Middle Ages the town was one of the Cinque Ports, along with Dover, Hythe, Romney and Sandwich. The Old Town's long, narrow High Street slants inland from the harbour between East Hill and West Hill, and is lined with half-timbered and weatherboarded houses. Tiny lanes and stepped paths climb the steep hillsides of the Old Town. Cliff railways climb to the summits of both hills.

Hastings Castle, on West Hill, was the first castle built by William after the Conquest; only fragments survive. A daily audiovisual show in the grounds re-creates the Battle of Hastings. St Clement's Caves burrow far into West Hill, and tableaux inside depict smugglers and their activities.

At the harbour, known as the Stade, fishermen winch boats ashore on the shingle. A few yards away are tall, black-painted wooden sheds, known as 'net shops', built for drying nets but now used for storage. Early morning fish auctions take place at the fish market above the shingle. Nearby are the Shipwreck Heritage Centre, the

ANCIENT PRIVILEGE *At the Stade in Hastings Old Town, local fishermen still have the right, as mariners of a Cinque Port, to beach their vessels without charge.*

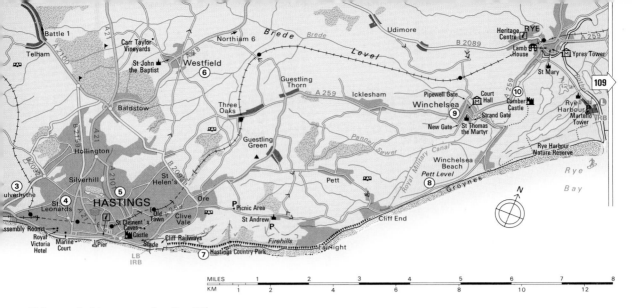

Fishermen's Museum and a Sea Life Centre with an 'ocean tunnel' which gives visitors a close look at rays, sharks and other marine creatures. West of the Stade are a traditional pier, and the Hastings and St Leonards beach, a continuous expanse that consists of shingle with low-tide sand and rock pools.

⑥ WESTFIELD
Weatherboarded houses line the by-roads off both sides of the main road through Westfield, whose massively buttressed, squat-towered Church of St John the Baptist is largely Norman. Visitors to the nearby Carr Taylor Vineyards can follow a vineyard trail or study the wine-making and bottling plant before sampling the products.

⑦ HASTINGS COUNTRY PARK
A superb open space of woods, grass-land and heath, cut by deep glens, extends along the clifftop from East Hill, in Hastings, eastwards to Fairlight. Birds to be seen there include woodpeckers, linnets, greenfinches and redpolls. A lane by Fairlight's tall-towered St Andrew's Church leads to the main car park and to a visitor centre. Below the car park, paths cross an area of heathland known, perhaps from its yellow-flowered gorse, as the Firehills. A small rocky cove at the foot of the cliffs is a naturist beach.

From Fairlight, a narrow road twists down to Cliff End, where the shingle beach is lined with groynes and rows of wooden stakes, which protect the coast

CASTLE ON THE MARSH *The drained expanses of Romney Marsh once lay beneath the sea, and Camber Castle stood on a spit of land. Today, sheep nibble the pancake-flat pastures.*

from erosion. Notices warn of mud-holes, rock falls, underwater obstructions and treacherous tides.

⑧ PETT LEVEL
An expanse of flat land, crisscrossed by watercourses and dotted with sheep, lies between the sea and the western end of the Royal Military Canal, dug in the early 19th century as part of the defensive system against Napoleon. Reedy ponds are a haven for herons and other waterbirds. The beach is shingle, with muddy sand uncovered at low tide; steps lead down to the beach from the road below the concrete sea wall.

⑨ WINCHELSEA
Weatherboarded cottages and tile-hung houses face each other across streets laid out on a grid pattern in this sleepy little town. Winchelsea now stands more than a mile inland, but during the Middle Ages it was one of the principal harbours on the south coast. From the 15th century the build-up of shingle along the shore gradually cut the town off from the sea. Winchelsea was repeatedly attacked by the French, who destroyed most of the Church of St Thomas the Martyr; only the choir and side chapels remain intact. Three medieval gateways survive, however,

as does the Court Hall, which contains a museum of the town's history.

At Winchelsea Beach, south of the town, there are chalets, caravans and camp sites, lying above a beach of shingle with low-tide sand.

⑩ CAMBER CASTLE
Crouching low amid farmland about a mile from the sea, Camber Castle (EH) is a solitary and impressive ruin, surviving virtually in its original form. It was one of a defensive chain built in the 1530s, at a time when Henry VIII feared invasion from the Continent, to a clover-leaf plan with rounded walls to deflect cannonballs. Visitors can see the interior of the castle by joining a guided tour that leaves from Rye Heritage Centre on Sundays, Wednesdays and Fridays, and involves a level walk of more than a mile across fields.

Strand Gate, Winchelsea

PLACES TO SEE INLAND

Battle, 6 miles NW of Hastings. Abbey and site of Battle of Hastings (EH); local history museum.

Great Dixter, Northiam, 11 miles N of Hastings. 15th-century hall house; gardens.

TOURIST INFORMATION

Bexhill (01424) 212023; Hastings (01424) 718888; Rye (01797) 226696

Marshy meadows and a birdwatchers' paradise

East of ancient Rye and the rolling Camber dunes lie Romney Marsh's flat farmland and, beyond, the shingle promontory of Dungeness. Farther north, bustling Dymchurch shelters behind a massive sea wall.

HAUNT OF SMUGGLERS *Many of the houses in Rye's Mermaid Street still retain the interconnecting attics through which smugglers could dodge the excisemen.*

① RYE
The gem of a medieval hilltop town is entered through an imposing stone gateway; its narrow streets, many of them cobbled, rise to the fine Norman Church of St Mary, distinctive for its 'quarterboys', gilded cherubs which strike the bells on the tower clock. Rye is surrounded by water on three sides, the Rother to the east, the Tillingham to the west, and the Royal Military Canal to the south. It has a small fishing fleet, and there are usually fishing boats moored in the Rother, where fresh fish can be bought at the quayside.

Lamb House (NT), built in the 18th century, was the home of the American novelist Henry James from 1897 to 1914. Steep, cobbled Mermaid Street, with its half-timbered Mermaid Inn, was once a haunt of smugglers. The 13th-century Ypres Tower, all that remains of Rye Castle, has a museum with exhibits that include one of the world's oldest fire engines. The tower overlooks the Gun Garden, where cannon still point out to sea. Rye Heritage Centre, on Strand Quay, not only traces the town's history with a sound and light show, but houses the Town Model, showing Rye as it was in the late 19th century.

② RYE HARBOUR
Reached through an industrial area, Rye Harbour, at the mouth of the Rother, consists of a Martello tower, a cluster of cottages and the prominent Victorian Church of the Holy Spirit. From the car park by the tower, a path leads to Rye Harbour Nature Reserve, an area of salt marsh and farmland that has some of the most varied coastal shingle vegetation in the south of England. Birds that can be seen from the hides include little and common terns, oystercatchers and ringed plovers.

③ CAMBER
The coast road from Rye zigzags past gravel pits and across golf links to this village of chalets, caravan parks and a holiday camp. The vast sand dunes that loom over Camber have been replanted with marram grass and shrubs to prevent erosion. Fenced footpaths lead across the dunes to Camber Sands, where the sea goes out for half a mile at low tide. Walkers should beware as there is a danger of being cut off by fast, incoming tides. East of Camber the dunes gradually give way to the shingle of Dungeness, where the currents become progressively more dangerous.

④ BROOKLAND
In common with all the villages that dot Romney Marsh, Brookland is surrounded by flat, reclaimed farmland. St Augustine's Church is unusual in having a detached octagonal wooden belfry, and a Norman lead font decorated with the signs of the Zodiac.

A mile west of Brookland, handicrafts ranging from chairs to earrings can be bought at the Philippine Craft Centre, housed in an old RAF camp. At nearby Brenzett, the Aeronautical Museum, which has restricted opening times, displays wartime memorabilia along with remains of World War II aircraft that crashed on the marsh.

⑤ LYDD
All Saints' Church, built in the 1440s, dominates the village. Known as the 'Cathedral of Romney Marsh', it is 200 ft long and has a tower 132 ft high. Lydd gave its name to the explosive lyddite, first tested there around 1890.

Lydd Ashford airport gives tours by light aircraft over Kent and Sussex, and flying instruction for the more adventurous. The Dungeness foreshore can be reached from Dengemarsh Road, which runs for 3 miles across the shingle, passing Herons Park leisure complex, which offers a variety of watersports such as jet skiing, water skiing and windsurfing on a flooded gravel pit.

⑥ DUNGENESS
The windswept shingle promontory, where thick fog can roll in suddenly, and whose coastline is forever changing, has been a constant danger to shipping. Two lighthouses stand on the foreshore. The graceful structure of Dungeness lighthouse throws a beam for 17 miles, while a short way across the shingle the tall, brick tower of the disused 1904 lighthouse has spectacular views round the coast from its parapet. Nearby, the base of Samuel Wyatt's lighthouse of 1792 has been converted into houses and flats. Scattered about the shingle are fishermen's huts, where fresh fish can be bought.

Behind the lighthouses loom the massive square blocks of Dungeness

RESIDENT BIRD *Despite its name, the common gull has in Dungeness its only regular breeding place in England.*

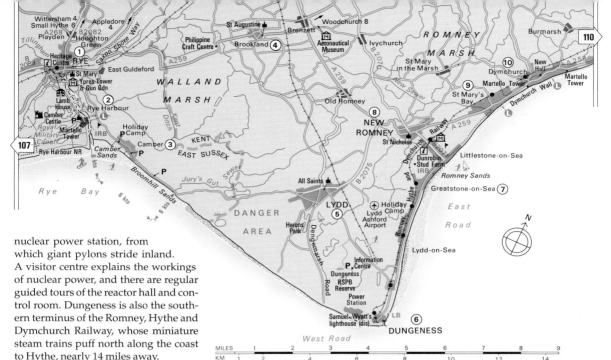

nuclear power station, from which giant pylons stride inland. A visitor centre explains the workings of nuclear power, and there are regular guided tours of the reactor hall and control room. Dungeness is also the southern terminus of the Romney, Hythe and Dymchurch Railway, whose miniature steam trains puff north along the coast to Hythe, nearly 14 miles away.

Dungeness RSPB Reserve, down a track off the Lydd-Dungeness road, has an information centre and waymarked walk. The reserve serves as a wintering ground for many migratory birds, and more than 300 species have been recorded there, including firecrests, little terns and stone curlews.

⑦ GREATSTONE-ON-SEA

The resort forms part of a straggling stretch of seaside development that runs for 3 miles from Lydd-on-Sea, past Greatstone to Littlestone, where tall Victorian houses face a stretch of grass above the sea. The beach is shingle, leading down at low tide to a broad expanse of sand. Low tide exposes a sunken section of a Mulberry artificial harbour, which was towed across the English Channel for use during the Normandy invasion of 1944.

The Dunrobin Stud Farm has a unique collection of stallions representing many British breeds. Summer visitors are asked to help to name new foals. Shire horses, donkeys and farm animals are also on show.

⑧ NEW ROMNEY

Until storms at the end of the 13th century diverted the mouth of the Rother to Rye, the river flowed into the sea there, and boats used to moor below the churchyard wall. As the shingle built up, Romney, the 'capital' of Romney Marsh and one of the original Cinque Ports, became stranded a mile from the sea. The superb St Nicholas Church is Norman in origin but was greatly enlarged in the 14th century. The station of the Romney, Hythe and Dymchurch Railway has a museum with a fully operational model railway.

⑨ ST MARY'S BAY

Holiday cottages and seaside amusements occupy much of this village. At the southern end the beach is shingle, leading down to pebbly sand; farther north it is sandy, protected by groynes. A breezy 3½ mile walk along the sea wall leads south to Littlestone.

⑩ DYMCHURCH

Lying more than 7ft below high-tide level, Dymchurch crouches behind the massive, possibly Roman, embankment known as Dymchurch Wall. This old Romney Marsh township is full of amusement arcades and funfairs, forming a lively contrast behind the sand and shingle beach with the dignified main street and imposing Martello towers. Tower Number 24 (EH), which has a cannon on its roof, has been restored and has displays illustrating the defences against Napoleon.

From as early as the 13th century to 1930 the complex Romney Marsh drainage system was run from Dymchurch by the grandly named 'Lords of the Level'. They operated from the Court Room in New Hall at the northern end of Dymchurch, where the present drainage board have their offices. The original court room is still on view in the museum at New Hall, along with relics from the town's past.

PLACES TO SEE INLAND
Appledore, 7 miles NE of Rye. Pretty village on Royal Military Canal.
Smallhythe Place (NT), 8 miles N of Rye. Timbered 16th-century house, home of actress Ellen Terry who lived there 1899-1928.
Stocks Mill, Wittersham, 5 miles N of Rye. Restored 18th-century post mill, small museum.
Woodchurch Windmill, 13 miles NW of New Romney. Restored smock mill with machinery and exhibition.

TOURIST INFORMATION
New Romney (01797) 364044 (summer); Rye (01797) 226696

SILENT SENTINEL *At Dymchurch a restored Martello tower, capped by a swivelling gun platform, shows how these 19th-century defences stood ready to repel Napoleon.*

The white cliffs of Dover, and a tunnel to France

Fortifications and reminders of war are found all along this stretch of coast, and especially at the historic port of Dover with its distinctive chalk cliffs. A new route to France plunges beneath the Channel.

① LYMPNE CASTLE
The castle, whose name is pronounced 'Limm', stands on a magnificent site at the edge of an inland cliff, and its tower offers panoramic views across Romney Marsh and over the English Channel to the French coast. Lympne Castle dates from early Norman times and has a superb panelled Great Hall.

② HYTHE
The town centre is half a mile inland, yet in medieval times Hythe was right on the sea and one of the Cinque Ports – the confederation of south-east coastal towns which supplied ships and crew for the defence of the realm in return for special charters and privileges. The older part of Hythe is separated from the largely Victorian resort area by the Royal Military Canal, dug during the early 19th century as part of the defensive system against Napoleon and now used by small pleasure boats.

In the old part of the town, on a steep slope above the canal, streets of mainly 18th-century houses run parallel to each other below the medieval Church of St Leonard. The church's crypt contains 1000 skulls and 8000 thighbones of people who lived between 1200 and 1400; the bones were probably placed there when the graveyard was cleared to make room for fresh burials.

Seaside Hythe has a long promenade above a shingle and sand beach protected by massive groynes. Fishing boats line the shingle below a Martello tower – a circular, early 19th-century fortress tower – that marks the eastern end of a military firing range extending along the coast for 2 miles.

Hythe is the northern terminus of the Romney, Hythe and Dymchurch Railway, a miniature steam railway that runs for nearly 14 miles to Dungeness. Brockhill Country Park, in hills northwest of the town, is the starting point for three waymarked country walks.

③ EUROTUNNEL EXHIBITION CENTRE
Outside the exhibition centre is the vast cutting head of a tunnelling machine used in the construction of the link with France. Inside, visitors can discover how the three 31 mile tunnels were built, and see a model reconstruction of the tunnel railway, its trains, and the terminal complexes on both shores. A viewing tower overlooks the long loading bays of the Channel Tunnel terminal on the other side of the M20.

④ SANDGATE
Rows of old fishermen's cottages are squeezed between the road and the sea at Sandgate. On the small esplanade are the battered remains of Sandgate Castle, which can be visited by appointment. The castle was one of a chain built by Henry VIII in the 1530s at a time of threatened invasion.

⑤ KENT BATTLE OF BRITAIN MUSEUM
In 1940, fighter aircraft that took off from Hawkinge Airfield played a crucial role in the Battle of Britain. The now-disused airfield is the base for a museum with a large collection of German and British aircraft remains and reconstructions, as well as wartime uniforms, weapons and photographs.

⑥ FOLKESTONE
A superb clifftop promenade with wide lawns and colourful flowerbeds stretches westwards from the town centre for more than a mile. The prome-

EARTH MOVER *A digger at the Eurotunnel Exhibition Centre; two of these machines took over four years to bore the tunnel.*

nade, called The Leas, is flanked on the landward side by tall stucco Victorian houses and a few large hotels, and on the seaward side by steeply sloping cliffs crossed by paths. Folkestone's old High Street slopes down to the harbour, where fishing boats lie stranded on the

BOAT TRAIN *The causeway across the inner harbour at Folkestone, which is used only by small craft, takes rail passengers to the catamaran terminal in the outer harbour.*

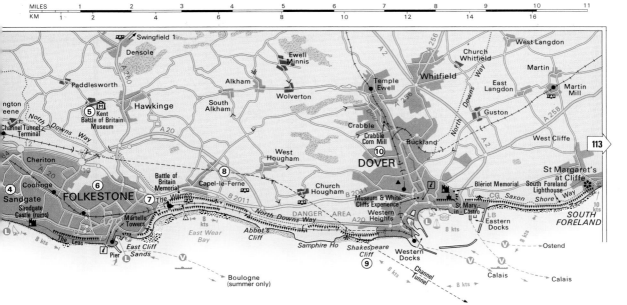

mud at low tide. Catamarans bound for Boulogne leave from the outer harbour. The main beach, East Cliff Sands, is reached from The Stade, the fish-market area by the harbour. Above the sands, a huge expanse of open grassland gives splendid views out to sea. One of the three Martello towers houses a visitor centre; guided walks start at the tower, and at the harbour.

⑦ THE WARREN

A wilderness of cliffs, scrub, grassland and woodland, The Warren is a favourite place for walkers, who can follow a waymarked trail that starts at the Martello tower visitor centre. More than 200 species of birds have been recorded at The Warren; chaffinches and yellow-hammers may be seen all year, and migrating birds, including blackcaps, chiffchaffs and nightingales, arrive in spring and autumn.

The hummocky land beneath the chalk cliffs has been created by landslips. A major slip, in 1915, sent blocks of chalk into the sea and buried the railway line that crosses The Warren.

⑧ CAPEL-LE-FERNE

From Capel-le-Ferne's clifftop road a steep footpath leads down over the railway line to the beach, where a concrete apron has been constructed above the shingle to prevent landslips.

Just west of the village, the RAF flag flutters above the clifftop Battle of Britain Memorial. The shape of a huge aircraft propeller, with blades 120 ft long, has been cut into the chalk; on the central boss of the propeller is a sculpture of a seated Battle of Britain fighter pilot, gazing at the sky.

⑨ SHAKESPEARE CLIFF

The most monumental of the white cliffs that guard Dover on both sides, this massive headland towers 300 ft above the sea. Its name comes from a scene in Shakespeare's *King Lear*, in which Edgar describes the cliff to his blind father Gloucester. Near the cliff,

the chalk spoil from the Channel Tunnel workings has been used to create a huge flat skirt called Samphire Ho, its name taken from the same speech in *King Lear*, in which Edgar describes the 'dreadful trade' of gathering the fleshy-leaved samphire plant from the cliffs.

⑩ DOVER

The Romans made Dover the headquarters of their northern fleet; in the Middle Ages the town was one of the Cinque Ports; and during both World Wars it was shelled and bombed from across the English Channel. Today, cross-Channel ferries and cargo ships come and go from the giant harbour, built at the beginning of the century.

On a hill above the eastern side of the town is the huge fortress of Dover Castle (EH). The castle's square keep was started in the 1180s; outer walls were added and remodelled in later centuries, and a labyrinth of underground tunnels was dug in Napoleonic times. During World War II some of the tunnels were used as an operations centre, where the evacuation of troops from Dunkirk was planned, and others were adapted as a hospital. Guided tours of the tunnels are available.

On a grassy mound beside the castle are the 40 ft high remains of a Roman *pharos*, or lighthouse, built soon after the Romans arrived in the 1st century AD. The Saxon Church of St Mary-in-Castro stands beside the lighthouse. In a clearing behind the castle, the granite outline of an aircraft sunk into the turf commemorates Louis Blériot, who landed there after making the first cross-Channel flight in 1909.

The White Cliffs Experience, in the town centre, uses special effects to bring to life scenes from Dover's history from Roman times to World War II. The town's museum tells the story of Dover since prehistoric times, and nearby are the remains of a Roman town house with wall paintings and a hypocaust. Dover Old Town Gaol, set in the town hall, reconstructs life in a Victorian

LOFTY LANDMARKS *A Saxon church and a Roman lighthouse look out from Dover's clifftop towards Cap Gris-Nez in France.*

prison. The hill known as the Western Heights, which was fortified in the 19th century, can be reached from harbour level by an ingenious triple spiral staircase known as the Grand Shaft.

A minor road from Dover to St Margaret's at Cliffe passes Langdon Cliffs, from where there is a bird's eye view of Dover's Eastern Docks. A 45 minute walk from Langdon Cliffs leads along the top of the white cliffs to South Foreland Lighthouse (NT), which can be visited but is no longer working.

Crabble Corn Mill, 2 miles north-west of the town centre, was built in 1812 to produce flour for the troops guarding Dover against Napoleon's threat of invasion. The mill has been restored to working order.

PLACES TO SEE INLAND

Butterfly Centre, Swingfield, 5 miles N of Folkestone. Free-flying butterflies, tropical plants.

Parsonage Farm Rural Heritage Centre, Elham, 7 miles NW of Folkestone. Farm with rare breeds of farm animals.

Port Lympne Wild Animal Park, 1 mile W of Lympne. Parkland with animals in natural surroundings; Dutch-style 1911 mansion.

TOURIST INFORMATION

Dover (01304) 205108; Eurotunnel Exhibition Centre (01303) 270547; Folkestone (01303) 258594; Hythe (01303) 267799 (summer)

A Royal Harbour on a coast stormed by invaders

Julius Caesar invaded Britain in 55 BC in this part of Kent, as did the Emperor Claudius in AD 43. As the line of the coast has altered much over 2000 years, their precise landing places cannot be identified.

① RAMSGATE
Graceful early 19th-century terraces line a busy harbour, served by ferry and jetfoil services to Dunkirk and Ostend. Known as the Royal Harbour since George IV embarked there on a voyage in 1821, it has a crowded marina, and a Maritime Museum based in the 19th-century Clock House, whose attractions include the steam tug *Cervia*. A Historic Harbour Trail identifies more than 30 points of interest in Ramsgate, from the dry dock of 1791 to the modern lifeboat. On West Cliff, above the ferry terminal, are a motor museum and a model village. The main bathing beach is at Ramsgate Sands, a wide strip of sand stretching north of the harbour.

② MANSTON
On high ground west of Ramsgate is RAF Manston, an airfield that played a crucial role in the fight against the Luftwaffe during World War II. The nearby Spitfire and Hurricane Memorial Building has superb examples of these two fighter aircraft, as well as uniforms and personal relics of the men who flew them – and often failed to return. From today's civilian Kent International Airport there are flights to the Channel Islands and to Cyprus.

③ MINSTER
A large village, whose name derives from the abbey founded there in AD 670, slopes gently down to the water meadows of the Stour. In 1027 building began on the present abbey, of which some Saxon and Norman stonework survives; it is now a Benedictine nunnery. The Agricultural and Rural Life Museum, next door, has a craft centre and a collection of farm implements of the past century.

④ PEGWELL BAY
A bay of sand and mud flats at the mouth of the Stour is fringed to the north by low chalk cliffs. To the west is the northern section of Pegwell Bay and Sandwich Bay Nature Reserve. Paths lead onto the reserve from a car park by the main road, with fine views across the bay. A short way to the north, a grassy picnic area offers a peaceful setting for the warlike *Hugin*, a replica of a dragon-prowed Viking longship. St Augustine landed in the bay in AD 597 on a mission to convert the pagans of Kent. He is commemorated by a stone cross outside the village of Cliffs End.

⑤ RICHBOROUGH CASTLE
In Roman times the Isle of Thanet was a true island, separated from Kent by a mile-wide channel. Richborough Castle (EH), at the southern end of the channel, was one of the Forts of the Saxon Shore, built about AD 285 to deter Norse raiders. Much of the outer wall survives, as do the foundations of a triumphal arch built soon after the Roman invasion of AD 43. Across the fields are the three huge cooling towers of Richborough power station, where guided tours are available.

⑥ SANDWICH
The northernmost of the Cinque Ports, Sandwich is a delightful old town with a complex network of streets and three medieval churches. Though the town is now almost 2 miles inland, it can be reached from Pegwell Bay by the winding 5 mile navigable channel of the River Stour. Boats can be launched from the quay at Sandwich, but only for two hours on either side of high tide.

The entrance to the town is guarded by the twin-turreted Barbican Gate, built in 1539 and facing north across a narrow bridge over the Stour. The stone Fisher Gate was built in 1384 at a time of savage raids by the French. Cinque Port treasures and other historic exhibits can be seen at the Guildhall Museum. Between the town and the river are the ponds and dykes of Gazen Salts, a small nature reserve that may be visited only by appointment.

⑦ SANDWICH BAY
The wide expanse of dunes between Sandwich and the sea provides the setting for three championship golf links – Royal Cinque Ports, Royal St George's (featured in the James Bond film *Goldfinger*) and Prince's.

A toll road from Sandwich leads through the opulent Sandwich Bay Estate to the Prince's clubhouse, now disused. From here a walk along the shingle foreshore leads to Pegwell Bay and Sandwich Bay Nature Reserve, which straddles the Stour estuary. The reserve represents Kent's last untouched complex of beach and foreshore, dunes and saltmarsh. It supports ducks, geese and large numbers of waders, and its salt-tolerant plants include sea holly and marsh orchids.

CABBAGE ON THE CLIFFS
Wild cabbage, the ancestor of garden cabbage, grows on chalk and limestone cliffs. Though it has fleshy leaves and no heart, it was once sold as a vegetable, but its bitter leaves needed boiling for a long time before they could be eaten.

Wild cabbage
Brassica oleracea
May-Aug

ST MARGARET'S BAY *From the foot of the chalk cliffs, cross-Channel swimmers set out in the wake of Captain Webb who, in 1875, became the first to swim the English Channel.*

CAREFUL TIMING Since 1854, Deal's Timeball Tower has signalled 1pm GMT when the ball, now electrically linked to Greenwich, drops down the central shaft.

⑧ DEAL

A quiet town with a steeply sloping shingle beach, Deal remains much as it was in the 18th century. In the days of sail, naval fleets and merchantmen anchored in The Downs – the stretch of water between Deal and the treacherous Goodwin Sands – waiting for favourable winds. That era is recalled by the Timeball Tower, whose timekeeping mechanism was used by sailors in The Downs to check their chronometers. The tower now houses a naval communications museum, while the Deal Museum explores the town's maritime history. Deal Castle (EH) was built by Henry VIII in the shape of a Tudor rose. In the west of the town, the Tides Leisure Pool complex has a 150ft high waterslide.

A roadside plaque just south of Deal Castle makes the doubtful claim that this was the point where Julius Caesar landed in Britain in 55BC.

⑨ WALMER CASTLE

Like Deal Castle, Walmer Castle (EH) was built by Henry VIII in 1540, when the sea came right up to its walls. The castle is now the official residence of the Lord Warden of the Cinque Ports. Its interior is elegantly panelled, with portraits and relics of the Duke of Wellington, who died there in 1852.

⑩ KINGSDOWN

Holiday homes and fishermen's cottages overlook a broad shingle beach dotted with boats and small huts. A range of high white cliffs begins at Kingsdown, and extends past Dover as far as Folkestone. Paths lead along the foreshore and up onto the cliffs, where there is a military range.

⑪ ST MARGARET'S BAY

The cove of shingle and rocks, with towering chalk cliffs on either side, is the English mainland's nearest point to France, 21 miles away, and is the traditional starting or finishing point for cross-Channel swimmers.

The bay can be reached by a narrow road that zigzags down from the town of St Margaret's at Cliffe, but heavy traffic during the holiday season makes it better to park at the top of the hill and walk down to the beach. The climate in St Margaret's is so mild that subtropical plants flourish. One public garden, The Pines, has a 9ft bronze sculpture of Sir Winston Churchill. Above the cliffs to the north, the tall, granite obelisk of the Dover Patrol Memorial commemorates naval personnel of two world wars who died while patrolling the Channel. Towards Kingsdown, a clifftop path, part of the long-distance Saxon Shore Way, takes walkers across an area of rolling heathland known as The Leas (NT).

PLACES TO SEE INLAND

Canterbury. Cathedral, site of Becket's murder in 1170; Heritage Museum; Roman Museum with mosaic floors in remains of Roman town house; Royal Museum and Art Gallery; West Gate Museum of Arms and Armoury.

Goodnestone Park Gardens, Wingham, 9 miles SW of Sandwich. Formal and woodland gardens.

Howletts Wild Animal Park, Bekesbourne, 10 miles W of Sandwich. Tigers, gorillas and other animals in natural surroundings.

Northbourne Court Gardens, 3 miles W of Deal. Tudor gardens on site of Saxon king's hunting lodge. Some Sunday afternoons in summer.

Wingham Bird Park, 6 miles W of Sandwich. Aviaries, lakes and adventure playground.

TOURIST INFORMATION

Deal (01304) 369576; Dover (01304) 205108; Ramsgate (01843) 591086; Sandwich (01304) 613565 (summer)

Holiday resorts fringing the eastern tip of Kent

A string of sandy bays stretches round the Isle of Thanet – an island now only in name – where the varied resorts of Margate, Broadstairs and Ramsgate form a holiday area that is almost continuous.

① HERNE BAY

An 80 ft clock tower dating from 1837 forms the seafront centrepiece of Herne Bay, a quiet seaside town laid out as a resort in the 1830s. The town's long pier was destroyed by storms in 1978, but the seaward end survives as a forlorn 'island' three-quarters of a mile offshore. The Pier Pavilion, at the landward end, is a leisure centre.

A curving harbour arm to the east of the Pier Pavilion shelters a sand and shingle beach, backed by neat gardens along the promenade. The beach to the west of the Pier Pavilion is shingle, with sand and some mud holes at low tide.

The village of Herne, 1½ miles inland, has the fine medieval Church of St Martin, and a tall black smock windmill built in the late 1780s. The mill has been restored and is open in summer on Sundays and Bank Holidays, and some weekday afternoons.

② EAST BLEAN WOOD

East Blean Wood is a remnant of the ancient Forest of Blean, which once covered much of north-east Kent. As well as oak, hornbeam and holly, there are areas of coppiced sweet chestnut trees where the rare heath fritillary butterfly may be seen. Birds found in the wood include woodpeckers, warblers, nuthatches and nightingales.

③ BISHOPSTONE GLEN

A small overgrown ravine cuts through the yellow-brown clay of Bishopstone Cliffs to a shingle beach where fossils may be found. A footpath to the glen starts at a small car park at the end of Bishopstone Lane; wooden steps descend to the beach.

Bishopstone Glen is at the western end of Reculver Country Park, whose clifftop grassland is ideal for walking, picnicking and birdwatching; skuas, terns and sandpipers are among the birds seen. There is an interpretation centre by the car park at Reculver.

④ RECULVER

Sharply etched against the sky, the twin towers of Reculver's ruined St Mary's Church are the main landmark along the 10 mile stretch of coast between Herne Bay and Margate. The grassy

SISTERLY BEACONS *Nicknamed the Two Sisters, these towers at Reculver have been a sailors' landmark for eight centuries.*

area round the towers is the site of the Roman fortress of Regulbium, built in the third century AD to guard the northern end of the Wantsum Channel, which once separated the Isle of Thanet from the mainland of Kent. In AD 669 King Egbert of Kent founded a monastery and church inside the fort; the towers on the site today date from a rebuilding in the 12th century.

Most of the church was demolished in the early 19th century, when the sea threatened to undermine it, but the towers were regarded as such an important navigational aid that they were restored by Trinity House. They now overlook a small resort of caravan parks and amusement arcades.

Alexanders, a plant about 1 ft high with sprays of yellow flowers, grows at the base of the towers; it was introduced by the Romans, who ate the celery-flavoured stems.

⑤ BIRCHINGTON

Though it forms part of Margate, Birchington is still recognisable as a separate village, grouped round the medieval Church of All Saints. The Victorian artist and poet Dante Gabriel Rossetti died at Birchington in 1882 and is buried in the churchyard. The Rossetti Memorial Garden in Sandles Lane commemorates his links with the town.

The most westerly of Birchington's four bays is Minnis Bay, whose wide

sweep of sand was once a landing place for smugglers. Grenham Bay, below a clifftop expanse of grass, has a wide undercliff promenade. Beresford Gap is a designated area for powerboats and water-skiing, and Epple Bay is a sandy cove surrounded by steep chalk cliffs.

The Powell-Cotton Museum, in the park of Quex House, has dioramas showing African animals in their natural habitats, and collections of antique firearms and Chinese porcelain. A tall bell tower in the park contains a peal of 12 bells and is crowned by a graceful wrought-iron spire.

⑥ WESTGATE ON SEA

The sedate western suburb of Margate is characterised by streets of red-brick Victorian and Edwardian houses, green open spaces, and two sandy bays, divided by a promontory laid out with landscaped gardens. At Westgate Bay, the cliffs dip sharply on either side of a gently sloping beach. Lively St Mildred's Bay is popular with swimmers and lined with beach huts.

A wide, grass-covered clifftop separates Westgate from Margate, and in the middle is a sheltered sunken garden that attracts many migrant birds in spring and autumn.

⑦ MARGATE

Margate's superb crescent of gently sloping sand has lured Londoners since 1753, when Benjamin Beale, a Margate glovemaker, invented the covered bathing machine. Before the arrival of the railway, visitors came to Margate from London by sea, in special boats called Margate hoys, which docked at the curving stone jetty known as Margate Pier. Confusingly, Margate's traditional seaside pier was known as the Jetty; most of it was destroyed by a storm in 1978, and only the rusty skeleton of the seaward end survives.

At the heart of Margate's seafront amusement arcades, gift shops and ice-cream parlours is Dreamland, a popular theme park, whose rides include Europe's largest big wheel, the oldest scenic railway in Britain, a water chute and picnic gardens. The town's other major attractions are underground: the Shell Grotto is made up of winding

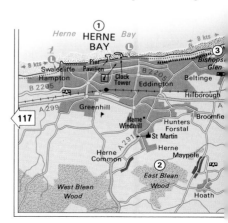

LITERARY BROADSTAIRS *The fort-like Bleak House, where Charles Dickens wrote* David Copperfield *and planned* Bleak House *itself, presides over the sands of Viking Bay.*

passages decorated from floor to ceiling with intricate shell designs; and Margate Caves, hewn out of the chalk more than a thousand years ago, have been used variously as dungeons, a church and a smugglers' hideout. In the old part of the town, centred on the Market Place, is the Old Town Hall, where a local history museum charts Margate's development as a major seaside resort. Visitors to the museum can also see Victorian prison cells.

Drapers Windmill, on the southern outskirts of Margate, is a restored black smock mill, built about 1850 and open to the public on Sunday afternoons all summer, and on Thursday evenings during July and August.

Drapers
Windmill

⑧ CLIFTONVILLE

A suburb of Margate with many hotels, Cliftonville is set well back from the cliffs behind a grassy expanse and has at its centre a wide garden and bandstand known as The Oval. At Cliftonville's Palm Bay, the wide, sandy beach is backed by a promenade. The clifftop Princes Walk leads eastwards round Foreness Point, an important site for migrating birds; footpaths continue along the coast to Kingsgate.

⑨ KINGSGATE

The sandy beach at Kingsgate's Botany Bay is reached by steps from the end of Kingsgate Avenue. On the cliff edge half a mile round the coast is the vast battlemented Kingsgate Castle, built about 1860 and now converted into flats; it once belonged to Lord Avebury, the politician who introduced Bank Holidays in 1871. Below the castle, another flight of steps leads down to the sheltered sands of Kingsgate Bay. The nearest car park is at sandy Joss Bay.

Inland from the promontory south of Joss Bay is the 85ft North Foreland Lighthouse, built to warn ships of the treacherous Goodwin Sands, 7 miles offshore. On clear nights, its beam is visible for 20 miles.

⑩ BROADSTAIRS

There are reminders of Charles Dickens at almost every corner of the narrow, twisting streets of the sedate town of Broadstairs, where the novelist spent many summer holidays. The battlemented Bleak House contains a maritime museum, furniture from Dickens's time and smuggling displays. A house on the seafront was once the home of Miss Mary Strong, the model for the character Betsey Trotwood in *David Copperfield*, and is now the Dickens House Museum. In June each year, Broadstairs holds a week-long Dickens Festival, when people dress up in Dickensian costume.

Viking Bay has a sandy beach, sheltered by the curving pier, where fishing boats land their catch.

PLACES TO SEE INLAND

Monkton Nature Reserve, 6 miles SW of Margate. Trails, field study centre, bat cave.

Sarre Mill Rural Heritage Experience, 7 miles SW of Margate. Restored early 19th-century smock mill producing flour.

TOURIST INFORMATION

Broadstairs (01843) 862242; Herne Bay (01227) 361911; Margate (01843) 220241

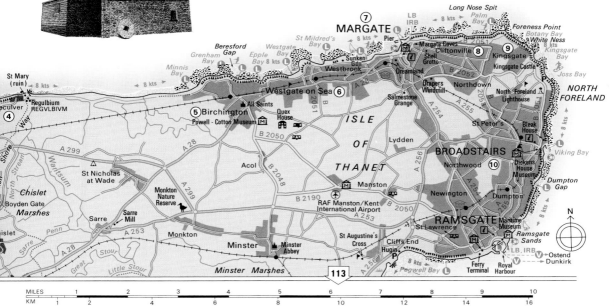

| MILES | 1 | | 2 | | 3 | | 4 | | 5 | | 6 | | 7 | | 8 | | 9 | | 10 |
| KM | 1 | 2 | | 4 | | 6 | | 8 | | 10 | | 12 | | 14 | | 16 | |

Salty creeks, an island of birds and an oyster bay

Samuel Pepys, overseer of the first Sheerness dockyard

The muddy channel of the Swale divides mainland Kent from the Isle of Sheppey, whose name is Anglo-Saxon for 'Sheep Island'. Faversham is an old town of real beauty, while Whitstable has the true tang of the sea.

① LOWER HALSTOW

Sailing dinghies moor in the village's small dock at Halstow Creek, and the tiny, partly Saxon, Church of St Mary of Antioch stands on a low mound above it. The coast road north of Lower Halstow joins the A249 just south of the monumental Kingsferry Bridge, which crosses The Swale.

② SITTINGBOURNE

Muddy Milton Creek winds its way into Sittingbourne, which was once a busy harbour town. Beside the creek the

SHEPPEY GATEWAY *Four towers house the mechanism that lifts Kingsferry Bridge to make way for craft on The Swale channel.*

Dolphin Yard Sailing Barge Museum recalls the great days of the sailing barges that traded on the Thames between 1850 and 1950. Visitors can watch barges being repaired in the old maintenance yard. Nearby is the southern terminus of the Sittingbourne and Kemsley Light Railway, whose steam trains carry passengers for 1½ miles on summer Sundays and Bank Holidays.

East of the town, the coast road to Faversham runs through some of Kent's most spectacular orchards.

③ QUEENBOROUGH

Named after Queen Philippa, wife of Edward III, Queenborough was built in the 14th century to guard the northern end of The Swale channel. Little of its historic centre remains, apart from Holy Trinity Church and the 18th-century Guildhall in the high street.

Deadmans Island, northernmost of the marshy islands nearby, was named in memory of victims of the Great Plague in 1665 who were buried there.

④ SHEERNESS

The north-west tip of Sheppey is largely concealed behind the high wall of Sheerness dockyard, constructed in

A DIARIST AND HIS DOCKYARD

Best known for his rumbustious diary of life in Restoration London, Samuel Pepys (1633-1703) held office as Charles II's Secretary of the Admiral. He carried out naval reforms and initiated new ship building; a superior referred to him as 'the right hand of the navy'. One of Pepys's duties was to supervise the construction of the first Sheerness dockyard in 1665, at the time of the second Anglo-Dutch war. Most of the present dockyard, however, dates from the 19th century.

Charles II's time. Much of the town consists of Victorian houses built for dockyard workers. A promenade, with wide views across the Thames to the Essex coast, backs the sand and shingle beach.

Barton's Point, on the eastern outskirts of the town, is a recreational and picnic area, offering windsurfing, fishing, boating and bowls.

⑤ MINSTER

The village clusters round the Church of St Mary and St Sexburga, built in the 7th century and one of the oldest places of worship in England. The imposing Abbey Gatehouse next to the church has a museum explaining Sheppey's history. East of the church, holiday houses stand on a hillside that slopes down to a wide beach of sand and mud scattered with stones, and backed by clay cliffs at its eastern end.

The broad sand and mud beach between Minster and Leysdown is noted

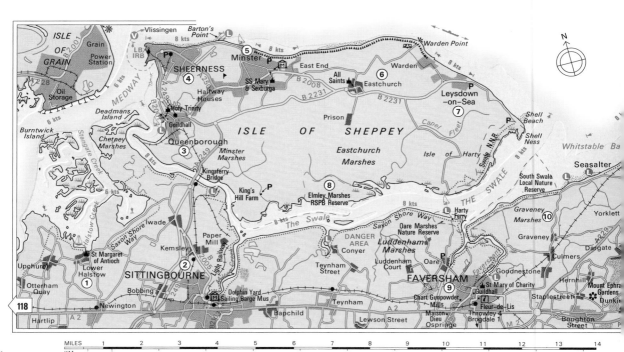

for its wide variety of fossils, including gigantic sharks' teeth. Visitors should beware of fast incoming tides.

⑥ EASTCHURCH
A stone memorial opposite All Saints' Church commemorates J.T.C. Moore-Brabazon, Thomas Sopwith and other aviation pioneers, who operated from Eastchurch aerodrome, now a prison, south of the village. Moore-Brabazon, flying at Shell Beach in the eastern corner of Sheppey in November 1909, was the first British pilot to achieve a circular flight of a mile.

⑦ LEYSDOWN-ON-SEA
At the end of the road crossing the Isle of Sheppey is a village of scattered caravan parks, chalets and holiday homes. Warden Point, just north of Leysdown, is an ideal spot from which to view shipping in the Thames estuary.

From Leysdown a road south, which soon becomes a potholed track, leads to a car park at Shell Ness, a spit of land largely made up of compressed cockle shells. Footpaths there lead across Swale Nature Reserve. From the hides visitors can watch lapwings, warblers, marsh harriers and many other birds.

⑧ ELMLEY MARSHES
Owned by the RSPB, the reserve is reached by a 2 mile track off the A249, a mile north of the Kingsferry Bridge. Wigeon, teal and white-fronted geese winter there, while breeding birds include redshanks, lapwings and shovelers. There is a car park at Kings Hill Farm, about a mile from the hide that overlooks the lagoons and mud flats.

⑨ FAVERSHAM
The town, at the head of a wide creek, has a harmonious blend of architectural styles. The main landmark is the carved stone steeple of St Mary of Charity

OYSTER HARBOUR *Fishing boats crowd beneath a line of oystermen's huts and sail lofts. In Whitstable harbour, oysters from a hatchery in Seasalter are graded, cleaned and sold.*

Church, but other notable buildings include the painted Guildhall and the large working brewery. Once a busy port, until the creek silted up, Faversham regained its prosperity through its gunpowder industry, whose heyday is vividly recalled at the restored Chart Gunpowder Mills. The mills, dating from the late 18th century, remained in use until the 1930s. The town's history is recalled at the Fleur-de-Lis Heritage Centre. Standard Quay, at the northern end of ancient Abbey Street, provides moorings for a spectacular array of colourful Thames barges.

In the southern suburb of Ospringe is Maison Dieu (EH), an unusual combination of hospital and pilgrims' hostel, little changed since the 16th century, which is open to visitors at weekends and Bank Holidays. To the north of Faversham is Oare Marshes Nature Reserve. A car park just outside Oare village gives access to the Saxon Shore Way, a 140 mile footpath, whose route skirts the reserve.

⑩ GRAVENEY MARSHES
Three miles of sea wall and foreshore extending from Faversham Creek to the Sportsman Inn, a mile north of Graveney, make up the South Swale Nature Reserve. In winter, the mud flats attract large numbers of waders and wildfowl, and the grassland beside the sea wall, part of the Saxon Shore Way, is abundant in flowering plants.

⑪ WHITSTABLE
There is a strong flavour of the sea in Whitstable, with its rows of weatherboarded fishermen's cottages, black-

tarred boat sheds and sailing dinghies. The busy harbour, once the port for Canterbury, has an active fishing fleet, and is lined with sheds where fresh fish can be bought. Whitstable's pebbled beach is flanked by a sea wall. For centuries Whitstable was famous for the quality of its oysters. The oyster trade gradually declined due to changes in climate and sea conditions; but in the 1960s it was revived and began to flourish again. At the far end of the harbour, the Oyster Fishery Exhibition tells the story of the industry, and Whitstable-grown oysters can be sampled there. In July the town holds an oyster festival.

The quiet resort of Tankerton is separated from Whitstable by a tree-covered hill topped by a ship's mast and a pair of cannons, marking its highest point. A wide grass bank slopes down from the village to the beach, from which a shingle finger, known as The Street, protrudes. It is dangerous to swim near The Street, but at low tide it is a favourite place for shell collectors.

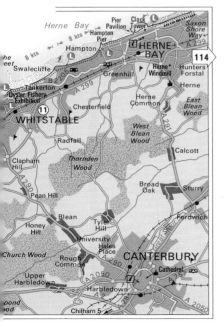

PLACES TO SEE INLAND

Belmont, Throwley, 4 miles S of Faversham. 18th-century mansion in parkland. Extensive collection of watches and clocks.

Brogdale Horticultural Trust, 2 miles S of Faversham. Collection of 4000 varieties of fruit trees and plants.

Chilham Castle Gardens, 13 miles S of Whitstable. Terraced gardens overlooking Stour.

Mount Ephraim Gardens, Hernhill, 6 miles SW of Whitstable. Rhododendrons and rose terraces.

TOURIST INFORMATION

Faversham (01795) 534542; Whitstable (01227) 275482

Castles and churches by the Thames and Medway

Forts and castles along the coast were built to protect the approach to London and the naval dockyard at Chatham. Rochester appears in novels by Charles Dickens, who spent much of his life in the area.

① TILBURY

The town's modern port is largely hidden behind a high wall, with only the tops of its cranes visible from outside. Large cruise ships still leave from the port, which also handles timber, grain and other cargo.

Tilbury can be reached from Gravesend by a passenger ferry across the Thames. It is a 10-minute walk from the ferry terminus to Tilbury Fort (EH), built in 1682 to defend the Thames against the Dutch and the French. A moat surrounds the fort on the inland side, and on the river side is an elaborate triumphal arch. Displays inside the fort show how London was defended against attack from the sea.

② GRAVESEND

In the 14th century, Gravesend ferrymen were granted the sole right to ferry passengers into London. Today, the town is the headquarters of the Port of London Authority's Thames Navigation Service, and tugs put out from the Royal Terrace Pier to guide ships into

Tilbury docks. St George's Church, which was rebuilt in the 18th century after one of the many fires which destroyed much of the older part of the town, is a striking feature of the waterfront. In the churchyard is a bronze statue of Princess Pocahontas, who married John Rolfe, an early Virginia colonist, and accompanied him to England in 1616. The next year Pocahontas died of fever as she was setting out to return to her native America, and was buried in the chancel of St George's.

Statue of Princess Pocahontas, in Gravesend

There are superb views of shipping on the Thames from the wide grassy expanse of Gordon Promenade, named after General Gordon, who died at Khartoum in 1885. In the late 1860s, Gordon supervised the construction of forts to defend the Thames against the threat of a French invasion, and also worked with the poor in Gravesend.

The town marks the northern end of the Saxon Shore Way, a 140 mile footpath which follows the coast round to Rye in East Sussex.

③ CLIFFE

Reclaimed land crossed by drainage ditches stands between the sea and Cliffe, which, as its name suggests, stands on higher ground. The massive 13th-century Church of St Helen is built of alternate bands of stone and squared flints, and has medieval wall paintings. West of the village are worked-out quarries and gravel workings, now full of water, and the stark remains of Cliffe Fort, built in the 1860s to guard against invasion from France.

④ COOLING

The remote little village of Cooling has links with both Shakespeare and Charles Dickens. Sir John Falstaff, the jovial knight of Shakespeare's *Henry IV* and *The Merry Wives of Windsor*, is thought to have been based on Sir John Oldcastle, who lived at Cooling Castle in the early 15th century. The castle gatehouse and part of the outer wall can be seen from the road, but they are not open to visitors. In the graveyard of Cooling's St James's Church are 14 lozenge-shaped children's tombstones, which Dickens described in *Great Expectations*; the children were all from

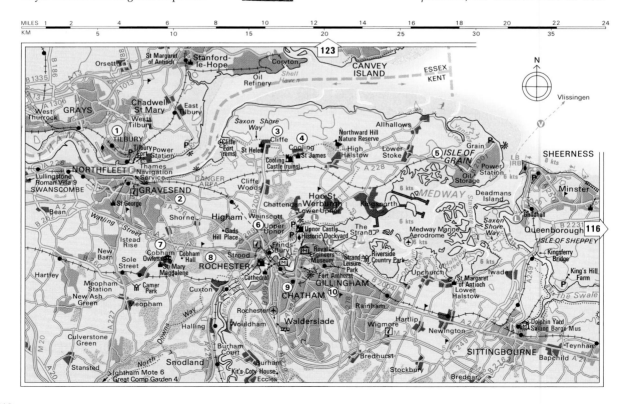

one family. An RSPB reserve at Northward Hill, 3 miles east of Cooling, has Britain's largest heronry, where herons can be seen from February to July. The reserve's other birds include nightingales, whitethroats and blackcaps.

⑤ ISLE OF GRAIN

The name of the peninsula – almost, but not quite separated from the rest of Kent by the Yantlet Creek – derives from the Old English *greon*, meaning 'sand' or gravel. Grain, on the eastern side of the 'isle', is reached through an industrial wilderness of gas and oil storage tanks. The village is dominated by a giant power station. Grain's small high street ends at an esplanade backed by grass, where there are wide views across the Thames to Essex, and over the Medway estuary to Sheerness.

⑥ UPPER UPNOR

The wedge-shaped defensive platform of Upnor Castle juts into the muddy waters of the Medway. The neat little castle was built in 1559 to guard the approaches to the naval dockyard at Chatham. Sharp wooden stakes protrude from the castle's battlements, and exhibits inside show the extent of the Medway's defences. The only time this defensive system was really put to the test was in 1667. It then failed completely, and the Dutch navy burned ten ships of the British fleet at Chatham.

Lower Upnor, just downstream, is a small sailing centre with fine views across the Medway to Chatham.

⑦ COBHAM

Tile-hung and weatherboarded houses line the main street in Cobham, whose 13th-century Church of St Mary Magdalene has a fine collection of medieval brasses. Charles Dickens was a frequent visitor to the village's half-timbered Leather Bottle Inn, and set part of *Pickwick Papers* there. Cobham Hall, a red-brick Elizabethan mansion with later additions by Inigo Jones, stands in parkland at the eastern end of the village; the house is a girls' school and is open on certain days at Easter and in summer. Owletts (NT), at the western end of the village, is a late 17th-century house with a fine plasterwork ceiling.

PLACES TO SEE INLAND

Great Comp Garden, 13 miles S of Gravesend. Formal areas with lawns and terraces, woodland paths, rare trees and shrubs.

Ightham Mote (NT), 15 miles SW of Gravesend. Medieval moated manor house.

Kit's Coty House (EH), 4 miles S of Chatham. Remains of prehistoric burial chamber.

Lullingstone Roman Villa (EH), 14 miles SW of Gravesend. Well-preserved remains including baths, underfloor heating, early Christian chapel.

TOURIST INFORMATION

Farthing Corner (M2) (01634) 360323; Gravesend (01474) 337600; Rochester (01634) 843666

CATHEDRAL OF THE MEDWAY TOWNS *Though altered and restored in later years, much of Rochester Cathedral dates from Norman times. It stands on the site of a Saxon church.*

⑧ ROCHESTER

For the last 12 years of his life, Charles Dickens lived at Gads Hill Place, 2 miles north-west of Rochester and now a school. He made this small cathedral city on the Medway the background for many scenes in *Great Expectations*, *Pickwick Papers* and other novels.

Rochester Cathedral, begun in 1077, has massive Norman pillars and a Norman crypt. Close by is the tall keep of Rochester Castle. The Guildhall Museum, in the high street, traces Rochester's history from pre-Roman times, and has a grim replica of one of the prison hulks which were moored in the Medway in the early 19th century. Farther along the high street are Watts Charity, built in 1579 to house poor travellers, and a gabled 16th-century house which has been converted into the Charles Dickens Centre and contains relics of the novelist and tableaux showing scenes from his novels.

Among Rochester's other historic buildings is Restoration House, where Charles II stayed in 1660 on the eve of his restoration to the throne. Dickens used the house, which is closed to visitors, as the model for Miss Havisham's house in *Great Expectations*. Rochester holds an annual Dickens Festival, when local people wear Dickensian costume and enact scenes from his novels.

⑨ CHATHAM

The town's long history as a naval dockyard began in 1547, when Henry VIII first maintained a storehouse to service his fleet at anchor in the River Medway. Drake, Hawkins and Nelson sailed from Chatham, and Nelson's flagship HMS *Victory* was one of 400 ships built there. The working dockyard closed down in 1984, but the site has been given a new lease of life as The Historic Dockyard, a museum covering more than four centuries of shipbuilding.

Among the many 18th and early 19th-century buildings in the dockyard is the Ropery, where, from a 'ropewalk'

VICTORIAN SLOOP *The gunboat HMS Gannet, now moored at Chatham, once patrolled the distant waters of the empire.*

that stretches for a quarter of a mile, visitors can watch ropes being made. Another exhibition recreates a day in 1758, and demonstrates how craftsmen built the wooden warship HMS *Valiant*. Cruises along the Medway can be taken on the paddle steamer *Kingswear Castle*, based at the dockyard. The Medway Heritage Centre, housed in a former church, describes the history of the river from prehistoric times. Fort Amherst, across the road, was built in its present form to defend the naval dockyard from attack by Napoleon's armies and has more than a mile of tunnels.

⑩ GILLINGHAM

At the western end of this mainly residential town, not far from Chatham's Historic Dockyard, is the Royal Engineers Museum, which tells the story of military engineering since 1066. Gillingham has a small shingle beach at the Strand Leisure Park, where there is an open-air swimming pool. Riverside Country Park, 2 miles east of Gillingham, is a varied area of meadow, woodland and tidal salt marsh.

FROM ROMAN FORTS TO 'HELLFIRE CORNER'

GENERATIONS OF INVADERS AND DEFENDERS have left their marks on the south-east corner of England. Romans, Saxons, Vikings, Normans: each wave laid down its own defences, and the area still abounds with the remains of fortifications built to strengthen the natural barrier of the English Channel.

Among the most impressive Roman relics is the fort at Richborough, near Sandwich, which guarded the Wantsum, the channel that once separated the Isle of Thanet from the Kentish mainland. A smaller fortress at Reculver shielded the Wantsum's northern end, while the coast between Hastings and Eastbourne was defended by the castle at Pevensey. The Romans established their main port at Dover, making it the headquarters of *classis Britannica*, the British fleet. They built a pair of lighthouses, one on either side of the harbour; the octagonal Pharos still stands high above the town beside the magnificent

COASTAL FIREPOWER *The castles built by Henry VIII, such as the one at Walmer, were made for the age of gunpowder. They had wide gun platforms within a Tudor-rose pattern with rounded corners less vulnerable to cannonballs.*

FORT WITHIN A FORT
Pevensey Castle's outer walls are those of the Roman fort of Anderida, used by King Alfred in the 9th century during his campaign against the Danes. William the Conqueror built a castle within the walls of the original Roman fort.

Norman castle. Other surviving Norman castles on the south-east coast are at Pevensey (inside the Roman walls), Hastings and Rochester. The Normans constructed their castles with huge keeps and massive outer walls to overawe the local population. During the Middle Ages, with the growth of enmity between England and France, they were gradually strengthened and enlarged. Meanwhile the south-east coast towns were erecting their own fortified gates and walls, which survive in part at Rye, Sandwich and elsewhere. In the 12th century five towns formed the defensive confederation of the Cinque Ports.

The next major drive to fortify the south coast was led by Henry VIII, whose aggressive foreign policy and defiance of the Pope had stirred fears of a Catholic invasion. Henry built a chain of 20 castles round the south coast, five of them – Camber, Sandgate, Walmer, Deal and Sandown – in what is now East Sussex and Kent.

Few major works were undertaken in the 17th and 18th centuries, but the growth of Napoleon's power after 1800 prompted the building of a string of small, closely set fortresses between Seaford and Folkestone known as Martello towers. The two-storey brick-built structures,

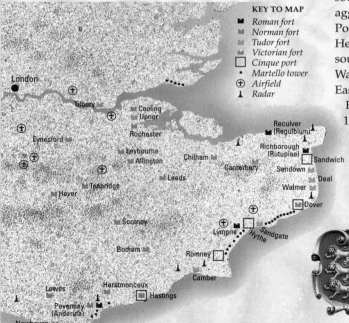

KEY TO MAP
- ◼ Roman fort
- ◼ Norman fort
- ◼ Tudor fort
- ◼ Victorian fort
- ▢ Cinque port
- • Martello tower
- ⊕ Airfield
- ⊥ Radar

London
Tilbury
Cooling
Upnor
Eynesford
Rochester
Reculver (Regulbium)
Leybourne
Allington
Chilham
Richborough (Rutupiae)
Sandwich
Canterbury
Sandown
Leeds
Deal
Tonbridge
Walmer
Hever
Dover
Scotney
Sandgate
Lympne
Hythe
Bodiam
Romney
Camber
Herstmonceux
Lewes
Hastings
Pevensey (Anderida)
Newhaven

ARMS OF THE CINQUE PORTS *The Cinque Ports – Dover, Hastings, Hythe, Romney and Sandwich – provided the king with ships and men in return for special privileges. Other ports joined the league later.*

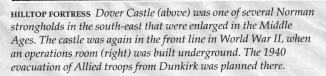

DEFENCE BY AIR AND LAND *The Spitfire (above) was one of Britain's most successful World War II fighting machines. Together with the Hurricane, it played a vital role in defeating the Luftwaffe during the Battle of Britain. Carrying eight machine guns, and reaching 362 mph, the Spitfire flew from south-east coastal bases. At the seaside, barbed wire (right) to deter seaborne invaders was a common sight.*

HILLTOP FORTRESS *Dover Castle (above) was one of several Norman strongholds in the south-east that were enlarged in the Middle Ages. The castle was again in the front line in World War II, when an operations room (right) was built underground. The 1940 evacuation of Allied troops from Dunkirk was planned there.*

many of which survive, each had a cannon on a rotating platform mounted on the roof.

Victoria's reign, though peaceful, saw much defensive building. At Dover, the Western Heights, across the harbour. from the castle, were fortified with huge walls and ditches, and a fort was built at Newhaven. Downstream from Gravesend, the Thames defences were substantially strengthened. By 1914 the Royal Navy had taken over the job of guarding the coast with its Dover Patrol ships. Fears of a German invasion in World War I were short-lived, but such fears revived at the start of World War II, and measures to defend the coast took on new forms. Giant radar pylons behind Pevensey

PROTECTIVE CHAIN *The Martello towers at Hythe were part of a chain of 74 built in the 19th century as a defence against Napoleon. The brick fortresses were about 35 ft high.*

and on the Dover cliffs warned of approaching German bombers, while Manston, Hawkinge and other RAF airfields were equipped with Spitfire and Hurricane fighters. The scene of fierce fighting in the air, and shelled by German long-distance guns, east Kent became known as 'Hellfire Corner'. At Dover Castle, early 19th-century tunnels dug 150 ft underground were turned into a command centre, later a key station for top-secret communications.

Playground for Londoners, and 'promontory of birds'

Away from the industrial sprawl of Shell Haven and the bright lights of Southend lie tranquil country parks and nature reserves. The vast wilderness of Foulness, closed to the public, is a haven for wildfowl.

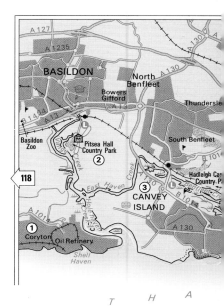

① CORYTON

Shell and Mobil's huge oil refinery of Shell Haven sprawls for some 3 miles along the north bank of the Thames estuary, processing more than half a million litres of crude oil each hour. The name Shell Haven derives not from the company but from an inlet, Shelf Haven, first used as a refinery site in the late 19th century by the Cory brothers, after whom Coryton is named.

② PITSEA HALL COUNTRY PARK

Covering a large area of tidal creeks, grassland, marshes and scrub, which attracts more than 160 species of bird, the park offers waymarked walks and several hides. At its southern end is a 100-berth marina. From here a narrow-gauge railway runs to the National Motorboat Museum, set in an exhibition hall at the park's entrance, where more than 30 boats are on display.

③ CANVEY ISLAND

Created from reclaimed land, Canvey is protected by a massive sea wall, built after floods swept across the island in 1953, drowning 58 people. From the top of the wall there are wide views across the Thames to the Kent shore. On its seaward side is a beach of muddy sand and shingle. A holiday club in the west of the island is open to day visitors.

④ HADLEIGH CASTLE COUNTRY PARK

The park is a patchwork of pasture, woodland, marsh and coast. Just to the east are the ruins of Hadleigh Castle,

STRATEGIC SITE *A round tower of Hadleigh Castle, built to guard against the French, watches over the Thames estuary.*

built for Edward III in the 1360s. The trim grassy area between the remains of the towers and the outer walls offers views of a sweep of coast from Southend to the stacks and tanks of the Coryton oil refinery.

Two 3 mile walks between Leigh and Benfleet stations cross the park. One follows the sea wall; the other takes an inland route past the castle.

⑤ TWO TREE ISLAND

An island of grassland and scrub is bisected by a narrow road from Leigh station which leads to a group of boat sheds and a concrete launching ramp. The western half of the island forms part of Hadleigh Castle Country Park, while to the east is a nature reserve incorporating large areas of salt marsh and mud flats. In autumn thousands of migrating Brent geese gather on the salt marsh to feed on eel-grass. There is a car park on the island, and waymarked paths cross the reserve and run alongside the marsh.

⑥ LEIGH-ON-SEA

A narrow street of cottages and shops, cut off on the landward side by the railway, retains an old-fashioned air, with stalls selling jellied eels, and cockles collected on Maplin Sands. A small sandy beach at the eastern end of the street is the start of a 7 mile walk along the seafront to Shoeburyness.

⑦ SOUTHEND-ON-SEA

Originally a village at the 'south end' of medieval Prittlewell Priory, Southend developed as a seaside resort in the early 19th century, and boomed during Victorian times, spreading to embrace surrounding villages. It is now also a major residential and working town.

Southend's pier – at 1.3 miles, the longest pleasure pier in the world – has regained some of its former glory after fire destroyed the pier-head buildings in 1976. An electric railway runs alongside the walkway, and a pier museum is open in summer. A tree-lined esplanade with a Victorian bandstand overlooks the resort's sand and shingle beach, which becomes muddy towards low-water mark. Seafront entertainments include a fairground known as Peter

AUTUMN MIGRANT *The dark-breasted Brent goose can often be seen in autumn feeding on the Two Tree Island salt marsh.*

Pan's Playground, a water theme park, and a Sea Life Centre, where visitors walk underwater through a glass tunnel, and enter a shark exhibition through the model jaws of a great white shark. Next to the pier is a half-size replica of Drake's *Golden Hind*.

Foremost among Southend's extensive parks and gardens is Priory Park in the north of the town, where visitors can follow a 'tree trail'. The park, with its lakes, bowling greens and tennis courts, surrounds the remains of Prittlewell Priory. The priory is now a local history museum with a section tracing the development of communications from the early days of printing to the invention of the pocket television. Horse-riders and golf enthusiasts flock to nearby Garons Leisure Park.

Among Southend's annual events are an air show, a carnival, and a race to Greenwich contested by 20 or more magnificent Thames sailing barges.

⑧ SHOEBURYNESS

At the eastern end of Southend, beyond Thorpe Bay, spiked railings extending into the sea mark the boundaries of a Ministry of Defence artillery range, which takes up the whole tip of Shoebury's 'ness', or promontory. The railings enclose about 1½ miles of beach. Round the Ness from Southend

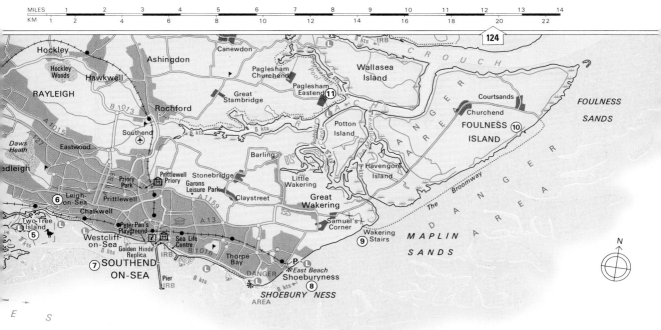

TEMPLES OF FUN *Much of Southend's seafront is geared to the pleasure-seeker; Peter Pan's Playground offers 'white knuckle' rides, and panoramic views from the Big Wheel.*

is the sand and shingle of the popular East Beach, backed by a car park and an open field of grass. Rampart Terrace, running behind the beach, has fine views of the Thames estuary.

⑨ WAKERING STAIRS

Beyond Samuel's Corner, a narrow road leads across Ministry of Defence land to Wakering Stairs. The road is usually closed, but when the barriers are open visitors can drive to the shoreline, and from there walk out onto the wide expanse of Maplin Sands. A track known as The Broomway, uncovered at low tide, is named after the wooden 'brooms' or poles that used to mark the route, which runs parallel to the shore

for 5 miles to Foulness Island. Walkers are not advised to follow the track, which can be very treacherous.

⑩ FOULNESS ISLAND

The low-lying island, whose name means 'promontory of birds', is owned by the Ministry of Defence and closed to the public, although a few people live in the isolated village of Churchend. In autumn up to 10 000 migrating Brent geese flock to the vast wilderness of Foulness and Maplin Sands.

⑪ PAGLESHAM EASTEND

An unpaved road from the hamlet of Paglesham Eastend provides the only proper access by land to the estuary of

the Roach. At the end of the road is a boatyard and a sailing centre, whose slipway is defended by a sturdy metal floodgate. There are walks along the sea wall in both directions, to Rochford and to Wallasea Island.

PLACES TO SEE INLAND

Basildon Zoo. Zoo with more than 100 species, including big cats, and an adventure playground.

Hockley Woods, 6 miles NE of Southend. Largest mature woodland in Essex, including waymarked walks and picnic area.

St Andrew, Ashingdon, 4 miles N of Southend. 11th-century hilltop church marking site where Canute defeated Edmund Ironside in 1016.

TOURIST INFORMATION

Southend (01702) 215120

Yachts on the creeks where Saxons once fought Danes

Between the sheltered creeks edging the Blackwater and the Crouch estuaries is a marsh-fringed peninsula whose shoreline, once a shifting wilderness of mud and saltings, has been reinforced by a long sea wall.

① MALDON

The town's ancient seafaring traditions live on at the Hythe, where restored Thames barges loom over the quayside. The quay leads onto a promenade, with a sweep of sloping grass that offers good views of pleasure craft thronging the Blackwater. The high street rises from the harbour to the Church of All Saints, with its triangular tower, and the 15th-century Moot Hall, which can be visited by appointment.

The 42 ft Maldon Embroidery, created in 1991 to mark the 1000th anniversary of the Battle of Maldon, is displayed at various sites at different times in the town, one of the oldest recorded settlements in Essex. In the grounds of St Peter's Church, of which only a tower remains, the Millennium Garden has an array of plants used in the 10th century for medicinal and culinary purposes. The Plume Library, next to the tower, contains 6000 antiquarian books.

② NORTHEY ISLAND

Surrounded by creeks and marshes, and screened by mature hedgerows, Northey Island (NT) resembles a secret garden. The secluded spot can be reached along a private road through South House Farm and over a causeway that is covered at high tide. A warden's permit is needed to visit the island, which is part farm, part nature reserve. A nature trail leads over fields to a hide from where herons, shelducks, pintails and curlews can be seen. Stone Age flint scrapers have been found there, and the causeway is probably Roman. In 991 an army of Danes crossed the causeway to defeat the Saxons, a story told in the epic poem *The Battle of Maldon*.

③ THE STONE

One of the few roads leading to the shore of the Blackwater estuary cuts through a large cluster of bungalows to a sea wall and concrete slipway at The

Stone. The beach is a strip of shingle and sand, becoming muddy as it sweeps eastwards around St Lawrence Bay.

④ BRADWELL WATERSIDE

A large marina and a group of houses overlook the narrow, sheltered creek separating the mainland from Pewet Island, which is covered by water at high tide. The village is also the base of an Environmental and Outdoor Education Centre run by Essex County Council. A salt marsh protected by a sea wall stretches northwards to the grey mass of Bradwell Power Station, which dominates this part of the coast. A visitor centre explains how the power station operates; there are guided tours.

⑤ BRADWELL-ON-SEA

A small village surrounded by marshes and reclaimed farmland, Bradwell is the start of 6½ mile circular walk taking in part of the long sea wall. The walk starts from a car park beside Westwick Farm, north-west of the village, and leads past Bradwell Power Station as far as St Peter's Chapel before turning inland. Bradwell's Church of St Thomas has a fine 18th-century brick tower, and a 14th-century porch transported in 1957 from Shapland, near Southend, to save it from demolition.

⑥ ST PETER'S CHAPEL

One of Britain's oldest churches occupies an isolated and beautiful spot on the site of the Roman fortress of Othona. St Cedd, who arrived there in AD 653 as a Northumbrian missionary to the East Anglians, later used stones

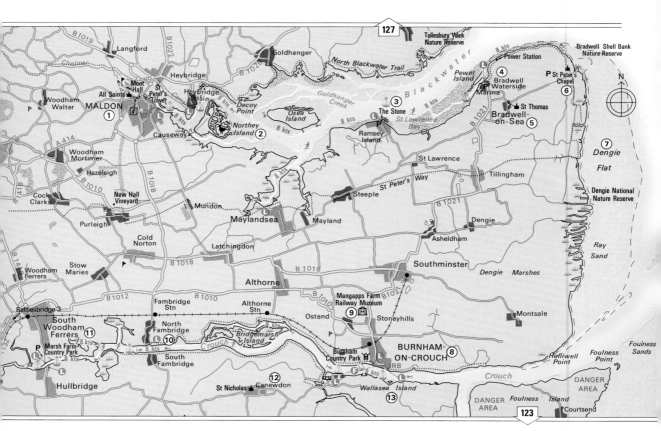

HISTORY AT THE HYTHE *Thames barges, with their rust-red sails, are a distinctive feature of Maldon's quayside. They relive past glories in the annual Blackwater Barge Match.*

from the fortress to build the chapel, whose full name is St Peter's-on-the-Wall. It stands on open grassland, and the last half mile from Bradwell-on-Sea must be walked. Footpaths lead along the sea wall in both directions.

SERVICE RESUMED *Before reconsecration in 1920, St Peter's Chapel had been used as a navigation beacon and as a barn.*

⑦ DENGIE FLAT

The sweep of low-tide mudflats between the Blackwater and the Crouch is a national nature reserve offering ideal breeding grounds for waders. At the northern end is Bradwell Shell Bank, a large area of sand, shingle and compacted cockleshells, protected by a line of sunken barges. The coastline is lined by a low sea wall, along which runs part of the St Peter's Way footpath. The path starts from St Peter's Chapel and runs 45 miles inland to Chipping Ongar.

⑧ BURNHAM-ON-CROUCH

A major yachting centre for more than a century, Burnham has an elegant Georgian high street and a neat, pedestrianised quayside whose buildings include the headquarters of two yacht clubs. The yacht harbour has berths for 350 boats. Burnham Country Park, west of the harbour, offers several riverside walks. Burnham hosts the annual South-East Boat Show in June, and at the end of August several hundred boats compete in Burnham Week.

⑨ MANGAPPS FARM RAILWAY MUSEUM

A working farm provides the setting for a fine collection of vintage engines, rolling stock and railway memorabilia of all kinds. A restored country station is the starting point for short rides in trains pulled by various engines, including an 1878 colliery steam-engine. An exhibit resembling Thomas the Tank Engine is popular with children.

⑩ NORTH FAMBRIDGE

Two small settlements face each other across the Crouch. At North Fambridge a scattering of old cottages and a 15th-century inn overlook a boatyard where a boardwalk leads 50 yd out into the river. From South Fambridge, on the opposite bank, paths skirt the river wall, for a mile upstream, and 5 miles downstream to Wallasea Island.

⑪ SOUTH WOODHAM FERRERS

This bright commuter town, with its brick-paved, pedestrianised centre, is separated from the Crouch by Marsh Farm Country Park, which is both a working farm and a nature reserve. A trail takes visitors through the farm, which raises cattle, sheep and pigs.

Weather-boarded cottages at Burnham

Beyond the farm, paths lead along the river round the reserve. The park includes an adventure playground.

⑫ CANEWDON

The 85 ft tower of St Nicholas's Church, once a landmark for Thames shipping, dominates the surrounding countryside. Beacon Hill, on which it stands, is said to have been the Danes' command post before the Battle of Ashingdon in 1016, when the Danish King Canute defeated the English Edmund Ironside.

⑬ WALLASEA ISLAND

Much of Wallasea is farmland, but a road across its north-west tip leads to a 500-berth marina and a boatyard. On summer weekends Wallasea is linked with Burnham by a passenger ferry.

PLACES TO SEE INLAND

Battlesbridge, 4 miles SW of South Woodham Ferrers. Largest antiques centre in Essex.

New Hall Vineyard, 4 miles S of Maldon. Wine-tasting and guided tours.

TOURIST INFORMATION

Maldon (01621) 856503

Popular yachting centres near Britain's oldest town

In the sheltered estuaries of the Colne and Blackwater, the hubbub of crowded sailing centres contrasts with the deep solitude of nature reserves. Colchester, the area's main town, thrives on its historical roots.

THE OLD OAK TREE *Fingringhoe oak supposedly grew from an acorn lodged in the nostril of a man hanged for smuggling.*

① HEYBRIDGE BASIN

A narrow road leads south from the B1026 to the banks of a basin at the end of the Chelmer and Blackwater Canal, which stretches inland for 11 miles to Chelmsford. The moorings above the lock are packed with sailing boats, from dinghies to 120 ft yachts. Running east along the sea wall is the 12 mile North Blackwater Trail to Tollesbury.

② TOLLESBURY

From the centre of the village, with its large market square and Norman Church of St Mary the Virgin, a narrow lane leads down past boathouses to a 250-berth marina. The nearby saltings, crisscrossed by boardwalks, include moorings for several hundred more craft. A 5 mile circular footpath, starting from the marina, skirts Tollesbury Wick Nature Reserve, a large area of former farmland and marshes. Part of the path follows the North Blackwater Trail.

To the north is the remote RSPB reserve of Old Hall Marshes. A permit must be obtained to enter the reserve, whose birdlife includes Brent geese, wigeon, shelduck, teal and short-eared owls. A public footpath runs round the edge of the peninsula.

③ WEST MERSEA

A causeway liable to high-tide flooding carries the B1025 across salt marshes to Mersea Island, where evidence of human habitation from about 10 000 BC has been found. West Mersea, a popular boating centre, includes a sweeping curve of densely packed boatyards, backed by a large residential area. There are two yacht clubs on the seafront, as well as a scattering of sailmakers, chandlers and oyster huts. A small museum specialises in local history. Oysters, once plentiful in the area, are now mostly brought in as oyster spat from elsewhere to be raised locally. There is a round-the-island yacht race each August, during Mersea Week.

④ EAST MERSEA

Compared with the bustle of West Mersea, the thinly populated farmland of East Mersea, favoured by caravanners, seems part of a different age. A narrow road leads to Cudmore Grove Country Park, which borders the Colne Estuary National Nature Reserve. Brushwood fences at the foot of low eroded cliffs protect the salt marsh and mud flats where knots, plovers, dunlins and oystercatchers flourish.

⑤ ABBERTON RESERVOIR

The road across the western end of Abberton Reservoir, one of Britain's finest waterbird sanctuaries, gives clear views of the country's largest colony of tree-nesting cormorants, numbering more than 1000 birds at the height of the breeding season. A wildfowl centre provides information about the cormorants, and about the reservoir's flocks of ducks, geese, swans and other waterfowl, and offers a panoramic view of a backwater where swans feed.

⑥ FINGRINGHOE

By St Andrew's Church stands a huge gnarled oak tree thought to be about 500 years old, making it one of the oldest oaks in Essex. Ferry Road leads down to the banks of the Colne, from where there are views of a tidal barrier, and of Wivenhoe across the river.

A woodland lane south of the village winds up to Fingringhoe Wick Nature Reserve, which stands on a rise overlooking the Colne and the flat sweep of Geedon Saltings. From a conservation centre, which is also the headquarters of the Essex Wildlife Trust, two trails pass through a large area of reclaimed gravel pits, woodland, heath, reedbeds, tidal mud and salt marsh. Eight hides allow visitors to see some of the 40 species of birds and 20 species of butterflies that have been recorded there.

⑦ COLCHESTER

A one-way system takes traffic swirling round the heart of Britain's oldest-recorded town, where the past, especially the Roman past, has been made part of the present. A trail marked with brass plaques links the main historic sights. Colchester was once an important port, but its quays at The Hythe are now little used. The town's traditional love of oysters is indulged each October at the Colchester Oyster Feast.

Colchester Castle, surrounded by grassy ramparts, lawns and rosebeds, is now a museum. The castle was built in the 11th century on the foundations of the Roman temple of Claudius, razed in AD 60 when Queen Boudicca of the Iceni led a revolt against Colchester, then the Roman capital. The attack is recalled in displays and video presentations inside the castle. Guided tours are available of the Roman vaults. The

TOLLESBURY BOATHOUSES *Overlooking a creek off the Blackwater estuary, these sail lofts date back to 1902, when Tollesbury had a fishing fleet of more than 100 sailing smacks.*

RICH LEGACY FROM ROMAN DAYS

A great Roman city was built at Colchester by the Emperor Claudius about AD 50, and many fine artefacts from the Roman period have been found in the area, some of them housed in the Castle Museum. The Romans introduced their gods into Britain, and some Britons accepted and worshipped them. Religion and myth are widely reflected in artistic creations such as statues and intricately patterned floor mosaics. Even before the invasion of AD 43, close links had been forged between Rome and the British tribes, as witnessed by the discovery of coins and medallions dating from the reign of the Emperor Augustus (29 BC–AD 14.)

Mythical 'seahorse' from a floor mosaic (left); medallion of 16 BC showing the head of Augustus (above); and a bronze statue of Mercury, messenger of the gods (right).

⑨ ALRESFORD CREEK

A lone weatherboarded house stands sentinel over a silent flood-plain, edged by an unpaved road linking two sloping shingle beaches. To the west looms rusting gear once used for loading cargo onto barges. Walkers can follow the creek inland for almost 2 miles, along a path that joins the B1029 between Brightlingsea and Thorrington.

⑩ BRIGHTLINGSEA

A broad, firm beach, overlooked by a hotel, yacht club and shops, makes Brightlingsea a popular boating centre. The beach-side road is cut off from the water by a sea wall, which is pierced by a launching ramp. In medieval times Brightlingsea was an important port and the only associate member of the Cinque Ports outside Kent and Sussex. The town prospered from boatbuilding and fishing, but it retains few vestiges of its historic past, apart from some fine old Essex fishing smacks cared for by the Smack Preservation Society.

town walls, 1½ miles of which still stand, were built some 20 years after Boudicca's rebellion. Outside the southern section of the wall are the impressive Norman ruins of St Botolph's Priory (EH). Other museums include Hollytrees, a Georgian house with collections of Georgian furniture, toys and costumes; the Tymperleys museum of Colchester-made clocks; and a social history museum based in the Saxon Church of the Holy Trinity.

Leisure World, in the north of the town, has a pool with water rides, spas and saunas. High Woods Country Park, which combines farmland, woods and wetland, has nature trails and a visitor centre. On the southern edge of Colchester is Bourne Mill (NT), a 16th-century fishing lodge converted to a watermill, which is open to the public two afternoons a week in high summer. Elephants, snow leopards and many rare breeds can be seen at Colchester Zoo, about 2 miles south-west of the town, near Heckfordbridge.

⑧ WIVENHOE

A lane leads away from the gaunt grey towers of Essex University through a maze of old streets to a waterfront of 18th and 19th-century houses and disused boatyards. Once a fishing and boatbuilding centre, the village is now largely residential. A quarter of a mile downriver is an immense concrete barrier, closed at exceptionally high tides. A passenger ferry runs to Rowhedge and Fingringhoe on summer weekends and bank holidays, tides permitting.

Three miles north-east of Wivenhoe, at Elmstead Market, are the Beth Chatto Gardens, where a thousand different species of plant grow.

PLACES TO SEE INLAND

Coggeshall. Paycockes (NT), Tudor merchant's house; Coggeshall Grange Barn (NT), oldest surviving timber-framed barn in Europe.

Layer Marney Tower, 6 miles SW of Colchester. Tallest Tudor gatehouse in Britain, with gardens, working farm and rare farm animals.

TOURIST INFORMATION

Colchester (01206) 282920

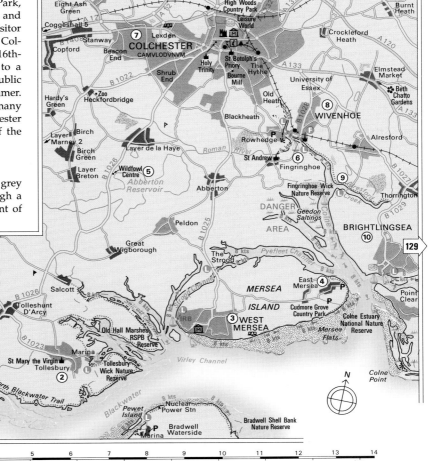

MILES 1 2 3 4 5 6 7 8 9 10 11 12 13 14
KM 1 2 4 6 8 10 12 14 16 18 20 22

Resorts and creeks near the historic port of Harwich

Family resorts, including lively Clacton and quiet Frinton, have grown up behind a long line of sandy beaches. North of The Naze are tranquil inlets, and Harwich, at the meeting of the Stour and Orwell estuaries.

① POINT CLEAR

A holiday village of caravans, chalets, bungalows and shops spreads across this small peninsula at the mouth of the River Colne. The beach is sand and shingle, with mud exposed at low tide.

South of Point Clear are the salt marshes and mud flats of Colne Point Nature Reserve, where many wildfowl and waders feed in winter. Permits are needed to visit the reserve.

② ST OSYTH

Old weatherboarded houses stand at the well-preserved centre of the village, named after a 7th-century abbess who was murdered by invading Danes. On the edge of the village is St Osyth's Priory, a beautiful house built over several centuries. Its massive gatehouse, built in the late 15th century and richly decorated with strips and squares of flint and stone, was the entrance to a medieval abbey. Most of the abbey buildings have disappeared, but the 13th-century Chapel of St Osyth survives. The house has a fine art collection, including paintings by George Stubbs. Peacocks strut across lawns and deer graze in the park.

Howlands Marsh Nature Reserve, west of the village, is an area of low-lying, hummocky grassland dotted with sheep. The road to Point Clear crosses St Osyth Creek, which has been

St Osyth's Priory Gatehouse

dammed to form a lake suitable for water-skiing and windsurfing. Two miles south of the village, holiday parks back St Osyth Beach, a sand and pebble expanse partly used by naturists.

③ JAYWICK

The small resort, with bungalows, chalets, caravans and seaside amusements, has a sand and pebble beach backed by a sea wall. Several Martello towers – circular, early 19th-century fortifications – stand on the coast to the west and east of Jaywick.

④ CLACTON-ON-SEA

A vigorous seaside resort in the old tradition, Clacton has a broad, 1180 ft pier flanked by long sandy beaches, and well-tended flower gardens backing a wide promenade. Amusements on the pier include a roller-skating rink and an aquarium; fishing from the end of the

pier yields bass, eel, whiting and cod. A nearby pavilion offers fairground rides. Fishing trips can be arranged, and pleasure flights from Clacton Airfield give panoramas of the surrounding countryside and nearby coastal resorts.

Until the 1860s the name of Clacton applied to two inland villages, Great Clacton and Little Clacton. The first pier, built in 1877 for goods and passengers, was rebuilt in the early 1890s, after which the town flourished as a resort.

The long beach and seafront continue north-eastwards past Holland-on-Sea, a residential area. Beyond is Holland Haven Country Park, a quiet expanse of marshland and grassland that is crisscrossed by a network of footpaths.

⑤ FRINTON-ON-SEA

Developed in the 1890s, Frinton retains the air of a genteel Victorian resort. It is free of conventional seaside entertainments, and is the only resort of any size in Britain without a pub. Red-brick houses flank wide tree-lined roads that lead to a long esplanade and a broad stretch of clifftop grassland called The Greensward. Below the cliffs, a fine sandy beach runs the full length of the town. A 1½ mile walk along the promenade, lined with beach huts, leads to Walton-on-the-Naze.

⑥ WALTON-ON-THE NAZE

A family resort, Walton has sandy beaches, which are almost covered at high tide, and a ¾ mile pleasure pier that is the second longest in Britain after Southend's. Amusements on the pier include tenpin bowling, and there is fishing for codling, skate and conger eel. The town developed as a resort from about 1830, and was once renowned for its sea holly, whose candied roots were sold for their supposed aphrodisiac qualities. A former lifeboat house next to the coastguard station is now a heritage centre.

North of Walton is The Naze, a wide clifftop area crowned by a brick tower built in 1720 as a navigational aid. The headland gives views of shipping going to and from Harwich and Felixstowe. A 1¼ mile nature trail leads to the tip of the headland, where a small area comprising blackthorn and bramble thickets, rough grassland and ponds is a nature reserve. It attracts migrant birds, including chats and warblers, during spring and autumn. Visitors should keep away from the eroding cliff edge.

⑦ KIRBY-LE-SOKEN QUAY

A lane from the small village of Kirby-le-Soken leads to Kirby-le-Soken Quay, a small inlet. Until the early 20th century, flat-bottomed Thames sailing barges transported coal, and horse manure from London's streets, to Kirby, and carried away grain and hay. A footpath along the sea wall gives views over the solitary Walton Backwaters. On rising tides in winter, avocets may be seen.

QUIET BACKWATERS *Kirby-le-Soken Quay overlooks the Walton Backwaters, a wilderness of reedy islands lying like the scattered pieces of a jigsaw puzzle behind The Naze.*

131
127

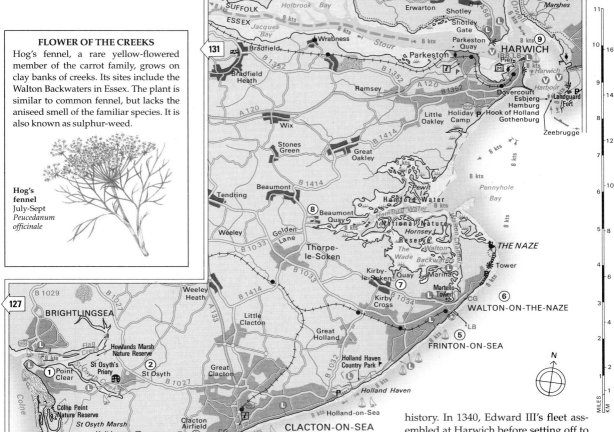

FLOWER OF THE CREEKS

Hog's fennel, a rare yellow-flowered member of the carrot family, grows on clay banks of creeks. Its sites include the Walton Backwaters in Essex. The plant is similar to common fennel, but lacks the aniseed smell of the familiar species. It is also known as sulphur-weed.

Hog's fennel
July–Sept
Peucedanum officinale

AID TO NAVIGATION *Harwich's Low Lighthouse, now flanked by beach huts, was one of two such beacons that guided sailors round difficult sandbanks from 1818 to 1863.*

history. In 1340, Edward III's fleet assembled at Harwich before setting off to defeat the French at Sluys, in the first major sea battle of the Hundred Years' War. Queen Elizabeth I, who stayed in Harwich in 1561, said it was a 'pretty place and wants for nothing'.

The Harwich Maritime Heritage Trail winds through the old town, where Georgian and Victorian houses line narrow streets and passageways. The trail starts at the Low Lighthouse, now a Maritime Museum, which is open on Sunday afternoons in summer. The High Lighthouse nearby, built in 1818, is now a private house. Near the Low Lighthouse is a unique 17th-century treadmill, designed to lift ammunition and stores; it was worked by two men walking inside twin wooden tread wheels. Ha'penny Pier, so called because when it opened the toll was a halfpenny, was originally the departure point for steamships to the Continent. A ferry to Felixstowe now operates from the pier, along with summer pleasure cruises along the Stour and Orwell rivers. St Nicholas Church, near the High Lighthouse, was rebuilt in the 1820s with cast-iron pillars, some of the first to be used; the church has a display of 17th-century Dutch tiles.

Dovercourt, to the south of Harwich, has a sandy beach backed by a sea wall. On the beach is a pair of disused lighthouses on stilts. The lighthouses, built in 1863, were fitted with gas lamps and were in use until 1917.

⑧ BEAUMONT QUAY

Fragments of a wall built of stone from Old London Bridge, demolished in 1831, are all that remain of Beaumont Quay. The lonely spot can be reached on foot by a lane, marked 'Private', to Quay Farm; cars are not allowed. From the quay there are views extending across Hamford Water, a national nature reserve made up of mud flats and dozens of inaccessible marshy islands.

⑨ HARWICH

The quayside in the old town of Harwich, at the tip of a narrow peninsula, is an ideal spot from which to watch shipping. By the quay itself there are pleasure craft and small fishing boats. Continental ferries go to and from Parkeston Quay, and large container ships berth at Felixstowe, on the opposite side of the Orwell and Stour estuaries. The town has a long maritime

Airy country, reedy waters where Constable painted

The Stour valley scenery inspired many of John Constable's best-known paintings. More colour enlivens the vista in the brightly painted barges that sail majestically along the estuaries of the Stour and the Orwell.

IPSWICH'S EYE-CATCHER *The elaborate plasterwork on the Ancient House, built in 1567, was added in the 17th century.*

① SUFFOLK YACHT HARBOUR
On the foreshore south-east of the village of Levington is a huge marina with launching and berthing facilities. It can be reached from the village along a road marked 'Private'. Visitors should declare their arrival at the marina office.

A 3 mile coastal path crosses the tranquil meadows of Trimley Marshes downstream to Felixstowe.

② NACTON
The road through the residential village leads to Orwell Park School, where a track meanders down to a peaceful spot at the edge of expansive tidal flats with panoramic views across the estuary. In the 17th and 18th centuries Orwell Park was the home of Admiral Sir Edward Vernon, nicknamed 'Old Grog', because of his suit of grogram cloth. Vernon introduced to the navy the daily rum ration known as 'grog'. Near the school is a domed 19th-century observatory, which is closed to the public. The medieval Church of St Martin lies on the other side of the lane.

③ IPSWICH
Suffolk's county town was one of England's most prosperous ports during the Middle Ages, exporting wool and trading in skins, leather and fish. The docks still thrive on the products of industries such as agriculture and brewing. A Wet Dock Maritime Trail explores a large area of the historic docks and the surrounding streets. Cardinal Wolsey was born in Ipswich in 1475; a few fine half-timbered buildings from the Tudor period survive, notably the Ancient House, once a merchant's house, which has fine pargetting, or moulded exterior plasterwork. Displays at the Ipswich Museum include replicas of treasures from the Anglo-Saxon burial site at Sutton Hoo near Woodbridge, north-east of Ipswich. A self-guided walk takes in Ipswich's 17 historic churches, while the Victorian Tolly Cobbold Brewery, rebuilt in 1896, offers conducted tours.

Near the town centre is Christchurch Mansion, built in 1548. Furnished in period styles from the 16th to 19th centuries, the mansion has paintings by Constable and Gainsborough.

④ WOOLVERSTONE MARINA
A private road off the B1456 leads through parkland to an extensive marina and sailing centre at Cat House, home of the Royal Harwich Yacht Club. In the 18th century a stuffed cat, placed at night in a lighted window, was the signal to smugglers that the coast was clear. A path along the foreshore leads a mile downstream to Pin Mill, and 2 miles upstream to Freston Tower, a 16th-century six-storey tower house built by Lord de Freston as a place in which to educate his daughter. On each level she was taught a different subject, culminating in astronomy at the top. The tower is not open to the public.

⑤ PIN MILL
The name Pin Mill is said to be derived from the wooden pegs or 'pins' that were made there and used in boat-building. This riverside beauty spot lies at the end of a narrow lane from Chelmondiston. High spring tides on the Orwell allow sailors to moor close to the walls of the Butt and Oyster Inn and order drinks without stepping ashore. The Pin Mill Barge Match, a dazzling display of ornately painted barges, is held annually in late June or early July.

The Cliff Plantation (NT), reached only from a short footpath east of Pin Mill, is an attractive area of pine woodland and open heath stretching along the bank of the river.

⑥ SHOTLEY GATE
At the end of Shotley Gate peninsula, which separates the Orwell from the Stour, a towering ship's mast marks what used to be the naval training base HMS Ganges. Since 1985 the base has served as the National Police Training Centre. At the end of the road by Shotley quay there are fine views of shipping entering and leaving the docks at Harwich and Parkeston.

⑦ ROYAL HOSPITAL SCHOOL
The original school was built at Greenwich in 1712 to serve the sons of disabled and retired seamen of the Royal Navy. Since 1933 the school has stood on its new site just outside the village of Holbrook, where its prominent stone pinnacle is a landmark on both sides of the Stour. Preference for admittance to the school is still given to the children of seafaring families.

To the south, footpaths lead round the shore of Holbrook Bay, and to isolated Stutton Church with its 15th-century tower, about a mile away.

WORKHORSE OF THE THAMES
The huge rust-red sails of the Thames sailing barges were a familiar and striking sight in Victorian times. They took grain, bricks and hay to London and returned to the ports of East Anglia with horse manure for agricultural land.

Thames sailing barge

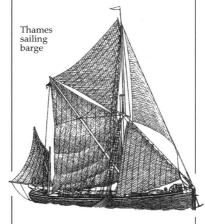

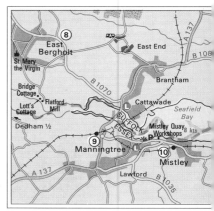

EAST BERGHOLT *Willy Lott's cottage looks much as John Constable saw it in 1816. His painting of this scene is now in the Christchurch Mansion Museum, Ipswich.*

⑧ EAST BERGHOLT

The landscape painter John Constable was born in the charming village of East Bergholt in 1776. The house where he lived no longer exists, but a plaque on railings near the Church of St Mary the Virgin marks the site. Constable's parents and his friend Willy Lott are buried in the churchyard, which has a free-standing, timber-built bell cage, whose bells are rung by hand.

Flatford Mill, south of the village, was owned by Constable's father. Both the watermill and nearby Lott's cottage are little changed since the artist's day; they are not open to the public. The National Trust property of Bridge Cottage includes a restored dry dock and a John Constable Exhibition. The willow-lined river and its surroundings make up the true heart of 'Constable Country', and guided walks round the sites depicted in the artist's paintings depart from the cottage in summer. The Granary Collection, nearby, is a museum housing an array of agricultural implements and vintage bicycles.

⑨ MANNINGTREE

A busy port and cloth-trading centre in Tudor times, Manningtree gradually lost its trade to neighbouring Mistley, but the town retains some attractive Georgian and Victorian buildings. In the 17th century Manningtree was the headquarters of Matthew Hopkins, who terrorised East Anglia in his role of 'Witch Finder General'. He was himself eventually accused of witchcraft, and later hanged. Every June or July, Manningtree holds a punt regatta with displays of flat-bottomed boats, and dinghy and yacht racing.

⑩ MISTLEY

The Swan Basin fountain is a symbol of the 18th-century attempt to turn Mistley into a spa. Now the town is a small but flourishing commercial port at the head of the Stour, with a Victorian malt-house and a resident population of mute swans. Visits can be arranged to the Mistley Quay Workshops, where craftsmen make pottery and musical instruments, and a showroom and teashop offer panoramic views of the river. On the road to Manningtree, the twin Mistley Towers (EH), in the middle of a graveyard, are the remains of a church built by Robert Adam as part of the unrealised spa scheme.

⑪ WRABNESS

All Saints' Church, on the village's north side, has a detached belfry – the single bell is housed in a wooden cage in the graveyard. From the rear of the church there is a fine view across the river to the Royal Hospital School. A narrow lane leads to one of the few sandy stretches on the Stour.

East of Wrabness is the Stour Estuary RSPB Reserve, an area of woodland and mud flats. Wildfowl are present all year round, but winter is an especially good time to see black-tailed godwits and Brent geese. Observation hides are reached along a path from the car park.

PLACES TO SEE INLAND

Castle House, Dedham, 4 miles W of Manningtree. Home of artist Sir Alfred Munnings, with many of his paintings.

Museum of East Anglian Life, Stowmarket, 10 miles NW of Ipswich.

Stonham Barns, nr Stowmarket, 10 miles N of Ipswich. Country leisure centre.

TOURIST INFORMATION

Harwich (01255) 506139; Ipswich (01473) 258070

Shingle beaches, and a sanctuary for avocets

Sutton Heath is all that remains of what was once a vast tract of open heathland east of the Deben. Today the river twists between marshes and wooded hills to the sea, which beats against red shingle shores.

HARNESSING THE TIDE *Woodbridge's tide mill is powered by the ebb and flow of tidal water trapped in a pool beside it.*

① FELIXSTOWE

A sedate Edwardian resort, stretching round a long, gently curving bay, is combined in Felixstowe with one of Europe's busiest container ports. In the resort part of the town a paved promenade is backed by a series of well-tended seafront gardens, one of which contains the curious Water Clock, whose mechanism is driven by water. Beyond the Spa Pavilion, with its lively programme of shows, is a sand and shingle shore with old-fashioned beach huts. Bathing is not safe a mile north of the pier, where the remains of a fort lie close to the waterline, although fishing is possible from the pier and the beach.

At the southern end of the town a road leads to Landguard Fort (EH), originally built in 1540 to guard the harbour entrance, and rebuilt in 1718. The chapel overlooking the Fort's gateway was the scene of a notorious scandal in 1763, when the acting governor held a dance there and used the altar as a bar. The fort has a museum explaining its history, and a nearby viewing area is a good spot for watching passing ships in Harwich Harbour. To the north of the fort is the Landguard Nature Reserve, whose less common visitors include barred warblers and black redstarts. Visits to the Landguard observatory must be arranged in advance with the wardens. West of the headland of Landguard Point is the huge Port of Felixstowe, from which there are regular ferry services to Zeebrugge, as well as a passenger ferry to Harwich.

② FELIXSTOWE FERRY

Huddled round one of the Martello towers that dot this stretch of coast, the village can be reached by road, or on foot across Felixstowe golf course. A ferry to Bawdsey Quay operates at certain times during the summer. Swift currents make swimming unsafe.

③ WALDRINGFIELD

The small but busy sailing centre on the Deben has a waterfront of muddy shingle, and a sandy beach, firm enough for launching boats. Chandlers and boatyards are scattered along a lane that skirts the edge of the foreshore, where teal, wigeon and shelduck can be seen. River trips along the estuary can be arranged from the boatyard in summer, and walks of about a mile lead both upstream and downstream. Parking at the waterfront is severely restricted, but there is a large car park behind the Maybush Inn up the hill.

④ WOODBRIDGE

Sail-making, rope-making and boatbuilding made Woodbridge prosperous between the 14th and 15th centuries. It is now one of the most attractive towns in East Anglia, with timber-framed and Georgian houses, and steep streets running down to the quayside. Dominating the centre of the triangular market place are the magnificent 15th-century Church of St Mary and the Dutch-gabled Shire Hall, built in the 16th century by Thomas Seckford, a wealthy courtier of Queen Elizabeth I. The hall contains the Suffolk Horse Museum, which illustrates the history of the world's oldest breed of working horse. Nearby Buttrum's Mill is a six-storey tower mill built in 1835 and fully restored. Four pairs of original millstones are on display. On the quayside, prominent among the jumble of boatyards, chandleries and yachts, is the white, weather-boarded Tide Mill. Built in the 1790s and operating until 1957 the mill is now in full working order.

Sutton Hoo, east of the town, is a group of grassy burial mounds on a heath where a Saxon king's treasure was excavated in 1939. The site is on private land, but conducted tours can be arranged in summer. Woodbridge Museum has an exhibition of archaeological findings from Sutton Hoo.

South of Woodbridge is Kyson Hill (NT), a finger of land projecting into the Deben, with panoramic views from the southern slopes across the river. A footpath leads to the muddy foreshore and follows the river bank northwards to Woodbridge quay a mile away.

⑤ SUTTON HEATH

The vast expanse of heath provides a valuable reminder of what the plateau east of the Deben was like a century ago, before modern forestry and farming swallowed up the land. Two large car parks give access to the heath. The one at the southern end has a picnic site, backed by gorse, conifers and bracken. Many footpaths crisscross the heath, including a circular nature trail that takes about an hour to walk.

Rendlesham Forest, nearby, is one such managed forest whose planting resulted in the loss of more heathland, and although much of it was lost in the 1987 storms, it has been replanted by the Forestry Commission. The Phoenix Trail, one of several waymarked footpaths, shows how foresters have set about creating a new woodland.

⑥ RAMSHOLT QUAY

Parking by the shingle foreshore of this pretty boating haven is limited, and the last part of the road down to the quayside is private, but a large car park at the top of the hill provides fine views

---

A SAXON KING'S TREASURE

At Sutton Hoo, near Woodbridge, lies a sandy heath where in 1939 the buried treasure of a Saxon king was found beneath a grave mound. The king may have been King Raedwald, King of East Anglia from around AD 599 to 625. Most of the priceless hoard of jewellery, coins and regalia unearthed are now on display in the British Museum.

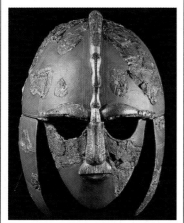

The remains of a fearsome bronze and iron helmet is part of the Sutton Hoo treasure.

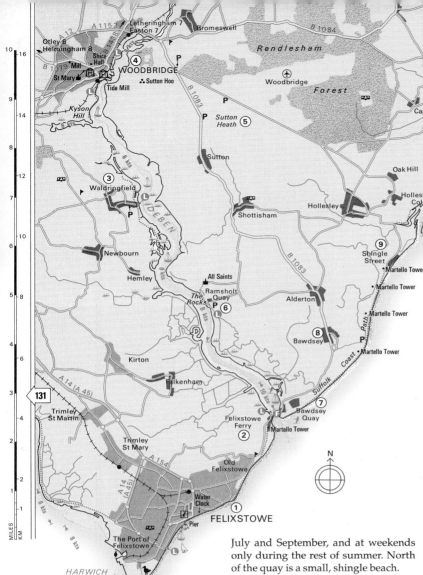

towards the Deben estuary. Nearby is a small, sandy beach known as The Rocks. The isolated All Saints' Church, with its distinctive Norman round tower, can be reached by a half-mile walk along a footpath north of the quay.

⑦ BAWDSEY QUAY

Although it is private property, the quay, which has a small parking area, is open to the public. A passenger boat to Felixstowe Ferry, on the opposite bank of the Deben, operates daily between July and September, and at weekends only during the rest of summer. North of the quay is a small, shingle beach.

⑧ BAWDSEY

A track leads down East Lane to a red shingle beach. A foreshore footpath, which forms part of the 50 mile Suffolk Coast Path, runs for 2½ miles northwards past a row of Martello towers to Shingle Street. Bawdsey College, beside the road to Bawdsey Quay, is the former base of RAF Bawdsey, where radar was developed before World War II.

⑨ SHINGLE STREET

Reached down a twisting, narrow road from Hollesley, Shingle Street is little more than a row of cottages built along a wide stretch of shingle thrown up by the sea into a high bank. A footpath from Shingle Street leads to the mouth of the Ore, opposite North Weir Point, which lies at the end of the 10 mile shingle bank that forms Orford Beach.

⑩ HAVERGATE ISLAND

The marshy island, lying in the long Ore channel that runs downstream from Orford to the sea, is an RSPB bird sanctuary. The water levels in the muddy lagoons are artificially maintained to provide the correct depth of water for Britain's oldest and largest breeding colony of avocets, who returned there to breed in 1947 after an absence of 100 years. Gulls, terns, redshanks and shelduck are also present. The island can be reached only by boat from Orford Quay, and permits must be sought in advance from the warden.

PLACES TO SEE INLAND

Easton Farm Park, 8 miles NE of Woodbridge. Working Victorian farm.

Helmingham Hall Gardens, 9 miles NW of Woodbridge. Moated and walled gardens, and parkland.

Letheringham Watermill, 8 miles NE of Woodbridge. 18th-century mill.

Otley Hall, 6 miles NW of Woodbridge. Partly moated 15th-century house.

TOURIST INFORMATION

Felixstowe (01394) 276770

PEBBLE VIEW *Shingle Street crouches beside a curving foreshore close to where the River Alde reaches the sea. High tides have left shallow lagoons in hollows in the stony expanse.*

Music and birdsong in the heaths and wetlands

Sandy cliffs are no match for storms and tides, which through the centuries have eaten away at this stretch of coast. Marshy creeks and slow-flowing rivers make the area a prime site for birdwatching.

① DUNWICH

Hidden in bushes near a shallow cliff is a fragment of a 1790 grave – the final link with All Saints' Church, which collapsed into the sea in about 1920. Saxon and Norman Dunwich flourished as a port, but in 1286, a huge storm threw tons of sand and shingle across the harbour mouth, diverting the River Blyth northwards. Trade was destroyed and Dunwich declined. By 1677 the sea had reached the market place, and the town became an estate village. Behind the Victorian Church of St James are the remains of a leper chapel, and nearby are the clifftop ruins of a 13th-century friary. The village museum chronicles the area's history from Roman times.

The long stretch of shingle beach is backed by sandy cliffs and heathland, protecting the low-lying meadows to the west. Dunwich Forest, to the north-west of the village, has woodland trails.

② WESTLETON

The quiet village has a large green, a tree-shaded pond and the thatched 14th-century Church of St Peter. To the north-east is Westleton Heath National Nature Reserve, one of the last surviving east Suffolk heathlands, which adjoins land owned by the RSPB and the Forestry Commission. There are delightful walks in the area, including one from the village to the Minsmere RSPB Reserve, 2 miles south-east.

③ DUNWICH HEATH

Two miles south of Dunwich, a stretch of National Trust heathland crowns the crumbling clifftops, beside which a waymarked walk provides panoramic views. Green woodpeckers and kestrels are among the heath's resident birds, and migrants include the nocturnal nightjar. The old coastguard cottages at the top of the cliffs serve as an information centre and a lookout point.

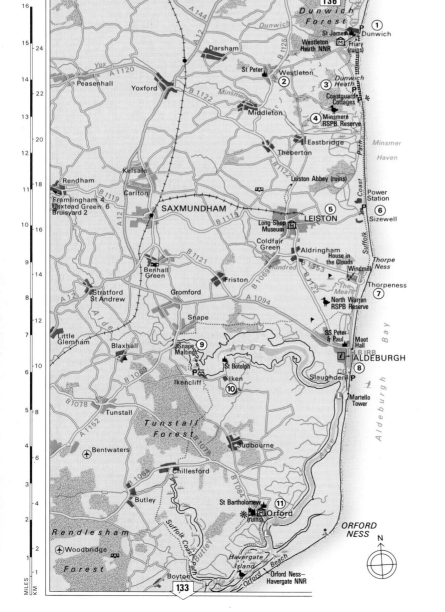

BIRDWATCHING AT MINSMERE

For almost 100 years avocets failed to breed in Britain, but they returned to the east coast in the 1940s when most of it was closed to the public because of the war. Now they breed regularly at the RSPB's Minsmere Reserve, which is also the home of the rare marsh harrier and up to 100 other breeding species.

Avocet
Recurvirostra avosetta

Marsh Harrier
Circus aeruginosus

WATERWORKS *Thorpeness's windmill stands over a 32 ft well that fed the House in the Clouds, built as a water tower.*

④ MINSMERE RSPB RESERVE

At the mouth of the Minsmere river is a nature reserve incorporating reedbeds, artificial lagoons and islands, heath and woodlands. The reserve shelters one of Britain's widest varieties of breeding birds, as well as many migrants; species to be seen include marsh harriers, avocets, sandpipers, meadow pipits and bitterns. The reserve has eight observation hides, for which permits must be obtained from the visitor centre. There is also a public hide on the beach, reached from the car park on Dunwich Heath immediately to the north.

⑤ LEISTON

The former village of Leiston, now a growing town, was built by Richard Garrett, the 19th-century railway pioneer whose workshops in Main Street form the excellent Long Shop Museum. The museum covers the history of the works, the town and the region.

A footpath leads from the northern outskirts of town to the brick-and-flint remains of Leiston Abbey, originally founded at Minsmere in the 12th century and reconstructed at its present site in the 14th century. A house built within the ruins, a neighbouring tithe barn and a 14th-century hall are now home to a music school.

⑥ SIZEWELL

The hamlet was a notorious smuggling village in the 18th century, but nowadays it is known for its twin power stations, the first of which opened in 1966, and the second in 1995. The site is dominated by a dome larger than that of St Paul's Cathedral in London, and by a network of enormous pylons. A visitor centre offers guided tours.

⑦ THORPENESS

A unique holiday village, centred on a shallow man-made lake called The Meare, Thorpeness was created by Glencairn Stuart Ogilvie when he inherited the family estate in the early 1900s. The houses are in varying styles, including Tudor, Jacobean and traditional 18th-century East Anglian tarred weatherboard. Small boats can be hired on The Meare. A track leads from the main village street to the distinctive House in the Clouds. Originally a water tower served by the nearby windmill, it is now a private dwelling. The restored windmill, first built at Aldringham 2 miles to the north-west in 1804 and moved to Thorpeness in the 1920s, is open to visitors in summer.

Shingle beaches stretch to the north and south. About a mile to the north, at Thorpe Ness, the beach is buffeted by strong winds and tides. To the south is North Warren RSPB Reserve, made up of wet meadows, woodland and heath.

⑧ ALDEBURGH

A main street of Georgian houses and older cottages, behind a wide shingle beach, reflects the elegance of this small historic town. Mentioned in Domesday Book, Aldeburgh was a prosperous port and fishing centre by 1600. Early in the 19th century the town became a popular resort, and in 1948 the composer Benjamin Britten and the singer Peter Pears established the annual music festival, now held at nearby Snape Maltings. The shingle beach, with a lifeboat station and a line of fishing boats, stretches north to Thorpeness.

The half-timbered Tudor Moot Hall, or Town Hall, is now almost on the shore, the three roads which originally separated it from the sea having been washed away over the centuries. The Moot Hall is open to visitors in summer and has a museum of local life. Britten and Pears are buried side by side in the churchyard of largely 16th-century St Peter and St Paul. Inside the church is a bust of the poet George Crabbe, who was born in Aldeburgh in 1754. Britten used Crabbe's pen-portrait of fisherman Peter Grimes in the poem *The Borough* as the basis of his first opera.

South of the town is a sea wall, wide enough for cars to park on. At Slaughden Quay boats can be launched into the River Alde. South of the Martello tower, the shingle tip known as Orford Ness is owned by the National Trust, and there is no public right of way along the shoreline. Orford Ness can be reached by ferry from Orford.

PLACES TO SEE INLAND
Bruisyard Vineyard, 12 miles NW of Aldeburgh. Winery and herb centre.
Framlingham Castle (EH), 14 miles NW of Aldeburgh. 12th-century landmark containing 18th-century poorhouse.
Saxtead Green Windmill, 16 miles NW of Aldeburgh. 18th century.

TOURIST INFORMATION
Aldeburgh (01728) 453637 (summer); Felixstowe (01394) 276770.

⑨ SNAPE MALTINGS

A group of magnificent Victorian buildings, formerly used to process barley for brewing, was converted in 1967 by various commercial businesses and the organisers of the annual Aldeburgh Festival into an international centre of music. The complex includes a craft centre, an art gallery, shops, bars and a teashop, and a School for Advanced Musical Studies dedicated to Benjamin Britten and Peter Pears, the founders of the festival. River trips in the Alde estuary start from the quay. The footpaths across the marshes to the village of Iken are sometimes impassable at high tide.

⑩ IKEN

Once a thriving fishing village, Iken is now a scattered hamlet set on high ground above the marshes of the Alde. Good views of the river can be had from beside the thatched Church of St Botolph, reached through a gate at the end of a narrow cul-de-sac.

At Ikencliff, a mile to the west, is a picnic site with wide views across the reeds and mud flats. Birdlife includes shelduck, redshanks and herons.

⑪ ORFORD

A prosperous port in the 12th century, Orford was cut off from the sea by the gradual growth of Orford Ness, a spit of shingle measuring some 10 miles. The village's past importance is symbolised by the imposing St Bartholomew's Church, parts of which date from Norman times, and by its large 12th-century castle keep (EH). A small museum tells the history of the village.

Waymarked paths include an hour's circular walk which starts at the quay. Boat trips can be taken up the River Alde or across to Havergate Island RSPB Reserve and Orford Ness.

TUDOR COUNCIL HOUSE *Aldeburgh's Moot Hall has hosted council meetings since the early 16th century.*

Ports ancient and modern at England's eastern tip

Gently undulating countryside and abundant birdlife are among the attractions of Suffolk's north-east corner. Lowestoft is a bustling port and holiday centre, while Southwold preserves old-fashioned charm.

① LOWESTOFT

The most easterly town in Britain is both a fishing port and a busy resort. A narrow strip of water called Lake Lothing divides the town, whose two halves are linked by a bascule bridge that is raised to admit fishing boats and pleasure craft to the main part of the port.

Lowestoft's fortunes were founded on the development of the Dogger Bank as a trawling ground in the mid 19th century. The main catch was herring, most of which was smoked and sent by rail to London and the Midlands. At the height of the herring boom, just before World War I, more than 700 drifters worked from Lowestoft. Today the fleet consists of about 30 trawlers, and the catch is largely plaice; a modern fish market has replaced the Victorian original. Though badly damaged during World War II, the old town retains a unique series of parallel lanes, known as 'scores', running steeply down from the high street to foreshore level. A Maritime Museum covers the history of the local fishing fleet, and nearby is a Royal Naval Patrol Service Museum. *Lydia Eva*, the world's last steam drifter, moors at Lowestoft for part of the summer, and can be visited; for the rest of the summer she is at Great Yarmouth. South of the bridge, at the head of a wide esplanade and the sandy sweep of South Beach, is the East Point Pavilion. An imposing glass building in Edwardian style, the pavilion has an exhibition of Lowestoft's heritage, and Discoverig, a children's play platform based on the theme of a North Sea gas rig.

② OULTON BROAD

Reed-fringed Oulton Broad, the southern gateway to the Broads, is one of the finest yachting lakes in Britain, and the only place on the Broads where powerboat race meetings are held. Nicholas Everitt Park, on its south bank, has tennis courts, a children's playground and a boating lake. The Lowestoft Museum in the park's Broad House has a fine collection of Lowestoft porcelain, toys, costumes and regalia from the recent past, as well as local Stone Age artefacts. Boat World shows the skills involved in repairing boats and building new ones. Mutford Lock is the starting point for boat tours along the Waveney to Beccles, 2 hours upstream.

③ PAKEFIELD

The southern suburb of Lowestoft has a sandy beach and a 14th-century church standing in a large churchyard on the edge of low cliffs. St Margaret and All Saints until 1748 was two churches in one, with two separate parishes and two rectors. Two miles inland, the East Anglian Transport Museum includes working vehicles such as a tram and a trolleybus set in a 1930s street scene.

④ BECCLES

An ancient, mellow town of narrow streets and Georgian-fronted houses, Beccles was once a prosperous port. Its most prominent landmark is the 14th-century detached bell-tower of the Church of St Michael. The William Clowes Museum describes the development of printing from 1800, and the Beccles Museum explains local history.

⑤ KESSINGLAND

The former fishing village has a wide shingle shore backed by holiday camps, and offers a variety of traditional beach amusements. South-west of Kessingland is the Suffolk Wildlife Park, which includes lions, cheetahs, camels and zebras, as well as a farmyard corner.

⑥ BENACRE NESS

The shingle headland may be reached only on foot, along the Suffolk Coast Path, or by a 1½ mile walk from outside the village of Benacre down a lane closed to cars. To the south is Benacre

SHINING LANDMARK *The white tower of Southwold lighthouse, a landmark for mariners since 1892, soars above Georgian brick-built cottages and the Sole Bay Inn.*

15th-century painted oak figure of a man-at-arms carrying a sword and a battleaxe; church services begin after the jack has struck a bell.

Several houses display a Dutch influence, including the little town museum, which is crammed with local memorabilia. The Sailors' Reading Room on the cliff and the Lifeboat Museum on Gun Hill both have mementos of tall ships and oil-skinned heroes, and offer reminders of the devastating power of the North Sea. Six 18-pounder cannons stand sentinel on Gun Hill.

Southwold is the home of Adnams Brewery, whose beer is delivered to local pubs by drays pulled by pairs of percheron horses. There are walks across the common, part of which is a golf course, to Southwold harbour, where fresh fish can be bought from fishermen's huts. From the harbour there is an iron footbridge, and a small passenger ferry in summer, across the Blyth to Walberswick. Boat trips up the river are available in summer.

⑨ WALBERSWICK

Its combination of sands, marshes, river and sea makes the somewhat isolated village of Walberswick a place of interest for young and old. On the western edge of this former port are the eerie ruins of the 15th-century Church of St Andrew, part of which has been rebuilt and restored to church use.

There is a road to Walberswick from the A12, but the village can be approached from Southwold by means of an iron footbridge or, in summer, by passenger ferry across the Blyth; there is also a footpath along the coast from Dunwich to the south.

The reedbeds of Westwood Marshes form part of Walberswick National Nature Reserve, whose regular visitors include the marsh harrier and bittern.

⑩ BLYTHBURGH

Now a little village set on the edge of marshes, Blythburgh was once a thriving port with its own mint and jail. Sharing the fate of many other river ports, it lost its trade when ships grew in size and the Blyth silted up.

Blythburgh's imposing Church of the Holy Trinity is floodlit at night and visible for miles around. Cromwell's men desecrated the church, using the great winged angels of the ceiling for target practice and screwing tethering rings for their horses into the pillars. Among the church's unusual features are carvings of the Seven Deadly Sins, and a clock 'jack', who strikes the bell with his axe and turns his head.

National Nature Reserve, a tranquil area of heath, dunes, broads and woodland, whose breeding birds include little terns and marsh harriers. Entry to the reserve is from the coast path, which can be dangerous in bad weather.

⑦ COVEHITHE

Lonely and dramatically sited, Covehithe's ruined Church of St Andrew is remarkable for the thatched chapel built in 1672 inside its roofless nave. The original, 15th-century church, whose fine tower survives, became too large for the parishioners to maintain, so they constructed the smaller church using materials from the old.

The road ends at a barrier a short way beyond the church. There is no public access to the beach from here because of the dangerously eroded state of the cliffs. A footpath starting just opposite the church leads under trees then across open heathland to low cliffs with a distant view of Southwold to the south. The sand and shingle beach stretches in both directions as far as the eye can see.

⑧ SOUTHWOLD

A small town of distinct character which has remained remarkably unchanged for the past century, Southwold is one of the jewels of the Suffolk coast. Its red-brick and flint cottages and colour-washed houses are built around a series of delightful greens, created after a fire had devastated the town in 1659.

Southwold Jack

The promenade is lined with some 250 brightly coloured beach huts.

The tallest buildings in Southwold are the brilliant white Victorian lighthouse, and the great flint Church of St Edmund. The church includes a fine hammerbeam roof and 'Southwold Jack', a

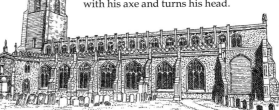

Blythburgh's Church of the Holy Trinity

+--+
| **PLACES TO SEE INLAND** |
| **Bungay Castle,** 6 miles W of Beccles. Norman |
| remains. |
| |
| **Otter Trust,** nr Bungay, 8 miles W of Beccles. |
| Otters in natural surroundings, rare waterfowl. |
| |
| **TOURIST INFORMATION** |
| Beccles (01502) 713196, Lowestoft (01502) |
| 523000, Southwold (01502) 724729 |
+--+

Glimpses of the past in colourful seaside towns

In Roman times much of the area round Great Yarmouth was a vast estuary and the sea heaved with fish. The town's status as the herring capital of the world declined after World War I, and it is now a resort.

① HEMSBY

The road to the coast from the Broadland village leads past holiday camps and amusement arcades to a wide, sandy beach scattered with stones and backed by a valley running between high sand dunes. To the south are the sandy beaches of Newport and California, which can be reached on foot along the shore and over the cliffs.

② CAISTER-ON-SEA

Dotted with holiday camps beside a broad sandy beach, Caister was once a thriving port, built around AD 125 to handle trade between Norfolk and the German Rhineland. The Roman Town (EH) is an excavated part of the old port that includes a defensive wall and the south gateway. In the village a lifeboat memorial lists the nine crew who lost their lives during a rescue operation in 1901, and a window in Holy Trinity Church has an inscription of a crewman's remark to King Edward VII: 'Caister men never turn back, Sir.'

Two miles west of the town is the splendid ruin of Caister Castle, built in the 1430s by Sir John Fastolf, who led the English archers at Agincourt in 1415. A Motor Museum with some 200 exhibits stands in the grounds.

③ GREAT YARMOUTH

East Anglia's biggest and brashest resort, with 4 miles of sandy beach, two piers and a lavish fairground, grew from a small fishermen's settlement on a sandbank in the estuary of three rivers. Fishing, especially for herrings,

SLENDER RUIN *Caister Castle was the first brick-built castle in England. Its 90 ft tower and much of the wall have survived.*

was the foundation of Yarmouth's wealth and prosperity from the Middle Ages until just after World War I, when foreign competition and overfishing led to a steady decline. The *Lydia Eva*, said to be the last remaining steam herring drifter in the world, is now a floating museum, berthed at South Quay for three months during the summer.

The 13th-century Tolhouse, once a courthouse and prison, is one of the oldest surviving civic buildings in England. It is now a museum of local history, with a brass rubbing centre and dungeons. At the northern end of the broad Market Place is the splendidly restored 12th-century Church of St Nicholas. From there it is a short walk to South Quay, with its network of alleys known as The Rows. The Elizabethan House, dating from 1596, is a museum of domestic life with panelled rooms and exhibitions of toys, games, china and civic plate. The Old Merchant's House (EH) is a 17th-century town house with splendid plaster ceilings, and nearby are the ruins of Greyfriars Cloisters. A shipwrecked sailors' home has become the Maritime Museum, which recalls the seafaring history of Norfolk, while a Sea Life Centre recreates a marine environment.

Set back from South Beach is Nelson's Monument, a memorial to Norfolk's greatest hero. On Sundays in July and August, visitors may climb its 217 steps to a viewing platform, which looks out over Yarmouth and Breydon Water.

④ BREYDON WATER

In summer the main channel through Breydon Water is busy with pleasure craft. The Breydon Water Nature Reserve is an area of mud flats, reached along footpaths from Great Yarmouth, that attracts many bird species. At the western end the grazing marshes and saltings of the Berney Marshes RSPB Reserve are another haven for wildfowl. The reserve can be reached by train, which stops at Berney Arms Halt, or by boat from Great Yarmouth, or on foot from either end of the water.

HERRING HERITAGE *A sign advertising bloaters (above) is displayed in Yarmouth's museum, housed on board the last of a once-sizable fleet of steam drifters (right).*

⑤ BURGH CASTLE

The village is mainly made up of caravan sites, but to the south-west are the impressive ruins of the mighty Roman fortress Gariannonum. When it was built in the 3rd century it stood on one bank of a huge estuary and a fleet of warships was probably based there. The ruins overlook Breydon Water and provide breathtaking views of the Broads and of 19th-century Berney Arms Windmill (EH), one of the highest and best preserved marsh mills in Norfolk. The mill can be reached from Berney Arms Halt station or from public moorings near the Church of St Peter and St Paul, which has a Norman round tower. A circular walk from the church takes about half an hour.

⑥ GORLESTON-ON-SEA

Quieter than neighbouring Yarmouth, the resort of Gorleston has amusement arcades and a flat, sandy beach. There are some lovely gardens and a golf course along the seafront. The harbour mouth is a good place from which to watch ships and boats sailing in and out of Yarmouth, and anglers catching a wide variety of fish. St Andrew's Church, dating from the 13th century, has one of the earliest and most interesting military brasses in England, representing a knight in chain-mail.

⑦ FRITTON LAKE

Formed by medieval peat-cutting, and stretching for 2 miles along the Norfolk and Suffolk border, the lake is one of the most beautiful expanses of water in East Anglia, attracting birds as varied as Egyptian geese and kingfishers. Fritton Lake Countryworld has boating, fishing and windsurfing, along with gardens, woodland walks and an undercover falconry with regular flying displays. Nearby is the hamlet of St Olaves, where the well-maintained ruins of St Olaves Priory (EH), and the Windpump, a boarded trestle drainage mill in working order, can be seen.

⑧ SOMERLEYTON

An attractive village near the River Waveney, Somerleyton has mock-Tudor thatched cottages clustered around its green. Somerleyton Hall is a Victorian mansion with a fine maze and miniature railway in its extensive grounds.

PLACES TO SEE INLAND

Broadland Conservation Centre, Ranworth, 13 miles NW of Great Yarmouth. Nature trail and floating gallery for bird watching.

Strumpshaw Fen RSPB Reserve, 14 miles W of Great Yarmouth.

Thrigby Hall Wildlife Gardens, 7 miles NW of Great Yarmouth. Collection of Asian animals, and landscaped garden.

TOURIST INFORMATION

Great Yarmouth (01493) 842195 (summer); Lowestoft (01502) 523000

⑨ BLUNDESTON

Passing the inland village on a walk from Yarmouth to Lowestoft, the novelist Charles Dickens misread the signpost, and subsequently gave the birthplace of his character David Copperfield as 'Blunderstone'. The Church of St Mary the Virgin, built in the 11th century, still has a sundial on the porch, but the one seen by young David from his bedroom window was replaced in 1983. The pretty churchyard remains largely unchanged, and Dickens recorded David Copperfield as saying of it: 'There is nothing half so green that I know anywhere, as the grass of that churchyard; nothing half so shady as its trees; nothing half so quiet as its tombstones.'

⑩ CORTON

Like Hopton on Sea, a mile to the north, Corton is a village of holiday camps with a beach of sand and shingle. Pleasurewood Hills, south-east of the village, is an American-style theme park with more than 50 rides and a variety of side shows.

FLOWER FROM MACEDONIA

In early spring roadsides leading to the sea are often fringed by alexanders. The flower is said to come from Macedonia, the country of Alexander the Great. The dark-green shiny leaves are embellished in summer by yellowish-green flowers, which develop into black fruits.

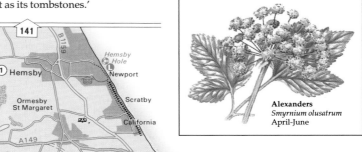

Alexanders
Smyrnium olusatrum
April-June

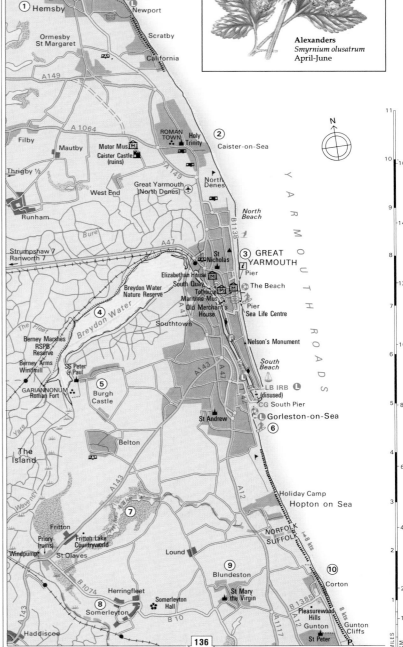

A gently curving coast of towering dunes and spires

Windmills and churches soar above the flat landscape of north-east Norfolk, noted for its fine sandy beaches. To resist the ceaseless assault of the sea, marram grass has been planted to stabilise the dunes.

① MUNDESLEY

A tranquil resort of wide sands backed by low cliffs, Mundesley, pronounced 'Munsley', is mentioned in Domesday Book. The poet William Cowper (1731-1800) lived in the high street, in a house now known as Cowper House, during his boyhood and towards the end of his life. He is said to have been inspired to write the hymn 'God Moves in a Mysterious Way' by the sight of a storm breaking over Happisburgh, 5 miles down the coast. Mundesley's historical connections with the sea are explored at the maritime museum, which includes a coastguard lookout tower.

South of Mundesley, past a millpond and waterwheel, is the four-storey brick tower of Stow Mill, built in 1827, with working fantail and sails.

② PASTON

The farming community of Paston entered literary history in the early 20th century with the publication of a remarkable series of letters providing graphic pictures of 15th-century English life. Most of the 'Paston Letters' were written by Margaret Paston, who went to live at Paston Hall in 1440. The hall she knew has long since gone, but St Margaret's Church, where she worshipped, has a number of family monuments. West of the church is a magnificent thatched barn some 160 ft long, built by Sir William Paston in 1581; it can be seen from the road.

③ BACTON

The sandy beach at Bacton is protected by groynes and a sloping sea wall. At the southern end of the village, tucked away off the coast road, is the ruined gateway of Bromholm Priory, a 12th-century place of pilgrimage, now a private farm. Bromholm was famous for its supposed possession of a piece of the 'True Cross' used in the Crucifixion, which was recorded as having raised people from the dead and restored sight. In Chaucer's 'Reeve's Tale', the miller's wife appeals for help to the 'holy cross of Bromholm'. The relic was lost after the Dissolution of the Monasteries, and Bromholm fell into decay. The considerable remains of the priory are in a private field, but they can be seen from the perimeter hedge.

Straddling the coast road to Bacton is the vast complex of gasholders, pylons and pipes of the Bacton Gas Terminal, where gas from North Sea wells up to 65 miles away is piped ashore.

④ WALCOTT AND OSTEND

Lined by fine, sandy beaches, the residential villages of Walcott and Ostend merge into one another, incorporating holiday camps and caravan sites. A launching ramp at Walcott Gap is usable only in settled weather.

South of Walcott is the isolated medieval Church of All Saints, which provides the main landmark in the surrounding flat countryside.

⑤ HAPPISBURGH

Soaring above the thatched roofs of Happisburgh, pronounced 'Hazeborough', are a red and white striped lighthouse and the 100 ft tower of the Church of St Mary the Virgin. The lighthouse warns mariners of the dangerous Hazeborough Sands, about 7 miles offshore. For centuries bodies of shipwrecked sailors, including 119 crew of HMS *Invincible*, wrecked on the sands in 1801, have been buried in St Mary's churchyard. Inside the church is a fine 15th-century font, carved with figures of lions and satyrs. In October 1940 German bombs fell in the churchyard, blowing out most of the windows and destroying a statue above the porch door. Shrapnel from the bombs is still embedded in pillars along the aisle.

A car park gives access to the village's sandy beach, where deep pools sometimes form as the tide comes in.

GUIDING LIGHT *Happisburgh Lighthouse warns mariners of the Hazeborough Sands, which run parallel to the coast for 9 miles.*

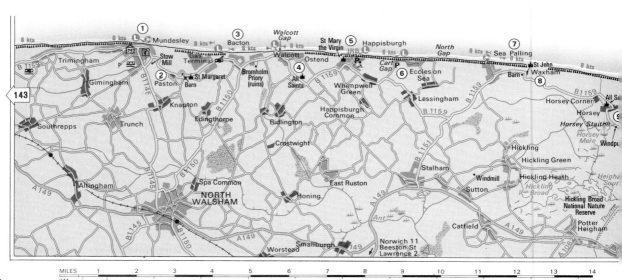

HORSEY WINDPUMP *The structure is a fine example of many seen in the Norfolk Broads, an area crisscrossed by waterways and reedy lakes popular with small-boat enthusiasts.*

⑩ WEST SOMERTON

A quiet village almost 2 miles from the sea, West Somerton is near peaceful Martham Broad, which can be reached along a footpath to the west of the village. East of West Somerton, up a steep lane, is the Church of St Mary the Virgin, whose nave has the remains of a 14th-century wall painting.

The village was the birthplace in 1820 of Robert Hales, the 'Norfolk Giant', who grew to 7 ft 8 in and weighed more than 32 stone. His remains are buried in a sarcophagus in the churchyard. The church itself is dwarfed by ten tall power-generating wind turbines that lie just outside the official Broads National Park.

The grave of the 'Norfolk Giant'

⑪ WINTERTON-ON-SEA

Norfolk is noted for its soaring church towers, and the 132 ft tower of Winterton's Holy Trinity and All Saints is one of the county's finest, dominating the countryside for miles around. Built between 1415 and 1430, the tower remains a landmark for sailors. The 'Fisherman's Corner' inside the church pays tribute to those who have died at sea with a cross made of ships' timbers, ropes, nets, a ship's lamp and an anchor. A road leads north-east from the village to a desert of sand and shingle.

North of the beach are the high, grassy sands of Winterton Dunes National Nature Reserve, where signs warn that adders are common in the area. Rare natterjack toads may also be seen there, along with many species of birds, including reed and sedge warblers, whitethroats and chiffchaffs. A car park at Winterton Beach provides access to the reserve.

⑥ ECCLES ON SEA

Holiday bungalows and beach chalets are strung out along a road which runs behind dunes planted with marram grass. The sea claimed the old village and its church in 1895, and boulders of flint masonry still lie on the beach. A narrow lane leads from Whimpwell Green to the sandy beach at Cart Gap.

⑦ SEA PALLING

A lane from the village of mostly modern houses and bungalows ends at a concrete ramp that leads over high dunes to the sandy beach. The dunes have been wired off to promote the growth of marram grass.

⑧ WAXHAM

The tiny village is best known for its 176 ft barn, the longest thatched barn in Norfolk, which stands just west of the partly ruined, weather-beaten Church of St John. Cars can be parked in the lane near the church, and from there it is a short walk to a seemingly endless beach of soft sand, backed by imposing dunes. The village's farmhouse, known as Waxham Hall, has an encircling wall with corner turrets and a splendid 15th-century gatehouse.

⑨ HORSEY

Lying little more than 3 ft above sea level, the former smuggling village of Horsey has fought a constant battle with the sea. The Saxon All Saints' Church, hidden beneath trees, has a thatched roof, and its round tower is one of 119 such towers in Norfolk. A 2 mile circular walk that takes in the church starts at Horsey Windpump (NT), built in 1912 to drain surplus water from agricultural land. The gallery at the top of the windpump offers views towards the sea, and inland across a wild, watery landscape.

Horsey Mere (NT), an offshoot of the Norfolk Broads, is a breeding ground for geese and many species of wildfowl and waders, which compete for space with small boats. A path leads round the northern edge of the mere.

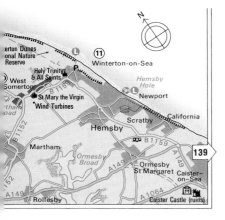

139

PLACES TO SEE INLAND

Hickling Broad National Nature Reserve, 3 miles W of Horsey.

Norwich. Norman Cathedral; Bridewell Museum of Local Industries; Castle Museum; Colman's Mustard Museum; Sainsbury Centre for Visual Arts at the University of East Anglia; St Peter Hungate Church Museum; Strangers Hall Museum of domestic life; Inspire Science Centre.

Sutton Windmill, 4 miles W of Sea Palling. 18th-century mill. Tallest in Britain at 68 ft.

TOURIST INFORMATION

Mundesley (01263) 721070 (summer); Norwich (01603) 666071

Birds in the salt marshes, crabs off sandy beaches

The marshes and shingle banks around Blakeney Point attract birdwatchers all the year round. To the east, set on low cliffs, are the resorts of Sheringham and Cromer, with their fine stretches of sand.

NORFOLK HUES *With its flint walls and red-tiled roofs, Blakeney is typical of the area's coastal villages. Boats moored at high water are left stranded on the mud at low tide.*

① MORSTON

From a car park north of the village, paths explore Morston Marshes, part of Blakeney National Nature Reserve (NT). The saltwater marshes are home to large numbers of redshanks, shelduck and Brent geese. From a quay near the car park, a ferry crosses to the bird sanctuary at Blakeney Point and beyond to sandbanks where seals bask.

② BLAKENEY

Until the 16th century the village was a thriving port, its vessels travelling as far as Iceland. But gradual silting has left a narrow channel that is accessible only to small craft at high tide. Blakeney is now a resort popular with pleasure boaters, birdwatchers and naturalists.

The high street runs steeply down to the harbour between cottages of brick and flint, behind some of which lie large and unsuspected gardens. The old Guildhall (EH) has a well-preserved 14th-century undercroft with an arched and vaulted brick ceiling. South of the village is the vast Church of St Nicholas, dubbed the 'Cathedral of the Coast'. Its western tower, rising to more than 100 ft, is a landmark for miles around; a smaller tower at the eastern end of the church was possibly built as a beacon to guide ships into Blakeney harbour.

From the village quay, a popular 3 mile walk follows the sea embankment to Blakeney Eye and continues back up the western side of Cley Channel to Cley next the Sea. Blakeney harbour is the departure point for boat trips to Blakeney Point.

③ BLAKENEY POINT

The centrepiece of Blakeney National Nature Reserve, a strange and lonely shingle spit stretches north-west for about 4 miles from Cley Eye to Blakeney Point. Most visitors reach the point by boat from Blakeney or Morston; there is also a footpath from Cley. Blakeney Point is home to nesting colonies of terns, ringed plovers and shelduck, and common and grey seals can often be seen from the boats. Plants among the marshes and dunes on the point's landward side include sea lavender and prickly sea-wort.

④ CLEY NEXT THE SEA

A former port left stranded by the receding sea, Cley, pronounced 'Cly', is on the edge of one of Britain's foremost nature reserves. Breeding species in Cley Marsh, a great bed of reeds dotted with brackish and freshwater lagoons, include bearded tits and bitterns, and many other visiting wildfowl can be seen in winter. There is a visitor centre and a large car park on the coast road east of the village.

In Cley itself, traces of the old quay remain along the narrow Cley Channel, dominated by an 18th-century tower windmill. This is now a guesthouse, but visitors can climb to the top for a view of the coast and the surrounding countryside. South of the village is ancient St Margaret's Church, rebuilt on a grand scale in the 14th century.

⑤ SALTHOUSE

Like nearby Blakeney and Cley, the attractive village of flint cottages is a former port cut off from the sea. Lanes lead across the bird sanctuary of Salthouse Marshes to the long-distance Norfolk Coast Path. Salthouse's Church of St Nicholas is a fine example of the late 15th-century style. About a mile inland, at Gallow Hill, are some impressive Bronze Age barrows.

⑥ WEYBOURNE

Just west of the village's Church of All Saints, a lane leads north to a car park by a stretch of shingle known as Weybourne Hope. The steeply shelving beach allows ships to anchor close inshore, and it was heavily defended at the time of the Spanish Armada. In

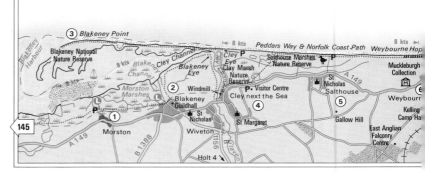

World War II, Weybourne Camp was an important anti-aircraft firing range and training camp. It is now the site of the Muckleburgh Collection, a museum of military equipment with a display of tanks, armoured cars and artillery. East of Weybourne, the shingle shore and marshland give way gradually to higher cliffs.

⑦ SHERINGHAM

A cluster of old cottages in the centre of the town dates from before the coming of the railway in 1887, which turned Sheringham into a popular resort. The busy high street comes to an end at a promenade, which overlooks a sand and shingle beach. A small fleet of fishing boats still goes out for crabs and lobsters, and when not at sea the boats are drawn up on the beach.

The local history museum, housed in three converted fishermen's cottages, contains fossils found in the area. The station is the headquarters of the North Norfolk Railway, called 'the Poppy Line' after the plant that thrives in this part of Norfolk. During the summer, steam and vintage diesel trains travel back and forth along the 5 mile line south-west to Holt. There are also displays of old locomotives and carriages. Sheringham has a golf course along the cliffs, and a leisure pool complex.

About a mile to the south-west is Sheringham Park (NT), designed by the landscape gardener Humphry Repton in 1812. A tower lookout gives panoramic views of the coast and surrounding countryside.

⑧ WEST RUNTON

South of the A149 at the village of West Runton is the Norfolk Shire Horse Centre, which has a museum of horse-drawn farm equipment and a collection of horses. Farther south is the so-called 'Roman Camp' on Beacon Hill – the highest point in Norfolk, at 329 ft. Heathland around the camp, much of it owned by the National Trust, is dotted with early medieval iron workings.

Half a mile west of the village, a track running beside a caravan park and over a level crossing leads to the solitary All Saints' Church. The church has a fine hammerbeam roof, and its tower dates from the 11th century.

⑨ CROMER

The self-styled 'gem of the Norfolk coast', popular as a resort since the end of the 18th century, stands on a low, crumbling cliff facing the North Sea. The long sandy beach, which turns to shingle at East Runton Gap, one mile to the west, is reached by a slipway from the promenade. Old flint cottages and winding streets surround the 14th-century Church of St Peter and St Paul, a grand structure even by Norfolk standards, with towers soaring to 160 ft. Behind the church, several cottages have been restored to create a museum that evokes the changing character of the town over the last 100 years.

Cromer is known for two things apart from its beach: the quality of its crabs and the brave deeds of its lifeboatmen. The most famous of all lifeboatmen is Henry Blogg, who was coxswain for the Cromer lifeboat from 1909 to 1947. During his years of service Blogg and his crew saved 873 people. Blogg is commemorated by a bronze bust in North Lodge Park, near the old lifeboat house, now a museum tracing the history of the station. The modern lifeboat station is housed above a slipway at the end of the pier.

Cromer lies at the eastern end of the long-distance Norfolk Coast Path to Hunstanton, and at the northern end of the Weavers' Way footpath, which travels inland through the Broads to Great Yarmouth, 56 miles to the south-east. A 2 mile clifftop walk east to Overstrand passes a squat lighthouse.

The Henry Blogg Memorial, Cromer

⑩ OVERSTRAND

The former clifftop crab-fishing village is now a popular little holiday resort. The wide sandy beach is reached either by steps or a slipway, both of which are very steep. Because of the dangerous state of the cliffs to the east of the village, there is no access to the sea or seafront between Overstrand and Mundesley, 5 miles along the coast.

PLACES TO SEE INLAND

Blicking Hall (NT), 10 miles S of Cromer. Jacobean mansion, gardens and parkland.

East Anglian Falconry Centre, 2 miles SW of Weybourne. Sanctuary for birds of prey, flight displays.

Felbrigg Hall (NT), 3 miles S of Cromer. Jacobean mansion, gardens and woodland.

Holt Country Park, 6 miles S of Blakeney. Mainly coniferous woodland, nature trail, visitor centre.

TOURIST INFORMATION

Cromer (01263) 512497; Sheringham (01263) 824329 (summer)

POPPY LINE *The North Norfolk Railway, based at Sheringham, was originally a branch line which ran from Cromer to Melton Constable, south-west of Holt.*

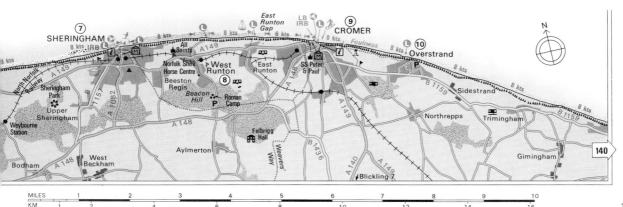

Tranquil Norfolk creeks, and a ridge of striped cliffs

East of Hunstanton is a series of flint-walled villages, cut off from the sea by sand dunes and wide expanses of salt marsh. A string of nature reserves borders a shoreline constantly reshaped by wind and tide.

LAYER-CAKE EFFECT *Hunstanton's crumbly cliffs display brilliant horizontal stripes, with red chalk sandwiched between white chalk and a brown sandstone known as carrstone.*

① HUNSTANTON

The only coastal town in East Anglia to face west has more than half a mile of horizontally striped 60ft cliffs, which have partly eroded into a litter of boulders on the sandy shore. On top of the cliffs an esplanade runs beside a broad grassy swathe, dominated by a disused lighthouse and the 13th-century ruins of St Edmund's Chapel. To the south, the esplanade drops away to gardens and an entertainment centre, including an adventure playground, set in the remains of a pier destroyed by a storm. Beyond is a fairground and a Sea Life Centre, where visitors are led underwater through a glass tunnel. Boat trips go to Seal Island, a sandbank in The Wash where seals bask at low tide.

Old Hunstanton, half a mile to the north, is a village of red-roofed cottages recalling fishing days. The sandy beach is backed by a golf course.

② RINGSTEAD

From the southern end of the village, with its cottages of local carrstone, a track leads along the foot of Ringstead Downs. The valley, cupped by open grassy slopes, hawthorn scrub and mixed woodland, is a small nature reserve. A mile to the east of Ringstead, Courtyard Farm is partly dedicated to organic farming. Trails lead through the estate, over chalkland and through native hardwood plantations.

③ HOLME NEXT THE SEA

This peaceful village, strung along narrow lanes, is where the 93 mile Peddars Way and Norfolk Coast Path meets the sea, after following a remarkably straight course from a point just over the Suffolk border, near Thetford. Holme's dunes and sandy beach lie beyond Hunstanton's championship golf links. Holme Dunes National Nature Reserve has a range of habitats, including environmentally sensitive dune systems. It is home to natterjack toads, now rare in Britain, and some 100 bird species can be seen there at peak migration times. Permits are available from the visitor centre.

The village of Thornham, a flourishing port until the late 19th century, is a starting point for walks along the Norfolk Coast Path; parking can be difficult. Walkers must keep to the path.

④ TITCHWELL MARSH RSPB RESERVE

A large car park and visitor centre serve the reserve, comprising a shingle beach, a reedbed and an area of marsh. Birds visiting Titchwell Marsh include avocets, marsh harriers and, in October, a wide variety of migrating waders.

⑤ BRANCASTER

A field marks the site of the 4th-century Roman fortress of Branodunum, whose name lives on in a different form as Brancaster. From the village centre, a road runs northwards for more than a mile to a beach car park bordered by dunes and a golf course. A sea wall protects some of the sandy beach.

⑥ BRANCASTER STAITHE

A small harbour – a 'staithe' is a bank, or landing stage, in Old English – stands on a channel almost choked with sand and mud. Small boats take visitors to the national nature reserve of Scolt Head Island when tides permit.

Brancaster Staithe has been known for its shellfish since Roman times; some 250 tons of oysters and mussels grown from imported seed are now gathered each year in the creek between the staithe and the sea. Brancaster Staithe merges into Burnham Deepdale, one of the villages in the area jointly

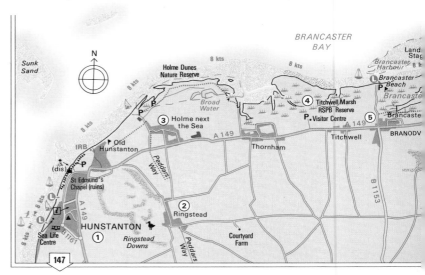

known as the 'Seven Burnhams'. Its Church of St Mary has a Norman font intricately carved with 12 illustrations of the countryman's working year.

⑦ SCOLT HEAD ISLAND NATIONAL NATURE RESERVE

Inaccessibility has contributed to the preservation of wildlife in this reserve. Colonies of common and Sandwich terns breed in a ternery at the western end, which the public may not visit between mid April and mid August.

⑧ BURNHAM MARKET

The small town was once three separate villages which merged after the railway opened in 1866. At its centre, Georgian houses and bow-windowed shops surround a long green. North of the town, Burnham Norton's solitary Church of St Margaret has a circular flint tower and a Norman font. Burnham Thorpe, to the south-east, was Lord Nelson's birthplace; the old rectory in which he was born was demolished in 1802.

⑨ BURNHAM OVERY STAITHE

A group of black-tarred cottages overlook a creek filled with small boats and flanked by a huge area of salt marsh. A mile-long path along the eastern sea wall leads to a boardwalk across dunes and to sands. In summer a ferry runs to Scolt Head Island. To the west of the village a six-storey tower windmill and a water mill are in view from the A149.

⑩ HOLKHAM GAP

A road runs seawards from the A149 to a car park, where a boardwalk through pines, planted to stabilise the dunes, leads to part of Holkham National Nature Reserve. One of Britain's largest coastal reserves, Holkham includes dunes and salt marshes, and a vast expanse of low-tide sands and mud flats that attracts many waders.

⑪ HOLKHAM HALL

The austere Palladian mansion was built for Thomas Coke (pronounced 'Cook'), Earl of Leicester, in the 18th

SAXON TOWER *St Mary at Burnham Deepdale is one of a number of Norfolk churches possessing a circular flint tower.*

century. Its paintings include works by Gainsborough, Rubens and Van Dyck. A Bygones Museum contains antique tools, tractors, cars and farm machinery. The surrounding parkland, landscaped partly by Capability Brown, has a 120 ft monument to a later Coke, known as 'Coke of Norfolk', who revolutionised farming by experiments in breeding, manuring and crop rotation. There is a walled garden, and visitors can wander through woodlands and a deer park.

⑫ WELLS-NEXT-THE-SEA

The old port has three distinctive parts: the quayside, the old streets behind it, and the beach area a mile to the north.

PLACES TO SEE INLAND

Binham Priory, 3 miles S of Stiffkey. Partly ruined 12th-century Benedictine monastery.

Little Walsingham, 5 miles S of Wells-next-the-Sea. Pilgrimage centre; abbey grounds, remains of 12th-century priory; Shirehall Museum.

Thursford Collection, 9 miles SE of Wells-next-the-Sea. Fairground organs, traction engines.

TOURIST INFORMATION

Hunstanton (01485) 532610; Wells-next-the-Sea (01328) 710885

The quay has cafés, shops and amusement arcades. Narrow streets lead up to The Buttlands, a tree-shaded green surrounded by dignified Georgian houses. The sandy beach, almost a mile deep at low tide, can be reached by road, on foot along the sea wall or from Holkham Gap, or by a miniature railway. On reclaimed marshland behind the sea wall is a caravan site and a boating lake. To the east are largely inaccessible salt marshes that form part of the Holkham National Nature Reserve.

On the Stiffkey road is the terminus of the Wells and Walsingham Light Railway, whose narrow-gauge steam trains run for 4 miles inland as far as the town of Little Walsingham.

⑬ STIFFKEY

A track opposite the Church of St John and St Mary leads down to Stiffkey Marshes, skirted by the Norfolk Coast Path. The marsh, forming part of Blakeney and Holkham national nature reserves, is one of the largest ungrazed salt marshes in western Europe.

RAKING IN THE 'BLUES'

As the tide retreats from Stiffkey Marshes, people stride out to the beach with rakes and buckets to gather the local delicacy – the prized cockles known as 'Stewkey blues' because of their bluish tinge. The pronunciation 'Stewkey' for Stiffkey has died out, but is still used to describe the cockles. The main season for cockle-gathering is August to October.

The tide yields its harvest at Stiffkey.

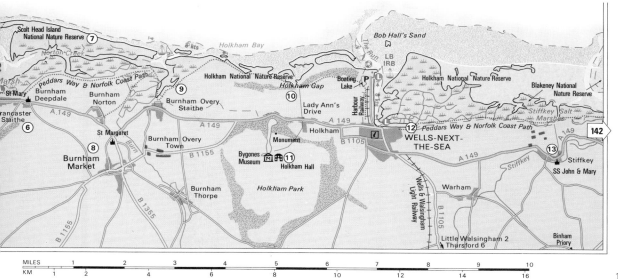

Ancient ports and wildlife havens around The Wash

Protective banks line The Wash's marshy shore, home to numerous wildfowl and waders. Inland, church towers and castles dominate the flat Fenland countryside, drained and reclaimed over the centuries.

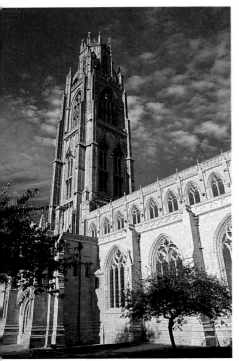

BOSTON SKYSCRAPER *The Gothic church tower known as the Stump soars to 272 ft, dwarfing St Botolph's Church.*

① FREISTON SHORE
A few houses huddle on the landward side of the sea wall which protects the 22 miles of shore from Boston northwards to Skegness. On the seaward side are marshes popular with birdwatchers. The full distance of the wall can be walked, but the marshes should not be explored without checking the tides.

② BOSTON
Cranes and other modern ironmongery around the busy docks share Boston's skyline with the lantern-topped tower of St Botolph's Church, a landmark for fenland travellers and sailors on The Wash for 500 years. A steep climb of more than 360 steps to the top of the tower, known as the Stump, yields panoramic views of the surrounding countryside. Inside the church are misericords dating from 1390, showing intricately carved satirical scenes such as a friar preaching to geese, and memorials commemorating the town's

association with early settlement in America. South of the vast marketplace outside St Botolph's is the 15th-century St Mary's Guildhall, now a museum featuring the cells where the earliest Pilgrim Fathers were held in 1607 before their trial for an illegal attempt to reach Holland and religious freedom. Next door is Fydell House, a fine early Georgian town house used as an adult education centre. Narrow lanes nearby follow their medieval lines, and some retain medieval buildings such as the 13th-century Blackfriars Hall, which suffered severe bomb damage during World War II. The building was renovated in the 1960s as Boston's arts and information centre.

North of St Botolph's, pleasure craft are moored along the shore at the Grand Sluice, built in 1766 to control flooding by the River Witham. Maud Foster Drain, a man-made waterway, runs parallel to the Witham, to the east. Beside it stands the seven-storey Maud Foster Windmill, said to be Britain's tallest in working order and a well-preserved example of a five-sailed Lincolnshire mill. It is open to visitors on Sunday afternoons and Wednesdays throughout the year.

③ HAVENSIDE COUNTRY PARK
A 2 mile strip along the north shore of The Haven, Boston port's link with the sea, has been set aside as a wildlife haven. The waterway is home to waders and sea birds including oystercatchers and cormorants. Inland, trees and shrubs shelter smaller birds such as

Pilgrim Fathers' Memorial

yellowhammers and bullfinches. In the south-eastern corner of the park, a stumpy granite pillar known as the Pilgrim Fathers' Memorial marks the spot where 13 Puritans were seized while attempting to flee to Holland in 1607. After a brief spell of imprisonment, several of them eventually made it to America aboard the *Mayflower* in 1620. Later migrants, who left Boston in 1630, founded Boston in Massachusetts. The memorial is reached on foot by the coast path, or by road through Fishtoft.

④ FRAMPTON MARSH
Miles of saltmarsh, mud flats and sandbanks, incorporating an RSPB reserve, stretch from the sea wall. Sea birds and waders, buntings and finches feed on the saltmarsh plants. They in turn are fed on by hen harriers, merlins and short-eared owls, hunters best seen at dusk as they fly inland to roost. In winter countless migrant waders and wildfowl take over, and the incoming tide drives them off the flats towards the sea wall. There is parking space by a path off the road 2 miles east of Frampton village.

⑤ SUTTON BRIDGE
The small village dates from the late 19th century, when a port was established on the Nene waterway. The docks collapsed a month after opening, and it was only in 1987 that the scheme was revived. Cargo ships draw up by Sutton Bridge golf course, on the west bank, said to be the place where King John lost his baggage train while crossing The Wash in 1216, shortly before he died. The west bank road continues north to a car park by the sea wall near the hamlet of Gedney Drove End. The wall walkway gives wide views over The Wash, whose quiet is shattered at intervals by low-flying military planes crossing the offshore sandbanks for bombing practice. Red flags are flown when training is in progress.

About 2 miles west of Sutton Bridge, Long Sutton's Butterfly and Falconry Park stages displays by birds of prey.

⑥ PETER SCOTT WALK
The road north of Sutton Bridge along the east bank of the Nene provides views over land reclaimed in the 19th century to a picnic site and a 'lighthouse'. Together with its twin across the river, the tower was built not for navigation but to mark the opening of the Nene's new channel in 1831. The buildings are now private houses.

The 10 mile Peter Scott Walk, named after the ornithologist who studied and painted wildfowl from the east bank 'lighthouse' in the 1930s, follows the outermost sea bank from the Nene to West Lynn. To the south, the rich farmland of the Fens is scored by a succession of banks marking centuries of reclamation from marsh and sea, culminating in the outer bank of 1974.

⑦ TERRINGTON ST CLEMENT

The magnificent Church of St Clement is known as 'the Cathedral of the Marshland'. Its unusual 15th-century tabernacle, or font cover, opens to reveal paintings of the baptism, fasting and temptation of Christ. The separate, massive tower has twice been a refuge for parishioners when the sea burst the banks, in 1613 and 1670.

⑧ KING'S LYNN

'Lynn', as locals call it, was called Bishop's Lynn until Henry VIII dispossessed the bishop. The town's eight centuries of prosperity are reflected in its architecture, from the large 13th-century Chapel of St Nicholas, now used as a venue for musical performances during Lynn's annual summer festival, to the spacious Tuesday Market, enclosed by elegant Jacobean and Georgian buildings. On the street known as Saturday Market is the 12th-century parish church of St Margaret. Its Georgian Gothic nave was built after a storm brought the spire crashing down on the medieval nave.

The 15th-century Holy Trinity Guildhall, checked with black flint and pale stone, is used for auctions. Housed in its undercroft are some of Lynn's treasures, including the unique 14th-century silver and enamel 'King John's Cup', and a historical display called 'Tales of the Old Gaol House'. St George's Guildhall (NT), dating from the early 15th century, is the largest ancient guildhall in England to have survived intact. Its upper part is a theatre where William Shakespeare is said to have performed. On Purfleet Quay, the Custom House

PERFUMED FIELDS *Lavender scents the summer air and colours the fields around Caley Mill, near Heacham, before the crop is harvested and its essence distilled.*

and Exchange of 1683, a potent symbol of Lynn's prosperity, is being restored to house a tourist information office. The quay is quiet, with only a few old boats moored alongside, but downstream on the Great Ouse is a busy port. Lynn also has a fishing fleet, and at True's Yard, by Alexandra Docks, the last two remaining traditional fishermen's cottages house a museum devoted to life in a fishing community. A ferry crosses the Great Ouse to West Lynn, where the Peter Scott Walk starts.

⑨ CASTLE RISING

The quiet hamlet is dominated by the ruins of a Norman fortress which was once one of the most important fortifications in East Anglia. The ruins of Castle Rising Castle (EH) rest on massive defensive earthworks reached by a bridge over a dry moat, and the 50 ft walls of the 12th-century keep remain standing. Some delicate and precise carving is still visible on the outer walls. There are fine views of the surrounding countryside from the ramparts. The

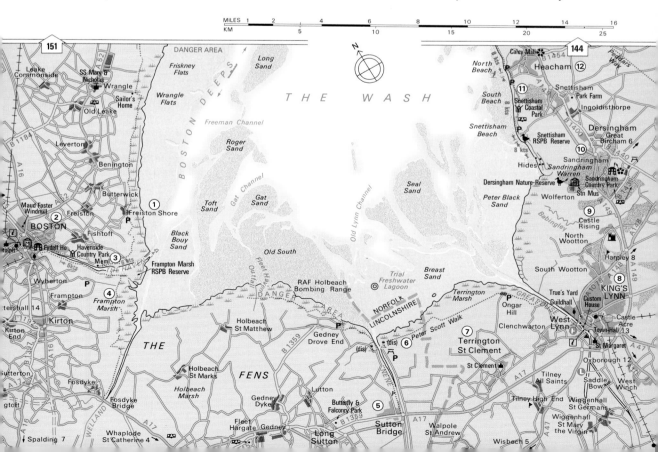

castle is said to be haunted by the ghost of Queen Isabella, wife of Edward II, who was banished there by her son, Edward III, for complicity in her husband's murder.

⑩ SANDRINGHAM

The royal country residence was bought by Queen Victoria for her son, Edward VII, when he was Prince of Wales. He rebuilt it in 1870, creating a cocktail of red brick, yellow stone, cupolas, turrets and gables. The house and grounds are open to visitors most days in summer, except for three weeks in July and early August.

Inside Sandringham are royal portraits and collections of porcelain, Fabergé jewellery, and silver and bronze objects set amid elegant furniture. A museum in the stables contains vintage cars, family photographs and other royal mementos. The spacious grounds have magnificent trees, lawns, shrubs, flowerbeds and lily-strewn lakes, and the estate includes a country park with nature trails and picnic sites.

To the west is the Dersingham Nature Reserve, whose peaty marshland supports rare plants such as round-leaved sundew and bog asphodel. A large nesting population of shelduck occupies its heathland. Birch, chestnut and Scots pine trees shelter fallow, roe and muntjac deer, and many species of bird.

At Wolferton, south of the reserve, the Edwardian royal railway station, disused since 1969, has been turned into a railway museum.

⑪ SNETTISHAM COASTAL PARK

North of the chalets and trailer parks at Snettisham Beach, and behind the sea bank, are stretches of open water, dense reedbeds, scrub and grassland. Among the resident birds are yellowhammers and reed buntings, and summer migrants include whitethroats. On the seaward side of the bank, where there is a hide, are the wildfowl, sea birds and waders for which The Wash is famous. South of Snettisham Beach is an RSPB reserve with four hides.

Near Snettisham village is Park Farm with a deer enclosure, farm animals and ponies, and craft workshops.

⑫ HEACHAM

The large seaside village has two sandy beaches, and there are walks along the sea bank and through riverside gardens. Heacham is Norfolk's lavender-growing centre, and fields turn mauve in July and August. Norfolk Lavender at Caley Mill provides tours of the lavender fields.

TRADING PLACE *At King's Lynn, yachts sail along the Great Ouse, a highway which brought the town prosperity in the Middle Ages as its merchants traded in wool and agricultural produce with the Continent. The twin grey towers of the Church of St Margaret look across Saturday Market Place to Holy Trinity Guildhall (right), one of the town's two 15th-century guildhalls.*

PLACES TO SEE INLAND

Castle Acre Priory (EH), 15 miles SE of King's Lynn. Remains of 12th-century priory.

Great Bircham Windmill, 7 miles NE of Sandringham. Restored windmill.

Houghton Hall, near Harpley, 13 miles NE of King's Lynn. Former home of 18th-century statesman Sir Robert Walpole.

Museum of Entertainment, Whaplode St Catherine, 19 miles S of Boston. Fairground organs and art.

Oxburgh Hall (NT), Oxborough, 14 miles S of King's Lynn. 15th-century moated manor.

Peckover House (NT), Wisbech, 12 miles SW of King's Lynn. 18th-century town house and Victorian garden.

Spalding, 16 miles SW of Boston. Ayscoughfee Hall, medieval manor and Museum of South Holland. Pinchbeck Engine, restored 1833 drainage engine.

Tattershall Castle (NT), 14 miles NW of Boston. 15th-century keep, an example of early brick building.

TOURIST INFORMATION

Boston (01205) 356656; King's Lynn (01553) 763044

A fragile coast protected by concrete and rock

Millions of people visit this flat and sandy part of the Lincolnshire coast each summer, but some stretches still offer quiet and solitude. Climbing a sea wall may suddenly reveal a vast panorama of sand, sea and sky.

① SALTFLEETBY TO THEDDLETHORPE DUNES

The sand flats, dunes and marshes of this national nature reserve support a great variety of animals and plants. In spring and summer the salt marshes are a blaze of sea lavenders and sea pinks. In autumn and winter migrating birds settle on the marshes after crossing the North Sea. A trail among marsh orchids has been constructed for the disabled and visitors wanting an easy route. A nearby RAF bombing range is clearly marked with flags and signposts.

② MABLETHORPE

Set among woodland, the first parish of Mablethorpe was swept away by the sea in 1289, and occasionally at spring tides it is possible to see the original shoreline and tree stumps. On a warm summer's day holidaymakers flock to Mablethorpe's long, sandy beach, funfair and amusement arcades. It is a scene far removed from the 1820s, when Lord Tennyson spent his summer holidays, in what was then a quiet village, roaming the sand hills and endless beaches for poetic inspiration. The Animal Gardens and Seal Trust, in the north of the town, has two rehabilitation pools for sick and injured seals. Ye Olde Curiosity Museum displays thousands of old items such as dolls, toys, kitchen utensils and furniture.

③ SUTTON ON SEA

During floods in 1953 the sea opened a 900 ft gap at Sutton and flooded the land for miles inland. A high, concrete promenade has been built behind the wide, firm sands to prevent another such disaster. To the south an 18-hole golf course hugs the shore.

④ HUTTOFT BANK

The large car terrace at Huttoft Bank is the only place between Mablethorpe and Skegness where it is possible to park a car within sight of the sea. The extensive sea defences comprise giant blocks of Norwegian rock, used to strengthen the sand and shingle beach as well as to resist the sea.

⑤ ALFORD

Although the cattle market no longer exists, Alford continues its tradition as a market town, with the emphasis on craft stalls, which are set up on Fridays in summer. The sails of Alford Mill are a striking landmark. Built in the 1830s and in full working order, the mill is one of only three five-sail mills in Britain. Another is at nearby Burgh le Marsh. The 17th-century Manor House has a folk museum, whose displays include reconstructions of a chemist's shop and schoolroom from the 19th century.

⑥ CHAPEL ST LEONARDS

A centre for smuggling during the 18th and 19th centuries, Chapel St Leonards is now a bright, modern seaside village of brick villas, interspersed with chalets and caravan parks. A 4 mile sandy beach extends to the north and south. There is an ornamental fish farm on the main Mablethorpe to Skegness road.

⑦ INGOLDMELLS

The 13th-century Church of St Peter and St Paul has a 600-year-old font, but the resort of Ingoldmells is more closely associated with Billy Butlin's first holiday camp, built there in 1936 and now known as Funcoast World. One of the original chalets stands in the grounds.

Hardy's Animal Farm, north-west of Ingoldmells, is a working farm where sheep, goats and ducks can be seen.

⑧ BURGH LE MARSH

Soaring above the centre of this old market town is the church tower of St Peter and St Paul. Equally noticeable at the eastern end of the town are the five sails of Dobson's Mill. The mill, built in 1816 and in working order, has a milling museum in its old granary, and is open on the second and last Sunday of each month in summer.

Gunby Hall (NT), 3 miles north-west of Burgh le Marsh, is a Georgian country house set in walled gardens.

MUSEUM PIECE *The labourer's cottage was moved from the village of Withern to Skegness's Church Farm Museum.*

RIDING HIGH *Funfairs are among the attractions for young visitors to Skegness, the latest in a flood of holidaymakers that started more than a century ago.*

CLASSIC OF POSTER ART *Skegness's Jolly Fisherman, created in 1908, advertised rail trips from King's Cross station in London.*

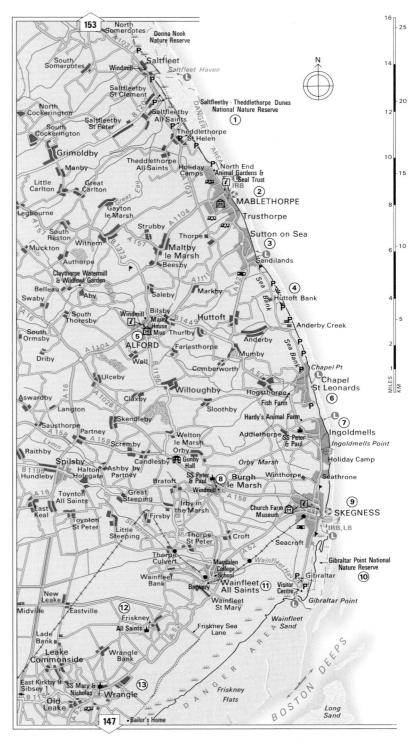

⑨ SKEGNESS

Familiarly known as 'Skeggy', the town is a product of the railway age. The track, which was laid and opened in 1875, provided a link with the industrial Midlands. Along the seafront are acres of formal gardens, as well as boating lakes, indoor fun centres and a model village. There are 6 miles of firm, sandy beach, whose size is gradually increasing each year as the sea recedes. Church Farm Museum shows how the land was farmed in the days before the arrival of tractors. The collection of faithfully reconstructed buildings includes a Lincolnshire 'mud and stud' thatched cottage, giving an insight into the living conditions of an agricultural labourer around 1790.

⑩ GIBRALTAR POINT
NATIONAL NATURE RESERVE

The reserve consists of dunes, rough grazing, fresh and saltwater marshes, and beach and foreshore. It extends for about 3 miles from the southern end of Skegness to the entrance to The Wash. There is a visitor centre, and a network of footpaths leads to hides and an observation platform. Visiting birds include Brent geese, fieldfares, twites and redwings. The reserve provides one of the few regular nesting places on the Lincolnshire coast for little terns.

⑪ WAINFLEET ALL SAINTS

Once an important seaport and market town, said to be on the site of the Roman town of Vainona, Wainfleet today is probably best known as the home of one of Britain's family-run breweries, Bateman's, which offers guided weekday evening tours. The red-brick Magdalen College School was built in 1484 by William of Waynflete, Bishop of Winchester, to prepare students for his other foundation, Oxford's Magdalen College. The school now accommodates a library.

⑫ FRISKNEY

With its 30 miles of roads, Friskney is a large and scattered farming parish. All Saints is an impressive church, begun in 1135. A rare feature of the church is the Georgian 'hudd', shaped like a sentry box and used to shelter a priest con-ducting a graveside funeral in bad weather. A footpath from Friskney Sea Lane leads to three sand banks, from where there is a footpath south-west to Wrangle, 3 miles away. Signs warn walkers to take care and to adhere to the track in order to avoid the RAF bombing range on Friskney Flats.

⑬ WRANGLE

Overlooking Wrangle's tiny green is the 14th-century Church of St Mary and St Nicholas with its medieval stained glass. A path from Sailor's Home, to the south-east, leads to the sea-bank, a wild, marshy area that borders the mud flats of The Wash.

PLACES TO SEE INLAND

Claythorpe Watermill and Wildfowl Garden, 8 miles SW of Mablethorpe. 18th-century mill with visitor centre and rare waterfowl species in landscaped grounds.

Lincolnshire Aviation Heritage Centre, East Kirkby, 13 miles NW of Wrangle. Aircraft museum based on 1940s airfield, with original control tower and air-raid shelter.

Sibsey Trader Mill, 6 miles W of Wrangle. 19th-century windmill. Last mill in Britain with six sails and six storeys.

TOURIST INFORMATION

Alford (01507) 462143 (summer); Louth (01507) 609289; Mablethorpe (01507) 472496; Skegness (01754) 764821

Trawlers and trippers on the Humber's southern shore

Between the Humber Bridge and Grimsby, much of the shore consists of mud flats spotted by the marks of modern industry. East of the traditional seaside resort of Cleethorpes, flat sands extend for miles.

① BARTON-UPON-HUMBER
On the south side of the Humber Bridge is a charming market town of tree-lined streets and Georgian houses. Barton-upon-Humber's greatest treasure is the Saxon Church of St Peter (EH), which retains its 10th-century tower and chancel. Nearby is the 13th-century Church of St Mary, which blends Norman and Gothic architecture. To the south is Baysgarth House, a Georgian mansion with a leisure park within its grounds, where a museum explains the geology and history of the district.

Several nature reserves dot the freshwater marsh of the Barton Clay Pits, former clay workings stretching for 7 miles along the riverbank, and the area attracts birdwatchers, anglers and walkers. The information centre east of the bridge is the start of the Viking Way, which heads west and south for some 130 miles to Oakham in Leicestershire. The Nev Cole Way follows the Humber east and south to Immingham, where it turns inland to skirt Grimsby, ending at Nettleton, some 50 miles from Barton.

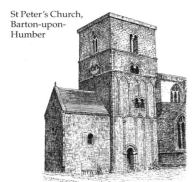

St Peter's Church, Barton-upon-Humber

② BARROW UPON HUMBER
Once a flourishing port, Barrow has the air of a forgotten town but retains some fine 18th-century houses. The road to Barrow Haven from the B1206 passes a mound where a Norman castle once stood. The Beck, a small muddy stream, follows the lane north to the Humber.

③ NEW HOLLAND
Before the Humber Bridge opened in 1981, the Hull car ferry departed from a wooden pier at New Holland, the decayed remains of which can still be seen. Beside an industrial area is a riverside parking spot and the Fairfields Pit nature reserve, which marks the end of the Barton Clay Pits, and there are good views to the bridge and the Hull docks.

④ GOXHILL
Flat pastureland surrounds Goxhill, a quiet village on the edge of a disused World War II American air base. South of the village is a moated farmhouse beside a ruined 14th-century priory; neither is open to visitors. About a mile to the south, partly ruined Thornton Abbey (EH) retains its 14th-century castellated brick gatehouse.

⑤ IMMINGHAM
It was from a small inlet at Immingham that the Pilgrim Fathers set sail for Holland in 1608 on the first stage of their voyage to America, where they arrived in 1620. A 20 ft monument to the pilgrims stands opposite the Church of St Andrew. The inlet where their boat was moored has disappeared under a huge docks and industrial complex. The docks are not open to visitors, but in a former chapel is a local history museum covering their development.

⑥ GRIMSBY
Until the mid 1970s, Grimsby was one of the world's great fishing ports, with a fleet of 200 trawlers which sailed as far north as the Barents Sea. The deep-sea fishing fleet has gone, but Grimsby remains one of Britain's major fishing ports, and there is also a large commercial dock. At the National Fishing Heritage Centre special effects are used to re-create the life and times of the Grimsby trawlermen. Moored outside are several fishing vessels, including the *Ross Tiger*, a trawler which fished off northern Scotland for 30 years. A marina forms part of the docks, which retain their 309 ft Dock Tower, a Victorian landmark visible for miles out to sea. The dockside wholesale fish market is not open to visitors, but there are tours of Alfred Enderby's fish-smoking factory, on Fish Dock Road.

Grimsby's green spaces include the large riverside Freshney Parkway, with a leisure centre nearby, and the People's Park with its classic Victorian gardens and floral hall. At Waltham village, about 4 miles south of Grimsby, a windmill built in 1880 is open to visitors on Sunday afternoons in summer.

GRIMSBY'S FOLLY *By the busy docks rises the Dock Tower, modelled on the tower of the Palazzo Pubblico in Siena, Italy.*

⑦ CLEETHORPES
The coming of the railway in the late 19th century prompted the rise of Cleethorpes as a holiday centre, and visitors arriving by mainline train can still step out of the station straight onto a 3 mile promenade. Family amusements line the walkway north of the pier. On Central Promenade stands Ross Castle, a 19th-century folly with a viewing platform over the Humber estuary.

The sea goes out almost a mile over the sands, but care should be taken with the fast incoming tides which can cut off walkers. Walkers along the seafront get a clear view of Bull Sand Fort and Haile Sand Fort, built during World War I as anti-submarine defences. At

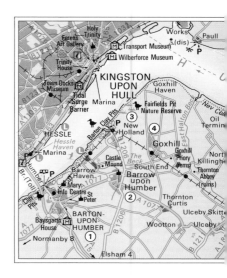

park that includes a lake for boating and fishing. Several lanes lead to the marshes and sand flats along the shore.

⑪ DONNA NOOK
A sprawl of marram-covered dunes, sand flats and marshes extending for 6 miles from Grainthorpe Haven to Salt-fleet Haven, the Donna Nook Nature Reserve is a stopping-off place for some 250 species of migrating birds. Breeding colonies include red-legged partridges and skylarks. Seals bask on far-off sand-banks at low tide, when the sea almost disappears from view. Signs warn visitors that part of the dunes is an RAF bombing range. Red flags fly when the range is in use.

⑫ SALTFLEET
A windmill converted into a private home overlooks the red-brick cottages of sleepy Saltfleet. A rough track along the narrow, muddy harbour of Saltfleet Haven leads to the shore, a vast expanse of flats and mud.

---

the southern end of the resort is the Lakeside leisure area, where a large boating lake with wildfowl is stocked with fish for anglers. The narrow-gauge Cleethorpes Coast Light Railway, which runs through the park, ends a mile to the south-east, near the Pleasure Island theme park and a plaque marking the Greenwich Meridian.

Urns and cremated remains discovered in a Bronze Age barrow at Beacon Hill, Cleethorpes's cemetery, are on display at the town's library.

⑧ TETNEY
A lane leads north-east from a quiet village past Tetney Oil Terminal's huge storage tanks to Tetney Lock, one of a series of locks on the 12 mile Louth Canal, which is now used only for drainage. Footpaths along the embankment on either side of the canal lead north-east to the sea wall which skirts the sand flats and salt marshes of Tetney Marshes, an RSPB reserve with a large breeding colony of little terns.

⑨ HORSE SHOE POINT
Reached from the A1031 by a long narrow road cutting across flat fields, Horse Shoe Point is no more than a spit of land above high-water mark. Low tide reveals almost 2 miles of sand flats. A 3 mile walk west leads to the Tetney Marshes RSPB Reserve.

⑩ NORTH SOMERCOTES
The village of North Somercotes, whose Church of St Mary dates largely from the 13th century, has a small holiday

PLACES TO SEE INLAND

Elsham Hall Country and Wildlife Park, 7 miles S of Barton-upon-Humber. Woodland walks, falconry and conservation centre, children's farm.

Normanby Hall Country Park, 10 miles W of Barton-upon-Humber. Regency mansion, costume galleries, farming museum, parkland.

TOURIST INFORMATION

Cleethorpes (01472) 200220; Grimsby (01472) 342422; Humber Bridge, North Bank (01482) 640852

OCEAN TRAWLER *Grimsby's National Fishing Heritage Centre includes the* Ross Tiger, *a side-winder trawler from which nets were towed and drawn in over the side of the boat.*

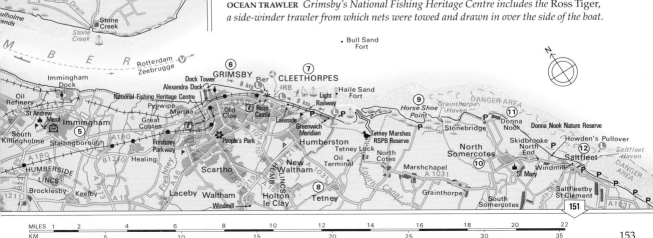

Flat fields and eroding sands north of the Humber

The fragility of low-lying Holderness, flanked by the Humber estuary and the North Sea, is most evident in the curving spit of Spurn Head, where land, water and sky seem to merge into one shifting wilderness.

① HUMBER BRIDGE
Unadornedly functional, the Humber Bridge has the longest single span of any bridge in the world, measuring 4626 ft, and its two towers stand 510 ft above their supporting platforms. The two-lane dual carriageway is used by some six million vehicles a year. There is a toll for motor vehicles, but the crossing is free for walkers and cyclists. The bridge offers magnificent views up and down the Humber estuary.

② HESSLE
The foreshore of the large residential village is a popular fishing spot. Just to the west of the bridge are woodland and meadow walks in the Humber Bridge Country Park. A disused chalk-crushing mill is a reminder of the hundreds of years of mineral extraction on Hessle foreshore. It is occasionally open for visits in summer. Hessle marks the end of the Wolds Way, a 79 mile footpath to Filey in North Yorkshire.

③ KINGSTON UPON HULL
Today a major industrial and commercial city, a modern port, and a centre of learning and research with two universities, Hull came into existence in the early 12th century. Its official name,

Kingston upon Hull, dates from 1299, when the port on the River Hull received a charter from Edward I. The first dock, built in the 1770s, has now been filled in, and is the site of Queen's Gardens, a large open space, and other former docks have acquired new identities. Princes Quay shopping centre has been built on stilts above the water of the former Princes Dock. The Humber Dock has been converted to a marina, where the restored Spurn Lightship is moored. The Town Docks Museum, highlighting Hull's contribution to Arctic whaling in the 19th century and its involvement in North Sea fishing, is housed in the former offices of the Hull Dock Company.

Hull suffered much bomb damage during World War II, but some buildings survive from the 18th century and earlier, especially around the narrow cobbled lanes and quays of the Old Town, on the western side of the River Hull. One house in the High Street was the birthplace in 1759 of William Wilberforce, who devoted his political life to the abolition of slavery. Wilberforce House has a unique collection of relics of the slave trade, as well as period costumes, furniture and silver. Wilberforce went to the old Hull Grammar School,

built in 1583, now a museum which holds changing exhibitions on the city's social history. The large Holy Trinity Church dates from the 14th century and contains some of the earliest English brickwork. Other nearby attractions include the Ferens Art Gallery, featuring old masters and marine paintings, and the Streetlife museum of transport, which covers 150 years of road and rail transport in the Hull area.

Walks along the foreshore and through the centre of the city include one which takes in the Tidal Surge Barrier by the mouth of the Hull, near the popular riverside viewing point of Victoria Pier. Hull's modern dockland, to the east of the city, handles fishing boats, containerised cargo ships and oil tankers, and ferries to Rotterdam and Zeebrugge sail from King George Dock.

④ HEDON
The attractive market town, founded in the 12th century, was once the most important shipping centre on the north bank of the Humber. The coming of larger ships, which could not sail up the narrow Hedon Haven, led to the port being abandoned. Many of the town's medieval buildings were destroyed by a fire in 1656, but among the legacies of its former glory is St Augustine Church, known as the King of Holderness, with a 129 ft high cruciform tower.

⑤ PAULL
From the Salt End roundabout on the A1033, the road to Paull runs between cornfields and a major BP chemical plant before continuing through farmland to the waterfront. A few houses and a neat little disused lighthouse built in 1836 provide the backdrop for a good view of Hull docks and boat traffic on the Humber.

A GIANT'S STRIDE *The gigantic Humber suspension bridge took eight years to be constructed. When it was opened in 1981, a new east coast road route was created.*

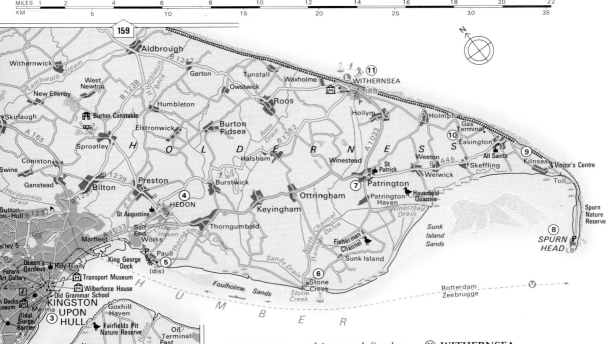

159

152

⑥ STONE CREEK

An isolated beauty spot, Stone Creek is at the end of a lane cutting across low-lying farmland. The hamlet is the base for a sailing club, but strong tidal currents pose a challenge to sailors. Nearby are nature reserves at Fisherman's Channel, an old creek, and at Haverfield Quarries, a large area of reedbeds. Both are home to wintering ducks and waders such as dunlins.

⑦ PATRINGTON

Known as the Queen of Holderness – the 'King' is at Hedon – the Church of St Patrick at Patrington is one of the masterpieces of medieval English architecture. Built between 1310 and 1420, it is designed like a cathedral, with a central tower and spire soaring 189 ft above the ground. The church has some 200 gargoyles, and there are many carvings on the capitals of the pillars. Now a quiet village, Patrington was once a busy market town used as a retreat by successive archbishops of York.

⑧ SPURN HEAD

The sand and shingle Spurn peninsula, some 3 miles long and in places only 30 ft wide, curves in a great hook into the mouth of the Humber. The peninsula, bordered by a sandy beach on the seaward side and by mud flats on the Humber side, is formed from material washed out from eroding shores to the north. Eroded and reformed over the centuries, it is held in its present precarious position and shape by sea defences built up over the last 150 years. Since 1960 the Spurn peninsula has been a nature reserve, and is now defined as Heritage Coast. The spit is a major site for observing bird migration, especially in autumn when visiting birds include Brent geese and Arctic terns. Seals and porpoises may also be seen. There is a charge for drivers using the road to Spurn Head, at the tip of the peninsula; to prevent disturbance to wildlife, dogs are not allowed on the reserve, even in cars. The remains of military defences can be seen near the car park.

The country's only full-time lifeboat crew and their families live at Spurn Head, and a jetty is the departure point for the pilots who accompany ships navigating the narrow and difficult shipping lanes into the Humber.

⑨ KILNSEA

A scattered community straddling the spit of land that ends at Spurn, Kilnsea has two shores. The eastern one is sandy and exposed to the North Sea; the western one is muddy and sheltered within the Humber estuary. The old Blue Bell inn has a plaque indicating that it was 534 yd from the sea when it was built in 1847. Now 190 yd from the sea, it has been converted to a visitor centre and tea room by the Spurn Heritage Coast Project.

⑩ EASINGTON

A few of the houses in this attractive little village are built of sea cobbles – large stones of various colours collected from the beach – and near the medieval All Saints Church is a 15th-century thatched red-brick barn. To the north of the village, however, there is a different scene. An industrial complex includes a British Gas terminal to which the first North Sea gas was piped ashore in 1967, a heliport and a large BP gas gathering station. The low clay cliffs and sand and shingle beach have suffered considerable erosion since the gas terminal was built, and rock defences are planned.

⑪ WITHERNSEA

Attractions at this traditional resort include a long sandy beach and a lively indoor leisure centre. Set well back from the sea, among rows of houses, is a handsome lighthouse, built in 1892. It is now a museum on the work of the RNLI and HM Coastguard, and has memorabilia of the 1950s actress Kay Kendall, who was born in Withernsea.

ROOM WITH A VIEW *The lamp room on top of Withernsea lighthouse is reached by a climb of 144 steps, and gives wide views.*

PLACES TO SEE INLAND

Beverley, 8 miles N of Hull. 13th-century Minster with heritage centre; 18th-century Guildhall; Army Transport Museum; Beverley Art Gallery.

Burton Constable Hall, 8 miles NE of Hull. Elizabethan mansion set in extensive parkland.

Skidby Windmill, 7 miles NW of Hull. Early 19th-century working mill, and museum.

TOURIST INFORMATION

Hull (01482) 223559; Humber Bridge (01482) 640852

THE CHANGING SHAPE OF THE SHORELINE

ALL AROUND THE COAST OF BRITAIN relentless tides and fast-flowing currents are gnawing at the land, and nowhere are the shores more vulnerable to attack than along England's east coast. Most fragile of all is the Holderness area, north of the Humber estuary, the most rapidly eroding stretch of coastline in Europe. The slow warming of the Earth over the past centuries has melted some polar and glacial ice and has made the oceans expand, causing a slight rise in sea levels worldwide. Meanwhile geological forces are causing the British Isles to tilt, with the east and south subsiding by a fraction of an inch each year as northern areas rise.

Over the centuries, Britain is estimated to have gained rather than lost total land area, but in many eastern areas the sea is wearing down the land, breaking up the softer rocks and pushing the eroded material along the coast. On some parts of the Suffolk coast the advancing sea has gained a quarter of a mile in four centuries. Its victims include Dunwich, an important medieval town that the waves' power had largely destroyed by around

VANISHING CLIFF *The potentially disastrous effects of erosion were illustrated by the fate of the Holbeck Hall Hotel in Scarborough, which collapsed into the sea in June 1993 after a huge landslip that sent hundreds of tons of earth slithering down onto the beach.*

1750. In Holderness, farther north, the crumbling white cliffs are retreating at an average of two yards a year, and more than 30 villages have been lost since Roman times. Because the shoreline consists of boulder clay, dumped there as the Ice Age glaciers retreated, it falls easy prey to the North Sea waves.

Man-made barriers can limit damage. Sea walls and groynes – steel, wood or stone walls usually erected at right angles to the coastline – deflect the power of the waves. Long stone barriers known as

MUD FLATS IN THE MAKING *Parts of the north Norfolk coast were reclaimed from the sea in the 17th and 18th centuries and are still used for grazing cattle and raising crops. At Blakeney Point (above) a shingle spit of wave-driven eroded material is still growing, and creates more creeks and mud flats as it moves westwards.*

HEAVY MEASURES
Boulders or specially designed concrete blocks are sometimes placed in front of a sea wall to deflect the force of the waves (below).

THE SEA AT BAY
Groynes (left) and breakwaters (above) can protect a limited area from attack by the sea, but they interrupt the natural movement of sand along the coast.

revetments can be built to protect cliffs or weak points in other defences. In Holderness, towns such as Hornsea and Withernsea are safe behind sea defences, but the coast between them is being eaten away. At Spurn, by the mouth of the River Humber, and at Blakeney Point in Norfolk, the movement of the waves is powerful enough to create and then re-shape large spits of land made of sand and shingle washed there from other parts of the coast. Groynes and sea walls have held Spurn in its present position for some 150 years, but such bar-riers cost millions of pounds to maintain and build up prob-lems for the future. In 1992

LAST MOMENTS *At Pakefield, on the fragile Suffolk coast, villagers empty their homes before watching them topple into the sea in the 1930s. Along many stretches of coast, signs (top) alert walkers to the dangers of crumbling cliffs.*

planners decided to allow natural flooding and as a result the spit will slowly move west, establishing a new natural balance with the sea.

Keeping the waves in check is always expensive. Sea walls cost as much as £8 million a mile to build and last 50-60 years; even a well-built groyne costs £250 000. Moreover, local defences often damage the shoreline as a whole. Groynes that work in one area can cause problems elsewhere by inhibiting the drift of sand needed to maintain beaches – and a beach is one of the best forms of natural defence.

The government, local authorities and conserva-tion bodies now favour 'soft engineering' policies, which emphasise the role of natural features such as beaches and ridges in controlling the sea. One form of this is 'managed retreat': existing sea defences are removed or modified, allowing the water to invade as far as a natural barrier or a new line of defences a little way inland. The flooded area forms salt marshes, absorbing the waves' force and creating a habitat for birds and other wildlife.

At places such as Blakeney Point, and Chesil Beach in Dorset, shingle ridges that were once incor-porated into man-made sea defences or used as a source of building materials are increasingly valued as natural flood barriers. Elsewhere, cliffs are being left to erode, providing rocks and sand for beaches along the coast. Some open countryside, including farmland, may be lost as a result of 'soft engineer-ing', but coastal towns will still be defended.

The programme is cheaper than traditional meth-ods of fighting the sea and helps to maintain a vari-ety of coastal habitats, but it is resisted by many landowners who oppose the loss of their property. Yet a strategy of working with nature rather than against it is gaining popularity given the prospect of rising sea levels over the coming decades, should forecasts of global warming prove to be accurate.

A receding coast near an arrow-shaped headland

As much as 16 ft of land are lost to the tide each year along parts of the coast between Bridlington and Aldbrough. Birds gather at the cliffs of Flamborough and Bempton, while tourists favour the sandy beaches.

① BEMPTON CLIFFS

A lane from the modern village of Bempton leads through cornfields to 400 ft perpendicular cliffs, which in summer are home to more than 200 000 birds. An RSPB visitor centre together with viewpoint information boards give information on the birds that can be seen there, including kittiwakes, gannets, razorbills and puffins. Corn buntings and meadow pipits breed in the grassland and fields on the clifftop. Cruises offering the best views of the cliffs leave from North Landing and Bridlington during the summer.

② THORNWICK BAY

Three tiny beaches, backed by icing-white cliffs topped with slabs of earth and grass, are reached from a rough track off the main North Landing road. A hazardous path zigzags over a triangular nose of land to a middle beach, blanketed by white boulders, where the chalk cliffs have slid onto the shore. Wooden steps lead to the chalk and sand of the western beach. Caves frame the cliffs of the easternmost beach of sand and shingle, where a short headland walk leads to North Landing.

BIRDS OF THE CLIFFS *Razorbills are named after the sharp upper mandible with which they grip their fish prey.*

③ NORTH LANDING

At one time as many as 80 fishing cobles used to go out for herring from the small but pretty cove. Cod and crab are still caught by a much reduced fleet. Fishing trips and excursions round the coast can be arranged in summer. A track from the car park leads to steep steps down a sand and pebble shore.

④ DANES DYKE

The deep 2½ mile gash through Flamborough Head was man-made during the Bronze Age from a natural ravine;

18 ft high and 60 ft wide in some places, the giant incision was intended to isolate the headland from the rest of England. The dyke's southern section forms a nature trail through woodland. Paths along the cliffs overlook a beach of smooth, white stones and lead west to Sewerby and east to South Landing.

⑤ FLAMBOROUGH HEAD

The arrow-shaped headland gets its name from the Saxon 'flean', meaning dart. In Flamborough village, a street of fishermen's cottages and a market place memorial are reminders of a fishing tradition that dates back to the 9th century. The road from the village passes the Old Tower, a lighthouse built in 1674, and continues to another lighthouse built in 1806, which is open to visitors in summer at the discretion of the keeper. Steep steps descend the slopes to the chalk beach of Selwicks (pronounced 'Silex') Bay, where the sea has carved inlets and sea stacks out of the face of the cliff. A mile walk over the headland leads to North Landing.

⑥ SOUTH LANDING

A path leading up steep steps from the boulder-strewn shingle beach is the start of a clifftop walk east across cornfields to Flamborough's lighthouse, 2 miles away. A nature trail begins at the Heritage Coast visitor centre next to the car park. There are picnic areas behind the car park and on the clifftop.

To the west, Beacon Hill was used as part of a chain of beacons built in 1588 to pass news of the approach of Spanish ships during the time of the Armada.

⑦ SEWERBY

At the end of the neat redbricked terraced high street, a road leads past Bondville Miniature Village to 18th-century Sewerby Hall, which houses a small art gallery, a museum and a collection of trophies and mementos of the

ENDURING BEACON *Flamborough Head's chalk cliffs may crumble, but its 85 ft lighthouse has defied winds and weather since 1806. Its present beam has a range of 29 miles.*

BOATS GALORE *A cheerful boating scene fills Bridlington harbour, the setting for a fishing festival every September.*

aviator Amy Johnson, who was born in Hull. A path from the east end of the high street leads behind the hall along the coast to Danes Dyke.

⑧ BRIDLINGTON

Originally two separate townships known as Burlington and The Quay, Bridlington is a bustling resort with donkey rides on the beach, summer shows at the Spa theatre, and a water park with four pools. Burlington, now known as the Old Town, includes the Bayle Museum of local antiquities and the 12th-century priory of St Mary. The North and South Parades, each with a mile-long sandy beach, are divided by the harbour, where there is a museum explaining the harbour's history. From a viewing point on the South Pier fishermen in their keel boats can be seen landing haddock, cod, lobsters and crabs. Fishing trips can be arranged, and there are cruises round the harbour and to the bird colonies of Flamborough Head and Bempton Cliffs.

Park Rose Pottery, 2 miles south-west of Bridlington, includes an owl sanctuary and an adventure playground.

⑨ SKIPSEA

After the Norman conquest, the village of Skipsea came into the possession of Drogo de Bevrere, who married a relative of William the Conqueror. All that remains of de Bevrere's castle is a grassy mound, which can be seen near All Saints' Church. The sand and shingle beach of Skipsea Sands is reached by steps down the sea-gnawed cliffs. There is also access from the holiday camp, 1½ miles to the south.

⑩ HORNSEA

The cobbled cottages and 15th-century Church of St Nicholas in Hornsea's main street are protected as a conservation area, which includes a folk museum housed in a 16th-century farmhouse. The old town is separated from the seafront with its amusements and leisure centre by the golf course and recreation area of Hall Garth Park. Hornsea Mere is Yorkshire's largest

freshwater lake and forms an RSPB reserve of international significance. A path beginning in Hull Road traces the south side of the Mere. The eastern side, where there is a car park, has rowing and sailing boats for hire. Honeysuckle Farm, to the north, has farm animals and a nature walk. Hornsea Pottery and Leisure Park includes 'Butterfly World' and a birds of prey conservation centre.

⑪ MAPPLETON

A recent protection programme, which involved tons of rock being deposited at the base of Mappleton's cliffs, has saved the village from the risk of falling into the sea. A grassy viewing and picnic area overlooking Mappleton Sands is reached by a wide path curving down to the shore. All Saints' Church, built in the 14th and 15th centuries, has long been a landmark for shipping.

⑫ ALDBROUGH

The village is set well back from the sea, but the end of the road to the coast has been torn up by the waves and has disappeared off the edge of the cliff. The sandy beach can be reached down steps that have to be rebuilt every year.

PLACES TO SEE INLAND

Burton Agnes Hall, 6 miles SW of Bridlington. Elizabethan house set in themed gardens.

Cruckley Animal Farm, 7 miles W of Skipsea. Working farm with rare farm animals.

Rudston Stone Monolith, 6 miles W of Bridlington. 25ft Bronze Age stone in All Saints' churchyard.

Sledmere House, 17 miles W of Bridlington. Georgian house, 'Capability Brown' parkland.

TOURIST INFORMATION

Bridlington (01262) 673474/606383; Hornsea (01964) 536404 (summer)

Rugged slopes flanking the beaches of Scarborough

Wild cliffs, prone to landslips, tempt walkers along the coast of the North York Moors National Park. To the south, gentler landscapes embrace the bucket-and-spade resorts of Scarborough and Filey.

① ROBIN HOOD'S BAY

Stone cottages with red pantiled roofs hug the steep slopes overlooking the bay with which the village shares its name. The narrow, cobbled streets and stepped paths twisting down to the sea were thick with smuggling activity in the 18th century. Today, visitors must park at the top of the village.

In the 19th century 'Bay Town', as it is also known, outranked Whitby as a fishing centre. The Fisherhead Museum recalls local seafaring and has displays of the area's fossils and wildlife.

A waymarked walk northwards from the village follows the Cleveland Way to join a disused railway track, making a 2½ mile circuit. 'Bay Town' is also the eastern end of the 190 mile Coast to Coast Walk from St Bees in Cumbria.

South-eastwards, the Cleveland Way leads along exhilarating clifftops. At low tide it is possible to walk along the sandy, rock-littered beach to Stoupe Beck Sands, 2 miles away.

② BOGGLE HOLE

The stream-chiselled valley owned by the National Trust is named after the boggle, or goblin, who was said to haunt its slopes. A steep 5 minute walk descends from the car park at the top of the valley, past a youth hostel housed in a former water mill, to a small cove.

③ STOUPE BECK SANDS

From the crossroads by the disused windmill near Ravenscar, a road cuts precipitously downhill over moorland, revealing the curve of Robin Hood's Bay. Steps lead from the car park behind Stoupe Brow Farm to a mosaic of seaweed, sand, pebbles and rocks.

④ RAVENSCAR

Raven Hall Hotel crowns 600 ft slopes, which plunge to a rocky shore. Built in 1774 as a private house, Raven Hall was visited by George III during his bouts of ill health. The hotel's grounds, with a swimming pool, a croquet lawn and a golf course, are open to non-residents.

In the 1890s, the hotel owner planned to turn the village into a fashionable seaside resort. Streets were laid out, but developers were deterred by the height and unstable nature of the cliffs.

A National Trust Coastal Centre marks the start of a path to the abandoned Peak Alum Works. Alum, produced here from 1650 to 1862, was used in textile manufacture and in tanning.

⑤ HAYBURN WYKE

Beetles, mosses, liverworts and a variety of land and sea birds are found in the secluded valley known as Hayburn Wyke, part of which is a nature reserve. Stone-laid paths, built in Victorian times for day-trippers who alighted at a long-vanished railway station, form a 20 minute circular walk. The trail leads over a stream which cascades onto a boulder-strewn shore, where fossils of liverworts and ferns can be found. Cars may be parked, with permission, in the car park of the Hayburn Wyke Hotel.

Staintondale Shire Horse Farm, to the north, offers cart rides, harnessing demonstrations and a picnic area.

⑥ CLOUGHTON WYKE

An uneven path from the parking area at the end of Newlands Lane, near the village of Cloughton, leads down to the rocky beach of Cloughton Wyke.

A 4½ mile circular walk leading from Cloughton's former station traces part of the defunct railway, and follows the Cleveland Way to Crook Ness and a disused coastguard lookout.

⑦ CROOK NESS

The rocky shore is reached along Rocks Lane from Burniston. There is a small parking area, from where a path drops to a beach of rocks, backed by broken cliffs. To the south, Scarborough Castle appears on the horizon.

⑧ SCARBOROUGH

The resort where sea bathing in Britain is said to have begun is set on slopes overlooking two wide bays. On the knob of land that divides the sands of North Bay and South Bay stands Scarborough Castle (EH), built by Henry II on the site of a Roman signal station. It retains high, buttressed walls and an impressive keep.

The 17th century saw the decline of Scarborough as a fortress town and its emergence as a spa resort. An ornate

OUTLAWS' BAY *No evidence exists to link Robin Hood's Bay with the outlaw after which it is named, but its days when smugglers handled brandy, tobacco and tea were real enough.*

iron bridge, built in 1826, provides a way to the beach from elegant clifftop hotels. St Mary's Church, dating from the 12th century, contains the grave of the novelist Anne Brontë, who, after

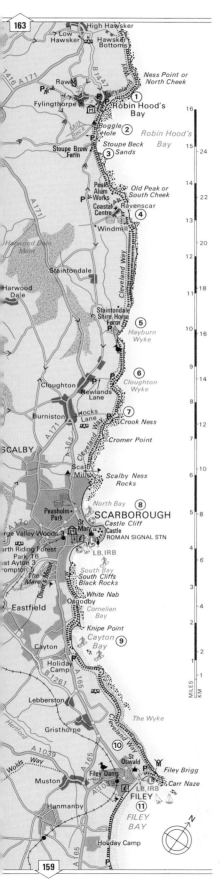

SCARBOROUGH FAIR *Fishing boats crowd the harbour, houses climb the slopes of a wooded cliff, and a Norman castle asserts its presence on the fair face of Scarborough's old town.*

several visits, died in the town in 1849. Cargo boats and fishing vessels berth in the inner harbour, while the outer harbour is reserved for pleasure craft. Rowing, fishing and motor boats can be hired from the harbour slipways. The Heritage Centre, on the seafront opposite the harbour, recalls Scarborough's history from 966 to 1966.

The town's indoor attractions include the Rotunda museum of archaeology and local history, the Art Gallery, the Wood End Museum of natural history and Sitwell family memorabilia, and The Spa complex on the South Bay, with its theatre and ballroom. On North Bay, Peasholm Park is the scene of reconstructed naval battles, using miniature craft, while the Sea Life Centre offers a window onto the life of the ocean. On the town's southern edge, a lake known as The Mere is watched over by Oliver's Mount, which gives views of the resort.

⑨ CAYTON BAY

The bay's northern headland of Knipe Point (NT) is reached along a footpath from the main road. The path begins behind a modern housing estate; there is very limited roadside parking. The short walk leads down to a rocky beach ribboned with sand. Cayton Bay can also be approached along a path starting near a car park by a holiday camp. A 3 mile walk along part of the Cleveland Way leads past the headland of White Nab to Scarborough's South Cliff.

⑩ CLEVELAND WAY

The 110 mile path traces a horseshoe-shaped route, starting inland at Helmsley and following the hills of the North York Moors before reaching the coast at Saltburn-by-the-Sea, 27 miles north of Robin Hood's Bay. The final section follows this glorious stretch of coast southwards as far as Filey Brigg.

⑪ FILEY

Victorian terraces and gardens look down over a promenade and 6 miles of sands. Gift shops and amusement parks cluster at the seafront's northern end. St Oswald's Church has Norman features and an unusual 13th-century effigy of a 'boy bishop'. The Folk Museum in Queen Street has exhibits relating to sea fishing and the lifeboat service.

Reached from the beach or from the North Cliff Country Park, the slender mile-long promontory of Filey Brigg, popular with anglers, marks the ends of both the Cleveland Way and the Wolds Way, a 79 mile route from Hessle Haven near the Humber Bridge. The area has hides for birdwatching at the Brigg and at the country park. Birds such as greenshanks, pochards, ruffs, mallards and teal may be seen from hides at Filey Dams Nature Reserve.

Fishing from a coble

VIKING VESSEL OF THE NORTH

The coble, the robust traditional fishing boat of north-eastern England, is thought to be a descendant of the Viking longship. Designed with a deep bow and a flat bottom suited to the rough waters of the North Sea, the vessel is used today to catch cod, crabs and lobsters. A modern coble is motorised and may have power winches, a radio and even a cabin.

PLACES TO SEE INLAND

Forge Valley Woods National Nature Reserve, 5 miles W of Scarborough. Oak and mixed deciduous woodland supporting varied birdlife.

Gallows Hill, Brompton, 6 miles SW of Scarborough. Home of Mary Wordsworth; Wordsworth and Coleridge exhibition; art gallery.

Honey Farm, East Ayton, 2 miles SW of Scarborough. Live honey bee exhibition.

North Riding Forest Park, 18 miles W of Scarborough. Waymarked walks; picnic sites; viewpoints; forest drive; Dalby Visitor Centre.

TOURIST INFORMATION

Filey (01723) 512204 (summer); Scarborough (01723) 373333

Harbours and relics of old industries among the cliffs

The Cleveland Way footpath snakes its way along the top of massive rockfaces scarred by centuries of mining and metal-working. Inland are secluded dales and the dramatic landscape of the North York Moors.

COVE OF INDUSTRY *On the cliffs by Hummersea Scar, grassed-over workings are relics of the alum industry that flourished along the Yorkshire coast for more than 250 years.*

① SKINNINGROVE

In the 1840s Skinningrove was a small fishing village. A few traditional flat-bottomed cobles still fish part-time from the rocky beach, but the discovery of ironstone in 1848 introduced more than a century of mining, iron-making and steel-making. British Steel Corporation's Skinningrove works, on the A174 near the museum, now makes specialised products from Teesside steel, such as the sculptures along the Cleveland Way footpath, just over a mile north of the village. The result of a local initiative linking sculpture and the environment, the works reflect the

Clifftop sculpture

social history of the area with images including fish, horses and hammers.

Although the area's last ironstone pit, at North Skelton to the west, closed in the mid 1960s, the small stream running through the village is still rust-coloured from iron-ore waste. The Tom Leonard Mining Museum, at the former Loftus ironstone mine, offers visitors an opportunity to experience the underground working conditions of the past.

② HUMMERSEA SCAR

The man-made channel cut into the flat rocks at the foot of the Hummersea Scar cliffs was used from the 17th to the 19th century as a harbour from which ships could carry away the output of local alum works. The rugged cliffside to the east as far as Boulby is scarred with remains of the workings, which supplied the wool, leather-tanning, candle-making and paper industries.

③ BOULBY

At 666 ft above sea level, Boulby Cliffs are the highest point on England's eastern coast. They descend to the sea by stages rather than in a vertical drop, but the summit footpath still affords an exhilarating view. In the spring the cliffs provide nesting sites for kittiwakes, fulmars and house martins. Like Skinningrove, Boulby had both alum and ironstone mines; and jet, a form of fossilised wood much valued by the Victorians for making jewellery, was also found here. A 5 mile trail traces the remains of the industrial sites. Inland is a large mining complex where potash is extracted and refined for use as an agricultural fertiliser. Workings extend 3774 ft underground and stretch for up to 2 miles under the seabed.

④ STAITHES

A narrow valley runs down to a small harbour, surrounded by high cliffs and protected from the open sea by a large breakwater and a protective wall of boulders. From the car park, at the top of the hill near the entrance to the village, streets of closely packed houses, separated by narrow alleys with names such as Slippery Hill and Gun Gutter, wind steeply down to the harbour. When James Cook was a haberdasher's

---

CAPTAIN COOK COUNTRY

The explorer James Cook was born in 1728 in the village of Marton, 2 miles south of Middlesbrough. The cottage where he was born no longer stands, but the site is marked by a granite vase in Stewart Park and nearby is a Birthplace Museum.

It was while he was working at Staithes that Cook first felt the urge to go to sea, but it is with Whitby that he is most closely associated. He was apprenticed to a Whitby shipowner, John Walker, in whose house he once lodged, and the house is now the Captain Cook Memorial Museum. All the ships used by Cook were built at the Fishburn shipyard in Whitby.

Captain Cook and his ship HMS *Endeavour*

apprentice in Staithes in the mid 1740s, 50 fishing cobles sailed out daily, and in the 19th century Staithes could fill three trains a week with cod, haddock and mackerel. Only a few cobles still fish regularly, but tourism now contributes greatly to the village's livelihood. Interest in Captain Cook is tapped by a heritage centre, sited in a refurbished former chapel built for Primitive Methodists in 1880. Near the centre is the start of a circular walk to Port Mulgrave, taking 2 to 3 hours.

⑤ PORT MULGRAVE

A row of cottages perched on the clifftop overlooks a dilapidated harbour, reached by a very steep flight of steps. The cottages were built in the 1850s for miners from the local ironstone mines, which were connected to the coast by a series of tunnels. An information panel by the path on the top of the cliffs reconstructs what the harbour looked like in 1911, at the peak of its activity. Most of the railway and pier were dismantled in the 1930s, and the breakwater was destroyed by Royal Engineers during World War II to prevent the harbour being used by an invasion fleet.

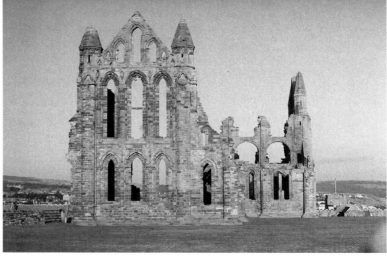

VICTIM OF HISTORY *Danes, Vikings and Henry VIII all had a hand in the destruction of Whitby Abbey. In 1914 it was shelled during a German warship attack on the coast.*

⑥ RUNSWICK BAY

In the 1680s an earlier village of Runswick slipped into the sea overnight, as no motorist grinding down the precipitous approach to the beach-side car park in low gear would find hard to believe. Modern Runswick consists of houses wedged into the unstable hillside at the northern end of a fine crescent of sand, and is popular as a small sailing resort and holiday village.

⑦ KETTLENESS

The entire village of Kettleness disappeared into the sea in 1829. The former rail station, built some 40 years later to serve the local farming community, is now a private residence, isolated in a windswept field. Nearby stands a half-ruined chapel, similarly marooned. On high ground between these buildings and the nearby hamlet of Goldsborough stood a Roman military post; excavated in 1919, it yielded the skeletons of three men, and the remains

of a dog which is thought to have died trying to protect its master from an attacker. Coins found on the site date this incident to some time after AD 423.

⑧ SANDSEND

The small but popular resort of Sandsend has a sandy beach that stretches for more than 2 miles to Whitby. The cliffs at Overdale Wyke and Sandsend Ness, to the north of the village, reveal some of the area's oldest alum workings, dating from 1607. In the early 19th century, a cement works was established at East Row, to the south of the village. Jet was also mined at Sandsend, to be worked by carvers in Whitby.

Part of the Loftus-Whitby railway line, which ran through the village until 1958, has been absorbed into the Cleveland Way footpath. The former Sandsend rail station is now a private house, but the foundation pillars of the viaducts which crossed two streams, Mickleby Beck and East Row Beck, can still be seen. A footpath beside each stream leads into the beautiful Mulgrave Woods, whose owner allows walkers to roam the paths on Saturdays, Sundays and Wednesdays, except in May. In the woods are the ruins of 13th-century Mulgrave Castle.

⑨ WHITBY

The harbour town's superb setting can be viewed in a sweeping panorama from the bridge carrying the A171 across the estuary of the Esk. The river divides the eastern side of the town from the Victorian West Cliff development. The East Cliff is surmounted by the majestic ruins of 13th-century Whitby Abbey (EH). The abbey was built on the site of an earlier monastery dedicated to St Hilda, which housed both monks and nuns and produced nine saints, five local bishops and the Saxon poet Caedmon. The large Church of St Mary, beside the abbey, has a Norman tower but was substantially altered in Georgian times. Inside the church is a variety of Georgian furnishings, including box pews and a triple-decker pulpit. The clifftop graveyard is

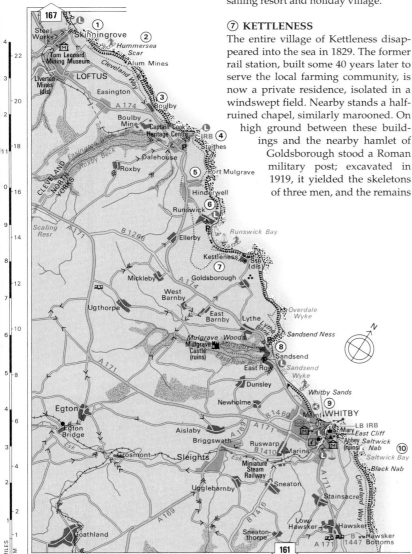

SHELTER FROM THE STORMY BLAST *Bluff headlands protect Staithes, bringing a backwater stillness to the creek where brightly painted cobles lie at rest. Beyond the bridge, the greystone lifeboat station stands at the head of its ramp. Between the jumble of tall houses and snug cottages runs a web of alleys, some little more than 18 in wide.*

set with straggling rows of headstones, pock-marked with salt erosion, and can be reached from the harbour below by a steep flight of 199 steps. Steps, graveyard and abbey ruins all feature in Bram Stoker's novel *Dracula*, and melodramatic tastes are catered for at the Dracula Experience on Marine Parade.

Surveying the lively harbour from the western side of the estuary is the statue of Captain Cook, whose great ships of exploration were all built at Whitby. The Captain Cook Memorial Museum, set in a house where Cook once lodged, has rooms containing furniture of the period, model ships, and drawings from artists who travelled on the explorer's voyages.

Near the statue of Captain Cook is an arch made from the jawbone of a whale, erected to commemorate what was one of Whitby's major businesses in the 18th and 19th centuries. Local captain William Scoresby, inventor of the 'crow's nest' ship's lookout, accounted for an extraordinary 533 whales in his career, almost a fifth of the entire catch brought in between 1753 and 1833. Whitby remains a working fishing port, and herrings are still smoked over oak to make kippers a local delicacy.

Whitby Museum in Pannett Park has one of Britain's finest fossil collections and also jewellery carved from the jet

found on the local shore, used in ornaments since the Bronze Age. The Museum of Victorian Whitby includes a gypsy caravan, the wheelhouse of a whaler, and reconstructions of a 19th-century drawing-room and of various workshops. The Lifeboat Museum in Pier Road contains the last rowing lifeboat to be used in the country.

Holiday activities include sailing from the marina in the harbour, sea and river fishing, and seaside amusements on the fine Whitby Sands. Two miles inland, at Ruswarp, visitors can hire rowing boats to explore the Esk, and a miniature steam railway travels round a half-mile circular track.

⑩ SALTWICK BAY

The Cleveland Way leads east from Whitby along the clifftop to a small stretch of sand between the rocky promontories of Saltwick Nab and Black Nab. Steep steps lead down the cliffside, which has been hollowed out by alum workings. Good fossils may sometimes be found in the rocks on either side of the bay.

PLACES TO SEE INLAND

Clarksons Wood Nature Trail. Starts at disused Liverton Mines in Loftus, 2 miles S of Skinningrove. Plantlife includes unusual orchids.

Egton Bridge, 8 miles SW of Whitby. Riverside moorland village.

Goathland, 9 miles SW of Whitby. Moorland village. Nearby are the Mallyan Spout waterfall and remains of Wade's Causeway Roman road.

Grosmont, 7 miles SW of Whitby. Terminus of 18 mile North York Moors Railway to Pickering.

TOURIST INFORMATION

Whitby (01947) 602674

Sandy havens in a stern landscape around the Tees

In an area of striking contrasts, previously despoiled landscapes are being reclaimed and restored. Windswept clifftops, fine sandy beaches and industrial heritage compete for the visitor's attention.

BRIDGES OVER THE WEAR *Sunderland's Wearmouth Bridge, dwarfing its railway counterpart in the foreground, was opened in 1929, replacing an earlier cast-iron bridge.*

① WHITBURN

A sandy bay stretches south of the neatly tended village of stone houses, whose Church of St Mary has been a coastal landmark since it was built in the 13th century. The clifftop path to the north, towards Lizard Point and South Shields, is edged with wild flowers. A stretch just north of Whitburn is closed occasionally for army firing exercises.

② SUNDERLAND

The industrial town's identity is symbolised by the parallel road and railway bridges spanning the River Wear, but the city's ancient origins are evident at sombre St Peter's Church, built in AD 674 as a monastery. It featured the first glass to be made in Britain, and Sunderland subsequently became a glass-making centre. A guided tour of local glass factories is combined with a visit to St Peter's, where scraps of 7th-century glass can be seen. Sunderland's history, including its six centuries of shipbuilding, is chronicled at the town's museum and art gallery.

Monkwearmouth Station Museum, to the north of the town, has a large collection of rail memorabilia. At Grindon Museum, to the south-west, are reconstructions of Edwardian homes and

shops. To the north-west is the 15th-century Hylton Castle (EH), with a fine display of medieval heraldry.

To the north of the city, on the seafront of suburban Roker, stands a memorial to the Venerable Bede, who was born in the area in AD 673. The cross commemorates in runic lettering the scholar's account of the growth of the Church in England, the first true work of English history. Nearby is St Andrew's Church, built in 1907 with fittings produced by artists of the Arts and Crafts movement.

③ SEAHAM

Modern Seaham developed around the cliffside harbour, built in the early 19th century as an outlet for local mines. In the old village, to the north, is the Saxon Church of St Mary, which contains a 13th-century font and 16th-century pulpit. North of Seaham is a clifftop promenade and a wide stretch of sandy beach; to the south, colliery waste still lies along the shore, although mining has now ceased in the area.

④ CASTLE EDEN DENE

The local nature reserve of Castle Eden Dene is an unusual feature in the former mining landscape south of

Seaham. A way-marked footpath runs 3 miles through a wooded ravine from the coast to the south-western edge of Peterlee, skirting a fast-flowing stream. The 18th-century castle in the centre of the forest is privately owned.

⑤ HARTLEPOOL

The town was a thriving shipbuilding centre until the early 1960s; the old docks are now a marina with several attractions of interest to visitors, including a collection of historic ships. A museum tells the story of Hartlepool from Saxon times, and next to it is a reconstruction of a seaport of the early 1900s, known as Historic Quay. The Headland museum explains the town's maritime past, and nearby is the fine early 12th-century Church of St Hilda.

To the south of the town is the popular resort of Seaton Carew. A long stretch of sandy beach leads onto North Gare Breakwater and the Teesmouth National Nature Reserve. The reserve's mud flats and sand dunes are a staging post for migrating waders such as knots and redshanks, and support a small population of grey seals.

Dividing the reserve into two separate areas is Hartlepool nuclear power station, whose information centre offers guided tours. Beyond the industrial complex of Seal Sands to the south-west lies the vast complex of oil refineries and chemical factories at Billingham.

⑥ STOCKTON-ON-TEES

The heart of the busy market town is its wide high street and the lanes and 'yards' that lead off it. Down one such lane is the Green Dragon Museum, whose exhibits include local pottery and mementos of the world's first true railway, the Stockton and Darlington, which began operations in 1825. The Castlegate Quay heritage centre stands on the river front, near the Tees Barrage and its watersports facilities.

To the north of the town, by the marshy valley of Billingham Beck, are a wetland country park and an ecology

---

SUNDERLAND LUSTRE-WARE
Sunderland's once-numerous potteries were noted throughout the 19th century for their pink lustre-ware. The potteries' iridescent patterns framed transfer-printed scenes, verses and emblems, and the original cast-iron Wearmouth Bridge was a favourite subject. A large collection of local lustre-ware can be seen at the Sunderland Museum and Art Gallery.

This lustre-ware jug dates from about 1820.

park with a visitor centre. The Preston Park Museum, on the southern edge of the town, features a reconstructed Victorian street. The grounds include an aviary and a butterfly farm.

⑦ MIDDLESBROUGH
Middlesbrough's prowess in engineering is reflected in two awe-inspiring bridges across the Tees. The Transporter Bridge, opened in 1911, ferries vehicles and pedestrians on a cantilever system. Newport Bridge was the first vertical lift bridge in Britain when it opened in 1934. The Dorman Museum near the river charts the city's history as a coal-shipping and metal-working town. The Captain Cook Birthplace Museum chronicles the explorer's career. Nearby are 18th-century Ormesby Hall (NT), and Newham Grange Leisure Farm, which gives demonstrations of farming skills. Lazenby Bank woodland, to the east of the town, offers fine views from the Iron Age hill-fort of Eston Nab.

⑧ SOUTH GARE BREAKWATER
The spit of muddy sand is a good place from which to observe shipping at the mouth of the Tees. It is also a haven for shoreline birds, and an oasis of solitude at the tip of an industrial sprawl. The small harbour has fishermen's huts, a yacht club, a coastguard tower and a lifeboat station.

⑨ REDCAR
A traditional 'bucket-and-spade' seaside resort, Redcar is also a busy working fishing port. The town's attractions include a race course and the RNLI Zetland Museum.

To the west is Coatham Marsh Nature Reserve, where sedge warblers are common in summer and herons can be seen throughout the year. The conservation area of Kirkleatham, to the south, features the Old Hall Museum of local history, opened in 1709 as a Free School, and the Owl Centre with flight displays by birds of prey.

⑩ MARSKE-BY-THE-SEA
A former fishing port, Marske-by-the-Sea has a fine stretch of sand that draws many holidaymakers. Errington Wood, on a prominent hillside in New Marske to the west, offers a woodland trail. A few miles to the south-west is Tocketts Mill, Cleveland's last working watermill; it is open to visitors every Sunday in summer.

⑪ SALTBURN-BY-THE-SEA
The advent of the railway in 1861 began Saltburn's transformation from a small fishing hamlet into a holiday resort. The town retains its (shortened) pier, Britain's oldest hydraulic cliff lift, built in 1884, and many fine examples of Victorian architecture. To the south, beside the wooded banks of Skelton Beck, lie the excavated remains of Marske Mill, an 18th-century watermill which went out of use in the 1920s.

GO BY RAIL *Some 70 years after trains brought the first tourists to Saltburn, a railway poster extols the resort's virtues.*

PLACES TO SEE INLAND

Gisborough Priory (EH), Guisborough, 10 miles E of Middlesbrough. Remains of wealthy Augustinian priory founded in 1119.

North of England Open Air Museum, Beamish, 13 miles W of Sunderland. Reconstruction of a colliery village, a farm and a railway station.

TOURIST INFORMATION

Hartlepool (01429) 869706; Middlesbrough (01642) 243425; Saltburn (01287) 622422; Sunderland (0191) 565 0960

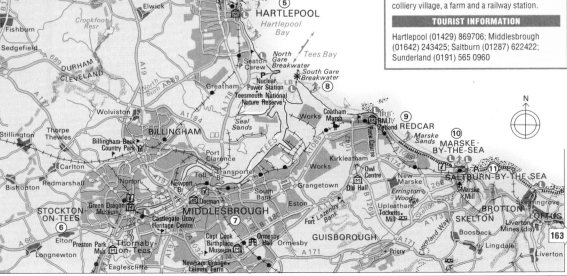

Deserted dunes on a coast where coal once ruled

For centuries coal was shipped south from the ports around the Tyne. Now old industrial scars and tideline coal-dust are disappearing, and lovely white sands fringe massive limestone cliffs and rocks.

① AMBLE

A busy coal-shipping port until the 1960s, Amble is now a small residential and resort town, with a marina, and a boatbuilder's yard beside the River Coquet. The north side of the harbour is formed by a spit of land jutting seawards from Warkworth, whose castle stands out on the skyline. The beach on the seaward side of the spit is a mix of sand, shingle and rock.

To the south of the town is the local nature reserve of Amble Dunes. A mile offshore, a lighthouse marks Coquet Island, the home of eider ducks, roseate terns and many other sea birds. The island is an RSPB nature reserve and cannot be visited, but boat trips round it can be taken from Amble.

② DRURIDGE BAY

The 6 mile crescent of magnificent sandy beach, backed by grass-covered dunes, is the setting for an environmental effort aimed at protecting and enhancing wildlife habitats.

Until 1989 Ladyburn Lake, in Druridge Bay Country Park, was an opencast mine; it is now a venue for watersports. The park, which has a large visitor centre, embraces 3½ miles of beach and dunes, with rocks and rock pools at its northern end.

③ LYNEMOUTH

The town is dominated by industry, in the form of an aluminium smelting works, a power station with pylons radiating from it, and a coal-processing plant. Though the underground pits are no longer mined, the beach is still black with coal dust washed from waste tips along the shore.

④ NEWBIGGIN-BY-THE-SEA

Once a working port, Newbiggin is now a haven for pleasure boats and a few fishing cobles. At the north end of the town's main street, the large Church of St Bartholomew stands alone on a windswept promontory. The sandy beach is backed by a wide promenade and a massive sea wall, while the tideline is black with coal dust and small nuggets of sea-coal.

Neighbouring Woodhorn is the site of a Colliery Museum reflecting what

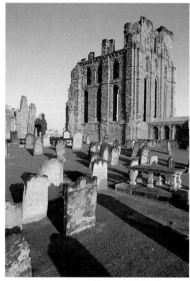

BENEDICTINE RUINS *Tynemouth Priory was built on the site of a monastery destroyed by the Danes in 865.*

life was like in the local mining communities. The former Woodhorn Colliery forms part of the Queen Elizabeth II Country Park, where one of Britain's largest spoil heaps has been turned into a leisure lake surrounded by extensive woodland. Woodhorn's Saxon church, said to be the oldest on the Northumberland coast, is now the Church Museum featuring carved stones and changing exhibitions.

⑤ BLYTH

The most eye-catching feature of this busy harbour town is the row of electricity-generating wind turbines lining the outer sea wall. Just to the north, the Cambois Power Station looms over the landscape. The River Blyth cuts deeply into the coastline, making it a journey of some 5 miles by road from the turbines to the town itself, though the harbour entrance is hardly 100 yd across. South of the harbour, a broad sandy beach extends for 2 miles to Seaton Sluice.

⑥ SEATON SLUICE

The tiny harbour at the mouth of Seaton Burn is lined with massive stones that were put in place in 1660, when a port was created for the export of coal and

salt. The harbour's name comes from a long-vanished sluice gate between the harbour and Seaton Burn.

One mile inland is the imposing mansion of Seaton Delaval, designed by Sir John Vanbrugh in the early 1700s; it is open two afternoons a week in summer.

⑦ WHITLEY BAY

Connected with Newcastle by the Metro railway, Whitley Bay is the city's main seaside lung. Hotels and guesthouses line the seafront, and gardens decorate the slopes between the road and the beach of Whitley Sands, sheltered from the open sea by rocks. The beach ends at St Mary's Island, which at low tide can be reached on foot across a causeway. There are fine views along the coast from the top of the lighthouse, which houses a visitor centre.

The former small fishing village of Cullercoats, just to the south, has been absorbed by Whitley Bay. A cluster of old houses survives round the stone walls of the tiny harbour.

⑧ TYNEMOUTH

The atmospheric ruins of Tynemouth Priory and Castle (EH) stand high on a grassy headland north of the Tyne. The fortified priory, built in 1090 on the site of a 7th-century monastery, had battlemented walls and a powerful gatehouse. It was in military use until after World War II, and the gun battery and magazine can still be seen.

Below the priory, a huge statue of Newcastle-born Admiral Collingwood, Nelson's second-in-command at Trafalgar, gazes out over the Tyne. A fine wide street of mainly 18th-century houses leads up to the priory gates, and there is a Sea Life Centre on the promenade, which extends northwards along the wide beach of Long Sands.

⑨ NORTH SHIELDS

Early in the morning, trawlers sell their catches from stalls on the Fish Quay of North Shields, a mile upriver from Tynemouth. Houses rise in steep tiers from the quayside. Tyneside's connec-

---

'BLOOD' ON THE CLIFFTOP

At the height of summer, large clusters of bloody crane's-bill bloom on the limestone cliffs and lime-rich dunes, creating patches of purplish-crimson, pink, or more rarely, white flowers. In autumn the rounded, deeply divided leaves turn a deep shade of blood-red; this and the small beak-like fruits explain the plant's name.

Bloody crane's-bill
Geranium sanguineum
July-Aug

tion with the pioneering days of the railway are recalled at the Stephenson Railway Museum, which includes one of the early locomotives of engineer George Stephenson. The museum is linked to the Metro railway network by the North Tyneside Steam Railway. The museum and the railway are open on summer weekends.

⑩ NEWCASTLE UPON TYNE
Though its shipbuilding days are over, Newcastle remains the thriving capital of north-east England. Six bridges across the Tyne link the city centre on the north bank with Gateshead on the south bank; they range from the soaring arch of the Tyne Bridge, built for road traffic in 1928, to the small Queen Elizabeth II Bridge, which carries the Metro. A Norman fortress towers high

MARSDEN ROCK *Offshore from the crumbling limestone cliffs of Marsden Bay, near South Shields, stands a huge natural arch where thousands of sea birds jostle for space.*

above the river; there are panoramic views of the town and the Tyne from its battlements. From the upper streets of the city, narrow lanes called 'chares' run down to the Quayside. Newcastle's shops and visitor attractions are concentrated in the pedestrianised streets round Eldon Square. Nearby is the Edwardian Central Arcade, built in elaborate neoclassical style.

North of the centre is the Town Moor, a large open area used for recreation, where freemen of the city still have the right to graze their cattle.

⑪ JARROW
The small riverside town has earned a place in history on three counts. The hunger marchers set out from Jarrow in

1936; the novelist Catherine Cookson was born there in 1906; and about 1200 years earlier the Venerable Bede lived and worked in the Saxon monastery that can still be traced among the ruins of a later Norman foundation. Above the chancel arch of St Paul's Church is the original Saxon dedication stone of AD 685, and one of the windows in the chancel contains stained glass of the same period, made in the monastic workshops. Nearby Bede's World tells the story of Northumbria in the early Middle Ages. The museum includes a reconstruction of an Anglo-Saxon farm.

⑫ SOUTH SHIELDS
The Romans built the fort of Arbeia on a hill commanding the south bank of the Tyne, where South Shields now stands. Digs at the site of Arbeia have revealed the foundations of the granaries that supplied the troops stationed along Hadrian's Wall, and one of the gates has been reconstructed.

At the foot of the headland, South Pier projects a mile into the sea, protecting the sands of Littlehaven Beach to the north. South of the pier, the long sandy beach of Sandhaven faces the open sea; strong currents at the northern end make swimming dangerous.

A path leads south across the grassy slopes of The Leas (NT), where the shore is rocky, and onto the sandy arc of Marsden Bay. Offshore is the spectacular arch of Marsden Rock. Souter Lighthouse (NT) is open to visitors.

PLACES TO SEE INLAND

Morpeth, 8 miles W of Newbiggin. Market town on River Wansbeck, town hall designed by Vanbrugh, 14th-century parish church, castle ruins, Bagpipe Museum.

Plessey Woods Country Park, 5 miles W of Blyth. Riverside and woodland walks.

TOURIST INFORMATION

Amble (01665) 712313 (summer); Jarrow (0191) 489 2106; Newcastle (0191) 261 0691; North Shields (0191) 257 9800; South Shields (0191) 454 6612; Whitley Bay (0191) 252 4494

Cobles and crab pots by the edges of sleepy quays

Great expanses of deserted shoreline are interspersed with tiny fishing villages, such as Craster, famous for its smoked herrings. The Farne Islands, once the hermitage of a saint, are now home to birds and seals.

FARNE ISLANDS VISITOR *The grey seal spends much of the year at sea, coming on shore to bask in fine weather and to breed.*

① FARNE ISLANDS
A scattering of rocky outcrops, within 4½ miles of the mainland, the Farne Islands (NT) form a nature reserve that attracts many nesting sea birds, including puffins, kittiwakes and most breeds of tern. The Farnes are also one of the grey seal's principal breeding grounds. Boats tour the islands from Seahouses harbour, but visitors can land only on Inner Farne and Staple Island.

The largest of 28 islands is Inner Farne, where St Cuthbert built himself in AD 676 a cell of stone and turf and lived alone there for eight years. A 14th-century chapel dedicated to him stands near Prior Castell's Tower, built in 1500, which may mark the site of the saint's cell. The lighthouse and small cottage on Longstone Island are associated with Grace Darling, heroine of a famous sea rescue in 1838.

② SEAHOUSES
Terraces of grey stone houses overlook the little port of Seahouses, where fishing cobles and a few larger vessels land their catches, and fish boxes and crab pots line the quayside. Trips to the Farne Islands leave from Seahouses in summer. The life of a Northumbrian fishing community at sea and ashore is vividly portrayed in the Marine Life Centre and Fishing Museum.

③ BEADNELL
Holiday villas line the coast road through Beadnell, which ends at a strange fortress-like structure beside the sea; the round, honey-coloured stone towers are actually 18th-century lime kilns (NT). The harbour, with an

entrance hardly wide enough for a dinghy, provides moorings for a small fleet of cobles; the fishermen stow their crab pots below the arches of the kilns. From the harbour, the sands of Beadnell Bay sweep south for 2 miles to the rocks of Snook Point. There is a 3½ mile walk beside the dunes to Low Newton.

④ LOW NEWTON-BY-THE-SEA
From the car park above Low Newton, the road leads steeply down to fishermen's cottages and a pub looking over a sandy beach. The Newton Pool Nature Reserve (NT) is a summer breeding ground for more than 30 species of bird, including black-headed gulls, little grebes and mute swans.

The sandy crescent edging Embleton Bay can be reached on foot from Low Newton, or across the golf course from Dunstan Steads. A coast path leads round the bay to Dunstanburgh Castle.

⑤ DUNSTANBURGH CASTLE
The only way to reach Dunstanburgh Castle (NT and EH), on its ledge of basalt rock, is by foot. Cars should be parked at Craster to the south, from which a walk of just over a mile leads to the brooding ruins. Begun by Thomas, Earl of Lancaster, in 1313, the original great gatehouse, with twin towers and walls several feet thick, was converted into the castle keep by John of Gaunt in

GAUNT RELIC *Siege and decay have rendered John of Gaunt's Dunstanburgh Castle a ragged but romantic ruin.*

1380. From the top of one of the towers there are panoramic views over the castle and down the steep incline of the castle rock to the rolling fields beyond.

⑥ CRASTER
Overlooking Craster's little harbour are the smoking sheds where the village's famous kippers are produced. The harbour, which empties of water at low tide, is now used by leisure boats and a few cobles that fish for lobsters and crabs. Behind the car park is the Arnold Memorial Nature Reserve, where bluethroats and other rare birds are sometimes seen in the lush woodlands.

⑦ HOWICK
The coast south of Craster is rugged, and the shore is dotted with rock pools at low tide. Past the Victorian hamlet of Howick, the road turns inland to Howick Hall, a classical 18th-century mansion overlooking a stream, whose superb terraced gardens are open to visitors. The gardens give way to an

FAIRWAYS BY THE SEA *Secluded Embleton Bay, near Low Newton-by-the-Sea, offers sand and solitude to the walker and invigorating sport to golfers on links among the dunes.*

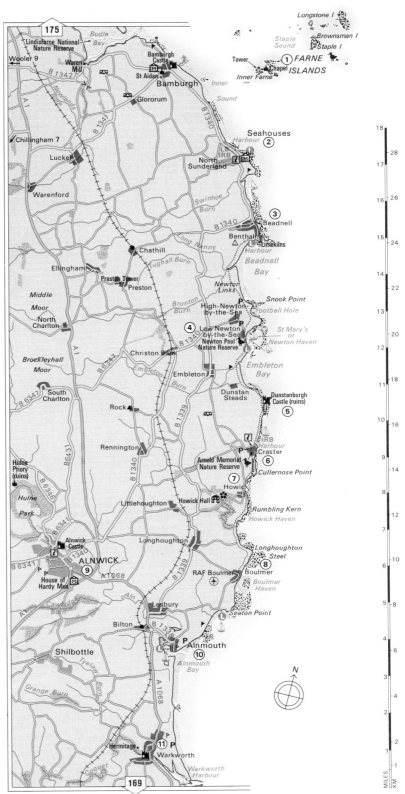

idyllic woodland, full of rhododendrons, through which a path follows the course of the stream as it meanders for 1½ miles down to the sea.

⑧ BOULMER

A gap in the offshore rocks between Longhoughton Steel and Seaton Point makes Boulmer a natural harbour. The hamlet is a fishing community, with fishing cobles moored off the beach overlooked by a row of fishermen's cottages. A large sandy beach is sheltered by a reef of rock offshore. A fighter aircraft stands menacingly at the gates of RAF Boulmer, whose yellow air-sea rescue helicopters can often be seen hovering over the coast.

⑨ ALNWICK

Alnwick's mighty Norman castle, reflected in the River Aln at its foot, contrasts with the sober streets of Georgian stone houses outside its gates. Since 1309 the castle has been the ancestral home of the Percy family, later the Dukes of Northumberland, whose best-known member was the gallant Harry Hotspur of Shakespeare's *Henry IV*. The castle is filled with fine paintings and porcelain, and the Abbot's Tower contains the regimental museum of the Royal Northumberland Fusiliers. In the spacious parkland behind the castle are the ruins of Hulne Priory, built in 1240.

On Alnwick's southern outskirts, the House of Hardy Museum recalls the history of one of the world's leading makers of fishing tackle.

⑩ ALNMOUTH

The village of colour-washed houses at the mouth of the Aln was an important port before the harbour silted up in 1806. Alnmouth is popular with golfers and sailing enthusiasts, as it has two golf links and a wide inland haven for small boats. The shore is sandy, but bathing is dangerous near the river mouth. South of the river is a 3 mile stretch of sand, bordered by dunes.

⑪ WARKWORTH

Enclosed by a horseshoe loop of the meandering Coquet, Warkworth's main street leads steeply up from the river to its splendid 15th-century castle (EH), set high on a grassy mound. Harry Hotspur was born there in 1364. A short walk upstream leads to a landing stage on the south bank of the Coquet, from where English Heritage's only ferry-man rows visitors to the Hermitage, a 14th-century chapel cut out of a cliff.

175

169

PLACES TO SEE INLAND

Chillingham Castle and Park, 13 miles W of Seahouses. Medieval fortress and park.

Preston Tower, Ellingham, 9 miles NE of Alnwick. 14th-century tower.

Wooler, 15 miles SW of Bamburgh. Market town on the edge of Northumberland National Park.

TOURIST INFORMATION

Alnwick (01665) 510665; Craster (01665) 576007 (summer); Seahouses (01665) 720884 (summer)

RESCUE AT SEA: THE INTREPID LIFESAVERS

A DISMASTED YACHT DRIFTING helplessly in a gale, an oil tanker savagely ripped apart by offshore rocks, a child bobbing out to sea on an airbed – dealing with such incidents is all in a day's work for the Royal National Lifeboat Institution, the oldest lifeboat service in the world.

The first purpose-built lifeboat, *Original*, was designed by William Wouldhave, the parish clerk of South Shields, and launched in 1790. *Original* operated off the Northumberland coast for more than 40 years, saving hundreds of lives. During those years lifeboat stations appeared all round the country, with boats paid for by local funds. In 1824, inspired by Sir William Hillary, a member of the lifeboat crew from Douglas, Isle of Man, the National Institution for the Preservation of Life from Shipwreck was founded. Thirty

A LESSON LEARNT *The effectiveness of the cork life jacket was proved in 1861, when the Whitby lifeboat capsized and all the crew drowned, except for Henry Freeman (left), the only man wearing a life jacket.*

years later it changed its name to the Royal National Lifeboat Institution. Then, as now, the RNLI was paid for wholly by public subscription. At about the same time a major item of lifesaving equipment, the cork life jacket, was invented by Captain John Ross Ward, whose contribution to safety at sea was recognised by the gift of a sculpture dedicated to 'the Hero of the Lifeboat'.

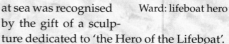

Ward: lifeboat hero

The earliest lifeboats were powered by oars ('pulling boats') or sails. Steam power was introduced in 1890, and superseded by petrol engines after 1904. The last sailing lifeboat remained in service at New Quay in Cardiganshire (Dyfed) until 1948, and a pulling boat operated from Whitby in North Yorkshire as recently as 1957.

Since World War II the number of small-boat sailors and swimmers who get into difficulties near the coast has increased steadily each year; the RNLI now answers an average of 15 calls for help each day. For rapid response to such incidents, small, fast, inflatable inshore lifeboats were introduced in 1963. These now account for about half the RNLI's fleet of

PRIZE-WINNING DESIGN *In 1789 a group of Newcastle businessmen offered a cash prize for a lifesaving boat. It went to the aptly named* Original, *built by Henry Greathead (top), a local shipwright.*

DARING EXPLOITS *One of Britain's best-known sea rescues took place in 1838 when Grace Darling and her father William, the lighthouse keeper on the Farne Islands off the coast of Northumberland, rowed out in a fierce gale to save the shipwrecked crew of the* Forfarshire. *The two became national celebrities, and the Shipwreck Institution awarded them its silver medal. The coble in which they rowed is at Bamburgh's Grace Darling Museum. A later hero was Henry Blogg of Norfolk, who spent 54 years with the Cromer lifeboat service. By the time he retired in 1948 he had taken part in 387 rescues, in which 873 lives had been saved.*

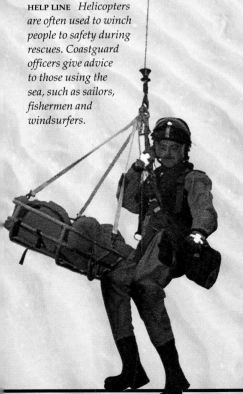

Since the RNLI's foundation, its volunteers have saved more than 126 000 lives. Some 400 lifeboat men and women have lost their lives while on duty; a recent tragedy occurred during a ferocious storm in 1981, when the eight-man crew of the Penlee lifeboat in Cornwall perished while attempting to rescue eight other people from the coaster *Union Star*.

The RNLI is only one of four organisations involved in search and rescue at sea. The others are HM Coastguard, the Royal Navy and the Royal Air Force. The Coastguard has its roots in the Preventative Water Guard, formed in 1809 to patrol coastal waters for smugglers. In 1856 the Coast Guard, as it was then called, assumed new roles, including defending the coast, helping vessels in danger and taking part in sea rescues. Today the Coastguard Agency is a highly sophisticated organisation, responsible for coordinating all civil search-and-rescue operations at sea, responding to marine pollution emergencies, and many other tasks.

Operating from 21 specially equipped centres round the coast, the agency monitors radio distress frequencies and takes 999 calls from the public. As soon as an incident is reported, officers can summon help from the RNLI, the navy, the air force or other ships at sea. The rescue coordination centre at Falmouth communicates by satellite with search-and-rescue centres round the world. The Dover centre monitors sea-going traffic in the Channel and provides a 24-hour radio safety service for vessels. Officers at Aberdeen give training in safety and emergency procedures for offshore oil and gas platforms.

some 280 lifeboats. There are eight different classes of seagoing lifeboat in service, each class named after a British river, and four different classes of inshore boat. Nearly all the men and women who serve in lifeboat crews are volunteers, unpaid except for a small sum to cover expenses. Many of them are fishermen, but they include other workers – people who are prepared to leave their jobs and homes at any time and in all weathers to help with rescues up to 50 miles offshore.

HELP LINE *Helicopters are often used to winch people to safety during rescues. Coastguard officers give advice to those using the sea, such as sailors, fishermen and windsurfers.*

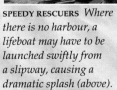

SPEEDY RESCUERS *Where there is no harbour, a lifeboat may have to be launched swiftly from a slipway, causing a dramatic splash (above).*

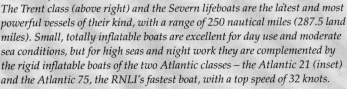

The Trent class (above right) and the Severn lifeboats are the latest and most powerful vessels of their kind, with a range of 250 nautical miles (287.5 land miles). Small, totally inflatable boats are excellent for day use and moderate sea conditions, but for high seas and night work they are complemented by the rigid inflatable boats of the two Atlantic classes – the Atlantic 21 (inset) and the Atlantic 75, the RNLI's fastest boat, with a top speed of 32 knots.

173

Prominent offshore castle and bridges on the border

The north Northumberland coast is characterised by huge tracts of sand, backed by empty grasslands. The only crowds visitors are likely to encounter are the flocks of birds which congregate on the mud flats.

PURPLE PATCHES ON THE DUNES
The clover-like flowers of purple milk-vetch bring striking colour to sand dunes along the shore, and to chalk and limestone grasslands. Some varieties of milk-vetch, so named because they are said to increase milk yield from goats, are added to salads on the Continent.

Purple milk-vetch
Astragalus danicus
May-July

① BERWICK-UPON-TWEED

Standing on a peninsula between sea and river, Berwick has the best-preserved Elizabethan town walls in Britain. During medieval times Berwick passed back and forth between the English and the Scots; today it is an English town situated north of the natural border of the Tweed, a superb salmon river. A small fishing fleet and a few commercial vessels are based at Tweedmouth. The stone pier north of the river, and the southern end of Spittal beach are good places from which to watch the fishermen at work. Three bridges cross over the Tweed at Berwick: the pink stone Jacobean Bridge (1611-35); the four-arched Royal Tweed Bridge (1925-8); and the grey Royal Border Bridge, built by Robert Stephenson in 1847, to take the railway.

Berwick Barracks (EH), constructed in 1721, houses the regimental museum of the King's Own Scottish Borderers as well as the borough's museum and art gallery. The Main Guard, the only survivor of four guard houses built in the 18th century, holds local history exhibitions. In the 18th-century Town Hall is a cell block with grim reminders of past punishments. The nearby Wine and Spirit Museum has displays of old brewing and bottling equipment.

Between the town ramparts and the sea is an open expanse of grassland called Magdalene Fields. The shore is mainly rocky, but just north of the pier there is a small sandy beach.

② SPITTAL

Flocks of swans haunt the mud flats at the mouth of the Tweed, which separates Berwick from the tiny resort of Spittal. The village has a grey-stone, Victorian main street, a promenade and a sandy beach. In season, fishermen net salmon off the beach. A coastal path leads 1½ miles south to Seahouse.

③ COCKLAWBURN BEACH

A turning off the A1 at the village of Scremerston leads over a level crossing to a sandy bay, with craggy outcrops and rock pools at both ends. Paths lead over the dunes down onto the beach. Cocklawburn Dunes Nature Reserve is visited by turnstones, oystercatchers and purple sandpipers. Near the shore are the huge remains of 18th-century limekilns. Lime-loving plants such as vetch grow on nearby spoil heaps.

④ CHESWICK

A few cottages and farmhouses make up the village, and a lane across the railway leads to dunes on the edge of vast sands that stretch at low tide for 4 miles across to Holy Island. Treacherous tides and currents make it dangerous to walk to the island, but walkers on the shore can enjoy exhilarating views.

⑤ BEAL

From a cluster of farm buildings, the road to Holy Island descends gently to the shore, where it becomes a causeway, impassable for about 3 hours either side of high tide. Tide tables stand beside the road. From the car park, visitors have a choice of footpaths round Lindisfarne National Nature Reserve.

⑥ LINDISFARNE NATIONAL NATURE RESERVE

A vast area of dunes, salt marsh and mud flats, Lindisfarne National Nature Reserve stretches from Goswick Sands in the north to Budle Bay in the south. The reserve is internationally known for the large flocks of wildfowl and waders that gather there. In winter the sheltered waters round Holy Island teem with ducks, geese – including pale-bellied Brent geese – and whooper swans. Bar-tailed godwits, redshanks and dunlin are among the more common waders that winter on the flats. Grey and common seals can sometimes be seen basking on the rocks and sands.

⑦ HOLY ISLAND

Cut off from the mainland for 11 out of 24 hours, at low tide Holy Island, or Lindisfarne, becomes the tip of a wide peninsula of sand, the feeding grounds of huge numbers of birds. Christianity came to the island in AD 634, when the monk Aidan crossed the sands to found a monastery, subsequently destroyed by the Danes in the 9th century. One magnificent relic has survived from the monastery, the Lindisfarne Gospels, a masterpiece of English Celtic art, now

HOME ON A ROCK *Impregnable as an eagle's eyrie, Lindisfarne Castle never fired a shot. It was built to defend Holy Island against Scottish raids, and was later converted to a house.*

one of the treasures of the British Museum. Lindisfarne Priory (EH) was begun in 1093. Its fretted and worn red sandstone ruins overlook the beach. The priory museum gives a vivid picture of the life of the Holy Island monks in their isolated community. Mead, once the monks' favourite tipple, is still made on the island.

Outside the priory walls, the tight-knit houses of Lindisfarne village look onto small squares and narrow streets. The jetty is still used by a few fishermen who go out after crabs and lobsters. Beyond the harbour, Lindisfarne Castle (NT) is dramatically sited on a cone of rock. Built in 1550, it was restored from a ruined site in 1902 by the architect Edwin Lutyens. East of the castle are the remains of limekilns, and on the north side of the island are wide strips of dunes backing fine sandy beaches.

⑧ ROSS BACK SANDS

To protect the environment, visitors are not widely encouraged onto this splendid sandy beach, which makes up part of the Lindisfarne National Nature Reserve, but it can be reached after a mile-long walk across the rolling dunes of Ross Links. The sands stretch for 3 miles, but are deserted on many days of the year. The view takes in the fairy-tale outline of Lindisfarne Castle to the north, and the looming bulk of Bamburgh Castle to the south.

⑨ BUDLE BAY

Almost cut off from the sea by a ridge of sand, Budle Bay consists at low tide of weed-covered mud flats that form a sanctuary for flocks of sea birds, which can be watched from roadside parking. It is dangerous to walk far out on the flats because of fast incoming tides. Swans and ducks visit the stream flowing into the bay at derelict Waren Mill, whose history goes back to Saxon times.

Grace Darling lies at peace in Bamburgh.

⑩ BAMBURGH

The village has a row of 18th-century cottages overlooking a tree-shaded green. In the churchyard of the fine Early English Church of St Aidan is a memorial to Bamburgh's own heroine, Grace Darling, who is also commemorated by a small museum run by the Royal National Lifeboat Institution. The museum's centrepiece is the fishing coble in which she and her father rescued the crew of the paddle-steamer *Forfarshire* in 1838.

An outcrop of rock rises 150 ft above the sandy bay of Bamburgh, and its upward sweep continues into the pink stone walls and battlements of majestic Bamburgh Castle, which towers above the village and the rolling dunes on either side. First fortified by the early kings of Northumbria, Bamburgh became the Northumbrian capital under King Oswald, who ruled in the 7th century. The castle was later pillaged by the Danes. A deep well, possibly dating from the 8th century, is Bamburgh Castle's oldest feature. The 12th-century keep retains its original walls, which are as thick as 11 ft in places.

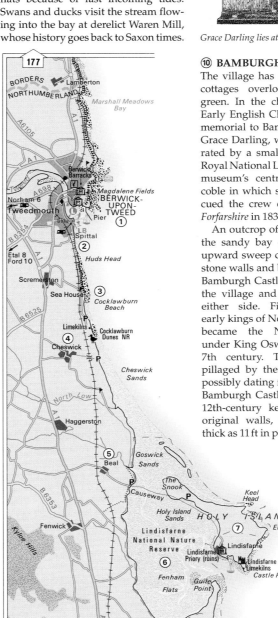

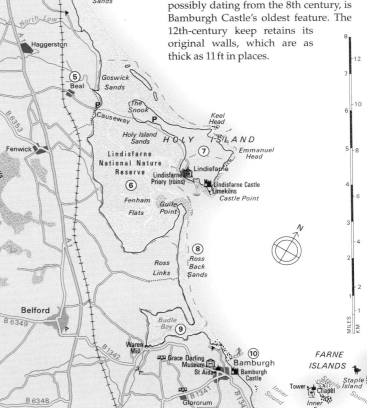

PLACES TO SEE INLAND

Etal, 10 miles SW of Berwick. Single-street village of whitewashed houses leading to ruins of 14th-century Border castle.

Ford, 12 miles SW of Berwick. Heatherslaw Corn Mill, 19th-century working water mill and museum of milling equipment; Lady Waterford Hall, Victorian school with biblical murals.

Norham Castle (EH), 7 miles SW of Berwick. Ruins of Norman keep and 14th-century castle overlooking River Tweed.

TOURIST INFORMATION

Berwick-upon-Tweed (01289) 330733

Fishing ports in the shelter of high, craggy headlands

Storm-sculpted sandstone cliffs, their ledges and clefts alive with many thousands of sea birds, rise to a peak at the magnificent national nature reserve of St Abb's Head, which towers more than 300ft above the sea.

VIEW FROM THE BRIDGE *Seen from one of its bridges, the deep gorge cut by Dunglass Burn is softened by cascades of greenery.*

① BARNS NESS

Scotland's biggest cement works and Torness nuclear power station are dominant landmarks on the south-eastern corner of the East Lothian coast. A short geological trail north from Barns Ness passes the Catcraig limekiln, relic of a once flourishing trade. To the south, Skateraw Harbour, whose breakwater has been pounded to rubble by the waves, is now a picnic area. A coast path skirts the power station, which supplies one quarter of Scotland's electricity, using 40 million gallons of seawater coolant every hour. A visitor centre explains how the system operates. Away from the industrial sites, tiny dune flowers brighten the grassland. Skylarks soar overhead, rock pipits take insects from the drying seaweed, and eiders can be seen offshore.

② OLDHAMSTOCKS

Tucked away in the green Lammermuir Hills, the village of Oldhamstocks has Saxon origins. Restored 18th-century cottages, some with red pantiled roofs, lead to a green where the older market cross and the village pump still stand. Remodelled in 1701, the parish church is the burial place of the Broadwood family, one of whom founded the well-known firm of piano-makers.

③ DUNGLASS

Five bridges cross the wooded ravine marking the boundary between East Lothian and Borders. A pleasant woodland path leads high above Dunglass Burn. Dunglass Collegiate Church dates from the 1440s; its east window was smashed in the 18th century, when the church was turned into a barn, but the building is now well cared for.

A mile to the south, at Cockburnspath, known locally as 'Co'path', is a pre-Reformation parish church whose 17th-century round tower has a stone spiral staircase leading to the gallery and the belfry. In 1503 James IV gave his English bride Margaret Tudor the lands of Cockburnspath as a wedding gift.

④ COVE

The tiny village on top of the cliffs was once linked to the harbour below by a steep road carved out of the rock. The road was closed to traffic in 1991 after a landslip, hastening the decline of Cove Harbour, where only small catches of lobsters are landed. The harbour's most unusual feature is a 60yd tunnel that cuts through the cliffs; wide enough for a horse and cart, it was built to give fishermen access to a curing house that still stands, disused, on the southern side.

The Southern Upland Way, which runs for 212 miles across country from Portpatrick in Dumfries and Galloway, reaches the east coast at Cove.

⑤ PEASE BAY

The cove of red cliffs and tawny sands is backed by a caravan park, beyond which lie the glorious wooded glens of Pease Dean and Tower Dean. Pease Dean is a wildlife reserve of predominantly oak and ash woodlands, where sun-dappled pathways follow the course of burns. Woodpeckers, warblers and wood pigeons may be heard above the chattering streams, and in spring and summer the reserve is covered in a carpet of wild flowers including campions, bluebells, primroses and tormentils, while the air is full of the garlic scent of ramsons.

⑥ ST ABB'S HEAD

Kittiwakes and guillemots, herring gulls, fulmars and puffins throng the cliffs and rock stacks of the superb national nature reserve of St Abb's Head (NTS). Swans, grebes and tufted duck are attracted to the reedy Mire Loch, in a low-lying geological fault. Footpaths and a road from the visitor centre lead to the large natural amphitheatre of Pettico Wick, and climb the sheep-cropped grassland towards Harelaw Hill, which offers wide views to the Cheviots and the Lomond hills of Fife. Scotland's only voluntary marine reserve lies offshore. It is run by local people with the aim of conserving the marine environment and increasing public awareness; wardens conduct 'rock-pool rambles' in summer, describing the wildlife found along the water's edge. On the cliffs to the north-west are the ruins of medieval Fast Castle.

WEATHERED ROCKS *Red sandstone pillars, carved by wind and sea, and washed by a summer shower, rise from a rocky promontory near the village of St Abbs.*

⑦ COLDINGHAM

The priory at Coldingham is one of the glories of this part of Scotland. Now used as a parish church, it evolved from the restored choir of a ruined medieval priory, most of which was demolished by Cromwell's cannons in 1648. The most notable interior feature of the building is the delicate arching and arcading of the north and east walls. In happier times, a thousand retainers of Mary, Queen of Scots, were accommodated in the priory during her 1566 progress through the Borders.

White-capped breakers roll in at Coldingham Sands, and beach huts line

EYEMOUTH QUAY *Trawlers crowding into the harbour carry on an industry dating from 1298, when monks from Coldingham Priory gained the right to fish in the local waters.*

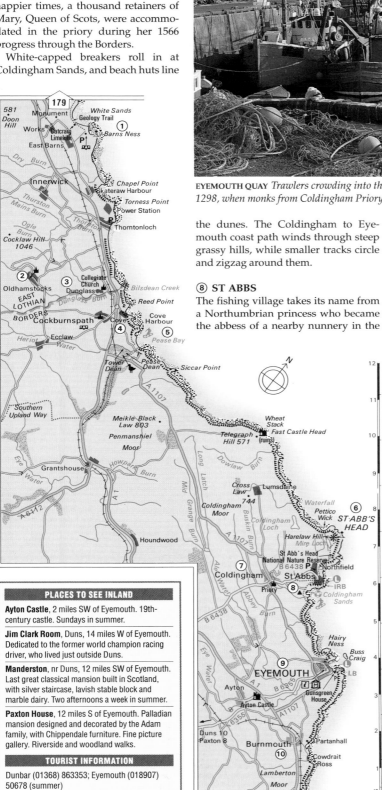

the dunes. The Coldingham to Eyemouth coast path winds through steep grassy hills, while smaller tracks circle and zigzag around them.

⑧ ST ABBS

The fishing village takes its name from a Northumbrian princess who became the abbess of a nearby nunnery in the 7th century. Rows of neat cottages overlook a harbour, and the towering reefs and rock stacks offshore are alive with sea birds. Fishing trips start from the harbour, which is used by sub-aqua divers as a base for the exploration of the marine reserve off St Abb's Head.

⑨ EYEMOUTH

Trawlers and seine-netters tie up at quaysides well back from the outer harbour in this major fishing port. White fish account for most of the town's multimillion-pound landings, but it also exports prawns, crabs and lobsters. The local museum tells Eyemouth's story since 1298, with a tapestry commemorating the 189 fishermen lost in a ferocious storm on October 14, 1881 – Eyemouth's 'Disaster Day'. Although local boats no longer catch herring, a week-long Herring Queen Festival is still held in July, when the fishing fleet, decorated with brightly coloured bunting, escorts the newly elected queen from St Abbs to Eyemouth.

An informative town trail identifies notable buildings such as the Georgian mansion of Gunsgreen House, once a smugglers' headquarters and now a golf clubhouse. The golf course spreads out over a breezy plateau, and there are coast walks in both directions.

⑩ BURNMOUTH

Intercity trains now thunder through the cutting which divides the upper part of Burnmouth in two, but from 1891 to 1962 the village was the junction for the short branch line to Eyemouth, used to transport fish. Burnmouth harbour lies at the foot of a steep hill, with crab and lobster boats operating off a rocky shore. The tiny settlements of Cowdrait, Ross and Partanhall face the sea; 'partan' is the Scots word for crab.

PLACES TO SEE INLAND

Ayton Castle, 2 miles SW of Eyemouth. 19th-century castle. Sundays in summer.

Jim Clark Room, Duns, 14 miles W of Eyemouth. Dedicated to the former world champion racing driver, who lived just outside Duns.

Manderston, nr Duns, 12 miles SW of Eyemouth. Last great classical mansion built in Scotland, with silver staircase, lavish stable block and marble dairy. Two afternoons a week in summer.

Paxton House, 12 miles S of Eyemouth. Palladian mansion designed and decorated by the Adam family, with Chippendale furniture. Fine picture gallery. Riverside and woodland walks.

TOURIST INFORMATION

Dunbar (01368) 863353; Eyemouth (018907) 50678 (summer)

Sea-fringed golf courses and a bird refuge on a rock

Muirfield's bunkers put top golfers to the test.

Sandy beaches are backed by rolling golf courses on this stretch of the East Lothian coast, which has been called 'the holy land of golf' because it has a tradition of playing the game that goes back to the 16th century.

① LONGNIDDRY

Some attractive older cottages recall the appearance of this trim commuter village before the arrival of the railway in 1846. To the north is a golf course, and the dunes and scrubland of Longniddry Bents, a D-Day training area. The village's western boundary is marked by a woodland path in Longniddry Dean. A 4½ mile walk along a disused railway track strikes east from Longniddry through farmland to Haddington.

② HADDINGTON

The town retains many elegant Georgian buildings, but the oldest mansion is 17th-century Haddington House. The house is closed to the public, but its quiet gardens, called St Mary's Pleasance after nearby St Mary's, the largest parish church in Scotland, are open daily. The Jane Welsh Carlyle Museum is based in the house where the Victorian writer Thomas Carlyle courted his future wife. A town trail explores Haddington's network of alleyways and courtyards, and there are riverside walks from Nungate Bridge.

③ ATHELSTANEFORD

The 18th-century model estate village was built on the site of a 10th-century battle in which King Athelstan of Northumbria was defeated by an army of Picts and Scots. The victors were heartened by the sight of a St Andrew's cross, symbol of Scotland's patron saint, formed by white clouds against the blue sky. That vision inspired Scotland's national flag, the saltire, an example of which flies in the village churchyard. Between Athelstaneford and East Fortune, where the airship R34 set off in 1919 on the first return crossing of the Atlantic, is a Museum of Flight and a motorcycle racing circuit. The long whinstone ridge of the Garleton Hills leads west from Athelstaneford to the 19th-century Hopetoun monument, built in honour of a local landowner. There are spectacular views from the tower.

④ ABERLADY

Among the maritime relics of Haddington's former seaport is the custom house beside Kilspindie golf course. The high street has distinctive 18th and 19th-century houses, many with Gothic detailing. A 'loupin'-on' stone outside the parish church allowed riders to mount their horses in a seemly manner.

Aberlady Bay, with its long wooden footbridge, is a nature reserve, whose visitors include ospreys and Montagu's harriers. South-west of the village, 18th-century Gosford House is bordered on its seaward side by dramatic banks of trees. It contains collections of porcelain and Italian Renaissance paintings. It is open three afternoons a week in June and July. Myreton Motor Museum stands inland among fields.

CAR OF YESTERYEAR *A rare 1923 Hillman sports car gleams among the memorabilia at Myreton Motor Museum, near Aberlady.*

⑤ GULLANE

The village's five golf courses include Muirfield, founded in 1891 by the Honourable Company of Edinburgh Golfers and several times host to the Open championship. Gullane is a dignified residential village, but ruined St Andrew's Church, abandoned in the 17th century after it was engulfed by wind-blown sand, is a reminder of natural hazards. The dunes at Gullane Bents have been stabilised thanks to the planting of coastal grasses and bushes, and the village has one of the finest beaches in the district. Footpaths skirt the private Archerfield estate.

⑥ DIRLETON

With its neat parish church and cottage gardens bordering a triangular green, Dirleton has been described as the most 'English-looking' village in Scotland. The tranquil scene is overlooked by the dramatic ruins of a castle, dating in part from the 13th century, whose grounds include a 16th-century dovecot.

Yellowcraig nature trail explores woodlands and shoreline dunes, and offers views of Fidra, a puffin colony island. To the south of Dirleton, the farm at Fenton Barns, which offers local produce, incorporates a golf centre, an archery centre and an archery museum.

⑦ NORTH BERWICK

Famous for its golf, North Berwick blossomed as a bracing holiday resort when the railway opened in 1850. The local museum recalls its Victorian heyday. There are sandy beaches on both sides of a restored harbour, crammed with yachts and lobster boats. In summer,

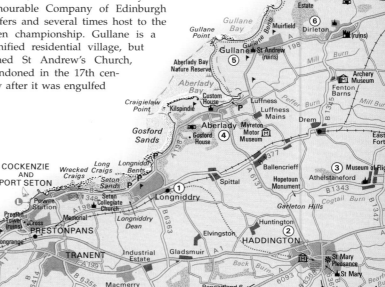

CASTLE OUTLOOK *Dating from the 14th century, Tantallon Castle perches on low cliffs close to the formidable 350ft high bulk of Bass Rock, populated by gannets and puffins.*

weather permitting, there are cruises round Fidra and Bass Rock. Steps and footbridges lead to a wave-lapped point on the narrow peninsula stretching north from the town; there are views of the rock of Craigleith offshore.

North Berwick Law is a towering volcanic remnant. Its magnificent summit viewpoint is marked by an archway made from a whale's jawbones. Tantallon Castle, to the east, was a stronghold of the Douglases until, like so many of the region's castles, it was bombarded by Cromwell during the Civil War.

⑧ BASS ROCK

The core of an ancient volcano, offshore Bass Rock is a mile in circumference with almost perpendicular cliffs. Noted for its gannetry, the rock gave the gannet its scientific name, *Sula bassana*. Among the other sea birds that can be seen there are fulmars, cormorants, razorbills and puffins. It has a light-house dating from 1902, the ruins of a 16th-century chapel and the remains of a fort which was used as a state prison from 1673 to 1701. Boat trips around Bass Rock start from North Berwick.

⑨ EAST LINTON

Although the little town has a colourful centre, its greatest attraction is Preston Mill (NTS), a restored 16th-century water mill. Phantassie Dovecot is a short stroll away. Nearby Tyninghame is a carefully preserved village built in the 18th century for old retainers of the earls of Haddington.

Whitekirk, 3 miles to the north of East Linton, was a medieval centre of pilgrimage, and an ecumenical pilgrimage from there to Haddington still takes place every year. The village's parish church of St Mary was burnt out in 1914, and rebuilt by public subscription. Behind the church is a monastic tithe barn, rare in Scotland.

⑩ JOHN MUIR COUNTRY PARK

Named after the Dunbar-born pioneer of the US National Parks movement, the park has 8 miles of beaches, dunes, salt marsh, pinewoods and open grassland. It is a recreational area as well as a wildlife sanctuary. Footpaths follow the coastline, where shelduck, mallard, teal plover and wigeon can often be seen.

⑪ DUNBAR

Exhibits at the 17th-century Town House show that the ancient burgh of Dunbar was inhabited in Iron Age times. Many of its buildings date from the 18th and 19th centuries. Most substantial of these is Lauderdale House, once a rich magnate's mansion and now divided into flats. John Muir's birthplace in the High Street is a museum, and a clifftop walk is named after him. The 19th-century Victoria Harbour was created by hacking through Dunbar Castle, now little more than a nesting cliff for gulls and kittiwakes. Harbourside dwellings and old warehouses built for a long-gone shipping trade have been restored, and there is a lifeboat museum. The Battery, raised in 1781 on natural basalt columns, is an excellent viewpoint. Sub-aqua divers and sea anglers frequent Dunbar, but the most popular recreation is golf.

PLACES TO SEE INLAND

Glenkinchie Distillery, Pencaitland, 8 miles SW of Haddington. Whisky distillery and museum.

Lennoxlove House, 2 miles S of Haddington. Displays related to Mary, Queen of Scots, and the 17th-century Duchess of Lennox, on whom the Britannia on British coins was based.

TOURIST INFORMATION

Dunbar (01368) 863353; North Berwick (01620) 892197; Pencraig (01620) 860063

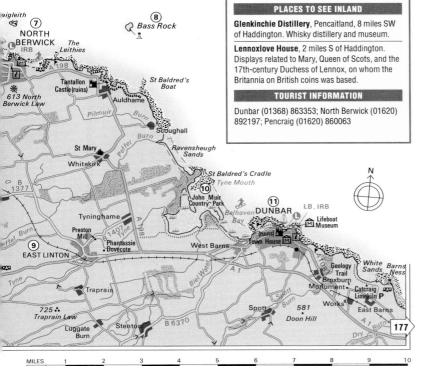

FATHER OF NATIONAL PARKS
John Muir, born in Dunbar in 1838, was a tireless campaigner for countryside conservation who inspired the US National Parks movement. Muir emigrated in 1849, and helped to establish America's first national park at Yosemite in 1890. Muir Woods near San Francisco is among 20 places in America to bear his name.

Proud and alluring skyline of Scotland's capital city

Built on crags and ringed by hills, Edinburgh has superb architecture and beautiful scenery. Container ships visiting its port of Leith share the Firth of Forth with fishing boats and yachts from nearby towns.

① CRAMOND

In AD142 the Romans built a fort near the mouth of the River Almond, whose excavated site can be seen behind Cramond Kirk. The long history of Cramond, now an attractive Edinburgh suburb, is recalled at a museum in an old malt house. Yachts share the narrow river with swans and mallards, and a wooded path follows the Almond upstream. Scotland's shortest ferry route crosses the mouth of the river, and from its western bank there is a 4 mile coastal walk north-west to Queensferry, passing through the Dalmeny estate and beneath the Forth bridges. Another walk along the breezy esplanade leads past picnic lawns to Granton, 2½ miles to the east. Uninhabited Cramond Island can be reached on foot across the mud flats at low water, but walkers should beware of fast incoming tides.

About half a mile inland is Lauriston Castle, a turreted tower house dating from the 16th century.

② GRANTON

Crammed with warehouses, seafood processing plants, boatyards, and storage and industrial sites, Granton is also the headquarters of two yacht clubs, including the Royal Forth, which occupy a fine harbour. Two Georgian mansions, housing the Royal Naval Reserve base of HMS Claverhouse and the old Custom House, face each other across Granton Square.

③ EDINBURGH

Set on a high crag above Princes Street, on a site fortified since prehistoric times, Edinburgh Castle (HS), home of the Scottish Crown Jewels, dominates the city centre. Edinburgh is, in fact, two cities, the medieval town strung

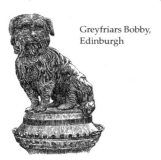

Greyfriars Bobby, Edinburgh

WHITE HORSE CLOSE *The 17th-century building off Edinburgh's Royal Mile, once a crowded slum, originally housed an inn.*

out along the Royal Mile between the castle and Holyroodhouse, and the elegant Georgian New Town. The Royal Mile has narrow closes opening out onto intimate courtyards, and historic buildings, including Gladstone's Land (NTS), a 17th-century house furnished in period style. The royal palace of Holyroodhouse was begun by James IV in the 15th century. In the New Town, the Georgian House (NTS) in Charlotte Square, furnished as it would have been by its original 18th-century owners, is an outstanding example of its period.

Edinburgh is the home of the Royal Museum of Scotland, the National Gallery, the National Library and a host of other art collections and museums. Huntly House is the city's local museum, while the Writers' Museum, in Lady Stair's House, commemorates Robert Burns, Sir Walter Scott and Robert Louis Stevenson. Smaller treasures include the statue of Greyfriars Bobby, a faithful dog which for 14 years guarded its master's grave in the cemetery of Greyfriars Kirk.

The Royal Botanic Garden, on the northern side of the city, displays major plant collections, while less formal outdoor areas include the volcanic hill range known as Arthur's Seat, which can be climbed for magnificent views across the city and the Firth of Forth. The Edinburgh Festival, in August, is one of Europe's great cultural events.

④ NEWHAVEN

Once celebrated for its handsome fish-wives and their distinctive dresses, Newhaven is centred on its old fishing

harbour that has been revitalised through the modernisation of the waterfront. Yachts, cruisers and inshore fishing boats make use of the little harbour, which is dwarfed by neighbouring Leith Docks. Newhaven Heritage Museum, in the restored fishmarket, explains the village's colourful history.

⑤ LEITH

The port of Edinburgh for centuries, Leith maintains flourishing docks, and the quaysides near the Water of Leith have been neatly restored. Sawmills and chemical industries have replaced the claret warehouses. The Clan Tartan Centre at Leith Mills has an exhibition of Highland dress. Visitors can discover if they have Scottish origins, and a clan name and tartan.

⑥ PORTOBELLO

Victorian and Edwardian day-trippers flocked to Edinburgh's beach resort, given its exotic name by its founder, a veteran of the 1739 battle of Puerto Bello in Panama. The town has been spruced up in recent years. The once polluted sands are now cleaned every day; several impressive buildings on the promenade have been refurbished; and funfairs and amusement arcades cluster at the promenade's western end.

⑦ MUSSELBURGH

Known as the 'honest town' since 1332, when its people cared for the dying Regent of Scotland, the Earl of Moray, without any thought of reward, Musselburgh retains a fine legacy of 18th and 19th-century buildings and monuments. A town trail recalls the many battles that Musselburgh was involved in, and explores the parts such men as Oliver Cromwell and Sir Walter Scott have played in its history. There is a

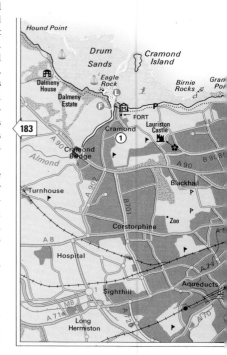

EDINBURGH EVENTIDE *Calton Hill gives a view of the floodlit castle. To the right is the silhouette of the Scott Monument.*

3 mile riverside walk along the Esk south-east to Whitecraig. The harbour at Fisherrow is popular with yachting enthusiasts. Formed round artificial lagoons, Levenhall Links has watersports areas, a bird reserve and a golfing practice ground. Inland, Inveresk is a quiet village where visitors can enjoy the gardens of Inveresk Lodge (NTS).

⑧ PRESTONPANS

A concrete promenade runs along the shoreline where the salt pans which gave the town its name were once located. The parish church looks seawards over gardens. Set back from the waterside, the 17th-century market cross is surmounted by a royal unicorn. There is a huge, well-preserved dovecot close by from the same era, and the ruins of 15th-century Preston Tower survive in a walled garden.

East of the town is a memorial to the 1745 Battle of Prestonpans. A nearby viewpoint looks across the Edinburgh skyline and the Firth of Forth. To the south-west is the industrial museum of Prestongrange, which includes a beam engine and several colliery locomotives, 'in steam' on summer Sundays.

⑨ COCKENZIE AND PORT SETON

Presiding over the twin villages is coal-fired Cockenzie power station. Cockenzie's harbour has a boat repair yard, while Port Seton's accommodates fishing vessels, where fish traders and curers do business. Peacocks parade on the lawns of Seton Collegiate Church (HS), which stands to the south-east.

PLACES TO SEE INLAND

Crichton Castle (HS), 9 miles SE of Musselburgh. Handsome, essentially 14th-century castle commanding the Tyne valley.

Dalkeith House Country Park, 8 miles SE of Edinburgh. Nature trails and Victorian buildings in riverside estate.

Edinburgh Butterfly and Insect World, 5 miles SE of Edinburgh. Displays of butterflies, scorpions, tarantulas and bees.

Scottish Mining Museum, Newtongrange, 9 miles SE of Edinburgh. Guided tours by former miners of the extensive Lady Victoria Colliery.

TOURIST INFORMATION

Edinburgh (0131) 557 1700; Old Craighall, Musselburgh (0131) 653 6172

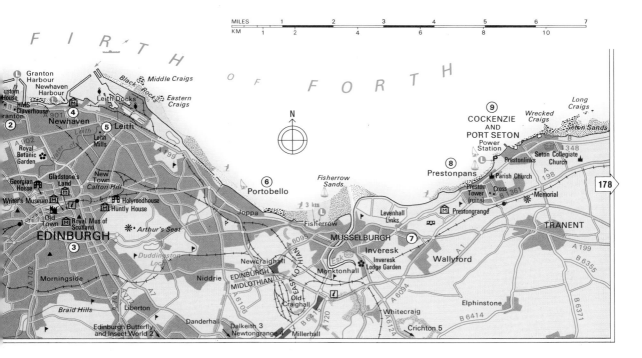

Mansions beside the Forth, and a king's island abbey

Though shipbuilding days are over, the Forth Rail Bridge remains as a symbol of the triumphs of Victorian engineering. In contrast, the elegant road bridge alongside is a testament to modern technology.

① GRANGEMOUTH

The town was established as the eastern terminal port of the Forth and Clyde Canal, which opened in 1790 but is now closed. Although shipbuilding has ended and dockside buildings have been cleared, Grangemouth still has considerable commercial traffic. Petrochemicals are now its main preoccupation, and the development of the industry is illustrated at the BP Exhibition Centre. The town's history, including that of its short-lived airport, which was used as a training ground during World War II, is described in the local museum. Half a mile away, the Museum Workshop displays restored vehicles, along with domestic, agricultural and industrial machinery.

Beside the golf course at Polmonthill, south-east of the town, a dry ski slope plunges down parallel to the course of the Antonine Wall, built by the Romans around AD142. The wall was a rampart of soil and turf on a stone foundation, which originally ran from Old Kilpatrick on the Clyde to Carriden on the Forth. Parts of it can still be seen.

② MUIRAVONSIDE COUNTRY PARK

The area of parkland and woods that makes up the Muiravonside estate includes a visitor centre and, among other buildings, a 17th-century dovecote. A footpath along the River Avon is flanked by oak, ash, beech, birch and hazel trees. More than 80 species of bird have been sighted in the park, including woodpeckers and dippers.

LINLITHGOW PALACE *The 19th-century parapet bears the badges of the four orders of knighthood to which James V belonged.*

③ LINLITHGOW

Founded in the 12th century, the burgh of Linlithgow is one of Scotland's oldest county towns. Linlithgow Palace (HS) was a residence of the Stuart monarchs. James V and his daughter Mary, Queen of Scots, were both born here. The palace stands on the banks of Linlithgow Loch, a natural loch where there is good fishing for brown and rainbow trout. The calm waters attract small-boat sailors and windsurfing enthusiasts. Careful management of the loch ensures that watersports do not interfere with the bird life that congregates there, including swans, coots, great crested grebes and cormorants. Beside the palace is the majestic, mainly 13th-century Church of St Michael. The nearby Renaissance-style Town House, built in 1670, has an intricately carved well outside, the work of a one-handed stonemason called Robert Gray.

④ UNION CANAL

A museum at Linlithgow's Manse Road Basin, run by the Union Canal Society, tells the story of Scotland's only contour canal, which has no locks. Opened in 1822, the canal runs between Edinburgh and Falkirk. Although blocked in some places, it is suitable for boating, angling and walking. The society operates weekend cruises to Avon aqueduct, south-west of the town.

⑤ BO'NESS

The town flourished during the Industrial Revolution, and became Scotland's third most important port. Its prosperity came from coal, iron-founding, salt, whaling and pottery-making, as recalled in Kinneil Museum in the Kinneil estate. Walks starting at the museum take in the sites of a Roman fortlet, a village which was abandoned as Bo'ness grew, and the ruined cottage, built in 1769, where James Watt experimented with steam engines.

A town trail in Bo'ness identifies many 18th and 19th-century houses and commercial buildings. Among the fascinating exhibits at the Museum of Communication is a 1928 Fultoscope, a forerunner of the fax machine. Walks by the pebbly shore and scrubland lead a mile east and 3 miles west along the

Firth of Forth, and cross the territory of birds such as skylarks and goldfinches. Terns fly offshore, while wildfowl and waders favour the tidal mud flats.

⑥ BO'NESS AND KINNEIL RAILWAY

On the northern outskirts of Bo'ness is Bo'ness station, created on a vacant site by the Scottish Railway Preservation Society. The station, now the society's headquarters, has a trail that introduces visitors to a collection of steam locomotives and rolling stock. A journey by steam train to Birkhill, taking 17 minutes, can be combined with guided tours of Birkhill Clay Mine, where fire clay used to make fire resistant bricks was processed until 1980. The fossils of giant tree ferns living 300 million years ago can also be seen in the mine.

BACK ON TRACK *The locomotive* Maude, *built in 1891, has been restored to working order at the Bo'ness and Kinneil Railway.*

⑦ BRIDGENESS AND CARRIDEN

These once-separate villages now form a large suburb of Bo'ness. A replica of a distance slab from the Antonine Wall can be seen in Harbour Street. Bridgeness Tower, built in 1750 as a windmill and later adapted as an observatory, has been restored. It is not open to visitors. In Kinningars Park an unusual 18th-century colliery winding-house remodelled as a dovecote is overlooked by modern homing-pigeon lofts. Carriden Church, the latest of four that have

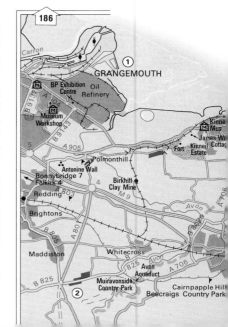

A KING'S THANKSGIVING *The Augustinian abbey on Inchcolm, reached from Queensferry, was founded by Alexander I after he had been rescued from a shipwreck on the island.*

occupied the present site, was built in the early 1900s but includes several Norman-style features.

⑧ BLACKNESS

The village's natural harbour became the seaport for Linlithgow in the late 14th century. Now it is used only by a sailing club. Blackness Castle (HS) was one of Scotland's most important artillery fortifications between the 16th century and World War I. After this time, the castle went out of use and was restored to its pre-1870 appearance. A ridge of parkland stretches from the village to the castle which, together with the beach beyond, make ideal picnic places. There are shoreline walks west to Bo'ness and east to Hopetoun House.

⑨ THE BINNS

In 1944 the 17th-century house was the first country mansion taken over by the National Trust for Scotland. Its name is from the Gaelic *beinn*, meaning 'mountain', although the house stands on only

a modest slope. This is the ancestral home of the Dalyell family, most noted of whom was Thomas or Tam, a royalist during the Civil War, who became a commander in the Russian Tsarist army and, finally, a scourge of the Presbyterian Covenanters back in Scotland. He founded the Scots Greys regiment at the Binns in 1681, and many mementos of him are preserved in the house. A short walk leads north-east to Tower Viewpoint, which looks out over the Forth and the surrounding hills.

⑩ HOPETOUN HOUSE

Completed in 1702, this elegant stately home is the seat of the Marquess of Linlithgow. The original house, built by Sir William Bruce, was later enlarged and extensively modified by William Adam and his sons. Many of the 18th-century furnishings, tapestries, portraits and porcelain are still in place, and several separate exhibitions are housed there. The grounds include walks through woodland, nature trails

and a beautiful, spacious park where red deer and Hebridean sheep can be seen. On the edge of the grounds, Abercorn Church dates partly from the 12th century, but masonry has been found from the 7th-century monastery

NOBLE GUESTS OF A GRAND PARK

The grounds of Hopetoun House are roamed by a flock of the rare black Hebridean sheep. These handsome animals are sometimes called St Kilda sheep because they originate from the St Kilda islands in the Outer Hebrides. The ram is a particularly magnificent creature with four horns framing an aristocratic head.

Hebridean ram

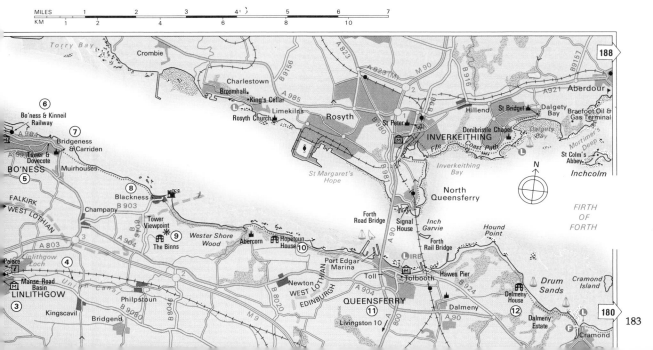

of Abercurnig which once occupied the same site when this area was part of the kingdom of Northumbria.

⑪ QUEENSFERRY

The town takes its name from a long-running ferry service across the Forth, which was in turn named after the 11th-century Queen Margaret. The ferry was superseded in 1964 by the Forth Road Bridge, an awesome structure just over 1½ miles long with a central span of 3300 ft. The skyline of Queensferry, often called South Queensferry, or Ferry, had already been dramatically altered in 1890 by the building of the magnificent Forth Rail Bridge. Trains still speed past its cantilevered girders. There is an attractive tolbooth in the high street, and a nearby yacht harbour gives the best views of the bridges. Queensferry Museum tells the story of the ferries, the bridges and the town. One display features the strange costume of the Burry Man, the central figure in the annual Ferry Fair, who is covered from head to foot in burrs and collects money for charity.

Robert Louis Stevenson wrote part of *Kidnapped* at Hawes Inn, and brought both it and Queensferry into the plot. To the west, at Port Edgar, is a large marina and watersports centre. Cruises, in summer, leave Hawes Pier for Inchcolm Island, where grey seals play and puffins nest in burrows near the atmospheric ruin of 12th-century St Colm's Abbey. Redundant gun emplacements are reminders of the peaceful island's sterner wartime role.

⑫ DALMENY HOUSE

Home of the Earl of Rosebery, the splendid Gothic Revival mansion, built in 1815, includes 18th-century porcelain,

FORTH GIANTS *Two bridges span the Firth of Forth north of Queensferry. In the 1880s, three huge cantilevered structures of steel were erected (right), as the Forth Rail Bridge took shape. The Road Bridge was completed around 80 years later.*

paintings by artists such as Gainsborough, and a room devoted to Napoleon. A 4½ mile waterside walk runs from Queensferry, past the oil terminal off Hound Point, to the little rowing-boat ferry at Cramond. To the west, 12th-century Dalmeny Church is probably Scotland's finest example of a Norman parish church.

PLACES TO SEE INLAND

Almond Valley Heritage Centre, Livingston, 10 miles SW of Queensferry. Displays on farming, milling and the shale-oil industry.

Beecraigs Country Park, 2 miles S of Linlithgow. Facilities for fishing, canoeing, archery and mountain biking. Trails through woodlands, and red-deer farm.

Cairnpapple Hill, 4 miles S of Linlithgow. Prehistoric hilltop burial cairns.

Rough Castle (HS), Bonnybridge, 6 miles W of Grangemouth. Site of Roman fort on Antonine Wall.

TOURIST INFORMATION

Bo'ness (01506) 826626 (summer); Falkirk (01324) 620244; Linlithgow (01506) 844600

Historic heartland on the Forth's northern shore

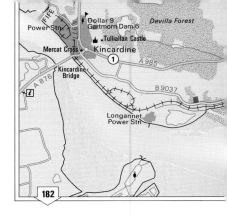

The gentle shore of south-west Fife is lined with villages and burghs that were once bustling ports, and the region's important role in history is recalled at Dunfermline Abbey, in Scotland's old capital.

COBBLED STREETS OF YESTERDAY *Time has passed by the 16th-century burgh of Culross, where narrow streets of red-roofed houses converge on the Mercat Cross.*

① KINCARDINE

Most traffic crossing the western end of the Firth of Forth speeds unheedingly past Kincardine, but this former fishing, trading, ferry and saltpanning port is an intriguing little town. Attractive groups of 18th-century houses in oddly angled lanes feature ornamental wall plaques and 'marriage lintels' marking the date when couples moved into their homes. There is a well-preserved 17th-century Mercat Cross, or market cross, indicating that the town was given a charter to hold a market. The green where cattle drovers grazed their herds before ferrying them to the great 'tryst', or livestock sale, at Falkirk across the Forth, survives as a public park.

The graveyard of the partly restored 17th-century Old Kirk of Tulliallan contains headstones carved with symbols of trades and professions. Tulliallan Castle, built as a mansion in the 19th century, is now a police training school.

② CULROSS

Salt and coal exports made a fortune for Sir George Bruce, the 17th-century laird of the well-preserved little burgh of Culross, pronounced 'Cooross'. Bruce's mansion, completed in 1611, was so grand that it became known as The Palace. Rare wall and ceiling paintings can be seen, as can the massive strongroom. In 1932, this was the first building bought by the National Trust for Scotland, at a cost of £700.

Much conservation work has been carried out in Culross, which retains the red-tiled roofs, crow-stepped gables and cobbled streets of its heyday in the 16th and 17th centuries. The NTS visitor centre, with an exhibition and video presentation outlining the burgh's history, is located in the Town House, and another restored house conceals an electricity substation. The House with the Evil Eyes takes its name from the window design high on its Dutch gable. Sir George Bruce and his family were buried in partly restored Culross Abbey, now the parish church, and many of the gravestones in the churchyard bear the royal warrant symbol of the Culross Hammermen, who for generations until the mid 18th century held the monopoly to make all Scotland's iron baking 'girdles', or griddles.

③ VALLEYFIELD WOOD

Footpaths follow the narrow valley of the Bluther Burn north of the former mining village of Valleyfield. The mansion of the Prestons of Valleyfield was knocked down in the 1940s, and the walled garden which was one of the features of an estate laid out by the English landscape gardener Humphry Repton in the early 19th century has returned to the wild. Overgrown as it is, the former estate is still Repton's 'deep, romantic and richly wooded glen'. The woodland is home to jays, coal tits, goldcrests and kingfishers, and walkers may catch glimpses of roe deer.

④ DUNFERMLINE

The town that was Scotland's principal place of royal residence for several hundred years stands on a rise of ground topped by the tower and spire of Dunfermline Abbey (HS). The building owes its foundation as a monastery in the 11th century to Queen Margaret, wife of King Malcolm III, and was given the status of an abbey early in the 12th century. Parts of the abbey have had to be rebuilt over the centuries, and its old nave is now attached to a 19th-century parish church. Just south of the abbey are the ruins of the monastic buildings. The abbey guesthouse, which developed into a royal palace, is now a visitor centre, and a heritage centre occupies 16th-century Abbot House, the oldest house in Dunfermline.

Dunfermline was the birthplace in 1835 of the American industrialist and philanthropist Andrew Carnegie, the son of a weaver. His simple boyhood home is a museum devoted to his life, and to his benefactions which at the time of his death in 1919 totalled some $350 million. His gifts to his native town included the first of the thousands of public libraries he endowed around the world, and the splendid Pittencrieff Park, from which he had been excluded as a child when it was a private estate. In the park is a conservation centre, and Pittencrieff House is a local history museum, with changing art exhibitions. A number of golf courses surround the town.

A statue of Andrew Carnegie stands in Dunfermline's Pittencrieff Park.

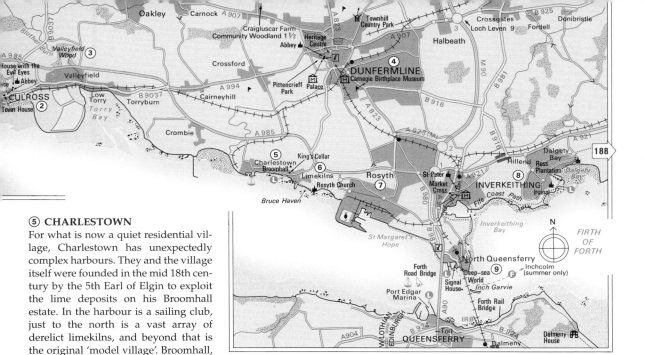

⑤ CHARLESTOWN

For what is now a quiet residential village, Charlestown has unexpectedly complex harbours. They and the village itself were founded in the mid 18th century by the 5th Earl of Elgin to exploit the lime deposits on his Broomhall estate. In the harbour is a sailing club, just to the north is a vast array of derelict limekilns, and beyond that is the original 'model village'. Broomhall, to the east of the village, is still the family seat, and not open to visitors.

⑥ LIMEKILNS

There are some fine cottages in the lanes of this old trading and ferry port, the location for an episode in Robert Louis Stevenson's novel *Kidnapped*. The village's oldest building, the 14th-century King's Cellar, once a store for the court at Dunfermline, is now a meeting hall. An embankment walk leads past Bruce Haven, an old harbour area, to the breezy site of ruined Rosyth Church.

⑦ ROSYTH

In 1909 the Admiralty bought a greenfield site by what was then the village of Rosyth to build one of Britain's largest Royal Naval dockyards, and a town to house the workers. Work still goes on, but Rosyth's scale of operations was drastically reduced in 1994. There is no public access to the docks.

⑧ INVERKEITHING

Rising steeply from its industrialised waterfront, Inverkeithing is one of Scotland's oldest royal burghs, receiving its charter in the early 12th century. Samuel Greig, the admiral who created the Russian Navy for Catherine the Great, was a native of the town, and temporary residents have included the 18th-century lawyer and author James Boswell, the 19th-century missionary and explorer David Livingstone, and Lord Raglan, commander of the British forces in the Crimean War.

The elegant 15th-century market cross is crowned by a royal unicorn carved in 1688 as a test for entry to the local company of masons. St Peter's Church was consecrated in 1244, and some Gothic elements survive in the present building. Part of the medieval friary houses the local history museum, and the friary gardens are an attractive public park. The gardens look across waterside sports fields, a busy paper works, and the old shipbreakers' yard where the German Grand Fleet, scuttled at Scapa Flow, was broken up for scrap after World War I.

⑨ NORTH QUEENSFERRY

Clustered below the Forth Bridge, the town was a busy ferry terminal until the road bridge opened in 1964. The piers are now used only by pleasure craft and by a summer ferry service to Inchcolm Island to the east. A town heritage trail takes in many places of interest from busier days, including inns, a hexagonal Signal House and a remarkable number of wells. From the centre of town, at the junction of Main Street and Old Kirk Road, the 7 mile Fife Coast Path heads north and east to Aberdour. An old quarry lagoon is now a Deep-Sea World aquarium.

PLACES TO SEE INLAND

Castle Campbell, Dollar, 10 miles N of Kincardine. 15th-century fortress in wooded glen.

Craigluscar Farm Community Woodland, 3 miles NW of Dunfermline. Remains of Iron Age hill-fort.

Gartmorn Dam Country Park, 7 miles NW of Kincardine. Nature reserve, visitor centre. Views to Ochil Hills.

Loch Leven, 12 miles NE of Dunfermline. National nature reserve, summer ferry to island castle, Vane Farm RSPB Reserve.

Townhill Country Park, 2 miles N of Dunfermline. Includes the Scottish National Water Ski Centre.

TOURIST INFORMATION

Dunfermline (01383) 720999; Forth Bridge (01383) 417759 (summer); Kincardine Bridge (01324) 831422 (summer)

SCOTLAND'S ROYAL SEPULCHRE *Among the kings buried in Dunfermline's magnificent abbey is Robert Bruce, whose name is written in letters of stone at the top of the tower.*

Quiet villages near a busy town on Fife's south coast

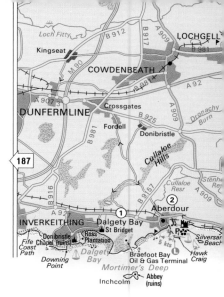

Bustling Kirkcaldy is at the centre of a cluster of small villages along the Firth of Forth, where catering to the needs of visitors has replaced traditional occupations such as coal-mining and fishing.

① DALGETY BAY

The first modern houses at Dalgety Bay, a residential town with a wide outlook across the Firth of Forth, were built in 1965, on the old Donibristle estate of the Earls of Moray. To the west, the Fife Coast Path runs past World War I gun emplacements at Downing Point, and a side path leads to the ruined 18th-century Donibristle Chapel.

The coast path skirts Ross Plantation, a half-flooded alder woodland where bulrushes and other moisture-loving plants thrive. Farther along the rocky bay is 13th-century St Bridget's Church, the burial place of the Seton Earls of Dunfermline. An oil and gas terminal lies over a wooded point to the east.

② ABERDOUR

Golf, yachting, windsurfing and walking are favourite activities in this trim resort. From the main beach, to the south of the town, there are views over the firth of Edinburgh Castle on its rock. In the foreground is Inchcolm Island with its ruined 12th-century abbey, which can be reached by a summer ferry service from North Queensferry, 6 miles to the west. Above Silversands beach, footpaths on the Hawk Craig headland end at the top of a vertical cliff. A driveway leads from the village

CASTLE WELL *A well 52 ft deep in the east courtyard supplied water for Aberdour Castle, which fell into ruins around 1700.*

to 14th-century Aberdour Castle, once a stronghold of the Douglases, and the castle's impressive garden terraces.

③ BURNTISLAND

At the little town's parish church in 1601 James VI of Scotland, later James I of England, announced his plan to publish a new version of the Bible, which became known as the Authorised Version. Some 30 years later, his son Charles I was highly indignant when many of his courtiers, and part of the royal treasury, were lost from a boat which foundered off Burntisland.

Above the sandy beach of Pettycur Bay is a large public park known as Burntisland Links. Overlooking a docks area busy with bulk containers from local aluminium works is Rossend Castle, a royal residence over several centuries, now restored as offices. An exhibition in the town hall, open in summer, explains Burntisland's history.

④ KINGHORN

South of Kinghorn's harbour conservation area are a sailing club and a small sandy beach, from which footpaths zigzag up a grassy hill towards the village. The old ferry port of Pettycur is used by fishermen as a base for, sea angling. The sands of Pettycur Bay stretch away to the west, below a vast caravan park. The lighthouse island of Inchkeith lies 2½ miles from the shore.

On the road to Burntisland is a monument to Alexander III, Scotland's last Celtic king, who fell from the cliffs to his death in 1286.

⑤ KIRKCALDY

Site of the Links Market, one of the biggest street fairs in Britain, held each April, Kirkcaldy has a generous supply of parks and green spaces. Ravenscraig Park, on a clifftop site with extensive sea views, includes ruined Ravenscraig Castle. Dunnikier Park is given over to sports fields and a golf course, while Beveridge Park to the south has a road network that once formed a car and motorcycle racing circuit. Nearby Raith Lake is stocked with rainbow trout and American brook trout.

Kirkcaldy was the birthplace in 1728 of the architect and interior designer

Robert Adam, and, five years earlier, of Adam Smith, the political economist who wrote *The Wealth of Nations*.

By the harbour is the restored 15th-century Sailors Walk, the oldest building in Kirkcaldy, now used as a bookshop; nearby are a modern maltings and a flour mill. Paintings from Scottish artists and local pottery feature in Kirkcaldy Museum and Art Gallery.

⑥ DYSART

From the northern end of the village, a lane called Hot Pot Wynd leads to Dysart's trim little harbour and its collection of pleasure craft and lobster boats. The 17th-century fishermen's houses in Pan Ha', another quaintly named street, have been restored by the National Trust for Scotland, and colourwashed houses surround the large 17th-century Tolbooth and the battlemented tower of the Church of St Serf. The John McDouall Stuart Museum commemorates the 19th-century explorer of the Australian interior, who

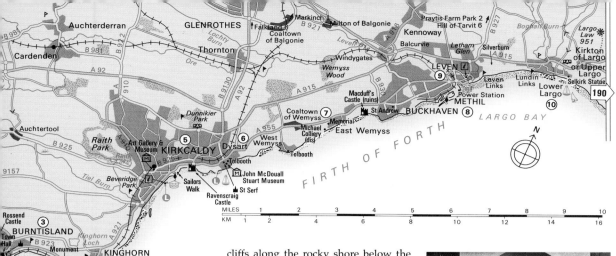

cliffs along the rocky shore below the castle, but rock falls make them and the path that leads to them hazardous.

was born in Dysart. A walk along the harbour cliff gives panoramic views of the village and the firth.

⑦ COALTOWN OF WEMYSS

Created as a model village in the mid 19th century to house local miners, Coaltown of Wemyss, pronounced 'weems', is one of a trio of similarly named villages on this strip of the coast. Many houses in Coaltown feature typical crow-stepped gables.

Colour-washed houses overlook a small disused harbour at West Wemyss, where fulmars nest on ledges in a cliff. The delicate Tolbooth has a gilded swan as its weather vane.

At East Wemyss, the disused Michael Colliery lies derelict above the sea, and nearby stands a memorial to the men who died in a fire at the colliery in 1967. At the north-eastern end of the village are the ruins of 11th-century Macduff's Castle. There are several caves in the

⑧ BUCKHAVEN AND METHIL

There is a substantial North Sea oil construction base at Methil, and its docks and power station complete the industrial seafront. To the south-west is the former sea-angling and lobster-fishing centre of Buckhaven. The town's theatre is housed in a redundant church which was originally located in St Andrews; local fishermen bought the church in 1869, then had it dismantled and brought in pieces by boat to Buckhaven where it was re-erected.

⑨ LEVEN

The little resort town has two excellent golf courses, one of which is a qualifying course for the Open championship. The broad sandy beach and promenade offer estuary views. Just north of Leven is Letham Glen, a public park with an enclosure of fallow deer. To the northeast, the Silverburn estate has a small farm and a walled garden; a crafts centre is in the old mansion house.

IMMORTAL CASTAWAY *A statue of Alexander Selkirk, erected in 1885, gazes from the site of his cottage at Lower Largo.*

⑩ LOWER LARGO

A statue in the old rivermouth port commemorates Alexander Selkirk, born in the town in 1676, whose adventures as a castaway on the deserted island of Juan Fernandez, off the coast of Chile, were the inspiration for Daniel Defoe's novel *Robinson Crusoe*.

The area is good for sailing and windsurfing, and dinghies can be launched from the shingle beach. Lower Largo merges with the resort of Lundin Links, where the Victorians built seaside villas and laid out gardens and a golf course.

From Kirkton of Largo, or Upper Largo, a footpath leads to the 952ft mound of Largo Law, which was once a volcano. The summit is a splendid point for views across the Firth of Forth.

VINTAGE PORT *An air of tranquillity envelops whitewashed stone houses at the old port of Lower Largo, ranged along a rock and seaweed-strewn shore by the Firth of Forth.*

PLACES TO SEE INLAND

Balbirnie Craft Centre, Markinch, 8 miles N of Kirkcaldy. Workshops for jewellery, leatherwork, pottery and furniture.

Falkland Palace (NTS), 12 miles N of Kirkcaldy. Renaissance palace of the Stuart kings and queens.

Hill of Tarvit (NTS), 8 miles N of Leven. Lavish Edwardian mansion with long, elevated views.

Praytis Farm Park, 4 miles N of Leven. Farm museum, deer park, country walks.

TOURIST INFORMATION

Burntisland (01592) 872667; Kirkcaldy (01592) 267775; Leven (01333) 429464

Handsome fishing villages, and city of a patron saint

St Andrews carries the distinction of being named after Scotland's patron saint, and is recognised as the cradle of golf. Away from the clubhouse, there is plenty to delight along the varied shoreline of East Neuk.

① ST ANDREWS

Named after Scotland's patron saint, St Andrews is internationally recognised as the home of golf, and has today the British Golf Museum and no fewer than six golf courses. The Old Course is on the northern edge of the town, in full view of several streets; a right of way called Grannie Clark's Wynd crosses the 1st and 18th fairways. Running parallel to the Old Course is West Sands, one of the town's two extensive beaches. East Sands stretches beyond the rivermouth harbour, which shelters lobster boats. South Street, entered through a 16th-century gateway, has narrow alleys known as 'rigs' branching off it. The street leads to the ruin of 12th-century St Andrews Cathedral (HS), whose tower can be climbed for a fine view across the city. Other attractions of St Andrews include the university, founded in 1410 and the third oldest in Britain, the Sea Life Centre, the Victorian Botanic Garden, and St Andrews Castle (HS), built around 1200, with a forbidding dungeon.

Two miles inland, Craigtoun Country Park features a Dutch-style model village, built in 1918 on a lake island.

The R&A clubhouse overlooks the Old Course.

② KINGSBARNS

The northernmost village in Fife's beautiful East Neuk, or east corner, used to store grain for royal residences in the county. The older houses in Kingsbarns display the neat proportions and delicate detail work for which the district is famous. There is a grassy picnic area down by the sea, and rock pools at low tide. Cambo Gardens were laid out in Victorian times beside a tumbling burn.

③ FIFE NESS

A World War II Royal Naval air station lies derelict beside the road to the rocky headland of Fife Ness. A kart racing circuit has been laid out there, and a side road leads to a shoreline picnic area. The coast path leads through grassland and wildflowers. Terns, eiders, puffins and gannets may be seen, as well as migratory birds in spring and autumn.

Balcomie golf course is at the far end of the Fife Ness road.

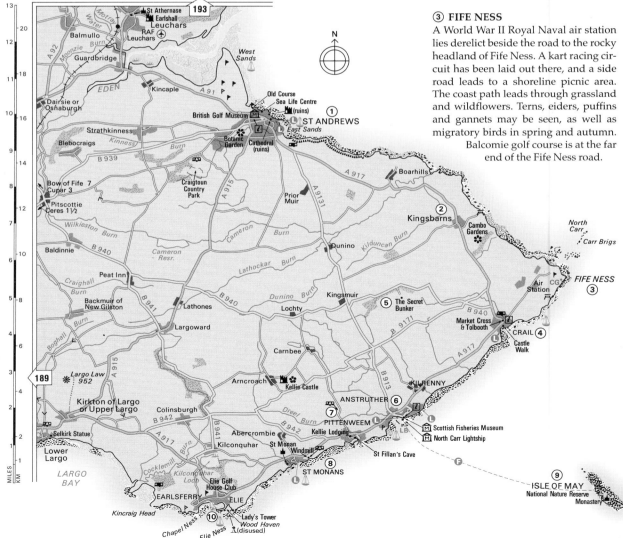

CASTLE OF BLOODSHED *Built by bishops, St Andrews Castle witnessed 400 years of turbulence as the city was embroiled in Scotland's political and religious turmoil.*

④ CRAIL

Individual property owners, and the National Trust for Scotland, have preserved the beauty of this little burgh. From the Tolbooth and the market cross to the pretty harbour area the townscape remains unspoiled. The local museum tells the story of Crail's involvement with royalty, fishing, golf and the air station on the road to Fife Ness. The parapet Castle Walk, which follows the remains of a castle wall along a cliff path, gives views of the harbour and, in clear weather, St Abb's Head, 30 miles to the south.

⑤ THE SECRET BUNKER

Marked on detailed maps simply as a communications mast, this astonishing place was revealed after its declassification in 1992 as a top-secret command centre, where Britain's government and military commanders would have been based in the event of a nuclear war. A simple and unobtrusive house, now part of a museum, hides the entrance to a 250 yd approach tunnel. Visitors can venture deep underground to explore the labyrinthine complex, built on shockproof foundations and protected by a 15 ft thick concrete ceiling.

⑥ ANSTRUTHER

Although its fishing fleet is now based at Pittenweem, Anstruther harbour is the location of the evocative Scottish Fisheries Museum, housed in 18th and 19th century buildings which were once used as a chandlery and net loft. The museum depicts the lifestyle of a fishing community and recalls the history of the industry.

⑦ PITTENWEEM

The 'weem', or cave, reputedly lived in by the 7th-century missionary St Fillan is carefully preserved in the stepped Cove Wynd, which descends from the high street to Pittenweem's harbour. The town is the home port of the East Neuk fishing fleet. The Kellie Lodging, built in 1592, was the town mansion of the Earls of Kellie. Their inland home, Kellie Castle (NTS), 2 miles north-west, was built in the 16th and 17th centuries and has a fine walled garden.

⑧ ST MONANS

Once a busy boat-building centre, St Monans' harbour is now a haven for yachts and shellfish boats. Overlooking the rocky shore, the sturdy, square-built Church of St Monan, with its many historic and heraldic features, stands on one of the oldest religious sites in Fife, dating from at least the 11th century. St Monans Windmill, near the coast path, was built in the 18th century to pump seawater into coal-fired salt pans. Partly restored, the mill includes displays relating to the salt-panning industry, which died in the 1820s.

⑨ ISLE OF MAY

Reached in summer by ferry from Anstruther harbour, the largest island in the Firth of Forth is an outstanding national nature reserve. Paths explore the narrow central plateau, where care should be taken as the clifftops are unstable in places. Guillemots, razorbills and kittiwakes nest in great numbers, and the island has a large puffin population. Eider ducks and grey seals can be seen around the shore. Scotland's first manned lighthouse was built there in 1636. From the 8th to 16th centuries the island was an important religious site. The ruins of a 12th-century monastery survive, as well as old military fortifications and domestic ruins.

⑩ ELIE AND EARLSFERRY

The former fishing port of Elie and the old market town and ferry port of Earlsferry have long been united as one burgh. Elie Golf House Club presides over a classic golf course, whose history goes back to 1589. The harbour is devoted to watersports of all kinds. A stroll along Wood Haven beach leads to Elie Ness, where there are walks, and a white 1908 lighthouse stands on one low headland. The Lady's Tower was the summerhouse of Lady Jane Anstruther, an 18th-century beauty who sent a bellman through the streets to warn the lower orders not to steal a look while she was bathing.

High basalt cliffs at Kincraig Head support ledge and grassland wild flowers, which attract many species of butterfly. Fulmars and house martins nest on the rock, while kestrels soar overhead.

PLACES TO SEE INLAND
Fife Folk Museum, Ceres, 8 miles SW of St Andrews. Exhibits on traditional trades, crafts and agriculture of the county, housed in 17th-century Tolbooth and Weigh House.
Scottish Deer Centre, Bow of Fife, 13 miles W of St Andrews. Audiovisual exhibition on deer, walks and winery.
Sir Douglas Bader Garden for the Disabled, Cupar, 10 miles W of St Andrews. Rose and rock gardens, waterfalls and aviary.

TOURIST INFORMATION
Anstruther (01333) 311073 (summer); Crail (01333) 450869 (summer); St Andrews (01334) 472021

VILLAGE HARBOUR *Crow-stepped gables, a characteristic Scottish style, add a distinctive touch to Crail's harbourside, which is bounded by giant walls of uncemented red boulders.*

Royal burghs and sailing resorts beside the Tay

The fertile Carse of Gowrie gently undulates between the ancient cities of Perth and Dundee, which stand beside the Firth of Tay. The Tay's banks are linked by the rail bridge of 1887 and the road bridge of 1966.

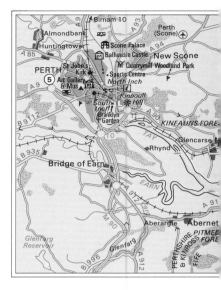

① CARNOUSTIE

The golfing centre providing three famous courses is also a holiday resort with long, sandy beaches and a sailing club. The War Memorial Gardens are an impressive blaze of colour in spring and summer. Barry Buddon, an army firing range, is closed to the public.

North-west of Carnoustie are Barry Mill (NTS), a 19th-century mill in working order, and Monikie Country Park, based on a reservoir.

② BROUGHTY FERRY

Many of Dundee's wealthiest Victorian businessmen built grand houses in this suburb, and helped to found both the Royal Tay Yacht Club and Forfarshire Cricket Club. Broughty Castle (HS), originally a 15th-century fortress, is now an excellent museum of local history, with displays on arms and armour, coastal wildlife and the old whaling industry. Extensive sandy beaches border the esplanade. There are pleasant public gardens, and Reres Park offers an unexpectedly wild wooded hill in the middle of a residential area.

③ DUNDEE

Once a city of 'jute, jam and journalism' Dundee retains only its magazine publishing industry. The royal burgh has not always been well served by modern planners, but some impressive older buildings survive. Claypotts Castle (HS) is an amazingly complete 16th-century tower house. The McManus Galleries, housed in a Victorian Gothic building, feature local history and Scottish paintings, while Barrack Street Museum concentrates on natural history. St Mary's Church dates partly from the 14th century. Tours may be made of the Verdant Works, a 19th-century jute and flax mill restored to celebrate the great days of the textile industry, and of Shaw's traditional Dundee Sweet Factory. The Mills Observatory, opened in 1953, is Britain's only full-time public observatory.

Dundee is home to two notable historic ships, both of which may be visited. The frigate *Unicorn*, launched in 1824, is one of Britain's oldest ships still afloat, while the Royal Research Ship *Discovery* was built in 1901 for Captain

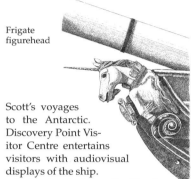

Frigate figurehead

Scott's voyages to the Antarctic. Discovery Point Visitor Centre entertains visitors with audiovisual displays of the ship.

In the heart of the city, Dundee Law, a 571 ft hill, offers a panorama extending across the city and its many open spaces, which include the university's Botanic Garden and Camperdown Country Park with its excellent wildlife centre. North of Camperdown lie Templeton Woods and the reservoir-based Clatto Country Park.

④ CARSE OF GOWRIE

The finest views of this low-lying landscape of fruit farms and agricultural land are from the hill roads. The roads serve villages such as Kinnaird with its dramatically placed parish church, and Rait with its antique shops. There is a Heavy Horse Centre at Glencarse, and a Railway Heritage Centre at Errol Station, which no longer has stopping trains. Inchture is an old stagecoach halt, and Baledgarno is an attractive 18th-century estate village at the gates of privately owned Rossie Priory.

⑤ PERTH

Described by Sir Walter Scott as the 'Fair City', the ancient royal burgh of Perth is a place of pleasant open spaces and notable buildings. At St John's Kirk, in 1559, John Knox's sermon lit the fires of the Reformation. During the 1745 Jacobite Rising Charles Edward Stuart lodged in the Salutation Hotel, where a plaque commemorates his visit. Perth has a large art gallery and museum of local history. Balhousie Castle houses the museum of the Black Watch, Perthshire's celebrated regiment. The early 20th-century Lower City Mills have been well preserved, complete with a working waterwheel. Branklyn Garden (NTS) has a fine collection of plants, including dwarf rhododendrons, while Cherrybank Gardens has Britain's largest collection of heathers.

Footpaths lead for about a mile up wooded Kinnoull Hill and continue to a clifftop folly tower. There are gentler walks in a narrow valley at Quarrymill Woodland Park, which has a visitor centre. Scone, pronounced 'Scoon', Palace, dates mainly from the 19th century, but incorporates details from the 16th century and earlier palaces. The palace, with its fine displays of porcelain and furniture, and the grounds are both

PALACE OF KINGS *The grounds of Scone Palace contain a replica of the Stone of Scone; more than 40 Scottish kings, including Robert Bruce, were crowned on the original stone.*

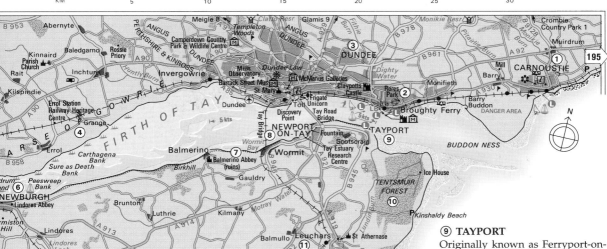

WATCH ON THE TAY *Overlooking the River Tay near Perth is 19th-century Kinnoull Tower, modelled by the Earl of Kinnoull on the Rhineland castles that had impressed him.*

open to visitors. Perth has three golf courses, a sports centre and a leisure centre with indoor and outdoor pools.

⑥ NEWBURGH

Originally a market town, the royal burgh of Newburgh was 'new' in the 13th century. Weaving and spinning, quarrying and fruit farming were some of many industries which brought prosperity to the town. The Laing Museum has displays on the town's ancient and modern history. Ruined Lindores Abbey, founded in 1178, stands on the town's eastern outskirts.

In hilly Pitmedden Forest, to the south-west, there are walks through larch, spruce and pine plantations with views of the Lomond Hills to the south.

⑦ BALMERINO

Set on a sweeping hillside of farms and woodlands overlooking the Tay, the village of Balmerino contains many neatly restored houses in peaceful lanes. Balmerino Abbey (NTS), founded in 1229, was on the pilgrim route from St Andrews to Arbroath. Its ruins stand in grounds noted for a 450-year-old Spanish chestnut tree. Coast paths lead west to Newburgh and east to Wormit, and outside the shooting season walks are possible on the Birkhill estate.

⑧ NEWPORT-ON-TAY

Bounded by the rail bridge and the road bridge, Newport looks directly across the Tay to Dundee. From the splendid Victorian fountain on top of a steep bank there are views over the redundant ferry pier, which now accommodates the Tay Estuary Research Centre, and is not open to the public. Beside the railway bridge stand the remains of an ill-designed earlier bridge, which collapsed during a storm in 1879. All 75 people on board a train which was crossing died as it plunged into the sea.

⑨ TAYPORT

Originally known as Ferryport-on-Craig, the burgh of Tayport was the southern terminal for the widest Tay ferry crossing until the opening of the Tay Road Bridge, which can be reached by a shoreline walk. Dundee stands in full view across the Tay, with the Sidlaw Hills on the skyline. Parkland and playing fields fringe Tayport's southern esplanade, and at Scotscraig, south-west of the village, there is a golf course.

⑩ TENTSMUIR FOREST

Extensive and almost entirely level plantations of Scots and Corsican pine are the home of roe deer, squirrels and crossbills. Special roosting sites have attracted several species of bat including pipistrelles, common long-eared bats and Natterer's. Walks leading from the car park by the beach at Kinshaldy Bay take in dunes, forests and open heaths. An abandoned 19th-century ice house survives beside an old salmon pond with a wildlife observation hide.

⑪ LEUCHARS

North of the Eden estuary, the massive RAF base at Leuchars was first used in 1911 for military balloon experiments. It is the scene, every September, of Scotland's biggest air show. In the attractive old part of Leuchars village, the Church of St Athernase, dating from about 1180, is one of the loveliest Norman churches in Scotland. Much of the arches, arcades and apse remain.

PLACES TO SEE INLAND

Beatrix Potter Garden, Birnam, 13 miles NW of Perth. Celebrates Beatrix Potter's time in the Birnam area, where she wrote the original 'picture letters' about Peter Rabbit and Jeremy Fisher.

Crombie Country Park, 5 miles NW of Carnoustie. Reservoir, woodland walks and wildlife hides.

Glamis Castle, 13 miles N of Dundee. Turreted red sandstone castle, which has been a royal residence since 1372. Extensive grounds.

Meigle Museum, 12 miles NW of Dundee. Stunning collection of Pictish sculptured stones.

TOURIST INFORMATION

Carnoustie (01241) 852258 (summer); Dundee (01382) 434664; Perth (01738) 638353

Sandy beaches flanking the busy town of Montrose

Most of the fishing fleets on the Angus coast, from Montrose to south of Carnoustie, have long gone, but Gourdon still thrives on traditional trawling methods, and Arbroath remains famous for its cured haddock.

① FOWLSHEUGH RSPB RESERVE
More than 100 000 kittiwakes, fulmars, razorbills, guillemots and other species make this reserve one of Britain's greatest sea bird colonies. A footpath from Crawton village leads to a grassy clifftop that looks down on inlets, towers and rock stacks, where the cries of sea birds constantly echo. Seals, porpoises and dolphins swim offshore.

② CATTERLINE
A grassy amphitheatre, bright with wild flowers in summer, plunges down to a tiny harbour in Catterline. Houses originally built for fishermen and coastguards stand on the clifftop. Catterline's fishing may have declined, but the village's charming setting is still popular with artists, and ornithologists come to photograph the sea birds on the cliffs and offshore islets. A clifftop path leads to Crawton, 1½ miles to the north.

③ OLD KIRK OF KINNEFF
Overlooking the sea, the Old Kirk outside Kinneff village dates from 1738, but there has been a church on the site since around AD 700. The church once held Scotland's best-kept state secret. In 1651 Cromwell's troops forced the surrender of Dunnottar Castle, 7 miles up the coast, where the Honours of Scotland – the royal crown, sword and sceptre – were thought to be in safe keeping. But they had been smuggled out by the parish minister's wife and hidden in the Old Kirk. Only in 1660, with peace restored, were the Honours returned to the state's ownership.

④ INVERBERVIE
The old market burgh, granted its charter in 1341, is now a small commuter town for Aberdeen. The most famous son of 'Bervie', as the town is known locally, was Hercules Linton, designer of the great tea-clipper *Cutty Sark*. A rose-garden memorial to him was opened by Sir Francis Chichester on the 100th anniversary of the ship's launch in 1869. The curving, wave-sculpted pebble beach of Bervie Bay is fringed by a picnic area, and behind it the old railway line between Inverbervie and Montrose is now a footpath which leads south to Gourdon and Johnshaven. The Grassic Gibbon Centre, 2 miles inland, commemorates James Leslie Mitchell who, using the pseudonym Lewis Grassic Gibbon, wrote *Sunset Song*, *Grey Granite* and *Cloud Howe*, an evocative trilogy of novels about The Mearns, the agricultural area around the town of Laurencekirk.

⑤ GOURDON
This is one of the last fishing villages in Scotland where 19th-century trawling methods are used, and one boat still uses baited lines. At the harbour a barometer built into a granite pillar is a Victorian memorial to the seafaring men of Gourdon. The old railway walk heads south towards Johnshaven past rocks where gulls gather offshore.

⑥ JOHNSHAVEN
In the early 18th century, Johnshaven was a highly productive fishing port. But many of its young men drifted away from the sea, partly because of the dangers of the coast, and partly because of the navy press gangs. Rows of cottages lead down to a working harbour, where lobsters and salmon are sold.

One mile north of the town, the Mill of Benholm, a restored working water-powered meal mill, is open to visitors in summer. Two miles inland, Damside Garden Herbs and Arboretum has seven gardens with displays of herbs, whose origins date back to Celtic times.

⑦ ST CYRUS
Riverbanks, salt marshes, sand dunes, cliffs and a sandy beach make up one of Britain's most fascinating national nature reserves. The visitor centre, originally a 19th-century lifeboat station, illustrates the wonderful variety of birdlife, wild flowers and butterflies within the reserve, which can be reached by a footbridge built in 1985 by a troop of Gurkhas, near the car park. Two salmon-fishing stations set out stake nets offshore. A short but steep path from the beach climbs to the village of St Cyrus, where a clifftop viewpoint looks out over the sea and to Montrose to the south. From the village an exhilarating path leads north to Woodston, where a tractor track swoops down to the sea again.

⑧ MONTROSE
The bustling town, and its neighbour Ferryden across the estuary of the South Esk, are centred on a port and a North Sea oil supply base. However, grassy expanses between the town and its sandy beach provide space for two golf courses, playing fields and strolling areas. Handsome Georgian buildings include the golden-domed Montrose Academy, which is closed to the public, and the Montrose Museum, recalling the town's history. The soaring spire of the 1834 parish church is a landmark for miles around. The Air Station Museum, which is only open on summer Sundays, has displays on

ROCK-STUDDED SANDS *Montrose Bay's dune-fringed beach extends between the Milton Ness headland and Montrose for 6 miles, broken only by the mouth of the North Esk.*

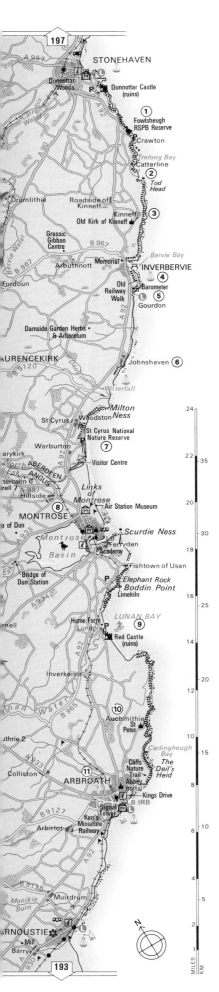

Britain's first military air station, established at Montrose in 1912. The brackish tidal waters of Montrose Basin are a reserve for many species of bird, including greylag and pink-footed geese during the winter.

Four miles west of Montrose, the House of Dun (NTS) is a stately mansion, designed by William Adam and built in 1730. The Caledonian Railway, nearby, operates steam-hauled trains on summer Sundays from Brechin, west of Montrose, to Bridge of Dun station.

⑨ LUNAN BAY
Stretching south from Boddin Point with its substantial limekiln and Elephant Rock, a rock eroded into the shape of an elephant's head, Lunan Bay has a long, sandy beach cut in half by the mouth of Lunan Water. Beyond Home Farm riding school, a car park gives access to a boardwalk over the sand dunes to the shore. The rust-coloured ruin of aptly named Red Castle, thought to have been built in the 15th century, stands on a hilltop overlooking a stake-net fishery, whose spare poles are stacked in wigwam form.

Just north of the bay, Fishtown of Usan's derelict coastguard tower rises from the middle of a row of roofless cottages. The beach is shingle with huge expanses of rock at low tide.

⑩ AUCHMITHIE
Until the beginning of the 20th century Auchmithie was one of the busiest fishing villages in the district of Angus. Farmlands sweep to the clifftop, where houses perch on the edge of a steep drop to the pebbly shore. A majestic red sandstone bluff rises sharply to the south. Modernised fishermen's cottages contrast with mellow St Peter's Church, built in 1885.

⑪ ARBROATH
Raucous calls of sea birds announce the early morning fish landings at a port famous for the Arbroath 'smokie', haddock cured slowly over a beechwood fire. Until the end of the 19th century,

BEFORE THE CATCH *Lobster pots stand on a harbour wall in Arbroath, home of the Arbroath 'smokie', a haddock delicacy.*

the town was principally a trading harbour. Today Arbroath is a holiday resort, with attractions such as Kerr's Miniature Railway, which has been operating since 1935. Beyond the Kings Drive promenade, Arbroath Cliffs nature trail, leading towards Auchmithie, takes in sea-bird nesting grounds, wild flower havens and spectacular rock formations. Arbroath Abbey (HS), now a well-preserved ruin, was built in 1178 and dedicated by the Scottish king William the Lion to his martyred friend Thomas Becket. The Declaration of Arbroath, signed at the abbey in 1320, was a re-affirmation of Scotland's independence. The Signal Tower, where messages used to be relayed to and from the Bell Rock lighthouse a dozen miles offshore, now houses a museum of Arbroath history.

SUMMER BELLES
In midsummer the lovely flowers of clustered bellflower daub patches of blue on dune grass and sea cliffs along the Angus coast. The bell-like flowers, large in relation to the size of the plant, are held in tight clumps with mouths uppermost on stems growing up to 2 ft high.

Clustered bellflower
Campanula glomerata
May-Sept

PLACES TO SEE INLAND

Edzell Castle (HS), 13 miles NW of Montrose. Beautiful formal garden at 16th-century tower house.

Fasque, nr Fettercairn, 13 miles NW of Montrose. Victorian stately home of Prime Minister William Ewart Gladstone.

House of Pitmuies, nr Guthrie. 8 miles NW of Arbroath. Walled gardens and riverside walk at 18th-century house.

TOURIST INFORMATION
Arbroath (01241) 872609; Carnoustie (01241) 852258 (summer); Montrose (01674) 672000 (summer); Stonehaven (01569) 762806 (summer)

A city of granite and a castle on a rocky spur

Aberdeen is the heart of the North Sea oil industry, as well as a seaside resort, a commercial centre and a fishing port. It is flanked by commuter towns, which were themselves once thriving fishing communities.

① BALMEDIE COUNTRY PARK

Between the Don and the Ythan estuaries, the park is a glorious stretch of vast sandy beaches and huge dunes. A visitor centre explains the area's attractions for waders, which include redshanks, ringed plovers and sanderlings.

② BRIDGE OF DON

The River Don, which flows through the Aberdeen suburb of Bridge of Don, is crossed by two bridges. The early 14th-century Brig o' Balgownie, which is reached from a row of restored cottages dating back to 1600, is closed to road traffic. Instead, vehicles use the Bridge of Don, built in 1829. The Scotstown Muir Nature Reserve is an area of heathland, gorse thickets, woodland and marshes, where a variety of birds and wild flowers can be spotted from a network of footpaths. The Donmouth Nature Reserve at the river mouth is visited by wildfowl all year round. A car park on the esplanade gives access to a footpath skirting the reserve's western end. A mile south-west of Bridge of Don, the Crombie Woollen Mills visitor centre tells the story of the renowned Crombie cloth, once made there.

③ ABERDEEN

Scotland's third largest city is the capital of the North Sea oil industry, and the harbour is crammed with oil-platform supply vessels. As well as being a popular seaside resort, Aberdeen is also a fishing, fish-processing and general trading port. Ferry services operate to Shetland and the Orkneys. Extensive public parks such as Hazlehead with its giant maze, and Duthie Park, with the largest Winter Gardens in Europe, provide expanses of green space. The local granite is evident in much of Aberdeen's imposing architecture, including Marischal College, part of the city's university, with its exuberant neo-Gothic frontage. Founded in 1593, the college has a museum devoted to its history. The Maritime Museum is in Provost Ross's House (NTS), while 16th-century Provost Skene's House contains the city museum. King's College Chapel, in the once separate burgh of Old Aberdeen, has a majestic 17th-century crown tower. Nearby St Machar's Cathedral (HS) originates from the 15th century.

Within the city boundaries, Cove is a fishing village, while Footdee, pronounced 'Fittie', has a sandy beach.

④ PORTLETHEN

Minor roads from the modern dormitory town of Portlethen lead to the three old fishing settlements of Portlethen Village, Findon and Downies. Most of the cottages at Portlethen Village have been restored as commuter homes, but lobster boats still work from a pebbly cove. 'Finnan haddie' – haddock split and smoked over a peat fire – was produced at Findon until the 1870s, although the method of smoking continues in other eastern coast towns in Scotland. Downies has a rocky shore, but two rusting winches on the steep, grassy cliff are reminders that fishermen once worked there.

⑤ NEWTONHILL

Though much developed in recent years, Newtonhill retains its original clifftop fishing village. Down a curving flight of steps, fishermen's huts stand out of sight of the village houses. A plank bridge over the Burn of Elsick forms part of a circular walk.

⑥ MUCHALLS

The original village of attractive 19th-century cottages has been obscured by modern housing. A clifftop path overlooks an imposing grass-covered natural arch, through which the tide pours.

A mile inland, along rough farm roads, heraldic lions guard the gateway of Muchalls Castle. Built in 1619, this laird's house with its turrets and fine plaster ceilings is now a hotel.

SEAFARING SCENE *Yachts cluster by Aberdeen's busy Regent Quay, presided over by the floodlit Harbour Board Office. A tithe was first levied in 1136 on craft using the harbour.*

SAINTLY FORTIFICATION *The 160ft rock on which Dunnottar Castle stands was first fortified in the 5th century. St Ninian, an early missionary, reputedly used it as a base.*

⑦ SKATIE SHORE

A path from the car park leads along the foot of cliffs to Skatie Shore, a sandy bay on an otherwise rocky coast. Garron Point marks the eastern end of the great Highland Boundary Fault, a fracture in the rock which runs almost arrow-straight across Scotland towards the Firth of Clyde on the west coast.

⑧ STONEHAVEN

Centred on the elegant Market Buildings of 1826, Stonehaven is a town of contrasts. The northern end with its amusement park, caravan site and sandy beach caters for the holiday-maker. A breezy promenade across Carron Water leads to the old town in the southern part of Stonehaven, where yachts and fishing boats shelter in the harbour. The Tolbooth Museum recalls that in 1748 a group of imprisoned Episcopalian ministers secretly baptised children brought to their cell window by fishermen's wives. A path climbs towards a war memorial, where there are fine views of the town and the surrounding hills and coast.

The old royal burgh of Cowie, north of Stonehaven, has a separate fishing quarter. Boatie Row, a seafront street of cottages, leads to a stake-net drying green. From there a stepped footpath continues along the clifftop to the ruins of 13th-century St Mary of the Storms Church and a dramatic sea view.

⑨ DUNNOTTAR WOODS

Shady paths run through this mainly broadleaved woodland. Gallow Hill, an old execution place, provides views of the woodlands to the south. On the Burn of Glasslaw, Lady Kennedy's Bath is a stonework bathing pool, created for one of the ladies of long-gone Dunnottar House. Sir Walter Scott once came upon a man restoring a memorial stone to a group of Covenanters near Dunnottar Kirk. The man, Robert Paterson, became the model for the hero of Scott's novel *Old Mortality*. The Covenanters' Stone is still in place.

⑩ DUNNOTTAR CASTLE

The ruined 14th-century fortress stands on an impregnable rock, separated from the mainland by a deep ravine. The castle was involved in many historical episodes, and was virtually demolished after the 1715 Jacobite Rising, before being partly restored in 1925. A tunnel entrance leads up towards the top level where the surviving buildings stand.

PLACES TO SEE INLAND

Crathes Castle and Gardens, 16 miles SW of Aberdeen. 16th-century castle with walled gardens, topiary hedges, woodland trails

TOURIST INFORMATION

Aberdeen (01224) 632727; Stonehaven (01569) 762806 (summer)

ISLANDS OF INDUSTRY
There are some 200 oil production platforms in British waters, most of which are to be found along the north-eastern coast of Scotland. Wells below the towering artificial 'islands' extract the oil from porous rock, which holds it like a giant sponge many hundreds of feet beneath the seabed. It is then pumped ashore in pipelines or loaded into tankers.

The Magnus platform was built to withstand winds of 100 knots.

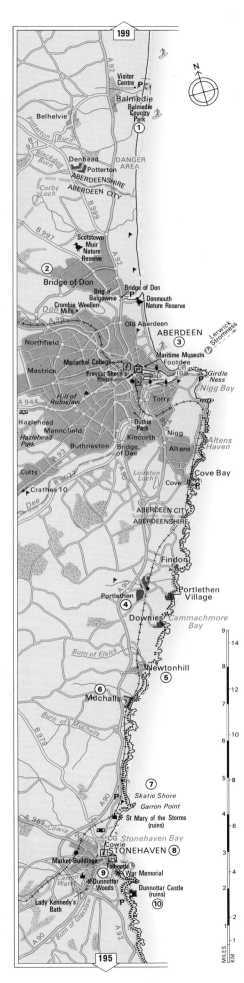

Imposing dunes north of a major white-fish port

Scotland's easternmost stretch of coast, where giant dunes edge sandy shores, is scarred with sea-hewn chasms and ravines. The novel Dracula *was reputedly inspired by Slains Castle, now an atmospheric ruin.*

① ST COMBS
Facing a rocky shore, and bounded by sandy beaches to the north and south, the fishing village of St Combs was founded in 1771, when the laird financed 20 fishermen to build houses there. A similar arrangement created the linked hamlet of Charlestown, just to the north. St Combs takes its name from a ruined medieval church dedicated to St Columba.

② RATTRAY HEAD
High, grassy dunes line miles of beach round Rattray Head, a fine place for watching wading birds and Arctic skuas. The lighthouse was built on a tidal platform, with an elegant shore station behind the dunes. Shoreline walks lead to Inverugie, 6 miles south, and St Combs, 5 miles north-west.

All that remains of Old Rattray is the ruined chapel of St Mary, dating from the 13th century. The village faded out 400 years later when shifting dunes silted up the harbour, although empty houses still survive from a later fishing settlement called Seatown.

③ CRIMOND
Surrounded by flat farmland, the village has a church clock which, due to an error by the clockmaker, shows 61 minutes in the hour. There is a rainbow trout fishery in the woodlands of Crimonmogate estate.

The Loch of Strathbeg RSPB reserve, north-east of Crimond, was a saltwater bay until its sea exit was blocked by the build-up of dunes in the 1720s. The reserve attracts birds such as tufted ducks and water rails. Its visitor centre at Starnafin has directions to four hides.

④ ST FERGUS
Europe's biggest gas terminal stands among farmlands just outside the village of St Fergus, named after an 8th-century bishop. At Scotstown, east of St Fergus, tussocky dunes give way to curving sands. Walkers can stroll along the shore for miles in either direction.

⑤ ADEN COUNTRY PARK
On the outskirts of Mintlaw, the beautiful riverside and woodland park is centred on a magnificent semicircular home farm complex with a square central tower. The park has a wildlife centre, and a heritage centre which illustrates 200 years of farming.

⑥ PETERHEAD
For a century until 1893, Peterhead was Britain's major whaling port. Today it is the largest white-fish port in Europe. The story of Peterhead's fishing and whaling industries, together with its political and historical associations, are explained in the Arbuthnot Museum. Peterhead Bay, which includes a North Sea oil base, a lido and a marina, is contained within the great Harbour of Refuge. The Fish House, near the mouth of the Ugie, dates from 1585 and still smokes trout and salmon. A statue of Field Marshal Keith, one of Frederick the Great's commanders, stands in front of the 18th-century Town House, built from the pink granite that characterises Peterhead. Nearby the Reform Monument's heraldic arms and Latin inscriptions celebrate the passing of the Reform Bill in 1832. The Reform Tower is another reminder of the same event.

⑦ BODDAM
The large, pink-granite village has a harbour which used to be filled with herring boats. Lobster boats still tie up there, but the major focus of activity is Peterhead Power Station, whose water supplies are pumped from Boddam harbour. On an all but island site linked to Boddam by a bridge, Buchan Ness is Britain's most easterly mainland lighthouse. A clifftop path follows the rocky Buchan coast towards Cruden Bay, 5 miles to the south.

⑧ BULLERS OF BUCHAN
Fishermen used to live in the tiny clifftop hamlet. Their boats were kept at the foot of frightening cliffs where ful-

OFFSHORE PERIL *A line of white water off Rattray Head marks the Rattray Briggs, a notorious reef where many ships were wrecked before the lighthouse was built in 1893.*

mars and kittiwakes nest. Visible from the cliff path, where walkers must take great care, the Pot is a huge granite cauldron into which the tide pours through a natural archway in the rock.

⑨ CRUDEN BAY

The original fishing village at Cruden Bay was transformed when the railway arrived in 1897. A palatial hotel was built, and excellent golf courses were laid out behind the magnificent sandy beach. Although the railway and hotel have both been dismantled, Cruden Bay remains an appealing holiday and golfing resort. Lobster boats use the harbour, and there are salmon nets offshore. The great stone font inside 18th-century St James's Church probably came from an earlier church, founded by Malcolm II in 1012. There is a monument in the main street to the pioneering Norwegian aviator Tryggve Gran, whose solo flight in 1914 from Cruden Bay to Stavanger in Norway was the first across the North Sea. Bram Stoker was a regular visitor to Cruden Bay, and it was there, in 1895, that he thought up the chilling story of *Dracula*. The novelist is said to have drawn inspiration for the book from the eerie clifftop ruins of Slains Castle, built in 1597, which can be reached with extreme care along a path from the car park at Cruden Bay.

North Sea oil is unobtrusively piped ashore to a terminal near the fishing hamlet of Whinnyfold, south of Cruden Bay. Helicopters fly overhead between Aberdeen airport and the oil platforms.

⑩ COLLIESTON

An amphitheatre of cottages encloses the harbour at Collieston, which used to be noted for 'speldings' – salted and sun-dried whiting. Footpaths meander round the village to clifftop viewpoints such as Cransdale, the site of an old quarry within the village bounds. The rocky inlet called St Catharine's Dub took its name from the *Santa Catarina*, a Spanish ship wrecked in 1590 while bringing arms for the Earl of Erroll's failed rebellion. Later, Collieston was a haunt of smugglers, one of whom, Philip Kennedy, was fatally wounded in a night-time ambush by excisemen in 1798. He crawled to the Kirk of Slains and died in the churchyard, where he lies under a non-committal gravestone.

BIRD HAVEN *The Forvie National Nature Reserve is home to some 4000 eider ducks. They breed in spring and early summer.*

⑪ FORVIE NATIONAL NATURE RESERVE

A visitor centre in the reserve describes this fascinating area of cliffs, beaches, salt marsh, mud flats and sandhills. The reserve, which has some of the largest dune systems in Britain, stretches from Collieston to the mouth of the River Ythan, with fulmars, kittiwakes and herring gulls on the cliffs near the remote salmon-fishing station at Rockend. Thousands of greylag and pink-footed geese winter there. Terns nest, together with the greatest concentration of eider ducks in Britain.

Footpaths from the car park on the reserve's western side lead for 3 miles east to the site of a lost village engulfed in 1413 by windblown sand. All that survives is ruined Forvie Kirk.

⑫ NEWBURGH

Some old quayside buildings are evidence of Newburgh's past as a trading and fishing port. Anglers and commercial fishermen are drawn to the sandy Ythan estuary, where gulls and oystercatchers gather on the shore.

PLACES TO SEE INLAND

Haddo House (NTS), 15 miles NW of Collieston. Adam mansion designed in 1731. Grounds form a country park.

Pitmedden Garden (NTS), 8 miles W of Newburgh. Elaborate formal garden first laid out in 1675. Museum of Farming Life.

TOURIST INFORMATION

Aden Country Park (01771) 623037; Ellon (01358) 720730 (summer); Peterhead (01779) 471904 (summer)

Formidable cliffs above a village at the sea's edge

The fishing towns and resorts along the Banff coast are hemmed in by spectacular cliffs. Crovie village, almost washed away by storms in 1953, presses up against the cliff face, just feet from the encroaching sea.

① CULLEN

A royal burgh since 1455, the cheerful resort of Cullen is built on two levels. Within the square of the upper village stands an ornate market cross, dating from 1696. Paths along disused railway viaducts provide views over restored Seatown, Cullen's lower village, where Cullen Skink – fish soup with a smoked haddock base – was devised. The Auld Kirk, dating from at least the 14th century, has fine 16th and 17th-century interior details. Sea-angling trips for mackerel, ling and haddock operate from the harbour. The coast path provides an easy stroll westwards along Cullen Bay and tackles rougher ground eastwards to remote Sunnyside Beach.

② FINDLATER CASTLE

A clifftop path from a car park at Barnyards of Findlater leads past a restored dovecote and overlooks the hazardous ruins of Findlater Castle, perched on a headland. This 15th-century fortress was abandoned soon after 1600. Westwards, the coast path dips down to the sandy beach at Sunnyside.

③ SANDEND

One of Scotland's smallest harbours is the focus of this traditional fishing village, whose short streets run at right angles to the sea. A fine, sandy beach occupies the head of Sandend Bay, where sea birds drink from the burn.

In Fordyce village, 3 miles inland, 13th-century St Tarquin's Church is an intriguing, partly restored ruin with elegant canopied tombs. Fordyce Joiners Workshop celebrates the expertise of Victorian rural craftsmen with displays of tools and machinery.

④ PORTSOY

Restored 17th-century warehouses stand tall by the waterside of the Moray Firth's oldest harbour, now used by pleasure craft and lobster boats. One of the warehouses is a workshop for 'Portsoy marble', a red and green serpentine used in the construction of parts of the Palace of Versailles. The track where the old branch railway once ran is now a short footpath climbing towards the boating pond at Loch Soy.

⑤ WHITEHILLS

The independent fishing village has not lost its livelihood to larger harbours and retains its own fish market. The ancient Red Well is fed by a spring containing iron salts. Immense cliffs rise to the east.

⑥ BANFF

A royal burgh and county town, Banff preserves many town houses of 17th and 18th-century landed families. The grand mansion of Duff House (HS), built around 1740, houses a magnificent collection of art from the National Galleries of Scotland. There are many impressive tombstones and memorial sculptures in the churchyard of ruined St Mary's. Banff Museum includes exhibits of local silverware, while Colleonard Sculpture Garden, just outside Banff, exhibits abstract sculptures that were created from living trees. James MacPherson, a notorious troublemaker, was hanged in 1700 at the Plainstones area of the town. The song he wrote in jail, starting 'I have spent my life in rioting', was rewritten by Robert Burns as *MacPherson's Farewell*.

⑦ MACDUFF

Set beyond the sandy mouth of the Deveron, Macduff is a major fishing port. Tours of the harbour, boat trips, sea-angling and diving expeditions can all be arranged. The town cross on the Hill of Doune stands in front of Doune Church, whose clock-tower has a blank face on its westward side. The clock was designed in this way as a gesture to the people of Banff, who had moved their own clocks forward on the day of James MacPherson's execution, to minimise the chance of a last-minute reprieve.

⑧ GARDENSTOWN

Built on a series of terraces set into the dramatic cliffs of Gamrie Bay, the village rises behind a well-maintained harbour. Gardenstown gained prosperity in the 19th century through its fishing industry, although most locally owned fishing boats operate from larger ports today. A clifftop path heads north to Crovie, pronounced 'Crivie', a 10 minute walk away. This village is crammed so tightly against the cliffs that there is no room for a public street. On the west side of Gamrie Bay, St John's Kirk was founded in the 11th century to mark the defeat of an invading Danish army, and is now in ruins.

⑨ PENNAN

Cliffs noisy with sea birds surround the handsome village of Pennan. The hotel and a red telephone box featured strongly in the film *Local Hero*. The box now has a preservation order on it and has become the most famous in Scotland. Cullykhan Bay's sandy beach is reached by a flight of steps.

A path leads from the car park at Cullykhan to the Bronze Age promontory settlement known as Fort Fiddes, from where walkers should proceed with caution to the intimidating sea cliff tunnel called Hell's Lum.

⑩ ABERDOUR BAY

The pebble beach of this popular tourist spot is backed by red sandstone cliffs, pierced by caves, that stretch beyond a grassy pass to Boat Shore. St Drostan's Well marks the spot where a 6th-century missionary from Caithness is said to have landed, and the Jane Whyte memorial commemorates the heroine of a shipwreck of 1884. The ruins of Old Aberdour Church, on a site consecrated

GRACIOUS LIVING *Duff House in Banff, one of Britain's finest Georgian baroque houses, was designed by William Adam.*

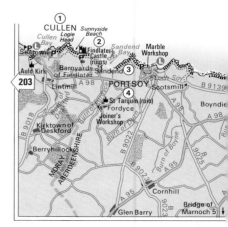

WITHOUT A STREET *The tiny village of Crovie is perched on the brink of Gamrie Bay, with virtually no room in which to expand, and at the foot of grassy cliffs that soar to 350 ft.*

in St Drostan's time, overlook Dour Burn. Part of the ruin dates from Norman times. A pleasant footpath runs for 3 miles inland over hills to Pennan. The village of New Aberdour, founded in 1798, replaced an earlier one on the shores of the bay. Northfield Farm Museum, about 3 miles to the south-west, has a collection of farm machinery and household implements.

⑪ ROSEHEARTY

Surrounding a peaceful harbour, the village was a flourishing fishing port from around the 14th century until the narrow entrance to its harbour could no longer cope adequately with larger vessels. Rosehearty's fleet is now based at Fraserburgh. The fine 15th-century ruin of Pitsligo Castle is preserved by a local

trust. Rosehearty war memorial, which looks across spectacular cliffs to the east and west, provides the district's finest viewpoint. More views can be taken in from the picnic site near the Mounthooly Dovecote of 1800. Pitsligo parish church, on the edge of Peathill, includes some beautiful woodcarvings that once adorned its 17th-century predecessor, whose ruins stand alongside.

⑫ SANDHAVEN

Fishing activity at Sandhaven and neighbouring Pittulie, once thriving ports, has declined since the late 19th century, although lobster boats still go out. Sandhaven Meal Mill, built in the late 18th century, has been restored as a visitor centre, with demonstrations of oats being processed into oatmeal.

⑬ FRASERBURGH

Named after its 16th-century founder, Alexander Fraser, Fraserburgh is the biggest fishing port after Peterhead on Scotland's north-east coast. The market cross, carved soon after the Union of Crowns in 1603, shows the royal arms of both Scotland and Great Britain. Kinnaird Head lighthouse, built into the structure of 16th-century Fraserburgh Castle, is a museum devoted to fishing and the lighthouse's history.

A sandy beach, fringed by dunes and reached from the Water of Philorth picnic site, stretches to the east. The line of the old light railway to the villages of Cairnbulg, Inverallochy and St Combs can still be made out and parts of it can be followed. Cairnbulg Boathaven is an excellent viewpoint over Fraserburgh Bay, and Cairnbulg Castle is open to visitors by appointment.

PLACES TO SEE INLAND

Cloverleaf Llama Farm, Bridge of Marnoch, 12 miles SW of Banff. Daily guided tours.

Delgatie Castle, nr Turriff, 10 miles SE of Macduff. 16th-century remodelling of an 11th-century tower house. Painted ceilings.

TOURIST INFORMATION

Banff (01261) 812419 (summer); Fraserburgh (01346) 518315 (summer)

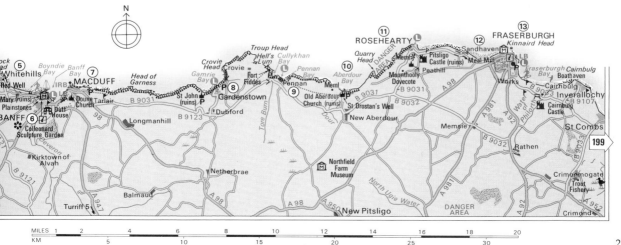

Fishing harbours where the Spey joins the Moray Firth

The villages of the Moray Firth owe their existence to fishing, though boats go out from only a few today. Walkers on the cliffs may see bottle-nosed dolphins out at sea; inland is the historic town of Elgin.

REBUILT IN STONE *A wooden tower once crowned the mound where the early 14th-century keep of Duffus Castle now stands.*

① DUFFUS

Like many of the villages along this coast, the quiet, pretty hamlet of Duffus was planned and built in the 19th century. The original village was centred on 13th-century St Peter's Church, now a ruin. In the churchyard, is a small gravewatcher's hut, built in 1830.

The ruins of Duffus Castle (HS), 2 miles south-east of the village, tower above a Norman mound set on the edge of flat land that was formerly a loch. There has been a castle on this spot since 1150; the most recent building was abandoned in the 18th century.

② LOSSIEMOUTH

Shellfish and some white fish are landed at this busy fishing town, and a fish market operates most weekday mornings. There are excellent sandy beaches to the east and west. The east beach often has good conditions for surfing. Britain's first Labour prime minister, Ramsay MacDonald, was born in Lossiemouth in 1866; a memorial, erected on the centenary of his birth, offers spectacular views over Spey Bay. The peace is sometimes broken by aircraft landing at and taking off from RAF Lossiemouth just outside the town.

Three miles inland are the ruins of 15th-century Spynie Palace (HS), once the home of the Bishops of Moray.

③ ELGIN

One of the principal market towns of the 'Granary of the North', as the fertile southern shore of the Moray Firth is known, Elgin has fine 19th-century neo-classical buildings and a few grand town houses from earlier centuries. Beside the River Lossie are the magnificent ruins of the cathedral, founded in 1224. Elgin Museum explains the history of the area from the days of the dinosaurs to the present. The Moray Motor Museum has a collection of veteran and vintage vehicles. A mile west of the town centre is Old Mills, a restored water mill dating from 1230.

④ LHANBRYDE

The name Lhanbryde means 'Church of St Bridget', and the original Victorian village, which has seen considerable housing development in recent years, was built around the church. Crooked Wood, just north of Lhanbryde, offers walks, and an orienteering course, for which information packs are available from Elgin tourist office. Nearly a mile south-west of the village is Coxton Tower, a small castle completed in 1644, open to visitors by appointment.

⑤ KINGSTON

No sign remains of the shipbuilding that once flourished in Kingston, at the mouth of the River Spey. The industry declined after cheaper iron-clad vessels

---

started to be made on the Clyde. Garmouth, nearly a mile to the south, was a busy port on the Spey estuary in the 18th century, but a great flood in 1829 altered the course of the river. Today both villages are peaceful places, with narrow winding streets. Walkers can follow the coast from the shingle beach at Kingston to the sands of Lossiemouth, some 7 miles to the west. A short stretch of shore immediately west of Kingston is sometimes closed to the public for military firing practice.

⑥ SPEY BAY

A collection of widely spaced houses at the mouth of the Spey make up the village of Spey Bay, once an important centre for salmon fishing. Inside Tugnet Ice House, a warehouse built in 1830 to store salmon before it was sold, displays explain the local fishing industry, and the way in which the river mouth has changed over the years. Although commercial fishing has ceased, salmon are still caught by individual fishermen.

The river estuary and long shingle beach are rich in slack and freshwater marsh vegetation, including coral-root orchid and burnet rose, and the area is good for viewing summer feeding birds such as ospreys. The village is at the northern end of the Speyside Way, a trail which follows the river inland for 45 miles to Tomintoul.

⑦ FOCHABERS

The town was laid out on a grid plan in the late 18th century, and many buildings from that time survive, including Bellie Kirk, which lends an air of Georgian elegance to the town square. The town's history is told in the Folk Museum, where exhibits include horse-drawn vehicles, costumes and toys. The former Milne's High School, a splendid example of Victorian architecture built in 1846, is now a primary school.

About a mile east of Fochabers, off the A98, are the Winding Walks, well-made paths through Whiteash Hill Wood. The top of the hill offers panoramic views of lower Speyside and the countryside east of Elgin. Eroded stacks of red sandstone, known as the Earth Pillars, can be seen on the banks of the Spey 1½ miles south of Fochabers.

Tours are available of the Baxters food-processing factory just across the river from Fochabers; a visitor centre tells the story of the company.

⑧ PORTGORDON

The late 18th-century village of Portgordon clusters round its tiny harbour, once used by salmon fishermen but now only by pleasure craft. A 2½ mile walk along the sand and shingle foreshore leads west to Spey Bay.

Just over a mile inland, at Leitcheston, stands a dovecot built to provide pigeon meat and eggs for a nearby castle, no trace of which remains. The dovecot is clearly visible from the A98.

> **THE NOBLE SALMON**
>
> To fishermen, the River Spey means salmon. The fish spend most of their adult lives, usually about 2-3 years, in the North Atlantic, but swim for thousands of miles back to the river of their birth to spawn, from November to early January. It is thought that some form of in-built 'compass' may enable salmon to steer by the Earth's magnetic field, or even by the stars. In coastal waters each fish can 'smell' its own river.
>
>
>
> *A salmon swimming home to its spawning grounds can leap waterfalls up to 11 ft high.*

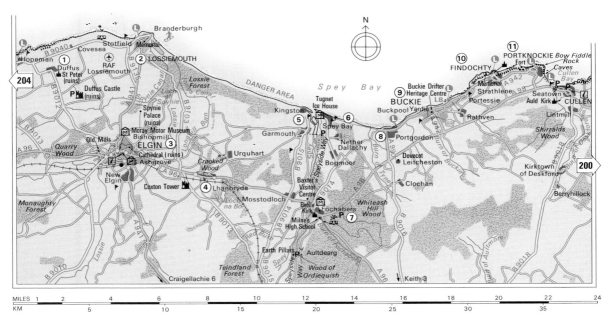

⑨ BUCKIE

Stretching for 2½ miles along the coast, from Buckpool in the west to Portessie in the east, Buckie is a thriving fishing port and one of the few places in Scotland where traditional fishing boats are still made. There is a morning fish market, at its busiest on Thursdays and Fridays. From the turn of the century to the 1930s Buckie was the base of a large herring fleet, but today the catch is mainly of shellfish, supplying markets in France and Spain, as well as in Britain. The story of herring fishing is told at the Buckie Drifter, a heritage centre where visitors can board a replica of a steam drifter. In summer boat trips are available round the harbour, or along the coast to observe bottle-nosed dolphins, which can often be seen in groups of 20 or more.

⑩ FINDOCHTY

The older part of Findochty, pronounced 'Finnechty', borders a little bay, overlooked by a World War I memorial to the west and the 19th-century Hythe's Church to the east. Brightly painted houses give a cheerful appearance to this former fishing village, which now attracts pleasure craft. Dolphin-watching boat trips leave from the harbour in summer. A coast path follows a smugglers' route westwards for a mile, past hidden coves and caves. To the east of the harbour is a sheltered sandy cove, from which a clifftop path leads eastwards to Portknockie.

⑪ PORTKNOCKIE

A quiet former fishing village, Portknockie consists mostly of closely packed houses sitting on a cliff high above the harbour, which provides an excellent haven for small boats. From the cliff path to the east strangely shaped rocks can be seen spearing out of the sea just offshore. Preacher's Cave, one of several caves along the rocky foreshore, was used as a church during the religious revival of the early 19th century. A 1½ mile clifftop walk west to Findochty offers superb views across the Moray Firth to the Black Isle.

PLACES TO SEE INLAND

Mill of Towie, nr Keith, 15 miles S of Buckie. Restored 19th-century mill producing oatmeal, using traditional machinery.

Speyside Cooperage, nr Craigellachie, 19 miles SE of Lossiemouth. Visitor centre explaining how coopers make casks for the whisky industry.

TOURIST INFORMATION

Elgin (01343) 542666

NATURAL ARTISTRY *Bow Fiddle Rock takes its name from the delicate shape suggested by its wave-sculpted arch. It can be seen from the clifftop walk east of Portknockie.*

A serene coast of sandy bays and quiet forests

*From the sheltered sands of Nairn, the shore sweeps east in a series
of open bays to the rocky headland of Burghead. Highland hills rich in
plants and wildlife are a backdrop to the shores of the Moray Firth.*

① NAIRN

The history of this popular holiday
town, which dates back to the 12th century, when Alexander I granted it a
royal charter, is explained in the Nairn
Museum, housed in a Georgian mansion. In the grounds of the museum is a
statue of Dr John Grigor, who did much
to promote Nairn as a health resort in
the 19th century. The early 19th-century
Old Courthouse, in the town centre, has
an impressive bell tower which was
added in 1860.

Nairn was once a prosperous herring
port, but the industry declined in the
1930s and the harbour is now used
mainly by pleasure craft. Behind the
harbour are the narrow streets and
tightly packed cottages of the old fishing district of Fishertown, where a
museum in the tiny Laing Hall charts
the history of the local fishing industry.
There is a sandy beach to the east of the
harbour, and another to the west, where
Nairn Leisure Park offers croquet, outdoor draughts and chess, a fitness trail
and a play area. There are walks along
both sides of the River Nairn. Highland
games are held in mid August.

② AULDEARN

A walk through the quiet village's
narrow streets leads to the 17th-century
Boath Doocot (NTS). The circular dovecote stands on the motte, or mound, of
an ancient castle, built as a stronghold
against Celtic attack. From the mound
there are wonderful views over the
Moray Firth, and of the nearby site of
the Battle of Auldearn, where in 1645
the Royalist Marquis of Montrose
routed a much larger force of Covenanters led by General Sir John Urry.

WINTER STOCK *The dovecote at Auldearn,
with hundreds of nest holes, supplied food
for the local laird's table during the winter.*

③ BRODIE CASTLE

Approached through dense woodland,
Brodie Castle (NTS) is an impressive
sight. A 16th-century tower with later
enlargements and alterations, the castle
has been the home of the Brodie family since it was built, and contains
collections of French furniture and fine
paintings. Just inside the eastern entrance to the beautifully landscaped
castle grounds is a well-preserved 9th-
century Pictish symbol stone known as
Rodney's Stone. The engraved 4 ft slab
was uncovered in the 18th century,
when the foundations were being dug
for the parish church of the village of
Dyke, just over half a mile away.

④ DARNAWAY FARM
VISITOR CENTRE

Visitors to Darnaway Farm can see a
dairy herd, as well as old tractors and
other farm implements. An audiovisual
display explains the history of the area
from ancient times to the present day.
Woodland trails explore the estate, and
in July and early August there are tours
of Darnaway Castle, the home of the
Earls of Moray since 1562. The castle
has a medieval hammerbeam roof.

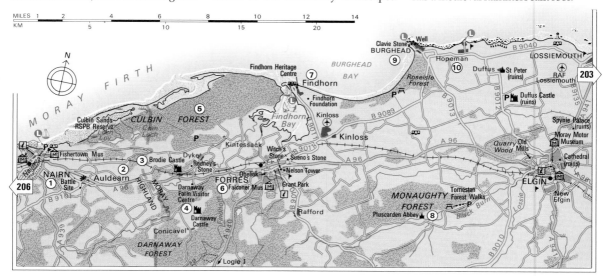

SEA, SAND AND SOLITUDE *From Findhorn, a 5 mile stretch of sand and dunes extends eastwards in a broad arc to the village of Burghead, situated on its stubby headland.*

⑤ CULBIN FOREST

For centuries, the area where Culbin Forest now stands was a desert of sand created by storms during the 17th century. The sands buried the village of Culbin, which had stood at the heart of rich farmland. In the 1920s the Forestry Commission started planting Scots and Corsican pines on the sands, and the forest now extends along some 9 miles of coastline. Its varied wildlife includes rare species such as ospreys, wildcats and capercaillies, Britain's largest game bird. There are walks through the forest to shoreline dunes. Bordering the forest on its north-western shore is the Culbin Sands RSPB Reserve, where birds such as bar-tailed godwits, knots, shelduck and greylag geese can be seen.

⑥ FORRES

The opening scenes of Shakespeare's tragedy *Macbeth* are set in Forres, an ancient royal burgh whose street layout dates from medieval times. At the centre of the town are the 19th-century tolbooth, or town hall, and market cross. The Falconer Museum explains aspects of the town's history. At the western end of the high street, an obelisk on Castle Hill commemorates James Thomson, a local surgeon who tended soldiers in the Crimean War regardless of their nationality. The Nelson Tower on Cluny Hill, at the eastern end of the town, was erected in 1806 to celebrate Britain's victory at Trafalgar; visitors can climb to the top for wide views of the Moray Firth. The extensive Grant Park, at the foot of Cluny Hill, is known for its floral displays.

North-east of the town is a 23 ft pillar known as Sueno's Stone (HS). The pillar is believed to be at least a thousand years old, and has carvings of warriors. Nearby is the Witch's Stone, thought to be a Pictish altar to the sun god.

⑦ FINDHORN

The former port at the entrance to Findhorn Bay is a centre for watersports and sailing. Grey and common seals live in the bay, and migrating wildfowl visit the extensive tidal mud flats. A heritage centre explains the natural and human history of the area. East of the village, paths lead from the long sandy crescent of Burghead Bay into Roseisle Forest.

At the southern end of the village is the base of the Findhorn Foundation, a spiritual community. Classes for non-residents are available in music, dance and the visual arts, and guided tours take place in the summer.

⑧ PLUSCARDEN ABBEY

A peaceful wooded valley is the setting for Britain's most northerly Benedictine monastery. A priory was established in 1230, but fell into disrepair after the Reformation. Restoration work started in the early 1900s, and a community of monks was established in 1948. The priory was given the status of an abbey in 1974, and rebuilding continues.

Two miles north-east of the abbey, a picnic site in Monaughty Forest marks the start of woodland trails known as the Torrieston Walks.

⑨ BURGHEAD

Stone-built granaries lining the harbour date from the time when Burghead was Moray's foremost grain-shipping port. Now the harbour is used by fishing boats and pleasure craft. The village is built on a promontory jutting into the Moray Firth, and near the tip is Burghead Well (HS), which may have provided water for a nearby Iron Age fort. The well is enclosed, but the key to the gateway is available from a neighbouring house.

Every January 11, a blazing tar barrel known as the Clavie is carried round the village. The event celebrates the New Year under the Julian calendar, which was replaced by the Gregorian calendar in 1752. The barrel's charred remains are placed on the Clavie Stone, not far from the well. In the window of the village library are panels explaining the Clavie tradition, as well as some Pictish stones engraved with the figure of a bull that were found in the area.

There are walks and a picnic area in Roseisle Forest, bordering the 5 mile sandy beach south-west of the town.

⑩ HOPEMAN

The quiet, unspoilt fishing village, founded in the early 19th century, is built on a gentle slope overlooking the sea, and the small sheltered harbour is used by pleasure craft. There are sandy beaches east and west of the harbour; a 5½ mile walk eastwards, mostly along cliffs, leads to Lossiemouth.

A BIRD OF THE PINE

The male capercaillie may be seen and heard in Culbin Forest showing off its tail feathers and uttering its gurgling mating call. The turkey-sized bird became extinct in Britain in 1783, but was re-introduced from Sweden in 1837. Its name may derive from the Gaelic word *capullcoille*, meaning 'horse of the woods'.

Aggressive males may threaten deer and sheep.

PLACES TO SEE INLAND

Randolph's Leap, nr Logie, 7 miles SW of Forres. Gorge on River Findhorn.

TOURIST INFORMATION

Elgin (01343) 542666; Forres (01309) 672938 (summer); Nairn (01667) 452753 (summer)

Where the Highlands sweep down to the firths

The Moray and Beauly Firths cut deep into the Highlands at Inverness, the region's unofficial 'capital', from which the Caledonian Canal heads south towards Loch Ness on its way to Scotland's west coast.

① FORTROSE

Lying at the foot of steep hills, the harbour of this former fishing village is often busy with pleasure craft. In the village are the ruins of Fortrose Cathedral (HS), which includes parts of the 14th-century south chapel and aisle, and of the 13th-century chapter house.

East of the harbour is a small beach, beyond which a long, narrow peninsula protrudes into the Moray Firth. Its tip, Chanonry Point, is approached by a road across a golf course. At the point, and next to a whitewashed lighthouse, stands the Brahan Seer Stone, which commemorates Kenneth MacKenzie, a 17th-century seer. Superb views extend from the point, across the firth to Fort George, and west towards Inverness.

② AVOCH

Old cottages cluster round the harbour of the bustling fishing village of Avoch, pronounced 'Ock'. The churchyard of Old Avoch Church contains the grave of Sir Alexander MacKenzie, the 18th-century Scottish-born explorer of Canada, who spent some time in the village after his retirement. Photographs and other items relating to the area can be seen at the Avoch Heritage Exhibition.

Avoch and Fortrose are linked by a 4½ mile circular walk, part of which follows a disused railway line near the banks of the Moray Firth.

③ MUNLOCHY

The quiet village is set on high ground at the head of Munlochy Bay, whose mud flats attract large numbers of birds, including herons and geese. Ornamental waterfowl are the principal attraction of the Black Isle Country Park, 2 miles south of Munlochy; sheep, llamas and wallabies can also be seen. From the park, a lane leads east to the hill of Craigiehowe, overlooking the bay's southern entrance. The hill is home to a herd of wild goats.

④ NORTH KESSOCK

The small village and its neighbour Charlestown mark the entrance to the Beauly Firth. Just north of the Kessock Bridge is a picnic area with fine views and a centre at which visitors can listen to dolphins and seals in the firth using underwater microphones. Paths nearby climb the 626 ft summit of Ord Hill.

A watersports centre at Craigrory, 2½ miles west of North Kessock, offers water-skiing, sailing and windsurfing.

⑤ MUIR OF ORD

The number of roads converging on Muir of Ord bear witness to the fact that it was once an important market town, which until the opening of the Kessock Bridge was the main gateway to the Black Isle peninsula. One of Scotland's major agricultural events, the Black Isle

Show, is held at Muir of Ord on the first Thursday in August. To the north-west of the town is the Glen Ord Distillery, where whisky has been produced since 1838. Tours are available, and a visitor centre traces the history of the area.

⑥ BEAULY

Set at the head of the Beauly estuary, the town grew up around 13th-century Beauly Priory (HS), whose ruins dominate the main street. To the west is a large crafts centre called Made In Scotland, where knitwear, jewellery, pottery and glassware are displayed.

South-east of Beauly is a winery based in a mansion known as Moniack Castle; products include wines made from elderflower and silver birch, and two liqueurs. The house is a private residence, but the fermenting rooms, vats and bottling room, which have been converted from the former stables and laundry, can be visited. A nearby walk follows a stream along Reelig Glen.

⑦ CRAIG PHADRIG

The 556 ft hill, just west of Inverness, can be explored by a network of paths through attractive woodland. On the summit are the remains of an Iron Age fort, from where there are superb views, eastwards across the Moray Firth and westwards over the Beauly Firth and to the mountains beyond. The easiest way to reach Craig Phadrig is from the car park at its southern end, approached by either the A82 or the A862.

⑧ INVERNESS

The Highlands' unofficial capital, straddling the Caledonian Canal and the River Ness, sits on a level plain fringed by tidal mud flats. On a hilltop overlooking the east bank of the Ness is the town's 19th-century castle, now the court house. The nearby Gothic-style Town House was the scene in 1921 of an emergency Cabinet meeting to discuss the Irish Treaty, called by the prime minister, David Lloyd George, who was on holiday in the area. Castle Wynd

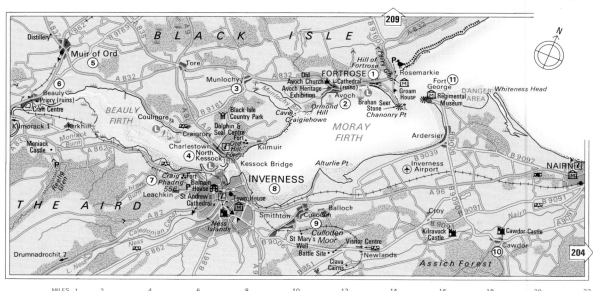

BONNY BANKS *Brushed with autumnal tints and framed by misty mountain peaks, Beauly Firth lives up to the Norman name* beau lieu, *a 'beautiful place'.*

houses an art gallery and a museum telling the history of the Highlands. On the river's west bank is the mid 19th-century St Andrew's Cathedral, which has fine stained glass. Just downriver is Balnain House, built in 1726, where Highland music is explained and performed. A pedestrian bridge crosses the Ness to the Old High Church, dating from the 14th century but substantially rebuilt 400 years later.

Inverness has many opportunities for gentle walks, such as around the Ness Islands south of the town. The islands are joined to each other and to the riverbanks by a series of bridges. Pleasure craft abound in this part of the Caledonian Canal, which links the Beauly Firth to Loch Ness; boats can be hired.

PRINCE'S SAVIOUR *At Inverness Castle is a statue of Flora MacDonald, who aided Bonnie Prince Charlie's escape in 1746.*

⑨ CULLODEN MOOR

Open farmland and dark forest cover Culloden Moor (NTS), the site of the bloody battle of 1746 in which the Duke of Cumberland's army defeated that of Charles Edward Stuart, Bonnie Prince Charlie, and ended the Stuart dynasty's last chance of regaining the English throne. A visitor centre explains the story of the battle. Guided tours of the moor can be arranged in summer. A pleasant forest walk of about 2 miles passes near the Prisoners' Stone, where 17 officers of the losing army were executed after the battle. Earlier historical remains can be seen south-east of the visitor centre at Clava Cairns (HS). The cairns, surrounded by rings of standing stones, are thought to be more than 4000 years old. On the western edge of the moor is ancient St Mary's Well, whose waters were once believed to have curative powers.

⑩ CAWDOR

A small river flows by the hamlet of Cawdor, separating it from the Cawdor estate to the east. Cawdor Castle, set amid woods of beech and oak, has been the home of the Thanes, later the Earls, of Cawdor for many centuries. The 14th-century keep was extended in the 17th century, and the mellow stone house now contains a superb collection of family portraits, as well as tapestries and some excellent furniture. There are nature trails in the impressive grounds.

West of Cawdor, on the north bank of the Nairn, is the 15th-century Kilravock Castle. The grounds are open to visitors in summer; on Wednesdays tours are given of the castle, which includes a small museum of clan-related objects.

Cannon line the ramparts at Fort George.

⑪ FORT GEORGE

Built after the Battle of Culloden as a garrison fortress for the Hanoverian army of George II, Fort George is one of the finest 18th-century artillery fortresses in Europe. It stands at the tip of a promontory jutting into the Moray Firth, and is protected by almost a mile of mighty ramparts. Every approach is covered by at least two cannon-lined walls. The fort is still an army barracks, but visitors may explore several buildings, such as the main guardrooms, a powder magazine, an armoury and the garrison chapel, and walk the ramparts for views of the Moray Firth. At the entrance to the fort is a visitor centre. In the grounds, but independently run, is the Regimental Museum of the Queen's Own Highlanders.

PLACES TO SEE INLAND
Cluanie Deer Farm Park, nr Kilmorack, 13 miles W of Inverness. Nature trail, picnic site.
Loch Ness Monster Exhibition, Drumnadrochit, 15 miles SW of Inverness. Guide to history of claimed monster sightings.

TOURIST INFORMATION
Inverness (01463) 234353; North Kessock (01463) 731505

Symbols of black gold in the towns of the Black Isle

Many of the towns on the Cromarty and Moray Firths have prospered from their links with the oil industry. Rigs form part of the landscape, but sparkling streams and shady woods offer countryside charm.

① INVERGORDON

Oil rigs are as much a part of Invergordon as the undulating hills behind it. The town prospered in the 1970s and 80s from both rig-fitting and aluminium smelting; the aluminium works are now closed. Although mainly used by cruisers, the harbour also has a yacht club. The stony foreshore, part of which forms the Nigg Bay RSPB Reserve, is a good place to spot wading birds, such as knots and dunlins. Walks from Invergordon can be taken along the shore for about 2 miles north-east to Saltburn and 4 miles west to Alness.

② ALNESS

The town has expanded greatly since the 1970s, as a result of the industrial growth brought by the oil business. It sits astride the River Averon, which flows through woodlands to reach a mud and shingle shore. Alness has two distilleries, one of which, Dalmore Distillery, is open to the public, though advance bookings are required.

③ EVANTON

The quiet village is overlooked by Cnoc Fyrish, a hill crowned by the Fyrish Monument. This structure, a replica of an Indian gate, was commissioned by General Sir Hector Munro in 1782, partly in celebration of his military success at Negapatam, in India, in 1781, and partly because its construction provided employment in the area. The monument can be reached from a forest walk that starts from the car park on the Boath road, off the A836.

Half a mile inland from Evanton lies the spectacular Black Rock Gorge, a 200 ft deep chasm carved by the River Glass as it storms down from Loch Glass towards the Cromarty Firth.

④ DINGWALL

There has been a settlement on this spot since Viking times. The name Dingwall comes from the Norse *Thing vollr*, meaning 'place of the parliament', and the market town continues to play a major administrative role in the district. The partly 18th-century Town House is now a museum illustrating the local history from the Bronze Age to the present day. It also includes information on General Sir Hector MacDonald, born locally in 1853. The pinnacle of his considerable military career, which began in the Gordon Highlanders, was in 1898 when he was recognised as the hero of the Battle of Omdurman. A tower erected in MacDonald's name in 1907, four years after his death, stands within the cemetery on top of Mitchell Hill. Cannons surround the tower, and the climb to the top gives excellent views over Dingwall and the Cromarty Firth; keys to the tower are available from the district council offices in the town.

⑤ STRATHPEFFER

The beautiful little town was distinctive in the 19th century for its spa, and it is still possible for visitors to sample the sulphurous waters in a pavilion in the town square. The former railway station building now houses a craft centre and the Highland Museum of Childhood, which has a dressing-up box for children, as well as displays of toys and photographs. A short walk through the eastern part of the town leads to the Eagle Stone, a fine example of Pictish art dating from the 7th century.

SECRETS OF THE SANDSTONE
Hugh Miller was a stonemason whose interest in geology began in the early 19th century when he was working in quarries on the Black Isle. He discovered many fossils that were unknown to science. In Old Red Sandstone at Eathie he found a winged fish, later named in his honour as *Pterichthyodes milleri*.

Hugh Miller and his Cromarty cottage

SAFE WATERS *Dingwall lies among low hills and deep in Cromarty Firth, a huge natural harbour which ancient map-makers called* Portus Salutis – 'the harbour of safety'.

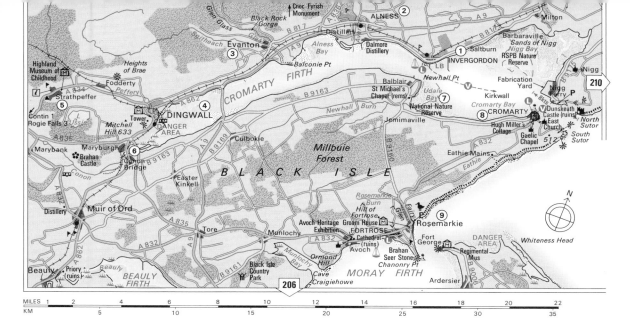

⑥ CONON BRIDGE

Once a separate community, Conon Bridge now merges with its neighbour Maryburgh, to form a large residential area. There is excellent fishing for salmon and sea trout on the fast-flowing Conon, and there are tranquil walks upstream along its southern banks.

The ruins of 17th-century Brahan Castle, 3 miles inland, lie within peaceful gardens that offer magnificent views extending along the Conon valley.

⑦ UDALE BAY

The national nature reserve of Udale Bay is an important resting point for migrating birds. From the RSPB hide in a lay-by to the west of the village of Jemimaville, large numbers of waders, ducks and geese may be viewed.

Inland, the remains of medieval St Michael's Chapel are situated in Kirkmichael burial ground, at the east end of the Newhall Point loop road. This road passes the cluster of pretty cottages that make up the village of Balblair, and provides a pleasant 2 mile circular walk, with good views of the nature reserve and the Firth.

⑧ CROMARTY

Before Dingwall, Cromarty was the administrative centre of the peninsula known as the Black Isle, so named according to one theory because it is seldom whitened by snow. Cromarty is presided over by oil rigs constructed at the Nigg Fabrication Yard to the north.

The town is notable for its variety of 18th and 19th-century architecture, and many of its old buildings have been restored. Hugh Miller's Cottage (NTS) was the birthplace of a remarkable 19th-century stonemason who was also a geologist, folk historian, accountant, newspaper editor and churchman. A memorial to Miller can be seen a short distance south of the cottage. The nearby Cromarty Courthouse, originally built in 1773, has been converted into a museum, complete with prison

NATURAL WONDERLAND *Silver birch trees stand tall by a trickling stream, nodding ferns beckon and a leafy path invites the walker into Fairy Glen, inland from Rosemarkie.*

cells, a trial room and exhibits detailing the history of the town. The East Church dates back to at least the 17th century and features a plaque commemorating the eccentric Sir Thomas Urquhart, the mid 17th-century Laird of Cromarty, who claimed to have traced his ancestry back to Adam and Eve. At the town's southern end is a chapel, built for the Gaelic-speaking worshippers who moved to Cromarty in search of work in the 1770s.

A walk along the foreshore leads to the South Sutor headland, which offers wide views of the North Sea and the Cromarty Firth, as well as over the narrow channel to the North Sutor on the Nigg peninsula. Another walk, starting at the village of Eathie Mains to the south of the town, leads to fossil beds on the shore of the Moray Firth, where Hugh Miller made several discoveries. Boat trips from the harbour explore the Cromarty Firth, where numbers of bottle-nosed dolphins may be seen, and a ferry runs to Nigg Ferry on the opposite bank.

⑨ ROSEMARKIE

The popular resort comprises a collection of small cottages and two-storey houses by a sandy beach. The Groam House Museum and Pictish Centre, in the tiny main street, recalls the history of the area. At the northern end of the village is a car park at the start of a walk leading through Fairy Glen Nature Reserve. Managed by the RSPB and local landowners, this wooded area extends some 2 miles inland along the Rosemarkie Burn, and features many varieties of woodland plant, and birds such as buzzards and willow warblers.

PLACES TO SEE INLAND

Contin Parish Church, 7 miles SW of Dingwall. Built in 18th century on site of older church destroyed in 1492.

Rogie Falls, 9 miles W of Dingwall. Forest walks and picnic site nearby.

TOURIST INFORMATION

North Kessock (01463) 731505; Strathpeffer (01997) 421415 (summer)

Pictish trail and place of pilgrimage in Easter Ross

The Dornoch Firth's wooded shores narrow into the salmon waters of the Kyle of Sutherland and its wild glens. To the south, symbol stones of a lost race unite abstract patterns with early Christian motifs.

① DORNOCH

The compact royal burgh has its roots in the 6th century, when a chapel was founded by St Barr, or Finbarr. The site of the chapel is marked at the east end of what is now the cathedral churchyard. The cathedral, originally built in the 13th century, was badly damaged by fire in 1580, but was much restored in the 17th and 19th centuries. The 16th-century Bishop's Palace across the road has been converted into a hotel. Next door is the Town Jail museum.

The Royal Dornoch Links attract many golfers, but the long, sandy beach backed by dunes remains relatively quiet. The sandbanks of Dornoch Firth draw many wintering wading birds and wildfowl, and common and grey seals can often be seen at low tide.

② SPINNINGDALE

From Dornoch the A949 passes the hamlet of Ospisdale and the tall Ospis Stone, which take their name from a Norse chieftain, on its way to the tiny village of Spinningdale. By the shore of an inlet stands, like some ancient castle, the ruin of an 18th-century cotton mill. To the north-west, down a small lane with limited parking, are Ledmore and Migdale Woods, where paths through pine and oak woods afford views of small Loch Migdale. On a promontory 2 miles south-west of the village stands the Iron Age fort of Dun Creich.

③ BONAR BRIDGE

The village lies on the north side of the Kyle of Sutherland as it enters the Dornoch Firth, and the river is spanned by a bridge of the same name. To the north-west are forest trails in Balblair Wood, while immediately south of the bridge is a picnic site with a riverside walk and an open-air display of types of rock found in northern Scotland.

Nearby Ardgay is the site of the Clach Eiteag, a massive white boulder that used to be moved from parish to parish to mark the site of local markets and fairs; it was finally set here on the site of an annual cattle market held throughout the 19th century.

④ EDDERTON

Ancient cairns and field systems in the gentle hills behind the small village suggest that this area was extensively settled in prehistoric times. In a field on the western edge of the village is a 10ft standing stone, probably of Bronze Age origin, featuring Pictish symbols in disc and Z-shapes. Permission to enter the field must be requested from the neighbouring farmhouse. In the old village churchyard is a cross-slab, a stone on which is carved the outline of a cross, with Pictish engravings of figures on horseback carrying shields and spears. Two miles to the east, a picnic area marks the start of an extensive network of woodland walks.

BRIDGING POINT *Bonar Bridge's bold and simple shape has earned it the nickname 'the coathanger'. In early summer, local hotels issue permits for salmon fishing upriver.*

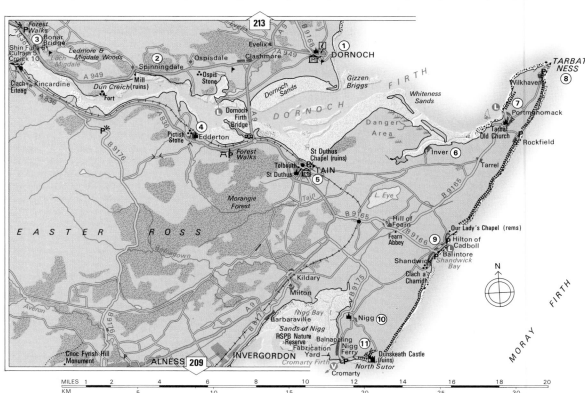

PENINSULA'S END *Waves toss up spray as they crash into jagged rocks at Tarbat Ness, at the mouth of the Dornoch Firth. The 134 ft lighthouse beams a warning light.*

⑤ TAIN

The town's importance as a place of pilgrimage dates from about AD 1000, when St Duthus, or Duthac, was born there. He established a chapel, whose ruins stand near the shore of Dornoch Firth. The 13th-century St Duthus Church, in the centre of the town, was frequented by James IV, who paid his last visit there only a few weeks before his death at the Battle of Flodden in 1513. The nearby Heritage Centre has a trail linking various aspects of the town's religious foundations.

Next to the 18th-century Tolbooth is the Court House, built in the 19th century with turrets and crenellations to match the Tolbooth's candle-snuffer pinnacles. The royal burgh's history is explained at the District Museum, which also houses the Clan Ross Centre. The Highland Fine Cheeses Factory offers guided tours.

⑥ INVER

The wide plain surrounding this quiet village is cluttered with the shells of disused military buildings. During World War II there were plans to use the area

for D-Day practice. Tidal shifts of sand and water channels made this impossible, and the idea was abandoned in favour of a shooting and tank training range. The area is still used for military exercises, and there is no access to the flatlands north-west of the village.

⑦ PORTMAHOMACK

The oddly domed tower of Tarbat Old Church dominates the village where, in the 18th century, Lord Tarbat built a pier beside what had been 'a handful of cottages on an empty heath'. An arc of houses looks out over tall marram grass and a sandy shore to a bay much used by windsurfers. At the northern end of the bay, a breakwater shelters craft engaged in lobster and crab fishing. Boats can be chartered for fishing trips, during which dolphins and porpoises may be spotted in the firth.

A short walk down a country road leads to the diminutive village of Rockfield, tucked away beneath imposing cliffs, and the ruined grandeur of 16th-century Ballone Castle.

⑧ TARBAT NESS

A finger of rolling farmland points towards the open sea, culminating in an area of heath and grassland and a rocky shore. At its tip, a tall slender lighthouse guides ships past the sandbar of Gizzen Briggs in the Dornoch Firth. Tarbat Ness is an important landfall for migrating birds from Scandinavia.

⑨ BALINTORE

Balintore is one of three seaside villages running into one another along a rocky foreshore that turns into a sandy beach at Shandwick Bay. At Hilton of Cadboll are the remains of the ancient Our Lady's Chapel (HS). The Pictish stone

The Pictish Clach a' Charridh stands by the shore near Balintore.

which originally stood next to the chapel is now in Edinburgh's Royal Museum of Scotland, but an information board features a site photograph.

To the south is Balintore and its massive harbour wall. Local boat owners provide fishing and sea bird viewing trips, and there are moorings for pleasure craft. South of Shandwick stands the magnificent Clach a' Charridh – a tall Pictish cross-slab with carvings of angels, huntsmen, warriors and animals, and abstract patterns.

⑩ NIGG

A room in Nigg Old Church, restored from near-dereliction, houses the Nigg Stone, a Pictish cross-slab which once stood in the churchyard. Engravings feature complex interlacing motifs, and the figures of St Paul and St Anthony.

⑪ NIGG FERRY

Under the shadow of the giant cranes stooping over the yards serving North Sea oilfields, a two-car ferry crosses the Cromarty Firth from Nigg Ferry to Cromarty. To the west, an RSPB reserve on the Sands of Nigg provides a haven for a wide range of ducks, geese and waders; a walk along the southern shore eventually climbs the cliffs of North Sutor, on which stand the ruins of 12th-century Dunskeath Castle.

PLACES TO SEE INLAND

Carbisdale Castle, near Culrain, 6 miles NW of Bonar Bridge. Forest walks.

Croick Church, 11 miles W of Bonar Bridge. Site of refuge for crofters evicted from their homes during 19th-century Highland Clearances.

Fearn Abbey, 2 miles NW of Balintore. Dates from 13th century.

Shin Falls, 6 miles NW of Bonar Bridge. Forest walks, spectacular waterfall and gorge.

TOURIST INFORMATION

Dornoch (01862) 810400; North Kessock/ Inverness (01463) 731505

Coastal valleys, and a vast moorland wilderness

Wild shores and towering cliffs are broken by coves in which small villages grew during the Highland Clearances, when crofters resettled on the coast. Inland are quiet glens rich in prehistoric remains.

ROCKY ASCENT *The womenfolk of Whaligoe used to climb the steep steps from the cove up to the clifftop, the first part of the journey to transport the catch north-eastwards to Wick.*

① WHALIGOE
From the tiny village of Whaligoe, a flight of some 360 often slippery flag-stone steps leads down to a minuscule quay bordering wave-lashed rocks. The boats of the 19th-century herring fishers had to be pulled into Whaligoe Cove stern first, and heavy gear and baskets of fish were carried up and down the steps by the women of the village.

About 3 miles to the south-west, on the Hill o' Many Stanes (HS), are hundreds of small Bronze Age standing stones.

② LATHERON
The village's 18th-century kirk now houses the Clan Gunn Museum, which documents the claim that a Gunn reached the Americas a century before Christopher Columbus did. Just north of Latheron are two fine Bronze Age standing stones. To the south, a side road descends to the snug harbour of Latheronwheel and a small picnic area, from which a path across a partly over-grown bridge leads to clifftop walks.

③ LAIDHAY CROFT MUSEUM
A traditional Caithness thatched long-house, standing on land worked as a croft until 1968, has been converted into a museum of local life. The building combines living quarters with stables and a byre, while agricultural imple-ments are displayed in a barn whose roof, incorporating driftwood and old oars, is supported by tree-trunk crucks known locally as 'Highland couples'.

④ DUNBEATH
The former fishing village has a heri-tage centre covering the history and wildlife of the area. From the centre there are views of the distant platforms of the Beatrice Oil Field, the only oil-field visible from the Scottish mainland. Dunbeath Castle, built on a sheer cliff south of the village in the 15th century, was one of the strongholds of the Earls of Caithness. It is still inhabited, and is not open to the public.

Dunbeath is the starting point for several walks, one of which follows Dunbeath Water for 4½ miles to a stand-ing stone and a cairn. The coast road south of the village passes the hamlet of Berriedale, where a trail follows Berrie-dale Water into a broad moorland.

⑤ BADBEA
A path by a lay-by leads to a ruined clifftop settlement, built in the early 19th century by families evicted from their homes during the Highland Clearances. A plaque on one building records that children and animals had to be tethered to stakes to keep them from being blown off into the sea. Most occupants eventually left for New Zealand, from where one descendant later returned to erect a tablet bearing the names of the emigrants.

⑥ ORD OF CAITHNESS
The coast road twists and climbs up the Ord of Caithness, where a narrow pass crosses a natural bastion of rock. From the 750 ft summit of the Ord, which marks the boundary between the dis-tricts of Caithness and Sutherland, the views of the coast in all directions are superb. Below its northern slope lie the workshops of Ousdale Weaving, open to visitors throughout the year.

⑦ HELMSDALE
Situated at the mouth of the Helmsdale salmon river, the former fishing village is surrounded by crofts and steep-sided hills. In the village is the Timespan Visi-tor Centre, where Highland history and lore is brought alive through tableaux and audiovisual presentations. Helms-dale is the starting point for a spectacu-

MOUNTAIN WATER *Berriedale Water takes a sinuous course through the high hills south of Dunbeath, on its way to the sea.*

lar 38 mile drive north-west to Melvich, following the Strath of Kildonan and Strath Halladale through the great expanse of peat bogs, known as the 'Flow Country', which covers much of north Sutherland and Caithness.

⑧ BRORA
The village had been a coal-mining centre from the 16th century when, in the early 1800s, the Sutherland estate evicted crofters from its land in the Strath of Kildonan. Many crofters settled in Brora, and the estate established, among other buildings, a whisky distillery. Coal-mining ceased in the early 1970s, but the Clynelish Distillery still produces a fine single malt, and can be visited. South of the harbour mouth, a large car park overlooks a rocky outcrop popular with gulls, gannets and basking seals. To the north a sandy shore stretches for more than a mile to Kintradwell Broch.

There is good fishing for salmon and trout in the area, as well as an 18-hole golf course, and impressive scenery along the shores of Loch Brora, 3 miles to the north-west.

⑨ CARN LIATH BROCH
Across the A9 from a parking spot, the well-preserved Iron Age Carn Liath Broch (HS) stands on a knoll looking out to sea. Some dwellings were built into its outer wall at the time of original construction, and others later, one of them from the remains of a fallen wall.

⑩ DUNROBIN CASTLE
Since the 13th century the castle has been in the hands of the Earls and Dukes of Sutherland, whose family played a leading role in the Highland Clearances. Its original massive keep has been embellished with turrets and pinnacles, first in the 19th century by Sir Charles Barry, architect of the Houses of Parliament, then by Sir Robert Lorimer

after a fire in 1915. The castle and its luxuriant formal gardens command far-ranging views. The castle museum contains Pictish stones and a number of mementos of the Victorian era.

⑪ GOLSPIE
The administrative centre of the district of Sutherland lies between a long sandy beach and a range of hills. On the 1293 ft summit of Beinn a' Bhragaidh, reached by a steep 2 mile track from the village, stands a huge statue of the first Duke of Sutherland. At the northern end of the village is the 19th-century Golspie Mill, once the meal mill for the Dunrobin estate, which is still used for milling flour. Next to the mill is the start of a mile-long walk along the tree-lined Golspie Burn to a waterfall, beyond which the path continues along the burn for another 3 miles. Highland rocks and crystals are displayed at the Orcadian Stone Company workshop.

⑫ LOCH FLEET
A causeway called The Mound crosses the narrow western end of this salt-water basin. When rising water shuts the sluice gates, visible from a car park north of the causeway, salmon moving in from the sea to spawn gather in a pool until the path upriver is open. Their main run is in July. Loch Fleet is a nature reserve, and common seals, terns, kittiwakes and cormorants can be viewed from a number of lay-bys. Above one of these, on the Embo road, stand the ruins of 14th-century Skelbo Castle, which is not open to the public. A car park in Skelbo Wood is the starting point for several forest trails.

DUCAL DOMAIN *Dunrobin Castle, seat of the Dukes of Sutherland, was rebuilt in the 19th century in the French chateau style.*

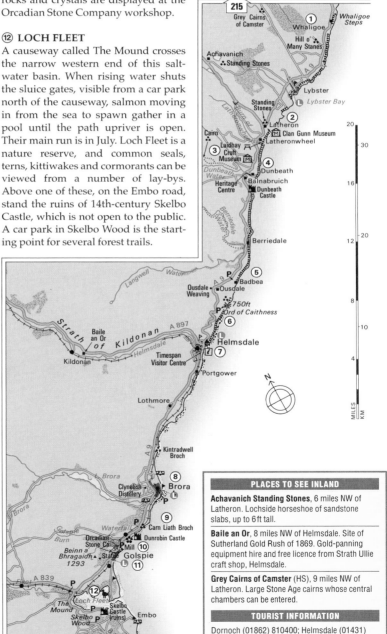

PLACES TO SEE INLAND

Achavanich Standing Stones, 6 miles NW of Latheron. Lochside horseshoe of sandstone slabs, up to 6 ft tall.

Baile an Or, 8 miles NW of Helmsdale. Site of Sutherland Gold Rush of 1869. Gold-panning equipment hire and free licence from Strath Ullie craft shop, Helmsdale.

Grey Cairns of Camster (HS), 9 miles NW of Latheron. Large Stone Age cairns whose central chambers can be entered.

TOURIST INFORMATION

Dornoch (01862) 810400; Helmsdale (01431) 821640 (summer); Wick (01955) 602596

Rock stacks and arches at the land's end of the north

John o'Groats is generally thought of as the most northerly point in mainland Britain, but Dunnet Head is 2 miles nearer the Arctic Circle. Sea-savaged rock formations stand isolated from red sandstone cliffs.

A broch's hollow wall contained a staircase.

① SCRABSTER
Originally developed for the export of Caithness flagstones, Scrabster's port today operates vehicle ferry services to Stromness on Orkney. It has been extended to accommodate a new fish market. Boats can be hired for sea anglers in search of shark, pollack, coalfish, skate and halibut. It was from Scrabster that Lord Kitchener set out in World War I aboard the ill-fated HMS *Hampshire*, which sank off Orkney.

② THURSO
Oats and barley were shipped from the town as far back as the 13th century; later beef, hides, fish and timber were transported. In the 1950s the population more than trebled with the opening of Dounreay nuclear power station, 10 miles to the west. The decommissioning of the plant has made Thurso's future uncertain. A statue in the main square commemorates Sir John Sinclair, a local landlord who played a major part in agricultural improvements in the 18th and 19th centuries. The skeletal 13th-century Church of St Peter stands near the restored fishing quarter of Fisherbiggins. A promenade has views north towards Orkney. Thurso Bay is often lively with windsurfers; on its east side is the ruin of Thurso Castle, which is closed to the public.

③ CASTLETOWN
In and round the small settlements of Scotland's north-eastern tip, walls of fields and even the smallest garden are typically made of Caithness flagstones. During the 19th century the easily split sedimentary rock of the area provided paving material for towns and cities throughout Britain, and as far afield as Calcutta and Melbourne, until the development of cheaper concrete virtually destroyed the trade. Workings in Castletown have closed, but an industrial trail from the Flagstone Centre follows the course of a stone from quarry to shipment from the harbour.

④ DUNNET BAY
There is a natural history visitor centre at the northern end of Dunnet Bay. Ranger-guided walks start at the centre and lead through the nearby forest, home to several species of butterfly. The walk continues through Dunnet Links Nature Reserve, where terns, gannets and auks can be seen. In Dunnet village, Mary-Ann's Cottage, named after a former occupant, is being restored as a working farm, and is open to the public.

A road from Dunnet winds over high moors to Dunnet Head and its lighthouse, the most northerly point on the British mainland. Standing more than 300 ft above the sea, the head offers superb views, and gives the visitor the feeling of being at the edge of the world.

⑤ BROUGH
The pier in the little rocky bay, reached by a steep path from Brough village, was built in the early 19th century to serve boats taking supplies to Dunnet Head and other isolated lighthouses. This task was superseded by helicopters until the lighthouses were automated. Thrusting up from the centre of the cove is Little Clett, a rugged sea stack noisy with sea birds.

DUNCANSBY HEAD *Wind and sea have chiselled the Duncansby Stacks to fine points, rising 200 ft from the sea. In the cliffs the sea has punched a hole known as Thirle Door.*

⑥ MEY

The Castle of Mey was built on the site of a stronghold of the Sinclairs in the 16th century. In 1952 it became a summer residence of Queen Elizabeth, the Queen Mother, and its gardens are open on certain days in summer. In the village of Mey, the Castle Arms Hotel displays colour photographs of the Royal Family taken during visits to Caithness. Off St John's Point the Men of Mey is a fearsome sight when the ebb tide throws gouts of roaring water 30 or 40ft high and blows spume far inland.

East of Mey, at Kirkstyle, is the Old Canisbay Kirk of St Drostan, whose oldest parts date from the 15th century. In the porch is a grave slab dedicated to the memory of members of the Groot, or Groat, family, who gave their name to the settlement 2½ miles to the east.

⑦ JOHN O' GROATS

A jumble of houses, hotels and shops, John o' Groats is named after Jan de Groot, an immigrant Dutchman who was commissioned by James IV in 1496 to set up a ferry service between the mainland and Orkney. De Groot's original octagonal house is now no more than a grassy mound supporting a flagstaff, but there is still a passenger ferry service to South Ronaldsay in summer. Birdwatching trips round the coast are available from the harbour. The Last House in Scotland Museum exhibits local memorabilia and photographs of shipwrecks in the Pentland Firth, and has displays relating to life on the nearby island of Stroma.

⑧ DUNCANSBY HEAD

The lighthouse on the headland guards the entrance to the Pentland Firth. A path from the car park, giving views of the chasms, arches and stacks carved out of the sandstone cliffs, descends to a shingle beach. At low tide it is possible to walk through a natural doorway in the rock towards Duncansby Stacks, remnants of an ancient cliff line eroded by the sea and rowdy with gannets, fulmars, skuas, guillemots and puffins.

⑨ KEISS

A quayside warehouse built in 1831 was once a store for salt, barrels, nets and fish. Newly delivered catches were preserved in the nearby ice-house. Crab fishing is now Keiss's main occupation.

PLACES TO SEE INLAND

Fossil Visitor Centre, Spittal, 10 miles SE of Thurso. Displays of fossils and exhibits related to the flagstone industry.

Lyth Arts Centre, 8 miles SE of Castletown. Craft exhibitions; artists and crafts people in residence, studio theatre for visiting drama, dance and music groups.

TOURIST INFORMATION

John o' Groats (01955) 611373 (summer); Thurso (01847) 892371 (summer); Wick (01955) 602596

Perched on the edge of a sheer cliff, 16th-century Keiss Castle, belonging like so many other properties in the area to the Sinclairs, was abandoned in 1755 in favour of a three-storey mansion, which can be seen just behind the original; the mansion is not open to the public. A 3 mile beach edging Sinclair's Bay forms the most extensive stretch of sands on the Caithness coast.

The Northlands Viking Centre at Auckengill covers local history from prehistoric times through the Pictish era to the late Norse period.

⑩ CASTLE GIRNIGOE AND CASTLE SINCLAIR

Two magnificent ruined fortresses balance precariously on a cliff overlooking Sinclair's Bay. Built by the Sinclairs, Castle Girnigoe dates from the 15th century; Castle Sinclair was added in the early 17th century. Neighbouring Ackergill Tower, another of the Sinclair strongholds, is one of the oldest inhabited houses in the north of Scotland. It is not open to the public.

⑪ WICK

The origin of the town's name is Viking, *vik* denoting a sheltered bay or creek in Old Norse. Wick consists largely of stone houses arranged according to a medieval street plan, most connected with the fishing trade which has been the community's mainstay. The heritage centre near the harbour includes a kippering shed and a fully functioning reconstructed lighthouse. Old Wick Castle (HS), on a peninsula to the south, dates from the 12th century and is one of Scotland's oldest castles. Near the airport, north of the town, is the Caithness Glass Visitor Centre and its factory.

GRIM RUINS *Castle Girnigoe, seen to the left of Castle Sinclair, was where the fourth Earl of Caithness held his son for treachery from 1570 to 1576 before putting him to death.*

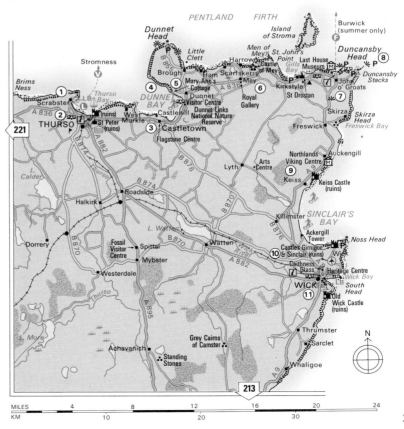

Fertile islands strewn with relics of early settlers

Only 18 of some 70 Orkney islands are inhabited, but sea birds abound and there are no fewer than 11 bird reserves. The birds feed on the fish that teem in the waters where the North Sea meets the Atlantic.

LONG FLIGHT *The Arctic tern is one of the summer visitors to Papa Westray. It winters far away in the Antarctic.*

① NORTH RONALDSAY
The flat cultivated land of Orkney's northernmost island is protected from the depredations of sheep by an enclosing stone dyke. The sheep feed on seaweed instead of grass. Near a broch, to the south, are the remains of an ancient dyke, a forerunner of the present one.

② WESTRAY
Farmsteads have occupied this fertile island for many centuries, as attested by the name of Noltland Castle (HS),

derived from the Old Norse word for 'cattle land'. In 1560 the castle's owner was Gilbert Balfour, who was implicated in the murder of Lord Darnley, husband of Mary Queen of Scots. He was forced to flee the country, only to be executed in Stockholm in 1576 for plotting against the Swedish king.

Neighbouring Papa Westray is called after the 'Papae', Celtic priests who once lived there. Its North Hill RSPB Reserve, together with the surrounding maritime heath and dunes, supports an abundance of wild flowers and is visited by ducks, cormorants, Arctic skuas and Arctic terns. Knap of Howar (HS), a prehistoric two-roomed farmhouse, is considered to be the oldest preserved dwelling in north-western Europe.

③ SANDAY
Seals bask on the skerries, or rocky isles, and there are seal colonies around the southern tip of this island of shining beaches. At Northwall, waders and ducks are joined in winter by whooper swans and goldeneyes. Many human societies have also flourished on Sanday. Tofts Ness has a prehistoric complex of 500 burial mounds, while Quoyness (HS) is a chambered tomb dating from 2000 BC. There are Viking graves by the Ness of Brough, and the ruined Cross Kirk stands on the site of another Viking settlement.

④ ROUSAY, EGILSAY AND WYRE
A vehicle ferry from Tingwall on Mainland links three neighbouring islands, whose main ancient sites are, like many others in Orkney, managed by Historic Scotland. Egilsay is dominated by the 12th-century round-towered church dedicated to St Magnus, who was martyred nearby. On Wyre is the castle of a 12th-century Norse chieftain known as Cubbie Roo. Along the southern shore of Rousay, the Westness Walk leads from the huge Mid Howe Broch to a chambered cairn known as 'The Great Ship of Death'. The shell of a church, together with Norse antiquities, including a cemetery and longhouses, have been uncovered. Sea birds and seals inhabit the Bay of Swandro.

⑤ BROUGH OF BIRSAY
During spring the Brough of Birsay (HS) is aglow with sea pinks. Reached by a causeway at low tide, it offers a wealth of historical remains, including Pictish and Viking farmsteads, and a 12th-century Romanesque church. The 16th-century Earl's Palace (HS) in Birsay village was built in Renaissance style, and has gardens, a bowling green and archery butts. Birsay Moors and Marwick Head are two of several RSPB reserves on Mainland.

⑥ LOCH OF HARRAY
The largest freshwater loch in Orkney offers plentiful fishing for brown trout. On its southern edge are the Stones of

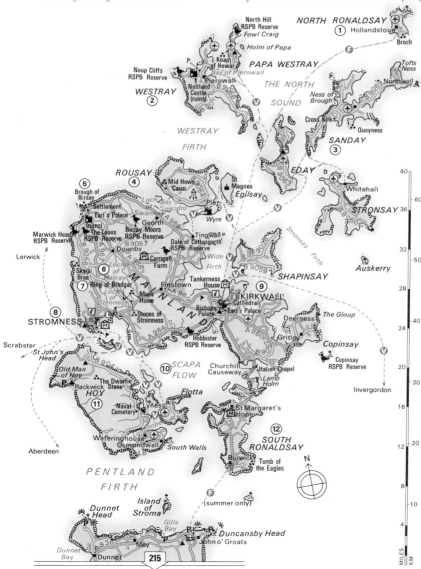

Stenness (HS), a 3rd century BC stone circle of which only four monoliths survive. The nearby Ring of Brodgar (HS) is a wider circle of 27 stones. To the south-east is Maes Howe (HS), a huge cairn with the world's largest collection of runic inscriptions in one place. Corrigall Farm Museum, off the A986, re-creates an 18th-century farmstead.

⑦ SKARA BRAE

For centuries the 4500-year-old village of Skara Brae (HS) was buried beneath dunes until it re-emerged during a storm in 1850. Sand had preserved the walls of stone houses and their domestic furniture, including food boxes lined with clay to act as refrigerators.

⑧ STROMNESS

Most of the harbourside houses have jetties and moorings for small boats. A plaque beside Login's Well recalls that for more than 200 years this port was the last watering place for vessels of the Hudson's Bay Company, who traded in fur with the North American Indians. Captain Cook's ships *Resolution* and *Discovery* made their first British landfall there after his death. The ill-fated Franklin expedition in search of the Northwest Passage set out from the port in 1845. Stromness Museum has displays of these and other historical records. Sea-angling trips operate to Scapa Flow or the Pentland Firth.

⑨ KIRKWALL

Centred on a busy harbour, Kirkwall is the 'capital' of Orkney. Its most impressive building is the Cathedral of St Magnus, dedicated to an 11th-century earl canonised after his murder. During rebuilding of the cathedral, an ancient skeleton was found with an axe cleft in its skull; the injury matched that from which the earl is believed to have died. The Bishop's Palace (HS) was founded around the same time as the cathedral, and neighbouring Earl's Palace (HS) is a fine example of a French Renaissance style building. Tankerness House is a museum with displays of Orkney life.

⑩ SCAPA FLOW

The great natural harbour was a British naval base during both world wars. Sunken German warships, scuttled there in 1919, are explored by diving enthusiasts. Early in World War II a

ACT OF FAITH *In 1943 Italian prisoners of war on Lamb Holm, by Scapa Flow, transformed two Nissen huts into a chapel.*

German U-boat torpedoed HMS *Royal Oak* at anchor in Scapa Flow. A large buoy marks as an official war grave the point where the vessel sank. The attack prompted Winston Churchill to order the building of concrete barriers to block the eastern approaches. A causeway constructed across the barriers now links three islands to Mainland. During World War II, prisoners of war converted Nissen huts on Lamb Holm into a place of worship, with medieval-style wall paintings. Today the majority of ships in the Flow are oil tankers serving the terminal on the island of Flotta.

⑪ HOY

Travellers passing the island by ferry from Scrabster are greeted by the sight of towering sandstone cliffs and the 450 ft sea stack known as the Old Man of Hoy, reached by a 2 mile footpath from Rackwick. The stack is within the North Hoy RSPB Reserve, notable for its spectacular scenery of high cliffs and heather moorlands. Rare red-throated divers can be seen there in summer. Hoy is also distinctive for its myriad wild flowers which grow at low altitudes. The Dwarfie Stane (HS), a tomb carved from a sandstone block around 3000 BC, stands beside the road to Rackwick. Lyness Naval Cemetery and Interpretation Centre recall events on Hoy during two world wars.

⑫ SOUTH RONALDSAY

In a clifftop setting 2½ miles east of Burwick is the excavated Tomb of the Eagles, so called because of the sea eagles' talons found there among the human burials. The fishing township of St Margaret's Hope takes its name from 7-year-old Margaret, 'Maid of Norway', who died there on her way to marry the son of Edward I of England. Its Wireless Museum covers military communication from 1930 onwards, while the Smiddy Museum displays blacksmiths' implements and metalwork.

NATURE'S CHALLENGE *The slender rock pillar known as the Old Man of Hoy was first climbed in 1966. In 1967 the BBC filmed six climbers tackling it by three different routes.*

TOURIST INFORMATION

Kirkwall (01856) 872856; Stromness (01856) 850716

Sea birds and seals by the fiords of Shetland

Shetland lies 110 miles north-east of Scotland's north coast, and the islands' traditions are more Norse than Scottish. Despite changes brought by North Sea oil fields, the islands retain their wild appeal.

① LERWICK
Shetland's capital, and the islands' only town, was a Dutch settlement in the 17th century. It became a thriving fishing port after Fort Charlotte was founded in 1653 to exploit the military potential of Bressay Sound. The oil boom of the 1970s brought dramatic growth to Lerwick, but the old town along the waterfront is intact.

A mile from the town centre, on an islet in the Loch of Clickimin, are the remains of a broch dating from the 4th century BC. The broch can be reached by a causeway. The Shetland Museum in Lerwick contains replicas of Celtic silver treasures and Norse artefacts. At Veensgarth, 5 miles to the north-west, the Tingwall Agriculture Museum explains the history of crofting in Shetland. The tourist centre issues permits for inland fishing, and boats for sea-angling can also be hired.

Traditions in Shetland show traces of Norse settlement between the 9th and 15th centuries. Lerwick's main annual celebration is the festival of 'Up Helly Aa', adapted from a Norse feast called Uphalliday. On the last Tuesday of January, a replica of a Viking longship is paraded and ceremonially burned as a prelude to a night of revelry.

② ISLE OF NOSS
The uninhabited island, a national nature reserve, is one of Europe's greatest sea-bird colonies. In the course of a walk around the small island, taking 2 to 3 hours, visitors can see eider ducks, Arctic terns and great skuas. Ledges provide nesting sites for gannets, kittiwakes and guillemots. The walk also includes the 594 ft Noup of Noss cliff.

③ MOUSA
This small uninhabited island, reached by boat from Sandwick, has on its west coast the most complete example of an Iron Age broch in existence today. The tower rises 43 ft on walls that are 12 ft thick at the base. Inside, a clan of Picts constructed a 'wheelhouse' of thatched wooden rooms set in a circle.

④ SUMBURGH
South of the village and its airport lies Jarlshof, one of Britain's most remarkable archaeological sites. Between trim, grassy hillocks are the remains of 3000 years of settlement, from the Stone Age through the Bronze and Iron Ages to Viking times. There is a small museum showing finds excavated at the site. At Boddam, to the north, is a 19th-century croft house restored as a museum.

At Sumburgh Head sea birds by the thousand roost, and seals clamber on and off the rocks below. To the west lies the sandy Bay of Quendale, and beyond towers a 900 ft hill, Fitful Head. An arduous walk leads to a radar dome at the summit, from where there are magnificent views over Mainland's cliffs,

JARLSHOF *A circular Iron Age dwelling is overlooked by the 17th-century Laird's House, near the village of Sumburgh.*

inlets and rolling inland hills. Nearby is the Loch of Spiggie RSPB Reserve, an important winter wildfowl refuge.

⑤ ST NINIAN'S ISLE
Despite its name, St Ninian's is not an island, but is linked to Mainland by a narrow isthmus formed by two beaches of pure sand back to back. On the hillside facing Mainland are the remains of a 12th-century chapel. There, in 1958, archaeologists found 27 Celtic silver pieces dating from around AD 800. Replicas of the coins can be seen at the Shetland Museum in Lerwick.

⑥ EAST AND WEST BURRA
The road to these islands leads south from Scalloway over a narrow causeway and provides dramatic views of Clift Hills on Mainland. Hamnavoe, a small fishing village, is the islands' principal community. In good weather there are views of the spectacular cliffs

OCEANS APART *Winding fiords in north Mainland cut deep into a boulder-strewn wilderness, almost meeting at Mavis Grind, the narrow isthmus at the tip of Sullom Voe.*

SHETLAND'S TOUGH LITTLE PONY
Measuring only 42 in high at the shoulder when fully grown, the Shetland pony was once in great demand for work in coal mines and on Scottish crofts. Now it is sold the world over as a pet, and is often the first mount ridden by pupils at riding schools.

Shetland pony

of Foula, 24 miles to the west, and its 1370 ft summit, The Sneug. An air service to Foula operates from Tingwall; passenger ferries leave from Walls in summer, and from West Burra Firth, near Burraview to the north, in winter.

⑦ SCALLOWAY

The former capital of Shetland is dominated by the towering, gaunt ruin of a castle built in 1600 by Earl Patrick Stewart, who forcibly replaced Norse law by Scottish feudal law. The key to the castle is available from a cottage opposite the entrance.

Close to the castle is the harbour, busy with fishing vessels. During World War II, Scalloway was the main base for Norwegian patriots who smuggled saboteurs in and refugees out of their homeland, an operation known as 'the Shetland Bus'.

⑧ WALLS

Set by a fine natural harbour visited by pleasure craft in summer, the village of Walls is western Mainland's principal settlement. The A971 from Lerwick cuts through moorland inhabited by sheep and dotted with inland lochs. The coast is reached by minor roads, such as the B9071, which heads south, passing a beach of red sand at Reawick before ending by granite cliffs around Westerwick. Towards Sandness is fertile crofting land. The area offers good walking, trout-fishing and birdwatching.

⑨ ESHA NESS

The headland is one of Shetland's many startling clifftop viewpoints, and one of the few accessible by car. The road leads to a lighthouse and car park over a high, barren, peat plain strewn with lava boulders. Fulmars soar over the ragged cliffs, and puffins burrow in the soil. North of the lighthouse are the Holes of Scraada, a series of blowholes carved out of the cliffs by the sea. There are fine walks over the springy turf. Ronas Hill, 7 miles to the north-east, is Mainland's highest point, at 1475 ft.

⑩ SULLOM VOE

In this deep, ice-scoured fiord, or 'voe' in the Shetland dialect, is the largest crude oil terminal in Europe. Pipelines from the East Shetlands Basin, emerging from the ocean 2 miles away across a peninsula, deliver oil to huge tanks, ready for transfer to tankers in the voe. Seals and otters can often be seen.

⑪ YELL

On the second largest island in Shetland, rolling peat hills are speckled with lochs and surrounded by cliffs. West Sandwick, however, has a fine sandy beach, and 3 miles north is Whale Firth, which has shingle beaches. The Lumbister RSPB Reserve, set amid moorland, has a thriving otter population. Frequent car ferries link Mainland to Yell, and Yell to Fetlar and Unst.

⑫ UNST

Britain's northernmost island is a place of screes and stony outcrops. Of all the islands, it has the densest population of Shetland ponies. In the south-east stand the ruins of 16th-century Muness Castle. At the island's northern tip is the Hermaness National Nature Reserve. The cliff ledges are crowded with guillemots and razorbills, while wheeling above are kittiwakes and fulmars.

⑬ FETLAR

The island is well known to ornithologists, particularly for its Arctic and great skuas and storm petrels. In 1967 a pair of snowy owls began to breed there, an event that caused a large part of Fetlar to be declared an RSPB reserve. In 1975 the only male vanished, and there are now no resident owls. Otters, common seals and grey seals abound.

⑭ FAIR ISLE

Fair Isle, 25 miles south-west of Sumburgh, is reached by air from Lerwick and by boat from Grutness, on Mainland. Its 70-odd inhabitants are still noted for their intricately patterned knitting. The island is owned by the National Trust for Scotland.

A lonely coast of plunging cliffs and secluded bays

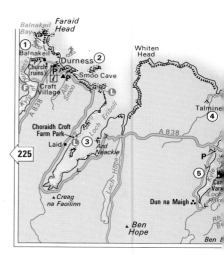

The coastline of one of the most sparsely inhabited regions of Britain is sprinkled with grey stone hamlets, set on inlets where golden sands are interspersed with gnarled, multicoloured rock formations.

① BALNAKEIL

At the southern end of the sandy bay, the ruin of a 17th-century church has a tombstone decorated with skull and crossbones built into a niche in a wall. It commemorates a highwayman said to have paid £1000 to be buried there, as protection against enemies who might desecrate a more exposed grave. In the churchyard is a monument to the Gaelic poet Rob Donn Calder, whose works were published after his death with a foreword by Sir Walter Scott.

Military installations that once formed part of an early warning system have been transformed into Balnakeil Craft Village, where visitors can watch workers creating leather goods, ceramics and other products.

A 3 mile walk north through the 'Faraid Desert', a long stretch of dunes edging the eastern side of Balnakeil Bay, leads to the narrow headland of Faraid Head, home of nesting puffins and other sea birds.

② DURNESS

The village stands on a limestone outcrop which supports richer grazing than the neighbouring moorlands. Outside the visitor centre, which houses the tourist information office, a geological display explains the region's rock formations. Inside, a mural painted by children depicts episodes from local history.

By the coast road east of the village, a curving flight of steps, followed by stepping stones, leads down to the vast Smoo Cave, whose name derives from the Norse word *smjuga*, meaning 'narrow cleft'. A wooden walkway extends into a second chamber, where the Allt Smoo burn falls 80ft from an opening in the roof. A third chamber is practically inaccessible by foot, but can be visited by boat trips in summer.

③ LOCH ERIBOLL

During World War II the deep loch, sheltered by steep hills, was an assembly point for North Atlantic convoys, whose crews dubbed it Loch 'Orrible. The small island in the middle was used as target practice by bombers assigned to destroy the German battleship *Tirpitz* in a Norwegian fiord of similar shape.

At the end of the war, crews of German U-boats surrendered to the British Navy in Loch Eriboll.

On Ard Neackie, a rugged outcrop protruding into the east side of the loch, stand four massive limekilns built in 1870 and a crumbling pier, which once served a nearby quarry.

At Laid on the loch's western shore is the Choraidh Croft Farm Park, where more than 30 breeds of rare and unusual farm animals include Soay sheep from the Outer Hebrides.

④ TALMINE

Some crofting families evicted during the Highland Clearances were resettled here and managed to scrape a livelihood by fishing and quarrying flagstones. The community survived for more than a century, but finally gave up the struggle against the inhospitable land. Holiday cottages have replaced the old crofts, looking out towards the uninhabited Rabbit Islands.

⑤ KYLE OF TONGUE

From parking spaces on the causeway crossing the long inlet known as the Kyle of Tongue, visitors can watch flocks of waders such as redshank and herons. On a ridge at the southern end of the kyle stands Dun na Maigh, a broch whose remaining wall rises clear of tumbled stones. Its entrance leads to a crumbling stairway and an inner cell. The bleak moorland west and south of the Kyle of Tongue is dominated by the mass of Ben Hope and the shapely peaks of Ben Loyal.

St Andrew's Church, Tongue

⑥ TONGUE

This surprisingly wooded oasis in an otherwise bleak landscape is a good centre for hill-walking, and for fishing in Loch Loyal, 4 miles to the south. In the village is a white-harled, or roughcast, church built in the late 17th century and dedicated to St Andrew. The church has a 'laird's loft', or raised gallery where the laird and his family worshipped, once used by chiefs of the Clan MacKay, who dominated the area.

From the village a footpath leads to Castle Varrich, a roofless tower reputed to have been a Viking lookout but more likely to be of 14th-century origin.

About 8 miles east of Tongue is the Forestry Commission's Borgie Forest, a conifer plantation with woodland and riverside walks passing some of the tallest trees in Sutherland.

⑦ BETTYHILL

Set on hummocks of rocky moorland, bright little Bettyhill developed largely as a result of the Clearances. One theory

---

TRADITIONAL TOIL

Crofting, or small farming, is one of the few ways of making a living from the land in the Highlands and Islands. The poor soil provides only a small income, which must be added to by other occupations. Today, the 18 000 registered crofters have security of tenure, government grants and the right to buy their crofts.

Crofters spread seaweed as fertiliser, 1885.

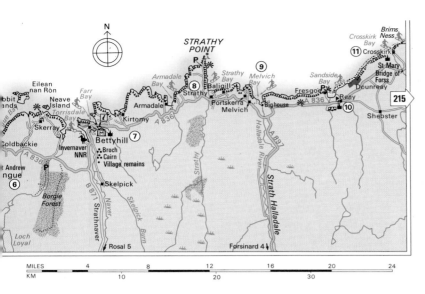

attributes its name to Elizabeth, Countess of Sutherland and the wife of the Duke of Sutherland, some of whose tenants were resettled there after being evicted from the Strathnaver valley in the early 19th century; but older tradition tells of one Betty 'Cnocan' who ran an inn at the top of the *cnoc*, the Gaelic word for 'hill'.

Bettyhill overlooks impressive sand dunes in Torrisdale Bay on one side, and Farr Bay on the other. Farr Bay is an expanse of unbroken golden sand which can be dizzying in bright sunshine, flanked by splintered rocks striped and inlaid with vivid colours and pastel shades.

The village's 18th-century church has become the Strathnaver Museum, with displays on the Clearances and the archaeological treasures of cairn, broch, and abandoned clachans, or hamlets, a few miles to the south in Strathnaver. The museum retains the church's handsome pulpit and reader's desk, and has a room with mementos of the Clan MacKay. In the churchyard stands the Farr Stone, a 9th-century Celtic cross-slab with carved patterns on one side only – possibly because it was once set against a wall.

On the western side of the Naver estuary is the Invernaver National Nature Reserve, where rare mountain plants grow almost down to sea level. The entrance to the reserve is on its western side, from the road leading north to Skerray off the A836.

About 3 miles south of Bettyhill, along a minor road leading to Skelpick, are chambered cairns, a ruined broch and remains of a pre-Clearance village.

A panel explains their history. The nearby B871 runs along Strathnaver, nearly deserted save for salmon fishers.

⑧ STRATHY

East of the scattered hamlet, a rough road runs north past heaps of peat piled outside grey stone cottages and a few barns. The road ends by a lighthouse at Strathy Point, where impressive cliffs offer views over miles of coastline. On a fine day it is possible to see Cape Wrath to the west, Dunnet Head to the east, and the Orkney islands to the northeast. The headland is on the migration route of many bird species, including gannets, skuas and storm petrels.

⑨ MELVICH BAY

The villages of Melvich and Portskerra run together above the dunes of a sandy bay and the Halladale River. There are clifftop walks, with a profusion of tiny wild orchids in the grass in early summer. A footpath down to the neck

WHERE MOORLAND MEETS THE SEA *Deep in the throat of the Kyle of Tongue, open moors sweep down to ragged cliffs, and to the water's edge on the sandy beach of Coldbackie.*

AT THE TIP OF THE TONGUE *A trawler passes the Rabbit Islands, which lie just outside the Kyle of Tongue, and on which a French sloop bringing gold to Charles Edward Stuart went aground in 1746. They are named after the suitability of their sandy soil for rabbits.*

of the strath faces the grey stone mansion of Bighouse, which was once home of a branch of the Clan MacKay.

⑩ REAY

In the 17th century, MacKay of Farr, chief of the clan and owner of vast tracts of mountains and deer forest in the area, took the name of the village and became Lord Reay. The village church, rebuilt in the 18th century after being buried by sand dunes for more than a century, still features the 'laird's loft'. Set into the wall of the chapel in the old burial ground is the Reay Stone, carved in relief with a cross and ornamental knot-work, probably dating from the 10th century. The key to the chapel is available from the village post office.

The shoreline to the east is dominated by the metallic sphere of Dounreay nuclear power station, now in the process of being decommissioned.

North of Reay is Sandside Bay, where an information panel by the car park tells of Pictish and Viking settlements lying buried deep beneath the shifting

dunes. On the western side of the bay is the hamlet of Fresgoe, whose boats fish mainly for cod, coley and lobster. Each year some 2500 salmon are taken from the bay by dragnets.

⑪ CROSSKIRK

From the hamlet of Bridge of Forss, on the A836 to the east of Reay, a minor road heads north to Crosskirk, a hamlet by a small pebbly bay. A footpath by a parking space crosses a stream to the 12th-century Chapel of St Mary, whose sturdy walls stand roofless. The chapel's sloping jambs and doorway lintel, unfamiliar in the Highlands, probably owe much to the influence of the Orkney Norsemen, who also ruled this part of Scotland. Just south of the little church is an ancient well, and the nearby fields are dotted with the remains of cairns and brochs.

PLACES TO SEE INLAND

'Flow Country' Visitor Centre, Forsinard, 15 miles S of Melvich. Information on northern Scotland's vast area of peatland.

Rosal (Forestry Commission), 14 miles S of Bettyhill. Pre-Clearance township.

TOURIST INFORMATION

Bettyhill (01641) 521342 (summer); Dornoch (01862) 810400; Thurso (01847) 892371

Expanses of wilderness in Scotland's far north-west

Mountainous Sutherland remains one of Britain's wildest regions. Narrow, twisting lanes lead to fishing villages and isolated crofting 'townships' on a rugged coast of cliffs and sandy bays.

① CAPE WRATH

Mainland Scotland's north-western tip is aptly named. The lighthouse, built in 1828, crowns a windswept headland battered by raging seas. To the east, the highest cliffs on the British mainland rise to 920 ft at Clò Mor. Cape Wrath can be reached only by a passenger ferry across the Kyle of Durness and then a track that crosses the huge wilderness known as The Parbh. In summer a minibus takes visitors along the 10 mile route. The cliffs and track lie within a Ministry of Defence bombing range, and walkers should check on restrictions at the Durness tourist information centre or post office before setting out.

② SANDWOOD BAY

A mile-long stretch of sands backed by rolling dunes makes Sandwood Bay one of the finest beaches in Britain. The bay's unspoiled nature owes much to its remoteness; the track from Blairmore is impassable to cars, and it is a 4 mile walk across the deserted peat and heather. On the southern edge of the bay, a finger of rock known as Am Buachaille rises sheer out of the sea.

③ KINLOCHBERVIE

The small village of Kinlochbervie has an impressive modern harbour where £15 million worth of fish was landed in 1994. To the north, at Oldshoremore and Oldshore Beg, wide sandy bays are backed by rolling grassland, with stunning views along the coast.

④ HANDA ISLAND

Some 30 species of bird, including puffins and guillemots, nest on this uninhabited cliff-girt sanctuary. A summer ferry from Tarbet crosses to Handa, and a bothy, or hut, is available for overnight accommodation. From Fanagmore, north of Tarbet, short boat trips explore the islands and seal colonies of Loch Laxford, which is also noted for its salmon.

⑤ SCOURIE

A sandy beach, hotels and a campsite make this village an attractive centre for visitors in an otherwise sparsely populated area. The wild and rocky shoreline can be explored on foot or by boat trips from the harbour, and there is trout fishing from nearby hill-lochs. In Loch a'Mhuilinn National Nature Reserve, to the south, woods of rowan, birch and oak slope down to the shore.

⑥ KYLESKU

The bridge across the narrows of Loch a' Chàirn Bhàin is a good place from which to appreciate an immense landscape of lochs and mountain wilderness. During World War II the loch was a training area for midget submarines. In summer, boat trips take visitors to view the spectacular waterfall of Eas a Chùal Aluinn, the highest in Britain with a drop of some 650 ft.

⑦ NORTH ASSYNT

South of Kylesku, a narrow road heads west to follow the spectacular coastline of Assynt, an area of low hillocks dotted with numerous lochs and lochans. West of the pink sands of Clashnessie Bay, a lane leads to the Stoer lighthouse. Climbers swim out 50yd laden with their kit to scale the Old Man of Stoer, a 200 ft sandstone pinnacle. Along the peninsula's southern shore are fine sands at Clachtoll and Achmelvich. Unusually for a Highland estate, North Assynt is owned by local crofters and run as a cooperative enterprise.

⑧ LOCHINVER

The heart of Assynt's largest village is its modern fishing harbour, and boats from as far afield as France regularly land their catches at Lochinver for sale at the evening fish market. There are craft shops and a visitor centre in the village, while at Baddidarach, on the loch's northern shore, there is a pottery. A path runs beside the River Inver, noted for its angling; the track up Glen Canisp is a starting point for climbers planning an assault on Suilven, one of Sutherland's most dramatic mountains.

⑨ LOCH ASSYNT

Two romantic ruins overlook the long loch, a magnet for anglers. Ardvreck Castle, built by the MacLeods in the 16th century, was seized in 1695 by the

SHORT CUT *Erected in 1984, the bridge at Kylesku enables road traffic to avoid an inland detour of nearly 100 miles.*

ANCIENT ROCKS *Ben Mór Coigach, south of Achiltibuie, soars to 2265 ft. Its rocks are among the world's oldest, and were sculpted into their present shape by Ice Age glaciers.*

MacKenzies, who later built nearby Calda House. Near the castle is a Stone Age chambered tomb. In Inchnadamph National Nature Reserve, to the south, are limestone caves thought to have sheltered hunters some 9000 years ago.

⑩ INVERPOLLY

Mountain wilderness and lochs stretching to the sea make up Inverpolly National Nature Reserve. The sandstone peaks of Cùl Mor, Cùl Beag and Stac Pollaidh offer challenging ascents to walkers and rock-climbers. From Knockan Visitor Centre, trails explore the diverse habitats of the reserve and the complexities of its geology. Nearby is Knockan Cliff, a site that revolutionised Victorian ideas of how mountain ranges were formed. To the north, at Elphin, Highland cattle are some of the traditional farming animals at the Highland and Rare Breeds Farm.

⑪ ENARD BAY

The 'Mad Road of Sutherland', following the coast south of Lochinver, offers views that are as breathtaking as many of its bends. From Inverkirkaig, a crofting village on a sand-and-shingle bay, a walk follows the river to the Falls of Kirkaig and the wild slopes of Suilven. The little road meanders on through woods and mountain glens until, beyond the River Polly, it enters barren moorland. Along the southern shore of Enard Bay, by the village of Achnahaird, an enormous sandy beach lies within a sheltered inlet.

TOURIST INFORMATION

Dornoch (01862) 810400; Durness (01971) 511259 (summer); Gairloch (01445) 712130; Lochinver (01571) 844330 (summer)

---

⑫ ACHILTIBUIE

Fishing nets hang out to dry along the shore at Achiltibuie, the largest of a string of crofting 'townships' that overlook the uninhabited Summer Isles. In the village is an experimental indoor garden, the Hydroponicum, where vegetables and flowers are grown without soil. There are cruises round the islands and deep-sea angling trips from the pier, situated about a mile north of the village. Farther north is the secluded harbour of Old Dornie.

The road leading south from Achiltibuie peters out at Culnacraig, where the shore is dominated by the towering peak of Ben Mór Coigach.

SPEEDY HUNTER *The pine marten, resident of the woodlands of Sutherland, uses its agility to catch small prey such as rabbits.*

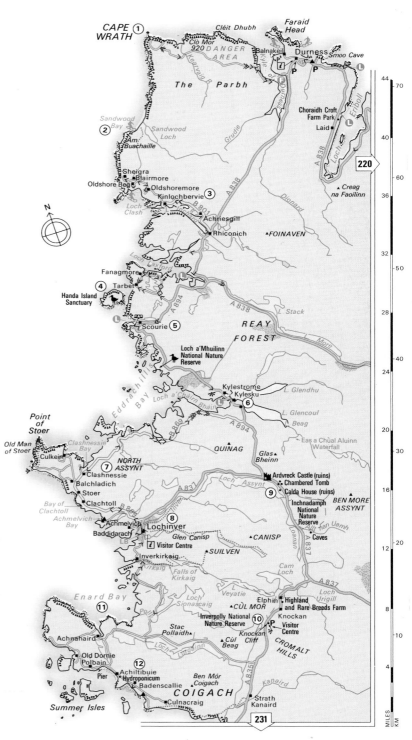

Golden sands and ancient stones of the Western Isles

On the linked islands of Lewis and Harris, the rugged landscape of moorlands, mountains, deep sea lochs and sandy beaches provides a dramatic background for prehistoric graves and standing stones.

① STORNOWAY

Car ownership per head in this island of scattered settlements is among the highest in Europe, and a large percentage of the Lewis and Harris population of 22000 comes into Stornoway to work. But the fishing port, ferry terminal and market town retains a gentle air.

Stornoway's architecture recalls the boom days of the late 19th century. A grandiose Edwardian town hall and wide avenues of imposing villas speak of more affluent times, when a herring fleet crammed into the harbour. Close to the town centre, a museum open in summer mounts varied exhibitions on the history of the Western Isles.

A small river feeds into the harbour mouth, and standing on its western bank is the mock-Tudor Lews Castle, now converted into offices, which was built in the 1840s by the business magnate Sir James Matheson. He brought in shiploads of soil in order to create the lush parkland surrounding the castle. This park, which now includes a golf course, is open to the public. Matheson spent a fortune on schools and new industries, but the islanders were resistant to his plans and the enterprise failed. In 1918, the industrialist Lord

TWEED – FROM HARRIS TO PARIS

Harris tweed, woven by hand in homes throughout the Western Isles, is famed for its quality and sturdiness. The introduction of a modern, double-width loom capable of producing finer, more intricately patterned material has led to a revival in the industry. Many weavers are happy to show off their skills to visitors, and tours are available of the Kenneth MacLeod mill in Siabost, on Lewis.

A Harris weaver works at a traditional loom.

Leverhulme bought the estate and tried to transform Stornoway into a great fishing port. In his turn, he met with indifference, and departed for Harris.

East of Stornoway, the road leads over the isthmus to the Eye Peninsula, passing the derelict 14th-century St Columba's Church and the graveyard of Ui, where 19 MacLeod chieftains are buried. From the Tiumpan Head lighthouse at the tip of the peninsula, basking sharks and whales can sometimes be seen. The B895 north of Stornoway, which peters out by Tolsta Head, runs through an area of green croft land, and sandy beaches dot the rocky shore.

② BUTT OF LEWIS

The northern tip of Lewis is a raw, exposed and windswept spot. Some 45 miles to the north is the island nature reserve of North Rona and beyond that are the Faeroes; to the east, the seas rage around Cape Wrath on Scotland's north-western tip; and 3000 miles due west lies northern Newfoundland and the entrance to Hudson's Bay.

In Eoropaidh, the island's northernmost village, is the 12th-century St Moluag's Chapel, built on the site of an earlier chapel. From nearby Port of Ness, where there is a sandy beach, each September the men of the parish sail to the island of Sulisgeir, 30 miles to the north, to harvest the young 'gugas', or gannets, which are a local delicacy.

In the village of Siadar, 10 miles to the south-west, are the ruins of a 12th-century chapel known as Teampull Pheadair, the Steinacleit stone circle and the vast monolith of Clach an Trushal.

③ ARNOL

The Blackhouse Museum at Arnol is the best example in the Hebrides of this traditional form of building, giving a picture of life in these thatched homes with stone walls up to 6ft thick. The house had no chimney, and the smoke from the peat fire in the centre of the floor stained everything a rich black. Straw mattresses in the box beds, the kettle hanging on a hook above the flames, and the neat crockery on the wooden dresser are all as they were when the house was last lived in, in the 1960s.

At Bragar to the west, a whale's jawbone, from an animal killed around 1920, arches over an otherwise humble gateway. In nearby Siabost, a crofting museum shows traditional agricultural, fishing and domestic equipment.

To the south-west of Arnol, lanes lead off the coast road to Dalbeg and Dalmore bays, where Atlantic rollers crash between jagged rocky headlands onto wide sweeps of sand.

④ CARLOWAY BROCH

The Iron Age broch, or fortified tower, standing on a crag by the hamlet of Dun Charlabhaigh is a testament to the skills of its masons. Some 2000 years after they were erected, the dry-stone walls are still 30ft high in some places. The central courtyard is 25ft across and surrounded by double walls containing galleries, chambers and flights of stairs.

In nearby Garenin, a traditional thatched 'blackhouse' has been renovated to provide a hostel.

MAGNIFICENT EMPTINESS *The view southwards across East Loch Roag from the stone circle at Callanish presents a spectacle of breathtaking beauty and remoteness.*

ENIGMATIC STONES *The purpose of the Callanish stones remains a mystery. It has been suggested that they may have formed part of a king's mausoleum, or of an observatory.*

the pieces can be seen in the National Museum of Antiquities in Edinburgh and the British Museum in London.

⑥ HUSHINISH

By the southern foothills of Clisham, at 2637 ft the highest peak in the Outer Hebrides, a roller-coaster road runs west through North Harris, past the remains of an old whaling station at Bun Abhainn Eadar and the privately owned castle at Abhainn Suidhe, pronounced 'Avinsooi'. The road ends at the Hushinish beaches and machair, the sandy lowlands unique to the western coasts of the Hebrides. In early summer the machair is covered in flowers. Across a narrow but treacherous stretch of water lies the island of Scarp, uninhabited since 1971.

⑦ TARBERT

Harris's capital is only a village but its ferry terminal, bank, shops and hotels give it the feel of a small town. To the east lies the island of Scalpay, served by a car ferry which is due to be replaced by a bridge in 1996. The island has just one road, along its south-western shore, and the lighthouse at Eilan Glas can be reached only on foot.

South of Tarbert, a narrow road runs round the inlets and sea lochs of South Harris's bare and rocky eastern coast, winding in and out of fishing villages where vegetables are still grown in 'lazy beds' – plots of earth created by hand, out of peat, manure, rotting seaweed and sand. By contrast, the west coast of Harris is a fertile expanse of machair, stretching between the breathtaking sandy beaches of Tràigh Losgaintir and Tràigh Sgarasta.

⑧ LEVERBURGH

In the 1920s Lord Leverhulme tried to turn a small township into a major fishing port by building a new pier and harbour, a fish-processing plant, a workers' hostel and a school. He died shortly after the work was completed, and the scheme was halted by his successors. Although it has some of the best housing in the island, Leverburgh retains a somewhat forlorn air. A passenger ferry runs to North Uist.

⑨ RODEL

The handsome little port at the very tip of South Harris is home to the finest example of ecclesiastical architecture in the Hebrides. The small Church of St Clement, built by the MacLeods of Dunvegan in the 16th century, contains three monuments to the family. The finest, carved in sparkling black local gneiss in 1528, shows the eighth chieftain, Alastair Crotach.

⑤ CALLANISH STONES

The standing stones outside the hamlet of Callanish rival those of Stonehenge and Carnac in the majesty of their setting – and in their inscrutability. Standing some 20 ft high on a hill above East Loch Roag, the Callanish Stones (HS) were quarried locally and erected about 4000 years ago in roughly the form of a Celtic cross, with a chambered cairn in the centre. Their meaning will probably never be known, but they appear to have astronomical significance and they align with other standing stones and circles in the area.

South of Callanish, the B8011 runs through rugged, near-deserted terrain. Where the road bends sharply round the tip of narrow Little Loch Roag, a rough and often muddy 2½ mile

path leads to the remains of a group of curious 'beehive' dwellings, a rare example of a primitive Hebridean form of housing in which stones were positioned to form a hollow hillock about 6 ft high. The B8011 continues to the huge sandy beach of Uig Sands, where in 1832 a set of Norse chess pieces were discovered in the dunes. Examples of

Rugged vistas in the 'long island' of the Hebrides

North Uist, Benbecula and South Uist are linked to one another by bridges and causeways to form a single 'long island', but each retains its own character, based on contrasts in scenery, history and religion.

① NORTH UIST

Ferries from Skye or Harris weave through a jumble of islands and headlands on their approach to Lochmaddy, the 'capital' of North Uist. A few yards from the ferry pier is the island's main hotel, and the nearby outdoor centre is often busy with walkers, climbers, sailors and divers. In the east of the island, where there is more water than land, hundreds of freshwater and saltwater lochs teem with trout.

Prehistoric remains abound on North Uist, as they do throughout this chain of islands. Three miles north-west of Lochmaddy, and half a mile from the road, is a group of stones called Na Fir

Bhreige, or 'The False Men' – according to one legend, they are wife-deserters turned to stone. Evidence of continuous occupation of the island from the Bronze Age has been discovered on the sandy peninsula of Machair Leathann in the north-west, and Dun an Sticar, a small Iron Age fortress near Newtonferry, is known to have been lived in until 1602. Passenger ferry services run from Newtonferry to Berneray and to Leverburgh on Harris.

The elusive corncrake and the rare red-necked phalarope are among the numerous birds than can be seen at the Balranald RSPB Reserve. A nature trail starts from the visitor centre at Hougharry. Near Carinish are the impressive remains of the 13th-century Teampull na Trionaid, or Trinity Temple, where the sons of medieval chieftains received their education. North of Clachan-a-Luib, just off the A867, is the 5000-year-old chambered cairn of

Barpa Langass, which contains a large burial vault. Otter-watching tours are run from Langass Lodge Hotel.

② BENBECULA

Causeways link the Uists to Benbecula, which is dominated, socially and economically, by the army rocket range headquarters, RAF base and airport at Balivanich. However, crofting and fishing activities continue to occupy many of the island's inhabitants, and there is a flourishing crafts industry.

On the southern slopes of Rueval is Prince Charlie's Cave – one of several caves of that name in the Hebrides – where Charles Edward Stuart managed to hide himself before fleeing to Skye with Flora MacDonald, on June 28, 1746, disguised as her Irish maid.

The vast community school at Liniclate houses a library, a museum, a restaurant and a theatre, as well as a swimming pool and sports centre, all of which are open to visitors.

③ SOUTH UIST

Whereas most of the Western Isles are Protestant, South Uist, like Barra, is Catholic, and small shrines, statues and votive offerings are scattered throughout the island.

On a hill beside the main road near West Gerinish is the 30 ft granite statue of Our Lady of the Isles, by Hew Lorimer, erected in 1957. She and the infant Jesus gaze over a rocket range, where test missiles are fired towards the Atlantic and tracked by a base on St Kilda, 45 miles to the west. The west coast of South Uist is a 20 mile beach

SHELTER AND WARMTH *On North Uist, blocks of peat (left) stand drying for crofters' fires. Peat is a fuel readily available on the treeless island. Wire netting weighted by stones holds down the heather thatch of a traditional Hebridean cottage (below).*

broken only by a few rocky headlands. The east is riven by deep fiords and lochs. One of the largest, the freshwater Loch Bee, almost bisects the island and is famed for its mute swans. Loch Druidibeg National Nature Reserve is a breeding ground for greylag geese, and a sanctuary for many other birds, including corncrakes.

Down a footpath behind a house on the main road north of Mingary a cairn marks the birthplace of Flora Mac-Donald. Nearby is the Kildonan School Museum, containing local artefacts and archaeological finds.

Lochboisdale is the main settlement and ferry port of South Uist, and a passenger ferry goes from Ludag to Barra.

④ ERISKAY

A vehicle ferry runs from Ludag in South Uist to this romantic island, famed for its beauty, for the haunting 'Eriskay Love Lilt', and for the farcical 'Whisky Galore' episode. In 1941 the SS *Politician*, bound for New York with 243 000 bottles of whisky, foundered in the shallow sea north of Eriskay. Most of the cargo was salvaged by locals, to be drunk, fed to livestock and used to light fires. Sir Compton Mackenzie's book on the incident was filmed on Barra. The fishermen, crofters and seafarers of Eriskay are renowned for their poetry and songs.

⑤ BARRA

The 14 mile road encircling much of this strikingly beautiful island makes it easy to explore. Several side roads wander off to the bays and beaches or into green glens beneath the central hills.

In the north is Tràigh Mhór, an immense cockle strand which, tides permitting, serves as a runway for planes to and from Stornoway, Benbecula, Tiree and Glasgow. A mile or so to the north, at Cille-bharra, is the 12th-century Church of St Barr, where a restored chapel contains a replica of a unique grave slab featuring both Norse runic markings and a Celtic cross. Sir

Compton Mackenzie is buried there. The main town and ferry port of Castlebay in the south is dominated by Kisimul Castle, which rises straight out of the waters of the bay. This is the home of the MacNeil of Barra, whose forebears were the terror of the western seas for hundreds of years until the 16th century. When they had dined, a bard would announce from the battlements: 'The MacNeil has supped; now the princes of the world may sit down to eat.' Guided tours of the castle are available in summer.

On the steep slopes of Heaval, which rises behind Castlebay, is a statue of the Madonna and Child, on a site offering spectacular views over the bay and beyond to Vatersay, Sandray, Pabbay, Mingulay and Berneray.

With a healthy income derived from tourism, fishing and seafood processing, Barra is one of the most prosperous communities in the Western Isles. Perfume is also made on the island, and shell grit is supplied for masonry paint. A Gaelic arts festival is held every July.

⑥ VATERSAY

The island is now linked to Barra by a causeway, making it easier for the inhabitants to get to and from the 'mainland', but leading to some loss of independent character. Vatersay won national fame in 1908 when a group of landless men from Barra 'raided' it, trusting in the old custom by which someone building a home and lighting a fire in it all in a day was entitled to tenure. The owner, Lady Cathcart, had ten of them put in prison, but the national outcry led to their release, and a year later the Congested Districts Board bought the island and divided it among the raiders.

On the dunes in the 'waist' of the island a monument records the tragedy in which all passengers on the *Annie Jane*, a ship taking victims of the Highland Clearances to America, were killed when their vessel was swept onto the surrounding rocks.

⑦ MINGULAY

Sailors used to sing the shanty 'Homeward Bound for Mingulay', but the only inhabitants of the island today are sea birds, seals and rabbits. Natural historians, artists and birdwatchers delight in the rugged surroundings, bordered on the western side by sheer 750ft cliffs, but the locals on Barra talk of ghosts rising from the moor of Macphee's Hill, and the abandoned village in the east bay is an eerie spot. Boat trips to Mingulay and to the neighbouring island of Berneray can be arranged from Castlebay harbour on Barra.

Quiet sea lochs with red sands and exotic gardens

Red sandstone hills shelter beaches of pink sand in Wester Ross, a region noted for its mountain walks and fishing. Warm waters from the North Atlantic Drift allow delicate plants to flourish along the shores.

NORTHERN OASIS *Subtropical trees and shrubs thrive in Inverewe Garden, which lies on the same latitude as Siberia.*

① ULLAPOOL
Shops and whitewashed cottages overlook Loch Broom in this lively little harbour town, established in 1788 as a herring port and curing station. Despite a major slump in the herring industry, fishing still continues around Ullapool, and in winter factory ships from eastern Europe anchor in Loch Broom to buy the local catch. A car ferry to the Isle of Lewis keeps the harbour busy, and there are local cruises and sea angling trips. Ullapool Museum, housed in the old parish church, has displays relating to local history.

② CORRIESHALLOCH GORGE
Beneath a gently swaying suspension bridge spanning the River Droma, the Falls of Measach thunder down 200 ft into a narrow gorge. From a viewing platform erected by the National Trust for Scotland, those with a head for heights can see ferns and mosses sprouting from the sheer rock walls of

the mile-long chasm. A few miles to the north is the Forestry Commission's Lael Forest Garden, an attractive arboretum of conifers and broad-leaved trees.

③ LITTLE LOCH BROOM
The massive crags of An Teallach tower above the loch's southern shore. One of many walks in the area starts from the hamlet of Ardessie and passes a series of waterfalls as it follows the course of a mountain stream.

About 2 miles south-east of Dundonnell, a narrow lane climbs north through a wooded glen before continuing through barren hills. From the road's end 6 miles away at the small village of Badrallach, on the loch's remote northern shore, a path leads to Scoraig, an 'alternative' community that relies on windmills for its power supply. The frequency of the passenger service between Scoraig and Badluarach varies from once a day to once a week, depending on the time of year.

④ GRUINARD BAY
A sweep of coves and sandy beaches, and a horizon of entrancing beauty, can be enjoyed from a viewpoint on Gruinard Hill. The largest beach, on the southern side of the bay, has pink sands formed of red sandstone. The sheltered waters, popular with canoeists and young families, are home to colonies of black-throated divers, and are sometimes frequented by porpoises. In the middle of the bay is Gruinard Island, used for experiments in germ warfare during World War II, when it was contaminated with anthrax. The island has now undergone decontamination and is considered safe, but it is privately owned and access is prohibited.

At Laide, on the bay's western shore, is a tiny ruined chapel said to have been founded by St Columba in the 7th century; the present building dates from the early 18th century. Nearby is a cave that was long used as a place of worship. A minor road from Laide leads

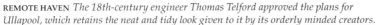

REMOTE HAVEN *The 18th-century engineer Thomas Telford approved the plans for Ullapool, which retains the neat and tidy look given to it by its orderly minded creators.*

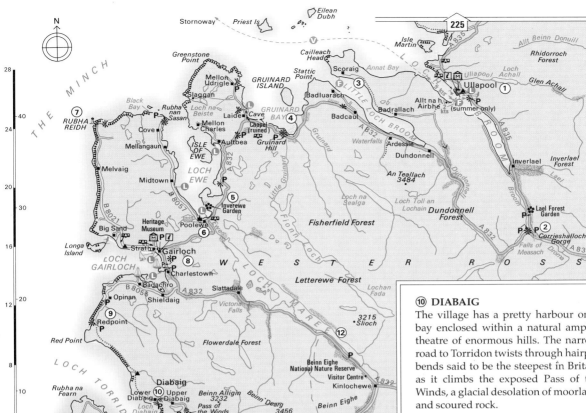

north to a wide beach of pure white sands at Mellon Udrigle. Halfway between Laide and Mellon Udrigle, by Loch na Beiste, a track heads west for 3 miles to the ruined village of Slaggan.

⑤ INVEREWE GARDEN

In 1862 Osgood Mackenzie inherited the Inverewe estate, then a barren wilderness of peat and rock. Taking advantage of the North Atlantic Drift, which gives the north-west coast of Scotland its mild, humid weather, Mackenzie planted trees as shelter-belts against the prevailing winds, improved the soil, and over the next 60 years created an environment in which sub-tropical plants could flourish. The gardens, now owned by the National Trust for Scotland, are crisscrossed by a maze of paths that meander through woodland, shrubberies and water-gardens. From a visitor centre, guided walks explore the wilder parts of the estate.

⑥ POOLEWE

With hotels, restaurants and a small indoor swimming pool, Poolewe is well geared to the needs of visitors. A minor road runs north along the western shore of Loch Ewe to superb pink sands at Mellangaun, continuing to the rocky headland of Rubha nan Sasan, where World War II gun emplacements once protected the Atlantic convoys that gathered in the loch.

⑦ RUBHA REIDH

From Melvaig at the end of the B8021, visitors can follow a private road which continues north along a clifftop route with views to the Outer Hebrides and Skye. The track ends at the Rubha Reidh lighthouse, whose buildings are the base of a holiday activity centre.

⑧ GAIRLOCH

The romantic scenery around Gairloch was much admired by Victorians, who travelled to the fashionable resort by steamer. Overlooked by a golf course is a long, sheltered sandy beach. Pleasure cruises and sea angling trips leave from the pier, and all-terrain vehicles can be hired to explore the surrounding hills. The Gairloch Heritage Museum has an excellent local history collection. Big Sand, to the north-west, is popular with watersports enthusiasts.

⑨ REDPOINT

About 2 miles south of Gairloch, a minor road leads west through woodland glens, passing a tranquil anchorage at Badachro where small boats can be hired. The road continues through moorland, descending to a sandy beach at Opinan before reaching the hamlet of Redpoint, where there are spectacular views across to Skye and Lewis. A footpath to the south of the car park passes magnificent sands before continuing for 9 miles along the coast to Diabaig.

⑩ DIABAIG

The village has a pretty harbour on a bay enclosed within a natural amphitheatre of enormous hills. The narrow road to Torridon twists through hairpin bends said to be the steepest in Britain as it climbs the exposed Pass of the Winds, a glacial desolation of moorland and scoured rock.

⑪ TORRIDON

Rising behind a scattered lochside village, the Torridon estate (NTS) is a wilderness of savage splendour, dominated by the massive quartz-capped peaks of Liathach, Beinn Alligin and Beinn Dearg. The Countryside Centre at Torridon has information on the region's walks and natural history, and tame red deer can be seen in enclosures at the nearby Deer Museum.

About 2 miles west of the village, on the north shore of Upper Loch Torridon, a waterfall near an NTS car park is the starting point for several way-marked hill walks. A short distance to the west is the former fishing harbour of Inveralligin, where whitewashed cottages huddle around a jetty.

⑫ LOCH MAREE

Densely wooded islands make Loch Maree one of the most attractive of Scotland's great freshwater lochs. There are pleasant walks in the Forestry Commission plantations around Slattadale on the loch's western shore, and nearby is a waterfall that was admired by Queen Victoria when she stayed in the area in 1877. At the south-western end of the loch is the wilderness of Beinn Eighe National Nature Reserve, whose ancient pinewoods are home to pine martens and wildcats. A visitor centre is the start point for several woodland and mountain trails.

TOURIST INFORMATION

Gairloch (01445) 712130; Ullapool (01854) 612135 (summer)

Mountain grandeur of Applecross and Knoydart

Isolated fishing and crofting villages line the wooded shores of lochs and bays along a wild indented coast. Inland, some of the world's most ancient mountain ranges form an awe-inspiring backdrop.

① SHIELDAIG

A waterfront of whitewashed cottages, a shop and a hotel face a wooded island in Loch Shieldaig. Boatyards and a village were established in the early 19th century as a potential source of recruits for the Royal Navy, but the area was 'cleared' of most inhabitants after the Napoleonic Wars in order to make room for sheep. Peaceful Shieldaig now appeals to yachtsmen and summer visitors seeking solitude.

② APPLECROSS

The coast road from Shieldaig to Applecross begins with splendid views across the loch to Torridon's spectacular mountains, composed of sandstone that, at more than 600 million years old, is among the oldest in the world. Crofts strung along the peninsula's western shore were extraordinarily remote until the road was built in the 1970s.

The little village is set on a sheltered bay, and wooded hills make it a haven in a bleak environment. The road east out of Applecross climbs into the lunar landscape of the 2000 ft high Bealach na

Bà, or Pass of the Cattle, where there can be blizzards even in midsummer. Following the hairpin bends that twist down to Loch Kishorn can be a memorable and challenging experience.

③ LOCH CARRON

In contrast to the wilds of Applecross, the landscape of sheltered Loch Carron is welcoming and gentle, with rose bushes by the cottages along its shore. The yard on nearby Loch Kishorn where oil rig platforms were once constructed closed in 1987, and the village of Lochcarron now relies for its income on visitors attracted by the tranquil beauty of the loch. The village has a golf course and a sailing club, as well as potters and weavers. The Smithy Heritage Centre has a local history section. South of the village are the ruins of Strome Castle (NTS), a MacDonald stronghold destroyed by the MacKenzies in 1602.

④ PLOCKTON

Palm trees line the waterfront of this delightful village, a favoured haunt of artists, naturalists and sailors. Small

---

HIGHLAND GAME

The Scottish Highlands are the domain of the red deer, which, along with the roe deer, is Britain's only native species of deer. The rarer fallow and sika deer were introduced to Scotland, becoming established in the wild after escapes from deer parks. All Scotland's deer species can cause extensive damage to growing trees and are culled to control numbers.

The red deer is Britain's largest wild animal.

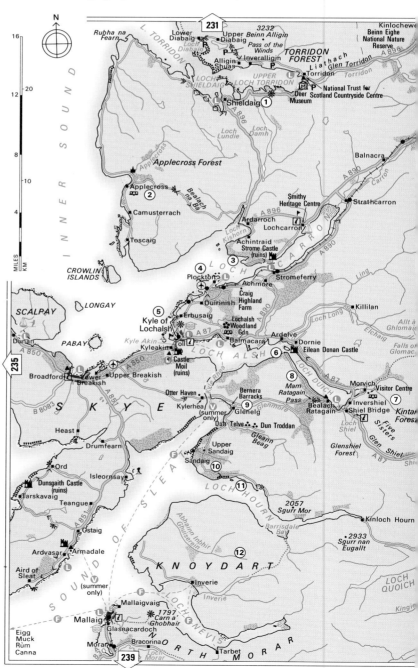

SEA-GIRT STRONGHOLD *Built on the site of an earlier fort, Eilean Donan Castle stands guard over the still waters of Loch Duich, Loch Long and Loch Alsh.*

boats may be hired, and there are trips to see the seal colonies on islands round the rocky headland. Pine martens and golden eagles can be spotted in the woods and hills south of Plockton. East of the village, the Craig Highland Farm has rare breeds of domestic animals.

⑤ KYLE OF LOCHALSH
A ferry point before the Skye bridge spanned Kyle Akin, the bustling little town has the air of a place of transit. The Lochalsh Woodland Garden (NTS) at Balmacara has exotic shrubs planted beneath magnificent old trees, and inland are several woodland walks.

⑥ EILEAN DONAN CASTLE
The battlements and turrets of a romantic castle rise from a rocky islet at the meeting place of three lochs. Eilean Donan was built in the 13th century as a Highland stronghold of the Scottish kings, and was later held by the MacKenzies and their loyal followers, the Macraes. After centuries of turbulent clan warfare, the castle was finally destroyed by British forces during the abortive Jacobite uprising in 1719. The ruins were fully restored in the early 1900s, and visitors can see Macrae portraits and furniture.

⑦ KINTAIL FOREST
The wild and mountainous estate of Kintail (NTS), which includes the dramatic but isolated waterfalls of Glomach, is open to walkers even during the deer-stalking season. An unmanned visitor centre at Morvich displays details of local walks. From Shiel Bridge, the A87 heads inland along Glen Shiel, overlooked by the peaks of the Five Sisters of Kintail.

⑧ MAM RATAGAIN PASS
The narrow road from Shiel Bridge to Glenelg, built as a military road in the 18th century, climbs 1100ft in a series of breathtaking zigzags to cross a wild pass. Through clearings in the forestry plantations there are views that might normally be seen only from the cockpit of an aircraft. The descent to Glenelg passes a string of working crofts.

⑨ GLENELG
North of the remote hamlet is a summer car ferry service to Skye. Just outside Glenelg are the crumbling ruins of Bernera Barracks, built by the English after the 1719 Jacobite uprising, and garrisoned until 1790. To the south-east, along Gleann Beag, are two of Scotland's finest Iron Age brochs, or fortified towers, Dun Troddan and Dun Telve. Their hollow dry-stone walls, which house stairs and galleries, still stand 30ft in height some 2000 years after they were built.

⑩ SANDAIG
From the tiny hamlet of Upper Sandaig, a 2 mile track through a forestry plantation leads to a rocky bay faced by small islands. Naturalist and author Gavin Maxwell, whose novel *Ring of Bright Water* told the story of his pet otters, lived in a waterside house dubbed Camusfeàrna in his books. The house has gone, destroyed in a fire, but visitors from around the world leave shells and pebbles on memorials to Maxwell and his otter Edal. Wild otters are often seen along this beautiful shore.

⑪ LOCH HOURN
The dark and claustrophobic 'Loch of Hell', flanked by high barren mountains, bites deep into the coast. A narrow road from Glenelg runs for some miles along the northern shore. Determined drivers can reach Kinloch Hourn at the head of the loch by a twisting lane through 30 miles of wilderness from Glen Garry to the east. At journey's end there is nothing but an eerie silence and total stillness.

⑫ KNOYDART
The Knoydart peninsula, between Loch Hourn and Loch Nevis, remains an utterly remote area of unspoilt wilderness. Inverie has a shop, a school, a restaurant and a pub, even a small library – but no road to connect it to the rest of the world. Day trips or longer visits must be made by boat from Mallaig. Quite unlike the landscape of Loch Hourn, the shoreline of Loch Nevis is an open and a bright place, a paradise for walkers and escapists.

TOURIST INFORMATION

Gairloch (01445) 712130; Kyle of Lochalsh (01599) 4276 (summer); Lochcarron (01520) 722357 (summer); Shiel Bridge (01599) 511264 (summer)

An 'Isle of Clouds', and the legend of a Fairy Flag

Skye is a gathering of peninsulas, composed mostly of mountains and moor. From the sea, the island's cloud-cap can be seen long before its dark peaks loom into view: the Norse called it Skuyo, 'Isle of Clouds'.

SKYLINE ON SKYE *Castle Moil at Kyleakin was never more than a miniature keep even when it was built, in the 13th century.*

① KYLERHEA

In summer Kylerhea is linked to Glenelg on the mainland by a six-car ferry with one ramp, whose deck revolves to allow cars to disembark. The 5 minute journey is romantic and exciting, often made across a fierce tidal flow which sweeps the ferry down the narrows like a twig in a stream. Incredibly, cattle were once swum across these straits.

Just north of the ferry is the Kylerhea Otter Haven, where a hide allows visitors to watch eagles, falcons, buzzards, herons, seals and a huge variety of sea birds, as well as otters.

② KYLEAKIN

For almost a century the landing point for the Kyle of Lochalsh ferry, the fishing village of Kyleakin is now bypassed by a toll bridge half a mile to the north. The bridge leapfrogs Eilean Ban, the lighthouse island where the author Gavin Maxwell lived for a year before his death in 1969. Watching over the bay is the ruin of 15th-century Castle Moil, said to have been built by a Norwegian princess called Saucy Mary who ran a chain across the straits to sink any ship failing to pay her toll. Seal-spotting cruises leave from Kyleakin in summer.

③ BROADFORD

The largest settlement in the south of Skye includes an environmental centre, incorporating the International Otter Survival Fund, which is open to visitors. A serpentarium has snakes, lizards and insects. Around 1745, Drambuie was first brewed at Broadford, following a secret recipe of Charles Edward Stuart, Bonnie Prince Charlie; the liqueur is no longer made on the island.

④ LUIB

Tourism has overtaken crofting as the principal industry on Skye, but the Folk Museum in Luib offers a glimpse of a typical crofter's life a century ago. The squat stone house, its thatched roof held down by ropes and rocks, contains old agricultural tools and household utensils, as well as a peat-fuelled range. The museum also features 'The Trail of the Fugitive', narrating the adventures of Bonnie Prince Charlie.

⑤ LOCH SLIGACHAN

With its large campsite and hotel, the head of Loch Sligachan serves as a base camp for mountaineers and hillwalkers venturing into the Cuillin Hills.

Climbers planning assaults on the fearsome crags and pinnacles of the Skye Ridge start from Glen Brittle, in the west of the island, where there is another campsite and a hostel. Anyone tempted to go into the hills without a professional guide should inform the Mountain Rescue Service in advance.

Visitors in search of gentler pursuits might prefer a round of golf at Sconser, near the mouth of Loch Sligachan. The Sconser Inn is believed to have been the place where MacDonald of Clanranald pleaded, unsuccessfully, with MacDonald and MacLeod chieftains to support the Jacobite uprising.

⑥ PORTREE

Edging a safe harbour, Skye's capital is the meeting point of several roads that reach out to the far corners of the island. The Royal Hotel stands on the site of McNab's Inn, where Bonnie Prince Charlie said farewell to Flora MacDonald in 1746 after the failed rebellion. The prince's story and the island's cultural history are explored at the Aros Heritage Centre just south of the town, which also has a lively arts centre.

The eastern coast of the Trotternish peninsula north of Portree is remarkable for its spectacular cliffs, such as Kilt Rock and the 300 ft Mealt Falls, and for the monstrous rock formations known as the Old Man of Storr and The Quiraing, both of which stab jagged spires into the bellies of the clouds.

ROYAL RENDEZVOUS *Portree's name means 'king's port', deriving from a visit in 1540 by James V, who chose it as a neutral place to meet the clan chiefs and seek their loyalty.*

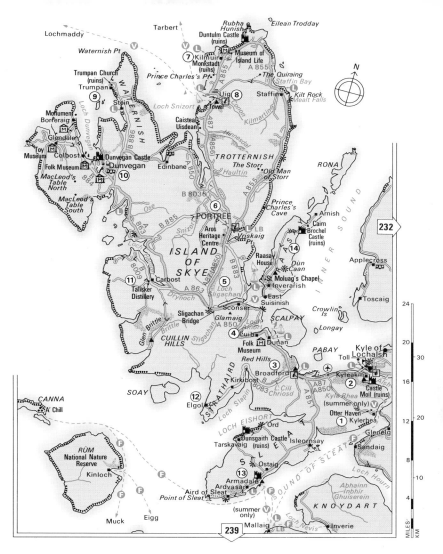

⑦ KILMUIR

It was at Prince Charles's Point, on the shore below Monkstadt house, that the fugitive prince hid after his journey in an open boat from Uist, while Flora MacDonald went to get help. Monkstadt is now a gaunt ruin, reached down an unmarked road. Flora is buried nearby. The Museum of Island Life is a group of refurbished 'blackhouses' illustrating the hardships and challenges faced by islanders 100 and more years ago. Perched on the cliffs to the north are the ruins of Duntulm Castle, home until 1730 of the MacDonalds of the Isles and haunted by the ghost of a child who was accidentally dropped to the rocks below by a nurse.

⑧ UIG

From this pretty, bowl-shaped bay, partly lined with trees, ferries leave for the Outer Hebrides. The only buildings of note are a bold white hotel and a 19th-century folly tower. The surrounding countryside is dotted with ruined brochs, duns and forts, standing stones and the remains of ancient settlements. Among these is Caisteal Uisdean, near the mouth of the Hinnesdal, a fortress built in the 17th century by the treacherous Hugh, a cousin of the MacDonald chieftain. It had no doors or windows, so that the only entrance was through the roof. Uig is a centre for canoeing, windsurfing and horse riding.

⑨ TRUMPAN

The ruins of Trumpan Church stand high up on the west coast of the Waternish peninsula. On a Sunday morning in 1578 a raiding party of MacDonalds from Uist set fire to the church, killing all but one of the congregation of MacLeods. But the ebbing tide beached the raiders' boats; they were caught and almost annihilated by a MacLeod force which, some say, was strengthened by spirits summoned by the waving of the Fairy Flag. The dead of both sides were buried beneath a toppled wall.

⑩ DUNVEGAN

For nearly 800 years the MacLeod chieftains have lived in Dunvegan Castle, making it the oldest house in Britain to have been continuously occupied by the same family. The imposing building has a clan exhibition, and many MacLeod treasures, including the Fairy Flag. There are boat trips to see Loch Dunvegan's seal colony. North of the castle are the coral beaches at Claigan.

A museum in Dunvegan is dedicated to Angus MacAskill, at 7ft 9in the tallest recorded true giant. On the peninsula to the west is Borreraig, home of the MacCrimmons, hereditary pipers to the MacLeods. A monument and museum mark their achievements. The Borreraig Park Exhibition Croft displays traditional farming implements and machinery. To the south, the ancient dwelling at Colbost Folk Museum, with a traditional peat fire in the middle of the floor and no chimney, makes it clear how 'blackhouses' got their name. Another museum, at Glendale, is devoted to toys. To the south are the flat-topped basalt mountains known as MacLeod's Tables. On Healabhal Bheag, one of MacLeod's Tables, a chieftain is said to have entertained to dinner some mainland lairds who had wagered that he could not provide a larger table than that in the king's court in Edinburgh.

⑪ TALISKER DISTILLERY

The only distillery on Skye stands on the shore of Loch Harport and is fed by the peaty waters of the Carbost Burn. Both the sea and the burn leave their mark on the smoky single malt whisky, which visitors are invited to sample before making a fascinating tour of the rambling, aromatic building.

⑫ ELGOL

The boulder-strewn bay at the end of the Strathaird peninsula is a fine point from which to view the Cuillin Hills to the north and the islands of Soay, Canna, Rúm and Eigg to the west and south. Boat trips round the peninsula and to the islands start from Kirkibost.

⑬ ARMADALE

A wooded road lined in summer with bluebells leads down the Sleat peninsula, the lush 'Garden of Skye', to

JAGGED AND GIGANTIC *Seen across Loch Slapin, to the east of Elgol, the formidable Cuillin Hills are characterised by an almost brutal beauty. The granite ridge rises to more than 3000 ft, and presents a daunting series of challenges to walkers and climbers.*

Armadale, where the Mallaig ferry docks. Armadale Castle houses one of Skye's major attractions, the Clan Donald Visitor Centre and its Museum of the Isles. Up the coast at Ostaig the flourishing Gaelic College runs short courses for visitors in Gaelic, music, and culture. From the Aird of Sleat in the south a 2 mile dirt track, for walkers only, leads to the remote hamlet, lighthouse and harbour at Point of Sleat.

On the northern coast of the peninsula are beaches of coral sand at Tarskavaig and Ord; between the two beaches stand the dangerous ruins of Dunsgaith Castle, the former residence of the MacDonalds of Sleat.

⑭ RAASAY

The beautiful, remote island of Raasay is reached by ferry from Skye. Only 13 miles long, it includes moorland, beaches, ravines, cliffs, woods, luxuriant gardens and fascinating buildings

and ruins. The islanders supported the Jacobite cause in 1745, and their houses were razed by the government. Raasay has a population of about 200, most of whom live near Inverarish.

Raasay House, former seat of the MacLeods of Raasay, is an outdoor pursuits centre and home to a local history society. Behind the house is a 13th-century chapel dedicated to Raasay's patron saint, Moluag. Remains of the island's iron industry can be seen at East Suisinish, near the ferry pier, and on the road leading east from Inverarish, at the foot of the track leading up to the flat summit of Dun Caan.

To the north are the ruins of Brochel Castle, and from here the track is known as Calum's Road. Calum Mac-Leod, who lived at Arnish, built a 3000 yd stretch of road to his village single-handedly but died in 1988, aged 77, soon after completing the task. A memorial cairn marks the route.

Shore where a prince's adventure began and ended

South of Mallaig, beaches of white sand sprinkle a ragged coast where tree-fringed sea lochs make sinuous courses between grand mountains. There are tales of Bonnie Prince Charlie, and legends of a monster.

① MALLAIG
The busy harbour village has a backdrop of dramatic hills and magnificent views over the Sound of Sleat to the jagged Cuillin Hills of Skye. The catch, mainly of shellfish, is landed on the quay for the evening market. Visitors can learn more about the fishing industry at Marine World, which displays sting rays, conger eels and other creatures. Mallaig's history is recalled at the Heritage Centre, which has exhibits and photographs. There are summer car ferries to Skye and to South Uist, and boat trips to Hebridean islands including Rùm, Eigg, Muck and Canna.

② MORAR
The hilly village looks out over the Morar estuary, which has pure white sands. Only half a mile in length, its river is an anchorage for pleasure craft. It flows to the sea from Loch Morar, which is 11 miles long, more than 1000 ft deep and said to be the lair of a monster called the Mhorag; venturesome fishermen can hire boats on the loch.

③ TRAIGH BEACH
Extensive sands, crystal-clear water and rock pools make Traigh one of the most attractive beaches on this stretch of coast. Both Traigh and the beach at Camusdarach, situated a mile to the north, are backed by dunes.

④ ARISAIG
In contrast to the nearby wilderness of high bare hills, the wooded glens round the village of Arisaig form a gentle landscape that encourages leisurely, undemanding exploration. In summer there are boat trips to Rùm, Eigg and Muck, which was a major harbour on a remote coast until the railway opened in 1894. An ancient ruined chapel by St Mary's Church has gravestones with medieval carvings, including scenes showing hunters. The ruined pier at Rhu, 3 miles west of Arisaig, is a good place for watching the seals or admiring sunsets over Rùm and Eigg.

⑤ LOCH NAN UAMH
A memorial cairn stands on the shore of Loch nan Uamh, where Charles Edward Stuart, or Bonnie Prince Charlie,

CAIRN OF DEFEAT *From near this cairn on Loch nan Uamh, Bonnie Prince Charlie sailed for France in September 1746.*

landed at the start of the 1745 rebellion, and departed 14 months later, following the Jacobite defeat at Culloden. Before the prince and his fellow fugitives left for France, they sheltered from the English redcoats in a cave below Arisaig House, now a hotel. On a headland to the south are traces of an Iron Age fort, whose stones were vitrified, or fused together by terrific heat – probably caused by the accidental burning of timbers used to strengthen the walls.

⑥ GLENFINNAN
Glenfinnan Monument (NTS), a tower topped by the statue of a kilted warrior, marks the spot where, on August 19, 1745, Charles Edward Stuart raised his standard to rally the clans to support him. An exhibition at the visitor centre relates the history of the uprising. Glenfinnan station, which serves trains on the spectacular West Highland Line, has a railway museum.

⑦ MOIDART
The A861 leads south from Lochailort into Moidart, the wild and sparsely populated area between Loch Ailort and Loch Shiel, offering an exhilarating coastal drive. A narrow lane branches off the main road by Glenuig Inn, and runs behind sandy beaches. At Kinlochmoidart, seven beech trees known as 'the Seven Men of Moidart' commemorate the band of Jacobites who landed with Bonnie Prince Charlie in 1745.

⑧ CASTLE TIORAM
A sand spit, occasionally covered by high water, connects the romantically sited island fortress of Castle Tioram with the wooded shores of Loch Moidart. The castle is said to have been built in 1353, though the curtain wall is probably far older, and for centuries it was the home of the chieftains of Clanranald. In 1715, Tioram was deliberately burnt down when the 14th chieftain departed to fight beside James Edward Stuart, the Old Pretender, convinced – rightly, as it turned out – that he would not return alive. The Silver Walk, along which buried treasure was once found, leads along the cliffs of Loch Moidart and then inland to the abandoned settlement of Port á Bhàta, whose inhabitants were transported to Australia in 1853 during the final stages of the Highland Clearances.

⑨ KENTRA BAY
On the northern side of the bay, beyond a bleak expanse of peat bog, are the sandy beaches of the Ardtoe peninsula and, at the end of the road, a fish farming research centre. A 3 mile track along the southern shore of Kentra Bay leads through forestry plantations to the Singing Sands of Camus an Lighe, so called because they are said to emit an eerie sound when trodden on.

HIGHLAND HERO *From the top of the tower at Glenfinnan a lone warrior gazes towards the hills from which, in 1745, 1500 Highlanders came to the aid of Bonnie Prince Charlie.*

RAIL ROAD TO THE ISLES *A steam train crosses the Glenfinnan Viaduct on the 164 mile journey from Glasgow to Mallaig, which takes in some of Britain's most dramatic scenery.*

⑩ ARDNAMURCHAN

The tip of this long peninsula, known as the Point of Ardnamurchan, is mainland Britain's most westerly point. A lighthouse stands on the clifftop. Local time, according to the sun, is 30 minutes behind Greenwich Mean Time.

From Salen, the road along the peninsula passes through lush woods and rhododendron thickets beside Loch Sunart before crossing desolate moors round Ben Hiant, the core of an extinct volcano. The Natural History Centre at Glenmore has displays relating to the local wildlife. From the scattered village of Kilchoan a car ferry operates to Tobermory on the Island of Mull.

Sanna Bay, north-east of the Point of Ardnamurchan, has a sandy beach sheltered from the winds by dunes covered by machair grass. Kilmory, on the peninsula's wild, isolated northern coast, has an ancient burial ground, and sandy beaches flanked by caves.

⑪ STRONTIAN

The lochside village gave its name to the metallic element strontium, which in 1808 was isolated from a mineral mined in the nearby hills. Silver, lead and zinc were also extracted there in the 18th and 19th centuries.

Nearly 2 miles inland is Ariundle Oakwood, a national nature reserve noted for its wild flowers and mosses, and with attractive walks leading to abandoned lead mines. The minor road through Scotstown leads up to a high mountain pass that gives extensive views across Loch Doilet.

⑫ LOCHALINE

The only road that crosses the lonely Morvern peninsula, bounded by great sea lochs, meets the coast at Lochaline. The village's sands are pure silica, and more than 100 000 tons are gathered every year for the ornamental glass industry. Intricate Celtic stone carvings are displayed inside the Church of Keil. At the head of Loch Aline, 3 miles from the village, Kinlochaline Castle is a 14th-century tower, once the seat of the chiefs of Clan MacInnes, which was restored in 1890. Its exterior can be seen from the grounds of Ardtornish House, a Victorian Gothic mansion; the house is not open to the public, but its woodland gardens can be visited.

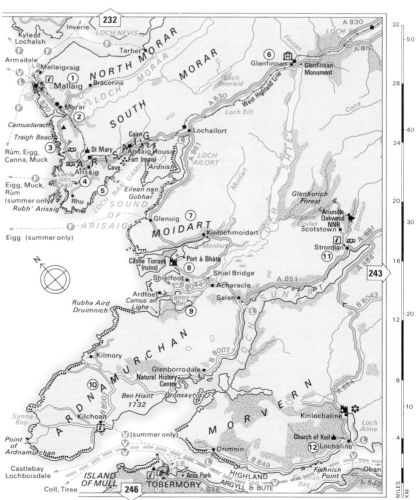

TOURIST INFORMATION

Fort William (01397) 703781; Kilchoan (01972) 510222 (summer); Mallaig (01687) 462170 (summer); Strontian (01967) 402131 (summer); Tobermory (01688) 302182

Solitude on the islands of the Inner Hebrides

Sunny and low-lying, or mountainous and forbidding, each of the Inner Hebrides has its individual character. The islands suffered greatly during the Highland Clearances, and are still sparsely inhabited.

GRAND MANOR *Rùm's Kinloch Castle, now a hotel owned by Scottish Natural Heritage, was built as a shooting lodge in 1901. Little has changed inside.*

① CANNA

The 5 mile long island of Canna (NTS) has a population of about 20, consisting of estate workers, crofters and lobster fishermen. Canna's deep-water harbour is popular in summer with small-boat sailors, despite its curious navigational hazards: the basalt rocks of the cliffs are so magnetic that they distort compass readings on craft as far as 3 miles away.

In the 1840s, during the Highland Clearances, about two-thirds of the inhabitants were shipped to Canada. Previously there had been a township on the island called A'Chill; its scant remains, which include a Celtic cross, a curious pink standing stone and a burial ground, can be seen near the pier.

② RÙM

Wild and mountainous, the island rises steeply from the sea to peaks of 2300 ft and more. Few people have lived there since 1826, when almost the entire population was shipped across the Atlantic to Newfoundland in Canada. In 1957, Rùm became a national nature reserve. Two signposted nature trails start from the ferry dock, near the head of Loch Scresort. One follows the loch's southern shore, part of which is frequented by otters, and ends 1½ miles away at Port nan Caranean, an abandoned village where eider ducks and gulls nest among the ruins. The other trail heads inland for about 2 miles.

Red deer are everywhere; there are also wild goats, and little Rùm ponies that are bred on the island to carry deer carcasses down from the hills. Golden eagles and, more rarely, sea eagles may be spotted. The sea eagle, which has a wingspan of 9 ft, became extinct in Britain early in the 20th century but was reintroduced to Rùm in the 1970s. Grey and common seals hunt for fish in the bay, and in the long summer evenings Manx shearwaters gather on the waves by the thousand, before returning to the mountain-top nests where they rear their young in burrows.

③ EIGG

With a population of about 80, Eigg is the most crowded island in the Small Islands Parish, which also includes Canna, Rùm and Muck. There are guest houses, self-catering cottages and a minibus service connecting the village of Galmisdale, where the boat comes in, with Cleadale. North of Cleadale, at

---

THE HIGHLAND CLEARANCES

Towards the end of the 18th century, Scottish landowners discovered that there was more profit in sheep than in people. Prices for wool and mutton were high, whereas crofters, struggling to scratch a living from the soil, were barely able to pay their rents. The failure of the potato crop in the 1840s aggravated the situation. Some chiefs and landlords went to great lengths to help their tenants, but many did not, and carried out large-scale evictions to make room for sheep. Crofters' homes all over the Highlands and Islands were put to the torch by landowners and many of their occupants were shipped overseas. The many roofless crofts scattered through the area bear witness to the extent of the Clearances.

Thomas Faed's painting The Last of the Clan *depicts the misery of eviction, when thousands of crofters left their homeland in emigrant ships. Others resettled on poor land near the coast.*

SWEET ISLE *Perhaps it was Coll's North Bay, with its craggy shores, that a Gaelic poet had in mind when he wrote of the island 'Fair gem of the ocean, sweet Coll of my song'.*

Camas Sgiotaig, are the Singing Sands, which squeak when walked upon, or even emit a long, continuous moan when the wind is in the right direction. There are sandy beaches to the south of the Singing Sands and to the north of Galmisdale. For visitors interested in geology there are fine walks round the cliffs of An Sgurr, the ridge at the southern end of the island. Bicycles, mopeds, ponies and dinghies may be hired.

④ MUCK

The small island's name comes from the Gaelic word *Muc*, which means variously a heap, a pig or a sea-pig, or porpoise. None of the meanings seems appropriate to the fertile, low-lying island, home to a few dozen people and where the meadows are bright with wild flowers in summer. Muck has a relatively mild climate, thanks to influence of the North Atlantic Drift and the island's sheltered position in relation to its higher and bigger neighbours. In 1828 Muck's landlord evicted most of the crofters and sent them to Nova Scotia in Canada, where some descendants still speak Gaelic.

⑤ COLL

From the deck of the Oban ferry, the eastern seaboard of the 12 mile long island looks inhospitably craggy. But once the boat penetrates Loch Eatharna to dock at Arinagour pier an expanse of gentle, heathery moorland, dotted with slaty-dark lochans, comes into view.

Much of the west coast is made up of bright shell-sand, blown into dunes of 100 ft and higher, their slopes knitted by grass to form what is known as machair, on which cattle graze.

There are plenty of sandy, secluded coves, and the bright township of Arinagour, which is ablaze in summer with flowers, includes shops and a craft centre. At the south-western end of the island is an RSPB reserve where corncrakes may be heard in summer. Otters live along the coast, and common seals are seen in many sheltered bays.

⑥ TIREE

Apart from three bumps at its western end, Tiree is so low-lying that it looks from a distance like a pencil stroke on the horizon. Closer inspection reveals empty beaches of pale sand, and especially in May, when Tiree has been the sunniest place in Britain, something of the air of a tropical isle. Conditions are good for surfing. There are carpets of wild flowers in early summer, but no trees; the 120 knot gales that come off the Atlantic Ocean in winter make their growth impossible. The island's name means 'Land of Corn', and the fertility of the machair helps

to support a population of about 750. Tiree's villages include Scarinish, south of sandy Gott Bay, and Balemartine on Hynish Bay. In the 1840s, labourers constructing the Skerryvore lighthouse, some 10 miles south-west of Tiree, were housed at Hynish, to the south of Balemartine; the granite buildings are now used as holiday accommodation. Balephuil, to the west, is set in a bay, attractively flanked by Ben Hynish and the steep headland of Ceann a' Mhara.

TOURIST INFORMATION

Fort William (01397) 703781; Kilchoan (01972) 510222 (summer); Mallaig (01687) 462170 (summer); Oban (01631) 63122; Tobermory (01688) 302182

241

Waterside castles near the wild hills north of Oban

Echoes of old battles and murders resound through the stern hills and the stones of ruined strongholds that lie between Fort William and the port of Oban. Offshore are the peaceful islands of Lismore and Kerrera.

① FORT WILLIAM

Oliver Cromwell established fortifications at Inverlochy, which were later expanded and renamed Fort William after King William III. The town is a busy holiday centre, attracting walkers and climbers; Ben Nevis, Britain's highest summit, is 4 miles east of the town and is bounded on its south side by the gorge of Glen Nevis, which is enclosed by dramatically plunging slopes. Other visitors come to cruise on the Caledonian Canal, which opened in 1847 to link the lochs of the Great Glen.

The West Highland Museum displays Jacobite relics, including a 'secret' portrait of Prince Charles Edward Stuart, or Bonnie Prince Charlie, which is revealed only when reflected onto a curved and polished surface. Treasures of the Earth, 4 miles north-west of Fort William at Corpach, is a collection of gemstones, crystals and fossils.

② GLEN COE

The dark summits lowering over 'the Narrow Glen' provide some of Britain's most testing challenges for mountaineers. Near the eastern end of the glen are ski slopes served by tows and by a chair lift, operating in summer as well as during the skiing season. Its 2400 ft high terminus gives wide views of the glen and over Rannoch Moor, a vast expanse studded with lochans.

In the village of Glencoe to the west, a folk museum is housed in a group of thatched cottages. Some of its displays recall the infamous massacre of February 1, 1692, when members of the MacDonald clan, who had been slow to renounce the Jacobite cause and to sign an oath of allegiance to William III, were butchered by Campbells of the Argyll militia. The killers had spent the previous 12 days accepting the unsuspecting MacDonalds' hospitality.

A National Trust for Scotland visitor centre, 2 miles south-east of the village, is the starting point for guided walks through the glen in summer.

③ LOCH LINNHE

Mountains rise steeply from the waters of Loch Linnhe, a long, straight inlet of the sea. The Corran ferry, which crosses the loch at its narrowest point, saves motorists approaching or leaving the mountainous Ardgour region from a long drive round the head of the loch.

At South Ballachulish, close by the bridge that spans Loch Leven's narrow outlet into Loch Linnhe, is a monument to James Stewart, hanged on this spot in November 1752 for complicity in the murder of Colin Campbell, a land agent employed by the English to evict suspected pro-Jacobites. Robert Louis Stevenson's novel *Kidnapped* presents the case that Stewart could not have been guilty, and was put to death only because his accusers and the jury were under Campbell domination.

④ PORTNACROISH

A yacht marina and wind-surfing centre look out towards Shuna Island. In Portnacroish churchyard a memorial stone recalls a battle in 1468 between the feuding Stewarts and MacDougalls 'in which many hundreds fell'.

Standing on an islet in the bay to the south is the tall rectangular Castle Stalker; the Gaelic name is *Caisted an*

ISLAND FORTRESS *Castle Stalker, in Loch Laich, was once given away by its Stewart owner in exchange for a Campbell boat.*

Stalcair, 'Castle of the Hunter', for it was often used by James IV as a hunting lodge. The castle is not open to visitors.

⑤ PORT APPIN

The little port is a harmonious collection of bright cottages, with a squat lighthouse and a diminutive pier house that has been expanded into a hotel. A passenger ferry runs from the pier across the narrow strait to Lismore. A footpath southwards from the car park follows the coast for nearly 2 miles.

⑥ LISMORE

The island consists of a narrow 10 mile strip of fertile grazing land. By virtue of its central position in Loch Linnhe, Lismore has far-ranging views, which include Ben Nevis, Mull and Morvern. The road that runs from end to end is joined roughly halfway along by a side road from Achnacroish, where the car ferry from Oban lands. Lismore can

NOBLE CROWN *Built to give work to unemployed masons, the granite replica of the Colosseum adds a fanciful touch to Oban's skyline and looks down to a bustling harbour.*

claim to have been one of the earliest Christian sites in the Highlands. The parish church of Kilmoluag was once the choir of a cathedral founded in the 13th century and dedicated to St Moluag, who was a contemporary of St Columba and arrived there in about 560; the rest of the building was destroyed during the Reformation.

⑦ OBAN SEA LIFE CENTRE

On the southern shore of Loch Creran is the earliest of Britain's Sea Life Centres, opened in 1979, where visitors can see sharks, octopuses, jellyfish and crabs. Other attractions include seal pools, a nursery for rescued seal pups, and shoals of herring. Near Barcaldine, 1½ miles east of the Sea Life Centre, there are waymarked forest walks.

⑧ LOCH ETIVE

The road along the northern shore of Loch Etive leads to Ardchattan Priory (HS), where a ruined chapel is all that remains of a 13th-century foundation. The priory was the scene in 1308 of a meeting of one of Robert Bruce's National Councils, the last to be conducted in Gaelic. Nearby, Ardchattan Garden has formal gardens overlooking the loch, and a wild garden with some 180 varieties of shrub.

Summer cruises to the remote head of the loch, which is dominated by the gaunt summits flanking Glen Coe, start from Loch Etive's southern shore, near Taynuilt village. Buoys mark the headlines, or ends, of ropes from which some 200 tons of mussels are harvested annually. Seals bask on a long tongue of rock. Bonawe Iron Furnace (HS), near Taynuilt, is a charcoal blast furnace, established in 1753 and now restored.

⑨ CONNEL

The village stands beside the narrow mouth of Loch Etive, which is crossed by a cantilever bridge built as a railway viaduct but now carrying road traffic. Below the bridge are the Falls of Lora, impressive rapids created by a submerged ridge over which, at ebb tide, the waters from Loch Etive thresh and swirl towards the Firth of Lorn.

⑩ DUNSTAFFNAGE CASTLE

Set upon a gnarled rocky outcrop in a commanding position near the mouth of Loch Etive, and defended by 10 ft thick outer walls, Dunstaffnage Castle (HS) was founded in the mid 13th century by the MacDougalls. In 1309 the castle was captured by Robert Bruce and for some years remained a royal property. Later it was granted to the Earls and then Dukes of Argyll, as hereditary Captains of Dunstaffnage. Flora MacDonald spent ten days there before being sent for trial in London for helping Bonnie Prince Charlie in his flight after Culloden. The nearby chapel dates from the 13th century and has intricate carving in its windows.

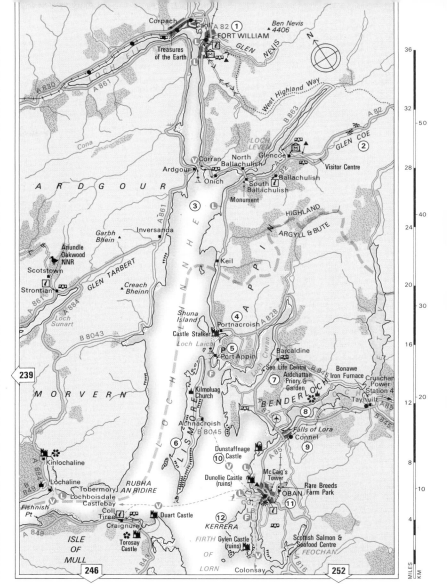

⑪ OBAN

The town rises steeply from its bustling waterfront to McCaig's Tower, built at the end of the 19th century by a local banker and resembling the Colosseum in Rome. The tower was to have been a museum and art gallery, but remains an unfinished shell around a pleasant garden, with a viewing platform looking out over the harbour. Beside the harbour is A World in Miniature, where visitors can examine scale models of furniture and paintings, which include Rembrandt's *Night Watch* and Van Gogh's *Irises*. Oban malt whisky distillery nearby provides tours. The Argyllshire Gathering, held each year in late August, features traditional Highland games such as throwing the hammer.

Tossing the caber at the Argyllshire Gathering

Ferries sail from the town to Mull and other Hebridean islands. Some of the ferries give dramatic views of Dunollie Castle, a ruined, creeper-choked tower house on a ridge to the north of Oban.

At Oban Rare Breeds Farm Park, 1½ miles east of the town, visitors can see pigs, sheep and cattle that are no longer found on modern farms.

⑫ KERRERA

Two miles south of Oban a passenger ferry leaves for the island of Kerrera, on which there are excellent walks, with fine views of Mull, Oban and Lismore. Perched on a pillar of rock in a bay of low cliffs at the southern end of the island, and a 2½ mile walk from the jetty, is the ruined Gylen Castle, a 16th-century MacDougall stronghold sacked by Covenanters during the Civil War.

PLACES TO SEE INLAND

Cruachan Power Station, 18 miles E of Oban. Guided minibus tours of hydroelectric power station deep within Ben Cruachan.

TOURIST INFORMATION

Ballachulish (01855) 811296 (summer); Fort William (01397) 703781; Oban (01631) 563122

High Drama in Location Scotland

Stories are sometimes heard of walkers in the Scottish Highlands who have come across a village that does not appear on any map, or seen a distant battle between hordes of kilted clansmen. Such strange events may be explained by the presence of a film crew, for the Highland landscape has long exerted a powerful appeal on film and television directors. If a film requires majestic scenery, islands, beaches or romantic castles, Scotland can offer locations that would be hard to match elsewhere in Europe. The light produced by northern latitudes and an unpolluted atmosphere astonishes many cameramen, and reclusive stars have occasionally been tempted out of Hollywood by the promise of some salmon fishing during idle moments on location. It is jokingly said that Fort William can rival Cannes as a place for spotting stars.

Scotland's history and literature have provided material for many film plots. Robert Louis Stevenson's novel *Kidnapped* has been filmed on four occasions, most recently in 1971 with Michael Caine as Alan Breck, using locations on the Isle of Mull. *Bonnie Prince Charlie* (1948) was a brave attempt by Sir Alexander Korda to challenge Hollywood's monopoly of epics, but despite a cast of thousands gathered in Glenfinnan to watch David Niven raise the Stuart standard, the paying public failed to rally to the cause.

FANTASTIC PARABLE *Eilean Donan Castle (right) was one of the west coast locations used in* Highlander. *The 1986 fantasy adventure, starring (above) Sean Connery and Christopher Lambert, was set in the medieval Highlands and present-day New York. In 1994 the third film in the series was partly shot in the Cuillin Hills on Skye.*

ISLANDERS WITH A SECRET *Film director Alexander MacKendrick turned* Whisky Galore, *Compton Mackenzie's whimsical fact-based novel, into a popular Ealing comedy, using the island of Barra for much of the filming.*

ANCIENT ROOTS *Australian actor Mel Gibson starred as the 13th-century Scottish patriot William Wallace in* Braveheart. *Though much of the film was shot in Ireland for financial reasons, no substitute was found for the isolated splendour of Glen Nevis (above right) to provide a suitably romantic setting for the hero's youth. Of all the Scottish glens, Glen Nevis and Glen Coe have most frequently been used as film locations.*

JACOBITE HERO *The glens of the western Highlands provide a dramatic backdrop to the tale of Celtic resistance in* Rob Roy, *about the 18th-century outlaw Robert MacGregor. Some of the locations used in the film, starring Liam Neeson and Jessica Lange, were so remote that the crew and cast had to be flown in by helicopter.*

Such heroic tales, especially those with wicked English villains, continue to inspire fascination, particularly in the USA. Films based on the life-stories of the Scottish heroes Rob Roy MacGregor (*Rob Roy*) and William Wallace (*Braveheart*), both released in 1995, made lavish use of Highland landscapes. More symbolic battles between good and evil have been fought out in the series of *Highlander* films, in which the Scottish glens represent the sophisticated hero's natural and unsullied homeland.

The Highland way of life, seemingly idyllic when contrasted with the urban rat race, is another theme that has long been popular. The heroes of *Whisky*

THE VILLAGE LIFE *Tranquil Plockton, at the mouth of Loch Carron on the west coast, was chosen to portray the fictional 'Lochdubh' in* Hamish Macbeth. *The 1995 BBC drama series, based on the stories of M. C. Beaton, related the exploits of a policeman (Robert Carlyle) in a sleepy Highland village.*

Galore, filmed in the Outer Hebrides in 1949, were the canny islanders who outwitted officials from the mainland in a race to salvage 20 000 crates of whisky from a wreck. *Local Hero* (1983) told of a young oil company executive who was seduced into abandoning his corporate values and his polished shoes on a west coast beach. The same ingredients of unspoilt landscapes and close-knit communities feature in television series such as *Hamish Macbeth* and *The Tales of Para Handy*, the 1990s remake of the 1950s stories about a Clyde cargo boat and its crew. All such interpretations present somewhat idealised visions of the lifestyle and the climate of the Highlands, but the locations often convey a magic that is far from illusory.

Filming in the Highlands places strenuous demands on cast and crew. Sudden changes in the weather can play havoc with the continuity, or rain and mist may shroud the scenery for days on end. Highland roads, furthermore, are few and far between, leaving many of the finest sites out of reach of the enormous convoy that usually accompanies a film crew. To stage a battle scene in an isolated glen may involve logistics on the scale of a military exercise, with the use of helicopters, artificial roads and self-contained encampments. That film companies are prepared to meet such daunting challenges is a measure of the lure of the unique and spectacular quality of the Scottish landscape.

The varied beauty of Mull, and a burial place of kings

The Island of Mull is a cheerful place, with its flower-filled upland meadows, waterfalls, and colourful houses at Tobermory. Offshore are Iona, and Staffa, with its amazing phenomenon of Fingal's Cave.

① CRAIGNURE

The 40 minute ferry trip from Oban to Craignure on Mull presents an ever-changing vista of mountains, islands and sea. Craignure itself is an attractive collection of houses, shops, a tea-room and an inn sandwiched between a wooded cliff, a pier and a coast path.

Just over a mile south of Craignure are Torosay Castle and Gardens. The castle, reached by road, woodland path or miniature railway, is a handsome Victorian mansion in the Scots baronial style. It contains family portraits from 1840, and photographic displays of life at the turn of the century. The terraced gardens and the Italian statue walk are glorious, with views of the Appin coast extending from Ben Cruachan to Ben Nevis. There is also a eucalyptus walk and a Japanese garden. At Fishnish

Point, 6 miles north-west of Craignure, a car ferry crosses to Lochaline, on the remote Morvern peninsula on the mainland. Otters may be seen from the picnic area near the ferry terminal.

② SALEN

A collection of snug stone cottages, a ruined pier, a general store and a post office make up Salen. The village was created at the beginning of the 19th century by Major General Lachlan MacQuarie, a native of the island of Ulva. He later became Governor of New South Wales; his mausoleum can be seen 3 miles south-west of Salen.

On a headland above a sandy bay to the north of Salen are the battered remains of Aros Castle, last occupied in 1608. The castle was one of a chain of great fortifications built in the 13th and

14th centuries throughout the Inner Hebrides and western mainland, and used by the Lords of the Isles, who were rulers of the Western Isles and part of the western mainland from the mid 14th century to the late 15th century.

③ TOBERMORY

The main town of Mull is a place of colour-washed houses and hotels, with shops selling items such as ship chandlery, fishing tackle, diving gear and guns. Tobermory was built in the 1780s, when the British Society for Encouraging Fisheries decided to found a port on the superb natural harbour. Fishing boats are now joined by pleasure craft and boats offering fishing trips for skate and mackerel, as well as by ferries to Coll, Tiree and, except in midwinter, to Kilchoan on the southern side of the Ardnamurchan peninsula. In Aros Park, about a mile south-east of the town, woodland walks lead past rhododendrons and waterfalls.

④ DERVAIG

The road from Tobermory to Dervaig is steep and single-tracked, and seems to wind through a hundred hairpin bends as it skirts small lochs or leaps over tiny stone bridges. Dervaig village, at the head of a narrow, rocky inlet, was built by Maclean of Coll in 1799, and consists mostly of low stone houses, some whitewashed, with brightly painted windows and doors. Cruises departing from the village give opportunities to

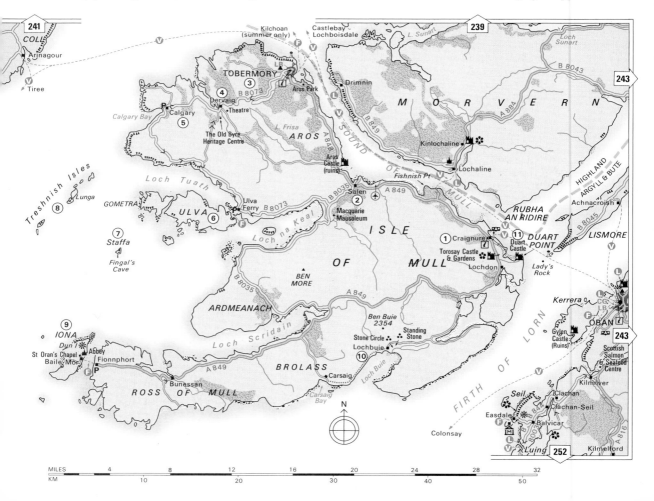

MILES 4 8 12 16 20 24 28 32
KM 10 20 30 40 50

CROFTING ON MULL *In the shadow of Ben Buie, near Lochbuie, a restored crofter's house contrasts with the roofless reminders of the Clearances found elsewhere on the island.*

THE MELODIOUS CAVE

Visitors to Fingal's Cave have for long marvelled at the remarkably regular hexagonal columns of basalt that ribbon the island of Staffa. About 50 million years ago, lava spread over the area to a depth of some 50 ft. After the lower layer of the basaltic lava cooled slowly and evenly, it cracked with geometric precision, leaving the six-sided columns seen today. The musical sound created by the sea flowing past the pillars inspired Mendelssohn's overture *The Hebrides*. The cave's Gaelic name, An Uam Binh, means the 'melodious cave'.

The cave's columns resemble organ pipes.

observe local wildlife, including sea birds, dolphins, porpoises and whales.

A byre on the road to Salen houses the Mull Little Theatre, which, with a seating capacity of 42, is reckoned to be Britain's smallest professional theatre. The Old Byre Heritage Centre, a mile south of the village, tells the history of Mull from the Bronze Age, with an audiovisual presentation and models of buildings and people of early times.

⑤ CALGARY
The tiny settlement stands on one of Mull's loveliest bays. The peace of its white sands and the grassy plain behind becomes a little less than infinite in summer, as the holiday crowds flock in, but the beauty of the bay remains unchanged. In 1822, during the Highland Clearances, the people of several townships round Calgary Bay emigrated to Canada after being evicted from their homes. The Canadian city of Calgary was named after the settlement on Mull, not by those who left in 1822 but more than 50 years later by a Colonel MacLeod, who had visited the

area. The views from the roads to and from Calgary are as grand as any in the Hebrides, embracing Coll and the Treshnish Isles to the west, and Skye and Ardnamurchan to the north.

⑥ ULVA
Scattered through Ulva are many ruins of settlements whose inhabitants were evicted in the late 1840s. An information centre explains the history of the island, which can be reached by passenger ferry from Mull. There are several waymarked trails around Ulva, including a 2 hour woodland walk and a 5 hour walk that leads across a bridge to the smaller island of Gometra.

⑦ STAFFA
In the first half of the 19th century, the lonely grandeur of the tiny uninhabited island attracted visitors such as Tennyson, Turner, Wordsworth and Queen Victoria. Mendelssohn wrote his overture *The Hebrides* after a visit to Fingal's Cave, at the southern end of Staffa. Legend has it that the giant Torquil MacLeod was building the

Giant's Causeway in Ireland and took home a sackful of his work, but the sack burst and rocks were scattered, the largest being Staffa. The island can be reached by boat cruises from Fionnphort, Ulva Ferry and Oban; landings are possible in good weather.

⑧ TRESHNISH ISLES
Puffins, skuas, gannets, guillemots and razorbills are among the many birds on the string of uninhabited islands. Day cruises from Oban and Ulva Ferry include landings on Lunga, the largest island at just over a mile in length; seals, black rabbits and rare varieties of orchid may be seen there.

⑨ IONA
St Columba called the 3½ mile long island 'Iona of my heart', and chose it as the site for his monastery. Of the original building of AD 563, which is thought to have been built of wattle and daub, nothing remains. In the Dark Ages the monastery was raided on several occasions by Vikings, and its community massacred. Because Iona was such a holy place, 60 kings were buried there, including

Ornamental designs embellish St Martin's Cross, outside Iona's abbey church.

TREASURE-HUNT TOWN *Within Tobermory's bay lies a galleon from the Spanish Armada. Doubloons from the wreck have proved elusive; the town's real treasure is its waterfront, lined with brightly coloured houses, while fishing boats reap the ocean's natural bounty.*

Macbeth and Duncan, the 11th-century Scottish kings on whom Shakespeare based the characters of his tragedy.

Iona's oldest building is St Oran's Chapel, built by Queen Margaret in 1080. The 13th-century abbey was restored in the 20th century and is the home of the Iona Community. Outside the abbey church is the beautifully carved St Martin's Cross, 17 ft high and more than 1000 years old. Ruins of a nunnery stand near the pier. The 328 ft

hill of Dun I gives views across the island and the Hebrides beyond. There is a ferry from Fionnphort, and day trips from Oban call at the island.

⑩ LOCHBUIE

A scattering of houses lies at the head of Loch Buie on a fertile plain where early settlers left standing stones and stone circles. A 5½ mile walk along the north side of the loch leads to massive cliffs at Carsaig Bay.

⑪ DUART CASTLE

Of all the fortresses in the Western Isles, none is more expressive of the power and majesty of the medieval chieftains than Duart Castle. The forbidding clifftop building dates from the 13th century, with additions made towards the end of the 14th century by the Macleans. In 1912 the castle was restored from a ruinous state to its former grandeur, and to its position as rallying place of the Clan Maclean. Inside

are family relics, an exhibition on chiefs of the clan, and a Scouting exhibition; the 27th clan chief was for many years leader of the Scout movement in the Commonwealth. The views from the Sea Room are especially breathtaking.

TOURIST INFORMATION

Craignure (01680) 812377 (summer); Oban (01631) 563122; Tobermory (01688) 302182

Whisky with a tang of peat from Jura and Islay

Wild, mountainous Jura and gentler Islay draw visitors interested in wildlife and unspoilt scenery. Palm trees grow in the mild, sunny climate of Colonsay, thanks to the influence of the North Atlantic Drift.

① COLONSAY

Almost alone among the Hebrides, the island suffered no forced evictions during the Highland Clearances and so is free of the sad, almost haunted quality that possesses so many other Scottish islands. Some 120 people live there.

Colonsay and Oronsay become one 10 mile island for 3 hours at each low tide, when they are linked by a sandy beach known as The Strand. Together, the islands enjoy almost as much sunshine as Tiree, the record-holder for Scotland, and a much lower rainfall than that of the mainland. Walking is rugged rather than difficult. There are white, empty beaches, standing stones and other antiquities to discover, and seal colonies on the islets and skerries. Wild goats live at the northern end of Colonsay, and on Oronsay; the long-horned, black-fleeced creatures are said to be descended from goats that swam to the islands from ships of the Spanish Armada, which were wrecked offshore in 1588. Rabbits abound, and golden eagles soar high and silently above.

Kiloran Bay, backed by dunes, is one of the island's finest beaches; a long headland protects it from the full force of the Atlantic, though strong westerly winds can provide rollers for surfing. At nearby Kiloran Gardens palm trees and rhododendrons flourish in the mild climate; there are woodland walks.

Only a handful of people live on Oronsay. St Columba is said to have landed there on his way from Ireland to Iona in the middle of the 6th century. Substantial ruins of a priory on the island date from the 13th century, and include a Celtic cross, a high altar and tombstones bearing the carved portraits of warriors and priests.

② JURA

Although the ferry crossing from Islay to Jura lasts only slightly longer than the time it takes to buy the ticket, there could hardly be a greater difference between the two islands. While Islay is well populated and largely flat, 27 mile long Jura is a wilderness of rock, moor and peat bog. Most of Jura's 200 inhabitants live in its south-eastern corner.

Craighouse, the island's only village, has a whisky distillery that can be visited by appointment. Jura House Walled Garden, 3½ miles south-west of the village, has plants from Australia and New Zealand that flourish in the mild climate of this part of the island. From the entrance to the garden a woodland walk leads to the shore.

Apart from this area, most of Jura is mountainous and inhabited only by deer. The creatures must have been well-known even in the days of the Vikings, for the name Jura comes from the Norse *Dyr Oe*, meaning 'Deer Island'. Three peaks in the south, rising to around 2500 ft and known as the Paps of Jura, are visible from much of the Argyll coast, as well as from many of the Hebridean islands.

One of the most difficult and winding A-class roads imaginable leads most of the way along Jura's east coast, and ends near the hamlet of Ardlussa. In the cemetery at Ardlussa are the graves of a woman who died aged 128, and a man 'who kept 180 Christmases'. A small track continuing beyond Ardlussa

ISLAND WILDERNESS *Beyond the deep-sea inlet of Loch Tarbert, open moorlands and peat-bogs climb towards the rugged peaks of Jura, one of the wildest of the Hebridean islands.*

ISLAY'S 'WATER OF LIFE'

Much of Islay consists of peat, and every year each of the island's distilleries burns some 800 tons of it, hand-cut from black trenches. The first stage in producing Islay's malt whiskies is to soak barley in water and leave it to germinate. The barley is then dried in a kiln over a peat fire whose smoke helps to give the whiskies their distinctive flavours. Later in the process are two stages of distillation, after which the spirit is matured in oak casks for several years.

The products of Islay's distilleries are world-renowned as being among the finest 'single malt' whiskies. Some of these are bottled and sold as a product of a single distillery, but most are used in the production of blended whiskies which may contain as many as 40 different grain and malt whiskies.

Before being distilled into malt whisky, the liquid is fermented in pine or larch vats.

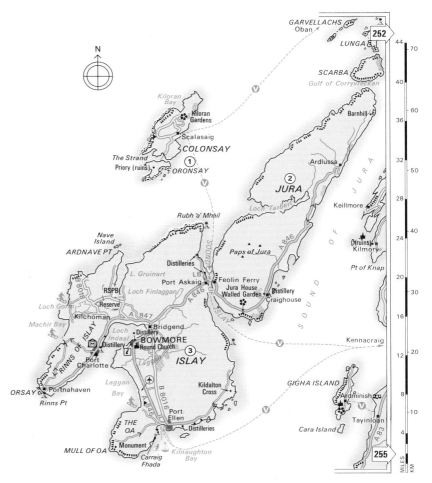

passes tiny Barnhill, where the author George Orwell wrote his novel *1984*.

To the north lies the roaring, seething whirlpool of the Gulf of Corryvreckan, which separates Jura from the small, uninhabited island of Scarba.

③ ISLAY

The island's healthy economy and the high level of employment among its 3500 people are almost entirely the result of a thriving whisky industry. Islay, pronounced 'I-la', has six distilleries, most of which are open to visitors. Three distilleries are near Port Ellen, one of the arrival points for vehicle ferries from Kennacraig. The other ferry terminal is Port Askaig.

Some 7 miles north-east of Port Ellen is the 9th-century Kildalton Cross, a magnificent example of Celtic carving. A mile's walk to the west of Port Ellen leads to the Carraig Fhada lighthouse and the Singing Sands, so-called because of the swishing noise created when people walk through the dry sand. To the south-west is a headland, whose name, The Oa, shares with Bu on Orkney and Ae in southern Scotland the distinction of being one of Britain's shortest place names. A monument at the tip of the headland was erected in memory of American sailors who were drowned nearby during World War I.

The long, straight road from Port Ellen to Bowmore, the island's administrative centre, runs inland from Laggan Bay, whose 5 miles of dune-backed sand is the largest of Islay's many beautiful beaches. Bowmore's unusual round

NO REFUGE *Bowmore's church, on Islay, was built in circular form so that the Devil would find no corners in which to hide.*

church was built in 1767. To the north-east, the main island on Loch Finlaggan was where the MacDonald chiefs held parliament from the 12th to the 16th centuries; excavations have revealed traces of buildings, a paved roadway and timber defences. A cottage near the loch houses an interpretive centre.

The island's history is explained in the Museum of Islay Life at Port Charlotte. Housed in a former church, the museum has exhibits about the island's prehistory, its impressive legacy of ancient monuments, and the story of the whisky industry.

In autumn, thousands of barnacle and Greenland white-fronted geese arrive to spend the winter at the Loch Gruinart RSPB Reserve. The marsh fritillary is among the butterflies to be seen there. Choughs and corncrakes breed on the reserve and elsewhere on Islay.

TOURIST INFORMATION

Bowmore (01496) 810254

251

An island fringe, and inlets cutting deep into Knapdale

Along the Argyll coast, land and sea interweave in an intricate web of hundreds of islands, promontories and lochs. Early settlers left behind many burial chambers, standing stones, rock carvings and hill-forts.

① SEIL

The island is reached by Clachan Bridge, which, although only some 50 yds long, is known grandiosely as 'The Bridge over the Atlantic'. On the west coast, Easdale has craft shops and art exhibitions, and gives views of the southern part of the Firth of Lorn and the islands. Just outside the village, An Cala is a small garden with streams, ponds and rockeries. From Easdale, a ferry makes the short journey to Easdale Island, whose folk museum evokes life in the heyday of the local slate industry, which existed until 1965. On the eastern side of Seil Sound, Ardmaddy Castle Gardens encompass woodlands and a walled garden, and have spectacular sea views.

Six miles north-east of Clachan Bridge, beyond Kilninver, the Scottish Salmon and Seafood Centre explains the life-cycle of wild salmon and the development of fish farming. Summer boat trips from the centre include excursions to study the wildlife and natural history of Loch Feochan.

② LUING

Grazed by a breed known as Luing cattle, and surrounded by backdrops of other islands – as well as by treacherous currents – Luing is reached by ferry from the south end of Seil. Once a slate-quarrying area, the island has rugged scenery in the north and gentler terrain farther south. Semi-precious stones may be found on the rocky shores.

③ ARDUAINE GARDEN

Rhododendrons, azaleas, shrubberies, lawns and a wilder woodland garden on the higher slopes make up Arduaine Garden (NTS). It is reached from the Loch Melfort Hotel by a path which has views of neighbouring islands and the marina at Craobh Haven.

④ INVERLIEVER FOREST

The huge conifer plantation cloaking the northern slopes of Loch Awe is a haunt of red, roe and sika deer, as well as of buzzards, ospreys and golden eagles. Along the road that runs parallel to the shore, several car parks provide starting points for walks that take in waterfalls and viewpoints.

DOUBLE IMAGE *Still waters at Crinan reflect masts in the harbour, and the jagged outline of the hills fringing Loch Crinan.*

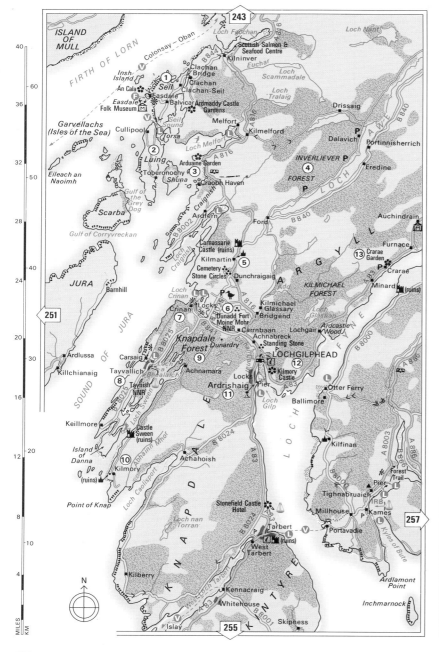

WATERY CORRIDOR *A yacht negotiates one of the Crinan Canal's 15 locks between the evergreen-clad slopes of Knapdale Forest.*

⑤ KILMARTIN

The Church of St Martin of Tours contains the 10th-century Kilmartin Cross, an early Celtic image of Christ. Housed in a shelter in the churchyard are a number of tombstones carved in the 14th and 15th centuries.

Kilmartin lies close to one of the largest concentrations of ancient ritual and burial monuments in Scotland, dating from before 3000 BC to about 1200 BC. A track leads south-westwards from the village past Nether Largie Linear Cemetery (HS), a series of burial chambers dating from 2300 BC and in use for about a thousand years. The graves' contents have been plundered, but piles of stones still cover the graves themselves. South Cairn, the best preserved, contains a large box made of stone slabs and divided into sections.

Nearby are the two Temple Wood Stone Circles (HS), erected before 3000 BC. Among the 17 uprights of the larger circle, an orange-coloured stone bears a spiral motif that is thought to have been connected with sun worship.

A mile north of Kilmartin are the imposing ruins of Carnassarie Castle (HS), a 16th-century fortified house.

⑥ DUNADD FORT

Strategically sited on a hillock, and defended by four tiers of walls, Dunadd Fort (HS) is believed to have been the inauguration site of the kings of the ancient kingdom of Dalriada, founded about AD 500. Enigmatic rock carvings on a slab at the summit depict a boar and a footprint. The fort is surrounded by a waterlogged peat bog, which once lay under the sea and is known as Moine Mhor. Part of the bog forms a national nature reserve.

To the east, Kilmichael Glassary (HS) is another ancient site, where mysterious 'cup and ring' markings – hollows surrounded by rings – were cut into rock in the Bronze Age.

⑦ CRINAN

The village lies beside a marina busy with sleek yachts and net-festooned fishing boats. Sweeping views extend over the Crinan Basin to the islands of Jura and Scarba. Boats leave in summer on seal and birdwatching trips.

Opened in 1801, the Crinan Canal forms a 9 mile short cut between Crinan and Ardrishaig, linking the Sound of Jura with Loch Fyne and saving a journey of 120 miles round the Kintyre peninsula. 'Clyde Puffers', vessels specially built for the Forth and Clyde and Crinan canals, used to transport cargo between Glasgow and the Argyll coast. One such craft carries passengers today.

⑧ TAYVALLICH

Tucked into a sheltered inlet among the heavily wooded promontories and bays that bound the upper end of Loch Sween, Tayvallich attracts small-boat sailors. At Carsaig, a mile to the west, a collection of houses huddles around a smaller, wilder bay with a dramatic view of the olive-dun hills of Jura.

South of Tayvallich, Taynish National Nature Reserve has Scotland's largest surviving remnant of oak forest. The reserve, which is crossed by a track, also has more open expanses that harbour orchids, butterflies, lichens and mosses.

⑨ KNAPDALE FOREST

The dense conifer plantations that cover the area known as Knapdale are dotted with small lochs, some of which are the focus of waymarked walks. One walk starts on the B841 a mile west of Cairnbaan and ascends Dunardry, a hill that gives a panorama northwards. The western side of Knapdale has some stretches of coast road with far-ranging views towards the mountains of Jura.

EFFIGIES IN STONE *Celtic grave slabs, remarkable for their detailed carvings, are housed in the ruined chapel at Kilmory.*

⑩ KILMORY

Farm buildings and holiday homes cluster around a ruined 13th-century chapel that contains more than 30 medieval grave slabs carved with warriors, chiefs and hunters. Outside stands the 15th-century MacMillan's Cross, with a crucifix on one side and a detailed hunting scene on the other.

To the south, the Point of Knap is a gentle jut of land that separates Loch Sween from Loch Caolisport. Two miles north-east of Kilmory, from the road to Achnamara, a path leads past a caravan site to the bleak ruins of Castle Sween, begun in the 12th century and retaining curtain walls which stand 40 ft high.

⑪ ARDRISHAIG

The port and fishing village, with its harbour and lighthouse, lies on the west bank of Loch Gilp, an inlet of Loch Fyne, and at the eastern end of the Crinan Canal. At the peak of the canal's activity Ardrishaig was a notably more bustling centre, busy with paddle-steamers and herring-boats.

⑫ LOCHGILPHEAD

A crescent of houses stands at the top of Loch Gilp, while straight, spacious streets characterise the inland part of Lochgilphead, a small market town that serves a large area and whose 19th-century growth was boosted by the Crinan Canal. A mile south-east of the town, the gardens of Kilmory Castle, now council offices, include rhododendrons, alpine plants and hardy ferns. Trails wind through the gardens.

⑬ CRARAE GARDEN

Within sheltered woodland gardens, by the northern shore of Loch Fyne, rhododendrons and azaleas bloom dazzlingly in spring and summer. Deciduous trees continue the colours into autumn. Paths climb the hillside, and footbridges span a plunging gorge. To the south, way-marked walks thread through the tranquil plantations of Kilmichael Forest.

TOURIST INFORMATION

Lochgilphead (01546) 602344 (summer);
Oban (01631) 563122; Tarbert (01880) 820429
(summer)

A remote peninsula within sight of Arran's lofty peak

Fishing villages are scattered along the narrow arm of Kintyre. The Isle of Arran has remarkable scenic variety, encompassing a low-lying plain studded with prehistoric sites, and a high mountain wilderness.

① TARBERT

A popular sailing centre, where Scotland's largest regatta is held each May, Tarbert was once the hub of the Loch Fyne herring industry. Although this activity has declined, Fish Quay is still busy in the morning as boats unload their catches. Much of the village is Victorian, but the castle's earliest visible remains date from the 13th century. An Tairbeart visitor centre has displays of the area and its wildlife.

Two miles north of Tarbert, the gardens of Stonefield Castle Hotel overlook Loch Fyne and contain Himalayan rhododendrons and exotic shrubs.

② GIGHA ISLAND

The island's gentle landscape is dotted with small farms, ancient duns, or forts, and prehistoric standing stones. South of the port of Ardminish, Gigha's only village, are the gardens of Achamore House, where azaleas, rhododendrons and palms flourish in the mild climate. The tiny ruined church dedicated to St Cattan dates from the 13th century.

③ GLENBARR ABBEY

Despite its name, Glenbarr Abbey is an 18th-century Gothic house, home to members of the Clan MacAlister, whose 500-year history is chronicled in a visitor centre in the building. Displays also include domestic mementos, china and antique toys. Walks and nature trails start from the house.

④ MACHRIHANISH

The hamlet of two-storey houses used to be a centre for the salt and coal industries. The main focus of activity today is a civilian and military airfield served by flights to and from Glasgow, but there is also a golf course, and a glorious 5 mile sandy beach running north to Westport.

⑤ MULL OF KINTYRE

A steep and twisting 7 mile drive through spectacular hill scenery leads from a point just west of Southend towards the peninsula's south-western tip. Visitors must walk the last few hundred yards to the lighthouse. The Antrim coast lies just 12 miles away, making the Mull of Kintyre the closest point to Ireland in mainland Britain.

⑥ SOUTHEND

A golf links lies between the quiet farming village and the sea. St Columba visited the area in AD561, two years before establishing a monastery on Iona. His name is given to a holy well near Keil Point, and to St Columba's Footsteps, carved in a rock in the churchyard, in which he is believed to have stood. Three small bays bite into the nearby coast, their sands coloured red. A track leads to the east end of Dunaverty Bay, where a headland gives a fine view of Sanda Island.

⑦ CAMPBELTOWN

Hills rise behind the harbour and a cluster of stone buildings. Herring fishing has declined since its 19th-century heyday, but the town is now a sailing and holiday resort. Whisky, too, has played a role in Campbeltown's history. More than 30 distilleries have operated in the area, but today there are just two. In summer there are tours of the Springbank distillery; these must be booked in advance. A small museum in the town's library explains the history and geology of the area, and displays finds from local Iron Age sites. The Campbeltown Heritage Centre delves into the town's industrial past. The Island Davaar, at the mouth of Campbeltown Loch, can be reached from the mainland by walking along a causeway which is exposed for 3 hours either side of low tide.

⑧ SADDELL

In a quiet glen just off the main road at Saddell stand fragments of a Cistercian abbey founded about 1160. Among gravestones protected under a shelter are examples of 14th to 16th-century stone-carvings. The nearby beach can be reached through the grounds of 16th-century Saddell Castle, but the castle itself is not open to the public. There is a car park at the castle gate.

⑨ CARRADALE

The tranquil holiday village and its small fishing harbour has sweeping views up the coast and across to Arran. Woodland walks can be followed from the Forest Centre, just west of the village, and in Carradale Forest to the north. Walkers may also venture southwards to Carradale Point, where there are remains of a fort dating from 1500 BC.

KINTYRE FISHING VILLAGE *Colour-washed houses line Tarbert's Fish Quay, a haven at the innermost recess of East Loch Tarbert, where fishing boats moor beside the pier.*

HIGH-SPEED HUNTER

At speeds of up to 180 mph the peregrine falcon dives on other birds and kills them with a single blow of its talons, then swoops down to retrieve its meal from the ground. The birds pair for life, and breed on island crags and sea cliffs on Kintyre and the Isle of Arran.

Peregrine falcon
Falco peregrinus

ACROSS THE WATER *Across Kilbrannan Sound from Skipness rise the mountains of Arran. Ten of the island's peaks thrust to more than 2000 ft in an area of 12 square miles.*

⑩ SKIPNESS

Roofless 13th-century Skipness Castle (HS), reached by a short walk from the car park, is one of the few buildings in this tiny village. There is a shingle and sand beach. In summer a ferry runs from Claonaig to Lochranza on Arran.

⑪ LOCHRANZA

Fringed by a pebbly beach and spread around the loch from which it takes its name, the village is a jumble of painted cottages set by the remains of twin-towered Lochranza Castle (HS), begun in the 13th century as a two-storey hall-house. The castle was rebuilt from its ruined shell 300 years later, but fell into disuse. On the other side of the loch, footpaths lead around the northern tip of Arran, offering views of Bute, and passing Ossian's Cave, named after a legendary Irish warrior and poet.

⑫ BLACKWATERFOOT

A 2 mile walk northwards along the coast from the small village leads to King's Cave, believed by some to have been the place where Robert Bruce was inspired by the perseverance of a spider weaving its web. On Machrie Moor, to the north, are a remarkable number of Neolithic and Bronze Age monuments, including Auchagallon stone circle.

⑬ WHITING BAY

A base for sea-fishing trips, with boats and rods for hire, the village of Whiting Bay is the starting point for two forest walks, one to the Glen-ashdale Falls, the other to the chambered cairns known as the Giants' Graves. Another chambered cairn, possibly dating from as long ago as 4000 BC, can be seen outside Lagg, on the south coast of the island. To its west, Cleats Shore is a naturist beach.

⑭ LAMLASH

The hamlet stands in a sheltered bay popular with small-boat sailors and anglers. Boats can be hired, and there are sea-fishing trips. Presiding over the scene is the towering mass of Holy Island, home to a community of Tibetan monks, and to feral ponies, sheep and goats. In summer, ferries cross to the island from Lamlash and Whiting Bay.

⑮ BRODICK

Arran's largest village is the port for the hour-long ferry crossing to Ardrossan, on the mainland. Dinghies, canoes and water skis can be hired near the broad sandy beach. The Isle of Arran Heritage Museum examines the island's past and its unusually complicated geology. About a mile to the north is 13th-century Brodick Castle (NTS), now the focus of a country park with extensive gardens, and craft and visitor centres.

Goat Fell, at 2866 ft Arran's highest peak, is a popular but quite demanding 2½ hour climb from Brodick. Other starting points are Corrie, where cottages look across to Bute and Little Cumbrae Island, and Sannox, close to a wooded cove with a picnic area.

TOURIST INFORMATION

Brodick (01770) 302140; Campbeltown (01586) 552056

255

Forested hills above the lochs of Cowal and Bute

The glass-clear waters of the Cowal peninsula are dotted with small sailing resorts and ruined fortifications. Inland, swift streams ripple through wooded glens and into lochs teeming with salmon and trout.

A POET'S LOVE *The statue of Mary Campbell gazes from Dunoon across the Firth of Clyde. Mary inspired some of Robert Burns's finest lyrics, including* Highland Mary.

① AUCHINDRAIN

Auchindrain's open-air museum is a monument to a communal farming system which was all but wiped out during the Highland Clearances of the 1830s. Twelve tenants paid their rent jointly to the Duke of Argyll, sharing the arable and grazing land at Auchindrain, and the practice continued in the same way until the 1930s. Cottages have been refurnished in period style, and barns, byres, a stable, a smithy and other buildings have been preserved.

THATCHED SURVIVAL *At the Auchindrain farm museum a stone-and-thatch cottage evokes the primitive life of the crofter.*

② INVERARAY

A splendid example of 18th-century urban planning, the town stands by the waters of a sheltered bay on Loch Fyne. Inveraray Castle was built at the same time as the town, as the home of the third Duke of Argyll, chief of the Campbells. Its magnificent interior is open to visitors, and in the grounds are woodland walks to a hilltop folly.

The old Inveraray Jail is now a museum of 19th-century crime and punishment. At the nearby pier, a small maritime museum is based in the schooner *Arctic Penguin*, a former Irish lightship. All Saints' bell tower, built in 1925 as the Clan Campbell war memorial, has a fine ten-bell peal and an exhibition on bell ringing.

The Combined Operations Museum, near the castle, recalls the days when Inveraray was a training base for the D-Day landings. South of the town is the Argyll Wildlife Park, populated by wildcats, deer and foxes.

③ LOCH FYNE

Measuring some 40 miles from its north-eastern tip to its mouth, Loch Fyne is one of Scotland's longest lochs. Its eastern shore provides dramatic views of forested ridges sweeping up from the water's edge. In Cairndow, by

the loch's head, the Strone Woodland Garden features a salmon leap. South of the 'Heart of Argyll', a traditional gypsy wedding site, are the quiet villages of St Catherines and Strachur, once served by steamer services.

An exhilarating lochside road continues south past the ruined hulk of 15th-century Castle Lachlan, skirting the rocky shoreline to Otter Ferry, named from the Gaelic *oitir*, the great shingle bar which is exposed at low tide. At Kilfinan, a pre-Reformation church stands near the village's restored stagecoach inn. From Millhouse, a small road heads west to Portavadie, an industrial 'ghost village' of the 1970s with a summer car ferry service to Tarbert. A picnic area just north of the village is the starting point for a hilly woodland trail.

④ TIGHNABRUAICH

A spectacular mountainous landscape surrounds Tighnabruaich and Bute's rumpled northern moorlands. The village dates from the 1850s, when a resort grew up as steamer traffic developed. This is a superb yachting area, with a busy sailing and windsurfing school, and pleasure cruises in the surrounding lochs. Other popular activities include golf, birdwatching, fishing, walking and shinty, a game similar to hockey.

To the north of the village on the A8003, a magnificent viewpoint overlooks Loch Riddon and both the eastern and western Kyles of Bute.

⑤ COLINTRAIVE

The airy village, whose name rhymes with 'strive', was once a place to which cattle destined for mainland markets swam over from Bute. Now the narrows are crossed by a vehicle ferry. To the east, Loch Striven lies among hill farms and forests. A wartime midget submarine training area, the loch is now a 'park' for redundant merchant ships, and there is a naval fuel depot.

⑥ DUNOON

As the town's heritage centre illustrates, in the Clyde steamer era Dunoon and its neighbours Kirn and Hunter's Quay were the Cowal peninsula's busiest resorts. Car ferries still operate to Gourock, and there are many summer cruises. Sea anglers tackle cod and coalfish, plaice and conger eel. There is inland loch and river fishing, as well as hill and forest walking, and golfing. South of the town are woodland walks in Morag's Fairy Glen.

The fragmentary remains of an ancient royal fortress lie in Dunoon's breezy park on Castle Hill. Nearby is a statue of Robert Burns's sweetheart, 'Highland Mary', or Mary Campbell, who was born in Dunoon in 1764.

Each year in late August, Dunoon is the site of the Cowal Highland Gathering, featuring athletics, Highland dancing competitions and heavy events such as tossing the caber.

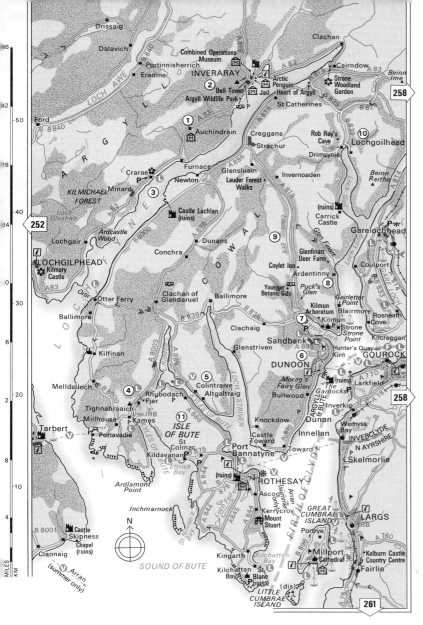

⑧ ARDENTINNY

Beautifully situated at the foot of Glen Finart, the hamlet faces the massive Trident missile base at Coulport on Loch Long's eastern shore, which is hidden from view from other angles. Gairletter Point, 2 miles to the south of Ardentinny, is a good location for bird-watching. There are guided tours of the Glenfinart deer farm to the north.

⑨ LOCH ECK

One of the grandest inland waterways in Scotland lies at the foot of the rugged hillsides of Cowal. Summertime cruises start from Coylet Inn. To the north, Lauder Forest Walks explore oakwoods and conifer plantations, and lead past waterfalls. To the south, an avenue of giant redwoods is a feature of the Younger Botanic Garden. Close by, footpaths and footbridges climb the spectacular 820 ft Puck's Glen.

⑩ LOCHGOILHEAD

Loch Goil curves through a fiord-like landscape, and the village at its head looks across small-boat moorings to a towering skyline. The holiday centre of Drimsynie includes the European Sheep and Wool Centre, where a stage show involves shepherds, sheepdogs, shearers and many breeds of sheep. A forest path leads north along a mossy glen to Rob Roy's Cave, named after an 18th-century highland rebel said to have hidden in the cave.

About 5 miles south, the village of Carrick Castle stands beside the ruins of the 14th-century Campbell tower which gave it its name. Herons can be seen along the shore.

⑪ ISLE OF BUTE

North and south lies wild moorland, but central Bute is a charming combination of Victorian coastal resort, farms, nature trails, angling lochs and western sea bays with superb views towards the granite peaks of Arran.

Rothesay, the island capital and car-ferry port, is flanked on either side by the Skeoch and Bogany Woods. Close to the shore are the substantial ruins of Rothesay Castle, dating from the 13th century. Bute Museum illustrates the history, archaeology and wildlife of a fascinating island. From the centre of the town, Serpentine Road climbs through 13 closely packed hairpin bends to viewpoint Canada Hill and colourful Ardencraig Gardens.

South of Rothesay is the 18th-century mansion of Mount Stuart, the hereditary seat of the Marquess of Bute, which is open to visitors. In the hills to the south of the island are the atmospheric ruins of the Church of St Blane (HS).

⑦ HOLY LOCH

The sailing village of Sandbank, on the southern shore of a sea loch which used to be a US Polaris submarine base, is where the boats *Sceptre* and *Sovereign*, Britain's unsuccessful challengers for the America's Cup sailing race in 1958 and 1964 respectively, were built. On the northern shore, footpaths through the broad-leaved trees and conifers of the Kilmun Arboretum, part of the Forestry Commission's Argyll Forest Park, climb a soaring ridge. Earls, dukes and the only Marquess of Argyll lie in the family mausoleum at the Church of St Munn, which has a curious water-powered organ. Off Strone Point, feeding gannets crash dive into the sea.

ROYALTY ON BUTE *Robert III was one of many Scottish kings to spend time at Rothesay Castle. He made his eldest son Duke of Rothesay, a title held today by the Prince of Wales.*

TOURIST INFORMATION

Dunoon (01369) 703785; Inveraray (01499) 302063; Rothesay (01700) 502151

Ports and resorts where the Highlands meet the Clyde

The Firth of Clyde earned a place in history during the great days of shipbuilding. Today the shipyards lie idle, though some are being redeveloped, and the firth itself is busy with pleasure boats and ferries.

① ARROCHAR

Set cosily among the mountains and forests at the head of Loch Long, the rural village of Arrochar was from around the 11th century the heartland of the MacFarlanes, notorious cattle-raiders. The clan territory was sold in 1784, and the family died out in 1866. Rock-climbers can enjoy scaling the 'Arrochar Alps', especially Ben Arthur, known as the Cobbler because of the silhouette of its summit. An easy walk over the range leads to the Cruach Tairbeirt path, which climbs through birchwoods to reveal views of Loch Lomond and Loch Long.

② LOCH LONG

The 17 mile fiord-like sea loch slices deep into the Arrochar mountains. Its steeply banked upper reaches attract sea-anglers. Cod, whiting, pollack, dab and eels are all caught there. Between Garelochhead and Arrochar, the West Highland Railway runs high above the lochside road. South of a Ministry of Defence jetty, the oil terminal at Finnart is one of the deepest-water tanker berths in Europe. Oil is pumped to Grangemouth's refinery, 57 miles away.

③ ROSNEATH PENINSULA

Much of the land on the peninsula, together with the modern road to Coulport, is Ministry of Defence property, although visitors are allowed to drive along the road. Buzzards, hen harriers and sparrowhawks patrol the high plantations and grazing pastures. Early-morning travellers may sometimes catch sight of roe deer. Cove Conservation Park, a mile south-east of Coulport, encourages ecological awareness through bird and animal displays, and includes hands-on exhibits that explain recycling, and wind and solar power. The park offers splendid views down into Loch Long.

The small villages of Clynder and Rosneath, on the eastern side of the peninsula, have a long history of boat-building. The rocky shores of Cove and Kilcreggan, to the south, are fringed with Victorian villas. Ferries and cruise boats, bound for Gourock, leave from Kilcreggan Pier in summer.

④ GARE LOCH

On the eastern bank of the Gare Loch are the attractive villages of Rhu and Garelochhead. The Royal Northern and Clyde Yacht club has its headquarters at Rhu, and uphill from the separate Rhu Marina is Glenarn, a woodland garden with scenic walks. A hillside viewpoint above Garelochhead reveals the huge Clyde submarine base at Faslane Bay.

⑤ HELENSBURGH

The town of tree-lined streets is set out on a grid pattern and tucked in behind a promenade. Gulls, oystercatchers, red-shanks, knots and turnstones feed along the water's edge among the yachts, sailboards and dinghies of Helensburgh's sailing club. Summer ferries, which call at the pier, sail to Kilcreggan and Gourock, and boat trips to Gare Loch and Holy Loch can also be arranged. A seafront obelisk commemorates Henry Bell, designer of the *Comet*, the world's first seagoing steamboat, launched in 1812. John Logie Baird, the television pioneer, was born at Helensburgh in 1888. There is a small

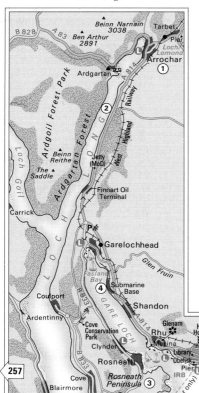

IN REMEMBRANCE *A monument on Lyle Hill pays homage to the Free French sailors who were based at Greenock and died in the Battle of the Atlantic in World War II.*

⑨ GREENOCK

As the birthplace, in 1736, of James Watt, who perfected the steam engine, Greenock was, in a sense, the cradle of the Industrial Revolution. The town prospered between the 17th and 19th centuries, but it has now declined as a port and shipbuilding centre. The Watt Library and the McLean Art Gallery and Museum tell the story of Watt and the town. The museum in the stately Georgian Custom House recalls literary figures from Chaucer to Burns who were once employed by the Customs and Excise service. Golf and a variety of watersports are available in Greenock, and sub-aqua divers can explore wrecks such as the sugar ship *Captayannis*, which sank in 1974. The Royal West of Scotland Amateur Boat Club is based at the Esplanade, while, on a smaller scale, the Model Yacht Club races radio-controlled yachts on Murdieston Dam. One of the district's finest viewpoints is above the World War II Free French memorial on Lyle Hill, where mountains and sea lochs dominate the scene.

⑩ GOUROCK

The association between this area of Strathclyde and James Watt is represented in jocular form by a giant yellow kettle, built into the wall of the Gourock tourist information centre. It recalls the old yarn that Watt's interest in the power of steam was roused when, as a boy, he watched a kettle boil. Ferries sail from Gourock to various points along the Clyde, and Prince's Pier has a direct rail link with Glasgow. Yacht races are held in summer off West Bay, the base of the Royal Gourock Yacht Club.

The 1897 drinking fountain in Gourock is a memorial to Queen Victoria's Diamond Jubilee.

STEAMBOAT OF THE CLYDE *At Port Glasgow is a replica of the* Comet, *which worked on the Clyde from 1812 to 1820.*

display explaining his life and works in the library, and a memorial window in the West Kirk. The Helensburgh Upland footpath, which starts at the top of Sinclair Street, passes through the car park of Hill House (NT), Charles Rennie Mackintosh's Edwardian masterpiece. The path soon broadens out to become the Hielandman's Road, with an exhilarating view over the Firth.

East of Helensburgh, the tidal bays at Ardmore provide fine opportunities for birdwatching. Large numbers of sea birds and waders congregate there.

⑥ DUMBARTON

The ancient town of Dumbarton became the capital of the kingdom of Strathclyde around the 6th century AD. Dumbarton Rock, which presides over the town from the shore, has steps and pathways leading to mainly 18th-century fortifications, while the higher summit of Castle Rock, next to it, offers commanding views of the Firth of Clyde. East of Castle Rock, a foreshore walk passes a launching ramp, which is all that remains of a wartime flying-boat factory. The pebbles, mud flats and reedbeds attract redshanks, shelduck and reed buntings. Denny's was a successful shipbuilding company also involved in the design and testing of model ships for the shipbuilding industry before the last yard closed in 1963 and whisky distilling took over as one of Dumbarton's main source of wealth. Denny's Ship Model Experiment Tank survives in the town centre as part of the Scottish Maritime Museum.

⑦ BOWLING

The village marks the western end of the Forth and Clyde Canal, opened in 1790. The canal is no longer used by water traffic, but is still enjoyed by coarse anglers, walkers and cyclists. Berths for pleasure craft are available at Bowling harbour, where locks, bridges and the old Custom House survive.

⑧ PORT GLASGOW

Originally the seaport for the city of Glasgow, until the Clyde was deepened in the 1700s, Port Glasgow was the building and launching site of Henry Bell's *Comet*. A replica of the steamboat is displayed in the town centre. Newark Castle (HS), nearby, is a 16th-century mansion. Shipbuilding at Port Glasgow has now dwindled to one fully operational yard, and parkland has replaced the demolished riverfront industries. Picnic sites at Kelburn, in the town's north-eastern area, overlook the rotting posts of tidal ponds where timber from North America used to be stored.

Finlaystone, off the road between Port Glasgow and Langbank, has gardens, woodland walks and picnic areas.

PLACES TO SEE INLAND

Balloch Castle Country Park, 4 miles N of Dumbarton.

Formakin, 7 miles E of Port Glasgow. Country park surrounding unusual Edwardian mansion.

Paisley, 14 miles SE of Port Glasgow. Abbey founded in 1163. Burial place of Stewart dynasty. Museum and Art Galleries, collection of Paisley shawls.

TOURIST INFORMATION

Balloch (01389) 753533 (summer); Dunoon (01369) 703785; Gourock (01475) 639467; Helensburgh (01436) 672642 (summer); Milton, Dumbarton (01389) 742306

Waterside retreats for Glasgow's city-dwellers

Holidays to resorts on the Firth of Clyde have long been cherished by Glaswegians. Most of the hydropathic hotels have gone, but water therapy can still be found in the form of sailing, fishing and bathing.

① INVERKIP

Larch and pinewood ridges swoop down to the village of Inverkip, once a smugglers' haunt and now marked by the pontoon moorings of the Clyde's oldest marina, built in 1971. Nearby Lunderston Bay has a sandy beach with rocky outcrops, and a picnic site.

East of the village, on a road signposted to Loch Thom, is the Cornalees Bridge Visitor Centre, where there are glen and moorland walks around a historic reservoir system.

② WEMYSS BAY

Once Glasgow's gateway to resorts along the Clyde, Wemyss (pronounced 'Weems') Bay is still a passenger port. A path from the elegant Grade A listed railway station descends to the departure point for the Rothesay ferries, where the paddle steamer *Waverley* also calls. A red sandstone cliff, dramatised by the deep ravine of Kelly Burn, is the bay's great landscape feature. Beyond it, Skelmorlie village has hotels and villas. A golf course and a trout fishery, open to visitors, occupy the hills above.

③ LARGS

The holiday and retirement town offers seafront walks, picnic spots, watersports and golf courses. Inverclyde National Sports Centre trains promising athletes. The local museum stands near the 17th-century Skelmorlie burial aisle, all that remains of the old parish church. The 'Pencil' monument, overlooking Largs Yacht Haven, commemorates the Scots' victory over the Vikings there in 1263, while the Víkingar! exhibition tells the story of the Viking influence in Europe, especially Scotland. Scandinavian visitors arrive every September for the town's Viking Festival. Monastic displays at the Christian Heritage Centre include embroidered vestments and models of old monasteries. There is a magnificent viewpoint at the top of Douglas Park, to the south-east of the town, from where, in clear weather, the peaks of Jura can be seen.

④ GREAT CUMBRAE ISLAND

One of the loveliest resorts on the Clyde, the island is reached by ferry from Largs. Visitors arrive at Cumbrae slip, sometimes amid the yachts, sailboards and dinghies of the two sailing schools. Millport, the only town on the island, is a traditional resort curving round an islet-studded bay of rocky and sandy coves. The 18th-century Garrison houses the Museum of the Cumbraes, and the Victorian Cathedral of the Isles, Scotland's smallest cathedral, stands close by. The house known as The Wedge, in Stuart Street, has a street frontage of only 47in, the narrowest in Britain. The Museum and Marine Biological Station, showing the underwater life of the Firth of Clyde, is at Keppel. Cumbrae's summit offers a superb panorama of the Firth and the surrounding country. Privately owned Little Cumbrae Island cannot be visited.

⑤ FAIRLIE

The pier at Fairlie has been transformed into a dinghy-launching, parking and picnic site, overlooking the sandy bay. Hunterston nuclear power station, to the south, offers guided tours.

Two miles north of Fairlie, Kelburn Castle and Country Centre occupy a wooded glen laced with paths.

⑥ SEAMILL

Long sandy beaches start near Seamill Hydro, last of the district's Victorian 'hydropathic' hotels, which were popular with middle-class Glaswegians as places to indulge in luxuries such as seawater baths. The coast road south to Seamill overlooks the boulder-strewn sands of Ardneil Bay. From a fine golf links, footpaths lead north to the farming settlement at Portencross, whose ruined castle lies south-west of a vitrified fort, dating from the Iron Age.

West Kilbride Museum has Ayrshire lace and period costumes. Blackshaw Farm Park, north-east of Seamill, is a working farm with farm animals.

LAST OF THE LINE *The 240ft long* Waverley, *the world's last seagoing paddle steamer, still serves the Clyde resorts and other points on Britain's coast in the summer months.*

⑦ ARDROSSAN

In 1806 the 12th Earl of Eglinton began to develop Ardrossan as a coal and cargo port. The town is now principally a car-ferry terminal for Arran and the Isle of Man. The ruins of 12th-century Ardrossan Castle, all but demolished to provide building material for Oliver Cromwell's citadel at Ayr, stand in a grassy park at Castlehill. From the ruins there are views of the Isle of Arran, and of Horse Island RSPB Reserve offshore.

⑧ SALTCOATS

The town's main activity in the 16th century was evaporating seawater in coal-fired salt pans. Today Saltcoats is a seaside resort with a sandy beach. The seafront has a harbour with a lookout tower and a walk along the sea wall. There is fishing for cod and flatfish both from the rocks and from boats. The local museum, in the former church, tells the story of the town and its neighbours, Ardrossan and Stevenston.

⑨ IRVINE

This old quayside town has close connections with the poet Robert Burns. The restored Glasgow Vennel, where he learned the flax-dresser's trade, houses a Burns museum, while the Burns Club and Museum, founded in 1826, is one of the world's oldest clubs dedicated to the poet, and features a collection of his manuscripts. The Scottish Maritime Museum overlooks Bogside Flats, a lonely spit visited by a variety of birds. Swimming and skating are among the activities offered by the Magnum Leisure Centre, while the Beach Park has watersports and boating. Eglinton Country Park, on Irvine's northern outskirts, includes a loch and a deer park.

⑩ TROON

Ringed by six golf courses, Troon is also a major sailing resort. Its marina occupies part of the old harbour where, in the early 19th century, the first railway in Scotland brought coal from inland. There is a pleasant stroll along a path backing the curving sands of South Beach. Out on the harbour peninsula, the grassy Ballast Bank was built in the 1860s as a wind-break and tide-break, and gives an exhilarating view across the water to the Isle of Arran.

⑪ PRESTWICK

The oldest burgh in Scotland, Prestwick was granted its status in AD 987. Old Prestwick was the first home, from 1860 to 1872, of the Open Championships. There are pleasant walks between the three golf courses and the sandy beach at Ayr Bay, popular with sailors and windsurfers. In one of the many public gardens is Bruce's Well, a 13th-century healing well. Robert Bruce is said to have drunk from it, and steps still descend to the underground cistern. Prestwick international airport has the best fog-free record in Britain.

'DOON THE WATTER'

The Firth of Clyde became the playground of Glaswegians after the launch of the first commercial steamboat service in 1812. By the mid 19th century the traditional day trip 'doon the watter' was well established, with a daily procession of steamers plying between the Broomielaw, Glasgow's harbour, and Clyde coastal resorts.

Holidaymakers of 1959 boarding a Rothesay ferry at Wemyss Bay.

PLACES TO SEE INLAND

Dalgarven Mill, 5 miles NW of Irvine. 17th-century mill and Ayrshire Country Life and Costume Museum.

Dean Castle and Country Park, 9 miles E of Irvine. 14th-century castle set in woodland.

Lochwinnoch RSPB Reserve, 13 miles E of Largs.

Weaver's Cottage, Kilbarchan, 16 miles NE of Largs. Restored 18th-century cottages recalling the life of local weavers.

TOURIST INFORMATION

Irvine (01294) 313886; Largs (01475) 673765; Millport (01475) 530753 (summer); Troon (01292) 317696 (summer)

RELIVING THE DAYS OF STEAM AND SAIL

A FAMILIAR SIGHT ON the west coast of Scotland for more than a century was the tough little workboats known as Clyde puffers. From mid-Victorian times the puffers steamed up and down the coast and plied between the many islands. They had flat bottoms to allow them to run straight onto the beaches, and a steam winch to help with the loading. Exhaust steam from the engine was sent up the funnel in a series of puffs which gave the vessels their name; later models ran on diesel.

The puffer was just one of the many small cargo boats that could once be seen all around the British coast, and of which a few examples still survive. These boats were designed in a striking diversity of styles to cope with various local conditions, such as swift tides, shallow estuaries or fickle winds.

Trade on the Humber, and on rivers and canals leading as far inland as Sheffield, relied on the keel, one of the simplest of sailing coasters. The hull

HUMBER CRAFT *The last of the working Humber keels,* Comrade, *sails out regularly from its base at South Ferriby.*

was shaped like a large date box, with bluff bows and a rounded stern. Its single mast carried a large square mainsail, which made the most of a following wind, and a smaller topsail. Out on open waters the keel proved itself to be a very effective sailing ship; in windless conditions it was hauled along the inland waterways by horse.

Altogether sleeker and more elegant than the keel, the Norfolk wherry was designed to negotiate the intricate network of waterways that make up the Norfolk Broads, though it was sturdy enough for short coastal journeys. The wherry had a huge sail set

NOSTALGIA TRIP *A coal-fired puffer, the* VIC 32 *(above), seen here on the Crinan Canal, allows passengers to relive the days of steam. The diesel-powered puffer* Spartan *(right) is preserved at the Scottish Maritime Museum at Irvine.*

STURDY BARGE *The two-masted Thames barge, or spritsail barge, was used in south-east England until well into the second half of the 20th century. The vessel had a short mast at the rear, known as the mizzenmast, a big mainsail, a topsail and one or more foresails in front of the larger mast.*

CORNISH WORKHORSE *Moored at Cotehele Quay and in use until 1970, the* Shamrock *is typical of the Tamar barges that used to transport cargoes of granite, coal and fruit.*

RESTORED TO USE *The restored* Hathor, *of 1905, is one of the few surviving Norfolk wherries. Her interior features Egyptian hieroglyphs, inspired by her owners' trip up the Nile in a boat of the same name.*

behind a single mast, in what is known as a 'gaff rig'. The wind could blow on either side of the sail, just as it does in a yacht or a sailing dinghy, making it possible to tack upwind, zigzagging along when the wind came from ahead of the boat rather than from behind. A 'vane', or streamer, flew from the top of the 40 ft mast to show which way the wind was blowing. When the wind dropped, the crew used long poles to push the boat along.

Restricted in size by the nature of its task, the wherry held a modest 25 tons. By contrast, the two-masted Thames barge, the largest coaster that could be managed by a two-man crew, bore loads of up to 150 tons. Another two-masted, or 'ketch-rigged', vessel was the Tamar barge, which traded along the river between Cornwall and Devon from the late 19th century; among its most lucrative, if unromantic, cargoes was animal manure. The Tamar barge, like other barges, had a flat bottom that allowed it to stand upright for loading at almost any point along the river bank.

One of the grandest and sturdiest of all sailing barges was the Severn trow, built to cope with the formidable currents of a river with the world's second greatest tidal rise and fall. The trow started as a square-rigged vessel rather like the keel, but the final version was ketch-rigged and capable of deep-sea voyages. The early vessels sailed as far up the Severn as Shrewsbury; later the vessels traded down the south Wales and Devon coasts. The classic sailing craft for longer runs was the schooner, which came in a variety of shapes and sizes. Most schooners were two-masted, but the biggest such boat ever built, the *Thomas W. Lawson*, had seven masts. The vessels originated in the USA, but many were built in British yards, notably at Appledore in Devon.

LAST OF THE SCHOONERS *The three-masted West Country vessel* Kathleen and May *was launched in 1900 and now rests in London, after 60 years of active service. She is one of the few survivors of hundreds of schooners which carried large cargoes around the British coast and across to Ireland.*

Sandy beaches and small resorts south of Ayr

Ruined strongholds and vivid legends recall the warlike past of this coast, while literary enthusiasts trace the footsteps of Robert Burns, and golfers flock to Turnberry. Offshore is the domed Ailsa Craig.

① AYR

The town described by Robert Burns in *Tam o'Shanter* as 'Auld Ayr wham ne'er a town surpasses for honest men and bonie lasses' is now Scotland's main west coast resort. It has 2 miles of sandy beaches and an esplanade backed by bowling greens and playgrounds. Seafishing trips from the harbour, at the mouth of the River Ayr, yield dogfish, tope, haddock and whiting; good shore fishing can be had along Newton Shore, north of the river mouth.

Of four bridges across the river, the 15th-century Auld Brig is for pedestrians only. Nearby are the New Bridge, rebuilt in 1878, and, beside it, Loudoun Hall, one of Scotland's oldest houses. The building dates from 1503 and is open to the public occasionally. Rozelle Estate, 1½ miles from the town centre in Alloway, has finely tended gardens and a sculpture park; 18th-century Rozelle House offers changing displays of fine art and permanent exhibitions of local history, especially military history.

② HEADS OF AYR

On cliffs south of Ayr Bay, where an Iron Age fort once stood, are the ruins of Greenan Castle, a 16th-century stronghold of the Kennedy family. Wonderwest World, to the south-west

Robert Burns

A POET'S BIRTHPLACE
Scotland's national poet was born in 1759 in Alloway, now a suburb of Ayr; visitors to his birthplace, Burns' Cottage, can see how the family lived. The Tam o'Shanter Centre, which has an exhibition of the poet's life and times, is near the Auld Brig o'Doon, where the witches' chase in the famous ballad *Tam o'Shanter* came to its wild close. The riverside Burns' Monument Gardens and the ruins of Alloway Kirk are also open to the public.

of the castle, includes a large indoor leisure pool, a go-kart track, a boating lake and a roller coaster. The nearby Heads of Ayr Farm Park is a working farm that also has llamas and owls.

③ DUNURE

Below a large car park and picnic site in this bright little village stand a well-preserved dovecot and the ruins of a castle that belonged to the Kennedy family, perched on a spur of rock above

the bay. Here in 1570 the lay abbot of Crossraguel Abbey, 5 miles south-east of Dunure, was slowly roasted alive over a fire in a successful attempt to persuade him to transfer his lands to the 4th Earl of Cassilis.

Robert Bruce is said to have landed at Dunure from Irish exile in 1307 to begin the campaign which freed Scotland from English rule for 400 years. At Pan Point, seawater was evaporated in salt pans to provide salt for preserving fish, until the harbour silted up.

④ ELECTRIC BRAE

Properly known as Croy Brae, this disconcerting stretch of road gives the south-east-bound driver the impression of going downhill when the vehicle is actually going uphill, and vice versa from the opposite direction. The road was dubbed Electric Brae because of a theory that the effect was due to magnetism. In fact it is an optical illusion, caused by the unusual configurations of the land on either side.

⑤ CULZEAN CASTLE

Until the mid 18th century Culzean, pronounced 'Cullain', was a simple medieval tower house perched on a cliff edge. In 1777 the 10th Earl of Cassilis engaged Robert Adam to transform the building and its interior. The finest features of Culzean Castle (NTS) include an oval staircase and the round drawing room with views over the Firth of Clyde. A flat at the top of the castle was given to General Eisenhower in recognition of his achievements during World War II; he stayed there on four occasions. An exhibition covers Eisenhower's career and his time in Britain.

A visitor centre in Adam's Home Farm is the focal point of a country park with a swan pond, deer centre, walled garden and adventure playground. Guided walks of the park are available.

⑥ MAIDENS

The small village takes its name from the treacherous offshore rocks that lie beyond the sand and shingle shore. A small modern harbour is used by fishing boats and recreational sailors. On the slopes above the present caravan sites once stood Shanter Farm, whose owner provided Robert Burns with the main character of *Tam o'Shanter*.

⑦ TURNBERRY

Fine silver sands stretch for 1½ miles at Turnberry, and behind them are the golf courses for which the village is best known. The Ailsa course has a tee close to the beach known as Woe-be-Tide, and the Arran course has fine views of the Isle of Arran, 14 miles away.

The fragment of castle north of the golf courses was the home of Robert Bruce's mother and, like several other sites, lays claim to having been his birthplace. In conflict with Dunure, it also claims to have been the place at

CLIFFTOP MASTERPIECE *Built in the Georgian Gothic style, Culzean Castle is recognised as one of the most spectacular achievements of the architect Robert Adam.*

HALFWAY HOUSE *Prominent from the mainland, the towering form of Ailsa Craig, which lies midway between Glasgow and Belfast, is known colloquially as Paddy's Milestone.*

which he landed before launching his campaign against the English. A lighthouse stands within the castle ruins.

Dowhill Mound, the motte of a long-vanished timber keep, thrusts up in a commanding position above the A77, 1½ miles south of Turnberry. Defensive ditches surround it on three sides. The motte can be reached, with difficulty, by scrambling up a steep slope from the lay-by immediately below it.

⑧ GIRVAN

More than a mile of sands lie to the south of the colourful harbour in this small resort, which has several floral gardens. Boat trips to Ailsa Craig, and for sea angling between Girvan and Bennane Head, leave from the harbour. Plaice and flounder can be caught from the town pier. A modern pontoon provides moorings for yachts.

⑨ AILSA CRAIG

Ten miles offshore, the huge plug of a long-extinct volcano dominates the view from most of this coastline. Ailsa Craig is more than 1100 ft high but measures only just over 2 miles in circumference. The island's granite was long used to make what were regarded as the finest stones for use in the Scottish sport of curling. Boats from Girvan land near the lighthouse, from which a path to the summit passes a fragment of castle that was already in ruins four centuries ago. The island is home to guillemots and kittiwakes, but they are outnumbered by thousands of gannets, which breed here every summer. Former tenants of the island used to pay their rents in gannet feathers.

⑩ LENDALFOOT

Above the tiny settlement with its shingle beach, a ruined tower of Carleton Castle rises from a hillside farm. There is an old tale that one of its owners, Sir John Cathcart, made a habit of marrying heiresses and then pushing them off a cliff at Games Loup, south-west of the castle; the eighth heiress, a Kennedy of Culzean, turned the tables by pushing Sir John off the same cliff. From

Lendalfoot, the coast road heads southwest towards Bennane Head. Below the car park and viewpoint at the top of the hill is Sawney Bean's Cave, once reached by a footpath that is now too dangerous to use. The cave was home in the 16th century to the Bean family, who were said to prey on travellers, killing and eating them. Around 1600 James VI had them hunted down and publicly dismembered in Edinburgh.

⑪ BALLANTRAE

The village's sand and shingle shore is flanked by a long green, suitable for picnicking. Dominating the southern end of the village are the jagged ruins of Ardstinchar Castle, where Mary, Queen of Scots, spent a night in August 1566; below the castle, a graceful old bridge, now closed to traffic, crosses the River Stinchar. When the water is low, salmon can often be seen in pools by the bridge, waiting for enough water to help them upstream to their spawning grounds.

The shingle spit and lagoons at the mouth of the river form the Ballantrae Nature Reserve; terns breed on the spit between May and July, when visitors are discouraged. In the 18th century Ballantrae was the headquarters of a ring of smugglers, who made regular use of several caves between Ballantrae and Bennane Head. An exhilarating walk leads high over Finnarts Hill to Finnarts Bay, 6 miles to the south.

PLACES TO SEE INLAND

Bargany Estate Gardens, Dailly, 5 miles E of Girvan. Woodland walks and picnic areas; azaleas.

Crossraguel Abbey (HS), 5 miles E of Maidens. Ruins of early 13th-century Cluniac monastery.

Doon Valley Heritage, Dalmellington, 15 miles SE of Ayr. Ironworks museum; visitor centre with reconstructed 18th-century weaver's room; industrial railway museum.

Souter Johnnie's House (NTS), 2 miles E of Maidens. Home of 18th-century village cobbler (souter) immortalised in Robert Burns's ballad *Tam o'Shanter.*

TOURIST INFORMATION

Ayr (01292) 288688; Girvan (01465) 714950 (summer)

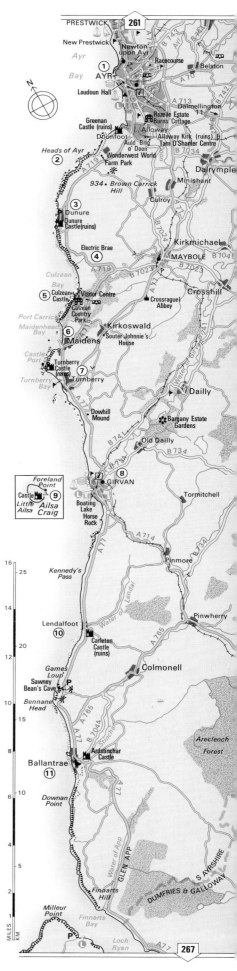

Exotic gardens on a hammerhead peninsula

Inland from a wild and rocky coastline, the influence of the warm ocean currents encourages the growth of subtropical plants in a number of carefully tended gardens, open to visitors, on the Rhins peninsula.

① CAIRNRYAN

During World War II Cairnryan became a military port handling supplies of food and ammunition from the USA. The wartime harbour has given way to a small ferry terminal for vehicle, passenger and freight services to Larne in Northern Ireland.

Finnarts Bay, to the north, offers some of the best local sea fishing, especially for tope and other types of shark.

② CASTLE KENNEDY GARDENS

Between the ivy-clad ruin of Castle Kennedy, mostly destroyed by fire in 1716, and the privately owned 19th-century Lochinch Castle, which is not open to the public, lie landscaped terraces, wooded gardens and tree-lined walkways. The gardens include grassy mounds and embankments created in the early 18th century by troops of the 2nd Earl of Stair to resemble contemporary military fortifications.

③ STRANRAER

In its sheltered position within Loch Ryan, Stranraer became, in 1872, the main terminal for steam packets to Northern Ireland. Today there are regular ferries to Larne, and a high-speed catamaran service to Belfast.

The Castle of St John in the centre of the town was built in 1500 beside a medieval chapel, demolished in the early 18th century. For a time, after 1682, it was the headquarters of 'Bluidy' Claverhouse during his persecution of Covenanters. The castle has also served as a courtroom and prison cells, and as a police station. Now it is a heritage centre demonstrating how law and order have been enforced through the ages. On the waterfront, the hotel known as North West Castle was built by Sir John Ross, 19th-century explorer of the Canadian Arctic. The Ryan Centre is a leisure complex that includes a swimming pool, steam rooms, a games hall and a theatre.

④ KIRKCOLM

The former fishing village sits inland from the bay of The Wig, where there is a slipway once part of a flying boat and seaplane base in both world wars. The slipway now serves Lochryan Sailing Club, and in summer is popular with small-boat sailors, water-skiers and windsurfers. The Wig and curving spit of The Scar attract nesting terns, eider ducks and oystercatchers.

To the north of Kirkcolm, Clachan Heughs woodland has trees planted in the exact formation of Sir John Moore's troops as they lined up to fight at Corunna in 1809. The Moore family lived nearby at Corsewall House, which is privately owned. Lady Bay has a sandy shore, car park and picnic area near salmon fishermen's huts.

LEADING LIGHT *Corsewall lighthouse was designed by Robert Stevenson, the father of the Scottish lighthouse system.*

⑤ CORSEWALL POINT

At the north-western tip of a wind-swept, almost treeless peninsula, deep-cut rock fissures bring the waves battering upwards into plumes of spray. On the headland above stands the white tower of Corsewall lighthouse; opened in 1816, it was designed by Robert Stevenson, the grandfather of the writer R.L. Stevenson.

⑥ PORTPATRICK

A holiday resort sparkling with colour-washed villas and hotels, Portpatrick has a small sandy beach, backed by cliffs, on the top of which are two golf courses. The northern cliff marks the western end of a coast-to-coast footpath, the 212 mile Southern Upland Way, which reaches the North Sea at Cockburnspath. For centuries boats sailed from Portpatrick to Donaghadee in Northern Ireland. In 1774 John Smeaton was commissioned to build a pier, lighthouse and breakwaters along the shore at Portpatrick, but storm tides wrecked his work. The later efforts of Thomas Telford and John Rennie were also defeated by the weather, and in the mid 19th century shipping to and from Ireland was re-routed via Stranraer.

A dizzying but well-fenced walk along the clifftop south of Portpatrick, with fine views out to sea, leads to the ruins of 16th-century Dunskey Castle.

⑦ PORT LOGAN

Stormy seas put an end to plans to develop a small harbour here in the early 19th century. Colonel Andrew

FORMER PORT OF CALL *Set around a cliff-girt inlet on a forbidding and exposed coast, Portpatrick served for almost 200 years as a port for packet-boats to and from Ireland.*

McDouall, a local resident who was behind the idea, had hoped to profit from the Irish cattle trade. The harbour was soon abandoned, though a few fishermen still go out in search of herring in June and July.

North of the village and its white-washed cottages there is a large car park from which wooden stairways descend to a sandy shore. A short walk along the shore leads to Logan Fish Pond, excavated in 1800 from the rocks behind the shore to provide a stock of fresh fish for the kitchen at nearby Logan House. The fish became so tame that they would answer a bell to be fed. The pond holds around 30 fish, mainly cod, and they are still so tame that they can be enticed to feed from visitors' hands.

⑧ MULL OF GALLOWAY

The southernmost tip of Scotland narrows between wave-beaten cliffs before rising to a high promontory from which one of Robert Stevenson's lighthouses looms 270 ft above the sea. The Mull of Galloway's cliffs form an RSPB reserve. In summer the rock ledges teem with crowds of rowdy sea birds such as guillemots, razorbills, kittiwakes and shags, which can be seen from certain lookout points along the clifftop.

⑨ DRUMMORE

Scotland's southernmost village originated in the early 19th century as a harbour for importing coal and lime from the north of England, and shipping out agricultural produce. Drummore is now a snug little holiday resort of whitewashed cottages overlooking a sandy beach, and the village is one of several local centres for tope fishing.

⑩ LOGAN BOTANIC GARDEN

An exotic walled garden has been arranged round the ruined keep of Balzieland Castle. The warm effect of the Gulf Stream enables many plants native to the southern hemisphere, such as eucalyptus, cabbage palms and tree ferns, to be grown.

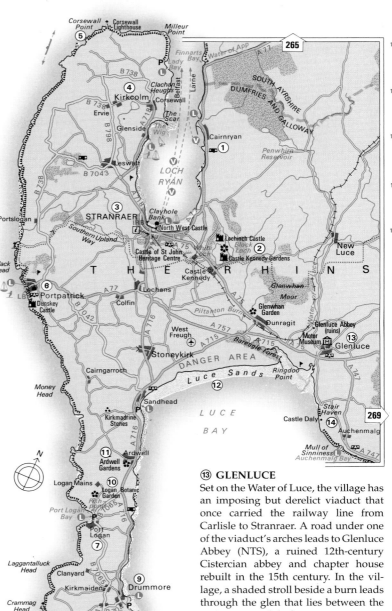

COASTAL LUSHNESS *In Logan Botanic Garden exotic plants grow in a mild climate amid an otherwise harsh landscape.*

⑪ ARDWELL GARDENS

Reached from the A716 south of Sandhead, the woodland gardens of Ardwell House offer seasonal displays of daffodils, azaleas, rhododendrons and a variety of other flowering shrubs. The gardens include three ponds, one giving views across Luce Bay.

⑫ LUCE SANDS

Sandhead's parking and picnic area overlooks an 8 mile stretch of golden sands, but a bombing range 2 miles to the east puts the sands beyond out of bounds to the public. Starting from the A715 towards Glenluce, a 1½ mile walk wanders through the spruces and pines of Bareagle Forest. The walk ends at a picnic area with a view over Luce Bay from Ringdoo Point.

⑬ GLENLUCE

Set on the Water of Luce, the village has an imposing but derelict viaduct that once carried the railway line from Carlisle to Stranraer. A road under one of the viaduct's arches leads to Glenluce Abbey (NTS), a ruined 12th-century Cistercian abbey and chapter house rebuilt in the 15th century. In the village, a shaded stroll beside a burn leads through the glen that lies between the main street and the bypass.

Just north of Glenluce is a motor museum with vintage cars and motor-cycles, period costumes, and old road and advertising signs.

⑭ STAIR HAVEN

Apart from its beach of rocks and sand, Stair Haven consists of little more than a lonely cottage, a small harbour and a ruined pier, now used only by local fishermen and visitors. Fishing boats can be hired from Castle Daly, a former schoolhouse. Species in the bay include crab, flounder, mullet, mackerel and skate. A narrow coastal road to Stair Haven from Glenluce gives uninterrupted vistas of Luce Sands and the bay.

PLACES TO SEE INLAND
Glenwhan Garden, 6 miles SE of Stranraer. Hilltop gardens and walks, with views over Luce Bay and the Mull of Galloway.
Kirkmadrine Stones, 8 miles SE of Portpatrick. Early Christian monuments in chapel doorway.

TOURIST INFORMATION
Stranraer (01776) 702595 (summer)

A saint's retreat on a coast of quiet sheltered harbours

Whithorn, where the Christian missionary Ninian founded a monastery in the 4th century AD, was a medieval place of pilgrimage. Fishermen, small-boat sailors and holidaymakers now outnumber the pilgrims.

AN ISLE ONLY IN NAME *The village of Isle of Whithorn, in fact situated on the mainland, originally served as the port for Whithorn. It is busy with small-boat sailors in summer.*

① AUCHENMALG BAY

At the northern end of a sandy bay stretching south to Craignarget is the hamlet of Auchenmalg, largely occupied by a caravan site. Boats can be hired for the fishing of crab, flounder, mullet and skate. Sinniness Barracks, a private house, was built in the 1820s to house a group of revenue men, sent to stamp out the Solway smuggling trade.

In a walled enclosure beside the road south to Port William are the low foundation walls of a 10th or 11th-century pilgrims' chapel dedicated to an Irish bishop, St Finian of Movilla.

② PORT WILLIAM

The village was established in the late 18th century as a shipbuilding and fishing centre, and became a haunt of smugglers. Near the shore of pebbles and splintered rock are parking and grassy picnic sites, and boats can be hired for tope and porbeagle fishing.

③ MONREITH

Trim cottages cluster round a sandy bay. On a headland, above the village and near a golf course, an otter sculpture commemorates Gavin Maxwell, author of *Ring of Bright Water*. Many of Maxwell's family are buried beside the ruins of Kirkmaiden Church, which cling to the cliff below.

A mile to the south is Lower Knock Waterfowl Rare Breeds Reserve, whose attractions include an otter family.

④ ST NINIAN'S CAVE

From a parking area at Kidsdale Farm, a path leads to the cave to which St Ninian retreated. The saint lived during the 4th and 5th centuries, and was the first Christian missionary to come to Scotland. Christian crosses have been carved into the cave walls.

⑤ ISLE OF WHITHORN

The village, a sailing and sea-angling centre with boats for hire, is the base of the Wigtown Bay Sailing Club. A causeway from the village leads to a rocky peninsula, once a genuine isle, where there is a 13th-century ruined chapel named after St Ninian.

Four miles inland at the town of Whithorn, archaeological finds associated with the saint, such as crosses and stones, are displayed at the Whithorn Museum (HS) and at the visitor centre. Both buildings are in the same complex.

⑥ GARLIESTON

Laid out around 1760 in two crescents of colour-washed cottages facing the sand and shingle bay, the village prospered from shipbuilding, sailmaking and cattle trade with Ireland. The harbour is used by small craft, and there are fishing trips for salmon. Walks to the shore join a short coastal path that leads past Galloway House Gardens to Cruggleton Castle ruins. The gardens have many fine old trees, and seasonal displays of azaleas and rhododendrons.

⑦ WIGTOWN

A royal burgh since 1292, Wigtown has a spacious town square, with a bowling green in the middle of it. The town's harbour silted up early in the 20th century, but it has been renovated with quays, parking and picnic areas along the River Bladnoch. In summer the flats and salt marshes of Wigtown's sandy bay are breeding grounds for lapwings, curlews and common terns. A path across a disused railway embankment leads to a grim memorial honouring two women Covenanters who in 1685, refusing to change their religious allegiance, were tied to stakes offshore and drowned by the rising tide.

⑧ KIRROUGHTREE FOREST GARDEN

The arboretum includes beeches, whitebeams and red oaks. There are forest trails, a wildlife pond and views of the heights of Cairnsmore of Fleet, which features briefly in John Buchan's novel *The Thirty-Nine Steps.* Beside the visitor centre is a car park and picnic site.

⑨ CREETOWN

In the 19th century the little port exported granite from nearby quarries. It is now used only by private craft. The Gem Rock Museum has a dazzling collection of gemstones, crystals and minerals. The Scottish historian and essayist Thomas Carlyle once assured Queen Victoria that the only road finer than that between Gatehouse of Fleet and Creetown was that between Creetown and Gatehouse of Fleet. The road, watched over by the relic of 16th-century Carsluith Castle (HS), 3½ miles south of Creetown, is still a visual delight, with magnificent seascapes on one side and lush greenery on the other.

⑩ CAIRN HOLY

Up a lane from the A75 are the two chambered cairns of Cairn Holy (HS). The larger one has an exposed burial

---

TRIBUTE TO AN AUTHOR

The statue of an otter at Monreith is a memorial to Gavin Maxwell (1914-69), who wrote about his pet otters in *Ring of Bright Water.* Maxwell spent his childhood near Port William, when his family owned the Monreith estate. He later moved to Sandaig, to a house called Camusfeàrna, where he kept the otters that inspired his writing.

A sleek bronze otter looks out from a clifftop site above the churchyard at Monreith.

chamber as well as a small courtyard in which ritual ceremonies took place between 4000 and 5000 years ago. The smaller cairn was much robbed for building stones in the 18th century.

⑪ GATEHOUSE OF FLEET

Planned on a grid pattern by James Murray of Broughton and Cally in the late 18th century, the town developed as a cotton manufacturing centre. Its history is explained at the Mill on the Fleet Heritage Centre. An exhibition of domestic life, 'As We Were', is housed in the hall of the original Free Church of Scotland building. On a rocky mound above the Water of Fleet, which divides the town in two, is the 15th-century tower of Cardoness Castle (HS).

South of the town, in the grounds of James Murray's old home, now the Cally Palace Hotel, the Fleet Oakwoods interpretative trail is a 2 mile walk through woodlands, where trees are identified by markers.

Two miles west of Gatehouse of Fleet, the small Skyreburn Aquarium has displays of sea, loch and river fish, and an exhibition of underwater photographs.

⑫ SANDGREEN

The bay is the most popular of a series of sandy coves, separated by grassy headlands, that stretch southwards along the coast opposite the Islands of Fleet. Between Sandgreen and the hamlet of Carrick, to the south, huts and chalets shelter behind shrubs and sandhills. At low tide walkers can cross from Carrick's bay to the biggest of the islands, Ardwall, inhabited in the late 18th century by a family who kept open house for smugglers.

⑬ BRIGHOUSE BAY

The deep, sandy inlet at Brighouse Bay is overlooked by a landscaped leisure centre, offering activities such

LOCAL ARTIST *William Stewart MacGeorge, born in Castle Douglas in 1861, studied abroad before returning home to paint scenes such as this, called simply* Kirkcudbright.

as golf, pony trekking and windsurfing. A walk east of about 2 miles leads round the coast to Ross Point, which looks out over Little Ross Island.

⑭ KIRKCUDBRIGHT

Pronounced 'Kirkoobree', the town's name probably derives from St Cuthbert who converted much of Scotland to Christianity. From the harbour, where boats land the small scallops known as 'Kirkcudbright queenies', visitors can book sea-angling trips. MacLellan's Castle (HS), a ruined 16th-century mansion, was built largely from the ruins of the neighbouring Greyfriars monastery. The medieval Tolbooth, in the largely Georgian high street, retains on its outer walls the manacles to which wrongdoers were fastened to receive public beatings. It now houses craft studios and an exhibition devoted to the town's long-established artists' colony. Broughton House (NTS), bequeathed to the town by the painter E.A. Hornel (1864-1933), has a collec-

tion of his paintings and sculptures. North of the harbour is the start of the 6 mile Dee Walk, which passes Tongland hydroelectric power station, where conducted tours are available.

The Wildlife Park, 2 miles northeast of Kirkcudbright, is involved with the conservation of rare breeds, such as Scottish wildcats, lynx and Arctic foxes, and offers guided tours.

PLACES TO SEE INLAND

Galloway Forest Park, 12 miles NE of Newton Stewart. A wild goat park, deer range and deer museum, with parking and picnic sites.

Glen Trool, 13 miles N of Newton Stewart. The Bruce stone above Loch Trool marks Robert Bruce's first victory over the English in 1307.

The Raiders' Road, 15 miles N of Kirkcudbright. A forest drive following old cattle rustlers' route.

Stones of Torhouse (HS), 3 miles W of Wigtown. Circle of 19 Bronze Age granite boulders.

TOURIST INFORMATION

Gatehouse of Fleet (01557) 814212 (summer); Kirkcudbright (01557) 330494 (summer); Newton Stewart (01671) 402431 (summer)

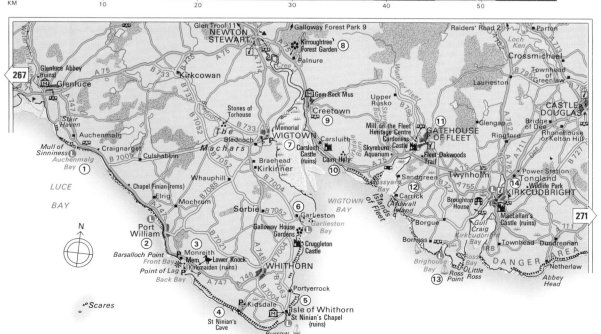

Fast tides and wide sands along the Solway Firth

Dividing the west coast of Scotland from England, the Solway Firth reaches into narrow inlets lined by quiet villages. Sheltered harbours provide safe anchorage from swift-flowing waters for small-boat sailors.

SHELTERED SECLUSION *Wooded hills shield the resort village of Kippford, sited at the head of Rough Firth and blessed with a mild climate. The sandy bay is a haven for small boats.*

① DUNDRENNAN ABBEY

A 13th-century chapter house and some Norman stonework are the remains of Dundrennan Abbey (HS), founded by Cistercians in 1142. It was here that Mary, Queen of Scots, having abdicated in favour of her infant son James VI, is believed to have spent her last night on Scottish soil, on May 15, 1568, before crossing the Solway to seek help from Queen Elizabeth I of England. Among the abbey's fine sculptures is a larger-than-life-size group depicting a murdered abbot and his assassin.

The shore at Port Mary forms part of a military firing range and is closed to the public when shooting takes place.

② AUCHENCAIRN

The steep little village of whitewashed cottages and pebble beaches was an iron-mining centre during the late 18th century, and also a haunt of smugglers. Hestan Island and its lighthouse lie a mile offshore. During the Middle Ages the island was owned by the monks of Dundrennan Abbey, and there are still traces of their fishpond near the causeway. A picnic site off the A711, 1½ miles south-west of Auchencairn, has a cairn

with a plaque identifying, in a 360-degree sweep, the most prominent hills and islets that can be seen from the spot.

③ BALCARY POINT

A byroad from Auchencairn leads to Balcary House, built by 18th-century smugglers as a headquarters and a storage place for contraband, and now a hotel. From the car park a signed footpath crosses the fields to Balcary Point, where sea birds such as oystercatchers, curlews, redshanks, dunlin and shelduck can be seen. In summer, common sandpipers abound.

④ PALNACKIE

The village was once a busy port on the Urr estuary, until its tiny harbour silted up. Several of the houses in Palnackie were built with two storeys to accommodate sailors from the trading ships that used to ply the coast. The estuary offers good fishing for flat-fish, and on a Saturday in late July or early August each year, the World Flounder Tramping Championships are held on the mud flats of the Glen Isle peninsula. Contestants may use only their feet and a three-pronged spear to catch the fish.

South-west of the village, 15th-century Orchardton Tower (HS) is the only surviving Scottish tower house built in the cylindrical style common in Ireland. A spiral staircase within its walls leads up to an airy parapet walk.

⑤ KIPPFORD

Hillside houses surround the small resort of Kippford and its pebble beach. The former shipbuilding centre is now the base of the Solway Yacht Club. A clifftop walk following the mile-long Jubilee Path (NTS) to the neighbouring village of Rockcliffe offers views of the Galloway Hills and, on clear days, St Bees Head in Cumbria and the peaks of the Lake District. On Scaur Hill beside the walk is the Motte of Mark, a 6th-century Celtic fort which was so savagely burnt by raiders that its stones vitrified.

A shingle spit leads at low tide from the southern end of the village to Rough Island (NTS), a bird sanctuary where terns and oystercatchers nest on the shingle during May and June. In the summer months, the National Trust for Scotland organises ranger-conducted tours of the shore and woodland from Kippford and Rockcliffe.

⑥ ROCKCLIFFE

With its shore of sand and rock pools, broken by jagged shoulders of rock in a sheltered bay, the village developed as a smart resort in Victorian times. A short footpath follows the edge of Rough Firth to the summit of Castlehill Point, which gives wide views across the Solway Firth to Cumbria. Shore and clifftop paths continue to Port o' Warren and Portling. At low tide, a number of smugglers' caves can be explored around Portling. Further east, at Sandy-

---

AMERICA'S MAN OF WAR

John Paul Jones became a hero to the Americans after he joined their naval forces during the War of Independence. He made daring raids on the British coast and, in 1779, won a singular victory over a superior British force in the North Sea. Generally regarded as the founder of the American naval tradition, he later served Catherine the Great in the Russian Navy.

John Paul Jones shoots a mutinous sailor.

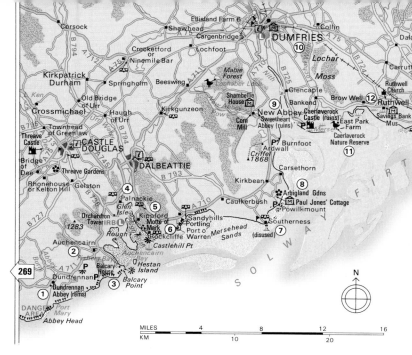

hills, there is a complex of offshore stake nets – a series of wide-mesh nets, secured by poles driven into the sand, and used for trapping salmon.

⑦ SOUTHERNESS

On the foreshore stands a lighthouse dating from the 18th century. The wide sands that surround it have given rise to a large holiday village with caravan sites, chalets, amusement arcades and a golf course. Walkers should take care when venturing seawards, as the tide can sweep in faster than walking pace.

⑧ ARBIGLAND GARDENS

The gardens reach down through a succession of glades, featuring a range of semi-tropical shrubs and trees, to a sheltered, sandy beach. In 1768 the head gardener's son, John Paul Jones, became the captain of a Dumfries trading vessel. Soon afterwards, he departed for America and became a founder of the American navy. His birthplace, Paul Jones' Cottage, is now a tiny museum on the bay. Beside it, a huge car park offers splendid vistas across the Solway Firth to the Lake District.

⑨ NEW ABBEY

Set among woods by the New Abbey Pow River, the village and surrounding landscape are dominated by Criffel, a hill that rises to 1868ft. The summit can be reached by a 1½ mile track that leads off the A710 at Ardwall, 2 miles south of New Abbey. From the top of Criffel can be seen the Nith estuary and the Isle of Man. Sweetheart Abbey (HS) was founded in 1273 by Devorgilla, the wife of John Balliol, a Scottish king. The abbey is so named because after Balliol's death Devorgilla carried his embalmed heart around with her, and had it buried with her.

Shambellie House (HS), at the northern end of the village, is a museum of mainly Victorian and Edwardian costume in period surroundings. In the 18th century the owner of the house built the nearby water-powered Corn Mill, now restored, which replaced an earlier one built by Cistercian monks. Bordering the road to Dumfries is Mabie Forest, with picnic areas and walks, including one through the nature reserve of Lochaber Loch, noted for its butterflies and old oak trees.

⑩ DUMFRIES

As southern Scotland's main town, Dumfries is known as the Queen of the South. Robert Burns was a resident of the town, and there are several memorials to the poet, including a visitor centre, along with the Burns House, where he lived from 1793 till his death in 1796, and his neo-classical mausoleum in St Michael's churchyard.

For centuries the first crossing of the River Nith north of its mouth was Devorgilla Bridge, which was built in the 15th century and took its name from the patroness of New Abbey. Today three vehicle bridges span the Nith, and Devorgilla Bridge is for pedestrians only. The Old Bridge House Museum of local life is set into its western end. The Ice Bowl in King Street is a major centre for skating, as well as the venue for ice hockey and curling competitions.

⑪ CAERLAVEROCK NATURE RESERVE

Barnacle geese from Spitsbergen come to spend autumn and winter on the nature reserve of the Caerlaverock Wildfowl and Wetlands Trust, along with pink-footed geese from Iceland, and other wildfowl. There is also a large colony of the rare natterjack toads. At East Park Farm, viewing towers and hides are open to the public all year round, and between May and August there are guided walks.

The deep red sandstone ruins of Caerlaverock Castle (HS), overlooking the Merse saltings, are reflected in its moat. Built in the late 13th century, the castle changed hands several times between English and Scots. One of its most remarkable features is a 17th-century row of interconnecting buildings that looks more like a Renaissance mansion than part of a fortress.

⑫ RUTHWELL

In the secluded village that lies at the foot of gently rising hills is a 7th-century stone cross carved with Biblical scenes and verses from the oldest-known English poem, *The Dream of the Rood*. Broken up as an idolatrous monument in 1640, it was later restored in 1820 by Dr Henry Duncan, the parish minister, and now stands in the apse of the church. Duncan also founded the first Trustee Savings Bank, remembered in the village's Savings Banks Museum.

West of the village is Brow Well, to which in early June 1796 Robert Burns

BORDER STRONGHOLD *Built in the shape of a triangular shield, with a tower at each corner, Caerlaverock Castle commanded a strategic landing point on the Solway Firth.*

FISHING NORWEGIAN STYLE *Commercial fishermen in the Nith use haaf-nets, named after the Norwegian* haaf, *meaning 'heave'. Nets are fixed to long wooden spars; when a sea trout or salmon swims into a net the fisherman flicks the net over the spar to trap the fish.*

came in the hope of curing his ailments by drinking the well waters which contain salts of iron; however, he died in Dumfries on July 21 the same year.

⑬ ANNAN

The village of red sandstone buildings stands on the eastern bank of the River Annan and is the main market town in the region. The tidal river provides anglers with good catches of salmon and trout. Commercial fishing is done from February to September with haaf-nets and stake-nets. South of the railway line an overgrown embankment is all that remains of the Solway viaduct, once used to transport iron ore from Cumberland to Lanarkshire steelworks.

⑭ GRETNA

Surrounded by low-lying marshland, Gretna evolved during World War I into a large estate for munitions workers. Beside the B721 on the western outskirts of the village, Alice's Wonderland is a collection of more than a thousand dolls, together with dolls' houses, clothing and soft toys. Overlooking the estuary of Kirtle Water is the 7ft high Lochmaben Stone, which may have formed part of a prehistoric stone circle.

From the mid 18th century, neighbouring Gretna Green flourished as a place for couples eloping from England to marry without parental approval and under the age of consent. In 1940, these 'anvil weddings', so called because they took place over the blacksmith's anvil, were made illegal. The Old Blacksmith's Centre is today a tourist complex with shops, and an anvil and coach museum. An old marriage register is displayed in the village hotel.

PLACES TO SEE INLAND

Carlyle's Birthplace (NTS), Ecclefechan, 6 miles N of Annan. Collections of letters and relics of historian and essayist Thomas Carlyle.

Clydesdale Horse Centre, 4 miles NE of Annan. Clydesdales at work. Photographic and video displays.

Ellisland Farm Farmhouse, 6 miles NW of Dumfries. Built by Robert Burns. Exhibits connected with the poet. Granary has exhibition of Burns as a farmer.

Threave Castle (HS) **and Threave Gardens** (NTS), 2 miles SW of Castle Douglas. Castle is a 14th-century tower on island in River Dee, reached by rowing-boat. Gardens have plant, rockery and heather displays, flowering trees, woodland walks; visitor centre (summer).

TOURIST INFORMATION

Castle Douglas (01556) 502611 (summer); Dalbeattie (01556) 610117 (summer); Dumfries (01387) 253862; Gretna (M74 service area) (01461) 338500; Gretna Green (01461) 337834 (summer)

Where Hadrian's Wall reached the western shore

Far-ranging views extend across mudflats left by treacherous tides. The Solway Firth and its low-lying hinterland have retained a timeless and secluded quality, a distinct contrast from the striking bustle of Carlisle.

A FORTRESS CHURCH

The squat tower of St John's Church in Newton Arlosh was built with stone walls 5ft thick and narrow window slits to serve as a defensive stronghold against border raiders, as well as a place of worship. The tower has no external door and can be entered only through a door inside the church at first-floor level.

St John's Church

① CROSSCANONBY SALTPANS

By the car park at the foot of Swarthy Hill, 2 miles south of Allonby, the square stone foundations of 17th-century salt-pans can be seen. Solway salt was made there by a process called 'sleeching', whereby salt was extracted from sand raked from the beach, rather than directly from seawater. On a mound across the road are the overgrown remains of the 'kinch', the circular stone enclosure where the sleech was processed. Steps lead up the hill to the remains of a small Roman fort, one of a chain of 'milefortlets' built to guard the Solway south of Hadrian's Wall.

② ALLONBY

Scattered along the coast road, Allonby is a quiet village of fishermen's cottages, with wide stretches of grass between the houses. The tide goes out more than a mile at low water, leaving vast areas of sand and rock pools, thronged with sea birds. It can be unsafe to venture far from the shore when the tide turns. The bay is popular with windsurfers.

③ SILLOTH

Wide, tree-lined streets give the small resort, with its sand and shingle beach, a spacious air. At the town's centre is The Green, an expanse of flowerbeds and rose bushes, fringed by pines and facing across the Solway Firth. Silloth became popular with holidaymakers after the railway arrived in the 1850s; the branch line is now defunct. The harbour, opened in 1859, was once a departure point for steamers to Liverpool and Dublin. Today it is used by pleasure craft and small coasters. The town's name dates from when monks of Holm Cultram Abbey cultivated grain on the fertile Cumbrian fields. Granaries, or 'laths', were used for storage. The granary by the sea became known as 'Sealath', altered down the years to 'Silloth'.

④ SKINBURNESS

Linked to Silloth by a mile-long promenade, Skinburness consists of a large hotel and a handful of houses. During his Scottish campaigns in the early 14th century, Edward I made the village his supply base. In 1303 a flood swept away most of the settlement, and the villagers moved inland to a safer site at Newton Arlosh. The sea has since retreated, leaving a tract of salt marsh on which sheep and cattle are put out to graze.

Grune Point, to the north-east, gives a wide view of the estuary. Antennae of the NATO radio station at Anthorn dominate the skyline to the east.

⑤ ABBEYTOWN

The farming village of Abbeytown gets its name from the Cistercian abbey of Holm Cultram, founded in 1150. As well as growing grain, the monks raised large flocks of sheep and established a thriving trade in salt from the Solway Firth. In 1322 the abbey was sacked by Robert Bruce, but was later rebuilt. It was dissolved by Henry VIII in 1538, but part of the nave survives and is still used as a parish church, dedicated to St Mary. To the south of the church, a series of grassy ridges and depressions marking the foundations give an indication of the size of the former abbey.

⑥ NEWTON ARLOSH

The straggling village was founded as a new settlement by the monks of Holm Cultram after Skinburness was flooded in 1303. It was for centuries under threat from Scottish marauders. St John's Church dates from the 14th century. During raids, cattle were driven inside its nave for safety.

⑦ HERDHILL SCAR

Until 1935, a mile-long railway viaduct connected the headland of Herdhill Scar to the Scottish shore. The line was opened in 1869 to link the iron-ore mines of Cumbria with the smelting furnaces of Lanarkshire. Trains ran across the viaduct until the 1920s.

Campfield Marsh RSPB Reserve, to the west of the promontory, is a huge area of tidal mudflats. A major site for a variety of water birds, including oyster-catchers and curlews, as well as a feeding ground for migrating pink-footed geese, the reserve can be viewed from lay-bys along the road.

⑧ BOWNESS-ON-SOLWAY

A compact village of narrow streets lined with sandstone cottages, Bowness was founded by the Romans as their fortress of Maia, at the western end of Hadrian's Wall, which was built across the neck of England to the Tyne at the northernmost limit of the Roman Empire. The present-day road through the village still follows the line of Maia's central thoroughfare.

From Maia, a chain of milefortlets and towers extended for a farther 40 miles down the Cumbrian coast. Two miles to the south of Bowness, on the

DISTANT HILLS *Across the Solway Firth from Silloth, the Scottish hills are seen at their best when cloaked in evening mists and as the sunset turns the water to shimmering gold.*

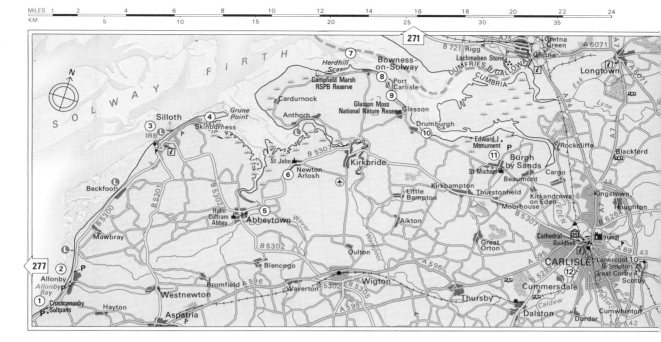

Kirkbride road, is the entrance to Glasson Moss National Nature Reserve, an expanse of peat bog and sphagnum moss, where insect-eating sundews and bog rosemary grow on the treacherous terrain. Visitors must have a permit.

⑨ PORT CARLISLE

The port was established in 1819 to provide a harbour, linked by canal to Carlisle, for coastal shipping. But in the 1860s the tidal currents changed and the harbour silted up. Today the village consists of little more than two terraces of handsome 19th-century cottages, and little remains of either the old harbour or the canal, apart from the stones that formed the harbour entrance.

⑩ DRUMBURGH

The small village originally marked the site of the next Roman fort to Bowness along Hadrian's Wall. Although the fort has gone, the road through Drumburgh still twists along the line of its outer walls. To the east, the sea wall follows the line of the original turf rampart.

⑪ BURGH BY SANDS

The stone and brick cottages of Burgh, pronounced 'Bruff', stand on the site of a Roman fort. St Michael's Church is built with stones from the Roman defences, but its Norman doorway is its earliest architectural feature. The building served as a refuge from marauders as well as a place of worship. Its 14th-century tower has no outer doorway.

A mile north of the village, the Edward I Monument is prominent amid the lonely saltings of Burgh Marsh. It marks the spot where Edward I died in 1307, aged 68, while setting out on a campaign against the Scots.

⑫ CARLISLE

Set on a bluff above the meeting-point of two rivers, the Eden and the Caldew, the red-brown sandstone walls and

RAIDERS' COAST *The salt marshes at Bowness-on-Solway face the Solway Firth. Between the 14th and 17th centuries, English and Scottish raiders feuded across the estuary.*

Norman keep of Carlisle Castle (EH) attest to the ancient role of the city as one of the guardians of northern England. Carlisle was built as a base by the Romans about AD 71. During and after the Middle Ages it was a crucial stronghold in the border wars between the English and the Scots. The castle was founded in 1092 by William II of England, who built the huge keep. Its gatehouse and ramparts date from about 1300. On the prison walls are prisoners' graffiti spanning several centuries. Behind the keep is the museum of the King's Own Border Regiment.

The nearby Tullie House Museum and Art Gallery, housed in a late 17th-century building, has displays on the Romans, as well as the feuding cattle thieves known as 'reivers' who terrorised the region in the Middle Ages and later. Dating from about 1130, Carlisle Cathedral is England's second smallest cathedral. It has magnificent

tracery in its east window, and beautifully carved 15th-century choir stalls adorned with painted backs.

Brightly coloured wooden carvings of human figures grimace from the upper storey of the 15th-century timber-framed Guildhall, which houses a small museum giving an introduction to the city's guilds. Carlisle is the terminus of the railway line that runs south-eastwards for 70 miles, across the spectacularly wild landscapes of the Pennine Hills to Settle in North Yorkshire.

PLACES TO SEE INLAND

Brampton, 10 miles E of Carlisle. Historic market town with Norman parish church and octagonal Moot Hall; Talkin Tarn Country Park nearby.

Lanercost Priory (EH), 12 miles NE of Carlisle. 12th-century priory ruins and church.

TOURIST INFORMATION

Carlisle (01228) 512444; Silloth (016973) 31944

Harbour towns that served Cumbria's coalfields

Dunes and grassland border the coast south from Allonby Bay. The breezy sandstone promontory of St Bees Head juts out between a trio of industrial ports and the sprawling Sellafield nuclear complex.

① MARYPORT

The town owes its name to Mary Senhouse, the wife of an 18th-century entrepreneur who built the docks and harbour to serve the Cumbrian coal trade. In the 19th century, ships from Maryport were loaded with iron rails, made in Cumbria for railways all over the world. The harbour is now home to the *Flying Buzzard*, a restored 1951 Clyde tug, and a World War II VIC (Victualling Inshore Craft), built as a naval supply vessel. There are guided tours of both boats. Near the harbourside is the Maritime Museum, where reminders of Maryport's seagoing past include several exhibits on Fletcher Christian, leader of the mutiny on board the *Bounty* in 1789.

High up on the north side of the town are the remains of the Roman fort of Alauna, built to prevent seaborne raiders from outflanking the defences of Hadrian's Wall. It is now no more than a faint outline in a field on private land. However, next to it the Senhouse Roman Museum has a magnificent collection of Roman inscriptions.

② COCKERMOUTH

Straddling the River Derwent, the market town has numerous colour-washed Georgian and Victorian houses. In 1770 William Wordsworth was born in Main Street, in what is now known as Wordsworth House (NT); it is furnished in 18th-century style, and contains many of the poet's personal effects. The town's other attractions include the Cumberland Toy and Model Museum, the Creighton Mineral and Fossil Museum, the Printing House Museum and tours round Jennings' brewery.

③ WORKINGTON

A grid of streets surrounds Portland Square, where 18th-century cottages overlook an expanse of tree-shaded cobbles. Much of the rest of Workington bears a distinctively industrial look. Mine tunnels once ran deep under the sea from the collieries around Workington, and Cumbrian coal used to be shipped from its deep-water harbour. Today, rails made by British Steel are exported worldwide from the town. In a public park above the Derwent stand

the imposing ruins of Workington Hall, where Mary, Queen of Scots, spent her last few days of freedom in May 1568, after fleeing from Scotland across the Solway Firth. Workington's past is conjured up inside the Helena Thompson Museum, a Georgian house across the road from the hall. Prints and models show the town as it was, and there are costumes, furniture and glassware.

A mile north of the town, the Siddick Pond Nature Reserve is a bird sanctuary with a lakeside hide, inside the perimeter fence of a paper mill.

④ WHITEHAVEN

Laid out in the 17th century on a grid pattern and retaining a Georgian elegance, Whitehaven was Britain's first post-medieval planned town. The docks and harbour, built in the 18th and 19th centuries, are used today by fishing boats, pleasure craft and coasters. The Whitehaven Beacon, a museum by the harbour, tells the stories of the town's sailors, miners, slave traders and tobacco merchants. Exhibits include a superb enamel goblet made in 1763.

⑤ ST BEES

The village takes its name from St Bee, or St Bega, an Irish princess who established a nunnery there around AD 650. Destroyed by the Vikings, the building was refounded as a Benedictine priory in 1120. St Mary and St Bega, the heavily restored priory church, has an elaborate Norman doorway. Across the road are the buildings of St Bees School, founded in 1583 by Edmund Grindal, Archbishop of Canterbury. St Bees is the western end of the Coast to Coast Walk, a 190 mile route across country to Robin Hood's Bay in North Yorkshire.

Looming over the village's long sandy beach is the high cliff of St Bees Head, reached by path from the car park at its foot. The RSPB Reserve on the headland has one of the largest sea bird colonies on England's west coast, and is the only breeding ground in England for black guillemots. On a clear day the Isle of Man can be seen some 30 miles to the west.

⑥ EGREMONT

A broad main street of colour-washed houses passes close to the ruins of Egremont Castle, which dates from the 12th century and is now within a public park overlooking the River Ehen. Part of the gatehouse, great hall and outer wall survive. The town's September Crab Fair is so called because, when it was founded in 1267, crab apples were given away to visitors. The fair's 'World Gurning Championship' is won by the contestant who pulls the ugliest face.

⑦ SELLAFIELD

In 1956, Calder Hall became Britain's first nuclear power station to generate electricity on a commercial scale. It is part of the Sellafield site, which can

A PORT REVIVED *The tide of trade has long since ebbed for Maryport, but the construction of a marina beside historic craft berthed there marks a renaissance in the town's fortunes.*

275

THE CUMBRIAN MUTINEER

Fletcher Christian, first officer of HMS *Bounty* and leader of the mutiny against Captain Bligh, was born in Cockermouth in 1764. Incensed by Bligh's harsh treatment of the crew, Christian and 25 other men set him adrift in a boat in the Pacific with a few loyal officers. Bligh's party reached Timor, 4000 miles away, while the mutineers landed on Pitcairn Island. Christian Street in Maryport is named after the leader of the mutiny.

Bounty mutineers turn Captain Bligh adrift.

be seen for miles around and includes the Thermal Oxide Reprocessing Plant (THORP), where spent nuclear fuel is recycled. There are tours of the site, and a visitor centre explains the development of nuclear power in Britain.

Two miles away, east of the village of Calder Bridge, are the riverside ruins of Calder Abbey, which date from the 12th century. The ruins are on private land and are not open to visitors, but may be seen from the road. The minor road climbing over the moors northwards towards Ennerdale Bridge gives far-ranging views of the coast.

⑧ GOSFORTH

Slate-roofed stone houses make up much of the village. St Mary's Church has a fine array of Norse and early Christian monuments; among them is an Anglo-Danish cross, erected in the churchyard around AD 1000. Its carvings are thought to combine Norse legend and Christianity, in a representation of the triumph of good over evil.

⑨ SEASCALE

The small residential village is just a mile down the coast from Sellafield. The sandy, boulder-strewn beach is regularly monitored for radioactivity.

Two miles to the south, a minor road through Drigg leads to a car park near the shore. A mile's walk leads to Drigg Nature Reserve, one of Cumbria's largest areas of sand dunes. The reserve forms part of a military firing range, and is closed when red flags are flying.

⑩ RAVENGLASS

The street of 18th and 19th-century houses that forms the nucleus of Ravenglass runs just above the tidemark beside a broad estuary. The village is the terminus of the Ravenglass and Eskdale Railway, along which

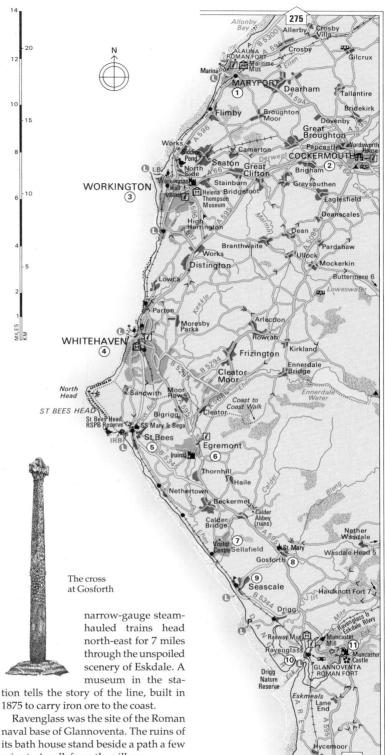

The cross at Gosforth

narrow-gauge steam-hauled trains head north-east for 7 miles through the unspoiled scenery of Eskdale. A museum in the station tells the story of the line, built in 1875 to carry iron ore to the coast.

Ravenglass was the site of the Roman naval base of Glannoventa. The ruins of its bath house stand beside a path a few minutes' walk from the village.

⑪ MUNCASTER CASTLE

Built on a hillside above the Esk, Muncaster Castle has 14th-century origins but was substantially rebuilt in the mid 19th century. The castle contains antique furniture, tapestries and portraits. Its gardens include azaleas, rhododendrons and a terrace almost a mile long. The Owl Centre in the grounds conserves endangered owls, and returns some to the wild.

Muncaster Mill, a mile to the north, is a restored 18th-century water mill which grinds and sells wholemeal flour.

279

PLACES TO SEE INLAND

Buttermere, 10 miles S of Cockermouth. Lake District hamlet; lake and fell walks.

Hardknott Fort (EH), 15 miles E of Seascale. Roman fort on magnificent hilltop site.

Wasdale Head, 9 miles NE of Gosforth. Hamlet in mountain setting by Wast Water.

TOURIST INFORMATION

Cockermouth (01900) 822634; Egremont (01946) 820693; Maryport (01900) 813738; Whitehaven (01946) 695678; Workington (01900) 602923

High dunes bordering the estuary of the Duddon

Southern Cumbria's wild and lonely beaches, dotted with outcrops of rock and separated by estuaries running far inland towards the lakes and fells, contrast with the industrial sprawl of Barrow-in-Furness.

HAVERIGG HEIGHTS *Dunes almost 70 ft high in places flank Haverigg Point, with marram grass binding the soft sand. The foreshore is more than a mile wide at low tide.*

① ANNASIDE

An unsignposted lane from Bootle winds seawards to the hamlet of Annaside, where it gives way to a track. Cars must be parked at the end of the road, from which it is a short walk to a 4 mile beach of rock-strewn sand. Sandwiched between the Lakeland hills and the sea, this coast is as lonely as any in England. Low tide reveals shallow rock pools.

Gutterby Spa, to the south, is a stretch of sand and shingle, backed by high cliffs, which can be reached either from the coast road or on foot from Annaside. The view inland is dominated by the looming bulk of Black Combe, which rises to almost 2000 ft.

② SILECROFT

The small, stone-built village is a mile inland from a sand and shingle beach that is popular with anglers. A large car park is the starting point for walks north and south along the shore.

③ HAVERIGG

A long expanse of low-tide sand is backed by broad dunes at the little resort of Haverigg. On one side of the village is an open prison; on the other stand the remains of old ironstone mines and quarries. Footpaths along the dunes give views across the estuary to Barrow and the Isle of Walney.

④ HODBARROW RSPB RESERVE

The dramatic stretch of brackish water was formed when the Hodbarrow iron mines were flooded after the last mine closed in 1968. Great crested grebes, tufted ducks, oystercatchers and little terns gather at the water's edge, while kestrels and barn owls hunt over the reserve. The sea wall on the south side of the reserve gives far-ranging views.

⑤ MILLOM

A quiet Victorian town on the western side of the Duddon estuary, Millom grew up around its 14th-century castle and 12th-century Holy Trinity Church, both of which are now isolated a mile north of the town centre. The castle is not open to the public. Millom grew prosperous from iron mining. During the late 19th century its mines had 11 working shafts, making them the largest and busiest in Britain; the last

workings closed in 1968. Displays at Millom's Folk Museum include a reconstruction of a miner's cottage kitchen, and a replica of part of the Hodbarrow iron mine at Haverigg.

⑥ BROUGHTON IN FURNESS

At the small town of Broughton, on the edge of the Lake District National Park, the fells crowd down to the Duddon. The neat square, lined by 18th-century houses and overhung by chestnut trees, was once a market place. It has a set of stocks, a slate table where fish were once laid out for sale, and an obelisk commemorating George III's golden jubilee in 1810. The Church of St Mary Magdalene dates from Norman times.

⑦ DUDDON SANDS

Low tide in the Duddon estuary reveals a stretch of sand 2 miles across at its widest point. In the estuary's upper reaches, footpaths link villages on opposite banks at low tide, but treacherous sands and fast incoming tides mean that visitors should not use the paths without local guidance. The mud flats on both sides of the estuary attract huge numbers of oystercatchers, lapwings and other wading birds.

⑧ DALTON-IN-FURNESS

The small town lies in an area honeycombed with old iron-ore quarries and mine workings. Dalton Castle (NT) is a squat 14th-century tower with a small museum, open only on Saturday afternoons in summer. Across the road from the castle is the huge Victorian Church of St Mary. The South Lakes Wild Animal Park includes wallabies, porcupines, antelopes, and exotic pheasants and ducks. Three miles north-west of Dalton is the Sandscale Haws Nature Reserve (NT), where natterjack toads breed in spring and Arctic birds visit in summer. Walks along the shore give superb views of Black Combe and other fells of the southern Lake District.

MONASTIC WEALTH *Furness Abbey, near Barrow, was in the 16th century England's second richest Cistercian house.*

⑨ BARROW-IN-FURNESS

Local deposits of iron ore transformed Barrow in the early 19th century from a country village into a thriving industrial and shipbuilding centre. High-grade ore was shipped to steelworks all over England, and by 1870 Barrow's own steelworks, now closed, were the biggest in the world. The town centre, with its wide streets and huge, red sandstone town hall, is a monument to Victorian civic pride. Though Barrow's great days of shipbuilding are over, Trident nuclear submarines are built there, in a hall whose vast white bulk looms over the port area. Across the road is the Dock Museum, which tells the story of Barrow's industrial past. In a peaceful green valley on the north side of the town are the sandstone ruins

HARBOUR GUARDIANS *Roa Island's lifeboat station watches over the huge harbour that played a role in Furness Abbey's trade, while the castle on nearby Piel Island kept vigil.*

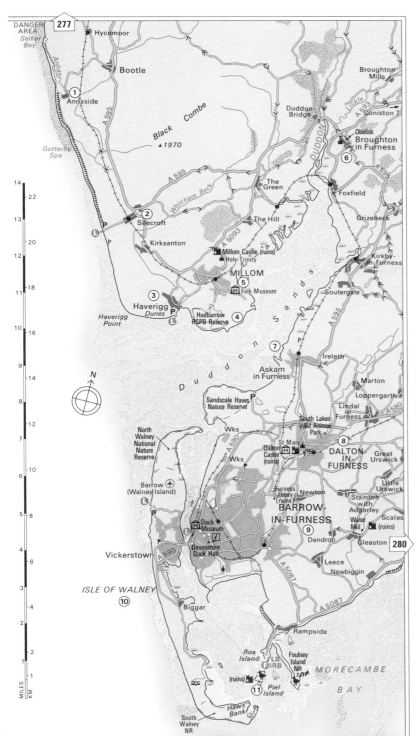

of Furness Abbey (EH), built by Cistercian monks in the 12th century. Remains of a warehouse used to shelter goods traded from the abbey, such as food, wine and wool, can also be seen.

⑩ ISLE OF WALNEY

The 12 mile strip of land provides the shelter which makes Barrow such a fine harbour. A wide expanse of water, dotted with rocks and islets, offers moorings for pleasure craft on the island's landward side. On the seaward side is a sandy beach more than 10 miles long.

The North Walney National Nature Reserve is an area of dunes and grassland where birds such as redshanks and stonechats congregate. The natterjack toad is also found there. At the island's southern end, a sand and shingle bank, with ponds formed by old gravel workings, forms another nature reserve, with one of Europe's busiest lesser black-backed and herring gull colonies.

⑪ PIEL ISLAND

Set midway between Roa Island on the mainland and the southern tip of the Isle of Walney, Piel played an important role in Barrow's defences from the 12th century. Piel Castle (EH) was built in the 16th century by the monks of Furness Abbey; parts of the massive keep and walls survive. The island can be reached on foot, with care, from South Walney at low tide, or by an irregular ferry service from Roa Island.

The narrow finger of land south-east of Roa Island is occupied by Foulney Island Nature Reserve, reached along a 1½ mile shingle causeway, flooded at high tide. The reserve attracts birds such as terns, eider ducks and dunlin.

PLACES TO SEE INLAND

Coniston, 9 miles NE of Broughton in Furness. Brantwood, home of Victorian sage John Ruskin; trips on Coniston Water aboard the restored 19th-century steam yacht *Gondola* (NT).

TOURIST INFORMATION

Barrow-in-Furness (01229) 870156

Vast expanses of low-tide sands in Morecambe Bay

Between the Lake District and the magnificent arc of Morecambe Bay lie the Furness and Cartmel peninsulas. The landscape combines gently rolling limestone hills with ancient woodland and gleaming estuaries.

① ALDINGHAM

Recorded in Domesday Book, the village has been gradually lost to the sea over the centuries. Little remains of the original Aldingham, except for the Church of St Cuthbert, protected from the sea by a wall, and 19th-century Aldingham Hall, which is not open to the public. Features of the 12th-century church include two carvings in the chancel portraying a demure bride and a bashful bridegroom.

② GLEASTON WATER MILL

Tucked away in peaceful farming country, Gleaston Water Mill was built in 1774. Its 18 ft waterwheel and machinery have been restored to working order. Archaeologists have unearthed flint tools, dating from 5000 BC, now displayed along with milling artefacts inside the mill. The 14th-century ruin of Gleaston Castle is not open to the public but can be seen from the road between Gleaston and Scales.

③ BAYCLIFF

The village is set on top of the low banks which border the west side of Morecambe Bay. North of Baycliff the elevated, bracken-covered expanse of Birkrigg Common gives panoramas of the bay and has a well-preserved Bronze Age stone circle.

④ BARDSEA COUNTRY PARK

The strip of coast beside the road from Baycliff to Ulverston, looking out across Morecambe Bay towards Heysham, has picnic spaces and waymarked footpaths. Sea Wood, where there is a nature trail, includes ancient woodland as well as oaks planted to provide timber for ships built at nearby Barrow-in-Furness. Conishead Priory stands in extensive grounds to the north of the country park. An Augustinian priory stood on the site in the 12th century, but the present mansion is a 19th-century Gothic fantasy run as a centre for Buddhist studies. It is open to the public most weekends in summer.

⑤ ULVERSTON

A market town since 1280, Ulverston flourished as a port in the early 19th century after the opening of a canal to the coast at Canal Foot. The comedian Arthur Stanley Jefferson, better known as Stan Laurel, was born in Ulverston in 1890 and is celebrated in the Laurel and Hardy Museum. On top of Hoad Hill, a 20 minute walk from the town centre, stands a 100 ft monument in the form of a lighthouse, erected in 1850 to commemorate Sir John Barrow, a distinguished explorer and Secretary to the Admiralty, who also was born in the town. There are exhilarating views of Morecambe Bay and the southern Lake District from the monument, which can be climbed by an interior staircase when a red flag is flying.

Just outside Ulverston, Swarthmoor Hall was in the 17th century a safe house for Quakers, who were a persecuted sect. The hall belonged to Judge Fell, a sympathiser. George Fox, the founder of the Quaker movement, stayed there. The staircase has one step deliberately made higher than the others, so that intruders would stumble over it and unwittingly alert the occupants. The hall, now owned by the Quakers, is usually open to the public.

⑥ GREENODD

Now a sleepy backwater, Greenodd was in the 19th century a busy harbour with a branch line of the Furness Railway linking it to Lake Windermere. All that remains of the track is a 3½ mile section from Haverthwaite, 2 miles to the north-east, along the Lakeside and Haverthwaite Railway. Steam locomotives proceed farther north-eastwards to Lakeside, where there is a steamboat connection on Lake Windermere.

To the east of Greenodd, Bigland Hall is set amid parkland, beside a lake. The hall and grounds are a centre for country pursuits such as riding and fishing.

⑦ HOLKER HALL

Although the oldest section of the hall dates from 1604, the part of the building that is open to the public was rebuilt in extravagant mock-Elizabethan style in 1874 after a fire. Its interior possesses a magnificent cantilevered oak staircase with intricately carved balusters. The grounds include

PAST PLEASURES *A visit to Holker Hall evokes various eras. The Elizabethan-style mansion (right) offers a glimpse of high living in the Victorian period, while the Lakeland Motor Museum (above), in the grounds, has a faithful reconstruction of a garage of the 1920s.*

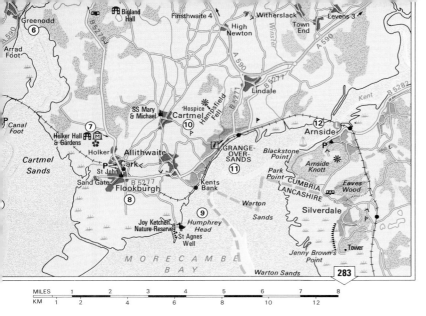

MILES 1 2 3 4 5 6 7 8
KM 1 2 4 6 8 10 12

formal and rose gardens, fountains and a splendid tree-lined, limestone cascade. There are picnic areas and woodland walks in the deer park, which has one of the oldest herds of fallow deer in Britain. Vintage Buicks and Bentleys, as well as an eye-catching array of antique motorcycles and car memorabilia, can be seen in the Lakeland Motor Museum, which is also in the grounds of the hall. The children's activities area has a toy and teddy bear exhibition.

⑧ FLOOKBURGH

Now separated from the sea by reclaimed marshland, Flookburgh was once so close to the shore that high tides would bring waves washing along the main street. It remains a fishing village, however, with shrimps and flukes – the local name for flounders – sold at local cottages. The fishermen cross the sands on tractors from nearby Sand Gate and Humphrey Head to net their catches.

⑨ HUMPHREY HEAD

Extending for about a mile into the flat expanses of Morecambe Bay, and rising to 172 ft, Humphrey Head is the only limestone cliff of any height on the coast of Cumbria. The head includes the Joy Ketchen Nature Reserve, which has a range of grassland plants and trees, including the rare Lancastrian whitebeam. At the foot of the cliffs is the holy well of St Agnes, celebrated by pilgrims for centuries for its curative powers.

⑩ CARTMEL

Dwarfing the village is the cathedral-like Priory Church of St Mary and St Michael, part of an Augustinian establishment founded in the 12th century. It has a huge east window, a fine set of misericords and an ornately carved tomb built to commemorate the first Lord Harrington, who died in 1347, and his wife; he is thought to have built the south choir aisle of the church. The

14th-century priory gatehouse, whose exhibition area shows work by local artists, flanks Cartmel's central square.

⑪ GRANGE-OVER-SANDS

Substantial Edwardian houses, arcades of shops, ornamental gardens, a lake and a bandstand recall a sedate age. There are children's amusements and bowling and putting greens near the mile-long waterfront promenade. Paths climb to Hampsfield Fell, whose 727 ft summit is capped by a 19th-century hospice, built as a refuge for travellers.

⑫ ARNSIDE

A holiday resort and sailing centre, the village hugs the lower slopes of Arnside Knott, whose summit is reached on foot and has wonderful views across the Kent estuary. A siren sounds at Arnside when the tide starts to come in. Under certain conditions, the tide rushes in at such a pace that it can be heard from the village as a distant roar. When tides are safe, guided walks head across the bay to Grange-over-Sands and Kents Bank. The train journey from Arnside to Ulverston crosses low viaducts, built over Warton Sands and Cartmel Sands, and gives superb coastal panoramas.

PLACES TO SEE INLAND

Levens Hall, Levens, 9 miles NE of Grange-over-Sands. Elizabethan house; gardens with topiary.

Sizergh Castle (NT), nr Levens, 11 miles NE of Grange-over-Sands. Country house, with peel tower, remodelled in Elizabethan times; gardens.

Stott Park Bobbin Mill (EH), nr Finsthwaite, 8 miles NW of Grange-over-Sands. Working museum of factory which provided bobbins for Lancashire's cotton mills.

TOURIST INFORMATION

Barrow-in-Furness (01229) 870156; Grange-over-Sands (015395) 34026 (summer); Ulverston (01229) 587120

BAYSIDE RESORT *Grange-over-Sands watches across Morecambe Bay, whose extensive areas of mud flats and quicksands are the haunt of many thousands of waders.*

A playground of the north lit by spectacular sunsets

North of the popular resort of Morecambe, the Lancashire coast echoes the unspoilt beauty of the nearby Lake District. The imposing city of Lancaster was in the 18th century one of Britain's busiest ports.

① SILVERDALE

At one time the village stood beside the River Kent and steamers cruised there from Morecambe, but in the 1920s the river changed its course northwards, leaving Silverdale high and dry.

The village has a long tradition as a resort, with the novelists Charlotte Brontë and Mrs Gaskell among its 19th-century visitors. A house above the shore was built as a bathhouse where Victorians could enjoy in comfort the fashionable benefits of immersion in the sea. The swathe of turf along the foreshore used to be harvested for bowling greens and tennis courts.

The winding lanes round Silverdale give occasional glimpses of the sea, and the village is an excellent centre for walking. Eaves Wood (NT), just north of Silverdale, includes ancient woodland with species such as oak, ash and small-leaved lime. The wood is a haven for rare butterflies including the high brown fritillary and pearl-bordered fritillary. A mile to the east of Silverdale is Leighton Moss RSPB Reserve, an area of reed beds, meres and woodland, where otters and red deer can be seen. Among the reserve's many birds is the elusive bittern, whose booming cry may be heard from late January to mid June.

② JENNY BROWN'S POINT

The point is strikingly solitary in character; its name is a mystery, but it is known that a man called Brown farmed there in the 16th century. This was once a centre for copper smelting, but the only remains of the industry to be seen today is an old stone chimney stack. It is reached from Silverdale by a lane signposted to a farm called Gibraltar.

③ CARNFORTH

Until 1931 the town had a steelworks which processed Cumbrian iron ore. After this closed, Carnforth remained a busy railway junction. The industrial heritage of north-western England is recalled in two of Carnforth's attractions. Steamtown, on the northern edge of the town, has a collection of locomotives and a short section of track along which trains run. The Lancaster Canal, on the other side of the town, is now used for recreation but was once

STATUS SYMBOL *Traditional heraldry was once imitated by railway companies, as in this crest at Carnforth's Steamtown.*

crowded with barges carrying sand and gravel. Completed in 1819, it connected Preston and Kendal; its towpath gives a 27 mile walk from Lancaster to Kendal.

④ BOLTON-LE-SANDS

The old village of Bolton-le-Sands lies to the east of the busy A6, which runs through the modern village. The Packet Boat Hotel was a stopping point on the canal for fast passenger boats capable of speeds of more than 10 mph. The newer village overlooks salt marshes that attract waders and waterfowl on their early autumn migrations southwards.

⑤ HEST BANK

West of Hest Bank, a residential suburb of Lancaster, is a wide expanse of open foreshore, where cars may be parked; the hills of the Lake District are visible on the other side of Morecambe Bay. Because of hazardous quicksands and a shift in the course of the river it is no longer possible to walk across the sands to Kents Bank, near Grange.

⑥ MORECAMBE

The resort was born with the coming of the railway, in the mid 19th century, providing cheap travel for thousands of workers from the industrial towns. Morecambe's success was built on sea, sand and entertainment, and the town remains a lively place today, with a 4 mile promenade whose attractions include a Wild West theme park and indoor leisure pools with waterslides. Sunsets are a memorable feature of Morecambe Bay. The town is vulnerable to storms; sea defences have been strengthened, and an old stone jetty, built in 1850, has been extended. Boats land catches of shrimps.

⑦ HEYSHAM

At the calm centre of Old Heysham, high on a headland looking across Morecambe Bay's sands, are the ruins of tiny St Patrick's Chapel, whose thick walls were built in the 8th and 9th centuries. Beside it are graves, including one of a child, cut into the rock. Just below the chapel is the Church of St Peter, dating from the 10th century.

BAROQUE FOLLY *Towering to 220ft and a landmark for miles around, the high-domed Ashton Memorial in Lancaster was erected in 1909 by Lord Ashton in memory of his wife.*

GRAVEYARD IN STONE *Their only roof the sky, these graves carved from the solid rock near the ruined St Patrick's Chapel near Heysham may date back to the 8th or 9th century.*

Modern Heysham is focused on the harbour, the starting point for a vehicle ferry to the Isle of Man, and the base of support vessels for the Morecambe Bay gas field, discovered in 1974. To the south of the harbour, and visible for miles, is the square block of Heysham's nuclear power station; there is a visitor centre, and guided tours are available. Beside the power station is a nature reserve where many butterflies and moths may be seen.

⑧ SUNDERLAND

It is difficult to imagine the simple huddle of houses at Sunderland as a busy shipping port, yet in the early 18th century cargoes from the West Indies were unloaded there and transferred to smaller vessels for the onward journey to Lancaster. Traffic declined with the growth of Glasson Dock, across the Lune estuary, and in the 19th century the village became known for sea bathing. The only road into Sunderland leads across a narrow causeway which is flooded at high tide; at low tide it traverses a maze of muddy channels. There is limited parking on the shore.

⑨ LANCASTER

State, church and commerce are represented in the three buildings that dominate the skyline of the handsome city of Lancaster. Sharing the same hilltop are the great medieval castle – used as a prison, though part is open to the public – and the Priory Church of St Mary, dating from the 14th century but with a history going back to before the Norman Conquest. Across the city, on Lancaster's highest point, is the Ashton Memorial, giving views as far as North Wales and the Isle of Man. It stands in Williamson Park, given to the city in the 19th century by Lord Ashton's father, a linoleum manufacturer.

Next to the memorial is an Edwardian Palm House with a collection of tropical butterflies. A footpath by the castle passes the site of a Roman bathhouse and drops to St George's Quay, beside the River Lune. The quayside Maritime Museum, housed in the former Custom House and an adjoining warehouse, relates the story of the port of Lancaster, which in the 18th century was one of the busiest in Britain, trading principally with the West Indies, until the silting of the Lune spelt the end for commercial shipping. Lancaster's Cottage Museum is furnished as an artisan's home of the early 19th century, just before Queen Victoria came to the throne. Judges' Lodgings contains a museum of childhood, and items made by Gillow, the Lancaster-based firm of furniture-makers.

⑩ GLASSON

Unlike many of the small ports in the area, Glasson, a port since the late 18th century, has not declined to become a historical curiosity but is a lively mix of working docks, a barge-lined canal and a yacht basin. Glasson's fortunes improved when it was linked to the main Lancaster Canal in 1826 and shipped raw materials for Lancaster's mills.

A 6 mile path leading along the Lune estuary as far as Lancaster offers excellent opportunities for birdwatching.

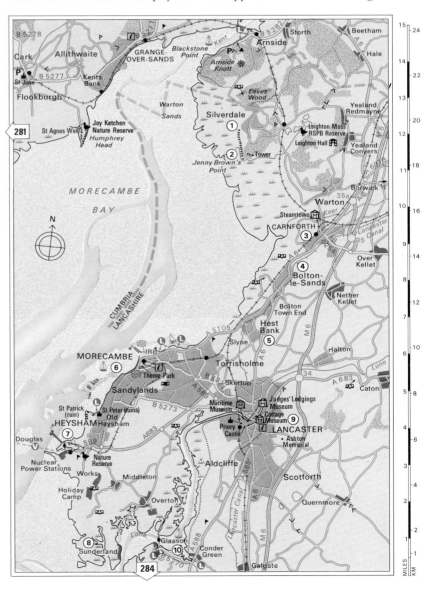

PLACES TO SEE INLAND

Leighton Hall, 3 miles N of Carnforth. Gothic revival house, home of the Gillow furniture-making family; maze; birds of prey.

TOURIST INFORMATION

Grange-over-Sands (015395) 34026 (summer); Lancaster (01524) 32878; Morecambe (01524) 582808

Holiday fun on the flat, broad Fylde peninsula

Between the estuaries of the Lune and the Ribble, the sandy beaches of the Fylde peninsula are lined with holiday resorts. Blackpool, whose famous illuminations brighten autumn evenings, still reigns supreme.

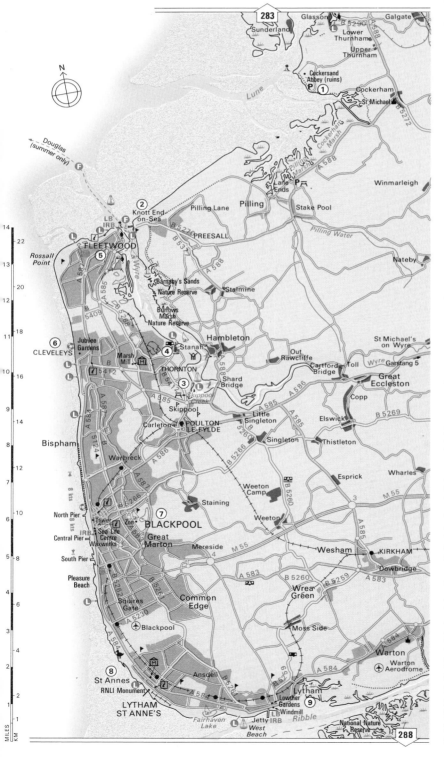

① COCKERSAND ABBEY

Cows graze placidly among the scattered ruins of Cockersand Abbey, once one of the great religious houses in north-west England. The squat tower of the 13th-century chapter house, and a few stunted walls, are all that remain of the abbey, built in the early 12th century on the tip of a remote tongue of land at the mouth of the River Lune. The remnants of a fish trap built by the monks can be seen at low tide.

A few hundred yards from the shore is a small lighthouse topped by a black cone. The bulk of Heysham nuclear power station looms on the far shore, and beyond are the Lakeland hills. A narrow lane, with limited parking space at the end, leads to the shore, from where it is a pleasant 10 minute stroll beside the bay to the abbey.

② KNOTT END-ON-SEA

Knott End is a small, quiet place with trim bungalows, a wide beach of sand and stretches of mud. Sailing boats are moored in the Wyre estuary, opposite Fleetwood docks, and beside the landing stage for the passenger ferry that in summer links Knott End and Fleetwood. From the quay, a path leads south along the riverbank past a golf course to the two nature reserves of Barnaby's Sands and Burrows Marsh, set in the last large areas of ungrazed salt marsh on the Lancashire coast.

A car park and picnic site at Lane Ends, 4½ miles east of Knott End, is an ideal spot for birdwatching, and gives broad views over Morecambe Bay.

③ SKIPPOOL CREEK

High tides on the River Wyre regularly reach up to 30ft in depth, filling a maze of creeks such as Skippool. The creek, a haven for birds, including herons, ducks and lapwings, is also a popular sailing centre, with moorings and jetties. There is a picnic area near the narrow path beside the creek; another path that floods at high tide leads north to Stanah, almost 2 miles away.

In the 16th century, Skippool was the port for the ancient market town of Poulton-le-Fylde, a mile inland. In the 1750s, the port's trade is said to have been greater than that of Liverpool. Imports included wine, tobacco, timber, and guano from Africa for use as fertiliser on Fylde farms.

④ STANAH

A visitor centre at Stanah, called the Wyreside Ecology Centre, located at the entrance to Wyre Estuary Country Park, provides information on the wildlife of the estuary, where many birds may be seen on the mud flats and sandbanks. In winter, there are large flocks of lapwings, golden plovers and redshanks, with oystercatchers near the estuary mouth. Just down river from Stanah, a large chemical works overlooks the marshes.

DRESSED TO IMPRESS *Ostrich-feather hats, cloth caps and bowlers were the headgear for strollers along Blackpool's North Pier in 1912, the heyday of seaside piers.*

⑤ FLEETWOOD

Once a major fishing port, Fleetwood could have been as elegant as Bath if plans for a new town, prepared in 1840 by the architect Decimus Burton, had been completed. Traces of his grand design survives, as does a great railway hotel, the North Euston; the hotel was built for travellers to Scotland, who took a boat from Fleetwood to Ardrossan and travelled on from there to Glasgow by train. The centrepiece of Burton's plan was The Mount, a grassy hill surmounted by a clock tower, which overlooks a long promenade with a boating lake, a pier, bowling greens and the Marine Hall entertainment centre, set in gardens.

Modern Fleetwood is a lively mix of resort, on the seaward side of the town, and working port, with extensive riverside docks and the Pharos Lighthouse located well inland. The beach is sand, with some shingle. Trams run between Fleetwood and Blackpool; in summer, there are passenger ferries to Knott End across the Wyre, and vehicle ferries to the Isle of Man.

⑥ CLEVELEYS

Cleveleys is quieter than neighbouring Blackpool and offers a more modest range of attractions, including amusement arcades, a children's play area, and the Jubilee Gardens behind the promenade with bowls and crazy golf. The beach is sand, with some shingle.

The red sails of Marsh Mill, turning slowly above the village of Thornton, 1½ miles inland, are a landmark in the area. Built in 1794, the 70 ft mill produced flour for bread, and crushed barley for animal feed, until 1922. The mill has been restored to working order, and also houses a clog museum. Beside the mill, shops are grouped round a courtyard where events such as brass band concerts are staged.

⑦ BLACKPOOL

Superlatives and statistics hardly do justice to the phenomenon of Blackpool, but they give an impression of the character of the place. More than 16.5 million visits are made to the town each year, by people drawn by the 518 ft 9 in Tower, and the huge Pleasure Beach, whose 150 rides include the world's tallest, fastest roller coaster. Every inch of the seafront between the North and South Piers is packed with hotels, bars, pubs and entertainments guaranteed to thrill, frighten, alarm, enrich or delight. There are 3500 hotels, guest houses and self-catering units in the resort, which has 120 000 holiday beds – more than the whole of Portugal. From early September to early November the illuminations dispel the autumn darkness with more than 500 000 lamps. The best way to see them is from one of the trams that trundle along the seafront to Cleveleys and on to Fleetwood. A Sea Life Centre, a zoo and a waxworks are further attractions.

⑧ ST ANNES

St Annes was built in Victorian times as a holiday resort for the better-off, offering traditional resort attractions. It has a pier, bandstand and sandy beach, as well as gardens, a toy and teddy bear museum, a miniature railway and trampolines. The flat sands are ideal for sand yachting. Fairhaven Lake is used for rowing, windsurfing and other watersports, and is also a good vantage point for watching migrant birds on the Ribble estuary. Sand dunes at the Blackpool, or northern, end of the town form a nature reserve with a small interpretative centre. A memorial in St Annes records a lifeboat disaster which took place in 1886, with the loss of 27 crew from two rescue boats.

Memorial, St Annes

⑨ LYTHAM

A windmill, built in 1805, stands on Lytham Green, a stretch of close-cropped turf behind the promenade. The mill produced flour until 1919, and now houses an illuminating exhibition of milling and of local life. The dramatic story of Lytham's lifeboat service is displayed in the former lifeboat house next to the mill; the new lifeboat house overlooks the wide Ribble estuary and the muddy beach. Placid and peaceful, the town has flower-lined walks, bowling greens and tennis courts in Lowther Gardens, and fine golf links, including the championship course of Royal Lytham and St Annes.

FACING THE ELEMENTS *Lytham's seafront windmill took advantage of the coastal winds. The old lifeboat house next to it is a reminder of the ever-present dangers of the sea.*

THE BRIGHT LIGHTS OF BLACKPOOL

BLACKPOOL IS AN ENGLISH INSTITUTION. Proudly bold and flashy, the resort offers the visitor a depth of character and informality that many of its rival holiday towns have lost. Blackpool has kept abreast of the times, and new and more sophisticated attractions spring up each year; but if the Victorians who created the town in the late 19th century could return they would still find Punch and Judy shows, seafront trams and horse-drawn carriages, elegant Gothic hotels and slender, iron-legged piers.

From its beginnings Blackpool has been the playground of the North. By the 1780s, well-off families from Manchester were arriving for the 'bathing season', and it was not long before day-trippers followed them; most came by carriage, but some even walked 40 miles for a breath of sea air on Sunday. When the railway arrived at Blackpool in 1846 it brought the seaside within easy reach of millions of people in the fast-growing textile towns, and it was the Lancashire cotton workers who shaped Blackpool's personality, making demands for fun that the town was quick to meet. From then on Blackpool's growth was checked only by the Depression of the 1930s and World War II. Many fires in recent years have changed the town's skyline and resulted in the loss of some of Blackpool's finest buildings, including

in 1991 the Art Deco Fun House on the Pleasure Beach, while the Tower Ballroom and North Pier have narrowly missed being entirely consumed by flames. Despite the setbacks, local planners and councillors have always kept faith in the potential and popularity of the resort, and have continued to invest in its future. The number of visitors grew from 3 million at the beginning of the 20th century

TRADITIONAL RIDES, MODERN RIDES *Donkeys (above) have walked the sands of Blackpool since Victorian times and are still hugely popular with children. Visitors looking for more exhilarating thrills can head for the Pleasure Beach where, among many funfair rides, there is the 'Big One' (left), the tallest, fastest roller coaster in the world, opened in 1994.*

RAZZLE-DAZZLE *Blackpool is a riot of lights during autumn nights. The Tower (far left) uses 10 000 light bulbs, and every year new features are added to the displays in the town (left) and on the Golden Mile (above).*

to some 8 million in the 1960s. Today, an estimated 6 million individuals visit the North's favourite holiday town each year, but because many of them return time and again, the total number of visits is more than 16 million a year. And while British weather may disappoint, Blackpool's traditional entertainment remains entirely dependable.

PIER PLEASURES *Central Pier (below) is distinctive for its spectacular big wheel. All three of Blackpool's piers have theatres, bars, and shops selling novelties such as balloons of every shape and size (left).*

STAGED ELEGANCE *The Tower Ballroom (above), with its elaborate plasterwork, painted ceiling and sumptuous gilding, set new standards for places of entertainment when it was opened in 1899. Blackpool excels at live seaside entertainment and has always attracted the top stars, as reflected in its eye-catching publicity posters (top).*

MOUNTAINS OF ROCK *Sticks of brightly coloured, candy-striped Blackpool rock (right) are produced by the ton at several factories in the town, and can be found piled high on the shelves of many shops and stalls all over the resort.*

287

Grassy dunes, and marshes where sea birds throng

The marshes and saltings on the southern side of the Ribble estuary are the home of countless sea birds. Farther south, the holiday resorts of Southport and Formby are fringed by miles of towering sand dunes.

① FRECKLETON

The sprawling village, set back from the narrow thread of the River Ribble, has a small brick church, built in 1837, with box pews and a fine Jacobean pulpit. A footpath leads from the village along the edge of an inlet to marshland that was the site of a battle in the Civil War. Nearby Naze Mount is thought to have been a Roman port. Freckleton is the site of a classical and folk music festival, which is held in December each year.

② PRESTON

The birthplace of Richard Arkwright, the inventor of the spinning frame, Preston was a centre of the cotton trade for much of the 18th and 19th centuries.

The docks have now been redeveloped as Preston Riversway, a marina with shops and leisure facilities, and wild habitats are being nurtured around waters recovering from a century of industrial pollution. A dock trail along the river takes about 2 hours.

Still mainly industrial, Preston has been a market town since Anglo-Saxon times; craft and pottery fairs are sometimes held in the Market Square. The Harris Museum and Art Gallery, an imposing building in the classical style, built in 1893, has changing exhibitions. Avenham and Miller parks include Victorian gardens stretching down to the banks of the Ribble. The County Museum, in the old Sessions House in Stanley Street, explains Lancashire's history and houses the galleries of three local regiments. The museum includes an audiovisual reconstruction of life in a World War I trench.

③ LONGTON BRICKCROFT

A wetland nature reserve occupies the site of a former brickworks, where ponds have been created from flooded claypits. The south pond is part of a recreation area popular for walking and picnics, while the north pond is a wildlife conservation area. Occasional guided walks start from a visitor centre.

④ RIBBLE MARSHES NATIONAL NATURE RESERVE

Stretching along the south bank of the Ribble estuary are the salt marsh, mud flats and sandbanks of the reserve. Thousands of ducks, geese, gulls and terns depend on the varied habitat for feeding and breeding. Each spring and autumn, up to 80 000 waders, including knots, dunlins and oystercatchers, arrive at Ribble Marshes on their way to and from Arctic breeding grounds. One of the best places from which to see the birds is the coast road known as Marine Drive, which skirts an RSPB reserve. To the north, a footpath leads along Banks Marsh embankment. Fortnightly spring tides can cause flooding, making the salt marsh dangerous.

ORNATE PORTAL *A canopy of glass and wrought iron has embellished a Southport shopping arcade since Victorian times.*

GRASS-COVERED DUNES *The tussocks of Formby Dunes are sculpted by the wind but held down by marram grass, which has been widely planted on them since the 18th century.*

HOW DUNES ARE FORMED

Dunes start to form when hardy plants such as sea rocket germinate on the shore, trapping wind-blown sand. Grasses, especially marram grass with its dense network of upright shoots, hold the dunes in place. A new series of dunes often forms to the seaward side of the original dunes, protecting them and allowing them to stabilise.

Regular planting of marram grass helps to conserve dune systems.

---

⑤ SOUTHPORT

Lined by a 7 mile stretch of sand, Southport has been a popular resort since the late 18th century, when a local man, William Sutton, made the first bathing house from local driftwood. There has been a pier there since 1860, and today a train takes holidaymakers from amusement arcades at the landward end to the sun decks and bars nearly a mile away. A Pier Festival is held each July. Stately Victorian buildings form a conservation area around the tree-lined Lord Street shopping centre. The Southport Railway Centre houses steam and diesel locomotives in an old engine shed.

The seafront includes a zoo and a marine lake where sailing, motor and rowing boats, jet skis and water skis can be hired. Victoria Park, to the east of the esplanade, is the site of the Southport Flower Show, held every August. Paths through the park provide access to a nature trail that explores part of the vast area of dunes running south to Crosby. It is possible to walk along the Sefton Coastal Footpath to Hightown, 11 miles away, and return by train.

⑥ AINSDALE SAND DUNES

High rolling dune ridges, valleys and hollows characterise the national nature reserve that lies at the centre of one of Britain's largest dune systems, stretching from Southport to Crosby.

A marked trail traces a circular route through the sands, where display boards describe the local wildlife and landscape. Natterjack toads live in the low hollows, known as slacks, in the dunes. On spring and summer nights the mating calls of the male toads create such a chorus that they have been nicknamed the 'Southport nightingales'. Waders flock to the beach and dune area, and the reserve supports many sand-loving plants, such as dune helleborine, and butterflies.

The 21 mile Sefton Coastal Footpath runs the length of the dunes, from Crossens in the north to Crosby Marine Park in the south. Industrial and urban development has destroyed part of the dunes, which once stretched all the way from the mouth of the Ribble to Liverpool. Repair work started in the late 1970s, and marram grass is still being planted to stabilise the dunes. Flood banks protect the land behind the dunes from tidal surges. Just inland from the reserve, large pine plantations dating from the early 1900s provide habitats for a variety of wildlife, including red squirrels. The Cheshire Lines path follows an old railway track for 10 miles from Ainsdale to Aintree.

⑦ FORMBY

High grassy dunes separate the town of Formby from its beach. From beachside car parks there are splendid walks with views of the ships entering and leaving the Mersey, backed by the distant mountains of north Wales. One of the lanes, Lifeboat Road, takes its name from Britain's first lifeboat station, built at Formby in 1776. The ruins of a later station built in 1809 can be seen on the beach. The sea has been steadily eating at the land south-west of Formby for more than 700 years. In 1730 the 12th-century Formby Chapel had to be abandoned and a new church built inland, where the present town was established at a safe distance from the sea.

In the porch of the 19th-century Church of St Luke is the gravestone of Richard Formby, the 7 ft armour-bearer to Henry IV and Henry V known as 'Richard the Giant'. Members of his family are buried in a group of ivy-covered altar tombs. A cross in the churchyard, which once stood on the village green, is believed to have been used during the Great Plague of 1665, when its hollows were filled with vinegar so that coins could be disinfected.

PLACES TO SEE INLAND

Astley Hall, Chorley, 10 miles S of Preston. Elizabethan house and gardens.

Beacon Fell Country Park, 11 miles N of Preston. Moorland and woodland with footpaths and orienteering course.

British Commercial Vehicle Museum, Leyland, 7 miles S of Preston.

Camelot Theme Park, Chorley, 10 miles S of Preston. Rides, shows.

Martin Mere, 9 miles E of Southport. Wildfowl and Wetlands Centre.

Rufford Old Hall (NT), 11 miles E of Southport. Timber-framed Tudor Hall; garden.

TOURIST INFORMATION

Charnock Richard Service Area (M6 northbound) (01257) 793773; Preston (01772) 253731; Southport (01704) 533333

Resorts and glens on the Isle of Man's east coast

Narrow glens plunge down to the sea on much of the Isle of Man's east coast, but north of Ramsey the coast is flat and low-lying, behind a sweep of dune-backed beach. The self-governing island is 32 miles long.

① BLUE POINT

A narrow turning off the A10 swings down the face of an ancient earthwork in a double hairpin to reach a small car park behind the dunes. A flat beach of sand and some shingle stretches south-westwards for 12 miles, and north-eastwards past Rue Point to the island's northernmost tip, the Point of Ayre.

The 4 mile stretch of coast between Rue Point and Point of Ayre is called The Ayres, from the old Norse meaning a bank of sand or gravel. A visitor centre, with a picnic site, is the starting point for a nature trail that illustrates the geology and natural history of this wild and lonely part of the island.

② POINT OF AYRE

A road from the village of Bride leads after 3 miles to the lighthouse on the point, from which there is a wide view of sea and low-lying land round three-quarters of the horizon, and behind to the frowning bulk of the mountains in the island's interior. The picnic site is a fine vantage point from which to watch ferryboats going to and from Douglas.

③ RAMSEY

The mild climate of Ramsey, and its sheltered position in the centre of the long sweep of Ramsey Bay, allows palm trees to grow on the seafront. Pleasure craft pack the harbour, in the estuary of the Sulby. There are sandy beaches on either side of the river mouth. Fishing from the pier, from the beach or from boats yields cod, flatfish and mackerel.

The Albert Tower on a hill behind the town was built to commemorate the visit of Queen Victoria and Prince Albert in 1847. Ramsey is the northern terminus of the Manx Electric Railway, whose trams run to Douglas.

④ MAUGHOLD HEAD

The pretty little village of Maughold is set back from the clifftops of Maughold Head. There is limited parking space near the entrance to the churchyard, from where a path leads to the top of the headland and the lighthouse. There are good views of the cliffs and coves off the island's eastern coast.

⑤ PORT MOOAR

A narrow lane that leaves the main road half a mile south-west of Maughold plunges down to this deep, funnel-shaped cove in the cliffs, where the waves roll up a beach of smooth pebbles. The high ground behind the cove shelters it from all but south-easterly winds. Cars can be parked on a broad grassy bank just above the beach.

⑥ DHOON GLEN

One of the most spectacular glens on the Isle of Man, Dhoon Glen is formed by a fast-running stream which cuts its way down through the cliffs to the sea at Dhoon Bay. The path to the shore crosses the glen by a series of rustic bridges, passing two steep waterfalls, each of which drops 60 ft or more. For those who find the climb back too steep, there is a less attractive but easier return path on the south side of the glen.

⑦ LAXEY

The compact village has a woollen mill, and a tiny harbour, full of yachts, which dries out at low tide. The short broad

LANDSCAPE CROSS-SECTION *The Isle of Man's scenic diversity is seen at Douglas, which shelters beneath a wooded hillside capped by moors speckled with brilliant yellow gorse.*

CAT WITHOUT A TAIL
A cross between a cat and a hare was once thought to be the origin of the tail-less Manx cat. It is now known, however, that the animal's lack of a tail is due to a genetic mutation, which was deliberately preserved by controlled breeding. The cat enjoys official protection on the Isle of Man, where it is still bred.

The Manx cat is also known as a 'rumpy'.

'Lady Isabella' at Laxey

promenade overlooks a beach of sand and pebbles; swimmers should keep away from the harbour mouth.

One of the Isle of Man's best-known sights is the huge Laxey Wheel, a mighty water wheel, also known as the 'Lady Isabella', which stands in a narrow valley at the top end of the village. The wheel was constructed in 1854 to pump water out of the lead mine workings under Snaefell, the island's highest mountain, and was named after the wife of the lieutenant governor who administered the island at the time. It has a diameter of 72 ft 6 in and a circumference of 217 ft. The wheel still pumps water, and when running at top speed it turns through a complete revolution in 30 seconds. Visitors can follow trails past former mine workings.

On the opposite side of the valley from the wheel, the Snaefell Mountain Railway runs in a long spiral up to the 2036 ft summit of Snaefell. The journey, which takes about half an hour, ends at a spectacular viewpoint.

⑧ GROUDLE GLEN

Paths descend narrow Groudle Glen through groves of beech, larch and pine and past rocky cliffs and rushing rapids. At the bottom is a small stony beach. The Groudle Glen narrow gauge steam railway runs through the glen on summer Sundays and Bank Holidays.

⑨ ONCHAN

The village of Onchan, virtually an extension of Douglas, spreads around the rocky mass of Onchan Head at the northern end of Douglas Bay. Electric trams of the Manx Electric Railway pass through Onchan on their route between Douglas and Ramsey. There are also regular services to Douglas by horse-drawn Victorian trams.

⑩ DOUGLAS

The island's capital and largest town spreads along the 2 mile curve of Douglas Bay, which forms a fine natural harbour. Ferries tie up at the docks at the southern end of the town, under the shelter of Douglas Head. The busy promenade looks out over a beach where sand is exposed at low water. In summer, horse-drawn trams, including a unique double-decker tram, run the length of the promenade; the service began in 1876, and uses about 35 horses.

Near the harbour is the terminus of the Isle of Man Steam Railway, a 3 ft gauge steam-hauled line which in summer runs to Port Erin on the south-west coast of the island. The railway was inaugurated in 1874.

The Manx Museum in Douglas recounts, with the aid of a film, the story of 10 000 years of turbulent Manx history, and has an extensive collection of artefacts covering all aspects of island life. In Nobles Park on the northern side

of the town are the grandstands that mark the start and finish of the annual Tourist Trophy motorcycle race.

⑪ PORT SODERICK

A turning off the A25 leads to an east-facing shingle beach. From the car park, walkers can follow a path for 1½ miles along Port Soderick Glen, where a small stream flows between grassy slopes.

PLACES TO SEE INLAND

Ballalheannagh Gardens, 2 miles SW of Laxey. Trees and shrubs, rocky valleys and ravines, section in oriental style.

Murray's Motorcycle Museum, Snaefell, 7 miles NW of Laxey. Motorcycles from 1902 to 1961, and memorabilia.

TOURIST INFORMATION

Douglas (01624) 686766

Harbour towns around the ancient Manx capital

Exposed to the Atlantic weather, the western side of the Isle of Man is wilder than the eastern half. Near Peel, itself dating back to pre-Viking times, is the meeting place of Tynwald, the island's ancient parliament.

① BALLAUGH

Ballaugh Bridge is a favourite viewpoint for spectators on the northern part of the Tourist Trophy motorcycle course. About 1½ miles to the north is a hamlet called The Cronk, whose Church of St Mary de Ballaugh dates back to before the 13th century. From The Cronk a winding lane leads to a small car park on the edge of miles of sandy beach and lonely dunes.

At the Curraghs Wildlife Park, about a mile east of Ballaugh, visitors can see tailless Manx cats and the multi-horned Manx sheep known as loaghtan, as well as monkeys, sea lions and otters.

② GLEN MOOAR

A narrow lane off the coast road, nearly a mile south-west of Kirk Michael, leads to a small car park in Glen Mooar. The beach at the seaward end of the glen is the southern limit of a long stretch of sandy cliffs that gives way to sand dunes beyond Jurby Head, several miles to the north. A lane on the opposite side of the coast road leads to the waterfall of *Spooyt Vane*, or 'White Spout', above Glen Mooar.

Cooildarry, a deep wooded valley just south of Kirk Michael, is a nature reserve with a variety of woodland habitats. Wood warblers are among the birds that can be seen there.

③ PEEL

An old fishing harbour, with narrow, winding streets, is dominated by the massive fortress of Peel Castle on St Patrick's Isle; the 'isle' is in fact linked to the mainland, forming a protective arm at the western end of the harbour. The castle's main walls date from the 14th century; within are a huge round tower and a ruined 13th-century cathedral.

On the eastern side of the harbour a promenade overlooks a sandy beach. There is good fishing for mackerel at the entrance to the harbour, and for mullet, skate, pollack, conger eel and flatfish from the breakwater beyond the castle. Manx kippers, cured over fires of oak woodchips, are produced in the town.

Tynwald Hill, 3 miles south-east of Peel at St John's, was the traditional meeting place of Tynwald, the island's parliament, which

has its origins in Viking times. Tynwald still meets there on July 5 each year, to hear details of the year's new Acts read in Manx and English by the island's two 'deemsters', or high court judges.

④ GLEN MAYE

The coast road running south from Peel leads into the steep, narrow valley of Glen Maye. In front of the Waterfall Hotel there is a large car park, from where a path winds down the glen past a magnificent waterfall, and follows the course of a stream that reaches a pebbly beach through steep cliffs. A footpath from the glen's lower end heads south along the coast over Contrary Head and on to Peel, 3 miles away, with superb views all the way.

⑤ NIARBYL BAY

A minor road from the village of Dalby reaches the sea at a small parking area by a group of cottages. A path climbs round the cliff face to the south, above Niarbyl Bay, eventually reaching a lane at the top of the slope. This lane rejoins the main road 3 miles farther south, near the summit of Cronk ny Arrey Laa.

⑥ FLESHWICK BAY
The road to Fleshwick Bay ends at a grassy slope overlooking a beach of shingle amid clusters of rocks. The bay faces northwards towards the cliffs which line the coast all the way to Peel.

⑦ PORT ERIN
Sheltered by the high cliffs of two headlands, the small resort of Port Erin is the western terminus of the Isle of Man Steam Railway, which runs round the southern end of the island to Douglas. Port Erin's Railway Museum includes the first and last engines to enter service on the line. The town also has a variety of seaside amusements.

A footpath round Bradda Head gives a panoramic view of Port Erin, and there are magnificent views out to sea from Milner's Tower, a monument built by a local locksmith in 1884 in the shape of a key. The path skirts the edge of Bradda Hill to the north, and eventually rejoins the road to Fleshwick Bay.

⑧ CALF OF MAN
The car park at the Isle of Man's southwestern tip overlooks the treacherous, rock-strewn passage of Calf Sound. To the south is the massive cliff of Spanish Head; straight ahead are the islets of

HARBOUR FORTRESS *Castle Rushen, at Castletown, stands on the site of a Viking stronghold, overlooking the mouth of the Silver Burn and defending Castletown Bay.*

Kitterland, and behind them is the uninhabited island known as Calf of Man. The island is a nature reserve supporting large colonies of guillemots, razorbills, kittiwakes and puffins; there are also smaller groups of hooded crows and choughs. In settled weather, there are boat trips to the island from Port Erin or Port St Mary.

⑨ CREGNEASH
The open air Cregneash Village Folk Museum recalls the old Manx way of life. From the car park, visitors walk to a group of old thatched cottages which include a smithy, a weaving shed and a turner's workshop with an old treadle lathe. Harry Kelly's Cottage is an old crofter's home, built more than 150 years ago and named after a Manx-speaking crofter. Demonstrations of wool spinning and smithying are given regularly in summer.

⑩ PORT ST MARY
Standing back-to-back with Port Erin, Port St Mary shelters between the twin headlands of Kallow Point and Gansey Point. Once a fishing village, it is now popular with yacht owners because of

MANX COTTAGES *At Cregneash Village Folk Museum, homes of crofters and fishermen evoke life in the 19th century.*

the deep-water moorings close inshore. Chapel Bay, and the wider sweep of Bay ny Carrickey, on the other side of Gansey Point, have sandy beaches.

Paths lead westwards to the spectacular cliff scenery of The Chasms and Spanish Head, and eastwards to Black Rocks. There is good sea fishing from boats off The Carrick, a rock in the bay.

⑪ CASTLETOWN
The town's narrow twisting streets seem to huddle for protection round the medieval fortress of Castle Rushen. Castletown was the island's capital until 1874, and a building now occupied by the local authority councillors was used for meetings of the House of Keys, the elected lower house of Tynwald, the Isle of Man parliament.

On the edge of Castletown's inner harbour is the Nautical Museum, which includes a sailmaker's workshop and model ships ranging from mid 18th-century sailing craft to modern diesel vessels. Among the exhibits is *Peggy,* last in a line of clippers made in the Isle of Man in the 17th and 18th centuries.

To the south of Castletown is the Scarlett Visitor Centre, where there are displays of the island's plants and animals, and a nature trail that follows part of the coastline.

⑫ DERBY HAVEN
A curving sandy bay, Derby Haven is separated from the larger Castletown Bay by the rocky headland of Langness. There are fine views of the island's coastal scenery from Dreswick Point lighthouse, at the southern end of Langness, and from the old fort on St Michael's Island, at the north-eastern tip of the headland. There is good sea fishing from boats off Langness.

THRILLS ON TWO WHEELS
Early in June, 38 miles of Isle of Man roads are closed to ordinary traffic for the annual Tourist Trophy motorcycle races. The gruelling course, which starts and finishes at Douglas, includes such testing hazards as the hump-backed Ballaugh Bridge, a sharp hairpin bend at Ramsey, and the road over Snaefell, which twists up to 1400 ft.

Tension rises as leading Tourist Trophy contenders negotiate the Gooseneck bend at high speed.

Shipping and industry on the shores of the Mersey

Port activity on the River Mersey has shifted downstream from the old docks of Liverpool to the container terminal at Seaforth, enabling the vast warehouses to be transformed into a stimulating heritage area.

① CROSBY

Now a suburb of Liverpool, Crosby was developed in the 18th and 19th centuries by wealthy local merchants who built the town's impressive Regency crescents and terraces. About a mile inland is the original hamlet of Little Crosby with its 17th-century cottages and the Georgian Crosby Hall, now used as an occasional venue for musical and theatrical performances.

An expanse of open grassland by the southern end of the sandy beach contains Crosby Marine Park, where beginners can learn to sail in the lake. Strong currents and the proximity of shipping lanes make swimming in the Crosby Channel hazardous.

North of the town is a large area of dunes, which have been cleared of their World War II fortifications. Parts of the dunes are a Ministry of Defence rifle range, and there is no public access north of the River Alt.

② SEAFORTH

The vast Royal Seaforth Container Terminal at the mouth of the estuary has taken over from the Liverpool docks as the focus for most of the Mersey's shipping. To the north of the busy docks area, by Crosby Marine Park, two lagoons form the centrepiece of a nature reserve where there are roosting colonies of cormorants and Arctic terns. Kittiwakes and Mediterranean gulls may also be seen.

③ BOOTLE

Bootle's huge, grey granite docks, built in the early part of the 19th century, are now used more by ship-breakers than for international trade.

The towpath of the Leeds and Liverpool Canal can be followed northwards for 7 miles as far as Aintree race course, and south for 2 miles to the locks of Liverpool's Stanley Dock. The four locks were built in the early 19th century by Jesse Hartley, who also built Liverpool's Albert Dock.

④ LIVERPOOL

When the silting up of the Dee in the early 18th century cut off the thriving port of Chester, Liverpool began to grow into one of the most important ports in the world. Between 1830 and 1930, 9 million emigrants from all over Europe began their voyage to America from Pier Head, and by the end of the 19th century some 40 per cent of the world's trade was carried in Liverpool ships. With the shift to containerisation and bulk-carriers, port activity moved north to the more modern docks at Bootle and Seaforth, and Liverpool's

Albert Dock was closed in 1972. Albert Dock is now a heritage area, and its huge Victorian warehouses include attractions such as the Tate Gallery Liverpool, a museum of 20th-century art, and the Beatles Story. The National Museum of HM Customs and Excise has a section on the trade in endangered animal species. The Maritime Museum, which features exhibitions on emigration and a gallery devoted to Liverpool's role in the Battle of the Atlantic during World War II, also has tall ships moored at the quayside.

The huge Royal Liver Building at Pier Head, built in 1908 by the Royal Liver Assurance Company, measures 322 ft from the ground to the top of the two statues of the fictitious Liver Birds. Its ground floor was once a shipping

BEATLEMANIA
Liverpool's Beatles Story features a reconstruction of The Cavern, the club credited with putting the band on the pop map in the 1960s.

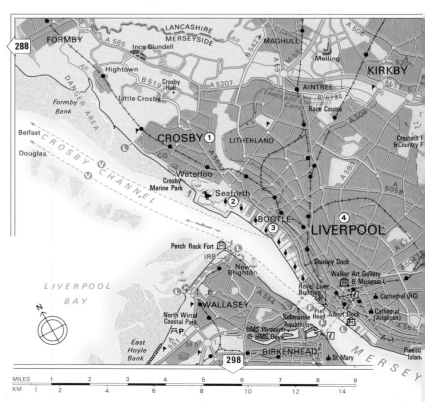

hall serving the major passenger liners. Part of it is open for visits, and there are tours to the top of the tower.

In the city centre are the Walker Art Gallery, with its collection of European art from the 14th century to the present day, and the Liverpool Museum, which includes a natural history centre and planetarium. Nearby is the 19th-century neo-classical building of St George's Hall, a former concert hall and Crown Court now housing temporary exhibitions and concerts. South of the city centre are two cathedrals. Liverpool's Anglican cathedral, the largest in Britain, took more than 70 years to build and was completed in 1978. Superb views of the city can be had from the top of the cathedral tower, which can be reached by means of two lifts, followed by a climb of more than a hundred steps. The Metropolitan Cathedral of Christ the King, a Roman Catholic cathedral completed in 1967, is remarkable for its circular design.

Two road tunnels and a train tunnel under the Mersey serve the many commuters who live across the water on the Wirral. There are also frequent ferry services, as well as longer cruises along the riverfront, and trips to the Isle of Man.

TUDOR ARTISTRY *Speke Hall, set in extensive gardens and woodland, is a superb example of the South Lancashire and Cheshire style of the 'black and white' timber-framed house.*

⑤ OTTERSPOOL

To the south of Liverpool, a 3 mile riverside promenade gives wide views across the Mersey to the Wirral shore. The large indoor amusement park of Pleasure Island has a laser-game area, a roller-skating rink, a bowling alley and a science centre with 'hands-on' exhibits. Inland are Sefton Park with its boating lake and Victorian palm house, and Sudley, a Victorian shipowner's home which contains paintings and furniture from the 18th and 19th centuries. Liverpool's Botanic Gardens, about a mile to the north-east, include a museum of Victorian artefacts.

⑥ SPEKE HALL

Construction of the intricately decorated, half-timbered Speke Hall (NT) began in 1490, but much of what is seen today dates from refurbishment in Victorian times. The Tudor Great Hall remains, and many panelled rooms contain furnishings and wallpaper designed by the 19th-century craftsman, poet and painter William Morris. In the courtyard are two ancient yew trees known as Adam and Eve.

⑦ HALE

At the centre of a great paw of land jutting out into the Mersey is a quiet village of whitewashed cottages and country gardens. In the 17th century, Hale was the home of John Middleton, better known as 'the Childe of Hale'. It is claimed that he grew to 9ft 3in, and that he won a contest with James I's champion wrestler. He is buried in St Mary's churchyard.

A lane leads south from the village to a stretch of mud flats and rocky sand. A lighthouse at the tip of the promontory is now part of a private riverside residence. About a mile north-east of Hale, a former waste tip has been reclaimed and the area has been transformed into the Pickerings Pasture Nature Reserve. Riverside and meadow walks explore the reserve, and there is a hide from which to watch the birds of nearby Hale Marshes, closed to the public.

To the north-west of Hale is the Halewood Country Park, where miles of walking and cycling routes have been developed along a disused railway track.

CATHEDRAL VISTA *Between the restored warehouses of Liverpool's Albert Dock, which was opened in 1846, appears the soaring 331ft sandstone tower of the Anglican Cathedral.*

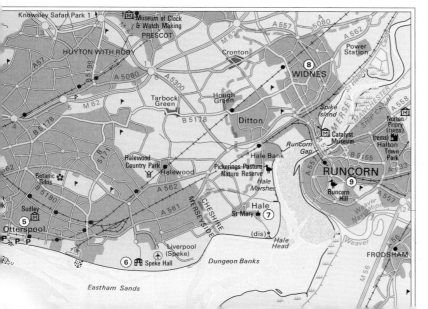

BIRDS' EYE VIEW *The ferry plying between Liverpool and Birkenhead provides spectacular views of the Merseyside skyline. Copper statues of the Liver Birds perch on the towers of the Royal Liver Building. It is said that the birds were the bungled creation in 1655 of the designer of Liverpool's corporate seal, which was supposed to show an eagle.*

⑧ WIDNES

Rail and road bridges now link Widnes and Runcorn at Runcorn Gap, where for centuries there was a ferry crossing. The two towns played an important role in the region sometimes referred to as the cradle of the British chemical industry. In 1845 a complex incorporating a railway, canals and docks was established in the area known as Spike Island, a strip of land separated from Widnes by the St Helens Canal, to develop soap and soda-ash works. The 'island' takes it name from the lodgings, known as spikes, built to accommodate the workforce. Until it fell into disuse in the early 20th century, Spike Island was busy with industrial activity, its canal and docks filled with cargo vessels. Now the works have been replaced by meadows and woodland, and paths follow the old railway lines. Birds of prey, including hen harriers and short-eared owls, hunt over the marshes to the east, and migrating birds such as teals visit in winter. A visitor centre explains the history and wildlife of the area. The nearby Catalyst Museum, which has an exterior glass lift offering views of Spike Island, explores the region's industrial heritage.

⑨ RUNCORN

Runcorn was once a resort which attracted daytrippers from Liverpool. Then the soap and chemical industries were established and, in the late 19th century, thousands of people arrived to work on the Manchester Ship Canal. Today, Runcorn is best known for its chemical works, which at night light up like a space-age city.

In the sandstone outcrops of the former quarry on Runcorn Hill, to the south of the town, fossilised dinosaur footprints were found in 1848. The area is now a nature reserve with a 'quarry trail', and a visitor centre containing an indoor hide for watching wildlife such as great spotted woodpeckers.

To the east of Runcorn, Town Park is the start of a 2 mile circular walk which takes in the remains of a 12th-century castle at Halton. Nearby are the ruins and gardens of Norton Priory, where a museum traces the development of the medieval priory into a Tudor manor house and then a Georgian mansion.

PLACES TO SEE INLAND

Croxteth Hall and Country Park, 4 miles NE of Liverpool. Edwardian country house, park, gardens and farm.

Knowsley Safari Park, 7 miles NE of Liverpool. Includes tigers, elephants, lions and camels; sea lion show.

Prescot Museum of Clock and Watch Making, 8 miles E of Liverpool. History of timekeeping.

TOURIST INFORMATION

Liverpool (0151) 708 8838

Victorian playgrounds by the Wirral's green fields

The Wirral peninsula, sandwiched between the estuaries of the Dee and the Mersey, is a patchwork of coastal grassland and wide sands which fostered Victorian resorts. 'Arcadia' is recaptured at Port Sunlight.

① THURSTASTON

North of the hamlet of Thurstaston, an area of woods, heath and parkland makes up Thurstaston Common (NT). Paths through the common take in a red sandstone outcrop known as Thor's Stone, from which there are wide views across the Dee to North Wales.

South-west of the village is the Thurstaston visitor centre, with information on the Wirral Country Park, which runs for 12 miles along a disused railway line from West Kirby to Hooton. Wading birds visit the shores of the park in winter, and dunlin and oystercatchers in autumn and spring. In summer there are cruises to observe the seals and sea birds at the mouth of the Dee estuary.

② WEST KIRBY

A large marine lake, stretching the length of the mile-long promenade, offers water-skiing, windsurfing and sailing. Lessons are available, and with a licence, obtainable from the office at the entrance to the lake, visitors can sail their own craft. Walking on the sands can be dangerous, because of the speed of the incoming tide. Walkers and lake users are asked to avoid disturbing the birds of Hilbre Island Nature Reserve.

③ HILBRE ISLAND

Hilbre is the largest of three small sandstone islands at the mouth of the Dee estuary, one of the most important sites in Europe for wintering wildfowl and waders. The island was used as an outpost by the Romans; Benedictine monks built a monastic cell there in the 12th century; and a signalling station was established in the 19th century. Hilbre Island Bird Observatory was formed in 1957, and the islands are now a nature reserve. The mud flats, marshes and sandbanks provide feeding grounds, while the high ground is used for roosting. Basking seals can often be seen.

Permits are needed to visit the reserve; these are obtainable from Thurstaston visitor centre and from an enquiry desk near the waterfront at West Kirby. It is an hour's walk from West Kirby to the islands, which are cut off by the tide for 3 hours either side of high water.

④ HOYLAKE

The Royal Liverpool Golf Links is Hoylake's main attraction, but a close second is its beach. From the 18th century, shifting sands filled the lake from which the small town takes its name, creating a broad sandbank which at low tide extends some 2 miles north from the promenade. At high water, deep channels and pools can be hazardous for swimmers. Fishing boats operate in good weather, some landing and selling their catch on the promenade.

⑤ LEASOWE

The village lies on the edge of the North Wirral Coastal Park, 4 miles of dunes and grassland between Hoylake and the New Brighton coastal defences. The most impressive dunes are found by the Gunsite picnic area to the east of the park. To the west is a 100ft brick lighthouse, built in the 18th century and now disused. It is open to visitors on two Sundays each month.

⑥ NEW BRIGHTON

The ferry from Liverpool brought thousands of Victorian daytrippers to New Brighton, and with the construction in 1898 of the 621ft New Brighton Tower, then the tallest structure in Britain, the town's future looked set.

However, the tower fell into neglect during World War I and was demolished in 1921, and the pier used by the ferries was closed some time later. The sands were scoured away by changes in currents caused by the building of the docks at Seaforth, on the opposite bank of the Mersey. The town still offers a range of seaside attractions such as a boating lake, and new breakwaters to

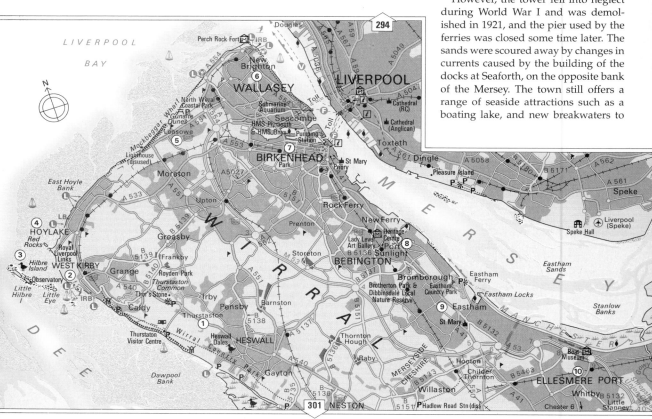

the north have encouraged the build-up of sand. At the mouth of the Mersey, a causeway leads to privately owned Perch Rock Fort, built in the 19th century. The fort's small museum, containing World War II aircraft wreckage, is open on occasional Sundays.

⑦ BIRKENHEAD

The first settlement on the site was attached to an ancient priory, and it was the monks who in the 12th century established a ferry to Liverpool. Birkenhead grew with the advent of a steam ferry service in the early 1800s, after which Liverpool merchants developed shipyards and docks, and built houses inland. The old Town Hall is being converted into a local history museum.

Most shipping activity has moved to Seaforth, north of Liverpool, but Birkenhead's industrial heritage is celebrated in a town trail starting at the

SUNLIGHT SOAP
By Appointment   soapmakers   to H.M. the King

VICTORIAN VISION *Birkenhead's old Town Hall was built in the 1880s by the shipbuilders William and John Laird.*

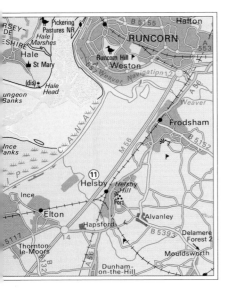

ferry terminus. The trail takes in a pumping station housing a large Victorian steam engine used to prevent flooding of the Mersey rail tunnel, and the 12th-century priory. The nearby Church of St Mary offers dramatic views of Liverpool and the Wirral from the top of its tower, reached by a climb of more than a hundred steps.

In the docks to the north of town, visitors can explore the frigate HMS *Plymouth* and the submarine HMS *Onyx*, both of which took part in the Falklands campaign. At nearby Seacombe, shark tanks are a feature of the Submarine Aquarium.

⑧ PORT SUNLIGHT

A splendid example of enlightened 19th-century town planning, Port Sunlight was created by soap magnate and philanthropist William Hesketh Lever, later Lord Leverhulme. His aim was to provide for his workforce 'a new Arcadia, ventilated and drained on the most scientific principles'. The village is now a conservation area; its heritage centre displays original building plans and offers details of a village trail. The nearby Lady Lever Art Gallery was built by Lord Leverhulme to display his collection of pre-Raphaelite paintings and Wedgwood china.

⑨ EASTHAM

East of the village is a small docks and oil storage depot area, but to the north is the Eastham Country Park, incorporating land that was once a Victorian

A VISION OF CLEANLINESS Port Sunlight, William Lever's soap factory and model village, was named after his Sunlight soap.

pleasure garden. A bear pit can still be seen in the woods. West of the park, in the ancient woodland of Brotherton Park and Dibbinsdale Nature Reserve, water voles and kingfishers can often be seen from the riverside path.

⑩ ELLESMERE PORT

The now little-used port stands at the junction of the Shropshire Union Canal and the Manchester Ship Canal, at the centre of an industrial area. In old warehouses by a disused dock basin is the Boat Museum, with the world's largest collection of traditional canal boats.

⑪ HELSBY

The sandstone outcrop of Helsby Hill (NT) is topped by an Iron Age hill-fort. Paths lead to the 462 ft summit, where there are sweeping views of the flatlands bordering the Mersey, and of the nearby refineries and chemical works. There is limited roadside parking.

PLACES TO SEE INLAND

Chester. Riverside cathedral city, with part-Roman, part-medieval walls, Cheshire Military Museum, Grosvenor local history museum, zoo.

Delamere Forest Park, 5 miles SE of Helsby. Visitor centre, waymarked paths and cycle trails.

TOURIST INFORMATION

Birkenhead (0151) 647 6780; Chester (01244) 318356

CANAL DAYS

The brightly painted canal boats of Ellesmere Port's Boat Museum lie at rest in waterside warehouses, set around a port built in the 1830s by Thomas Telford. The buildings also contain old pumping engines and a restored boat-builders' workshop. Visitors can take a trip on the canal in a narrow boat.

The Friendship *carried coal and timber between 1925 and 1959.*

Beach resorts near the mud flats of the Dee estuary

The holiday coast of north Wales comes to an end by Point of Ayr, at the entrance to the Dee estuary. Access to the shore is restricted along the estuary, where mud banks and marshes are home to countless birds.

A VIKING MEMORY *On the Point of Ayr, named after the Norse word for shingle, stands the disused Talacre Lighthouse.*

① RHYL

Pleasure craft and a scattering of fishing boats moor at Foryd Harbour, the oldest part of the busy holiday resort. A wide range of attractions lines Rhyl's 3 miles of sand, from a marine boating lake and the Ocean Beach amusement park to the west, to a Sea Life Centre and an indoor swimming centre with surfing pool half-way along the promenade. Nearby is a local history museum and an arts centre. Strong currents by the mouth of the River Clwyd, at the western end of the beach, make swimming dangerous there.

The slender 240 ft Skytower on the waterfront offers sweeping views down the coast and inland towards the distant hills of Snowdonia, and the promenade and sea wall provide a 5 mile walk eastwards to Prestatyn.

② PRESTATYN

Rhyl's quieter neighbour relies for its popularity on its three sandy beaches. At Ffrith Beach, to the west, steep dunes overlook the low stone sea wall and the groynes which help to stabilise the broad sweep of sand. Inland, at Festival Gardens, are an indoor bowling green and other amusements. At Central Beach is an indoor swimming pool complex with restaurants and bars. Barkby Beach, to the east, is dominated by a large holiday camp.

Prestatyn marks the northern end of the 168 mile Offa's Dyke Path, which heads south to Chepstow on the Severn estuary. The path follows in part the great bank and ditch built as a boundary between England and Wales by Offa, King of Mercia in the 8th century. Information on the path is available from the Offa's Dyke Interpretative Centre in Prestatyn. Other walks in the surrounding hills include one to Gop Hill, about 3 miles inland, where there is a large Bronze Age cairn.

③ TALACRE

The area around Talacre is dominated by holiday camps and caravan parks, but out towards the Point of Ayr is a lonely area of salt marshes, with wide views across the broad Dee estuary to the Wirral. A footpath along the top of the sea wall leads south towards the

last working coal mine in North Wales. The excavations stretch far out under the estuary, and a new industrial process is being developed there to liquefy the coal and convert it into oil.

To the south-east, the coast all the way to Flint is lined by large industrial units, and high sea walls separate the shore from inland areas.

④ HOLYWELL

The name of the small inland town is derived from St Winefride and her well. According to legend, a local chieftain cut off the 7th-century saint's head after she had spurned his advances, and where her blood fell a well sprang up which developed a reputation for healing properties. St Beuno, Winefride's uncle, cursed the murderer, who was swallowed up by the earth, and miraculously brought his niece back to life.

The well is just north of the town, in the Greenfield Valley Heritage Park; it is in the ornate 15th-century St Winefride's Chapel, the second chapel to have been built on the site. At the northern end of the park, near the coast, are the ruins of Basingwerk Abbey, thought to have been founded in 1132 by the Savigny order of monks but transferred to the Cistercians soon afterwards. In the 15th century, guests attracted by Winefride's shrine were so numerous that there were two sittings at meal times. Between these two ecclesiastical sites is an area which once resounded to the hammers and wheels of industry. There are remains of old copper works and of a cotton mill, a farming museum and a visitor centre.

KING'S LODGINGS *Holywell's Basingwerk Abbey was Edward I's base while Flint Castle was being built, in the 13th century.*

⑤ FLINT

Tower blocks now dwarf the castle, begun in 1277, that once formed the centrepiece of the town. Flint Castle was the first of the string of fortifications designed by Edward I to subdue and hold Wales. The castle is in ruins, but the great keep with its circular gallery is still an impressive feature.

⑥ CONNAH'S QUAY

The silting of the River Dee over the centuries resulted in port facilities being moved ever closer to the sea. The river was converted to a canal in the 18th century and a port was founded at Connah's Quay, but nothing stemmed the inexorable march of the sands, and these docks also fell into disuse.

To the south is Wepre Country Park, containing the ruins of ancient Ewloe Castle (Cadw), built by Welsh princes and extended in the 13th century by Llywelyn ap Gruffudd. To the east, a ruined Norman fortress stands near 18th-century Hawarden Castle. For many years the home of the Victorian prime minister

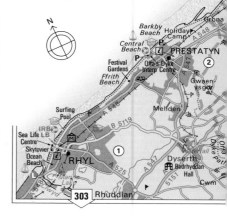

the estuary. To the south are Ness Gardens, which have a large collection of heathers and willows, as well as conservatories housing exotic plants.

⑩ PARKGATE
The sea has left the former seaside town stranded, and the promenade and harbour wall now look out over a large stretch of salt marsh. Parkgate was once one of the main departure points for Ireland, and 18th-century houses along the waterfront are reminders of the days when it was a fashionable resort.

In the marshes and mud flats west of Parkgate is the Gayton Sands RSPB Reserve, where large flocks of wintering waders include pintails and bar-tailed godwits. Peregrines, merlins and hen harriers hunt along the foreshore. There is a good viewpoint by a car park to the north of Parkgate, where the B5135 bends east towards the A540.

⑪ HESWALL
To the west of the large town, a number of little streets run right down to the shore, offering views out across the sands and mud flats of Dawpool Bank. The Wirral Country Park provides an attractive coastal walk to the resort of West Kirby, 6 miles to the north.

William Gladstone, the castle is still the Gladstone family seat and not open to visitors. Gladstone founded St Deiniol's library, in Hawarden village, in 1896 and endowed it with his books and papers.

⑦ QUEENSFERRY
Until 1897, when the first bridge was built there, Queensferry was the last ferry crossing on the Dee before the river widened into its estuary. The modern town has a large leisure centre which includes an ice-skating rink.

⑧ BURTON
A port in medieval times and now set well inland as a result of silting, Burton is an attractive village with a mixture of black and white timber-framed houses

and sandstone cottages. The Church of St Nicholas, which was largely rebuilt in 1721, features a single-handed working clock on its western tower.

⑨ NESTON
From the small town, a path skirting the edge of the flats and marshland to the south offers wide views over the Dee estuary to the hills of North Wales. East of Neston, the Wirral Country Park follows a disused railway line, offering footpaths and bridleways through tranquil farmland. The former Hadlow Road station has been preserved much as it was when the last train operated in 1956. The line ran 12 miles north-west from Hooton to West Kirby, and the park continues north of Heston along

PLACES TO SEE INLAND

Dyserth, 2 miles S of Prestatyn. Bodrhyddan Hall, 17th-century manor house and gardens; Dyserth waterfall, once a pilgrimage centre.

Loggerheads Country Park, Cadole, 9 miles S of Flint. Woodland walks, nature trails, limestone crags and water mill. Nearby is 1820ft Moel Famau, the highest of the Clwydian Range.

TOURIST INFORMATION

Birkenhead (0151) 6476780; Ewloe (01244) 541597; Prestatyn (01745) 854365 (summer); Rhyl (01745) 355068/344515

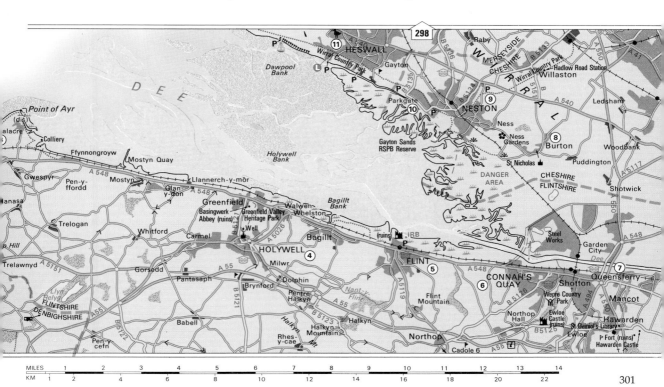

Castles, hills and long beaches in North Wales

West of the holiday coast around Colwyn Bay, ancient copper mines dot the summit of Great Ormes Head. Conwy's proud, gaunt castle and the spectacular mountains of Snowdonia provide a dramatic backdrop.

① PENMAENMAWR

The little resort is squeezed into a gap between the mountains and the sea. The coast road dives through tunnels at either side of the town, while a relief road swings right across the end of the promenade on tall concrete legs. When Robert Stephenson built the railway line along this stretch of coast in the mid 19th century he had to protect it with avalanche shelters and a strong sea wall; a later sea wall lines the promenade along the pebbly beach.

The tall hills south of the town have been worked for their granite since prehistoric times, and an industrial trail leads to the site of a Stone Age axe factory. Nearby is the impressive Maenie Hirion Bronze Age stone circle, also known as the Druid's Circle.

② CONWY

Between 1283 and 1289, around 1500 craftsmen constructed a massive castle for Edward I, with a barbican at either end and eight tall towers. The town and garrison that grew up next to Conwy Castle (Cadw) were enclosed by almost a mile of immense walls. The castle and its walls remain extremely well preserved, making Conwy one of the finest medieval fortified towns in Europe.

There is a good view from the ramparts down to the crowded streets below and out over the Conwy estuary.

A wealth of old buildings within the walls includes 14th-century timber-framed Aberconwy House (NT) and 16th-century Plas Mawr (Cadw), distinctive for its ornate plaster work. On the quayside, overlooking a collection of fishing boats, is what is said to be the smallest house in Britain, with a frontage just 8 ft 4 in in height and 6 ft across. Pleasure cruises and sea-fishing trips leave from the quay.

Four crossings link the two banks of the river: Thomas Telford's 1820s suspension bridge, now used by pedestrians only; a tubular rail bridge designed by Robert Stephenson in the 1840s; a road bridge; and a road tunnel carrying the Conwy bypass. North of the town is a marina with a residential development, and the wide sands of Morfa Beach. On the north bank of the Conwy estuary at Llandudno Junction is an RSPB reserve; access is from the A55.

③ DEGANWY

A fortress crowned the hill above the estuary at Deganwy 600 years before Conwy Castle was built on the opposite bank. To save it falling into English hands, the Welsh prince Llywelyn ap Gruffudd had it destroyed in 1260, as part of his campaign against Edward I. The castle was fought over, destroyed and rebuilt over the centuries, and the ruins still loom over the town. Towards the end of the 19th century, Deganwy developed as a slate-shipping port, but the town is now a small seaside resort. It faces south-west, ensuring maximum sunshine as well as protection from the winds. Strong estuary currents can make swimming from the shingle beach hazardous.

④ GREAT ORMES HEAD

The headland which stands at the western end of Llandudno Bay rises as a great rocky pile to a 679 ft summit. Those wanting to reach the top without walking have three alternatives: to go by car along the Marine Drive toll road; to take the cable car; or to use Britain's last cable-hauled street tramway, which was opened in 1902.

Copper was mined at Great Ormes Head in the 18th and 19th centuries, but recent excavations have uncovered mines that were first worked around 1800 BC, during the Bronze Age. The tramway stops at the mines, where visitors can explore the old workings.

At the summit is a country park with a visitor centre offering tremendous views over Snowdonia to the south and,

---

TINY WINGS ON A HEADLAND
Along the cliffs of Great Ormes Head flits the dwarf grayling, a sub-species of the grayling that is found only in this part of north Wales. It is smaller than other graylings, with a wingspan up to 1½ in. It is also duller in colour and flies late in June, a little earlier than most English graylings.

Dwarf grayling   Wing underside
Hipparchia semele thyone

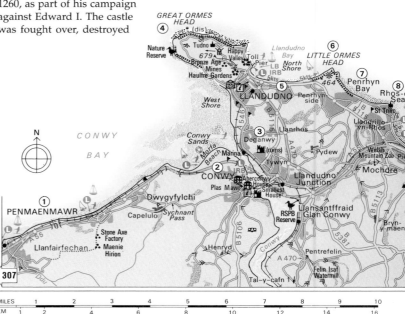

TIGHT QUARTERS *Conwy's smallest house has only two rooms – distinctly cramped for a former occupant, who was 6 ft 3 in tall.*

Lewis Carroll is remembered as the creator of such immortal characters as the griffon and the mock turtle.

DOMINATING WALLS *Taking its shape from the rock on which it is built, Conwy Castle was part of Edward I's 'iron ring' of fortresses designed to control Wales.*

on clear days, to the mountains of Cumbria some 60 miles to the north. On the sheltered eastern slopes are the public gardens of Haulfre, from where there are good views of the sands of both Llandudno and West Shore, and of Happy Valley, with its artificial ski slope and toboggan run. On the exposed northern face is the little 7th-century church and well of St Tudno, after whom the town of Llandudno was named. The strip of land and rock around the base of the headland is a local nature reserve.

⑤ LLANDUDNO

The bustling resort is a child of the railway age. In 1850 the population was around 1000, but by the time the branch line opened in 1858 a new town was being developed with wide streets, large houses and a promenade along the North Shore. The completion of the pier with its ornate pavilions brought still more visitors by paddle steamer.

Llandudno has never lost its elegance, and today's pavement cafés give it an almost Continental air. Its major attractions remain the beaches, offering such traditional amusements as donkey rides and Punch and Judy shows. West Shore's sand and shingle beach faces south over Conwy Bay. The sea recedes a long way at low tide and walkers should take care not to be trapped when the tide turns. North Shore is a 2 mile crescent of sand stretching eastwards from the pier to Little Ormes Head. There are boat trips round Great Ormes Head and fishing trips from the North Shore promenade jetty.

Llandudno's local history museum covers the area's history from the Bronze Age to Roman times. The Alice in Wonderland Visitor Centre explains the town's connection with the writer Lewis Carroll.

⑥ LITTLE ORMES HEAD

Unlike visitors to Great Ormes Head, those who want to reach the top of the 464 ft headland marking the eastern end of Llandudno Bay have no option but to use their feet. They will be rewarded with peace, solitude and superb views. Several paths climb to the summit, most of them starting on the Penryhn Bay side of the headland.

CREATOR OF A WONDERLAND
An association between Llandudno and the works of writer Lewis Carroll is commemorated by a statue on the town's West Shore, depicting the White Rabbit from *Alice's Adventures in Wonderland*. Lewis Carroll – the Rev. Charles Dodgson – was a friend of Henry Liddell, an Oxford dean, and records in his diary telling stories to the dean's daughter on a punt on the Isis. Young Alice spent many summers in the 1860s in the Liddells' holiday home in Llandudno, but it is unlikely that Carroll visited them there.

⑦ PENRYHN BAY

A shingle beach with rock pools to explore is backed by rows of seaside villas, most of them dating from the 1930s. There are impressive sea defences, consisting of immense boulders.

⑧ RHOS-ON-SEA

The resort stands at the western, more peaceful, end of the great sweep of Colwyn Bay. At the western end of the promenade is a tiny chapel, just 12 ft by 6 ft, built in the 16th century and dedicated to 6th-century St Trillo. The chapel stands in the grounds of an ancient monastery, whose monks constructed a fish trap on the sands; this consisted of a rough triangle of stone walls in which fish were caught as the tide went out, as if in a giant rock pool. The remains of the large trap can be seen at low tide.

This is a popular area for watersports and sailing, and family amusements include a puppet theatre.

⑨ COLWYN BAY

Three miles of sand backed by a promenade stretch from Rhos-on-Sea to the town of Old Colwyn. Residential areas are largely separated from the beach by the busy A55 and the main-line railway. Nonetheless, the area remains an excellent centre for watersports from sailing to jet-skiing, and there is a wide range of seaside attractions, such as the Eirias Park amusement park and an indoor

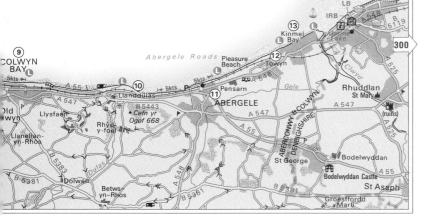

GREAT ORME TRAMWAY · LLANDUDNO ·

LASTING APPEAL *For more than a century Llandudno, seen here from the top of craggy Great Ormes Head, has attracted holidaymakers. The elegant bow-windowed and balconied hotels still look much as they did in Victorian and Edwardian times. The Great Orme Tramway, opened in 1902, still runs to the 679 ft summit every day in the summer.*

swimming pool with a water chute. On a hillside overlooking the bay is the Welsh Mountain Zoo, which has a large section devoted to chimpanzees.

⑩ LLANDDULAS

The elevated coast road sweeps over Llanddulas, where a long beach of sand and shingle is punctuated by groynes. The town has been beset by railway dis-

asters. In 1868, several wagons loaded with paraffin came loose and rolled downhill into a mail train, engulfing it in flames and killing more than 30 people. In August 1879 floods swept away the stone viaduct carrying the railway; engineers erected a replacement, made of steel, within a month. In 1950 a mail train collided with an engine and six people died. Inland,

narrow lanes follow the course of the River Dulas, and there are fine views of the coast from the cave-pitted limestone hill of Cefn yr Ogof.

⑪ ABERGELE

The small market town, set about a mile back from the coast, and its seaside neighbour Pensarn sit at the centre of a 7 mile beach of shingle and low-tide

sand. It was around Pensarn that Captain Matthew Webb trained before going on to become, in 1875, the first person to swim the English Channel. There is a seaside amusement area at Pensarn Pleasure Beach.

⑫ TOWYN

In 1990 high seas broke through the coastal defences and flooded the town. The damage has been repaired and the resort has been restored to its former popularity, so that the sand and pebble shore is again lined with an almost solid rank of caravan parks. Trotting races are held on the Tir Prince Raceway.

⑬ KINMEL BAY

A wide expanse of sand, backed by a development of holiday bungalows and caravan parks, ends at the point where the River Clwyd meets the sea. The beach is popular with bathers, but strong currents make swimming dangerous near the estuary.

PLACES TO SEE INLAND

Bodelwyddan Castle, 4 miles SE of Abergele. Victorian mansion; includes an annexe to London's National Portrait Gallery; 19th-century marble church nearby.

Bodnant Garden (NT), Tal-y-Cafn, 7 miles S of Llandudno. Terraced grounds with sweeping views of Snowdonia.

Felin Isaf Watermill, Pentrefelin, 6 miles S of Llandudno. 18th-century working watermill.

Rhuddlan, 5 miles E of Abergele. Ruins of 13th-century Rhuddlan Castle (Cadw); 13th-century St Mary's Church.

St Asaph Cathedral, 7 miles SE of Abergele. Mainly 13th-century cathedral, built on site of an earlier Norman structure.

TOURIST INFORMATION

Colwyn Bay (01492) 530478; Conwy (01492) 592248; Llandudno (01492) 876413

From Snowdonia's peaks to Anglesey's sandy bays

Two great 19th-century bridges span the turbulent waters of the Menai Strait, joining the mountainous mainland to the island of Anglesey, where glorious beaches are backed by low-lying hills and meadows.

① RED WHARF BAY
Low tide exposes some 10 square miles of sand, backed by dunes and low grassland and enclosed by rounded headlands. There is ample scope for beachcombing, but walkers should beware of the incoming tide, which rushes along a multitude of small channels to flood the beach. Bathing is hazardous when the tide is going out. From the little harbour known as Red Wharf Bay, at the western end of the bay of the same name, a path leads north to the earthen ramparts of the old Celtic fort of Castell-mawr.

② LLANDDONA
From the hilltop village a lane leads precipitously down to the sea. Halfway down the hill the road forks, the lane to the west going straight to the sands of the more remote, eastern end of Red Wharf Bay. The lane heading east leads to the hamlet of Pentrellwyn, where the sands give way to a rocky, hilly shore.

③ PUFFIN ISLAND
Half a mile out to sea from the Trwyn Du lighthouse on Anglesey's eastern tip lies uninhabited Puffin Island, known in Welsh as Ynys Seiriol after St Seiriol, who founded a settlement on the island in the 6th century. Remains can be seen of the monastery, which was abandoned in the 13th century, and of a 19th-century telegraph station. Access is restricted to naturalists with permits, but there are boat trips around the island from Beaumaris. Puffins are now rare on the island, but shags, cormorants and seals are regular visitors.

④ PENMON
According to tradition, a priory was founded at Penmon in the 6th century by Cynlas, St Seiriol's brother. The original building was destroyed by Viking raiders, and rebuilt in the 12th century. A good deal of Norman architecture survives, as well as earlier remnants, including elaborately carved Celtic crosses and a 1000-year-old font. Nearby are the spring of St Seiriol's Well, a cell said to have been used by the hermit saint, and a 17th-century dovecote.

A toll road leads past some disused quarries to the point of Trwyn Du and

TUDOR LARDER *Penmon dovecote was built around 1600 to supply birds for the table of Sir Richard Bulkeley.*

spectacular views across Conwy Bay. Currents around the point make swimming from the pebbly beaches unsafe.

⑤ BEAUMARIS
The fine little town and sailing centre is dominated by 13th-century Beaumaris Castle (Cadw), built by Edward I. The castle is one of the most sophisticated examples of medieval military architecture in Britain. Its moat was originally linked to the sea, and two rings of walls are punctuated by defensive towers.

Other interesting buildings in the town include the Grammar School of 1603, now used as a community centre, and the Courthouse of 1614, still in use and open for visits in summer. Nearby is the early 19th-century jail, where cells have been restored. At the Museum of Childhood, by the castle, displays span two centuries of toys and games. Strong currents make the shingle beach unsuitable for bathing.

⑥ MENAI BRIDGE
Parliament approved the building of a bridge over the Menai Strait in 1819, and the engineer Thomas Telford opted for a suspension bridge – a new concept in his day. The village on the strait's northern bank, which at the time was called Porthaethwy, was renamed in honour of the bridge, and has developed into a small town.

The bridge is best seen from the north bank shoreline promenade, at the western end of which is Church Island and the 14th-century church of St Tysilio. The island can be reached by a causeway exposed at low tide.

North-west of the town is the Pili Palas butterfly and bird house, which also includes many reptiles and insects.

⑦ LLANFAIRPWLLGWYNGYLL
In the 19th century, the Victorian equivalent of today's tourist board invented the name Llanfairpwllgwyngyllgogerychwyrndrobwllllantysiliogogogoch, literally translated as 'St Mary's Church in the hollow of white hazel near a rapid whirlpool and the Church of St Tysilio near the red cave'. The name has attracted visitors ever since, though it is commonly shortened to Llanfair P.G. When British Rail closed the station in 1966 there was an uproar, and it was officially reopened in 1973. The platform ticket with the town's name in full is an attraction in itself. Near the station is an old road tollhouse with its original list of charges, starting at three halfpennies for a horse carrying a load of lime.

Llanfair P.G. is linked to the mainland by the Britannia Bridge, built by Robert Stephenson in 1850 to carry the Holyhead Railway. The bridge was

EDWARD'S LAST CASTLE *Beaumaris Castle was named after the French* beau marais, *meaning 'beautiful marsh'. Its strong, concentric walls have never fallen to an enemy.*

GRACEFUL DESIGN *Spanning the treacherous waters of the Menai Strait, Thomas Telford's Menai Suspension Bridge remains as proudly elegant as the day it was opened in 1826.*

damaged by fire in 1970 and was reconstructed as a double-decker, with a road on the upper level and the railway underneath. On the shoreline is a statue of Admiral Nelson, erected in 1873 as a navigation aid. In the village is an 88ft column that serves as a monument to the first Marquess of Anglesey; inside the column is a spiral staircase which can be climbed for stupendous views of Snowdonia and the strait.

⑧ PLAS NEWYDD
The imposing mansion of Plas Newydd (NT) was built in the 1790s in a mixture of classical and Gothic styles, by James Wyatt and Joseph Potter for the Paget family, later the Marquesses of Anglesey. Among the relics on display is the artificial leg of the first Marquess of Anglesey, Wellington's second-in-command at Waterloo, where he lost his limb. In the dining room an immense mural painted by Rex Whistler in the 1930s shows members of the Paget family, with the painter sweeping leaves.

⑨ BANGOR
The university city dates from the foundation of the cathedral by St Deiniol in AD 548. Near the cathedral is the Bible Garden, so called because it was created to show plants mentioned in the Bible. The Museum of Welsh Antiquities covers the development of north Wales from prehistoric times to the present day. To the north of the town, an ornate pier reaches out more than halfway into the Menai Strait. Pleasure boats

moor at nearby Porth Penrhyn, developed in the 19th century for the export of slate from local quarries.

⑩ PENRHYN CASTLE
An extravagant example of the early 19th-century taste for neo-Norman architecture, the castle was designed for the Pennant family in 1820 by Thomas Hopper. Inside the castle are elaborate stone carvings and an exhibition of paintings by old masters such as Rembrandt and Canaletto. The stables house a museum of dolls from all over the world, and a collection of industrial locomotives. The lush grounds include a ruined medieval chapel and the Pennant pet cemetery.

Kingfishers, peregrine falcons and firecrests can be seen at the Spinnies Nature Reserve, to the east of the castle.

⑪ LLANFAIRFECHAN
The unassuming town sits between the hills and the sea, in a narrow gap which also accommodates the railway and the main coast road. There is a substantial sea wall, and groynes reach out into the Lavan Sands. Llanfairfechan is a good centre for exploring the foothills of Snowdonia a few miles to the south.

PLACES TO SEE INLAND

Aber Falls, Coedydd Aber National Nature Reserve, 8 miles E of Bangor. 3 mile nature trail to spectacular waterfalls; visitor centre.

Snowdon National Nature Reserve, nr Llanberis, 12 miles S of Bangor. Rugged terrain with remains of copper mines and slate quarries.

TOURIST INFORMATION

Bangor (01248) 352786 (summer); Llanfair P.G. (01248) 713177

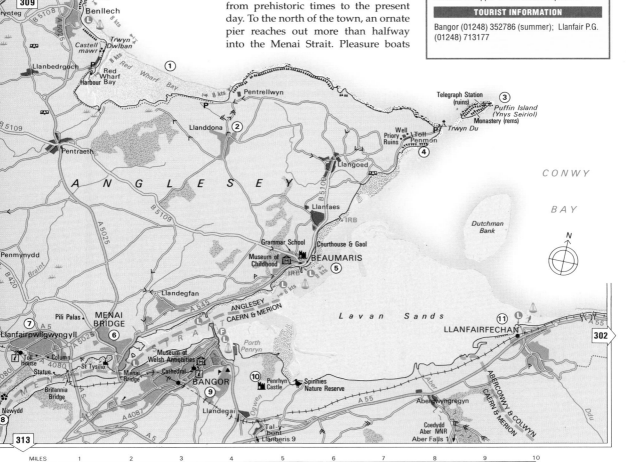

A golden coast under the gaze of a copper mountain

The indented coastline of northern Anglesey shelters remote coves and harbours, while to the east are gentler shores and large, flat sands. Both coasts are notorious for their history of smuggling and shipwrecks.

① CEMLYN BAY

Grassy headlands overlook a rocky bay, in which a shingle ridge shelters a salt-water lagoon. The ridge and lagoon form the Cemlyn Nature Reserve, home to a wide variety of sea birds and water-fowl, including red-breasted mergansers and several species of tern. On the western edge of the bay, a memorial stone records the launch in 1828 of Anglesey's first lifeboat. A path heads west to a sand and shingle beach at the secluded cove of Hen Borth.

② WYLFA HEAD

The twin reactors of the Wylfa nuclear power station stand out on the western shore of a low headland. Guided tours of the station start from the visitor centre. From the nearby car park, paths lead north to Wylfa Head and east to a woodland nature trail.

③ CEMAES BAY

Northern Anglesey's main harbour until the development of Amlwch in the 18th century, Cemaes Bay and the village of Cemaes were once a centre for fishing, shipbuilding, and a good deal of smuggling. Today pleasure craft outnumber the few fishing boats sheltering behind the harbour breakwater.

Cemaes sits at the centre of the bay's five sheltered beaches; the biggest and sandiest of these, to the east of the harbour, is separated from the village by the small Afon Wygyr river. A car park is reached by a lane from the hamlet of Llanbadrig to the north. To the south-east of Cemaes is a set of electricity-generating

wind turbines. The clifftop footpath north of the village leads past 14th-century St Padrig's Church, dedicated to St Patrick, who is said to have been shipwrecked nearby, and continues on to the cove of Porth Llanlleiana. Dotted around the cove are the ruined buildings of a former china-clay works. Nearby are the remains of the Celtic hill-fort of Dinas Gynfor and the dramatically named inlet of Hell's Mouth.

④ PORTH WEN

Lack of road access to the deep bay makes its sandy beach more secluded than most in the area. The easiest way to reach the beach is by a 1½ mile clifftop walk from the village of Bull Bay to the east. The structures resembling huge beehives on the western side of the bay are the remains of an old brick works.

⑤ BULL BAY

The holiday village, built around a rocky cove, was in the 19th century a busy little fishing port and shipbuilding centre, and a depot for pilot boats which met ships making for Amlwch harbour. The village is now the base for a sailing club. The falling tide leaves a multitude of pools on the rocky beach, and there are caves to explore at the foot of the cliffs to the west. There is sea fishing from the rocks around the village, and an 18-hole golf course on the road to Amlwch.

⑥ AMLWCH

A fishing village until the mid 18th-century, Amlwch was developed as a port and shipbuilding yard to serve the copper mines of Parys Mountain, a few miles inland. There had been mining in the area as far back as Roman times, but the great boom began in the late 18th century; by 1780 the Parys Mountain Copper Company employed 1500 men, women and children. The company endowed the town's Church of St Eleth, built in 1800, and even minted its own coins for local use. Examples of the coins, which had the company's initials on one side and a druid's head on the other, can be seen at the National Museum of Wales in Cardiff. By 1815 Welsh copper mining was in decline, and the industry was destroyed by competition from African and American mines in the 1900s, after which the harbour fell into disuse.

'Druid' coin

Pleasure craft now fill the harbour, and boats offer fishing trips and cruises. Inland is the eerie landscape of the old Parys Mountain mines, where paths explore a rocky and unstable wilderness surrounded by ore-stained pools. On the hill are the stump of an old wind-mill and the ruins of an engine house.

⑦ LLANEILIAN

In the hilltop village overlooking the cove of Porth Eilian is the largely 15th-century Church of St Eilian, built on the site of a 5th-century hermitage. Inside are some fine wood carvings.

From the church, a lane leads down to a sand and shingle beach sheltered by lichen-covered cliffs. The path continues to a lighthouse on the narrow rocky headland of Point Lynas. In 1766 the Liverpool Pilotage Service was

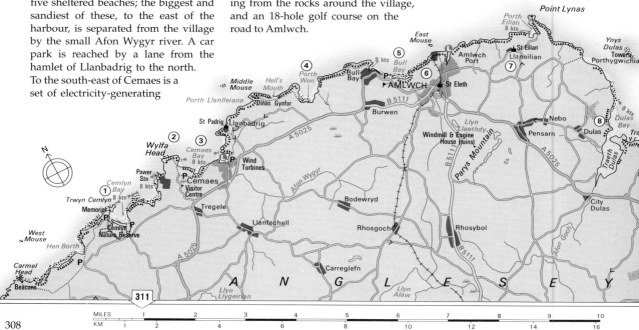

A BUSTLING PAST *Small boats shelter at Amlwch harbour, where once ships of up to 100 tons would anchor to load up with copper from the nearby Parys Mountain mines.*

established on the point, to send out six-oared gigs to meet ships heading for the Merseyside docks.

⑧ DULAS

Scattered farms make up the hamlet of Dulas, from where lanes lead to the wide estuary of the Afon Goch. Gulls wheel over the pleasure boats moored on the mud flats, where traces remain of brick works and limekilns that once lined the shore. Parking is limited on the western side of the bay, but the east side is accessible from Traeth Lligwy. North of the bay is the rocky island of Ynys Dulas, where a tower serves as a landmark for sailors. Grey seals can often be seen basking against its walls.

⑨ TRAETH LLIGWY

Wide flat sands and ample car parking make the large beach a popular spot for holidaymakers. A path heads north to the more secluded sandy bay of Traeth yr Ora, while to the east it follows the line of the cliffs to Moelfre. The lane leading south-east from Traeth Lligwy to the hamlet of Llanallgo passes two archaeological sites, both managed by Cadw. The older is Lligwy Chambered Barrow, a Bronze Age tomb consisting of eight upright stones supporting a massive capstone. Nearby is Din Lligwy, a native settlement dating from between the 1st and the 4th centuries AD, where remains of stone huts and iron-smelting hearths can be seen.

⑩ MOELFRE

The small holiday resort and its sheltered pebbly beach are popular with bathers, sailors and other watersports enthusiasts. North of the village is a Sea Watch Centre with displays on marine life, ships and shipwrecks, which is open in summer and at other times by arrangement for groups.

The headland that shelters the harbour presents a dangerous obstacle to shipping in stormy weather. In October 1859 the steam clipper *Royal Charter*, bound for Liverpool from the Australian goldfields with a cargo of gold, ran aground on the rocks, and all but a dozen of the 450 passengers were lost. About two-thirds of the gold was later recovered. Charles Dickens visited Moelfre two months after the disaster and adapted the story of the wreck for a tale in *The Uncommercial Traveller*. There is a memorial to the victims in nearby Carmel Church, and another on the cliffs above the site of the tragedy.

⑪ TRAETH BYCHAN

The small sandy bay flanked by rocks and banks of shingle is the base for a sailing club, and is often busy with power boats and water-skiers. There are good clifftop walks to the south.

⑫ BENLLECH

A popular holiday resort, Benllech has a long, sandy beach lined by a row of shops and cafés, and offering traditional seaside amusements such as donkey and pony rides. The cliffs that back the beach are studded with fossils, including corals – showing that this was once a subtropical seabed.

PLACES TO SEE INLAND

Llyn Alaw Reservoir, 6 miles SW of Amlwch. Visitor centre, woodland walks, angling.

TOURIST INFORMATION

Holyhead (01407) 762622

WRITING ON THE WALL *In Llaneilian's quiet Church of St Eilian, the rood screen shows a skeleton below the grim warning* Colyn angau yw pechod *– 'the sting of death is sin'.*

The clamour of sea birds above a remote lighthouse

In north-western Anglesey are many tiny coves, hidden at the foot of imposing cliffs. Travellers using the Holyhead ferry may unknowingly bypass one of the wildest and most attractive areas of the island.

① CARMEL HEAD
Anglesey's remote north-western corner, a treacherous area for shipping, drops away to the sea in steep cliffs. Two navigation beacons stand on the headland, and a third is set offshore on the rocky islet of West Mouse. Farther out are The Skerries with their lighthouse, built in 1841 to replace a fire in a brazier kept burning by a man and wife who lived out on the rocks to maintain this lonely duty. Carmel Head (NT) is reached by a footpath from a car park sited by a sharp bend in the road north of Llanfairynghornwy. The cliffs are popular with birdwatchers, who may spot choughs, now rare, and peregrine falcons. On the head is a pine forest where pheasants are reared by a local landowner; the nearby coast path is closed during the shooting season, from mid September to early February.

② CHURCH BAY
Among the sand and shingle of this fine, long beach are reefs where rock pools are exposed at low tide. High red cliffs flank the wide bay, and the bulky mass of Holyhead Mountain rises up across the water. From Church Bay, paths explore the countryside and follow the cliffs to the north and south.

③ PORTH TYWYN MAWR
A lane heading west from Llanfwrog travels across rolling grassland before ending by a wide, dune-backed sandy beach with a scattering of rocky islets offshore. There is very limited parking space along the side of the road.

④ PORTH PENRHYN MAWR
The quiet shingle beach is backed by low grassland dotted with old farm buildings and a caravan park. It is a good place from which to watch ships and ferry boats sailing in and out of Holyhead harbour.

⑤ VALLEY
Set in a cutting made through a hill in the early 19th century during the construction of what is now the A5, the town is a transit point for people travelling to and from Holy Island. The area is dominated by an RAF station 2 miles to

RAF trainer Hawk

the south that serves as a training school for jet pilots and a base for sea and mountain rescue helicopters.

⑥ PENRHOS COASTAL PARK
Woodland and coastal paths crisscross the estate of Penrhos, bordered on its western side by the A5 and an aluminium smelting works. The Penrhos woods were created in the early 1900s with some 15 000 broad-leaved trees, but most of the original trees were replaced in the 1960s with commercial forestry species. The park is a refuge for birds such as kestrels, reed buntings, linnets, terns and shelducks. Freshwater lakes flooded by seawater during exceptionally strong storms in 1990 are slowly recovering. The old tollhouse built in the 19th century at the start of Thomas Telford's new road from Holyhead to London has been moved from its original position, and re-erected in the park as a tearoom.

⑦ HOLYHEAD
Anglesey's largest town is called Caergybi in Welsh. 'Caer' refers to a fortress built in the 4th century AD by the Romans, and much of its surrounding walls remain, encircling the 13th-century Church of St Cybi (Cadw). In the south-west corner of the churchyard is the small chapel of Eglwys-y-Bedd, marking the grave of Seregri, leader of a band of Irish raiders in the 6th century.

A large port from the 16th century, Holyhead acquired a direct link with London on the completion in 1821 of a new toll road from the capital engineered by Thomas Telford and now the A5. Its opening in the presence of George IV is commemorated by a triumphal arch, situated on the harbour. The road was soon joined by the railway, and a 1½ mile breakwater was built. There are good views of harbour activity from the lighthouse at the tip of the breakwater, reached by a promenade. A ferry service to and from Dun Laoghaire and Dublin in the Republic of Ireland operates from Holyhead.

SEA BIRD ISLAND *Choughs nest on South Stack, a rocky fist below towering cliffs. The lighthouse was built in 1808 by David Alexander, who also built Dartmoor Prison.*

IRISH CONNECTION *From Holyhead, modern ferries ply a route to Ireland that was first established in the 16th century.*

⑧ HOLYHEAD MOUNTAIN

From the road heading west from Holyhead to South Stack, rough tracks lead through gorse and heather to the stony grandeur and stupendous views of Holyhead Mountain, at 720 ft the highest hill in Anglesey. On the summit are the remains of the Iron Age fort of Caer y Twr (Cadw), which houses the ruins of a 4th-century Roman watchtower or beacon. Just off the road on the lower slopes to the west is the settlement of Cytiau'r Gwyddelod (Cadw), inhabited during the 3rd and 4th centuries. The low stone walls of 20 huts survive, some showing where the inhabitants placed their fires, their seats and their beds.

On the north-eastern slopes of Holyhead Mountain is the small Breakwater Country Park, a former quarry used for the building of Holyhead's breakwater and now the home of choughs and peregrine falcons.

⑨ SOUTH STACK

Holy Island's north-western tip consists of a huge rock crowned by a 90 ft lighthouse and overlooked by 200 ft cliffs. Before the lighthouse was automated in 1984 and the island closed to visitors, it was reached by a precipitous flight of some 350 steps and a short suspension bridge over turbulent waters. There are plans to allow visitors onto the island. The cliffs above South Stack, part of an RSPB nature reserve, are noted for their vast numbers of sea birds, including a large colony of puffins. Standing on the rockface to the south of the lighthouse, crenellated Twr Elin, or Ellen's Tower, built in the 18th century as a summer-house by the Stanleys of Alderley, is now the reserve's visitor centre. There are spectacular clifftop walks north-east around Gogarth Bay to the promontory and islet of North Stack.

PLACES TO SEE INLAND

Llynnon Mill, Llanddeusant, 6 miles NE of Valley. 18th-century working windmill.

Trefignath, 2 miles SE of Holyhead. Stone Age burial chamber.

TOURIST INFORMATION

Holyhead (01407) 762622

---

⑩ TREARDDUR BAY

The bay cuts deeply into the narrow neck of Holy Island, an area of rocky coves and small sandy beaches. Watersports activity at the main beach, a long stretch of sand with rocky outcrops, includes surfing, canoeing and windsurfing. Porth Diana Nature Reserve, at the southern end of the bay, is based on a rocky escarpment which in late spring is covered in the blossoms of rockroses.

To the north-west of Trearddur Bay is the sandy, cliff-girt cove of Porth Dafarch, a popular spot for watersports such as skin-diving and canoeing.

⑪ RHOSCOLYN

A narrow lane leads from the scattered farming village of Rhoscolyn to sandy Borthwen Bay, from where several footpaths follow the rocky coast. To the east are the sands of Silver Bay, and to the west is the ancient St Gwenfaen's Well, whose waters were once thought to have curative powers. A beacon warns ships of the outlying rocks.

⑫ RHOSNEIGR

The little town with its narrow streets of whitewashed cottages, once a base for shipbuilding and for shipwrecking gangs, developed as a resort towards the end of the 19th century. To the north are the broad sands of Crigyll Beach

and Cymyran Beach. Holiday activities include windsurfing, horse riding in the gorse and dunes, and sea fishing. There is an 18-hole golf course.

⑬ PORTH TRECASTELL

The small sandy beach, which often has ideal conditions for surfing, is also known as Cable Bay, after the transatlantic telegraph cable which comes ashore there. On the headland is the burial chamber of Barclodiad y Gawres (Cadw), built around 2500 BC. Its top was destroyed by quarrying, but the passage and side chambers of the tomb have been recovered. The abstract patterns carved on the walls are similar to those found in Irish tombs of the same period. The key to the chamber is available from the Coastal Heritage Centre at Aberffraw, 2 miles to the south-east.

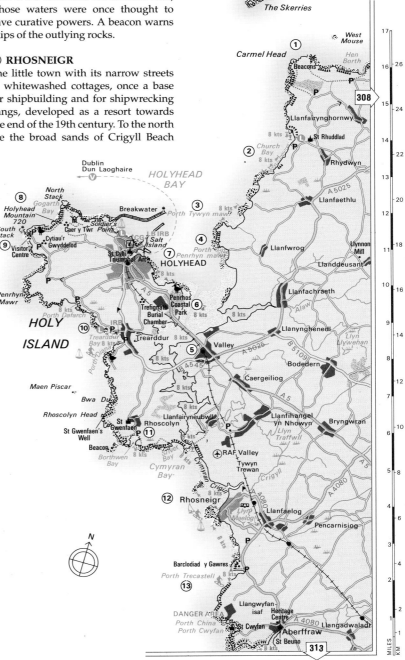

Havens of solitude and peace by the Menai Strait

From Anglesey's southern tip, once the centre of a Welsh kingdom, long sandy beaches backed by high dunes look across the Menai Strait to the Lleyn Pensinsula and the towering mountains of Snowdonia.

BASKING SEAL *Atlantic grey seals can often be seen on the rocky tip of Llanddwyn Island, which shelters the waters of Llanddwyn Bay from the rolling breakers of Malltraeth Bay.*

① ST CWYFAN'S CHURCH
On an islet set between two tiny coves sits the disused Church of St Cwyfan, reached on foot by a causeway at low tide. The first church dedicated to the Irish saint was built in the 7th century, but the present building was begun some 500 years later. The islet can be approached by road as well as by a 2 mile clifftop walk from Aberffraw.

② ABERFFRAW
The quiet little village was once the capital of Gwynedd, the kingdom of North Wales. Its period of greatness began in AD 870 under Rhodri the Great, and continued until Llywelyn ap Gruffudd was killed by the forces of Edward I in 1282. Some of the stonework in the 12th-century Church of St Beuno is said to be

Aberffraw's humpback bridge

remains from the royal palace, thought to have been nearby. There are exhibitions on the area's history and wildlife in the Llys Llywelyn Coastal Heritage Centre. The broad, swift-flowing Afon Ffraw passes under the village's 18th-century stone bridge before skirting the western edge of a large area of sand dunes, and reaches the sea by the sandy beach of Traeth Mawr. There are good views of the Lleyn Peninsula.

③ MALLTRAETH
The long inlet of the Cefni estuary gave the village its name, which means 'salt marsh' in Welsh. Flooding was a regular occurrence until 1818, when Thomas Telford built the great embankment known as Malltraeth Cob, and the river was canalised.

There are no paths along the estuary's western shore, but the great sweep of marsh and dunes which stretches southwards along the eastern side are part of the Newborough Warren National Nature Reserve. Redshanks, godwits, ruffs and shelducks are frequent visitors to the area, and there are hides from which the birds can be observed by small Parc Mawr lake, at the northern tip of Newborough Forest.

④ LLANDDWYN BAY
A 4 mile stretch of sand, between Abermenai Point and the start of Llanddwyn Island, is bordered by a vast area of dunes to the east and the Newborough Forest to the west. The sands offer spectacular views across the Menai Strait to the mountains of Snowdonia. The car park at the end of the road from Newborough is the starting point for a number of forest walks.

Llanddwyn Island, technically a peninsula rather than an island, forms part of the Newborough Warren National Nature Reserve. The island is named after St Dwynwen, patron saint of Welsh lovers, who founded a convent there in the 5th century. Crosses commemorate the saint and her followers, and ruins survive of a Tudor church built on the site of her chapel. At the tip of the island is a disused 19th-century lighthouse, standing beside the cottages that once belonged to pilots who guided vessels over the sandbars at the entrance to the Menai Strait. One of the houses has been restored to show how it would have been around 1900, and another has exhibitions on wildlife and the environment. Both houses are open for visits in summer.

⑤ NEWBOROUGH WARREN
Violent storms in the Middle Ages covered a huge area of farmland in southern Anglesey with sand. In Tudor times the dunes were stabilised by planting marram grass, and more recently Newborough Warren, as the area became known, was home to a huge colony of rabbits, until the animals were almost wiped out by myxomatosis in 1954. The warren has now given its name to a national nature reserve, and paths lead through the dunes and their wet hollows. Plants that thrive in the reserve include thyme and marsh orchids. The small lake of Llyn Rhos Ddu attracts ducks, grebes, coots and moorhens, which can be observed from a hide.

⑥ DWYRAN
Dotted around the small farming village are numerous places of interest to visitors. Walk-in aviaries are a feature of Bird World, which has a collection of exotic birds from around the world. The Model Village reproduces buildings and sites of Anglesey such as Beaumaris Castle and Aberffraw's main street, at a scale of 1in to the foot. Bryntirion Working Farm offers guided walks round its dairy farm and displays a collection of 19th-century agricultural machinery. The lane heading south-east from the farm peters out on the pebbly shore of the Menai Strait, from where there is a superb view across the water to Caernarfon Castle.

About 3 miles to the north-east is the Anglesey Sea Zoo, where many species of local marine life such as dogfish and dahlia anemones can be seen. There are walks along the nearby foreshore.

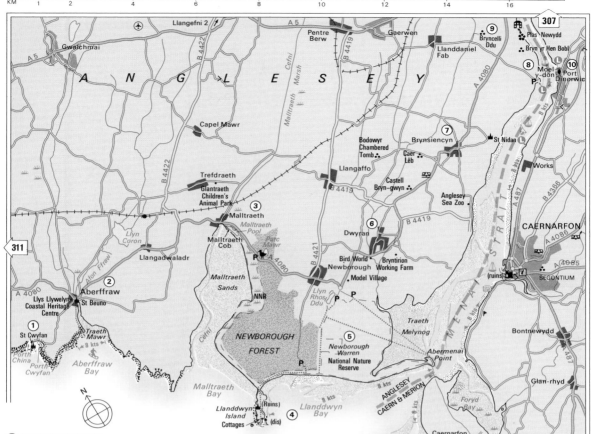

⑦ BRYNSIENCYN

Near the compact farming village is the derelict Church of St Nidan, which marks what would have been the area's centre of habitation in the early Middle Ages. The saint visited the area in the 7th century, but the present structure dates from the 14th century.

On a lane to the west is Caer Lêb, where there are banks and a ditches of a 3rd-century settlement, and the Stone Age chambered tomb of Bodowyr, consisting of four stone uprights crowned with a huge capstone. At Castell Bryngwyn, to the south, are the Stone Age remains of a circular bank and ditch. All three sites are managed by Cadw.

⑧ MOEL-Y-DON

From the A4080 about 2 miles north of Brynsiencyn, a narrow road leads south to a scattering of houses along a mud and shingle shore. A ferry once crossed the strait from Moel-y-don to Port Dinorwic, and the slipway that served it survives. This peaceful spot is believed to be the place where the Roman invasion of Anglesey began in AD 60.

⑨ BRYNCELLI DDU

A track off the road heading south-east from the village of Llanddaniel Fab leads to Bryncelli Ddu (Cadw), one of the best-preserved of Anglesey's many prehistoric sites. The large Bronze Age burial chamber, dating back some 4000 years, is set within a circular ditch which once contained 14 standing stones, all now fallen. At the end of a stone-lined passageway inside the great earthen mound is a chamber 10 ft long

BURIAL MOUND *The Bronze Age tomb at Bryncelli Ddu is crowned by a cairn that was originally 160 ft across. In the chamber is an upright stone, probably used in rituals.*

and made of six huge upright stones, one of which has linear carvings.

To the south-east is another well-preserved chambered mound of the same period, Bryn yr Hen Bobl (Cadw). Excavations in the 1930s of its small burial chamber revealed a cremation urn and the bones of some 20 people.

⑩ PORT DINORWIC

A popular anchorage for 8th-century Viking raiders, Port Dinorwic later developed as a small fishing village. It entered a period of prosperity with the opening of the Dinorwic slate quarries early in the 19th century. Quays were built, and a railway linked the port to the workings at Llanberis, in the mountains of Snowdonia. Today pleasure boats tie up where slate schooners once moored, and ocean-going yachts use the dock facilities. Sailing boats can be hired, with or without a crew, and there are fishing trips for bass and flounder.

PLACES TO SEE INLAND

Glantraeth Children's Animal Park, 2 miles NE of Malltraeth. Animals include Shetland ponies.

Oriel Ynis Môn, Llangefni, 7 miles NE of Malltraeth. Anglesey's main heritage centre, with displays on druids, princes and wildlife.

TOURIST INFORMATION

Caernarfon (01286) 672232; Llanfair P.G. (01248) 713177

Ancient hill-forts near the splendour of Caernarfon

An ancient pilgrims' route winds its way along the north coast of the Lleyn Peninsula, crossing a wild and remote area characterised by prehistoric remains, secluded coves, old churches and quiet villages.

① NEFYN

In 1284 the former fishing village was chosen by Edward I as the site of a tournament held to celebrate the downfall of Llywelyn ap Gruffudd and the conquest of North Wales. Throughout the Middle Ages, Nefyn was a stopping place for pilgrims travelling along the coast to Bardsey Island. The medieval Church of St Mary houses the Lleyn Historical and Maritime Museum, a record of the life of the local community from the 19th century. The long beach has firm sand backed by shingle, and rock pools appear at low tide. Boat trips and shore fishing are available; and when the waves roll in from the north there is surfing in the bay.

② PISTYLL

Like Nefyn, Pistyll was a stopping place for Bardsey Island pilgrims. The hamlet's small Church of St Beuno, which dates from the 7th century, is set in a

St Beuno's Church, Pistyll

grove of trees overlooking the sea, down a lane off the coast road. The stream which flows noisily past the church leads to a long shingle beach.

③ YR EIFL

The three peaks of Yr Eifl, Welsh for 'the fork', are known in English as 'the rivals'. Until the early 1970s, granite was quarried from their flanks, leaving giant terraces, especially on the seaward side. There are paths around the peaks, the tallest of which rises to 1849 ft. The track from Trefor to the north passes disused quarries.

From the village of Llithfaen, to the south, a lane winds steeply down to the valley of Nant Gwrtheyrn. The lane ends at a car park about a mile from the sea, and from there a woodland track leads to the former quarrymen's village of Porth y Nant, abandoned in 1959. The buildings have been restored as a centre for the teaching of Welsh. A nature trail follows the stream that flows behind the centre.

④ TRE'R CEIRI

Paths up the heather-covered inland slopes of Yr Eifl lead to the magnificent Iron Age hill-fort of Tre'r Ceiri, or 'giants' town'. A massive stone wall, some 15 ft thick in places, surrounds the foundations of 150 stone dwellings. On a nearby summit is a Bronze Age cairn.

The shortest walk to the site, taking some 40 minutes, starts from a lay-by on the B4417 south-west of Llanaelhaearn. In clear weather there are awe-inspiring views of the Lleyn Peninsula, and north-east towards Snowdonia.

⑤ TREFOR

A steep lane from the village of Trefor leads down to a small harbour protected by a short breakwater. Formerly used for loading ships with granite

MEDIEVAL TRADITION *At Easter, harvest time and Christmas, Pistyll's Church of St Beuno is strewn with rushes and herbs.*

from the Yr Eifl quarries, the harbour is now visited by pleasure craft. Nearby is a small sand and pebble beach. Sea and shore fishing are available.

⑥ CLYNNOG FAWR

The village of small whitewashed cottages has one of Wales's best-known churches, a stopping place for pilgrims on the road to Bardsey Island since its foundation by St Beuno in the 7th century. The present building dates from the 16th century. Inside is St Beuno's Chest, a medieval wooden trunk which held money paid to the church by the owners of lambs or calves born with 'Beuno's Mark' – a split in the ear.

At the foot of the hills by the roadside south of the village is St Beuno's Well, whose waters were thought to have curative powers. Sufferers from various ailments drank its water, and completed the remedy by spending the night on the saint's tomb in the church.

⑦ ABERDESACH

Low tide reveals a strip of sand at the pebble beaches of Aberdesach, where holiday chalets fringe the shore, and its neighbour Pontllyfni. Fishermen can catch bass from the beach in late summer and autumn. There is little parking space at Pontllyfni, but the village is easily reached on foot from Aberdesach's car park. Offshore to the north is the rock of Caer Arianrhod, visible only at low tide.

⑧ PARC GLYNLLIFON

By the A499 south of the village of Llandwrog, an imposing stone gateway marks the entrance to a small country

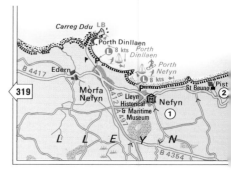

park. Parc Glynllifon is set in the grounds of a mansion built in the 1840s for the 3rd Lord Newborough. Outbuildings house craft workshops, but Glynllifon Mansion is now an agricultural and sixth form college and not open to visitors. The gardens and woodlands are crisscrossed by a network of marked paths, one of which passes a small 18th-century fort.

⑨ DINAS DINLLE

The small holiday village is named after the Iron Age hill-fort on the crest of the 100 ft hill which dominates this flat stretch of coast. Erosion makes the summit dangerous for walkers, and there is no public right of way to the fort. To the north is a 3 mile sandy beach, backed by a shingle bank constructed to protect the low-lying land from floods. The road skirting the beach ends by Caernarfon Airport, a former RAF airfield now used for pleasure flights along the Menai Strait and over the Snowdonia mountains. The airport's Air World Museum includes a collection of old RAF aircraft and a 'hands-on' flight simulator.

East of the airfield, a path borders Foryd Bay, a wide expanse of sand, mud and shingle, teeming with wildfowl and wading birds. Quicksand and fast currents make walking on the flats and swimming in the estuary dangerous.

⑩ CAERNARFON

Begun by Edward I in 1283 and completed some 40 years later, Caernarfon Castle (Cadw) was one of the most powerful fortresses in the chain built to keep the Welsh under English domination. Exhibits in its towers include an audiovisual display telling the story of the castle; the Queen's Tower houses the regimental museum of the Royal Welch Fusiliers. Caernarfon Castle was in 1969 the scene of the investiture of Prince Charles as Prince of Wales. The oldest part of Caernarfon town is enclosed by the medieval town walls that extend from the castle and surround a maze of narrow streets lined with 18th and 19th-century houses.

The quayside next to the castle is the departure point for pleasure boat excursions and fishing trips on the Menai Strait; there are walks along the foreshore westwards towards Foryd Bay. At Victoria Dock, outside the city walls, a

THE JEWEL IN THE CROWN *Modelled on the Roman walls of Constantinople, Caernarfon Castle was the finest of Edward I's Welsh castles. Today it is a World Heritage Site.*

museum charting Caernarfon's industrial history, and the Seoint II, a restored steam dredger, are open in summer.

Twthill, to the east of Caernarfon, was the site of a pre-Roman Celtic fortress; and in AD 78 the Romans built the fort of Segontium (Cadw). The foundations of the barracks where a thousand troops were housed can still be seen, and coins and pottery found on the site are shown in a small museum.

PLACES TO SEE INLAND

Llanberis, 8 miles E of Caernarfon. Small lakeside town, terminus of Snowdon Mountain Railway to Snowdon's summit.

Penygroes, 7 miles S of Caernarfon. Former slate-quarrying village, gateway to Nantlle valley.

TOURIST INFORMATION

Caernarfon (01286) 672232; Pwllheli (01758) 613000

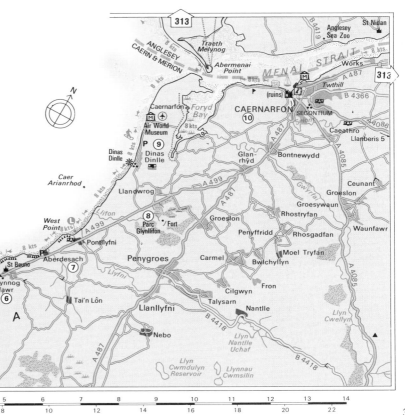

MIGHTY CASTLES THAT RING WALES

$\mathcal{A}$ROUND THE COAST OF NORTH WALES, from Ewloe to Aberystwyth, stand some of the finest medieval castles in the world. Some, like Ewloe, were the strongholds of the Welsh princes Llywelyn ap Iorwerth (Llywelyn the Great) and his grandson Llywelyn ap Gruffudd (Llywelyn the Last), but most were built by Edward I of England after his crushing defeat of the Welsh in 1282.

The first true castles in Wales were built by the Normans, especially in the southern lowlands, where Norman lordships were most powerful. The earliest fortified buildings were of the motte-and-bailey type, which consisted of a mound crowned by a timber tower or keep, and an adjoining enclosure. The Great Tower of Chepstow Castle, built of stone, was completed in 1071, but masonry castles were not common until the 12th century. In central and northern Wales, the Welsh kept the Normans and English at bay for 200 years.

Edward was a brilliant commander, and when he launched his armies into Wales in 1277, five years after his accession to the Crown, a series of swift victories brought Llywelyn ap Gruffudd to his knees, stripping him of most of his lands and leaving him Prince of Wales only in title. Five years later Llywelyn led a new revolt, but was killed in a

DEFIANT PRINCE OF WALES *Welsh leader Llywelyn ap Gruffudd resisted Edward I's attempts to control Wales. Llywelyn's death in 1282 spelt the defeat of the Welsh struggle for independence.*

Edward I of England

skirmish near Builth. Determined to crush the threat of any further uprising, Edward built a chain of massive castles in Wales, with walls 15 ft thick, deep moats and fortified barbicans. Many of them were built on the coast so that they could be provisioned by sea, and each was situated and fortified in such a way that it could be held by a garrison of fewer than 100 men. Their cost brought Edward to the verge of bankruptcy. But the fortresses served their purpose well, and never again was Edward's rule seriously threatened.

The castles of Wales saw action again during a new Welsh bid for independence, led by Owain Glyndwr, early in the 15th century. Glyndwr seized Harlech and made it the centre of his court

NORMAN FORTRESS *Cardiff Castle, set on the site of an earlier Roman fort, was throughout the Middle Ages the headquarters of the Norman lordship of Glamorgan. The castle keep (above) dates from the 12th century. The separate halls and towers were almost entirely rebuilt in the 19th century.*

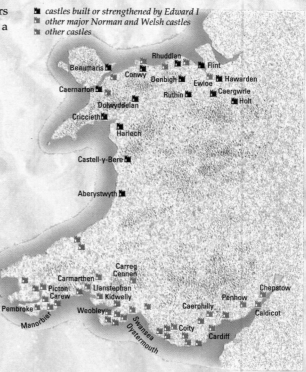

🏰 *castles built or strengthened by Edward I*
🏰 *other major Norman and Welsh castles*
🏰 *other castles*

Rhuddlan
Beaumaris
Conwy   Flint
Denbigh   Ewloe   Hawarden
Caernarfon   Ruthin   Caergwrle
Dolwyddelan   Holt
Cricieth
Harlech
Castell-y-Bere
Aberystwyth

Carreg Cennen
Carmarthen
Picton   Llanstephan
Carew   Kidwelly
Pembroke   Weobley
Manorbier   Swansea   Coity
Oystermouth
Caerphilly
Penhow
Caldicot
Chepstow
Cardiff

SURVIVOR OF A KING'S REVENGE *Caernarfon Castle had a Parliamentary garrison at the end of the Civil War, and on the restoration of the monarchy Charles II ordered that it be destroyed. But his instructions were ignored and the castle survived, to be extensively restored in Victorian times.*

for five years, before his rebellion was crushed. Conwy was also captured, but Caernarfon held out. The Wars of the Roses, 50 years later, saw Harlech as a Lancastrian stronghold, defended for eight years by the famed 'Men of Harlech'. During the Civil War, Beaumaris was among the castles held by the Royalists which surrendered to Cromwell's forces only when Charles I's cause was all but lost.

MILITARY MIGHT *Beaumaris Castle, the last fortress to be built by Edward I in Wales, was virtually impregnable until the invention of the cannon in the 14th century. Round towers gave archers an all-round view of the walls, and the huge gatehouses stood at an angle to the outer gateways, exposing any intruder to intense archer fire.*

CONWY CASTLE *Thomas Telford's 19th-century bridge reaches over the River Conwy to the castle and walled town. Edward I, who built the fortress, was himself besieged there in 1295 during a Welsh revolt.*

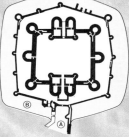

PROTECTED ENTRANCE *Beaumaris Castle was originally ringed by a broad moat, now partially filled in. A tidal dock (A) enabled supply ships to sail right up to the moat (B) from the Menai Strait.*

Beaches and coves along the Lleyn Peninsula

One of the least-changed parts of Wales, the thin finger of the Lleyn Peninsula is a land of narrow, twisting roads, which suddenly reveal distant mountains, or the sun sparkling on blue water in a sandy cove.

TRANQUILLITY PRESERVED *Porth Dinllaen is now a calm backwater, but in the early 19th century it was considered as an alternative to Holyhead as the main port for Ireland.*

① PORTH DINLLAEN
Once the home of a small fleet of herring boats, the little village of Porth Dinllaen sits among the rocks at the western end of a sandy bay, its crescent of fishermen's cottages facing a sandy cove. Strong currents sometimes surge against the rocks north of the beach. Visitors may not park in the village, but must leave their car in Morfa Nefyn, to the south, and walk about a mile along the edge of a golf course. Morfa Nefyn has a long, curving sandy beach.

② TUDWEILIOG
North of the village of Tudweiliog, a narrow road branching off the B4417 gives access to several secluded beaches and coves. From a car park beside solitary Towyn farmhouse, a path crosses a field to the sandy cove of Porth Towyn. A footpath hugs the coast, leading west past the even smaller cove of Porth Ysglaig to Porth Ysgaden, where two rock-studded beaches are separated by a small headland. Porth Ysgaden often has good surfing waves, but treacherous currents around the headland can make swimming unsafe.

③ TRAETH PENLLECH
The winding road from Penllech Bach to Pen-y-graig dives into a valley where a stream flows through a wooded ravine. From the bottom of the hill, a 5 minute walk beside the stream leads to a sandy beach backed by low cliffs. To the south is the sandy cove of Porth Colmon, and a 15 minute clifftop walk leads north to the tiny rocky bay of Porth Ychain.

④ PORTH IAGO
The deep cleft in the shoreline, containing a small crescent of sand backed by grassy slopes, is signposted from the road between Pen-y-graig and Carreg. The descent from the car park to the beach is difficult in wet weather. The bay offers good surfing, and diving from the rocks round its edge.

⑤ PORTH OER
This sandy cove is also known in English as Whistling Sands, because footsteps cause dry sand grains to make a squeaking or whistling noise as they rub against each other. A steep track near a picnic area by the cliffs leads down to the long sandy beach, pro-

tected by rocky promontories. At low tide, rock pools form by the cliffs at the southern end of the beach.

⑥ MYNYDD MAWR
The Lleyn Peninsula's south-western tip is crowned by the 524 ft Mynydd Mawr. The narrow winding road up the hill has two car parks, the smaller one at the top beside a disused coastguard lookout point. From the lower car park, a rough track leads down to a tiny cove, from where medieval pilgrims used to embark on the crossing to Bardsey Island. Nearby St Mary's Well has fresh water, though it is covered at high tide.

⑦ BARDSEY ISLAND
NATIONAL NATURE RESERVE
The remote mass of rock, dominated by a 548 ft hill, is 2 miles from the mainland across a sound seething with strong currents. In Welsh, Bardsey is called Ynys Enlli, or 'Island of the Eddies'. It became a refuge for early Christians after the Romans left Britain, and later was an important pilgrimage site. So many pilgrims were buried on the island that it became known as the Isle of Twenty Thousand Saints.

The island is now a national nature reserve, and farmhouses have been converted into accommodation for holidaymakers and those taking part in religious retreats. Day visits can be made from Aberdaron only by arrangement with the warden.

⑧ ABERDARON
A fishing village of whitewashed cottages stands snugly in a fold of rugged coastline. The twin-naved Church of St Hywyn was built at a safe distance from the sea 1400 years ago, but erosion has taken its toll, and the church now has its own sea wall to protect it. The long sand and shingle beach is sheltered from winds except those from the south and south-west. The bay is popular with surfers and divers, and offshore fishing trips can be arranged.

⑨ PORTH YSGO
The sheltered little bay, which faces south-west, is reached by a 10 minute walk from the road heading east from

---

BIRD OF THE WESTERN SHORES
On the coasts of Wales, Ireland, western Scotland and the Isle of Man, colonies of choughs nest in caves, on ledges and in cliff crevices. In flight they often perform aerobatics, displaying their flight feathers like outspread fingers and dive, soar and roll in spectacular fashion.

Chough
Pyrrhocorax pyrrhocorax

Aberdaron. From a small car park by a deserted farmhouse, a path follows a valley of ferns, gorse and foxgloves, down which a stream cascades to the sea in a series of small waterfalls. Wooden steps lead to the sand and shingle beach, which is covered at high tide. At low water, it is studded with blue-black rocks from a disused manganese mine on the hills behind the bay.

⑩ PLAS YN RHIW

Built on a steep slope overlooking the vast expanse of Porth Neigwl bay, Plas yn Rhiw (NT) is a small 17th-century manor house set in a large woodland garden crammed with fuchsias, roses and hydrangeas. Inside are furnishings, books and paintings collected by the former owners, who refurbished the house in the late 1930s.

⑪ PORTH NEIGWL

A 4 mile sweep of sand and low cliffs, Porth Neigwl frequently has rolling waves which provide perfect conditions for surfing. The English name for the bay is Hell's Mouth, because of the threat it posed to sailing ships blown inshore. The sands are most easily reached from a car park west of Llanengan, at the southern end of the bay.

Inland is a flat stretch of farmland. A 3 mile circular walk from the northern end of the bay takes in the disused Church of St Gwyninin, standing in the fields by Llandegwning farmhouse.

⑫ ST TUDWAL'S ISLANDS

A 5th-century Breton saint founded a priory on the more easterly of these two offshore islands, as a refuge after the collapse of the Roman Empire. The ruins of a later, medieval chapel can still be seen from boats which cruise round the islands from Abersoch. St Tudwal's Islands are privately owned, and landing on them is not allowed.

⑬ ABERSOCH

The once-quiet fishing village is now a centre for powerboat and sailing enthusiasts. Abersoch's two sandy beaches are separated by a headland crowned with houses. The southern beach is backed by high dunes and a golf course; to the north the sands run for 2 miles to the headland of Trwyn Llanbedrog.

Two nearby villages have interesting churches. The twin-naved Church of St Engan at Llanengan, to the south-west, was founded in the 6th century and has a beautifully carved rood screen. The Church of St Cian at Llangian, to the north-west, has a small triangular stone pillar on its south side with a Latin inscription, now illegible, dating from the 5th century. It commemorates 'Melus the doctor, son of Martinus', providing the earliest surviving mention of a doctor anywhere in Wales.

⑭ LLANBEDROG

A lane leads down from Llanbedrog village to a curving beach of sand and shingle, sheltered by the wooded headland of Trwyn Llanbedrog to the south. From the hill's 430 ft summit, known as Mynydd Tîr-y-cwmwd, there are fine views out to sea to St Tudwal's Islands, and along the coast east to Pwllheli. South of the village is the restored Victorian Gothic manor house of Plas Glyn-y-weddw, now an arts gallery and a centre for residential arts courses.

<table>
<tr><td colspan="2">PLACES TO SEE INLAND</td></tr>
<tr><td>Carn Fadryn, 6 miles NW of Llanbedrog. Iron Age hill-fort.</td></tr>
<tr><td>Mynydd Rhiw, 7 miles W of Llanbedrog. Panoramic views of Lleyn Peninsula from 1000 ft summit.</td></tr>
<tr><td colspan="2">TOURIST INFORMATION</td></tr>
<tr><td>Pwllheli (01758) 613000</td></tr>
</table>

BRIEF LIFE *The isolated 19th-century Church of St Gwyninin, inland from Porth Neigwl, has been closed for 50 years.*

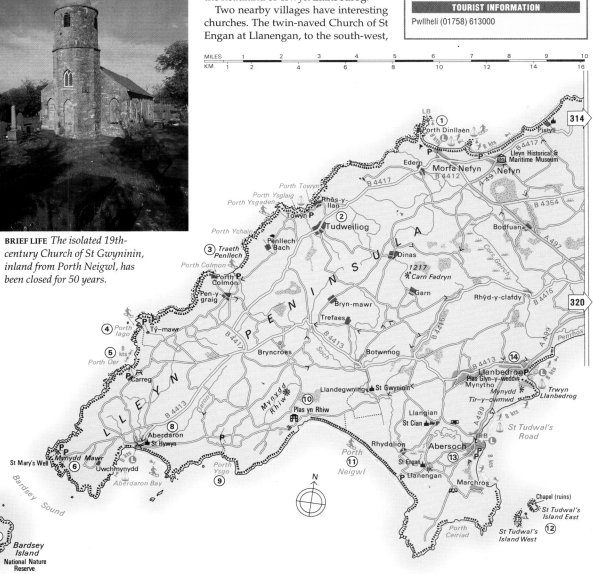

Castles and a fantasy village on a sheltered shore

The sandy beaches on the southern coast of the Lleyn Peninsula are washed by waters warmed by the North Atlantic Drift. Beside the Glaslyn estuary, narrow-gauge trains run along mountain valleys.

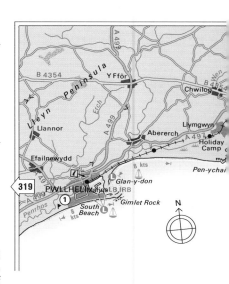

① PWLLHELI

The port and market town is the biggest and busiest settlement on the Lleyn Peninsula. Pwllheli's inner and outer harbours have both been developed, and a marina is situated in the inner harbour. A promenade lined by small hotels and boarding houses runs along South Beach, a long strip of sand backed by shingle. East of the harbour, sandy Glan-y-don beach extends for almost 4 miles towards the headland of Pen-ychain, site of a large holiday camp and leisure complex.

② LLANYSTUMDWY

Set on the banks of the turbulent little Afon Dwyfor, the village of Llanystumdwy is where the Liberal prime minister David Lloyd George grew up. His simple and dignified grave, marked by a single massive boulder inscribed 'DLG 1863-1945', lies within a stone enclosure in a glade beside the river. On the main village street is the Lloyd George Museum, which displays photographs, personal effects and political cartoons. The museum also contains a reconstruction of a Victorian schoolroom. Nearby is Highgate, the small stone cottage where he lived until 1880.

South-east of the village, the Afon Dwyfach joins the Dwyfor to form a long estuary. A riverside walk of about a mile leads to a pebbly shore where rock pools form at low tide. It is possible to walk along the shore to Criccieth.

TWENTIETH-CENTURY WIZARD
David Lloyd George, Liberal politician and Britain's prime minister from 1916 to 1922, was known as the 'Welsh Wizard' because of his spellbinding oratory. He retired from political life in 1944 and died a year later at Llanystumdwy, where his bronze bust stands outside a museum devoted to his life and times.

③ CRICCIETH

The ruins of Criccieth Castle (Cadw) stand high on a towering headland, overlooking the Victorian terraces of the little town of Criccieth on one side and the open sea on the other. Constructed by the Welsh prince Llywelyn ap Gruffudd in the middle of the 13th century, the fortress passed into English hands when Edward I captured it in 1283, but it was retaken by Owain Glyndwr during his rebellion in 1404. Some of the cracks and splits in the stonework probably date from the final siege, when the castle was sacked and burnt by the Welsh. The castle's visitor centre has an exhibition on the castles built by the Welsh princes, and another on Giraldus Cambrensis, or Gerald of Wales, the 12th-century churchman and Welsh historian.

West of the headland is a pebbly beach protected by groynes, and a high sea wall shelters a line of hotels. To the east, beyond a short breakwater, a curving sweep of sand and pebble stretches towards Morfa Bychan.

④ MORFA BYCHAN

The Welsh name of this village means 'Little Marsh'. Its huge sandy beach, Black Rock Sands, is backed by dunes stretching east to the Glaslyn estuary. There are caves among the rocks on the headland at the western end of the beach. The bay provides good surfing, but strong currents make swimming dangerous at the estuary end of the beach. The small Morfa Bychan Nature Reserve, set in dunes beside a golf course east of the village, is a nesting site for moorhens, larks and partridges.

⑤ BORTH-Y-GEST

Trim cottages, many of them colour-washed, fringe a small sheltered bay on the bank of the Glaslyn, reached by a road from Porthmadog to the north-east. To the north-west are the towering crags of Moel-y-Gest, from where there are splendid views across the estuary towards Harlech and the mountains inland. According to Welsh legend, Prince Madog, son of the king Owain Gwynedd, set sail from Borth-y-Gest in 1170 and reached America more than 300 years before Columbus.

⑥ PORTHMADOG

The harbour town was created early in the 19th century, with the building of the mile-long embankment called The Cob across the Glaslyn estuary, which reclaimed 7000 acres of land from the river's mud flats. Porthmadog grew prosperous from the slate trade, when stone from the quarries of Blaenau Ffestiniog was brought down on the narrow-gauge Ffestiniog Railway to be loaded onto ships. An old slate warehouse is now the Maritime Museum, which traces the town's history.

The town is now a centre for rock-climbing, hill-walking, riding and fishing, and small boats anchor by The Cob. The Ffestiniog Railway, whose terminus is by the harbour, has been restored to provide a 13 mile scenic trip through

ITALIANATE CAPRICE *The holiday village of Portmeirion was the light-hearted masterpiece of the architect Clough Williams-Ellis.*

MILES 1 2 3 4 5 6 7 8 9 10
KM 1 2 4 6 8 10 12 14 16

paths cross high dunes to a large sandy beach. Nearby is the championship golf course of Royal St David's.

⑩ LLANDANWG
Part of this village, including the church of St Tanwg, has been half buried by the shifting sands of the Artro estuary. Strong currents round the sandy beach, on Llandanwg's seaward side, make bathing dangerous on the falling tide.

⑪ LLANBEDR
The village sits on the southern bank of the Artro, and lanes head east towards the rugged peaks of Snowdonia. In the 16th-century Church of St Peter is a stone found in the nearby hills, marked with a spiral design that is thought to date from the Bronze Age. South of the village, converted from a World War II RAF living quarters, is Maes Artro, a complex of visitor attractions including an exhibition on traditional farming implements, an RAF museum with old fighter planes, and crafts workshops.

From Llanbedr, a road heads west to Shell Island, known in Welsh as Mochras. A peninsula rather than an island, it is covered in more than 200 different kinds of shell carried there by peculiarities of the offshore currents. The 'island' can be reached across a causeway at low tide; a notice board indicates when it is safe to cross.

STEAMING AGAIN *The little engines of the Ffestiniog Railway, based at Porthmadog, operate on a line first opened in 1836.*

the mountains as far as Blaenau Ffestiniog. Porthmadog is also a terminus for the narrow-gauge Welsh Highland Railway, which goes inland on a mile-long return journey.

⑦ PORTMEIRION
Inspired by a visit to the Italian resort of Portofino in the 1920s, the architect Clough Williams-Ellis returned home determined to create a 'dream village'. Built in stages between 1925 and 1972, Portmeirion is a fantasy folly on the grandest scale, consisting of 50 buildings arranged around a central plaza, and a tiny harbour. Buildings in extravagant Italianate style rub shoulders with architectural oddments brought to Portmeirion from all over Britain. The buildings include a tall bell tower, built by Williams-Ellis, and an 18th-century colonnade salvaged from Bristol. The village sits on a hillside overlooking the Dwyryd estuary, and footpaths lead through gardens of subtropical plants and trees to a wide sandy beach. Strong currents and swift tides make swimming dangerous. In the 1960s Portmeirion was used as the setting for the television series *The Prisoner*.

⑧ MORFA HARLECH
South of the broad sandy estuary of the Glaslyn and the Dwyryd is a wide stretch of flatland reclaimed from the sea, now mainly grazing land. South and east of Harlech Point is an expanse of dunes and salt marshes, now a nature reserve with colonies of wading birds. Visitors may walk along the foreshore of the reserve, but access to the dunes themselves is by permit only.

The sands of Traeth Bach, along the northern edge of the Morfa, are unsafe for bathing because of strong currents and fast incoming tides.

⑨ HARLECH
One of Edward I's string of fortresses, Harlech Castle (Cadw) stands dramatically on a 200 ft rocky bluff. In 1404 it was captured by Owain Glyndwr, who based his court there until it was retaken by the English five years later. During the Wars of the Roses it was held by the Lancastrians and withstood a seven-year siege by the Yorkists before falling to them in 1468. The song 'Men of Harlech' is said to have been inspired by the Lancastrians' resistance. From the top of one of the turrets there are magnificent views of the coast and inland towards Snowdonia. The small town of Harlech is built along a ridge behind the castle bluff, and to the west

PLACES TO SEE INLAND
Llechwedd Slate Caverns, nr Blaenau Ffestiniog, 13 miles NE of Porthmadog. Underground tramway, miners' village.
Sygun Copper Mine, nr Beddgelert, 8 miles NE of Porthmadog. Tours of mine disused since 1903.

TOURIST INFORMATION
Harlech (01766) 780658 (summer); Porthmadog (01766) 512981; Pwllheli (01758) 613000

STANDING STRONG *Harlech Castle overlooks ground that was once a tidal creek. Its massive twin-towered gatehouse makes it a striking example of 13th-century architecture.*

Wide sands and mountain views off Barmouth Bay

Around the holiday town of Barmouth, soft wide sands, wild mountain scenery where gold is still mined, and wooded estuaries create the varied landscape of the Snowdonia National Park's south-western tip.

① DYFFRYN ARDUDWY

The little village stands midway along the 7 miles of sandy beach, backed by grass-covered dunes, which stretches from Shell Island to Barmouth. To the south, caravans and holiday developments predominate, but to the north-west is the unspoilt wilderness of Morfa Dyffryn National Nature Reserve. Visitors can walk along the foreshore up to Shell Island, but entry to the main part of the dunes is by permit only.

On the southern outskirts of the village are the remains of a prehistoric burial chamber, managed by Cadw, and many other sites lie in the nearby hills. Pony-trekking is available. Ysgethin Museum, at Tal-y-bont village, contains reconstructions of 19th-century shop interiors, and agricultural machinery.

② LLANABER

A narrow village squeezed between the mountains and the sea, Llanaber has a superb example of early Gothic architecture in its Church of St Mary and St Bodfan, which dates from the early 13th century. In the church is an inscribed monolith known as the Caelixtus Stone, dating from the 5th century AD. Old slate tombs in the churchyard are said to have been used by smugglers as hiding places for their contraband.

③ BARMOUTH

The seafront of this popular holiday resort has sandy beaches, donkey rides and bright arcades. The old town, clinging to the hillside above the harbour at the mouth of the Mawddach estuary, is a maze of cottages and slate-stepped alleyways. On the quayside is Ty Gwyn, a small museum containing artefacts from a local Tudor shipwreck, housed in a 15th-century building. Nearby Ty Crwn is a circular lock-up house built in 1834. A trail leads from the old town to the viewpoint of Dinas Olau, which in 1885 was the first piece of land to be acquired by the National Trust. A 4 mile track dubbed the Panorama Walk skirts the hills overlooking the estuary and leads to the hamlet of Cutiau.

The railway bridge across the estuary has a pedestrian walkway, and a ferry service connects with the Fairbourne and Barmouth Steam Railway.

④ PENMAENPOOL

Water, woods and mountains surround the hamlet of Penmaenpool on the south bank of the upper Mawddach estuary. A signal box beside a disused railway, offering a good vantage point for bird-watchers, houses a Wildlife Centre, from which 7 miles of level track-bed provide a peaceful walk along the estuary to the Morfa Mawddach station.

⑤ DOLGELLAU

Built on a strategic crossing point by the Afon Wnion, and with valleys snaking deep into the hills behind, Dolgellau has for centuries been an important market town; a livestock market is still held on Fridays. Narrow winding streets of dark stone houses converge upon a busy and spacious central square, where the tourist information centre houses an exhibition explaining the region's links with the 17th-century Quaker movement.

In the 19th century, Dolgellau became the centre of a gold rush after the precious metal was discovered in the surrounding hills. Tours of the one mine still producing gold depart from the Welsh Gold Visitor Centre. The town is a good place from which to explore the surrounding hills. Apart from a stiff climb to the 2927 ft summit of Cadair Idris, the centrepiece of a nature reserve 3 miles to the south, gentler strolls include the 3 mile Torrent Walk along the wooded gorge of the Clywedog to the east. To the north-west, on the east bank of the Mawddach, are the ruins of Cymer Abbey (Cadw), founded by the Cistercians in the 12th century.

⑥ LLYNNAU CREGENNEN

A lane from the village of Arthog climbs abruptly in a series of hairpin bends through the tree-line to two lakes set in wild and open mountain scenery. A network of footpaths explores the area, and fishing permits are available from a National Trust warden, based at a farmhouse by the car park.

⑦ FAIRBOURNE

Two miles of sandy beach front this small but sprawling resort. In summer, the Fairbourne and Barmouth Steam Railway runs along the shore to connect with a ferry across the estuary to Barmouth. Built in 1890 as a horse-drawn tramway, the line was equipped with steam locomotives to run on its 12½ in-gauge tracks in 1916. Today the train is powered by half-scale replicas of vintage engines.

⑧ LLWYNGWRIL

Steep mountains loom above this busy village, from whose sand and shingle beach there are fine views northwards to the Lleyn Peninsula. At Llangelynnin to the south is the clifftop Church of St Celynnin, dating from the 11th century, which retains traces of medieval frescoes on the chancel wall. The track leading to the church soon becomes too narrow to accommodate cars; there are parking lay-bys at the side of the A493.

BARMOUTH SANDS *A busy fishing port in the 18th century, Barmouth now attracts many holidaymakers and sailors with its 2 miles of golden sands and spectacular views.*

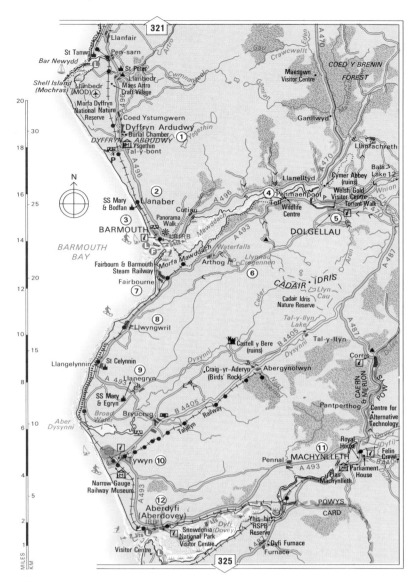

CENTRE POINT *Resembling a rocket on its launching pad, Machynlleth's 78ft clock tower straddles the main street.*

⑫ ABERDYFI

The attractive little resort, also known as Aberdovey, is a popular centre for sailing and watersports at the mouth of the Dyfi, and miles of sandy, dune-backed beach line the seashore to the north. An exhibition in the Snowdonia National Park Visitor Centre explains the town's shipping and shipbuilding activities in the 19th century, and tells the legend of a land lost beneath the sea, remembered in the Victorian song 'The Bells of Aberdovey'.

There are fishing expeditions and boat trips from the harbour. An 18 hole championship golf course occupies a magnificent position on the dunes.

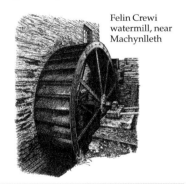

Felin Crewi watermill, near Machynlleth

PLACES TO SEE INLAND

Bala Lake, 15 miles NE of Dolgellau. Watersports, fishing, narrow-gauge railway.

Coed y Brenin Forest, 7 miles N of Dolgellau. Visitor centre, forest trails, craft demonstrations.

TOURIST INFORMATION

Aberdyfi (01654) 767321 (summer); Barmouth (01341) 280787 (summer); Dolgellau (01341) 422888; Machynlleth (01654) 702401; Tywyn (01654) 710070 (summer)

---

⑨ LLANEGRYN

The small village overlooks the fertile Dysynni valley, known for the ancient Welsh Black cattle. On a hill just north of the village is the 13th-century parish Church of St Mary and St Egryn, which contains an intricately carved oak rood screen, one of the finest in Wales.

A few miles upstream, colonies of cormorants populate the gaunt cliffs of Craig-yr-Aderyn, or Birds' Rock. A lane continues to the melancholy ruins of Castell y Bere (Cadw), a small fortress built on a precipitous crag by the 13th-century Prince Llywelyn ab Iorwerth.

⑩ TYWYN

'Tywyn' is the Welsh word for sand dune, reflecting the nature of the coast around this busy little town from where 4 miles of sand stretch south to Aberdyfi. Tywyn is a terminus of the narrow-gauge Talyllyn Railway, which runs north-east through 7 miles of spectacular mountain scenery to Abergynolwyn and the former quarries at Nant Gwernol, the starting point for several waymarked woodland walks. Tywyn station houses a museum with vintage steam locomotives.

⑪ MACHYNLLETH

Set at the head of the Dyfi estuary, Machynlleth has been a market town since the 13th century, and is still graced by many fine old buildings. The late medieval Parliament House has an exhibition devoted to the Welsh rebel Owain Glyndwr, who is said to have summoned a parliament in 1404 on a neighbouring site which now accommodates a tourist information centre. It is thought that the 15th-century Royal House was Glyndwr's home.

Dominating the town centre is a clock tower built in 1873 by the 5th Marquess of Londonderry, whose former mansion, Plas Machynlleth, houses an exhibition of Welsh myths and culture known as Celtica. The nearby leisure centre has a swimming pool with slides. The Dyfi offers good fishing for salmon and sea trout in season, and there is pony trekking in the hills.

To the east of the town is the 16th-century Felin Crewi watermill, still used to produce flour. To the north is the Centre for Alternative Technology, where solar and wind-driven electricity generators, organic gardens and low-energy housing are on display.

A university town, and a railway into the hills

Dunes and bogs near the Dyfi estuary give way to a long line of cliffs. At one of the few breaks in the cliffs, where the Rheidol and Ystwyth rivers meet the sea, is the resort and university town of Aberystwyth.

① YNYS-HIR RSPB RESERVE

A variety of habitats, including woodland, salt marsh, peat bog and reed beds, means that a wide range of birds can be seen in the reserve. Spring is the best time for spotting woodland birds, including pied flycatchers and redstarts, while in May, and from October to December, Ynys-hir is host to great numbers of estuary birds such as whimbrels, dunlins, wigeons and curlews. Winter birds of prey include red kites and peregrines. The reserve is one of only a handful of places in England and Wales to be visited in winter by the Greenland white-fronted goose.

② DYFI FURNACE

The charcoal-burning blast furnace that stands by a gushing waterfall on the River Einion, in the village of Furnace, is probably the best preserved in Britain. Dyfi Furnace (Cadw) was built about 1755 for smelting iron ore, and operated for about half a century. The huge water wheel attached to the outside of the building is similar to the one

FULL CIRCLE *After a period of use as a sawmill and a barn, Dyfi Furnace has been restored and a water wheel turns again.*

that originally powered the furnace's giant bellows. Visitors may look inside the blast furnace and bellows room.

③ HEN GAPEL

A former chapel in the tiny village of Tre'r-ddôl houses a folk museum with a collection of Welsh furniture, crafts and a range of domestic and farm objects. There is also a display on religion.

④ YNYSLAS

The tip of the peninsula that extends into the flat, watery expanses of the Dyfi estuary is made up of sand dunes that are constantly changing and moving, as well as of extensive areas of salt marsh. A visitor centre at Ynyslas explains how dunes are formed, and describes their plants and wildlife. The centre is the starting point for guided nature walks on Sundays. Polecats and weasels are among the animals resident in the vicinity. Orchids grow in the damp, low-lying areas between the dunes, and ringed plovers lay their well-camouflaged eggs on a shingle ridge along the west side of the dunes.

Ynyslas is part of the Dyfi National Nature Reserve, which includes the estuary of the River Dyfi, and Cors Fochno, a raised bog to the south dotted with numerous pools. Cors Fochno was dug for peat for many centuries until the 1950s and is not open to the public. Low tide on the beach between Ynyslas and Borth reveals the remains of a forest that grew after the end of the Ice Ages, 10 000 years ago, and was gradually submerged as the sea level rose.

⑤ BORTH

A mile-long line of houses straggles behind Borth's sea wall and its long sand and pebble beach, popular with bathers and surfers. Visitors to the Animalarium, located towards the southern end of the village, can see a variety of creatures, including lemurs, wallabies, snakes and tarantulas.

To the south of Borth, a coastal path passes a war memorial and follows exhilarating clifftops for some 5 miles. Halfway to Aberystwyth, the path descends to a remote sand and shingle beach at Wallog. Walkers can return from Aberystwyth to Borth by train.

ACADEMIA ON THE SEAFRONT *Seen from Constitution Hill, the chateau-style old building of the University of Wales, founded in 1872, heads a parade of buildings at Aberystwyth.*

THE RAILWAY THAT SERVED THE MINES

Steam trains of the Vale of Rheidol Railway take summer visitors through 12 miles of magnificent scenery from Aberystwyth to Devil's Bridge. The 1 ft 11¾ in gauge railway opened in 1902 to transport ore from the mines of the Rheidol valley and timber to the harbour at Aberystwyth. Silver and lead were mined in the area from the Middle Ages until World War I. Some local mines supplied silver for Charles I's mint at Aberystwyth Castle. The industry peaked in the 1860s, when nearly 100 mines were being worked and the ore was carried out on horseback and in sledges. The restored Llywernog Silver-lead Mine, in operation from 1745 to 1910, is open to visitors.

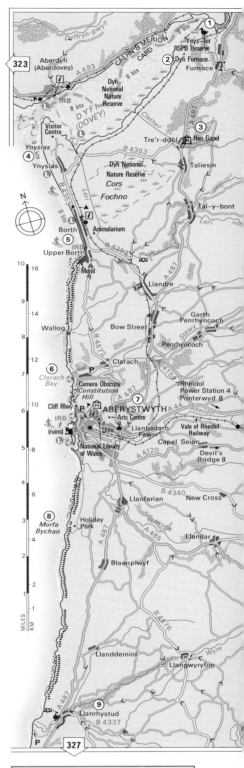

⑥ CLARACH BAY

At low tide the bay has a pleasant sandy beach, but swimmers should beware of strong currents round the headlands both to the north and south. Chalets and caravan sites are spread along the seafront, and inland. Visitors seeking solitude can head in either direction along steeply rising clifftop paths.

⑦ ABERYSTWYTH

Bay-windowed guesthouses and hotels stretch round the curved promenade of the Victorian seaside resort and university town, whose name means 'mouth of the River Ystwyth'. There are panoramic views of Aberystwyth and its sand and shingle beach from the top of Constitution Hill, which can be reached by a stiff climb from the northern end of the bay or by Britain's longest electrically powered cliff railway. At the top of the hill is a camera obscura offering a bird's eye view of the surrounding landscape on a white concave surface.

Substantial castle ruins stand on a headland at the southern end of the bay. Begun in 1277 by Edward I, the castle was captured in 1404 by Owain Glyndwr, and suffered a pounding by Oliver Cromwell's cannons in the Civil War in 1649; much of the rubble was removed by local residents to build houses. Aberystwyth's old harbour, at the mouth of the River Rheidol, offers fishing trips and boat tours for wildlife enthusiasts. A marina has berths for visiting small-boat sailors.

A restored Edwardian theatre houses the Ceredigion Museum, which has relics of the area's lead-mining and seafaring days, as well as domestic items and a reconstruction of a traditional cottage. On the first floor of the railway station, the Aberystwyth Yesterday exhibition documents the development of the town up to the 1940s. The station is the starting point for the narrow-gauge Vale of Rheidol Railway.

The main campus of the University of Wales is on Penglais Hill. Nearby is the National Library of Wales, where an exhibition chronicles Welsh Methodism and Welsh history from the 13th century. Close by, the Arts Centre includes galleries with exhibitions of ceramics, photography, paintings and crafts. The university's first constituent college was housed within a prominent Gothic revival Victorian building, designed as a grand hotel, on the seafront.

Llanbadarn Fawr, a mile south-east of Aberystwyth, has a long history as a religious settlement. In the 6th century Padarn, a Celtic saint, arrived there from Brittany with 847 monks and founded a religious order. The early 13th-century Llanbadarn Church has several carved Celtic crosses, some dating from the 10th century.

⑧ MORFA BYCHAN

High cliffs stretch southwards from Aberystwyth, and the only access to the sea for more than 7 miles is at Morfa Bychan. The road to the coast ends at a holiday park, where cars may be parked with permission from the office. A short walk to the north leads to steps descending to a stony beach. A hilly coastal path leads northwards before dropping down to Aberystwyth.

⑨ LLANRHYSTUD

Hills rising to more than 400 ft shelter the compact village. North and south of the mouth of a broad stream flowing into the sea are shingle and sand beaches flanked by caravan sites. The southern beach, near Morfa caravan site, is the easier to reach, with a road ending at a car park behind the shore.

PLACES TO SEE INLAND

Devil's Bridge, 12 miles E of Aberystwyth. Three bridges at the meeting of two rivers; waterfalls; terminus of Vale of Rheidol Railway.

Llywernog Silver-lead Mine, Ponterwyd, 11 miles E of Aberystwyth. Restored mine, with working water wheels, indoor exhibits, panning for silver, guided underground tour.

Rheidol Power Station, 8 miles E of Aberystwyth. Information Centre, guided tours, fish farm, reservoir walk past fish ladder and falls.

TOURIST INFORMATION

Aberystwyth (01970) 612125; Borth (01970) 871174 (summer)

Whaleback promontories giving glimpses of sea life

Remote cliffs, small resorts and secluded beaches characterise this strikingly indented coastline. Porpoises often appear offshore, along with bottle-nosed dolphins, rare in the waters of England and Wales.

① CARDIGAN

The busy town stands on gentle slopes above the east bank of the River Teifi, which is crossed by two road bridges. In the 18th and 19th centuries Cardigan was a thriving port serving the valley. Today pleasure craft and small fishing boats moor at the quays.

② GWBERT

Sand dunes, which support some 160 plant species, give way just north of the village of Gwbert to rocky cliffs that stretch as far as New Quay. The beach at Gwbert is shingle, with muddy sand exposed at low tide; river currents make swimming dangerous.

At the Coastal Farm Park and Waterfowl Centre, on the headland almost a mile north of Gwbert, visitors can see rare breeds from many parts of the world. The headland provides good views of Cardigan Island, a nature reserve inhabited by Soay sheep and not open to the public. Bottle-nosed dolphins, Atlantic grey seals, shags, black-backed gulls and herring gulls can be seen round the island.

When a steamer was shipwrecked off Cardigan Island in 1934, a number of brown rats came ashore and destroyed the island's colonies of puffins and Manx shearwaters. Lures to tempt these species to return to the island include dummy puffins and a machine that imitates the call of the shearwaters.

③ MWNT

A drive along a narrow, tortuous lane ends at a spectacular sandy cove, enclosed by high cliffs. Near the clifftop car park is the 14th-century Church of the Holy Cross, formerly used by pilgrims on their way to Bardsey Island, off the Lleyn Peninsula.

④ ABERPORTH

The quiet resort of Aberporth clusters round two sandy beaches. Bathing is unsafe when the wind blows from the north and causes currents to funnel round the bay. Until the beginning of the 20th century, Aberporth was a centre for herring fishing. Huge shoals spawned in the waters round Cardigan Island, and during one night in 1808 some nine million fish were caught. A short distance west of Aberporth is a Ministry of Defence missile testing centre. Felinwynt Butterflies, 3 miles west of the village, has exotic butterflies in a simulated tropical environment.

⑤ TRESAITH

The stone-built hamlet lies at the foot of a hill by a beach of firm sand below a strip of shingle. Walkers can head west along the cliffs to Aberporth or, when the tide is out, east along the sands for a mile to the beach at Penbryn. It is advisable to park at the top of the hill.

⑥ TRAETH-PENBRYN

The National Trust owns this small sandy beach, tucked between low cliffs at the end of a wooded combe. A narrow road leads to the sea, but cars must be parked in the hamlet of Penbryn, a 10 minute walk away.

⑦ LLANGRANOG

Approached along a narrow valley, the village is a small but bustling resort. From its sand and pebble beach, a path climbs onto the headland of Ynys-Lochtyn, overlooked by a 541ft hill, crowned by the site of a prehistoric fort. In the evening the dry ski-slope at the Urdd Centre, a youth centre a mile east of Llangranog, is open to the public.

SURF AND SAND *Spume-flecked waves race into Tresaith's sandy cove, with its ranks of seaweed-covered rocks and a waterfall tumbling down at the foot of a 400ft headland.*

FEEDING THE LAND

Limekilns on the Welsh coast are relics of the days in the 19th century when coasters called in with cargoes of limestone. The lime was burned in the kilns to make fertiliser for farmlands whose soil was acid through lack of underlying chalk.

Stone limekilns stand by a Welsh shore.

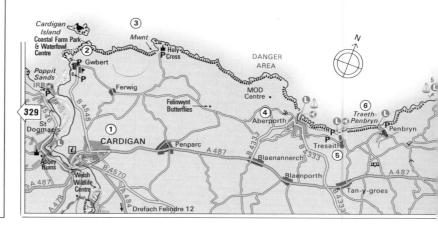

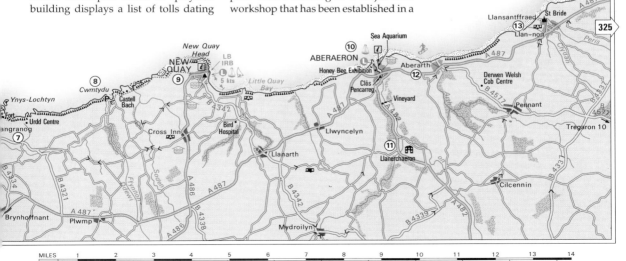

COASTAL COLORATION *A path leads over a clifftop brightly carpeted with purple heather and yellow gorse, and gains a view of Llangranog, lying in its steep-sided green valley.*

⑧ CWMTYDU

A long drive along narrow lanes leads to this secluded shingle beach, where the remains of an old lime kiln overlook the shore by the small car park. The layers of rock in the grey shale cliffs near Cwmtydu are strikingly buckled and tilted. On the eastern side of the cove, a path climbs steeply onto a grassy slope and passes the site of Castell Bach, a promontory fort occupied by a small Celtic community about 2000 years ago. The path continues along the coast to New Quay.

⑨ NEW QUAY

Streets wind down to a harbour filled with fishing boats and other craft, near a sandy beach. The quay after which the village was named was built in the early 19th century, providing the only safe harbour along this whole stretch of coast; a thriving port and shipbuilding centre developed there. A quayside building displays a list of tolls dating from the days when there was also a busy coastal trade at New Quay. Mackerel can be caught from the shore, and boat trips to watch dolphins leave from the harbour in summer. The poet Dylan Thomas lived in New Quay in the 1940s. The Bird Hospital, south-east of New Quay, treats oiled and injured sea birds and seals. It is open to visitors on Tuesday, Thursday and Saturday afternoons in summer.

⑩ ABERAERON

Terraces of pastel-shaded early 19th-century houses give Aberaeron's streets something of a Mediterranean flavour. Pleasure craft and fishing boats use the harbour. There are shingle beaches near the harbour mouth.

On the quay is the Aberaeron Sea Aquarium, and the nearby Honey Bee Exhibition gives a glimpse inside a beehive and has a display of antique honey pots. Clôs Pencarreg is a major craft workshop that has been established in a former farm. The crafts demonstrated there include pottery, glass-blowing, etching and painting in watercolours.

⑪ LLANERCHAERON

The 18th-century house was bought by the National Trust after the death in 1989 of its previous owner, who had made hardly any changes to the property for nearly half a century. The building is now being restored, but the walled garden, the ornamental garden and the farm buildings are open to the public.

⑫ ABERARTH

A tight knot of lanes lined with 19th-century terraced cottages recalls the busier days of Aberarth, once a port at the mouth of the Arth. A shingle beach can be reached from the east side of the river. Parking in the village is difficult. At the Derwen Welsh Cob Centre, east of Aberarth, visitors can see the versatile horses at close quarters; a museum explains their agricultural role.

⑬ LLANSANTFFRAED

The coast road between Aberarth and Llan-non gives fine views towards Aberystwyth. A lane from Llan-non leads to Llansantffraed, a neighbouring village on the coast. Cars can be driven as far as St Bride's Church, from where it is a few minutes' walk to a shingle beach. Parking space is limited.

PLACES TO SEE INLAND

Cors Caron National Nature Reserve, nr Tregaron, 16 miles E of Aberaeron. Raised peat bog whose diverse bird life includes herons, kestrels, ospreys and red kites.

Museum of the Welsh Woollen Industry, Drefach Felindre, 14 miles SE of Cardigan. Tools and machinery; demonstrations of weaving and spinning; working mill.

TOURIST INFORMATION

Aberaeron (01545) 570602; Cardigan (01239) 613230; New Quay (01545) 560865 (summer)

Shores where Britain's last invaders met their match

The northernmost section of the Pembrokeshire Coast Path climbs and dips along a switchback route, onto high vantage points and past tiny, chisel-shaped coves. Inland, early settlers left monuments on the hills.

ESTUARY TOWN *Lower Town, the oldest part of Fishguard, lies at the mouth of the steep-sided valley of the River Gwaun. The valley was carved out by Ice Age glacial meltwater.*

① STRUMBLE HEAD

Approached along a network of lanes, the remote headland gives splendid views of the nearby cliffs and of the lighthouse on Ynys Meicel, an island just offshore. In very clear conditions the Irish coast can be seen. Strumble Head's car park is a popular starting point for walks along the coast path.

② CARREGWASTAD POINT

An inscribed stone at Carregwastad Point commemorates the most recent invasion of Britain, which took place in 1797 during the Napoleonic Wars. A ragged, drunken force of some 1200 men, made up of Frenchmen and convicts, came ashore, led by an elderly American; they surrendered only a few days later. It is said that the attackers took fright when they saw local women dressed in Welsh costume, and mistook their red shawls and tall hats for the uniforms of British soldiers. The invaders seized Tre-Howel, a farmhouse still standing a mile inland, as their headquarters. Carregwastad Point can be reached only on foot; there are paths from Tre-Howel and Llanwnda.

③ GOODWICK

Sited at the western end of Fishguard Bay, the village retains a distinctly Victorian character. A creation of the Great Western Railway, it was intended to be a terminal for liners sailing to and from New York, but the transatlantic trade later shifted to Southampton. Today ferries leave the harbour for Rosslare, in Ireland; there are day trips to Dublin, Waterford and Cork.

④ FISHGUARD

The hub of the town is a hilly area of narrow streets centred on The Square, on one side of which is an inn, the Royal Oak, where the French surrender of 1797 was signed. In the pub are a captured French musket and other battle memorabilia. Lower Town, set round the mouth of the River Gwaun, preserves the character of a fishing village. From a car park by the coast road just north of Lower Town, a short path leads to the ruins of Old Fort, which was constructed in 1781 and gives views towards the ferry terminal.

South-east of Fishguard, lanes lead along the unspoilt Gwaun valley, where waymarked walks start at Sychbant car park, 3 miles east of Cilrhedyn Bridge.

⑤ DINAS HEAD

Jutting out between Fishguard Bay and Newport Bay, the stubby peninsula of Dinas Head provides a 3 mile circular walk along cliffs and through Cwm Dewi, the sheltered valley that divides it from the mainland. Cwm-yr-Eglwys, the village at the eastern end of Cwm Dewi, has a sandy beach and is a good starting point for walks. The village's ruined St Brynach's Church was a victim of a great storm of 1859, which in a single night wrecked more than 100 ships off the Welsh coast. Pwllgwaelod, at the western end of Cwm Dewi, is a beach of sand and rocks.

⑥ NEWPORT

St Mary's Church overlooks the small town's most attractive corners, including its castle, dating from Norman times and now a private house. Carreg Coetan Arthur burial chamber, erected round 3500BC, stands among modern houses. The sandy Parrog Beach, on the south side of the Nyfer estuary, retains a small quay, a vestige of Newport's days

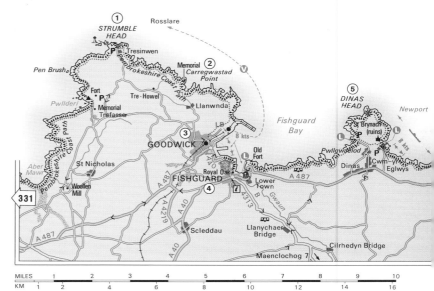

CELTIC CROSS *At Nevern the Great Cross of St Brynach stands 13 ft high. Its intricate carvings show an Irish influence.*

as a port. A mile-long walk beside the north side of the estuary, or a 3 mile drive, leads to Newport Sands, which are backed by dunes. The town has an information centre for visitors to the Pembrokeshire Coast National Park, which extends round the coast from Poppit Sands to Amroth, near Tenby.

⑦ NEVERN

The tranquil village sits in the valley of the Nyfer, whose birdlife includes the scarce avocet. A stone cross carved in the 10th or 11th century stands in the churchyard of ancient St Brynach's Church. Sticky red sap oozes from what is known as the 'bleeding yew', in an avenue of yews leading to the church porch. Of the nearby Norman castle little remains except for grassy humps overshadowed by trees.

⑧ PENTRE IFAN

The Neolithic burial chamber known as Pentre Ifan comprises a 17 ft capstone supported by three upright stones. From its elevated site views extend northwards towards the sea and southwards to the 1760 ft Mynydd Preseli. Pentre Ifan is reached by a footpath from a parking space on a remote lane.

Nearby there are many other relics of early settlers. Carningli Common, west of Pentre Ifan, is studded with ancient hut circles. To the south of Newport, a track along the ridge of Mynydd Preseli passes stone circles, cairns, standing stones and burial chambers. The exposed ridge gives magnificent views as far as Dunkery Beacon in Somerset and Snowdonia in north Wales.

⑨ CASTELL HENLLYS

Circular huts with large thatched conical roofs are part of a reconstructed Iron Age village, built as it might have been 2400 years ago, on the site of a hill-fort, with plunging slopes on three sides. Occasional re-enactments show how the inhabitants lived and worked.

⑩ MOYLGROVE

Lanes dip down steeply into the peaceful one-street village. To the north-west at the narrow inlet of Ceibwr Bay, low tide reveals a shingle beach beneath imposing cliffs. The bay is the only point that can be reached by road on the 11 miles of coast from Newport Bay to Poppit Sands. A mile's walk south-west

---

ANCIENT CRAFT ON THE TEIFI

Coracles are used for salmon fishing on the River Teifi, mainly between Cilgerran and Cenarth. Sea-bass fishing takes place after dusk. Easily carried, the boats are made of intertwined laths of willow and hazel covered with fabric and pitch. The bowl-shaped design is unchanged since the Iron Age, except that ancient Britons used animal hide to cover the craft.

A fisherman paddling a coracle

---

along the coast from the bay passes a dramatic blowhole called Pwll-y-wrach (the Witches' Cauldron). Beyond the blowhole, the coast path can be treacherous in places as it follows high cliffs.

⑪ POPPIT SANDS

Dunes flank the wide, popular sandy beach at the mouth of the Teifi estuary. Swimmers should beware of currents at mid-tide and avoid the deep-water channel farther out at all times. There is a testing uphill walk from the beach to Cemaes Head. South-west of the headland cliffs rise to more than 500 ft.

The beach lies at the northern end of the 168 mile Pembrokeshire Coast Path, which follows the inlets and headlands of the coast to Amroth, north of Tenby.

⑫ ST DOGMAELS

The sloping village above the River Teifi grew up round St Dogmaels Abbey (Cadw), which was established by the Welsh, probably in the 7th century. The ruins date from the 12th century. Next to the abbey is the Church of St Thomas, which has a stone whose inscriptions provided the key to an early alphabet.

On the River Teifi, a few fishermen use seine nets to catch salmon. One end of the net is held on shore, and the other by a boat. The seine is cast in a semicircle and the ends are pulled together.

⑬ WELSH WILDLIFE CENTRE

Woodland, freshwater marsh and salt marsh are all found in this extensive nature reserve along the tidal stretch of the River Teifi, and reached by a lane from Cilgerran. Disused slate quarries and lime kilns are relics of 19th-century industry. The reserve has one of Britain's largest colonies of Cetti's warblers, as well as numerous bitterns; otters may also be seen. There are birdwatchers' hides and several trails, and daily guided walks in summer.

⑭ CILGERRAN

The impregnable-looking Cilgerran Castle (Cadw/NT) perches above a wooded gorge on the winding River Teifi. The castle was founded by the Normans, but most of it dates from the 13th century, and in 1387 it withstood a siege by the Flemish. There is a fine view of the castle from the river, which is popular with canoeists. Cilgerran hosts a Coracle Regatta in August.

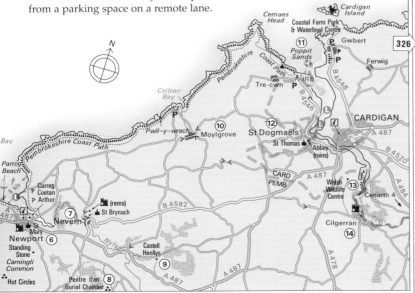

PLACES TO SEE INLAND

Cenarth, 7 miles SE of Cardigan. National Coracle Centre, with coracles from Wales and elsewhere; trips in the boats can sometimes be arranged. 17th-century mill. Smithy and museum.

Penrhos Cottage, Maenclochog, 11 miles SE of Fishguard. Single-storey thatched cottage, little altered since the 19th century, with Welsh oak furniture.

TOURIST INFORMATION

Cardigan (01239) 613230; Fishguard (01348) 873484

A wild coast of forgotten ports, and a pilgrim city

Founded by the patron saint of Wales in the 6th century, St David's is Britain's smallest city. The sea was once the only highway on this rugged coast, where pleasure craft now anchor in the ancient harbours.

① PWLLDERI

A narrow lane from Trefasser leads past a memorial to Dewi Emrys, an early 20th-century poet of the Pembroke coast, to a clifftop viewpoint above the rocky cove of Pwllderi. On a clear day St David's Head can be seen 21 miles to the south-west. A dramatic stretch of the coast path winds north-east to Strumble Head, while a steeper route ascends to the Iron Age fortress of Garn Fawr. The fort can be reached more easily from the car park on the landward side. In clear conditions the coast of Ireland can be seen from ramparts on the summit.

② ABER MAWR

Low tide exposes tree stumps lying in the sand and shingle of this isolated beach. Perfectly preserved by the salt water, they are the remnants of a forest drowned by a sudden flood 8000 years ago as the European ice-sheets melted. Melin Tregwynt, a mile to the east, is an 18th-century working woollen mill.

③ ABERCASTLE

From Tudor times until the 1930s Abercastle was a thriving port and boat yard, but only limekilns, an old granary

Carreg Sampson, near Abercastle

and a few cottages now line the quiet creek, where some sand is revealed at low water. Half a mile to the west, at Longhouse Farm, Carreg Sampson is a magnificent 5000-year-old cromlech, an open-sided tomb of massive stones.

④ TREVINE

The elegant hilltop village has a broad high street lined with pretty cottages. Aber Draw Mill had, until recently, stood as a ruin since 1918. It was the subject of a Welsh poem, called 'Melin Trefin', by Crwys Williams, who was born in Trevine in 1875 and predicted its decline. The mill has been restored and visitors can watch weavers at work on a 300-year-old hand loom.

⑤ PORTHGAIN

Immense brick walls tower over the harbour of Porthgain. Constructed in the 19th century, the walls once formed storage bins for granite roadstone, 40 000 tons of which were loaded into coastal steamers every year. The crushing plant and quarries closed in 1932, but the village remains a thriving community, whose harbour is used by fishing boats and a few pleasure craft.

⑥ ABEREIDDY

Slate-grey sands create an unusual beach on this fine west-facing bay. A short path leads from the car park past ruined cottages to the Blue Lagoon, a deep sheer-sided pool that was formerly a slate quarry and now provides a sheltered and romantic anchorage for small boats. Farther north, along the coast path, there are isolated sandy beaches beneath the cliffs at Traethllyfn.

⑦ ST DAVID'S HEAD

Stone outcrops rise above wild but beautiful moorland on this peninsula. An ancient route that once linked Pembrokeshire with Salisbury Plain and Ireland leads down to the shore, and there is a Neolithic cromlech on the skyline. An Iron Age fort on the headland stands near a stone rampart known as The Warrior's Dyke.

⑧ WHITESANDS BAY

One of the most popular beaches in Pembrokeshire, Whitesands Bay is divided into different areas for surfing, canoeing and swimming. There is a fine expanse of sand, and the views across to Ramsey Island from the beach, particularly at sunset, are spectacular.

⑨ ST JUSTINIAN

The appealing but rockbound cove is named after a 6th-century Breton saint. A ruined chapel stands on the spot where he was buried, overlooking St

A SECLUDED INLET *Solva's creek was once busy with coasters, and steamships sailing as far as America. Today the smooth, glass-like waters provide an ideal anchorage for yachts.*

LIFEBOAT AWAY! *St David's lifeboat is launched from its haven on Ramsey Sound. The frequent storms along the rocky coast mean that the lifeboat is often called into action.*

Justinian's lifeboat station, which was used as the location for the television drama series *Lifeboat*.

⑩ RAMSEY ISLAND
RSPB RESERVE

Boats to this superb bird sanctuary of cliffs and mountain heath depart in summer from St Justinian. Guillemots, razorbills and kittiwakes nest on 400 ft precipices above isolated coves where grey seals breed, while fields grazed by sheep and deer provide a perfect habitat for birds such as lapwings.

⑪ PORTHCLAIS

Only fishermen and pleasure craft now use this narrow tidal inlet that was once the port of St David's and an important base for trade with Ireland. Limekilns by the water's edge recall the days when local farmers used slaked lime to sweeten the acidic soil. A hillside path leads from the car park to the late medieval harbour walls.

⑫ ST DAVID'S

The smallest of all cathedral cities, St David's was the birthplace of the patron saint of Wales. St David founded a monastery there during the 6th century, and the city became a place of pilgrimage in the Middle Ages. The present cathedral dates largely from the late 12th century, but incorporates

later features such as the carved Renaissance ceiling in the nave. The building has a superb setting in a valley by the massive and ornate ruins of Bishop's Palace (Cadw), which date mainly from the 14th century. St David's has an Oceanarium and a Marine Life Centre, and rare breeds of livestock can be seen at St David's Farm Park. There is an attractively sited golf course on the road to Whitesands Bay.

St Non's Chapel (Cadw), south of the city, is traditionally identified as the birthplace of St David's mother, and has a healing well that still attracts visitors.

⑬ CAERFAI BAY

A lane from St David's leads to a clifftop car park with sweeping views across St Brides Bay. The climb down to the beach at Caerfai is steep, but low tide reveals extensive sands beneath the cliffs of red, mauve and green stone. The purple sandstone used for St David's Cathedral came from nearby quarries at Caer Bwdy.

⑭ SOLVA

Set on a narrow, sheltered inlet that winds inland beneath steep hills, Solva has a history of sea trade, piracy and smuggling dating back to the 7th century. By the early 19th century the village had a population of 1200 and a fleet of 30 ships. There were even scheduled crossings to America. Its last steamship was torpedoed by a U-boat in the harbour mouth in 1915. Today, the harbour is thronged with pleasure craft.

⑮ NEWGALE

Two miles of sand attract surfers and swimmers to Newgale. At high tide waves break against a shingle bank thrown up by violent storms. Brandy Brook, at the northern end of the beach, is said to mark the divide between English-speaking Pembrokeshire and Welsh-speaking country to the north.

PLACES TO SEE INLAND

Treffgarne, 15 miles E of St David's. Moorland walks, wooded gorge, craft shop in converted water mill.

TOURIST INFORMATION

St David's (01437) 720392 (summer)

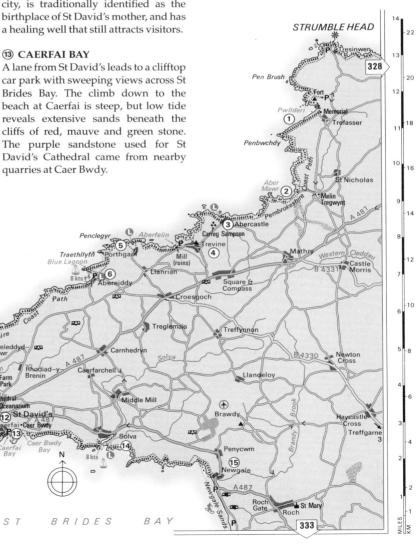

Shimmering sands curling round St Brides Bay

Beautiful beaches such as pristine Marloes Sands and the watersports centre of Dale cluster round this coastline. Offshore are the bird islands of Skomer, surrounded by Wales's first marine reserve, and Skokholm.

GOLDEN BLAZE OF SUMMER
From high summer to late autumn, the clifftops of west Wales are vivid with the yellow flowers of western gorse. Though gorse is common throughout Britain, western gorse is a different species, with smaller flowers and shorter spines, and is found only on the west coast of Britain and southern Scotland.

Western gorse
Ulex gallii
July-Sept

① ROCH
The village centre remains unspoilt despite some sprawling outskirts. Farm buildings and the Church of St Mary stand around the gates of Roch Castle, a 12th-century tower perched upon a rocky pinnacle. The castle was the birthplace, in 1630, of Charles II's mistress, Lucy Walter, mother of the tragic Duke of Monmouth, who was executed for his rebellion against James II. It is now rented out as holiday accommodation.

② NOLTON HAVEN
Few traces remain of the coal industry that once brought prosperity to the pretty village of Nolton Haven, but tunnels from abandoned workings run out deep beneath the sea. Remnants of a landing quay overlook a sandy cove backed by grassy slopes.

③ DRUIDSTON HAVEN
Narrow lanes with little opportunity for parking, and a steep climb down a cliff path ensure that this isolated beach is seldom crowded. It consists of a pebble bank at high tide, but the low water reveals a mile of sand.

④ BROAD HAVEN
A wide expanse of sand with easy access from the road has ensured the popularity of this lively resort. Shops and hotels overlook the little esplanade that runs behind the attractive beach. Natural arches and other interesting rock formations can be seen in the cliffs to the north and south.

⑤ LITTLE HAVEN
Steep hills backing a small harbour have restricted development in this pretty fishing village. Narrow lanes wind past charming old cottages, and engaging pubs overlook the quay, with ample parking nearby. At low tide it is possible to walk along the shore across the sandy beaches at The Settlands to Broad Haven, less than a mile away.

⑥ ST BRIDES HAVEN
The remote sandy cove has a gentle beauty that contrasts with the wilder seascapes of the area. There are rock pools to explore and the evening tide attracts sea anglers. The ancient Church of St Bride, with its churchyard of old stone monuments, overlooks the beach. Remains of early Christian graves can be seen in cliffs beyond the ruined limekiln on the headland. The Gothic mansion to the west, known as St Bride's Castle, was built in 1800 by Lord Kensington, a former local MP, and is now divided into flats.

⑦ MARTIN'S HAVEN
The departure point for summer trips to the islands of Skokholm and Skomer, Martin's Haven consists of little more than a few houses and a car park. An old stone wall, cutting off the headland from the rest of the peninsula, encloses an area of wilderness known as the Deer Park (NT). The deer, if they were ever there, have long escaped, but walks across uncultivated grassland take in clifftop scenery with superb views of the coast, and offer the chance to glimpse rare birds such as the chough, a member of the crow family that is now extinct in most of Britain.

⑧ SKOMER ISLAND
NATIONAL NATURE RESERVE
Skomer, reached by boat from Martin's Haven, is the breeding ground of almost half the world's population of Manx shearwaters, with an estimated 165 000 pairs nesting in clifftop burrows. Puffins, guillemots and razorbills are also common, while grey seals breed in shoreline caves and dolphins fish the tidal races. Wild flowers such as sea pinks and yellow samphires are spectacular in spring and early summer. The seas, seabed and shore around Skomer form a marine nature reserve, whose range of habitats support a great number of creatures and plants, including corals, sponges, sea firs, sea slugs and dogfish.

⑨ SKOKHOLM ISLAND
Smaller and more remote than Skomer, Skokholm was the site of Britain's first bird observatory in 1933. The observatory is now an old farmhouse. Manx shearwaters, puffins and storm petrels are abundant, and the island is a resting place for many migrant species.

⑩ MARLOES SANDS
A 10 minute walk from the car park west of Marloes village leads to one of Britain's finest beaches. Golden sands and colourful, dramatic cliffs contribute to the setting, though bathing can be dangerous in heavy seas, and parts of the beach are cut off by the rising tide. Marloes Mere, at the western end of the beach, was once famous for its leeches, which were profitably gathered for sale to London doctors in the 18th century.

⑪ ST ANN'S HEAD
A lighthouse, a coastguard station and a scattering of whitewashed cottages stand isolated on this windswept headland, whose cliffs provide splendid views of Skokholm Island and the shipping lanes of Milford Haven. In 1485 Henry Tudor, having previously fled from Wales to Brittany, landed at Mill Bay and within a fortnight won the English crown at Bosworth Field.

⑫ DALE
Yachting gear and wet suits are the summer fashions in this village on a sheltered bay that gives distant views of Milford Haven's oil refineries. The shingle and sand beach is not for bathers or surfers, but ideal for every other form of watersport, and on breezy days the waters of Dale Roads are alive with brightly coloured sails. To the west of the Church of St James the Great a short path descends to Westdale Bay, an isolated, sandy cove beneath a huge Iron Age fort. Visitors should beware of strong currents and unstable cliffs.

FIRST LIGHT *Built in 1714, the lighthouse on St Ann's Head was the first to operate on the west coast of Wales.*

romantically abandoned gardens to a tiny cove at Monk Haven, where low tide exposes a thin strip of sand below the pebble beach. A rugged clifftop route continues to an Iron Age fort on Little Castle Head.

⑭ SANDY HAVEN

A blend of subtly coloured muddy sand and abstract shapes of driftwood along a beautiful tidal creek provided the inspiration for many scenes painted by the 20th-century artist Graham Sutherland. The eastern shore is occupied by a caravan and camping site.

PLACES TO SEE INLAND

Pembrokeshire Motor Museum, Simpson Cross, 2 miles SE of Roch. A private collection of classic cars, motorcycles and toys.

TOURIST INFORMATION

Broad Haven (01437) 781412 (summer)

FLAT-TOPPED BLUFFS *Clifftops along the south Pembrokeshire coast, such as those at Marloes Sands, are strikingly level.*

⑬ ST ISHMAEL'S

The village was once the site of a Norman castle, now marked by a roadside mound. The Norman Church of St Ishmael, tucked away in a wooded valley to the south, is the village's secret gem. From the fascinating, overgrown churchyard, a short path winds through

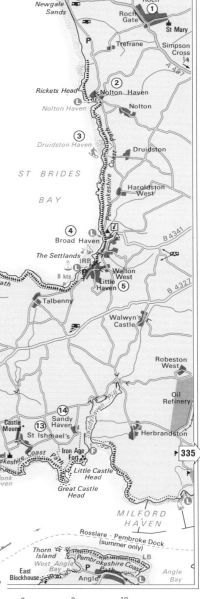

Lonely creeks and a great oil port by Milford Haven

Huge tankers berth in Milford Haven's deep-water harbour, while pleasure craft sail upstream into a maze of tidal creeks edged with gentle countryside that has been dubbed 'Little England beyond Wales'.

① MILFORD HAVEN

During a brief visit in 1802, Lord Nelson pronounced Milford Haven to be the finest natural harbour in the northern hemisphere. His enthusiasm may well have been encouraged by his mistress, Emma Hamilton, whose husband Sir William was involved in building a new town that was given the same name as the waterway it borders. Together with Charles Greville, Hamilton developed Milford Haven as a whaling station and a naval dockyard, but the venture failed to prosper and the town faced a decline until the 1880s, when large new docks became the centre of a thriving fishing industry. In the 1960s, Milford Haven entered its third age, developing as one of the biggest oil ports in Europe, and prospering until the ending of the oil boom in early 1980s.

The docks have been renovated to provide a variety of entertainments and attractions for visitors. The Heritage and Maritime Museum has displays of local history, and the Kaleidoscope Discovery Centre features 'hands-on' scientific toys. Among the boats on display in the marina are a working lightship and a gaff-rigged schooner.

② NEYLAND

The terraced streets of the little town were built in the 1850s around the terminus of Isambard Brunel's South Wales Railway. Brunel had planned a port for ocean-going steamers, but Neyland never quite lived up to expectations. The town lost its rail link in the 1950s, and the ferry service to Pembroke Dock ceased operating after the opening of the Cleddau Bridge in 1975. The focus of modern development is a large marina. To the west, past Llanstadwell's castellated Church of St David, the rock and shingle shore of Hazelbeach affords views of Pembroke Dock and its power station, and upstream towards the Cleddau Bridge.

③ LLANGWM

The name of this compact riverside village is said to be not Welsh, but Flemish, a corruption of *lang heim*, meaning 'a long way from home'. Llangwm was indeed a Flemish settlement, established in the 12th century by Henry I in an effort to undermine Welsh influence and create a culture loyal to the English throne. The village is a good starting place for walks through the rolling countryside and along the Daugleddau, and a 6 mile circular walk leads south from the village green.

④ HAVERFORDWEST

Until the railway arrived in the 1850s, ships came up the Western Cleddau at high tide to dock at this important

AN ARTIST IN WALES

The artist Graham Sutherland (1903-80) is perhaps best known for his tapestry *Christ in Glory* in Coventry Cathedral, and for his controversial portrait of Winston Churchill. However, the Pembrokeshire coastline was a constant source of inspiration to Sutherland, and many scenes he painted in the area are displayed in the Graham Sutherland Gallery at Picton Castle.

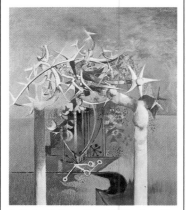

Sutherland's Thorn Trees *(1946) reflects his impressions of trees along the riverbanks.*

OIL AND FISH *Oil refining replaced fishing as the main industry at Milford Haven in the 1960s. Now it too is in decline, but the sewin, a unique local sea-trout, is still fished.*

market town. Founded by the Normans as a garrison, Haverfordwest was settled by Flemish immigrants, threatened by Welsh princes and sacked by the French in 1405 in the course of Owain Glyndwr's rising, though all attemps to take the castle failed. For centuries the town flourished as a port with a reputation for illicit trade and piracy.

The substantial but neglected castle ruins overlook the lively high street and 13th-century St Mary's Church, which has a splendid arcade of pointed arches with elaborately decorated pillars. Remains of an Augustinian priory, founded in the 13th century, can be seen off Quay Street along the river, where old quays have been redeveloped.

⑤ PICTON CASTLE

Built late in the 13th century on the site of an earlier fortification, Picton Castle has been for the past 500 years the home of the Philipps family, who transformed it from a fortress to a country house. The extensive grounds include landscaped gardens and woodland walks. The house can be visited by guided tour on some afternoons each week. A gallery behind the house is devoted to the works of Graham Sutherland, who painted many pictures of the lonely tidal creeks along the Daugleddau and its tributaries. The Eastern Cleddau can be reached along the lane that runs south from the castle gates.

⑥ LANDSHIPPING QUAY

Early in the 19th century, 6000 tons of coal were loaded at Landshipping Quay each year, but mining ceased in 1844 after floods swept through a local pit at a cost of some 40 lives. It is hard to imagine the industry and hardship that once characterised life on this peaceful stretch of river, where wading birds feed off the mud flats and otters may occasionally be seen.

⑦ LAWRENNY

Pleasure boats congregate around the moorings at Lawrenny Quay, 12 miles from the open sea. On high ground above the quay, bordering National Trust woodland, the terrace of a long-demolished country house provides a picnic site with views across the maze of tidal waterways.

⑧ CAREW

The ruined shell of Carew Castle, part medieval fortress, part Elizabethan mansion, overlooks the river crossing. The castle was besieged and slighted in the Civil War, but remains a fascinating and romantic place.

Next to the bridge by the castle is an intricately decorated 14 ft Celtic Cross, one of the finest early Christian monuments in Wales. Downstream, opposite one of Britain's few remaining working tidal mills, a stone causeway serves as a footbridge to the north bank of the Carew and a hillside picnic site. To the

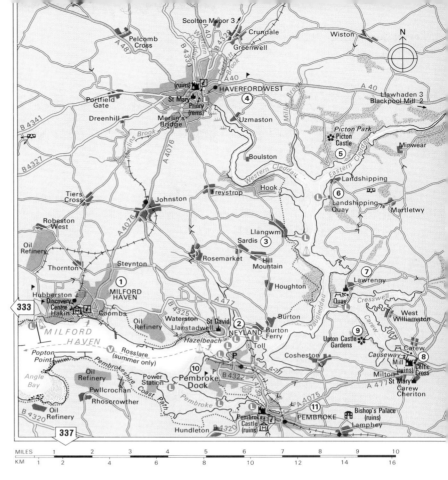

south, in Carew Cheriton, the early 14th-century church of St Mary includes medieval tiles from the castle.

⑨ UPTON CASTLE GARDENS

The large grounds, in which stand a privately owned 19th-century Gothic mansion, consist of formal terraces and woodland walks leading to a tree-lined riverside path. A small medieval chapel within the grounds contains some fine carved effigies dating from the 13th to the 15th centuries.

⑩ PEMBROKE DOCK

During the Napoleonic Wars, entrepreneur Charles Greville charged increasingly high prices for building warships in his dockyard at Milford Haven, and in 1814 the Admiralty established its own yards at Pembroke Dock, with Martello towers and barracks to defend them and rows of terraced houses for the shipyard workers.

Shipbuilding ceased in 1926, but during World War II the town was an important base for flying-boats and the starting point for Atlantic convoys, and consequently suffered many air raids. The docks are used by both military and commercial ships, and a vehicle ferry runs from Pembroke Dock to Rosslare in the Irish Republic.

⑪ PEMBROKE

First settled by the Normans, the town is dominated by its massive castle, which stands on a butt of rock surrounded on three sides by water. The castle was badly damaged during the

Civil War before being captured by Cromwell's forces – the first occasion on which it had fallen during a long and bloody history. The rounded keep is almost 80 ft in height and battlemented walkways link the many towers. Beneath the Northern Hall is the Wogan Cavern, an enormous natural cave overlooking the river. The small town includes a pleasing hotchpotch of old buildings. In Westgate Hill, opposite the castle entrance, the Museum of the Home displays domestic bygones.

Pembroke Castle

PLACES TO SEE INLAND

Blackpool Mill, 8 miles E of Haverfordwest. Renovated iron foundry and watermill. Riverside walks through Minwear Woods.

Llawhaden Castle, 9 miles E of Haverfordwest. Impressive ruins of 13th-century castle.

Scolton Manor, 5 miles NE of Haverfordwest. Georgian mansion housing a museum of local history. Located in a country park.

TOURIST INFORMATION

Haverfordwest (01437) 763110; Milford Haven (01646) 690866 (summer); Pembroke (01646) 622388; Pembroke Dock (01646) 622246 (summer)

Coves and sea stacks of South Pembrokeshire

The rugged cliffs on the western side of the Pembroke peninsula are lashed by Atlantic waves. Eastwards, a string of sandy bays leads to the resort town of Tenby and the sheltered waters of Carmarthen Bay.

① ANGLE

The peaceful, end-of-the-road village keeps its greatest treasures hidden from view. Behind St Mary's Church is a fortified tower, probably Norman, of a type common in the Scottish borders but rare in Wales. Nearby is the tiny 15th-century Seamen's Chapel, with a painted vault and stained-glass windows depicting scriptural sea scenes. A rough track leads down from the church to an inlet of Angle Bay, where a few boats are laid up on mud and shingle, and there is a good view over the Milford Haven waterway.

About a mile to the west of the village is West Angle Bay, where a large beach of soft sand and gently rolling surf offers views of the fortifications that once protected Milford Haven. The original Elizabethan East Blockhouse totters on the edge of a cliff at the southern extremity of the bay; its 19th-century replacement is close by. West Blockhouse can be glimpsed across the Milford Haven estuary. The fort on Thorn Island at the northern edge of West Angle Bay is now a hotel.

SWEET SMELL OF SUCCESS

Gorse blooms and fragrant herbs grown on Caldey Island are used by Cistercian monks to make perfumed sachets which are sold to visitors. Natural essences are blended to make the well-known Caldey Island perfume. The thriving monastery farms most of the island's 600 acres, with dairy and sheep farming the main enterprises. Dairy produce from the Jersey herd is used and sold on the island.

Monks gather gorse blooms on Caldey Island.

② FRESHWATER WEST

High dunes, a vast expanse of flat, sandy beach and crashing surf combine to make this a spectacular bay. It is also a dangerous one, with a strong undertow on the ebb tide and low-water quicksands at the northern end of the beach. Halfway along the beach, at Little Furzenip, a small thatched hut dates from the time when seaweed was brought here for storing and making into laver bread, a South Wales delicacy.

③ CASTLEMARTIN

The most conspicuous feature of this village is what appears to be a walled traffic island, but is in fact an 18th-century cattle pound. The stone enclosure now contains a small public garden. Another curiosity is the Church of St Michael and All Angels, which stands in isolation at the bottom of the hill. Its immense castellated tower may have been built as a defensible strongpoint against local pirates, a tradition throughout the south-west. An army training range occupies the south-west of the peninsula, sending the Pembrokeshire Coast Path inland and along the B4319 through Castlemartin. The eastern side of the range is accessible most weekends, when the coast path between Elegug Stacks and St Govan's Chapel can be walked.

④ ELEGUG STACKS

Two great limestone pillars rear up out of the waves beside high cliffs. In the summer breeding season guillemots arrive in great flocks, perching on any available ledge and jostling for space with an array of auks, razorbills, ful-

CHAPEL OF MYSTERY *Little is known about St Govan, whose tiny chapel stands on a rocky ledge. Some say he was the Arthurian knight Sir Gawain, who became a hermit.*

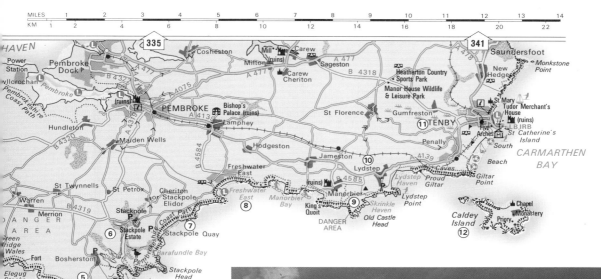

mars and kittiwakes. Just to the west, a natural rock arch, known as the Green Bridge of Wales, thrusts out from the cliffs. The headland immediately to the east shows traces of the defensive ditches and ramparts of an Iron Age fort. When Castlemartin Range is not in use, visitors can enjoy an exhilarating walk along the dramatic cliff path east from Elegug Stacks to St Govan's Head.

⑤ ST GOVAN'S CHAPEL

A flight of steep, well-worn stone steps lead down to a tiny church squeezed into a cleft in the rocks. According to tradition, St Govan was being pursued by pirates when the rocks split open to provide a hiding place, and he stayed here preaching and praying until his death in AD 586. The present chapel, however, dates from the 11th century. Outside is a small well, now dry, whose waters were thought to have healing powers. Legend is also behind the naming of nearby Bell Rock. The church bell, stolen by pirates, was said to have been saved by angels, who set it in the rock; when St Govan struck the boulder, it sounded as loud as a mighty cathedral bell. Just to the west is a great gash in the cliffs known as Huntsman's Leap; a huntsman is reputed to have jumped his horse over this 180 ft cleft – and then, on looking back, to have died of fright.

⑥ STACKPOLE ESTATE

The estate, parts of which are a nature reserve, is centred on a vast area of lily ponds created in the 18th century to enhance the now-demolished Stackpole Court. From car parks at Stackpole and Bosherston, tree-shaded walks at the water's edge and over footbridges enable visitors to watch the waders and waterfowl that congregate on the ponds. There is a walk out across the dunes to the sandy bay of Broad Haven, a sheltered south-facing bay almost enclosed by a horseshoe of rocks and

'AGREEABLE TENBY' *In his* Tour through Great Britain *of 1724, Daniel Defoe described Tenby as 'the most agreeable town on all the south coast of Wales, except Pembroke'.*

dunes. Stackpole Estate is owned by the National Trust, as is the stretch of coast to Freshwater East to the north-east.

⑦ STACKPOLE QUAY

The quay, now disused, was built to ship local limestone and to bring in fuel for the Stackpole Estate, and the dunes and grassland to the west of the bay form part of the estate's nature reserve. A clifftop walk leads south-west past an area of grey limestone stacks and arches to the fine sandy beach of Barafundle Bay. To the south is Stackpole Head, around which are several caves that have collapsed into blowholes. North-east of Stackpole Quay, the limestone cliffs give way to rich orange sandstone.

⑧ FRESHWATER EAST

Wide sands backed by dunes and good road access make Freshwater East a popular family beach. The crescent-shaped beach faces east, and is thus sheltered from the prevailing winds.

⑨ MANORBIER

When the traveller and writer Giraldus Cambrensis, or Gerald of Wales, was born there in 1146, the new stone castle built by his family, the powerful de Barris, was noted for its sumptuous

baronial hall and living quarters. The Norman edifice is still sternly impressive, with its solid towers and gatehouse and high curtain walls. The stout ruins look out over a popular sandy beach, noted for its good surf. Bathers should beware of powerful undertows in rough weather.

On the headland south of the beach are the remains of a 5000-year-old burial chamber, known as King's Quoit, which consists of a massive capstone supported on two uprights. Farther along the coast, past a firing range on Old Castle Head, a steep flight of steps leads down to the sandy beach of Skrinkle Haven and its high rock arch striding out into the sea.

⑩ LYDSTEP

A toll road serving a caravan site leads to the sheltered, sandy beach of Lydstep Haven. There are beachside amusements, and watersports include water-skiing. A short clifftop walk south leads to the headland of Lydstep Point (NT).

⑪ TENBY

The resort's great appeal for holiday-makers lies in its beaches, together offering over a mile of fine sand and sheltered bathing, and in its beautiful

SEA-TOWERS OF BABEL *Home to multitudes of raucous sea birds, the Elegug Stacks are carved from limestone by the relentless tides. Guillemots crowd the stacks and upper ledges (elegug means guillemot in Welsh), while razorbills and fulmars nest below.*

little harbour crowded with boats. In the town's narrow streets, Georgian villas with intricate iron balconies jostle with fishermen's cottages.

Much of Tenby's present character comes from its development in the 19th century as a watering place by Sir William Paxton, but its origins are much older. Little remains of the Norman castle; most of it was destroyed by Cromwell's forces during the Civil War. But much survives of the 13th-century town wall, including the old west gate, now known as Five Arches. The medieval St Mary's Church is enlivened by carved figures looking down from the nave roof, and by ornate chancel vaulting. The town's past prosperity is reflected in the refurbished Tudor Merchant's House (NT) and in displays at the local museum, where there is also a section devoted to the work of the Tenby-born artist Augustus John. Other attractions include an aquarium and an indoor swimming pool.

On St Catherine's Island, which can be reached on foot at low tide, is a 19th-century fortress, an outpost of the protective ring that once defended the military dockyards of Milford Haven.

⑫ CALDEY ISLAND

The first monks came to Caldey Island in the 6th century, and memories of those days survive in a cross with an inscription in the Celtic ogham alphabet. The Benedictines arrived in the 12th century and remained on the island until the dissolution of the monasteries by Henry VIII. Surviving buildings that date from that time include the gatehouse and the Prior's Lodging. Monastic life resumed in 1929, and the rebuilt monastery is now home to monks of the Cistercian order.

Caldey Island can be visited by boat from Tenby during the summer. Visitors can see the churches, buy the perfume and chocolate made by the monks, or simply enjoy the calm of this wooded island. There are splendid views of colonies of seals and sea birds from the top of the hill which crowns the island. Only male visitors are allowed into the monastery itself.

PLACES TO SEE INLAND

Bishop's Palace (Cadw), Lamphey, 8 miles W of Tenby. Ruins of 13th-century palace of the archbishops of St Davids.

Manor House Wildlife and Leisure Park, 3 miles NW of Tenby. Wildlife, wooded grounds, 18th-century manor house, amusements. Nearby is the all-weather Heatherton Country Sports Park.

TOURIST INFORMATION

Pembroke (01646) 622388; Tenby (01834) 842402

Flat sands and a poet's home on Carmarthen Bay

Wide, sandy bays give way to broad estuaries and maze-like creeks that were once protected by a string of castles. Inland, meandering rivers flow through the rich agricultural area surrounding Carmarthen.

SANDS OF TIME *Large caves mark the western end of Pendine Sands, the site of dramatic events such as Malcolm Campbell's land-speed record of 146 mph in 1926.*

① SAUNDERSFOOT
At the northern end of the lively little resort's long sandy beach is an attractive harbour full of pleasure boats. Saundersfoot has its origins in the 19th century, when its harbour was built to export coal from nearby mines, but there are few traces left of the industrial past. The Stepaside Heritage Park, on the grounds of a former colliery and ironworks about a mile inland, contains a bird park and a craft village.

② WISEMAN'S BRIDGE
The roads to this little hamlet from both Saundersfood and Stepaside, on the A477, wind through a wooded valley, while the coast path from Saundersfoot follows a disused railway track. The firm sandy beach, which affords good views south-east towards the Gower Peninsula, was used for exercises in preparation for the D-Day landings.

③ AMROTH
The little village overlooks a vast sandy beach backed by shingle and rocks, and protected by wooden groynes. Exceptionally low tides reveal the stumps of trees belonging to an ancient forest, long since drowned by the waves.

A tiny stream meandering down to the beach marks both the old county boundary between Pembrokeshire and Carmarthenshire, and the southern end of the Pembrokeshire Coast Path, which starts near Cardigan some 180 miles away. In a secluded valley just to the north of Amroth is Colby Woodland Garden (NT), where a stream cascades down a hillside through a series of pools and ponds. In spring bluebells and daffodils cover the grounds.

④ PENDINE SANDS
Firm, flat sands stretch for 6 miles from the holiday village of Pendine to the Taf estuary. At low tide the sea can be a mile or more away from the foreshore, while the long expanse of shallow water at high tide makes Pendine Sands very popular with young families. The beach, a corner of which is used as a vast car park, was used in the 1920s in several attempts to break the land-speed record, and was the site of Parry Thomas's fatal crash in 1927. East of Pendine is a Ministry of Defence firing range, but the sands are open to the public most weekends and from mid afternoon on weekdays.

⑤ LAUGHARNE
A generous sprinkling of handsome 18th-century houses gives the neat and quiet town of Laugharne, pronounced 'Larne', an air of solid respectability. The old castle, home in the 12th century to the Welsh prince Rhys ap Gruffud, stands guard over the salt flats of the Taf estuary. Two towers are all that remain of the original structure; the rest was rebuilt as a fortified mansion in the 16th century. The castle is open to the public.

Laugharne is best known for its association with the writer Dylan Thomas. The town is said to have been the model for the fictional village of Llaregub in his classic work, the play for voices *Under Milk Wood*. A walk northwards out of the town passes Sea View, where Thomas lived before World War II, and continues to the Boat House, where he spent the last years of his life and which now contains a collection of Thomas memorabilia. Nearby is the poet's 'writing shed', from where there are superb views over the estuary; the inside of the shed can be viewed through a window. Thomas and his wife Caitlin are buried in St Martin's churchyard. A likeness of the poet appears on the sign hanging outside Brown's Hotel, where the poet was a regular visitor.

SEMI-ROYAL RESIDENCE *Most of Laugharne Castle dates from the 16th century, when it became the home of Sir John Perrott, reputedly the illegitimate son of Henry VIII.*

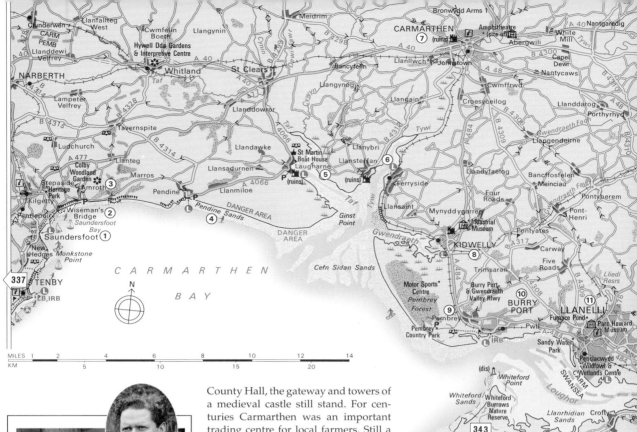

MILES 1 2 4 6 8 10 12 14
KM 5 10 15 20

A POET AND HIS WORKSHOP

A wooden hut overlooking the River Taf has been restored to look exactly as it did when Dylan Thomas (1914-53) wrote many of his poems there. He described its view of the 'mussel pooled and heron priested shore' in his *Poem in October*. There, too, he wrote much of his play *Under Milk Wood*, which follows a day and a night in a Welsh fishing village and gives life to a gallery of local characters including Captain Cat, Polly Garter and Mrs Ogmore-Pritchard.

⑥ LLANSTEFFAN

The peaceful little village stands at the mouth of the Tywi, where the river's muddy banks give way to soft sands. This important strategic site was probaby fortified by the Normans, but the present castle ruins, whose massive walls rise above the old earthworks, date from early in the 13th century; its gatehouse remains impressive. Upriver from the castle is a wide sandy beach, where strong currents make bathing hazardous except at high tide.

⑦ CARMARTHEN

The Romans established the fort of Moridunum on this site in the 2nd century, and the decayed remains of an amphitheatre can by seen by the A40 to the north-east of the town. Beside the County Hall, the gateway and towers of a medieval castle still stand. For centuries Carmarthen was an important trading centre for local farmers. Still a busy market town, it also holds regular livestock sales. The old Bishop's Palace, at Abergwili to the east of the town, is now the Carmarthen Museum, a local history collection set in parkland.

⑧ KIDWELLY

The town is dominated by its well-preserved castle, begun in the 12th century by Roger, Bishop of Salisbury, and extended in the 13th and 14th centuries. In the 18th century, Kidwelly found a new prosperity as a tin-plating centre. The old works, with their steam engine and nearby colliery, have been converted into an industrial museum. Kidwelly Quay on Kymers Canal, built in the late 1760s, has been restored as a waterside picnic area.

⑨ PEMBREY

The area of dunes, woodland and sandy beach between the estuaries of the Tywi and the Loughor was not always as peaceful as it is now. In 1881 works were set up at Pembrey to produce explosives, and the site eventually became a Royal Ordnance factory. The factory closed in the 1960s, and in its place is the Pembrey Country Park, offering family attractions such as a miniature railway and a falconry centre. Also in the park are an equestrian centre and a dry-skiing slope. Paths through the park lead to 7 miles of sandy beach. To the north are walks in Pembrey Forest and a motor sports centre.

⑩ BURRY PORT

Developed in the early 19th century for the export of coal, Burry Port is now a quiet little town whose harbour provides safe moorings for pleasure craft and a few fishing boats. To the west of the harbour, tracks through the dunes lead to Pembrey Country Park.

⑪ LLANELLI

In this busy market town, a tin-plating centre in the 19th century, many sites of heavy industry have been reclaimed and put to new uses. Furnace Pond to the north, where an 18th-century blast furnace once stood, has countryside walks, while the site of a former steel-works to the west has become the Sandy Water Park, a watersports venue. Parc Howard, the former home of a tin-plate magnate, Lord Stepney, houses the local history museum. Just to the north of town are the Lliedi Reservoirs, offering woodland walks in an area known as 'Swiss Valley'.

In the shadow of the British Steel Trostre Works to the south-east is the Penclacwydd Wildfowl and Wetlands Centre, which attracts more than 1000 species of wildfowl from around the world, including Asian white-winged wood ducks and Hawaiian geese.

PLACES TO SEE INLAND

Gwili Railway, Bronwydd Arms, 3 miles N of Carmarthen. Restored stretch of valley line.

Hywell Dda Gardens and Interpretive Centre, Whitland, 14 miles W of Carmarthen. Medieval site with displays of the 10th-century codified Welsh laws of King Hywell Dda.

Narberth, 21 miles W of Carmarthen. Wilson Museum of Welsh history; Landsker Visitor Centre, focusing on medieval Welsh folk tales.

TOURIST INFORMATION

Carmarthen (01267) 231557; Kilgetty (01834) 813672; Llanelli (01554) 772020

Secluded beaches at the foot of the Gower's high cliffs

Pushing out into the sea like a clenched fist, the Gower peninsula offers a wide variety of scenery: superb sandy beaches, immense cliffs, rolling dunes, salt marshes and a maze of narrow, winding village lanes.

① PEN-CLAWDD
Little creeks meander through salt marshes to the mud flats of the Loughor estuary, overlooked by the cockling village of Pen-clawdd. This is a dangerous area of cloying mud and swift river currents, but each day the cocklers go out as they have done since the 16th century. Donkeys and carts were the traditional transport used by the cocklers, but tractors are today being introduced.

② WEOBLEY CASTLE
A fortified manor house, Weobley Castle (Cadw), dates from the 13th century and has towers of different shapes, from square to octagonal. Its powerful owners, the De la Bere family, lived there until the Welsh uprising in 1400.

③ WHITEFORD SANDS
A glorious sandy beach stretches south from Whiteford Point. Whiteford Burrows National Nature Reserve can be reached on foot along a track near St Madog's Church in Llanmadoc village.

④ BROUGHTON BURROWS
Immense sand dunes heave up at the southern end of Broughton Bay. Sandy paths snake through and over the dunes

to the offshore island of Burry Holms, which can be reached at low water. The island has remains of an Iron Age fort, a ruined chapel associated with the 6th-century hermit St Cenydd, and a beacon that has replaced the old lighthouse on Whiteford Point.

⑤ RHOSSILI BAY
A magnificent crescent of flat sand, with a creamy edge of curling surf, is set against a background of imposing cliffs. The steep climb down to the shore from Rhossili village ensures that the beach is never as crowded as some of the more easily reached beaches on the Gower. It provides good surfing conditions. The surrounding cliffs are popular with paragliders and hang-gliders. Heather and bracken-covered Rhossili Down (NT), rising up behind the cliffs, is an excellent area for walks.

⑥ WORMS HEAD
The line of rocks snaking out from a headland forms part of the Gower Coast National Nature Reserve, which stretches east as far as Port-Eynon. Worms Head can be reached with care during the four hours either side of low tide. The best starting point for a walk is

the National Trust visitor centre just outside Rhossili village. From there a path leads for 3 miles over the cliffs, with superb views across Rhossili Bay. The two islands at the seaward end of the head are joined by a rock arch called the Devil's Bridge, where in high winds an eerie booming noise can be heard. This is caused by air rushing through the hole.

⑦ MEWSLADE BAY
Backed by dramatic cliffs, the secluded, sandy bay can be reached by a short walk from Pitton village. The lack of any approach road makes Mewslade and adjoining Fall Bay havens of peace.

⑧ PORT-EYNON
St Cadoc's churchyard, in Port-Eynon village, has a memorial to three local lifeboatmen who died in 1916 trying to save the survivors from the SS *Dunvegan*, which foundered in heavy seas at Oxwich Bay. The road through the village leads to a sandy beach. The abandoned cottages of Salthouse fishing hamlet and the fortified 16th-century Salt House stand on Port-Eynon Point, whose cliff caves were inhabited in prehistoric times. One of them, Longhole Cave, can be reached from a path overlooking Overton Cliff. The great cleft of Culver Hole, walled up with medieval masonry, is thought to have been a dovecote for a now vanished castle.

⑨ OXWICH
Standing at the western end of broad Oxwich Bay, this charming village of stone cottages and thatched roofs has a popular sandy beach offering waterskiing, windsurfing, sailing and canoeing. Oxwich National Nature Reserve, an area of dunes, marshes and woodland, provides habitats for a variety of plants, such as the carnivorous lesser bladderwort, and lizards, dragonflies

CLIFF-HEMMED BAY *Threecliff Bay, flanked by limestone cliffs, is one of the most beautiful on the South Wales coast. The pale sands are traversed by a stream on its way to the sea.*

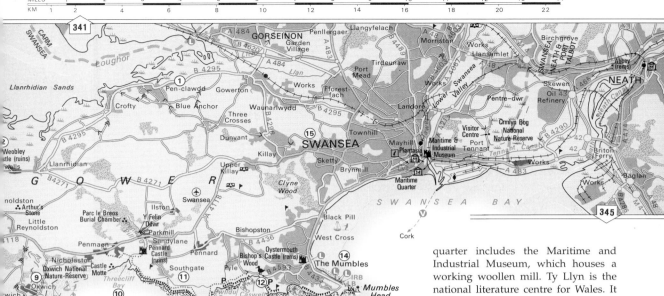

and birds. Oxwich Castle (Cadw) dates from the 14th century, but has been much altered since. Its impressive gateway is emblazoned with the crest of the Mansel family, the original owners.

⑩ THREECLIFF BAY
Like several of the most scenic bays along the Gower peninsula, Threecliff can be reached only on foot from either Parkmill or Southgate. The name comes from the three crags that rear up above the beach, one of which has been pierced by the sea to form a rock arch. The motte of a medieval castle can be seen on the western side of the valley.

⑪ SOUTHGATE
The residential village is a good starting point for exploring the southern Gower. To the west there is a gentle walk along the cliffs to the ruins of 13th-century Pennard Castle. A more rugged clifftop path leads east for 2½ miles to Pwlldu Head and a sandy cove at Pwlldu Bay.

A mile north-west of Southgate, at the village of Parkmill, is Y Felin Ddwr, a restored water mill, dating from the 17th century, with a craft centre.

⑫ CASWELL BAY
Rocky headlands shelter the sandy bay, which has good surfing. Bishop's Wood Nature Reserve is an area of grassland scrub and woodland that stretches up a valley from the coast. A car park gives access to a visitor centre and to paths round the reserve, where many species of birds and butterflies may be seen.

⑬ LANGLAND BAY
Houses and hotels line the cliffs that back the bay. The sand that characterises Gower beaches gives way to sand and shingle at Langland. The bay is popular with surfers.

⑭ THE MUMBLES
The Mumbles headland pokes out in a triple hump like a serpent's back to the lighthouse on the point. To the east is the immense sweep of Swansea Bay. The Mumbles town is a cheerful resort, which developed after the building of the Swansea and Mumbles Railway in 1804. The railway has gone, but the pier along which it ran remains, with its pavilions and lifeboat station. Overlooking the town are the substantial ruins of Oystermouth Castle, rebuilt in stone around 1280 after the original timber castle had burnt down.

⑮ SWANSEA
Once a major industrial centre, Swansea has undergone a complete transformation in recent years. The copper smelters have gone, and the old dock area on which Swansea's prosperity was founded has become the Maritime Quarter, where a waterfront village has grown up around a marina and historic craft can be seen out on the water. The quarter includes the Maritime and Industrial Museum, which houses a working woollen mill. Ty Llyn is the national literature centre for Wales. It holds literary readings, performances and interpretive exhibitions and includes a book shop. The centre is the only one of its kind in Britain.

Swansea is a popular seaside town, whose other attractions include sandy beaches, the city museum, a leisure centre and Plantasia, a glass pyramid with more than 5000 plants of a thousand different varieties.

About a mile to the east of Swansea is Crymlyn Bog National Nature Reserve, an unspoilt area supporting a wealth of plants, insects, and birds such as reed buntings, water rails and marsh tits.

PLACES TO SEE INLAND

Arthur's Stone, 12 miles W of Swansea. Bronze Age chambered tomb.

Neath, 8 miles east of Swansea. Cistercian abbey ruins (Cadw); Resolven Basin; boat trips on restored 4 mile canal section; Borough Museum.

Parc le Breos Burial Chamber (Cadw), 10 miles W of Swansea. Stone Age tomb.

TOURIST INFORMATION

Swansea (01792) 468321

THE KEY TO GOWER *The Normans built Oystermouth Castle, north of The Mumbles, to control the Gower peninsula.*

High dunes giving way to a ridge of striped cliffs

Towering dunes, sandy beaches with pounding surf, popular resorts and heavy industry all come together on Swansea Bay. To the south, crumbling cliffs give sweeping views of the Bristol Channel.

① ABERAVON AND PORT TALBOT

Established in the early 1900s, the steel-works remain a dominant feature of Port Talbot, although their operations were scaled down in the early 1980s. As the works developed, they outgrew the old dock and a new deep-water harbour was built. Other industries, notably a large chemical business, were attracted to the town. But between the chemical works to the north and the steel mills to the south an area of sand dunes was levelled to create a wide, flat beach, and along the sands grew up the resort of Aberavon.

Holiday activities in Aberavon are focused on the 2 miles of beach, which is pounded by rolling surf. Seaside amusements line the promenade, at the southern end of which is a leisure centre with an indoor swimming pool.

② MARGAM SANDS

The quiet stretch of sandy beach is tantalisingly hard to reach. One route to the sands follows a lane with very little parking from exit 38 on the M4, passing a crematorium and an industrial area. A more satisfactory approach is on foot from Kenfig Sands to the south.

Away from the beach, to the east of the motorway, is 12th-century Margam Abbey. All that remains of the Norman building is the monastery nave, now a parish church. Earlier Christian memories are evoked by the intricately carved Celtic crosses in the nearby Stones Museum. The museum stands just outside Margam Country Park, a large estate featuring an Iron Age hill-fort, a 19th-century Gothic-style mansion house and an elegant orangery built in 1789. Other attractions in the grounds include a putting green, a rare breeds farm, a boating lake and a sculpture park.

Celtic cross at the Stones Museum, Margam

③ KENFIG SANDS

High dunes now cover an area once occupied by a medieval town, complete with castle, church, guildhall and markets. By the 17th century the settlement had been abandoned to the rising sands, blown in from the seaward side by the wind. The scant remains of the castle can be seen rising out of the dunes near the motorway. The sands form a national nature reserve noted for its orchids, butterflies and moths. The reserve's large pool, fed by springs, attracts a variety of birds, including coots and swans. The archaeology and natural history of the area are explained at a visitor centre, from which footpaths lead through the dunes to the sea.

④ REST BAY

Easy access and a large car park make Rest Bay very popular with holiday-makers. The stretch of sand is one of the best surfing beaches in South Wales, backed by wide, smooth rock ledges.

⑤ PORTHCAWL

The bright, cheerful seaside resort started life as a 19th-century coal port, before new docks at Barry to the south-east and Port Talbot to the north killed the trade. Much of the old port has disappeared under a car park, and the slides and rides of the Coney Beach funfair stand on the old ballast tip.

The 1932 Grand Pavilion theatre is the heart of the long esplanade, which is lined with viewing galleries and kiosks overlooking the sea. There are good beaches, such as the rock-fringed Sandy Bay and Trecco Bay east of the town. Swimmers should avoid the waters near the headlands, where there are dangerous currents. Newton Point is the start of an 18-mile Heritage Coast Walk south to Gileston.

CANDY-STRIPED ROCKFACE *Horizontal layers of rock rise in tiers towards the fragile cliffs of Dunraven Bay, once a smugglers' haunt.*

PERIOD SURVIVAL *This thatched, stone-built cottage is typical of many in the unspoilt hamlet of Merthyr Mawr.*

⑥ MERTHYR MAWR

A delightful hamlet of old cottages scattered along tree-shaded lanes by the banks of the River Ogmore, Merthyr Mawr lies hidden away from the sea by immense sand dunes known as the Merthyr-mawr Warren. A narrow lane leads down through the village to a car park by Candleston Castle. This 15th-century fortified manor house is now largely ruined, but interesting details survive, such as the elaborately carved fireplace of the great hall. There are paths through the desert-like dunes to the sandy beach of Traeth yr Afon. Currents near the mouth of the Ogmore make swimming dangerous.

Just south of Merthyr Mawr are the lonely ruins of Ogmore Castle, reached by stepping stones across the river. The castle was built by the Norman invader William de Londres in the 12th century. The keep, built of massive boulders, is slightly later.

In Ewenny, a riverside village about a mile to the east, are the remains of a fortified priory founded in the 12th century, and the workshops of the Ewenny Pottery, one of Wales's oldest.

⑦ OGMORE-BY-SEA

The village perches on the towering clifftops at the mouth of the Ogmore river, with wide views across the entrance of the Bristol Channel. A short walk from the car park at the southern edge of the town leads down to a sandy beach backed by flat rock ledges, where there are clearly marked bathing areas away from the estuary currents.

⑧ SOUTHERNDOWN

The clifftop village of modest stone houses has developed into a popular little holiday centre. Footpaths can be followed north towards Ogmore-by-Sea, and south to Dunraven Bay.

⑨ DUNRAVEN BAY

Extraordinary 'striped' cliffs of alternating layers of limestone and shale back a popular holiday beach of wide stone ledges and firm sand. Visitors are advised to keep well clear of the unstable rockface, and to confine their swimming to inshore waters at high tide, clear of the strong currents that swirl around the Trwyn y Witch headland.

The Heritage Coast Walk passes Dunraven Bay, and a heritage centre explains the wildlife and history of the area, notorious for its tales of smuggling and shipwrecking.

⑩ MONKNASH

From this tiny village set back from the coast, a lane meanders down to a car park by the deep, wooded valley of Cwm Nash, from where it is a pleasant stroll to the coast of high crumbling cliffs and flat stones resembling a manmade pavement. North of the valley are two remote and lovely beaches, Traeth Mawr and Traeth Bach, Welsh for 'big beach' and 'little beach'. The beaches are tide traps at high water, and bathing can be dangerous.

⑪ NASH POINT

The lane from Marcross runs down to a grassy headland above a small sand and shingle bay with low-water rockpools. The two lighthouses on the point, only one of which is in use, were built in the 1830s after the wreck of a passenger ship. A clifftop saunter offers splendid views across the Bristol Channel.

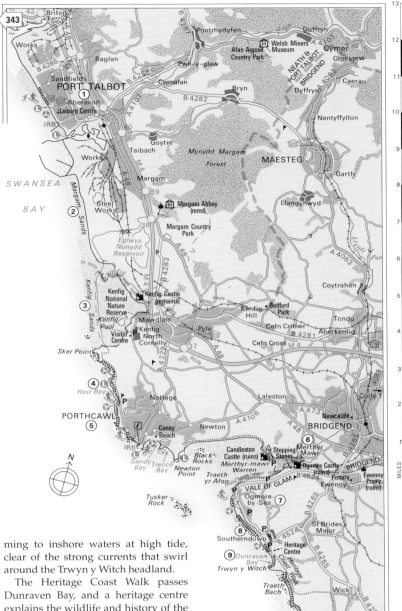

343
346

PLACES TO SEE INLAND

Afan Argoed Country Park, 7 miles NE of Port Talbot. Welsh Miners Museum, Forestry Interpretation Centre.

Bedford Park, 6 miles NE of Porthcawl. Rural grounds centred on 18th and 19th-century Cefn Cribwr Ironworks.

Bridgend, 6 mile E of Porthcawl. Market town with 12th-century fortress and church.

Coity Castle (Cadw), 9 miles E of Porthcawl. Medieval remains and Norman keep.

TOURIST INFORMATION

Porthcawl (01656) 786639/782211 (summer); Sarn Park Services, Junction 36, M4 (Bridgend) (01656) 654906

Resorts west of Cardiff where coal was once king

Around the town of Llantwit Major is a lonely coast of cliffs and bays, backed by quiet rolling countryside. To the east, pleasure boats ride at moorings in what were once some of the world's busiest coal ports.

NEW-BUILT WALLS *St Donat's Castle today gleams as if new, thanks to restoration in the 1920s. It now has 30 bathrooms.*

① ST DONAT'S CASTLE

What appears to be a mock-Norman fantasy castle overlooking a bay is in fact a 14th-century fortress, turned into a more comfortable residence during the Elizabethan era with the addition of an inner courtyard and great hall. The castle became neglected in the 18th century, but in 1925 the US newspaper magnate William Randolph Hearst took it over and restored it, installing such features as a magnificent dining-room ceiling rescued from a Lincolnshire church. St Donat's Castle is now an international sixth-form college, but guided tours are given in June and July. The castle shares grounds with a refurbished 14th-century tithe barn housing an art gallery and a theatre, and a public footpath leads down past the church to a small bay and a stony beach.

② LLANTWIT MAJOR

The ancient town of narrow crooked streets was founded around AD 500 as Caer Wogan, becoming the site of Britain's first Christian college. St David, St Gildas and, according to legend, St Patrick were educated there. The parish church of St Illtud, to the west of the town, has a 1000-year-old font and some crosses from the 8th and 9th centuries. From Llantwit Major, a road leads through a wooded valley to a sand and shingle beach at Col-huw Point, where there are extensive rock pools.

③ SUMMERHOUSE POINT

A lane from Boverton village, on the eastern edge of Llantwit Major, passes privately owned Boverton Mill Farm before it becomes an unsurfaced track ending at a car park. A short walk leads to the rocky headland of Summerhouse Point, from where there are clifftop walks and excellent views over the Bristol Channel. The Seawatch Centre, housed in a former coastguard station, has displays of weather-forecasting instruments and radar.

④ LIMPERT BAY

The bay marks the end of the Heritage Coast Walk which starts just outside Porthcawl, 18 miles to the north-west. The shoreline, although dominated by the tall chimneys of Aberthaw power station, is attractive, with rock ledges descending to a sand and shingle beach.

⑤ PORTHKERRY COUNTRY PARK

Nature trails and bridle paths crisscross an estate of rolling grassland and woodland edging a pebbly beach. Striding over the park is the impressive viaduct built in the 1890s for the Vale of Glamorgan Railway. North of the park, across the A4226, the Welsh Hawking Centre has daily flying displays.

⑥ BARRY

In the 1880s the mine owners of the Taf and Rhondda valleys built a new harbour and railway for exporting coal, joined Barry Island to the mainland by a causeway, and built the Barry Railway. By the late 1890s, Barry was one of the busiest coal ports in the world. Now the mines have closed, leaving the docks empty, and Barry has found a new role as a brash and cheerful resort.

Holiday activity is focused on the southern side of Barry Island, where the large sandy beach of Whitmore Bay is backed by a promenade and pleasure park. A holiday centre occupies the eastern headland, and beyond it is the smaller but equally sandy beach at Jacksons Bay. To the west is The Knap, a long pebbly beach overlooked by landscaped gardens containing a boating lake and an open-air swimming pool.

⑦ SULLY BAY

A small offshore island, accessible by a causeway at low tide, lies off a south-facing pebbly beach. The bay is popular with holidaymakers seeking to avoid the more crowded beaches of Barry

TOUGH ELEGANCE *Despite being damaged by a fire in 1931, and again by a ship which collided with it in 1947, Penarth Pier proudly celebrated its 100th birthday in 1994.*

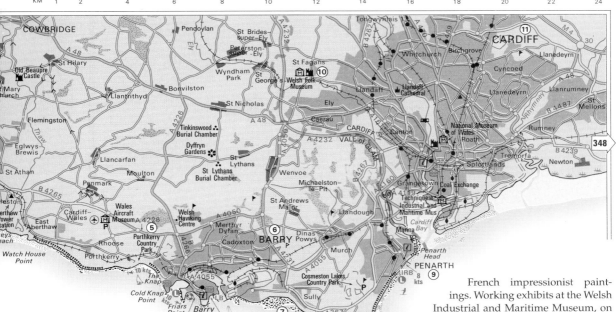

Island. Currents that swirl in between the island and the mainland make bathing hazardous at the eastern end of the beach.

⑧ LAVERNOCK POINT

Approached by a narrow lane from the B4267 near Cosmeston Lakes Country Park, Lavernock Point stands at the eastern end of the wild and inaccessible St Mary's Well Bay and its crumbling cliffs. In 1897 the first radio message across the sea was received at the point, sent by Guglielmo Marconi and Post Office engineers from the island of Flat Holm in the Bristol Channel, whose lighthouse is visible in the distance.

⑨ PENARTH

Like Barry, Penarth developed from a dock area created in the 19th century, and it too has adopted a new identity as a seaside resort. A great sweep of promenade, with a fine pier and quirky 1930s pavilion, overlooks a shingle beach, and in the old docks area is a thriving marina. Clifftop walks north from the town to Penarth Head and south to Lavernock Point give superb views of the bay, thronged in summer with watersports enthusiasts, and across the Bristol Channel to the Somerset coast.

South of Penarth is Cosmeston Lakes Country Park, whose centrepiece is a reconstruction of a medieval village, built on its original site.

⑩ ST FAGANS

The parkland of St Fagans Castle is home to the Welsh Folk Museum, which has a collection of old buildings from all over Wales that have been rescued and carefully re-erected. They include farmhouses, cottages, a Victorian shop complex, a moorland mud dwelling and a whole Celtic village. Traditional skills are demonstrated in working buildings ranging from a woollen mill to a bakery.

⑪ CARDIFF

Roman legions built the first fortress on the site of what is now the Welsh capital in the 1st century AD, and 1000 years later the Normans incorporated these defences into their own castle. Cardiff Castle grew and developed over the centuries, but owes its present form to the Marquess of Bute who in the 1870s, with the architect William Burges, restored the building in an extravagant mock-Gothic style.

Cardiff's prosperity was founded on the export of coal. In 1830 the Bute family obtained permission to build what was to become Bute West Dock on Cardiff Bay, and the docks continued to grow until World War I. As at Barry and Penarth, the decline of the coal trade has brought new developments, and ambitious long-term plans. Work has begun on a barrage that will turn Cardiff Bay into a vast freshwater lake by sealing off the estuary of the Taff and Ely rivers, creating some 8 miles of new waterfront along the mudbanks. New buildings are planned, including an opera house, and old buildings have been renovated and put to new uses: the handsome dock buildings have been converted into apartments; the sumptuous Coal Exchange has become a venue for musical performances, art exhibitions and other public events, as has a restored wooden church once used by visiting Norwegian sailors.

Near the castle are the lawns and gardens of riverside Bute Park, and to the north is the Civic Centre, whose complex of dazzling white neoclassical buildings, begun in 1897, include the splendid City Hall and the National Museum of Wales. The museum has a large archaeological section, an industrial gallery, and a fine collection of French impressionist paintings. Working exhibits at the Welsh Industrial and Maritime Museum, on the edge of Cardiff Bay, include a replica of the first steam locomotive. Next to it is Techniquest with 'hands-on' science displays.

On the western side of Cardiff is Llandaff Cathedral, built on a site first occupied by a religious community in the 6th century. Restored after extensive bomb damage in World War II, it is the home of Sir Jacob Epstein's giant sculpture, *Christ in Majesty*.

STEAM AGE *A saddle-tank locomotive at the Industrial and Maritime Museum, Cardiff, was once used for colliery shunting.*

PLACES TO SEE INLAND

Castell Coch (Cadw), Tongwynlais, 5 miles NW of Cardiff. Victorian folly, part medieval.

Old Beaupre Castle (Cadw), 3 miles NE of Llantwit Major. Elizabethan mansion remains.

St Lythans, 5 miles N of Barry. Iron Age burial chambers (Cadw): Tinkinswood chambered barrow and St Lythans chambered long barrow. Dyffryn Gardens: landscaped grounds, butterfly house, summer open-air theatre.

Wales Aircraft Museum, 4 miles W of Barry. Collection includes Vulcan bomber.

TOURIST INFORMATION

Barry Island (01446) 747171 (summer); Cardiff (01222) 227281; Penarth (01222) 708849 (summer)

Roman relics, and bridges at the mouth of the Severn

SALMON TRAPS *Wild salmon are still caught in conical nets at Goldcliff, as they try to swim upstream from the sea.*

Where the Severn meets the Bristol Channel, man-made flood banks protect the land against the effects of the world's second highest tidal fluctuation. Spring tides have an average rise and fall of almost 41ft.

① PETERSTONE WENTLOOGE

Although the village is set half a mile from the sea, a plaque on the wall of St Peter's Church recalls the day in 1606 when flood waters rose up its walls to a height of 6ft. A walk down the path beside the churchyard reveals the measures taken to prevent a recurrence of such flooding: a chequerboard of fields divided by drainage channels. The path reaches a high sea wall that stretches right along the coast as far as Newport. Beyond the wall is the nature reserve of Peterstone Wentlooge Marshes, whose visitors include locally rare species such as avocets and spotted crakes.

② NEWPORT

Prosperity came to Newport with the opening of the Monmouthshire Canal in 1796, which brought iron and coal from the valleys, and grew with the expansion of the docks in the 19th century. Although Newport still handles timber and bulk cargo, parts of the docks are being transformed into an area for leisure and arts. A visitor centre stands beside the flight of 14 locks, which raise the canal 168ft up a watery

staircase. The Transporter Bridge, built in 1906 and currently being restored as a visitor attraction, used to carry cars on a platform across the River Usk. Its unusual design was made necessary by the low river banks and the need to clear the tall masts of ships. The ruins of 13th-century Newport Castle (Cadw) can be seen in the city centre. Newport's role in the Chartist uprising of 1839 is the subject of a display in the Museum and Art Gallery, whose other exhibits include a collection of 500 teapots.

To the south-west of the city is Tredegar House, built in the 17th century and set in magnificent parkland.

③ CAERLEON

The legionary fortress at Caerleon (Cadw) was one of three principal strategic bases built in Britain by the Romans; the other two were at Chester and York. The modern town's streets still follow the grid pattern laid down when Caerleon was Isca Silurum, home to around 6000 Roman soldiers. Many traces of Isca survive, but the most spectacular relic of Roman times is the amphitheatre. The old town's history is told in the Roman Legionary Museum, alongside which stands the Capricorn education centre for children.

④ GOLDCLIFF

Although set well back from the coast, Goldcliff was inundated in the great floods of the 17th century. Its defensive wall of giant boulders has a walkway along the top that follows the coastline east for almost a mile. A beacon and a huge anchor stand on the headland, and a row of stake nets for trapping salmon can be seen offshore.

⑤ MAGOR

The delightful village is centred on a square of elegant houses and the fine old Church of St Mary the Virgin, known as the 'Cathedral of the Moors'. Dating from the 13th century, with 15th-century additions, the church stands at the edge of Caldicot Level, an area of grassland running down to the coast. Magor Marsh Nature Reserve, off the Redwick road, has been established in the last vestige of what was once all undrained farmland. The reserve provides a variety of habitats for many species of plant and wildlife.

⑥ CAERWENT

The market town of Venta Silurum was established by the Romans on this site in the 1st century AD. The modern village of Caerwent has grown up over the

ROMAN ARENA *Gladiatorial contests took place in the Caerleon amphitheatre, which could seat the fortress's entire garrison.*

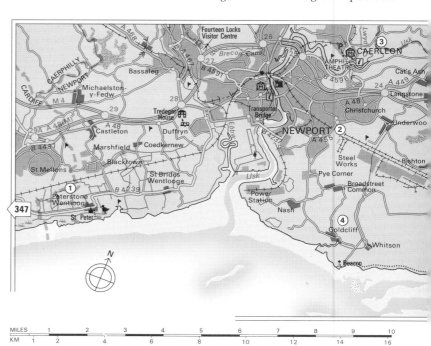

| MILES | | 1 | | 2 | | 3 | | 4 | | 5 | | 6 | | 7 | | 8 | | 9 | | 10 |
| KM | 1 | | 2 | | 4 | | 6 | | 8 | | 10 | | 12 | | 14 | | 16 |

BRIDGING THE SEVERN *First conceived in 1845, the Severn Bridge was finally started in 1961 and opened in 1966. It replaced a ferry which plied between Beachley and Aust.*

Roman town (Cadw), but the old ramparts are still visible and modern roads pass through what were once chariot gateways. Foundations of some of the original Roman houses have been found. The most impressive building is the octagonal temple outside the walls.

⑦ SUDBROOK

The town was built to accommodate the men who dug the railway tunnel under the Severn. Work began in 1873, but the tunnel was not opened until 1886. In 1883 the whole works were flooded and 83 men, trapped below ground, had to be rescued by boat. To remove the water, steam pumping engines were installed; one of the old engine houses still dominates the town. Sudbrook lies at the northern end of a new engineering marvel, the second Severn Bridge. Long before anyone thought of bridges

over or tunnels under the tidal Severn, the village of Black Rock, east of Sudbrook, was a passenger ferry terminus. It is now a quiet spot with a picnic area and views out to both bridges.

Two miles north-west of Sudbrook is 14th-century Caldicot Castle, set in gardens and a beautiful country park.

⑧ CHEPSTOW

Once a port and shipbuilding centre, Chepstow most recently has been involved in the building of the new Severn road bridge. The town's development is recalled in the Chepstow Museum. Of all the great Norman castles that line the frontier between England and Wales, few can claim a more dramatic location than Chepstow Castle (Cadw), which glowers down

from its clifftop perch. Begun in 1067, the castle saw its last military action in the Civil War, almost 600 years later.

The River Wye, which flows through the town centre, is spanned by three bridges: a high-arched cast-iron span of 1814, the railway bridge of 1962 and the modern road bridge. Chepstow is the gateway to the spectacular Wye valley, with its towering limestone cliffs.

Offa's Dyke, an earthen ditch and bank built in the 8th century to divide off Mercia from the Celtic kingdoms, begins near Beachley, to the south-east of the town. A long-distance footpath follows part of its course for 168 miles to the north coast of Wales.

⑨ SEVERN BRIDGE

Before the building of the first Severn Bridge, the only way to cross the river with a vehicle was by a long road detour or by ferry. The bridge has a main span of 3240 ft, and towers that reach 445 ft in height. The new bridge, downriver, is due to open in 1996. It will be about 3 miles long and its highest point almost 450 ft.

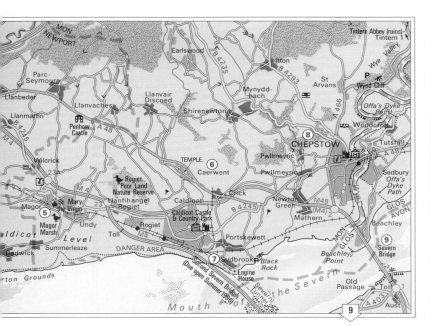

PLACES TO SEE INLAND

The Old Station, Tintern, 7 miles N of Chepstow. Former Victorian railway station.

Penhow Castle, 8 miles E of Newport. Oldest lived-in castle in Wales, dating from 15th century.

Rogiet Poor Land Nature Reserve, 9 miles E of Magor. Variety of plants in wooded grasslands.

Tintern Abbey (Cadw), 6 miles N of Chepstow. Ruined Cistercian abbey.

Wynd Cliff, 3 miles N of Chepstow. Two viewpoints of horseshoe bend of River Wye.

TOURIST INFORMATION

Caerleon (01633) 430777 (seasonal); Chepstow (01291) 623772 (summer); Magor (01633) 881122; Newport (01633) 842962

EXPLORING THE LIVING WORLD OF OUR SEASHORE

*How to recognise the plants and animals of sandy shores
and rock pools, shingle beaches and estuaries.*

Our varied coastline is the product of millions of years of erosion by wind and waves. Beating and tearing at the original rocks – some hard, some soft – the elements have shaped them into sheltered bays or exposed headlands, sheer cliffs or shifting sand dunes. Working on the fallen rocks, the same elements have slowly ground them down into particles of various sizes, producing the four clearly distinct types of foreshore that occur round our coastline.

A visitor to the seaside can recognise the type of coast by a glance at the surface underfoot. In descending order of the size of their particles the four types are: rocky shores, shingle beaches, sandy shores, and muddy estuaries and salt marshes.

Living organisms 'recognise' and are adapted to the different types of coastline, or 'habitats'. If they are rooted plants or immobile animals, it is possible to predict fairly accurately where particular species will be found on the shore. The identification section which follows commences with four double-page paintings showing where to look for particular species on the four main types of coastline.

Amateur naturalists looking at shore-life for the first time may find it easiest to start by searching for and becoming familiar with the organisms illustrated in these habitat paintings. In the illustrations showing a rocky shore, a sandy shore and an estuary, additional species which may occur – sometimes at 'zones'

or levels higher up the shore – are shown in inset panels. In the painting of a shingle beach, the panel illustrates a variety of pebbles which the beachcomber may discover.

Many organisms, however – especially those of the open sea and the air – are not so rigidly fixed to any particular part of the shore. Though they may use one habitat rather than another in which to breed or feed, it would be misleading to regard them as being confined to that habitat.

For this reason the remaining pages in this section are devoted to identification charts of clearly defined groups of more mobile animals: fish and mammals, birds and butterflies, hard-bodied creatures and soft-bodied creatures.

Many marine organisms lose their shape or colour if removed from the water. To appreciate their beauty to the full, and to assist identification of species, it is wise to use a rectangular white enamel dish in which any animals caught in a simple shrimping net can be watched and identified before they are returned to the sea. In addition, on the coast as anywhere else, the complete naturalist would also carry a pair of lightweight binoculars, a single-lens reflex camera and a powerful zoom lens.

With this equipment, and the help of the following pages, it should be a simple task to identify most of the common plants and animals of the seashore.

THE ROCKY SHORE: LIFE ON BOULDERS AND IN POOLS

Rocky shores range from wave-battered boulder beaches on which few species can survive to quiet protected corners with crevices and rock pools where thousands of species of animals and seashore plants may occur. The number of species also depends on the types of rock and the steepness of their slopes. Horizontal soft rocks such as sandstone that weather to a smooth surface provide fewer footholds or sheltered fissures than inclined hard rocks such as limestone, shales and slates.

Species are found in distinct zones on the shore according to the extent of exposure between tides. On unsheltered coasts species colonise zones higher up the shore to avoid the salt spray thrown up by breaking waves and carried on the wind. This 'zonation' can be seen in miniature where vertical rocks surround a tidal pool. On the sheltered face of the rock, a broad band of channelled wrack at the top may give way to a zone of spiral wrack, with the pool harbouring a number of red seaweeds.

These red seaweeds provide food and shelter for a multitude of animals. Some, such as periwinkles, live by grazing the seaweeds. Others, including barnacles and sponges, feed on particles floating in the water. A pool left at lower water may also contain predators such as sea anemones, crabs and several species of shoreline fish.

Sea bootlaces
Chorda filum

Oarweed
Laminaria digitata

Dog whelk
Nucella lapillus

European cowrie
Trivia monacha

Beadlet anemone
Actinia equina

Thongweed
Himanthalia elongata

Common limpet
Patella vulgata

Grey topshell
Gibbula cineraria

Keyhole limpet
Diodora graeca

Flat periwinkle
Littorina obtusata

Bladder wrack
Fucus vesiculosus

Beadlet anemone
(Strawberry form)

Breadcrumb sponge
Halichondria panicea

LIFE ON THE MIDDLE AND UPPER SHORE

On the middle shore, which is exposed by the tide twice a day, animals shelter at low water beneath seaweed or in cracks in the rocks. Plants and animals living around the high-tide level are adapted to withstand extremes of weather conditions, when they may not be covered by the sea for many days.

English stonecrop
Sedum anglicum
Acid rocks,
mainly in W

Thrift
Armeria maritima
Rocks and coastal
grassland

Rock sea-spurrey
Spergularia rupicola
Higher rocks, mainly
in S and W

Sheep's bit
Jasione montana
Acid rocks, rare
in N and E

Sea black-shields
Lecanora atra
Just above high-
water mark

Black lichen
Verrucaria maura
Rocks above
highest tides

Lichen
Lichina confinis
Just above high-
water mark

Orange lichen
Xanthoria parietina
Higher rocks
and cliffs

Rough periwinkle
Littorina saxatilis
Crevices on upper
shore

Small periwinkle
Littorina neritoides
Crevices on upper
shore

Painted topshell
*Calliostoma
zizyphinum*
Lower shore
downwards

Thick topshell
Monodonta lineata
Middle shore,
SW and W

Edible winkle
Littorina littorea
Middle shore
downwards

Chiton
Lepidochitona cinerea
Middle shore
downwards

Acorn barnacle
Balanus perforatus
Rocks on upper
shore, S and Wales

Star barnacle
Chthamalus stellatus
Middle shore,
SW and W

Channelled wrack
Pelvetia canaliculata
Near high-water
mark

Knotted wrack
Ascophyllum nodosum
Middle shore
upwards

Dulse
Palmaria palmata
Middle shore
downwards

Green seaweed
Cladophora rupestris
Middle shore
downwards

Coral weed
Corallina officinalis

Serrated wrack
Fucus serratus

Red seaweed
Hildenbrandia rubra

Common mussel
Mytilus edulis

Common whelk
Buccinum undatum

Purple topshell
Gibbula umbilicalis

Acorn barnacle
Chthamalus montagui

SHINGLE BEACHES: WHERE LIFE CLINGS TO THE STONES

Shingle beaches fringe many miles of Britain's coast, especially in southern and eastern England. Formed by the interaction of waves and currents, the beaches are constantly moving and changing shape. They are composed of water-worn rounded stones of various sizes derived from hard rocks or from flints formerly embedded in chalk.

Although the most common type of shingle shore borders the coast – as for example at the foot of chalk cliffs – remarkable 'moving' shingle spits are formed where currents flowing along the shore meet the mouths of rivers. Examples of these can be found at Spurn Head on the Humber's north side and at Orford Ness on the Suffolk coast.

Shingle spits sometimes build up across bays, forming a bar and cutting off an area of water to form a brackish lagoon or, if fed by a stream, a freshwater lake. Slapton Ley in South Devon is a good example.

Fringing beaches made entirely of large stones and boulders are almost barren, but when the stones are smaller and mixed with sand or mud they can be rich in plant and animal life. On spits and bars such as Chesil Bank in Dorset, which largely encloses the tidal lagoon known as The Fleet, the sheltered and more stable land-facing sides provide habitats for a wide range of species.

Vegetation seldom covers a shingle shore completely. The bare areas between the clumps of plants are often the breeding sites for a number of ground-nesting birds, particularly ringed plovers and terns whose pebble-coloured eggs are hard to detect.

Yellow horned poppy
Glaucium flavum
Rare or absent in north and east

Rock samphire
Crithmum maritimum
South and west

Cuttlefish bone
Remains of internal shell of
Sepia officinalis

Hornwrack
Leaf-like frond of colonial animal
Flustra foliacea

Whelk egg mass
Egg capsules of common whelk
Buccinum undatum

Mermaid's purse
Egg-case of dog-fish
Scyliorhinus caniculus

PEBBLES OF OUR SHORES

Fragments of rock are broken by rivers and waves from mountains and cliffs and then pounded by ferocious seas until their rough corners become sand and the remains are rounded into pebbles. Quartz, jasper and sandstone pebbles can be seen along many parts of the coast, while jet and serpentine, for example, are found in only a few particular areas.

Basalt
W Scotland

Quartz
Widespread

Chalk
Mainly S and E England

Granite
Cornwall, Wales, E Scotland

Carnelian
Cornwall and East Anglia

Jasper
Widespread

Flint
Mainly S and E England

Limestone
Mainly W coasts

Serpentine
Lizard, Anglesey and Ayr

Jet
Whitby, N Yorks

Amber
Lincolnshire and Norfolk

Quartzite
S Devon and Dorset

Shale
Mainly N and E coasts

Red sandstone
Widespread

Citrine
Cornwall and East Anglia

Agate
Widespread

Sea-kale
Crambe maritima
Absent from
N Scotland

Red fescue
Festuca rubra

Curled dock
Rumex crispus var. trigranulatus

Sea campion
Silene maritima

Arctic tern's nest

Sea spleenwort
Asplenium marinum
Absent from east and south-east

THE SANDY SHORE: HIGH AND DRY AS THE TIDE EBBS

The millions of grains of sand which make up the typical sandy shore are the product of many centuries of erosion by weathering of sandstone or other soft rocks forming the coastline. As the tide recedes the sand dries, then becomes loose and is blown up the beach. When it meets an obstacle, the sand settles and begins to form small dunes.

The first obstacle may be the strand line, at the high-water mark, where shells accumulate. Here nutrients from the decay of seaweeds enrich the sands, and annual plants such as salt-wort and various oraches grow.

These mini-dunes are invaded by perennial plants, particularly by grasses such as lyme grass and marram, whose extensive systems of roots and underground stems bind and compact the sand. Within the shelter of these grasses, other pioneer species such as sea holly and sand-dune moss become established.

On exposed coasts these primary dunes are easily destroyed by gales and stormy seas. But on more sheltered shores they become stabilised, often creating a series of ridges which attract such sand-loving plants as viper's-bugloss and lady's bedstraw. The hollows between the ridges are called 'slacks'; they are frequently wet, supporting marshland plants and animals.

On the north-west Scottish islands, Atlantic rollers pound shells into fragments, incorporating them into the lime-rich sands of the 'machair', where wild flowers grow.

Lugworm casts
Arenicola marina

Sea potato
Echinocardium cordatum

Curved razor shell
Ensis ensis

Common otter shell
Lutraria lutraria

Large sunset shell
Gari depressa

Thick trough shell
Spisula solida

Spiny cockle
Acanthocardia aculeata

Common necklace shell
Lunatia alderi

Thin tellin
Tellina tenuis

Warty venus
Venus verrucosa

Rayed trough shell
Mactra stultorum

Common cockle
Cerastoderma edule

Striped venus
Venus striatula

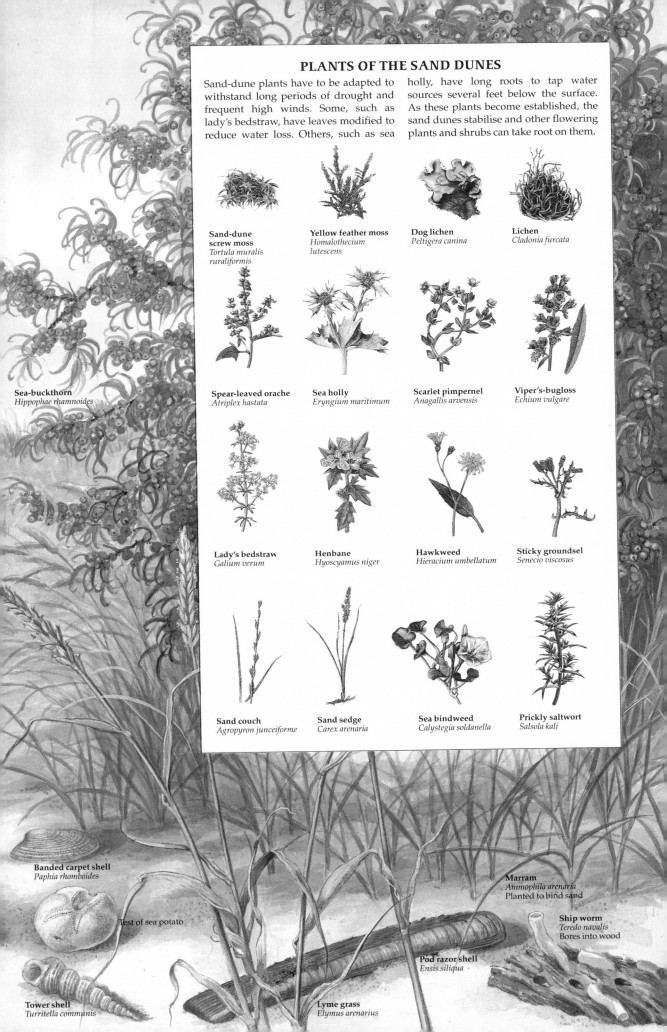

PLANTS OF THE SAND DUNES

Sand-dune plants have to be adapted to withstand long periods of drought and frequent high winds. Some, such as lady's bedstraw, have leaves modified to reduce water loss. Others, such as sea holly, have long roots to tap water sources several feet below the surface. As these plants become established, the sand dunes stabilise and other flowering plants and shrubs can take root on them.

Sand-dune screw moss
Tortula muralis ruraliformis

Yellow feather moss
Homalothecium lutescens

Dog lichen
Peltigera canina

Lichen
Cladonia furcata

Spear-leaved orache
Atriplex hastata

Sea holly
Eryngium maritimum

Scarlet pimpernel
Anagallis arvensis

Viper's-bugloss
Echium vulgare

Lady's bedstraw
Galium verum

Henbane
Hyoscyamus niger

Hawkweed
Hieracium umbellatum

Sticky groundsel
Senecio viscosus

Sand couch
Agropyron junceiforme

Sand sedge
Carex arenaria

Sea bindweed
Calystegia soldanella

Prickly saltwort
Salsola kali

Sea-buckthorn
Hippophae rhamnoides

Banded carpet shell
Paphia rhomboides

Test of sea potato

Tower shell
Turritella communis

Lyme grass
Elymus arenarius

Pod razor shell
Ensis siliqua

Marram
Ammophila arenaria
Planted to bind sand

Ship worm
Teredo navalis
Bores into wood

Estuary and Marsh: Where the Tides Invade the Land

Salt marsh in sheltered bays and estuaries forms a transitional zone between land and sea. It is an area where land organisms must be adapted to frequent immersion in salt water at high tide and where marine organisms must tolerate long periods of exposure at low tide.

Plants that are adapted to the periodic inundation and the high salt content of the sediments round their roots either have mechanisms that excrete salt from their leaves, such as sea-lavender, or are succulents, such as glasswort, able to limit salt concentration.

The first plants to colonise salt marshes are often glassworts and eel grass, though in very sheltered estuaries cord-grasses are more likely. The stems of these plants slow down the movement of water, encouraging the deposition of fine particles from the sea, and gradually elevating the level of the land. As the land rises, it is exposed for increasing periods between tides, and species which are less tolerant to immersion, such as annual seablite and sea aster, are able to grow.

Higher up the shore, salt marsh is dominated by sea-lavender and, particularly on the south coast, by sea-purslane. At the top of the marsh, where the land is flooded only during high spring tides, a grassy area develops where plants such as sea rush and salt-marsh grass can flourish.

Common cord-grass
Spartina townsendii

Sea-purslane
Halimione portulacoides
Rare in Scotland

Sea aster
Aster tripolium

Common sea-lavender
Limonium vulgare
Rare in Scotland

Common shore crab
Carcinus maenas

Common mussel
Mytilus edulis

Glasswort
Salicornia europaea
With laver spire shells

Acorn barnacle
Balanus improvisus

Spiral wrack
Fucus spiralis

Laver spire shell
Hydrobia ulvae

PLANTS OF THE UPPER MARSHES

Plants whose names include the prefixes 'sea' or 'salt-marsh' are highly adapted to endure the special conditions of the narrow strip between sea and land. Many have thick, succulent leaves which supply water for growth when it is difficult to draw moisture from the saline soils. Most such plants can be found only in marshy habitats but some, such as common reed and common scurvygrass, are more widespread.

Shrubby seablite
Suaeda fruticosa
Dorset to Wash

Sea milkwort
Glaux maritima

Sea-heath
Frankenia laevis
Hants to Wash

**Greater
sea-spurrey**
Spergularia media

Sea plantain
Plantago maritima

**Common
scurvygrass**
Cochlearia officinalis

Sea arrowgrass
Triglochin maritima

**Common
salt-marsh grass**
Puccinellia maritima

Common reed
Phragmites australis

Sea club-rush
Scirpus maritimus

Salt-marsh rush
Juncus gerardii

Sea rush
*Juncus
maritimus*

Annual seablite
Suaeda maritima

Eel grass
Zostera marina
Leaves lie flat at low tide

BIRDS OF THE SEA AND SHORE

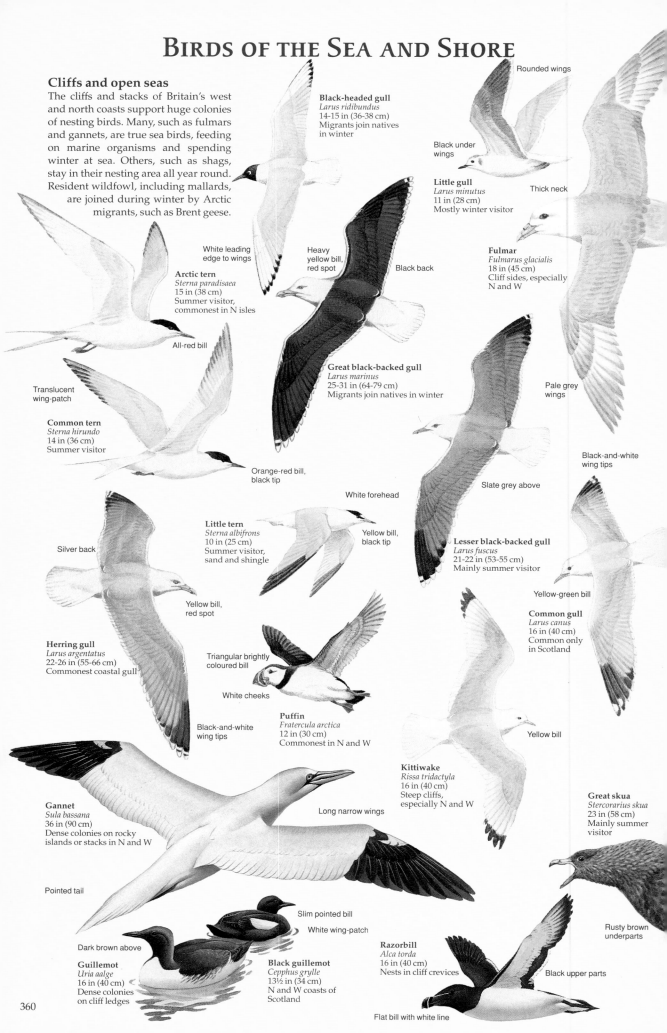

Cliffs and open seas

The cliffs and stacks of Britain's west and north coasts support huge colonies of nesting birds. Many, such as fulmars and gannets, are true sea birds, feeding on marine organisms and spending winter at sea. Others, such as shags, stay in their nesting area all year round. Resident wildfowl, including mallards, are joined during winter by Arctic migrants, such as Brent geese.

Rounded wings

Black-headed gull
Larus ridibundus
14-15 in (36-38 cm)
Migrants join natives in winter

Black under wings

Little gull
Larus minutus
11 in (28 cm)
Mostly winter visitor

Thick neck

Fulmar
Fulmarus glacialis
18 in (45 cm)
Cliff sides, especially N and W

White leading edge to wings

Heavy yellow bill, red spot

Black back

Arctic tern
Sterna paradisaea
15 in (38 cm)
Summer visitor, commonest in N isles

All-red bill

Great black-backed gull
Larus marinus
25-31 in (64-79 cm)
Migrants join natives in winter

Pale grey wings

Translucent wing-patch

Black-and-white wing tips

Common tern
Sterna hirundo
14 in (36 cm)
Summer visitor

Slate grey above

Orange-red bill, black tip

White forehead

Little tern
Sterna albifrons
10 in (25 cm)
Summer visitor, sand and shingle

Yellow bill, black tip

Lesser black-backed gull
Larus fuscus
21-22 in (53-55 cm)
Mainly summer visitor

Silver back

Yellow-green bill

Yellow bill, red spot

Common gull
Larus canus
16 in (40 cm)
Common only in Scotland

Herring gull
Larus argentatus
22-26 in (55-66 cm)
Commonest coastal gull

Triangular brightly coloured bill

White cheeks

Puffin
Fratercula arctica
12 in (30 cm)
Commonest in N and W

Black-and-white wing tips

Yellow bill

Kittiwake
Rissa tridactyla
16 in (40 cm)
Steep cliffs, especially N and W

Great skua
Stercorarius skua
23 in (58 cm)
Mainly summer visitor

Gannet
Sula bassana
36 in (90 cm)
Dense colonies on rocky islands or stacks in N and W

Long narrow wings

Pointed tail

Slim pointed bill

White wing-patch

Rusty brown underparts

Dark brown above

Razorbill
Alca torda
16 in (40 cm)
Nests in cliff crevices

Black upper parts

Guillemot
Uria aalge
16 in (40 cm)
Dense colonies on cliff ledges

Black guillemot
Cepphus grylle
13½ in (34 cm)
N and W coasts of Scotland

Flat bill with white line

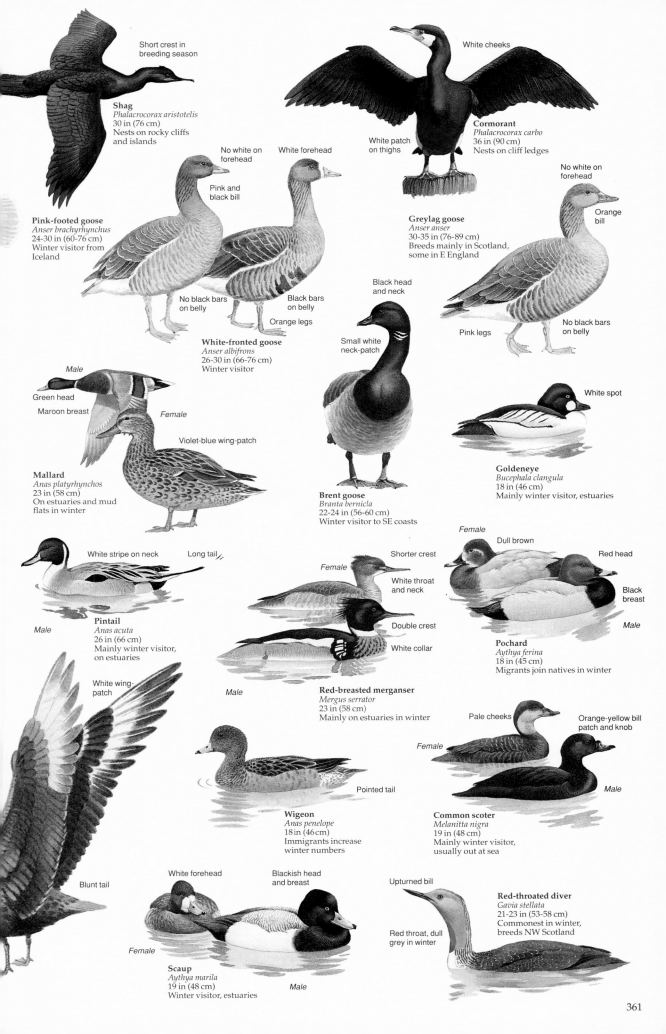

Shag
Phalacrocorax aristotelis
30 in (76 cm)
Nests on rocky cliffs
and islands

Short crest in
breeding season

White cheeks

Cormorant
Phalacrocorax carbo
36 in (90 cm)
Nests on cliff ledges

White patch
on thighs

No white on
forehead

White forehead

Pink and
black bill

Pink-footed goose
Anser brachyrhynchus
24-30 in (60-76 cm)
Winter visitor from
Iceland

Greylag goose
Anser anser
30-35 in (76-89 cm)
Breeds mainly in Scotland,
some in E England

No white on
forehead

Orange
bill

No black bars
on belly

Black bars
on belly

Orange legs

White-fronted goose
Anser albifrons
26-30 in (66-76 cm)
Winter visitor

Black head
and neck

Small white
neck-patch

Pink legs

No black bars
on belly

Male

Green head

Maroon breast

Female

Violet-blue wing-patch

White spot

Mallard
Anas platyrhynchos
23 in (58 cm)
On estuaries and mud
flats in winter

Brent goose
Branta bernicla
22-24 in (56-60 cm)
Winter visitor to SE coasts

Goldeneye
Bucephala clangula
18 in (46 cm)
Mainly winter visitor, estuaries

White stripe on neck

Long tail

Shorter crest

Female

White throat
and neck

Double crest

White collar

Female

Dull brown

Red head

Black
breast

Male

Pintail
Anas acuta
26 in (66 cm)
Mainly winter visitor,
on estuaries

Male

White wing-
patch

Red-breasted merganser
Mergus serrator
23 in (58 cm)
Mainly on estuaries in winter

Pochard
Aythya ferina
18 in (45 cm)
Migrants join natives in winter

Pale cheeks

Orange-yellow bill
patch and knob

Female

Male

Pointed tail

Male

Wigeon
Anas penelope
18 in (46 cm)
Immigrants increase
winter numbers

Common scoter
Melanitta nigra
19 in (48 cm)
Mainly winter visitor,
usually out at sea

Blunt tail

White forehead

Blackish head
and breast

Upturned bill

Red-throated diver
Gavia stellata
21-23 in (53-58 cm)
Commonest in winter,
breeds NW Scotland

Red throat, dull
grey in winter

Female

Scaup
Aythya marila
19 in (48 cm)
Winter visitor, estuaries

Male

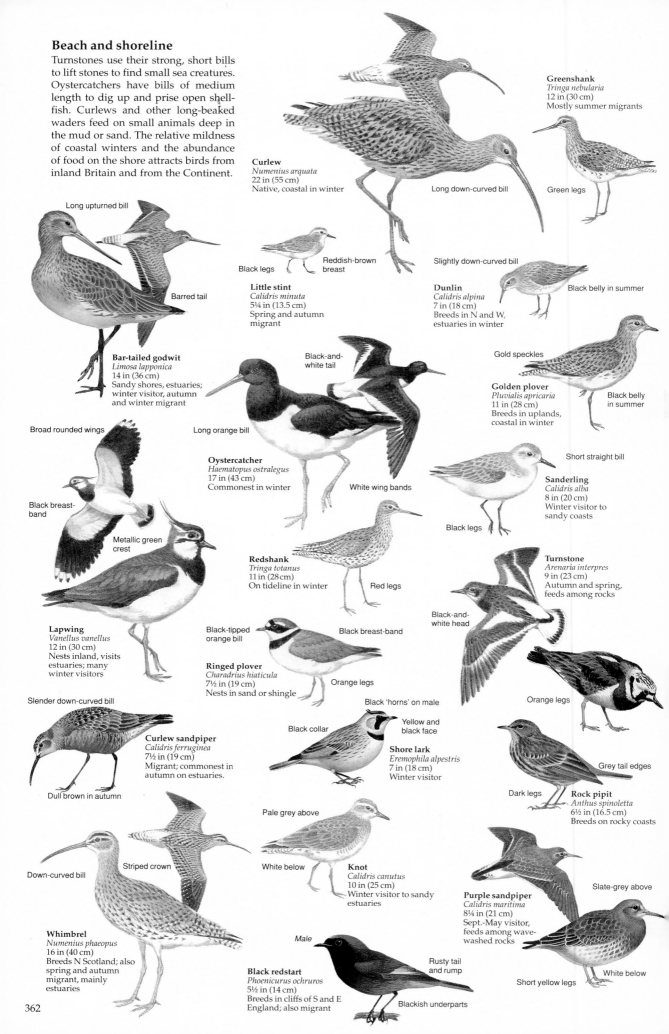

Beach and shoreline

Turnstones use their strong, short bills to lift stones to find small sea creatures. Oystercatchers have bills of medium length to dig up and prise open shellfish. Curlews and other long-beaked waders feed on small animals deep in the mud or sand. The relative mildness of coastal winters and the abundance of food on the shore attracts birds from inland Britain and from the Continent.

Curlew
Numenius arquata
22 in (55 cm)
Native, coastal in winter

Long down-curved bill

Greenshank
Tringa nebularia
12 in (30 cm)
Mostly summer migrants

Green legs

Long upturned bill

Barred tail

Black legs

Reddish-brown breast

Little stint
Calidris minuta
5¼ in (13.5 cm)
Spring and autumn migrant

Slightly down-curved bill

Dunlin
Calidris alpina
7 in (18 cm)
Breeds in N and W, estuaries in winter

Black belly in summer

Bar-tailed godwit
Limosa lapponica
14 in (36 cm)
Sandy shores, estuaries; winter visitor, autumn and winter migrant

Black-and-white tail

Gold speckles

Golden plover
Pluvialis apricaria
11 in (28 cm)
Breeds in uplands, coastal in winter

Black belly in summer

Broad rounded wings

Long orange bill

Black breast-band

Metallic green crest

Oystercatcher
Haematopus ostralegus
17 in (43 cm)
Commonest in winter

White wing bands

Short straight bill

Sanderling
Calidris alba
8 in (20 cm)
Winter visitor to sandy coasts

Black legs

Redshank
Tringa totanus
11 in (28 cm)
On tideline in winter

Red legs

Lapwing
Vanellus vanellus
12 in (30 cm)
Nests inland, visits estuaries; many winter visitors

Turnstone
Arenaria interpres
9 in (23 cm)
Autumn and spring, feeds among rocks

Black-and-white head

Black-tipped orange bill

Black breast-band

Ringed plover
Charadrius hiaticula
7½ in (19 cm)
Nests in sand or shingle

Orange legs

Orange legs

Slender down-curved bill

Black 'horns' on male

Black collar

Yellow and black face

Curlew sandpiper
Calidris ferruginea
7½ in (19 cm)
Migrant; commonest in autumn on estuaries.

Shore lark
Eremophila alpestris
7 in (18 cm)
Winter visitor

Grey tail edges

Dull brown in autumn

Dark legs

Rock pipit
Anthus spinoletta
6½ in (16.5 cm)
Breeds on rocky coasts

Pale grey above

Striped crown

Down-curved bill

White below

Knot
Calidris canutus
10 in (25 cm)
Winter visitor to sandy estuaries

Slate-grey above

Purple sandpiper
Calidris maritima
8¼ in (21 cm)
Sept.-May visitor, feeds among wave-washed rocks

Whimbrel
Numenius phaeopus
16 in (40 cm)
Breeds N Scotland; also spring and autumn migrant, mainly estuaries

Male

Black redstart
Phoenicurus ochruros
5½ in (14 cm)
Breeds in cliffs of S and E England; also migrant

Rusty tail and rump

Blackish underparts

Short yellow legs

White below

BUTTERFLIES OF THE COAST

Clifftops and woods

Britain's coasts offer areas of grassland, mixed scrub and woodland clearings, in which butterflies abound. Exposed clifftops, especially in the west, are covered in gorse and blackthorn, interspersed with kidney vetch and thrift. Sheltered valleys harbour plants which provide food for both caterpillars and mature insects. In woods, fritillary species occur, but are hard to identify as they move fast and settle infrequently. Marbled whites are easier to pick out. In open areas common blues are often seen with other small butterflies such as small coppers and small heaths. They are joined in midsummer by medium-sized gatekeepers.

Pearly margin on hind wings

Small pearl-bordered fritillary
Boloria selene
Woodland clearings; locally common in Wales, W England and Scotland, mid May, June and August

Dark-green fritillary
Argynnis aglaja
Meadows and woodland clearings, downs, dunes and grassland; mostly S and W, mid June–early Sept

Yellowish-green on underside

White spot on forewings

Small tortoiseshell
Aglais urticae
Open country; widespread, mid June–Oct

Lilac-blue upper side

Male

Silvery blue

Grey scales on veins

Common blue
Polyommatus icarus
Grassland; widespread, May–Sept

Chalk-hill blue
Lysandra coridon
Chalk or limestone grassland; S and E England, mid July–mid Sept

Brown

Female

Green-veined white
Artogeia napi
Clifftops and meadows; widespread, June–Sept

Large 'eye' on wings

No orange patch

Female

Orange patch on forewings

Jagged shape

Peacock
Inachis io
Open country; England and Wales, mid July–Sept

Orange tip
Anthocharis cardamines
Meadows and woods; England and Wales, late April–June

Male

Comma
Polygonia c-album
Open country; Wales and S England, July and August

Grey border to wings

Black apex to forewings

Small heath
Coenonympha pamphilus
Open country, dry grassland; very common, May–Sept

Lemon-yellow

Brimstone
Gonepteryx rhamni
Open country; Wales and S England, early spring and midsummer

Male

Faint greyish marks on forewings

Large white
Pieris brassicae
Widespread, some from Europe, April and May, July and August

Small white
Pieris rapae
Meadows; absent Shetland and W Isles, very common elsewhere April–Sept

Long dark line on forewings

Small skipper
Thymelicus sylvestris
Widespread, S and central England and Wales, June–August

Thick black marks on forewings

Black-eye spot

Gatekeeper
Pyronia tithonus
In brambles, woodland and hedgerows; England and Wales, mid July–mid Sept

Black eye-spot, white centre

Male

Twin spots on hind wings

Large skipper
Ochlodes venatus
Chalk downs; England and Wales June–August

Female

Small copper
Lycaena phlaeas
Grassland; widespread except far N, May–Oct

Female

Meadow brown
Maniola jurtina
Dry grassland; very common, mid June–mid Sept

Dark spots and border

Orange markings

Clouded yellow
Colias croceus
Migrant from south, May–Sept

White spots on forewings

White spots

Eye-spots on forewings

Painted lady
Cynthia cardui
Open country; immigrant, widespread, June–Sept

Red admiral
Vanessa atalanta
Migrant from south and south-east, May–Oct

Scarlet band

Grayling
Hipparchia semele
Open heaths, dry hillsides, coastal grasslands and dunes; widespread, July–Sept

FISH AND SEA MAMMALS

Shoreline fish

Many fish species are almost confined to the shoreline. They tend to be of unusual shapes, from the long narrow pipefish to the flattened lumpsucker, and move up and down with the tide, sheltering in pools at low water. Those that feed on plankton – small water-borne plants and animals – have small teeth or none at all. The shrimp and small-fish eaters have large teeth.

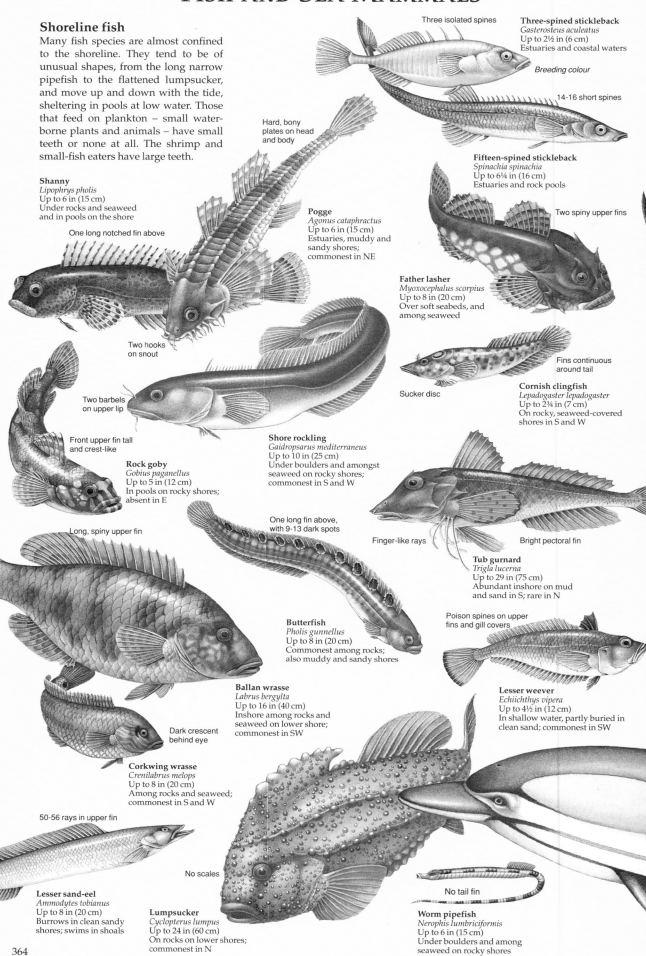

Three isolated spines

Three-spined stickleback
Gasterosteus aculeatus
Up to 2½ in (6 cm)
Estuaries and coastal waters

Breeding colour

14-16 short spines

Hard, bony plates on head and body

Fifteen-spined stickleback
Spinachia spinachia
Up to 6¼ in (16 cm)
Estuaries and rock pools

Two spiny upper fins

Shanny
Lipophrys pholis
Up to 6 in (15 cm)
Under rocks and seaweed and in pools on the shore

Pogge
Agonus cataphractus
Up to 6 in (15 cm)
Estuaries, muddy and sandy shores; commonest in NE

One long notched fin above

Father lasher
Myoxocephalus scorpius
Up to 8 in (20 cm)
Over soft seabeds, and among seaweed

Fins continuous around tail

Two hooks on snout

Sucker disc

Cornish clingfish
Lepadogaster lepadogaster
Up to 2¾ in (7 cm)
On rocky, seaweed-covered shores in S and W

Two barbels on upper lip

Front upper fin tall and crest-like

Rock goby
Gobius paganellus
Up to 5 in (12 cm)
In pools on rocky shores; absent in E

Shore rockling
Gaidropsarus mediterraneus
Up to 10 in (25 cm)
Under boulders and amongst seaweed on rocky shores; commonest in S and W

One long fin above, with 9-13 dark spots

Finger-like rays

Bright pectoral fin

Long, spiny upper fin

Tub gurnard
Trigla lucerna
Up to 29 in (75 cm)
Abundant inshore on mud and sand in S; rare in N

Butterfish
Pholis gunnellus
Up to 8 in (20 cm)
Commonest among rocks; also muddy and sandy shores

Poison spines on upper fins and gill covers

Ballan wrasse
Labrus bergylta
Up to 16 in (40 cm)
Inshore among rocks and seaweed on lower shore; commonest in SW

Lesser weever
Echiichthys vipera
Up to 4½ in (12 cm)
In shallow water, partly buried in clean sand; commonest in SW

Dark crescent behind eye

Corkwing wrasse
Crenilabrus melops
Up to 8 in (20 cm)
Among rocks and seaweed; commonest in S and W

50-56 rays in upper fin

No scales

No tail fin

Lesser sand-eel
Ammodytes tobianus
Up to 8 in (20 cm)
Burrows in clean sandy shores; swims in shoals

Lumpsucker
Cyclopterus lumpus
Up to 24 in (60 cm)
On rocks on lower shores; commonest in N

Worm pipefish
Nerophis lumbriciformis
Up to 6 in (15 cm)
Under boulders and among seaweed on rocky shores

Offshore fish

Fish that normally inhabit the open sea come inshore and up estuaries at particular times of the year. Often more regularly shaped than shoreline fish, they include such species as herring and mackerel. A variety of horizontally flattened fish live on the seabed, including rays and plaice. Seldom seen from the shore, they can often be identified on fishing harbour quaysides.

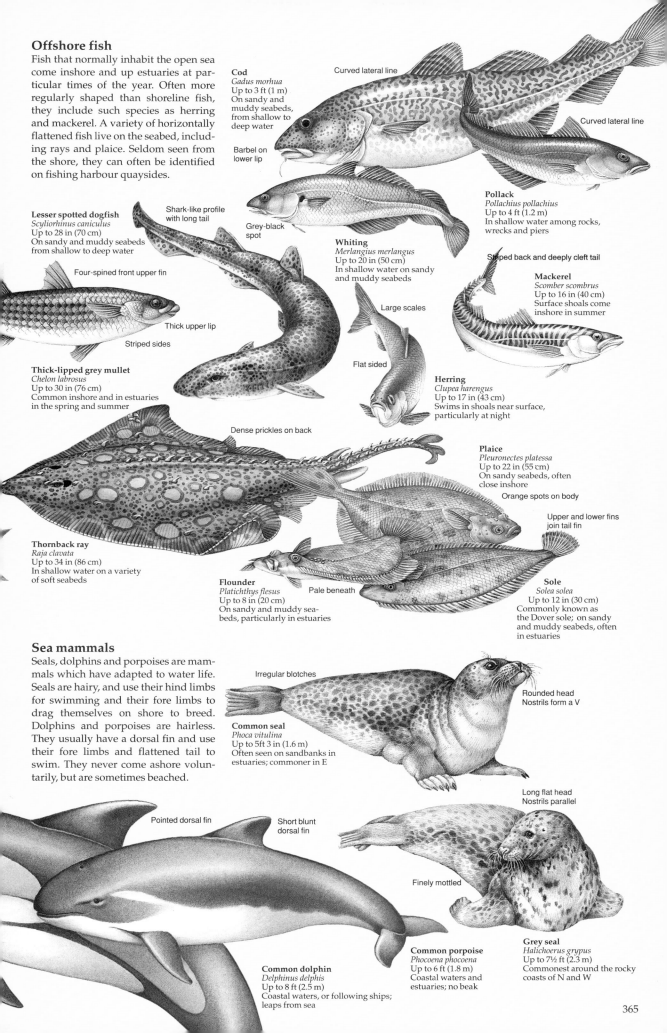

Curved lateral line

Cod
Gadus morhua
Up to 3 ft (1 m)
On sandy and muddy seabeds, from shallow to deep water

Barbel on lower lip

Curved lateral line

Pollack
Pollachius pollachius
Up to 4 ft (1.2 m)
In shallow water among rocks, wrecks and piers

Lesser spotted dogfish
Scyliorhinus caniculus
Up to 28 in (70 cm)
On sandy and muddy seabeds from shallow to deep water

Shark-like profile with long tail

Grey-black spot

Whiting
Merlangius merlangus
Up to 20 in (50 cm)
In shallow water on sandy and muddy seabeds

Striped back and deeply cleft tail

Mackerel
Scomber scombrus
Up to 16 in (40 cm)
Surface shoals come inshore in summer

Four-spined front upper fin

Large scales

Thick upper lip

Striped sides

Flat sided

Thick-lipped grey mullet
Chelon labrosus
Up to 30 in (76 cm)
Common inshore and in estuaries in the spring and summer

Herring
Clupea harengus
Up to 17 in (43 cm)
Swims in shoals near surface, particularly at night

Dense prickles on back

Plaice
Pleuronectes platessa
Up to 22 in (55 cm)
On sandy seabeds, often close inshore

Orange spots on body

Upper and lower fins join tail fin

Thornback ray
Raja clavata
Up to 34 in (86 cm)
In shallow water on a variety of soft seabeds

Flounder
Platichthys flesus
Up to 8 in (20 cm)
On sandy and muddy seabeds, particularly in estuaries

Pale beneath

Sole
Solea solea
Up to 12 in (30 cm)
Commonly known as the Dover sole; on sandy and muddy seabeds, often in estuaries

Sea mammals

Seals, dolphins and porpoises are mammals which have adapted to water life. Seals are hairy, and use their hind limbs for swimming and their fore limbs to drag themselves on shore to breed. Dolphins and porpoises are hairless. They usually have a dorsal fin and use their fore limbs and flattened tail to swim. They never come ashore voluntarily, but are sometimes beached.

Irregular blotches

Rounded head
Nostrils form a V

Common seal
Phoca vitulina
Up to 5ft 3 in (1.6 m)
Often seen on sandbanks in estuaries; commoner in E

Long flat head
Nostrils parallel

Pointed dorsal fin

Short blunt dorsal fin

Finely mottled

Grey seal
Halichoerus grypus
Up to 7½ ft (2.3 m)
Commonest around the rocky coasts of N and W

Common porpoise
Phocoena phocoena
Up to 6 ft (1.8 m)
Coastal waters and estuaries; no beak

Common dolphin
Delphinus delphis
Up to 8 ft (2.5 m)
Coastal waters, or following ships; leaps from sea

HARD-BODIED CREATURES

Insects and insect-like animals

Only a few insects live on the seashore. Centipedes and false scorpions may be found in rock crevices or among rotting debris on the shoreline. Sea spiders occur low down the shore among seaweed, often attached to sea anemones on which they feed. Slaters and sand hoppers, resembling insects, are in fact crustaceans. Slaters are marine forms of woodlice, with bodies flattened from above. Sand hoppers are compressed sideways and usually appear curled up.

Antennae two-thirds length of body

Sea-slater
Ligia oceanica
Up to 1 in (2.5 cm)
In crevices in sea walls and under stones on the upper shore

Upper and lower antennae same length

Pill-bug
Gammarus locusta
Up to ¾ in (2 cm)
Under stones and seaweed on middle and lower shore

Bores holes in wood

Gribble
Limnoria lignorum
Up to ⅛ in (3 mm)
Often in timber washed ashore

Sea-spider
Pycnogonum littorale
Body up to 1 in (2.5cm)
Under stones on lower shore

Thick body and legs

Bristle-tail
Petrobius maritimus
Up to ½ in (13 mm)
On rocks on upper shore; jumps when exposed

Legs on each segment   Feelers on head

Short upper antennae

Long hair-like point

Centipede
Strigamia maritima
Up to 1½ in (4 cm)
In rock crevices on upper shore

Sand hopper
Orchestia gammarella
Up to ¾ in (2 cm)
Among decaying seaweed on upper shore; jumping animal

False scorpion
Neobisium maritimum
Up to ¼ in (6 mm)
In deep rock crevices on upper shore

Scorpion-like pincers

Land snails

Tall plants growing on sand dunes, particularly on dunes of the west coast which have a high calcium content in the sand, often carry large numbers of snails. Species with alternating bands of varied colours are prominent, but after death they become bleached white by the elements.

Broken, blotchy bands

Variable colour and banding

Dark brown lip

Grove snail
Cepaea nemoralis
Up to 1 in (2.5 cm)
Absent from far N Scotland

Wrinkled snail
Candidula intersecta
Up to ½ in (13 mm)
Common, except in N Scotland

Pointed snail
Cochlicella acuta
Up to 1 in (2.5 cm)
Absent from E coast

Barnacles

Closely related to crabs, barnacles fix themselves head downwards on rocks or wood. Their bodies are protected by a series of plates and their feathery legs, which continuously protrude and retract into the shell when immersed, are adapted to catching food.

Lump attached to underside of shore crab

Long stalk

Goose barnacle
Lepas anatifera
Up to 2 in (5 cm) long
Attached to boats and driftwood

Parasitic barnacle
Sacculina carcini
Up to 1½ in (4 cm)

Five white plates

Prawns and shrimps

All these decapods have five pairs of 'walking' legs, the front pair of which are adapted for feeding. Prawns and shrimps have light, vertically flattened bodies and can swim. The head and body are fused and shielded by a shell with a forward-pointing extension, called a rostrum, between the eyes; this is prominent and toothed in prawns, but much reduced in shrimps. There are two pairs of antennae.

Six to eight teeth

No teeth

Common prawn
Palaemon serratus
Up to 2¾ in (7 cm)
In pools among seaweed, especially in SW

Common shrimp
Crangon crangon
Up to 2 in (5 cm)
Shallow water and pools

Norway lobster
Nephrops norvegicus
Up to 6 in (15 cm) long
On mud and sand, lower shore downwards

Seven to ten teeth

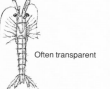

Often transparent

Slender shape

Chameleon shrimp
Praunus flexuosus
Up to 1 in (2.5 cm)
Shallow water and pools, among eel-grass and seaweed

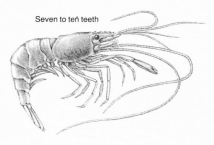

Prawn
Palaemon elegans
Up to 2 in (5 cm)
In pools, among seaweed

Crabs and lobsters

These creatures are called decapods because they have five pairs of legs; the first pair are usually conspicuous pincers. They have broad shells and horizontally flattened bodies. Lobsters have long antennae and a prominent 'fan' tail which they contract to dart backwards through the water. Crabs have shorter antennae, and no obvious tail.

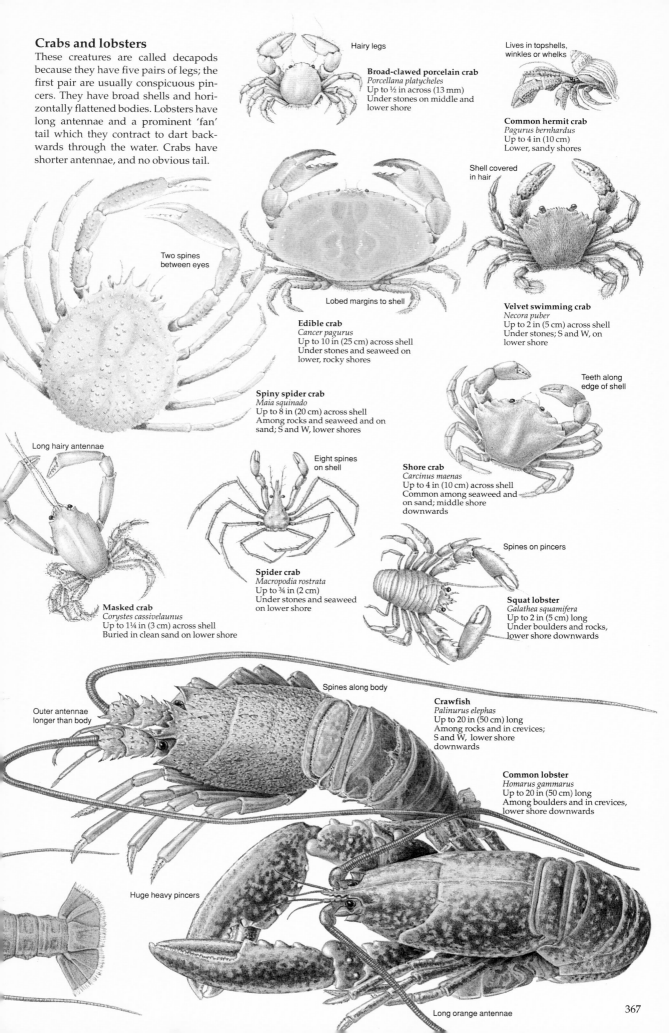

Hairy legs

Broad-clawed porcelain crab
Porcellana platycheles
Up to ½ in across (13 mm)
Under stones on middle and lower shore

Lives in topshells, winkles or whelks

Common hermit crab
Pagurus bernhardus
Up to 4 in (10 cm)
Lower, sandy shores

Shell covered in hair

Two spines between eyes

Lobed margins to shell

Edible crab
Cancer pagurus
Up to 10 in (25 cm) across shell
Under stones and seaweed on lower, rocky shores

Velvet swimming crab
Necora puber
Up to 2 in (5 cm) across shell
Under stones; S and W, on lower shore

Spiny spider crab
Maia squinado
Up to 8 in (20 cm) across shell
Among rocks and seaweed and on sand; S and W, lower shores

Teeth along edge of shell

Long hairy antennae

Eight spines on shell

Shore crab
Carcinus maenas
Up to 4 in (10 cm) across shell
Common among seaweed and on sand; middle shore downwards

Spines on pincers

Spider crab
Macropodia rostrata
Up to ¾ in (2 cm)
Under stones and seaweed on lower shore

Masked crab
Corystes cassivelaunus
Up to 1¼ in (3 cm) across shell
Buried in clean sand on lower shore

Squat lobster
Galathea squamifera
Up to 2 in (5 cm) long
Under boulders and rocks, lower shore downwards

Spines along body

Crawfish
Palinurus elephas
Up to 20 in (50 cm) long
Among rocks and in crevices; S and W, lower shore downwards

Outer antennae longer than body

Common lobster
Homarus gammarus
Up to 20 in (50 cm) long
Among boulders and in crevices, lower shore downwards

Huge heavy pincers

Long orange antennae

367

Soft or Spiny-skinned Creatures

Worms

Four main worm groups occur in the sea. Flatworms are leaf-shaped and glide with the assistance of hair-like cilia beneath rocks. Ribbon worms are flat and burrow in mud or sand. Bristle worms are round and their bodies are divided into bristly segments; they include many of the most commonly seen worms, such as fishermen's ragworms. Bristle worms that live in shell or stone tubes are known as tube worms.

Two tentacles on head

Wavy flatworm
Prostheceraeus vittatus
Up to 1¼ in (3 cm)
Under stones or gravel on lower shore

Head wider than rest of body

Red ribbon worm
Lineus ruber
Up to 6¼ in (16 cm)
Under stones or gravel on middle and lower shore

Four pairs of tentacles

Green leaf worm
Eulalia viridis
2-6 in (5-15 cm)
In rock crevices on middle and lower shore

Green triangular paddles

Four antennae and four tentacles

Yellow leaf-shaped paddles

Paddle worm
Nereiphylla paretti
6-12 in (15-30 cm)
Under stones on lower shore

Mat of hairs on upper surface

Sea mouse
Aphrodita aculeata
4-8 in (10-20 cm)
On sandy lower shore or washed up

Red line down back

Ragworm
Neres (Hediste) diversicolor
Up to 4¾ in (12 cm)
Burrows in sand or mud on middle and lower shore

King ragworm
Nereis (Neanthes) virens
Up to 16 in (40 cm)
Burrows in sand; mainly N and W on lower shore

Thick body

Scale worm
Harmothoë impar
Up to 1 in (2.5 cm)
Under stones and seaweed on lower shore

Scales with bristles

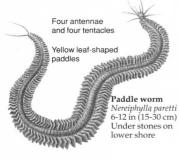

Tube larger towards trumpet-shaped entrance

Serpulid worm
Serpula vermicularis
2¾-4 in (7-10 cm)
Attached to rocks and shells on lower shore, or washed up

Spirorbid worm
Spirorbis spirorbis
Up to ⅛ in (3 mm)
Attached to brown seaweeds on middle and lower shore

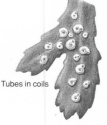

Tubes in coils

Cat-worm
Nephtys caeca
4-10 in (10-25 cm)
Burrows in sand on middle and lower shore

Lugworm
Arenicola marina
4-8 in (10-20 cm)
In sand on middle and lower shore

Thread at tail

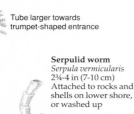

Colonies of tubes made of large sand grains

Smooth tube of fine mud

Posterior lacks bristles or gills

Tube of coarse sand and shell

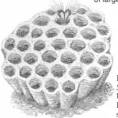

Honeycomb worm
Sabellaria alveolata
Up to 1¾ in (4 cm)
Encrusts rocks and shells on lower shore

Peacock worm
Sabella pavonina
4¼-10½ in (11-26.5 cm)
In mud or muddy sand on lower shore

Sand mason
Lanice conchilega
6-12 in (15-30 cm)
In sand on middle and lower shore

Sea slugs and sea squirts

Sea slugs are molluscs which have lost their shells; sea lemons are closely related. Sea cucumbers and sea gherkins are echinoderms which lack obvious spines or a tough skeleton; the skeleton is embedded in the skin. The primitive-looking sea squirt is in fact an advanced animal, with tadpole-like larvae.

One pair of tentacles

Sea lemon
Archidoris pseudoargus
Up to 2¾ in (7 cm)
Feeds on sponges on lower shore

Grouped like stars

Star sea squirt
Botryllus schlosseri
Up to 6 in (15 cm)
On rocks, stones and seaweeds on lower shore

Transparent with two openings

Tube sea squirt
Ciona intestinalis
Up to 4¾ in (12 cm) high
On rocks, seaweeds and piers on lower shore

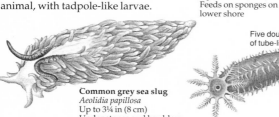

Common grey sea slug
Aeolidia papillosa
Up to 3¼ in (8 cm)
Under stones and boulders between tide marks; feeds on anemones on middle and lower shore

Two pairs of tentacles

Five double rows of tube-like feet

Sea gherkin
Trachythyone elongata
Up to 6 in (15 cm)
Among mud and stones on lower shore

Warts on upper side

Sea cucumber
Holothuria forskali
Up to 8 in (20 cm)
Among rock and seaweed; S and W on lower shore

Starfish and sea urchins

The group of marine animals known as echinoderms is notable for its unique form of radial body symmetry. The body may be globe-shaped, as in sea urchins, or it may branch off into five or more arms, as in starfish. Seawater enters the animal through a pore at the centre of its body. The changing water pressure controls the movement of tube-feet which enable the animal to move. The brittle skeletons, or tests, of dead sea urchins are often washed up.

Ridged margins with spines

Sand star
Astropecten irregularis
Up to 4¾ in (12 cm) in diameter
Burrows in sand; below low water, or washed up

Common brittle star
Ophiothrix fragilis
Disc up to ¾ in (2 cm) in diameter
Under stones and seaweed on lower shore

Spiny starfish
Marthasterias glacialis
Up to 32 in (80 cm) in diameter
Among rocks and stones; in S and W on lower shore

Thick spines

Thin arms with short spines

Brittle star
Amphipholis squamata
Disc up to ¼ in (6 mm) diameter
Under rocks and seaweeds on lower shore

Blunt spines on upper surface

Spherical from above, flattened at poles
Strong spines

Long smooth spines

Test

Violet tip to spines

Test

Common sea urchin
Echinus esculentus
Up to 4 in (10 cm) in diameter
On seaweed-covered rocks on lower shore

Rock urchin
Paracentrotus lividus
Up to 2½ in (6 cm) in diameter
Often in large groups on rocks; SW only, on lower shore

Weak spines

Purple heart urchin
Spatangus purpureus
Up to 4¾ in (12 cm) in diameter
Burrows in coarse sand on lower shore

Test

Test

Green sea urchin
Psammechinus miliaris
Up to 2 in (5 cm) in diameter
Under stones on lower shore

Squids and octopuses

The most obvious feature of the cephalopods, the group to which cuttlefish, squids and octopuses belong, is the four or five pairs of tentacles which surround the mouth. They are used for catching prey, which they reach by darting forward suddenly, ejecting a jet of water through a funnel formed from a modified foot. The eyes are as efficient as those of backboned animals.

Common octopus
Octopus vulgaris
Up to 40 in (100 cm)
Pools among rocks; southern coasts, on lower shore

Arms with two rows of suckers

Common cuttlefish
Sepia officinalis
Up to 12 in (30 cm)
Over sand in sheltered bays or estuaries, on lower shore

Broad oval shape

Common squid
Loligo forbesi
Up to 24 in (60 cm)
Free swimming, rarely close to shore

Long pen-like shape

Jellyfish

When in water, jellyfish are umbrella-shaped. They often have a central mouth surrounded by long tentacles that trail behind them as they swim. These tentacles paralyse prey with stinging cells, and then pass the food to the mouth. The Portuguese man-of-war is not a true jellyfish, but a siphonophore; unable to swim, it floats on the surface by means of a gas-filled bladder. Its tentacles have stinging hairs.

Four frilly mouth arms

Common jellyfish
Aurelia aurita
Up to 10 in (25 cm) in diameter
Often in sheltered bays; most common species, also known as moon jellyfish

Portuguese man-of-war
Physalia physalia
Up to 12 in (30 cm) long
Open sea, and SW coasts after persistent SW winds

Umbrella dome-shaped

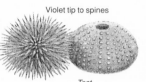

Long tentacles, often missing when washed up

Jellyfish
Rhizostoma octopus
Up to 24 in (60 cm) in diameter
Open sea, S and W coasts; uncommon

Compass jellyfish
Chrysaora hysoscella
Up to 12 in (30 cm) in diameter
Open sea, mainly S and W coasts; uncommon

Umbrella with 24 compass-like markings

SAFETY AT THE SEASIDE: HOW TO AVOID DANGER

The main hazards facing a visitor to the coast are weather, tides and currents. Risks can be minimised by checking local weather forecasts and tide tables; and by asking a lifeguard or the nearest coastguard rescue centre about particular dangers. Most sporting activities, such as sailing and water-skiing, have codes explaining how to avoid danger and what to do if you get into distress.

EXPLORING THE SEASHORE

Scrambling across rocks and seeking out the shells, stones and pools left by the tide is an absorbing activity, making it easy to lose track of time and distance. Some tides turn very quickly and can sweep up hidden channels, cutting off the retreat of walkers who have ventured too far from the high-tide line.

Make sure you know the times of the tides and other local conditions before setting out, and allow plenty of time to get back before the tide turns. Particularly high tides, called spring tides, occur just after the new moon and full moon. Neap tides, which have the lowest range between high and low water, occur during the moon's first and last quarters. Wear footwear suitable for climbing over slippery rocks, such as rope-soled shoes.

DO NOT *go exploring alone.*
DO *check tide tables.*
DO *wear appropriate footwear.*

WALKING

On coast paths fog and mist may appear unexpectedly and severely reduce visibility; on the shore, tides can turn quickly and cut off unprepared walkers. A few basic precautions will help you to cope with any emergencies.

Familiarise yourself with the weather forecast and local tides before you set off, and take a first-aid kit and map with you. Keep to paths and stay away from cliff edges. Special care is needed where cliffs have been eroded and there may no longer be footpath access. When walking in remote areas, notify someone of your planned route and arrival time. Wear appropriate footwear and clothing, and take refreshments.

DO *check weather forecasts and tide tables.*
DO *take a first-aid kit and map with you.*
DO *be careful along clifftop paths.*

FURTHER INFORMATION The Ramblers' Association, 1/5 Wandsworth Road, London SW8 2XX (0171) 582 6878

SWIMMING

Wait until one hour after a meal before going into the sea and be aware that your swimming ability will be affected by waves, tides and water temperature. Never swim out to sea; it is safer to swim parallel to the shore, staying within or close to your depth.

Swim with others if possible and off a beach patrolled by lifeguards. If you do get into difficulties, follow the advice on emergency procedures provided by the Royal Life Saving Society. If you cannot swim, do not go into the sea above waist height. The best place to learn is in a pool, with expert tuition.

Swimming in polluted seas threatens health. Selected beaches are monitored for contamination by sewage and other pollutants, and results of tests can be obtained from local National Rivers Authority offices. Flags are flown to identify beaches that have been granted annual awards for bathing water quality and facilities for visitors, but such flags can be misleading. The European Blue Flag and the Premier Seaside Award indicate beaches whose water has passed high standards for the previous bathing season, but the ordinary Seaside Award can be given to areas with far lower water quality, in some cases the legal minimum, which is far from rigorous. Both 'Seaside' awards are given by the Tidy Britain Group, which also administers the European Blue Flag award. The Marine Conservation Society campaigns to improve the quality of seawater and compiles an annual *Good Beach Guide*.

When diving into the sea, check the water depth and look for obstacles first. If you plan to go snorkelling, seek professional advice on the equipment needed and its use. Airbeds and inflatable toys, though fun on the beach, can be dangerous on the water, where they may be swept out to sea by currents.

DO NOT *swim when red flags are flying.*
DO NOT *go swimming alone.*
DO NOT *use airbeds on the water.*

FURTHER INFORMATION Amateur Swimming Association, Harold Fern House, Derby Square, Loughborough LE11 OAL (01509) 230431

SURFING

Surfing is for experienced swimmers only. Before you go out, contact the leisure or recreation department of the local authority, or ask a lifeguard, about restricted areas, and check for tide movements, underwater obstacles and rip currents. Insure yourself against public liability in case you accidentally injure someone. Choose the right board for your experience and body weight. A board that is too long will be hard to control, while one that is too short will not support you properly.

Some beaches have separate areas for surfing, indicated by black-and-white quarter flags. You must surf between these markers, and avoid swimming areas, which may be indicated by red-and-yellow flags. When paddling out, manoeuvre around the surfing area to avoid incoming riders, and in crowded conditions watch out for fallen riders and loose boards. If you and your board part company, try to hold onto it, especially in a rip current. An ankle leash is an important part of your equipment. Familiarise yourself with safety procedures in case of emergency.

DO *use the right length board.*
DO *leave the water before becoming tired.*
DO *avoid swimming areas.*

FURTHER INFORMATION British Surfing Association, Champions Yard, Penzance TR18 2TA (01736) 60250

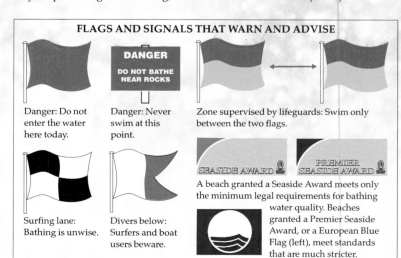

FLAGS AND SIGNALS THAT WARN AND ADVISE

Danger: Do not enter the water here today.

DANGER DO NOT BATHE NEAR ROCKS — Danger: Never swim at this point.

Zone supervised by lifeguards: Swim only between the two flags.

Surfing lane: Bathing is unwise.

Divers below: Surfers and boat users beware.

SEASIDE AWARD — PREMIER SEASIDE AWARD

A beach granted a Seaside Award meets only the minimum legal requirements for bathing water quality. Beaches granted a Premier Seaside Award, or a European Blue Flag (left), meet standards that are much stricter.

WATER-SKIING

Water-skiing requires expert training to ensure safety and enjoyment. Your boat should be insured to pull a water-skier, and the driver should have completed a water-ski driving course. There should always be two people in the boat, one to drive and one to watch the skier. Learn and use the approved signals between skier and crew. Always wear a life jacket (or a buoyancy aid, if you are a good swimmer) that meets EU standards. Check skis for loose wing nuts, loose binding, splinters and sharp metal.

Do not ski in water less than 3 ft deep, and watch the water ahead for obstacles such as rocks and breakwaters. Do not ski within 200 yd of the shore or near other water users.

DO *take lessons before attempting to ski.*
DO *avoid other water users.*
DO NOT *ski in water less than 3 ft deep.*

FURTHER INFORMATION British Water Ski Federation, 390 City Road, London EC1V 2QA (0171) 833 2855

CANOEING

Like all watersports, canoeing – or kayaking, as it is often known – can be dangerous if you are not well prepared. Joining a recognised club will give you access to advice and instruction which could save your life. Even when you feel confident, do not go out alone; the recommended minimum number for a canoeing trip is three people who can handle their craft competently.

Make sure that you are familiar with local hazards, the weather, tides and currents, and plan your movements accordingly. Wear warm clothing, a waterproof cagoule, and a life jacket (or a buoyancy aid, if you are a good swimmer). It is advisable to carry a compass, towing line, flares and a spare paddle.

Register your canoe with the nearest coastguard rescue centre and mark it on the inside with your name and an emergency telephone number. If you do get into trouble, stay with the canoe so that you can use it for additional buoyancy and to help rescuers to pinpoint your whereabouts in any search.

DO *register your canoe with the coastguard.*
DO *mark your name and an emergency telephone number inside the cockpit.*
DO *tell someone on shore of your intended movements and planned time of return.*

FURTHER INFORMATION British Canoe Union, Adbolton Lane, West Bridgford, Nottingham NG2 5AS (01159) 821100

WINDSURFING

There are fewer restrictions on windsurfing than on other forms of sailing, but be careful to keep clear of bathing areas, busy harbours and anglers. Wear

---

WHO TO CALL UPON WHEN DANGER THREATENS

The absence of a warning sign on a beach does not mean there is no danger. Most beaches have no such signs and no facilities for immediate rescue, but many of the more popular beaches are supervised by lifeguards, and HM Coastguard maintains a network of permanently manned rescue centres. Each rescue centre will give information on tides and local weather, coastal conditions and safety for sea users.

Coastguard
HM Coastguard, a 999 service, coordinates all civil maritime search-and-rescue operations for people and vessels. In 1994 it was merged with the Marine Pollution Control Unit to form the Coastguard Agency. The Coastguard has a small fleet of patrol craft, but in rescues can call upon Royal Navy and Royal Air Force helicopters, RNLI lifeboats, ships at sea, and police and fire services.

Lifeguards
Lifeguards may be trained volunteers or professionals employed by local councils. All lifeguards have lifesaving equipment; many also have inshore rescue boats and oxygen-powered resuscitation equipment. They can call out other rescue services if required. Areas of beaches supervised by lifeguards are marked with red-and-yellow flags.

Royal National Lifeboat Institution
Lifeboat stations are manned by trained volunteer crews, whose craft range from inshore high-speed inflatables to all-weather vessels. The appropriate vessel can be called quickly into service by the Coastguard.

---

appropriate clothing, such as a wet suit and light windproof jacket, as well as a life jacket (or a buoyancy aid, if you are a good swimmer) which meets EU standards. Carry a flare, and a spare length of line.

Check tide times and weather forecasts. Do not sail in an offshore wind unless you are very experienced. Contact the Royal Yachting Association for advice on emergency procedures.

DO *keep clear of other water users.*
DO *wear a buoyancy aid.*
DO NOT *sail in an offshore wind.*

FURTHER INFORMATION UK Board Sailing Association Ltd, PO Box 28, Fareham PO14 3XD (01329) 664779

SMALL-BOAT SAILING

Lessons with a club or with a training establishment recognised by the Royal Yachting Association will give instruction in emergency actions, such as capsize drill and 'man overboard' drill, as well as the 'rules of the road' for boat users. Small-boat sailors should also be able to swim at least 50 yd in light clothing and in a life jacket.

Before setting sail, obtain information on local weather conditions and tides. The local authority or the nearest coastguard rescue centre can give details of hazards such as rocks or wrecks, harbour bylaws and any restricted areas. Ensure that all your equipment, life jackets and flares are in good order. Tell someone on shore where you are going and when you expect to be back, and report your safe return.

If you are launching from the beach or from a slipway, an offshore wind will soon speed you on your way, but you may have difficulty turning back. If you are inexperienced, it is better to launch into an onshore wind. Launching and landing in breakers and surf poses special problems, and expert advice is needed. It is inadvisable to sail in winds above force 4 on the Beaufort Scale; never sail in winds above force 6.

If you capsize, and all your efforts to right the boat fail, it is important to stay with the boat. Climb onto the boat if you can and wait for help.

DO *check weather forecasts and tide tables.*
DO *observe harbour bylaws.*
DO *tell someone where you are going and when you expect to return.*

FURTHER INFORMATION Royal Yachting Association, RYA House, Romsey Road, Eastleigh SO50 9YA (01703) 629962

WHAT TO DO IN AN EMERGENCY

Helping yourself
If you fall into the water and are unable to reach safety:
• *Keep calm and try not to struggle.*
• *Turn over and float on your back.*
• *Attract attention by waving one arm and shouting for help.*
• *When help arrives, remain calm and do not clutch hold of your rescuer.*

Helping others
If you see someone in difficulties, don't go into the water to help, if you can avoid it. Other methods of rescue are usually safer for the rescuer and the person in distress. Try to find someone who will help you. One person can then seek expert assistance from a lifeguard, or by dialling 999 and asking for 'Coastguard'. While waiting for help, consider other methods of rescue.
• *Near shore, if conditions allow, several rescuers may link hands to make a human chain to reach the victim.*
• *If you cannot reach the person in distress, throw a floating object, such as a life buoy or a spare wheel, to be held onto.*
• *If a boat is available, row it to the victim stern first so that it does not capsize when the person in distress grabs it.*

Further information
Royal Life Saving Society, Mountbatten House, Studley, Warwickshire B80 7NN, (01527) 853943

LAW AND THE COAST: WHERE YOU MAY GO, WHAT YOU MAY DO

Most of Britain's shores and coastal waters can be freely used by anyone for any normal form of recreation. Though the foreshore nearly always allows public access, the beach above it may be privately owned and closed to the public. In certain areas even the foreshore may be closed for special reasons. And although beachcombing can be fun, removing objects from the beach may in some cases be against the law.

VISITING THE SEASHORE

Q *Where does the land end?*

A The land ends where the sea starts at low water on the lowest ebb of the tide. Land that can be privately owned usually ends at the average high-water line. The area in between is known as the foreshore. Most of Britain's foreshore is the property of the Crown and is managed by local councils or port authorities. Normally the public has the right to walk on it.

Q *When is the foreshore private?*

A In some cases a stretch of foreshore may be owned by a government department, such as the Ministry of Defence, which can exclude the public from the beach and prevent boats from landing there. Other stretches of foreshore may be owned privately – if, for example, quarrying takes place on or near the shore. Some parts of the foreshore are leased for private use, mainly by holiday companies who may deny access or charge an entrance fee. The National Trust also owns stretches of foreshore to which there is normally public access.

Q *What laws apply on the foreshore?*

A Most British laws remain in force as far as the outer edge of British territorial waters. These extend 3 nautical miles (3.4 land miles) from low-water level. They also include any estuary or bay less than 24 nautical miles (27.6 land miles) wide, and water between the mainland and islands.

Local authority bylaws may regulate the use of a beach for up to 1000 m out to sea from low-water level. For instance, swimming may be restricted to certain areas, either for swimmers' safety or to safeguard a nature reserve; or a stretch of beach may be closed because of a rock fall.

Q *Can I do what I like on the shore?*

A No council or other authority will stop you from swimming, sunbathing, picnicking or building sandcastles on any beach in Britain, provided you have reached the beach by a legal route. Increasingly, however, local authorities lay down bylaws to control the public

use of beaches. Such laws may prevent people from taking dogs, lighting fires, using transistor radios, or playing certain games on parts of the foreshore.

Bylaws are sometimes used to divide the beach into sections, with different parts set aside for different purposes. For example, part of a beach may be set aside for nude bathing or sunbathing. Water-skiing or speedboating may be banned in some areas, and car parking or camping may be restricted.

Q *What if there is no beach?*

A In places where the land falls vertically into the sea – as with a steep cliff or a harbour wall – there may be no foreshore even at low tide. In such cases there are no general public rights of use, even for fishing from the harbour wall or a convenient rock.

WALKING ON THE COAST

Q *Where am I allowed to walk?*

A A public footpath, bridleway, or byway (a road used as a public path or a public road) are all rights of way. They are not always signposted and you may need a map to follow them. Although anyone can use these rights of way at any time, this does not mean you can walk freely over the land they cross. A 'permissive' path is not a public right of way but can be used with the permission of the owner.

Q *What am I allowed to do?*

A You may stop to rest, admire a view or to eat a picnic on a public right of way so long as you do not stray from the route or cause an obstruction. If you deliberately disturb people or animals or do anything that is not part of your journey on a public right of way you may be trespassing. Although trespass is rarely a criminal offence, if you cause loss or damage on someone else's land you may be prosecuted.

If a public right of way is blocked, you have the right to remove enough of the obstacle to get by. However, you must be careful not to allow livestock to escape from their enclosures.

Local councils in England and Wales must keep 'definitive maps' showing all public paths in their areas. It is also the

responsibility of the councils to erect signposts at every point where a public footpath leaves a road.

Q *How can I reach the shore?*

A Although the foreshore itself is open to the public, to get to it you must use a public right of way, such as a public road or a footpath. If you need to cross private property, you must seek permission from the landowner, who may charge you for crossing the land.

Anyone may land on the foreshore by boat, and may walk across it to and from the boat, even when public access from the landward side is not possible.

BEACHCOMBING

Q *What can I take from the beach?*

A Anything forming part of the beach, including pebbles, sand and seaweed, is the property of the owner of that section of the shore. Above high-water mark the owner may be a private individual or a body such as the National Trust; below high-water line it is usually the Crown. Although in practice nobody will stop you removing small quantities of sand or seaweed, any abuse of this freedom can be stopped.

Lost or abandoned objects which have become buried in the sand also belong to the landowner. While metal detectors can be used on beaches, permission from the landowner is needed to disturb the ground to remove an object. Valuable objects deliberately hidden by their owner belong to the Crown; any finds should be reported to the police. Property found on the surface of a beach, rather than buried in it,

---

THE RIGHTS ABOUT WRECKS

The term 'wreck' applies not just to a shipwrecked vessel, but to any property or parts of a ship or aircraft found on or near the shore. It may be cargo or equipment or valuable gold coins, and is defined by the following categories:

FLOTSAM *Property that has floated off a shipwreck.*
JETSAM *Property deliberately thrown overboard to lighten a vessel in distress.*
DERELICT *Either a vessel or cargo abandoned at sea without hope of recovery.*
LAGAN *Items thrown into the sea but marked by buoys to locate them at a later date.*

Anyone finding a wreck or derelict property is required by law to hand it over, or report it, to the Receiver of Wreck. If you fail to report a finding, you may be prosecuted and fined. Finders may receive a salvage reward if an owner is identified. After one year, if the property has not been claimed, it passes to the Crown and may be auctioned or sold, although often the finder may keep the wreck in lieu of a salvage reward. Some wreck sites are protected by law and may only be investigated under a government licence.

belongs to the finder only if it has been genuinely lost, and if after proper enquiries have been made the true owner cannot be identified. If you find an object on the beach that appears to be of any value, hand it to the police, who will return it to you if it remains unclaimed after a few months. While driftwood and normal debris can be removed, a wreck or derelict property belongs to the Crown.

FISHING

Q Can I fish where I like?

A Sea-fishing by rod and line is largely unrestricted, though local bylaws may limit it in some places – for example, to protect a marine nature reserve or a fish farm. There is no close season for sea-fishing, and no ban on night fishing. Burbot, sturgeon, allis shad and vendace are all protected, making it an offence to kill, injure or disturb any of these species.

No licence is necessary for anglers either on shore or in boats using rod and line, though you may need permission from the landowner before fishing from a jetty or harbour.

WATERSPORTS

Q How are watersports controlled?

A Sports such as surfing, windsurfing and water-skiing are subject to local authority control. In addition to imposing bylaws, councils may enforce restraints such as denying powerboats access to the shore where there is no public right of way.

Anybody taking part in these sports should have insurance to cover accidents caused by them to others. This would cover, for example, a swimmer injured by a water-skier. Personal injury and damage to property caused when taking part in these sports is excluded from normal household insurance.

Q Are there any restrictions on skin-diving?

A The seabed out to the edge of the territorial sea belongs to the Crown, like the foreshore, and many of the same rules apply. Diving may be prohibited in marine nature reserves, fish farms and historic wreck sites. Ask for local advice. Taking fish from nets belonging to others is theft.

SAILING AND BOATING

Q Do I need a licence?

A Boats intended for private use around the shores of Britain do not need a licence, nor do their helmsmen or drivers. Licences are required only for vessels used commercially for fishing or for carrying passengers or cargo.

Q Where may I take my boat?

A There are few restrictions on sailing in tidal waters, including the tidal sections of estuaries and rivers, and the waters that cover the foreshore at high water. Occasionally boats may be banned from military training areas, or excluded from marine nature reserves. Powerboats may be subject to speed limits within 1000m of the shore, usually off busy beaches, and water-skiing may be limited to defined areas. Regulations are usually displayed by the waterside, or can be obtained from local council offices.

Q Where may I launch, land and moor?

A Boats may be launched only where there is a public slipway or other public access to the sea for boats; in other situations the landowner's permission must be sought. If there is no public right to launch a boat at a particular spot, an owner who provides a public launchway may charge for its use.

Once at sea, boats may be landed anywhere on the foreshore, except in prohibited areas, and launched again. Bylaws sometimes restrict powerboats from approaching busy beaches.

Boats may be anchored freely at sea, but to moor in a harbour permission is normally needed from the harbourmaster, and a fee is often payable. Helmsmen must follow the harbour-

master's instructions while navigating in and near the port. If an accident occurs as a result of the negligence of anyone owning or using a boat, he or she is liable for damages and the payment of compensation, in the same way as someone responsible for a car accident. Boats and crews should therefore be adequately insured against accidents and liability to others.

When hiring a boat, check that the owner is insured against any accident that might happen while you are in the vessel. If no such arrangement exists, make your own insurance provision, as the owner could hold you responsible for any accident.

ACCIDENTS AT SEA

Q What happens when there is an accident at sea?

A When accidents occur, the coastguard or police should be informed as soon as possible. To summon assistance in an emergency, dial 999 and ask for 'Coastguard'. Any vessel able to do so has a duty to help to rescue any person or vessel in distress.

Air-sea rescuers and coastguards make no charges for the service they provide. But anyone voluntarily rescuing a person or property in real and appreciable danger, including those people who set the rescue in motion, may be entitled to a salvage reward.

FURTHER INFORMATION

Whether you plan a trip to a nature reserve or to a historic building, contacting the appropriate organisation in advance will help you to get the most from your visit. Some national bodies preserve our countryside and heritage for public enjoyment, while others can offer safety advice.

TOURIST OFFICES

The Tourist Information Centres (TICs) listed for each section of the coast will send you leaflets and maps of the area, accommodation lists and programmes of forthcoming events, and also answer telephone queries. Before visiting a historic building or other attraction, it is advisable to check its opening times with the local TIC. Some TICs and tourist attractions are open for the summer season only, which generally runs from Easter to the end of October.

MARINE SAFETY

The Coastguard Agency, which incorporates the Marine Pollution Control Unit, is responsible for organising all civil search-and-rescue operations at sea. Its Maritime Rescue Coordination Centres at Aberdeen, Clyde, Dover, Falmouth, Swansea and Yarmouth are subdivided into a number of district rescue centres, which give information on tides, local conditions and safety.

Coastguard Agency,
Spring Place, 105 Commercial Road, Southampton SO15 1EG
(01703) 329100

Aberdeen MRCC, Marine House, Blaikies Quay, Aberdeen AB1 2PB
(01224) 592334
Forth, Fifeness, Crail, Fife KY10 3XN
(01333) 450666
Pentland, Cromwell Road, Kirkwall, Orkney KW15 1LN (01856) 873268
Shetland, The Knab, Lerwick, Shetland ZE1 0AX (01595) 692976

Clyde MRCC, Navy Buildings, Eldon Street, Greenock PA16 7QY
(01475) 729988
Oban, Boswell House, Argyll Square, Oban PA34 4BD
(01631) 563720
Stornoway, Battery Point, Stornoway, Isle of Lewis
HS1 2RT (01851) 702013

Dover MRCC, Langdon Battery, Swingate, Dover CT15 5NA
(01304) 210008
Solent, Whytecroft House, 44 Marine Parade West, Lee on Solent PO13 9NR (01705) 552100
Thames, East Terrace, Walton-on-Naze, CO14 8PY (01255) 675518

Falmouth MRCC, Pendennis Point, Castle Drive, Falmouth TR11 4WZ
(01326) 317575
Brixham, Kings Quay, Brixham TQ5 9TW (01803) 882704
Portland, Custom House Quay, Weymouth DT4 8BE (01305) 760439

Swansea MRCC, Tutt Head, Mumbles, Swansea SA3 4EX (01792) 366534
Holyhead, Prince of Wales Road, Holyhead, Anglesey LL65 1ET
(01407) 762051
Liverpool, Hall Road West, Crosby, Liverpool L23 8SY (0151) 9313341
Milford Haven, Gorsewood Drive, Hakin, Milford Haven SA73 3ER
(01646) 690909

Yarmouth MRCC, Havenbridge House, Great Yarmouth NR30 1HZ
(01493) 851338
Humber, Lime Kiln Lane, Bridlington YO15 2LX (01262) 672317
Tyne Tees, Priory Grounds, Tynemouth NE30 4DA (0191) 2572691

The other main organisations involved in maintaining safety at sea are:

Royal National Lifeboat Institution, West Quay Road, Poole BH15 1HZ
(01202) 671133
Seeks to preserve life following accidents at sea, and promotes sea safety.

Royal Society for the Prevention of Accidents,
Cannon House, The Priory Queensway, Birmingham B4 6BS
(0121) 200 2461
Promotes and provides information on water safety.

Royal Yachting Association,
RYA House, Romsey Road, Eastleigh SO50 9YA (01703) 627400
Offers advice on training and law relating to all types of recreational craft.

Surf Life Saving Association,
Verney House, 115 Sidwell Street, Exeter EX4 6RY (01392) 54364
Coordinates volunteer lifesavers who patrol beaches and carry out rescues.

CLEAN BEACHES

The quality of the sea water at selected bathing beaches is monitored throughout the summer by the National Rivers Authority and, in Scotland, the River Purification Board. The water is tested for its contamination by sewage and other pollutants, and the results of tests made during the previous bathing season are available to the public.

Sea water quality is assessed in accordance with the EC Bathing Water Directive, which stipulates two standards for measuring cleanliness. The Mandatory standard represents the minimum level of cleanliness that all bathing beaches are supposed to attain, but many beaches in Britain still fall below this standard; many others are not regularly monitored. The much stricter Guideline standard, which all European Union member states must strive to meet, has been consistently maintained at only a few British bathing beaches. Beaches with the best record for water quality are identified in the *Reader's Digest Good Beach Guide*, an annual survey compiled by the Marine Conservation Society and published by David & Charles.

Beach awards are presented annually by the Tidy Britain Group, an organisation largely funded by the Department of the Environment. 'Resort' beaches close to towns are assessed for water quality, safety provisions and beach management. 'Rural' beaches, in more remote locations, are tested for water quality, ease of access and general cleanliness. Beaches eligible for the Seaside Award need to have passed only the lower, Mandatory standard for water quality. Those eligible for the Premier Seaside Award or the European Blue Flag must have passed the higher Guideline standard.

All these awards are based on tests conducted during the previous bathing season, and a beach that wins an accolade one year may lose it the next.

Marine Conservation Society,
9 Gloucester Road, Ross-on-Wye HR9 5BU (01989) 566017
Works to conserve the marine habitat for wildlife and for future generations.

National Rivers Authority,
Rivers House, Waterside Drive, Aztec West, Almondsbury, Bristol BS12 4UD (01454) 624400
Protects the water environment, monitors water quality, providing information through its nine regional offices.

River Purification Board,
1 South Street, Perth PH2 8NJ
(01738) 627989

Tidy Britain Group,
The Pier, Wigan WN3 4EX
(01942) 824620

NATIONAL HERITAGE

Many historic houses, castles and other heritage sites are owned or maintained by national bodies. These organisations will provide lists of their properties and details of opening times.

Cadw,
Welsh Historic Monuments, Brunel House, 2 Fitzalan Road, Cardiff CF2 1UY (01222) 500200
Protects and preserves ancient monuments and historic buildings in Wales.

English Heritage,
23 Savile Row, London W1X 2HE
(0171) 973 3000
Preserves England's architectural and archaeological heritage.

Historic Scotland,
Longmore House, Salisbury Place, Edinburgh EH9 1SH (0131) 668 8600
Manages monuments of historic interest for public enjoyment in Scotland.

Landmark Trust,
  Shottesbrooke, Maidenhead
  SL6 3SW (01628) 825925
Restores buildings of historical or architectural interest, and lets them to the public for holiday use.

Maritime Trust,
  2 Greenwich Church Street,
  London SE10 9BG (0181) 858 2698
Preserves maritime heritage.

National Trust,
  36 Queen Anne's Gate, London
  SW1H 9AS (0171) 222 9251
Preserves lands and buildings of historical interest or natural beauty.

National Trust for Scotland,
  5 Charlotte Square, Edinburgh
  EH2 4DU (0131) 226 5922

COUNTRYSIDE

Many stretches of coast in England and Wales fall within areas of protected countryside, or have been identified as worthy of special management to conserve their natural qualities or enhance their recreational possibilities. Designated or defined areas include Heritage Coasts, Areas of Outstanding Natural Beauty (AONBs) and National Parks. They are identified and managed by national bodies such as the Countryside Commission and its Welsh equivalent, the Countryside Council for Wales.

Campaign for the Protection of Rural Wales,
  Ty Gwyn, 31 High Street, Welshpool
  SY21 7YD (01938) 552525

Council for the Protection of Rural England,
  25 Buckingham Palace Road,
  London SW1W OPP (0171) 976 6433

Countryside Commission,
  John Dower House, Crescent Place,
  Cheltenham GL50 3RA
  (01242) 521381

Countryside Council for Wales,
  Plas Penrhos, Penrhosgarnedd,
  Bangor LL57 2LQ (01248) 370444

NATURE RESERVES

A nature reserve is an area protected for the purpose of conservation. It may have rare plants or wildlife, or unusual geological features. National Nature Reserves are sites of national significance designated and usually managed by English Nature, Scottish Natural Heritage or the Countryside Council for Wales. Local nature reserves may be managed by local authorities, local trusts, or in some cases by the RSPB or the National Trust. Many reserves are open to the public, but check in advance what restrictions apply to visitors and whether you need to obtain a permit. The waters around Lundy Island form Britain's only statutory marine nature reserve, where bylaws and a 'zoning' arrangement have been introduced to safeguard the marine environment.

Voluntary marine reserves are managed by local groups for the purpose of research, education or conservation.

English Nature,
  Northminster House, Northminster
  PE1 1UA (01733) 340345
Promotes conservation and enjoyment of the countryside and protects wildlife.

RSPB (Royal Society for the Protection of Birds),
  The Lodge, Sandy SG19 2DL
  (01767) 680551

Scottish Natural Heritage,
  12 Hope Terrace, Edinburgh
  EH9 2AS (0131) 447 4784

Scottish Wildlife Trust,
  Cramond House, Kirk Cramond,
  Cramond Glebe Road, Edinburgh
  EH4 6NS (0131) 312 7765
Conserves wild plants, animals, birds and their habitats in Scotland.

Wildlife Trusts,
  The Green, Witham Park, Waterside
  South LN5 7JR (01522) 544400
County Wildlife Trusts' national office.

WALKING

Ramblers' groups will provide details of the many footpaths, long-distance paths and nature trails along the coast.

Ramblers' Association,
  1/5 Wandsworth Road, London
  SW8 2XX (0171) 582 6878

Ramblers' Association Scotland,
  23 Crusader House, Haigh Business
  Park, Markinch KY7 6AQ
  (01592) 611177

Forestry Commission,
  231 Corstorphin Road, Edinburgh
  EH12 7AT (0131) 334 0303
Manages forest areas for recreation and conservation.

The waters round the British Isles are divided into named areas used by the Meteorological Office in giving details of sea conditions, visibility and wind speeds. Forecasts of gales or storms use the Beaufort Scale, which defines the wind force by a number. For instance, force 4 refers to a moderate breeze of 13 to 18 mph, and force 6 is a strong breeze of 25 to 31 mph. Small boats may be unsafe in conditions of force 4 upwards. When winds of force 8 (39 to 46 mph) are expected within 6 hours, gale warnings are issued.

Index

Page numbers in **bold** type indicate a main entry, often accompanied by an illustration on the same page. Page numbers in *italics* indicate other illustrations. Page numbers in roman type indicate shorter text references. The abbreviation NNR denotes a National Nature Reserve.

Acknowledgments

The great majority of the photographs and illustrations in this book were specially commissioned by Reader's Digest from the photographers and artists whose names appear on page 4.

Other photographs were provided by the sources listed below.

The position of the illustrations on each page is indicated by the letters after the page number: T=top; B=bottom; L=left; C=centre; R=right

17 Bruce Coleman Ltd/Paul Meitz **20** CL The Mary Rose Trust BR Skyphoto's Collection/R J Larn **20-21** E T Archive **21** TR F E Gibson BC NHPA/Jane Gifford BR Brioney East/Rex Features Ltd **26** CR Eigentum des Germanischen National Museums **38** CL (tea salt mustard) Anthony Blake Photo Library/Paul Grater CL (pepper) Anthony Blake Photo Library TR Mermaid Inn, Rye CL CR Mary Evans Picture Library BR The Bridgeman Art Library/Fitzwilliam Museum, Cambridge **39** TR The Mansell Collection TR The Bridgeman Art Library/Victoria and Albert Museum, London **40** TL BR Robert Harding Picture Library/Adam Woolfitt **41** Robert Harding Picture Library/Adam Woolfitt **46** CR RSPCA/Stuart Harrop **56** T National Maritime Museum, London C The Bridgeman Art Library BR *The Departure of the Pilgrim Fathers from Plymouth, 1620* by B F Gribble/City Museum and Art Gallery, Plymouth, reproduced by permission of the owner **57** T E T Archive/National Maritime Museum BC Press Association Ltd BR Associated Press **68** BL Tate Gallery, London **71** BL Bruce Coleman Ltd/Jens Rydell **76** CL Robert Harding Picture Library/Philip Craven **77** TL Images Colour Library BR Collection/Alain Le Garsmeur **78** Guernsey Tourist Board **79** TR Collections/Alain Le Garsmeur **82** BL The National Trust/Joe Cornish **82-83** The National Trust/Derry Robinson **83** TR The National Trust/Derek Harris CL NHPA/G I Bernard BC BR The National Trust **87** BL The National Motor Museum, Beaulieu **94** Michael Holford **95** NHPA/Laurie Campbell **98** Reproduced by permission of the Trustees of the Victoria and Albert Museum, London **100** CL The Mansell Collection C Mary Evans Picture Library CR Angelo Hornak BC Mary Evans Picture Library **100-1** Valentines of Dundee/J S Gray **101** TR Hulton Deutsch CL The Mansell Collection CR Brighton Central Reference Library BL BC Science and Society Picture Library/NRM **103** Robert Harding Picture Library/R Tomlinson **108** BR Bruce Coleman Ltd/George McCarthy **116** TR Hulton Deutsch **120** TR Skyscan C B Sheila and Oliver Mathews **121** TL Jason Hawkes Aerial Collection TR Hulton Deutsch C Imperial War Museum CR Popperfoto **122** CR Bruce Coleman Ltd/L R Dawson **132** BL Michael Holford **154** TL Kingston upon Hull Museums and Art Gallery **156** TC Rex Features Ltd/Ross Parry B The National Trust **157** TR Landform Slides C Environmental Picture Library/Robert Brook BL Popperfoto **158** TC Bruce Coleman Ltd/Uwe Walz GDT **160** Roger Scruton **162** C National Maritime Museum, London Artist: Nathaniel Dance **164-5** Roger Scruton **166** BR Tyne and Wear Museums **167** Science and Society Picture Library **170** TL Bruce Coleman Ltd/Jeff Foott **172** T A photograph from work by Frank Meadow Sutcliffe © Sutcliffe Gallery, Whitby CL (INSET) CL Royal National Lifeboat Institution CR The Bridgeman Art Library BR Mary Evans Picture Library **173** TL Network/Barry Lewis C CR Royal National Lifeboat Institution BL Network/Barry Lewis BR Royal National Lifeboat Institution **179** BR Sierra Club **184-5** Patricia Macdonald **185** Hulton Deutsch **187** Scotland in Focus/G Thomson **190** Images Colour Library/R Parker **192** BR Edinburgh Photographic Library/Peter Davenport **194** Scotland in Focus/E D Lee **195** TR Images Colour Library **196** Scotland in Focus/R G Elliot **197** B Photographs by British Petroleum **199** BL Bruce Coleman Ltd/RinieVan Meurs **201** TL Images Colour Library TR NHPA/Laurie Campbell **205** BL Bruce Coleman Ltd/Eckart Pott **08** T National Galleries of Scotland B Charles Tait **210** Charles Tait **211** T Scotland in Focus/Napier **212** Scotland in Focus/A Gordon **214** B Comstock Photofile Ltd/Simon McBride **215** Scotland in Focus **216** Bruce Coleman Ltd/Gordon Langsbury **217** TR Scotland in Focus/J Weir BL Hamish Brown **220** Reproduced by permission of the George Washington Wilson Collection, Aberdeen University Library **224** Images Colour Library **225** NHPA/Laurie Campbell **226** C Scotland in Focus/R G Elliott B Alastair Scott **228** CL Mike Briggs B Scotland in Focus/R G Elliott **230** TR National Trust for Scotland/Brian Chapple B Scotland in Focus **232** RSPCA/Colin Carver **233** Scotland in Focus **236-7** Scotland in Focus **238** T Alastair Scott **239** Scotland in Focus/J MacPherson **240** T CL David Paterson BR © Glasgow Museum and Art Galleries **241** T Images Colour Library **244** L British Film Institute TC CL Ronald Grant Archive CR © 1994 MGM United Artists CR Scotland in Focus/J MacPherson BC 20th Century Fox/Andrew Cooper **244-5** British Film Institute **245** TR The Kobal Collection C Zenith Films/Charlie Crawford CR Ronald Grant Archive BL Scotland in Focus **247** CR Bruce Coleman Ltd/Rodney Dawson **248** BL Neville Fox-Davies **248-9** Neville Fox-Davies **250** Scotland in Focus/A G Johnston **251** CL Morrison Bowmore Distillers Ltd CR Scotland in Focus/A G Johnston **261** Caledonian Newspapers Ltd/Glasgow Herald and Evening Times **262** BL Scottish Maritime Museum BR Peter Reeves **263** TL Collections/Paul Watts TR C Broads Authority BR The Maritime Trust/Shell (UK) **264** C Scottish Tourist Board/Doug Corrance **269** The Bridgeman Art Library/City of Edinburgh Museums and Art Galleries **270** BR Mary Evans Picture Library **277** TL National Maritime Museum, London **280** C Holker Hall Lakeland Motor Museum **282** BR Northern Picture Library/Abraham Cardwell **285** TL Blackpool District Library **286** BR Hulton Deutsch **286-7** Robert Harding Picture Library/Charles Bowman **287** C (POSTER GROUP) First Leisure Corporation BR W S Slater and Co Ltd **289** C Sefton Coast Management Scheme **90** BL Images Colour Library **293** CL Robert Harding Picture Library/Margaret Collier BL Don Morley **294** C The Beatles Story Ltd **295** CL Merseyside Tourism and Conference Bureau Ltd **299** TR Robert Opie **303** (INSET) TR Mary Evans Picture Library **311** Irish Ferries **312** TL Paul Kay **316** TR Wales Tourist Board C Mary Evans Picture Library BL Robert Harding Picture Library **317** T Mary Evans Picture Library CR Robert Harding Picture Library/Adam Woolfitt BL The Mansell Collection **326** BL Mick Sharp/Jean Williamson **334** CR The Bridgeman Art Library/The British Council, London **336** BL Photo Precision C Hulton Deutsch **350** Lupe Cunha Photos **370-1** Colorsport **372-3** All-Sport (UK)/Stephen Munday

The publishers would like to thank Tourist Information Centres, Heritage Coast officers, National Parks officers and local reference libraries for their help in the preparation of this book. The following organisations and individuals also made valuable contributions:

Amateur Swimming Association; British Surfing Association; British Trust for Ornithology (Jim Flegg); British Water Ski Federation; Broads Authority; Cadw; Kenneth Clark; The Coastguard Agency (Phil Rogers); Countryside Commission; Countryside Council for Wales; Dover Museum (Mark Frost); English Heritage; English Nature (Jonathan Wray); Forestry Commission; Hartland Point Museum (Mark R Myers); Heritage Coast Forum (David Masters); Marine Conservation Society; The Mary Rose Trust; National Maritime Museum; National Rivers Authority; The National Trust; The National Trust for Scotland; Natural History Museum (David George); Norfolk Coast Project; Northern Lighthouse Board; Oxford University Museum (George McGavin); Ramblers' Association; Royal National Lifeboat Institution; Royal Society for the Protection of Birds; Royal Yachting Association; Scottish Film Council; Scottish Maritime Museum; Scottish Natural Heritage; Shipwreck Heritage Centre, Hastings (Peter Marsden); Douglas C Smith; Southampton University Dept of Archaeology (John Adams); Tidy Britain Group; Trinity House; UK Board Sailing Association; Water Services Association; Wildlife Trusts.

MAP ORIGINATION Cartographic Department of the Automobile Association
MAP REVISIONS Cosmographics, Watford, England
TYPESET AND SEPARATED IN ENGLAND
PAPER Townsend Hook Paper Company Ltd, Snodland, England
PRINTING AND BINDING Jarrold and Sons Ltd, Norwich, England

40-520-1

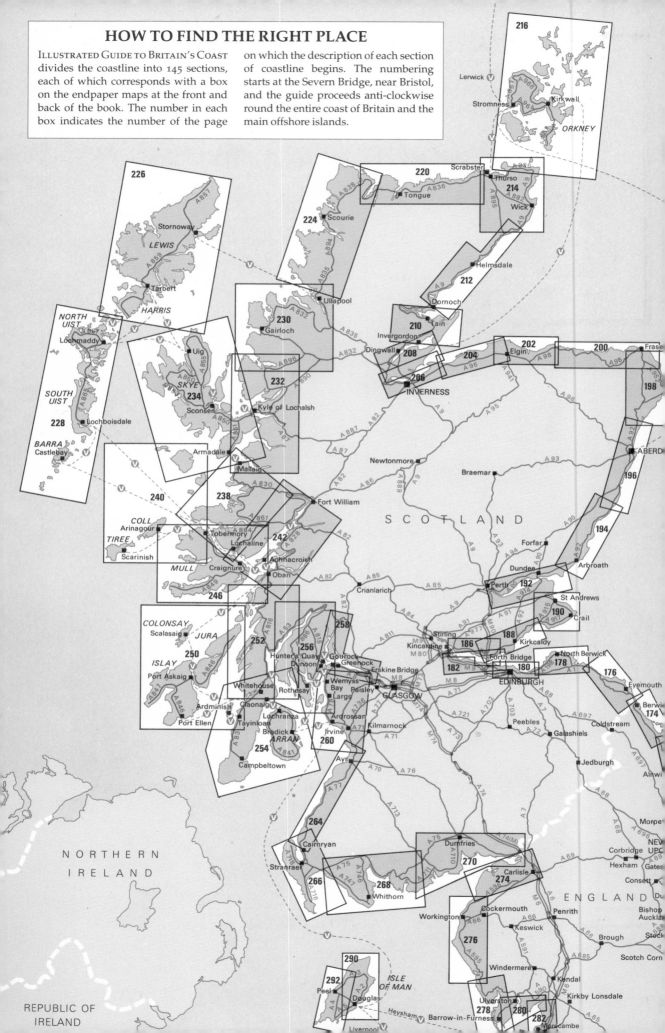

HOW TO FIND THE RIGHT PLACE

ILLUSTRATED GUIDE TO BRITAIN'S COAST divides the coastline into 145 sections, each of which corresponds with a box on the endpaper maps at the front and back of the book. The number in each box indicates the number of the page on which the description of each section of coastline begins. The numbering starts at the Severn Bridge, near Bristol, and the guide proceeds anti-clockwise round the entire coast of Britain and the main offshore islands.